Review of the
CRIMINAL
COURTS

OF ENGLAND AND WALES

REPORT

OCTOBER 2001

By the Right Honourable
LORD JUSTICE AULD

London : THE STATIONERY OFFICE

Published with the permission of the Lord Chancellors
Department on behalf of the Controller of Her Majesty's
Stationery Office.

© Crown Copyright 2001

First published 2001

ISBN 0 11 702547 X

Printed in the United Kingdom for The Stationery Office.
TJ005620   C45   65536   10/01

CONTENTS

Chapter 6 – The judiciary

Chapter 7 – A unified Criminal Court

Chapter 8 – The criminal justice system

Chapter 9 – Decriminalisation and alternatives to conventional trial

Chapter 10 – Preparing for trial

Chapter 11 – The trial: procedures and evidence

Chapter 12 – Appeals

Appendices

FOREWORD

SCOPE OF THE REVIEW

1   On 14th December 1999 the Lord Chancellor, the Home Secretary and the Attorney-General appointed me to conduct this Review into the working of the Criminal Courts and to report within a year. My terms of reference were to inquire into:

> "the practices and procedures of, and the rules of evidence applied by, the criminal courts at every level, with a view to ensuring that they deliver justice fairly, by streamlining all their processes, increasing their efficiency and strengthening the effectiveness of their relationships with others across the whole of the criminal justice system, and having regard to the interests of all parties including victims and witnesses, thereby promoting public confidence in the rule of law."

2   The Lord Chancellor, in announcing my appointment, said:

> "The Government's aim is to provide criminal courts which are, and are seen to be:
>
> - modern and in touch with the communities they serve;
>
> - efficient;
>
> - fair and responsive to the needs of all their users;
>
> - co-operative in their relations with other criminal justice agencies; and
>
> - with modern and effective case management to remove unnecessary delays from the system."

3   The Review is primarily of the practices and procedures of the criminal courts. But it also goes beyond their workings. They are the focal point of

the criminal justice system of which a number of agencies, voluntary bodies and legal practitioners also form part. How well or badly they all work together has a significant and highly public effect on the daily working of the courts, both in the quality and in the efficiency of the justice they dispense. This is an important area in which the public appears to have little confidence in the system, despite strenuous efforts over recent years to improve it.

4   The Review is thus concerned with how the criminal justice system works insofar as it involves the courts, but not with criminal justice policy or philosophy or principles of sentencing. It is nevertheless a broad inquiry into how the criminal courts should do their job so as to combine fairness with efficiency, while also having regard to the interests of all involved in or exposed to their process. This involves practical questions about the structure and composition of the courts, their relationship with other parts of the criminal justice system, their procedures before and at trial and on appeal, some aspects of the rules of evidence they apply and the process of sentencing.

5   I was asked to take a radical and long-term look at the working of the whole of the criminal courts system and to make broad recommendations, where necessary, for its improvement. That I have attempted to do, considering the structural context along with the processes and their effect on each other, looking for short and medium term improvements as a path to long term reforms. I have not been asked to provide a costed blue-print for change and have, therefore, left to others the task of detailed examination of feasibility and costing of any of my proposals that the Government may wish to develop.

6   I have interpreted the Review's terms of reference as including:

- the management and funding of 'the criminal justice system', including the relationship of the courts with others concerned in it;

- the structure and organisation of the courts and the distribution of work between them;

- their composition, including the use of juries in the Crown Court and of lay and professional judges in magistrates' courts;

- case management, procedure and evidence and the contribution to all three of information technology;

- treatment of all those concerned with criminal justice and securing public confidence in it; and

- appellate structures and procedures.

GENERAL APPROACH

7 My general approach has been to explore under those main headings whether there is a clear need for change and, if so, what change might be feasible and sufficiently worthwhile to justify the disturbance of well established structures and procedures. In recommending change or no change, I have borne in mind the often ill-defined boundary between procedural and substantive law. Procedure and practice may have significant effects on substantive rights and duties, particularly now that our ancient common law principle of 'due process of law' has become underpinned by Articles 5 and 6 of the European Convention on Human Rights.

8 I thought at first that I could conduct the Review, as well as write the Report, in a structured way, starting by examining present case management, trial procedures and evidence against criteria of fairness and efficiency, and only moving on to consider larger questions, such as management and funding, structure, jurisdiction and composition of the courts if procedures under the present system demanded change of that order.

9 But I rapidly concluded that such an approach would be blinkered. It could have left undiscovered improvements in the system that might flow from the reshaping of it by structural, managerial and/or jurisdictional change and new information technology. It could also have discouraged consideration of improvements necessary to meet increasing public expectations. These include, for example, modern and higher standards of court accommodation, witness and victim care and proper provision for diversity and the likely demands of Human Rights on the trial process. I have, therefore, examined, as an aid to improvement of the courts' practices and procedures, their structure, jurisdiction and management in the context of the criminal justice system as a whole, including the various government departments and agencies involved and their relationship one with another.

CONDUCT OF THE REVIEW

10 During the Review the Lord Chancellor, with the agreement of the Home Secretary and the Attorney-General, appointed twelve consultants to assist me. Each is highly distinguished and experienced in his or her respective field. They were: The Honourable Mr. Justice Crane, Jane Hickman, David Perry, QC, Sir David Phillips, QPM, His Honour Judge Pitchers, Andrew Prickett, CBE, Dame Helen Reeves, Professor John Spencer, Lord Stevenson of Coddenham, CBE, Professor Richard Susskind, OBE, Beverley Thompson, OBE, and Rosemary Thomson, CBE. I take this early opportunity to record

my gratitude to them all for their guidance in the conduct of the Review and their considerable contribution to this Report.

11   I must also mark my appreciation of, and give thanks to, the Review Secretariat, led first by Michael Kron, CBE, and then Edward Adams, for their dedicated and skilful support at every stage of the Review. The other members were Betty Blatt, Simon Boddis, Sarah Jameson, Amanda Jeffery, Shelley Johnston, Helen Journeaux, Nasrin Khan, Sarah McAdam and Barbara Saunders. They and my trusty clerk, Sylvia Slater, worked prodigiously throughout the Review, each in his or her field making valuable contributions to the Report. I could never have completed the task without them.

12   I have consulted widely. In the first instance I sought views under my interpretation of the terms of reference by letter, media advertisements and the Review's website. This resulted in written submissions from over 1,000 individuals and organisations in the United Kingdom and other Commonwealth Countries, Europe and the United States of America. Appendix 1 contains a list of all those who made written submissions. Many others expressed their views to me in meetings, conferences and seminars held for the purpose or concerned with subject matters of the Review. I have also visited many courts and criminal justice agencies and related bodies to observe and discuss their workings.

13   As a second stage of consultation, I circulated and published on the Review website a list of issues prompted by the submissions received. This generated supplemental and additional submissions and formed the basis for discussion at 20 Review Seminars that I held around the country for, among others, representatives of local criminal justice agencies, leading academics and others with local experience of or exposure to the system. With the assistance of the Cambridge University Law Faculty's Centre for European Legal Studies, and under the direction of Professor Spencer, one of the Review's Consultants, I convened a conference in Cambridge of distinguished European judges and jurists to learn something of their respective systems. And I have visited a number of court centres in Scotland, Northern Ireland, the United States of America (Miami, Philadelphia and New York) and Canada (Calgary and Ottawa) to view and discuss their practices and procedures.

14   I have attempted to thank individually all who have so generously contributed their time, knowledge and experience in these various ways to assisting me in the Review. I take this public opportunity to repeat those thanks and to offer them to any contributors to whom I or the Review Secretariat may not have written or spoken personally.

15   I have also drawn on the work of previous inquiries and reviews and commissions, including: Lord Morris of Borthy-y-Gest's 1963-1965 Departmental Committee on Jury Service;[1] Lord Beeching's 1966-1969 Royal Commission on Assizes and Quarter Sessions;[2] Lord Justice James' Committee on the Distribution of Business between the Crown Court and Magistrates' Courts in 1975;[3] Sir Cyril Philips' 1978-1981 Royal Commission on Criminal Procedure, whose task was to review the criminal process from the start of investigation to the point of trial;[4] Lord Roskill's Fraud Trials Committee, 1986;[5] Mr Julian Le Vay's 1989 Home Office Efficiency Scrutiny of the organisation of Magistrates' Courts;[6] Viscount Runciman's 1991-1993 Royal Commission on Criminal Justice,[7] the focus of which was the integrity of investigation and trial of alleged offences in the Crown Court, rather than the organisation and efficiency of the criminal courts as a whole; Martin Narey's 1997 Review of Delay in the Criminal Justice System;[8] Sir Iain Glidewell's 1997-1998 Review of the Crown Prosecution Service;[9] Sir William Macpherson of Cluny's Stephen Lawrence Inquiry;[10] and Professor Rod Morgan's and Neil Russell's research in 2000 for the Lord Chancellor's Department and Home Office on the judiciary in the magistrates' courts.[11]

16   My reference to other inquiries and reviews has not been confined to those in this country. In recent years there has been much impressive work in this field in the Commonwealth and the United States of America, on which I have drawn for guidance in the Report where appropriate and which I have listed in Appendix 2. I owe a considerable debt to this large body of overseas research, as I do to the many Commonwealth and United States Judges who have been so generous of their time and hospitality.

17   In the time available to the Review I have only been able to commission a few limited projects of research. However, over the same period Government Departments have continued to conduct and/or have commissioned many, and sometimes overlapping, reviews, inquiries and research and pilot projects on various matters within my terms of reference. These, and those that I have commissioned, are listed in Appendix 3. The Law Commission has also had in hand a number of related projects, notably codification of the criminal law,

---

[1] Cmnd 2627 (HMSO 1965)

[2] Cmnd 4135 (HMSO 1969)

[3] HMSO, 1975

[4] Cmnd 8092 (HMSO 1981)

[5] HMSO, 1986

[6] HMSO, 1989

[7] Cmnd 2263 (HMSO 1993)

[8] Home Office, February 1997

[9] Cmnd 3960 (HMSO 1998)

[10] Cmnd 4262-1 (HMSO 1999)

[11] RDS Occasional Paper No 66 (Home Office, December 2000)

fraud, double jeopardy, bail and human rights, evidence of previous misconduct, prosecution appeals and sentencing. And the Government has continued to enact or attempt to enact legislation to introduce further legislative proposals covering Review issues, the most notable of which have been: the unsuccessful Mode of Trial Bills, designed to remove an accused's right to elect jury trial in 'either-way' cases the Powers of Criminal Courts (Sentencing) Act 2000, consolidating sentencing legislation; the Criminal Justice and Court Services Act 2000, which includes provision for a national probation service and various methods of dealing with offenders; and the Criminal Justice and Police Act 2001 which deals with a number of matters, including the treatment of vulnerable and intimidated witnesses.

18   In February of this year, the Government published a major policy paper, *Criminal Justice: The Way Ahead*[12] setting out its proposals for a comprehensive overhaul of the criminal justice system. This paper contained important commitments relating to the management of the Crown Prosecution Service, to law reform and to the criminal courts and the trial process. Finally, in July the Home Office published the Report of the sentencing review carried out by John Halliday CB.[13] Although not within the subject matter of this Review, some of its recommendations have implications for the allocation of work within the courts structure thatI consider in the Report.

19   I have regarded this wealth of emerging material as valuable information for the Review and have drawn on it where I have considered it helpful to do so. I have also taken into account recent and current initiatives within Government, including those concerning over-all planning, management and funding of the criminal justice system, case management, diversity, information and communications technology, witness and victim care and youth justice. In doing so, I have not sought to duplicate those initiatives, but to examine whether and in what way they support or conflict with candidates for reform suggested in the Review.

---

[12] Cmnd 5074 (The Stationery Office, February 2001)

[13] *Making Punishments Work: Report of a Review of the Sentencing Framework for England and Wales* (Home Office, July 2001)

CHAPTER 1

INTRODUCTION

1   The scheme of the Report is to examine the purpose, structure and working of the criminal courts in the criminal justice system and to consider:

- re-structuring and improving the composition of the criminal courts, introducing new criteria and procedures for allocating work between them and better matching of courts to cases;

- introducing a new structure for direction and better management of the criminal justice system as a whole, with a view to improving the quality of justice, efficiency and effectiveness of the criminal process;

- removing work from the criminal process that should not be there, and providing within it alternative forms of disposal for certain types of case;

- improving preparation for trial and trial procedures, and reform of the law of criminal evidence ; and

- simplification of the appellate structure and its procedures.

2   Throughout, I have tried to keep an eye on our newly acquired domestic law of human rights, the potential of information technology, not only to improve existing and familiar ways of doing things, but to re-shape our practices and procedures, and to the urgent need to enhance public confidence in the criminal justice system as a whole. I add that the last of those - public confidence - features in almost every issue raised by the Review. It includes among its many aspects, questions of diversity, civilised treatment of all involved in or exposed to the criminal justice system, public accessibility to the courts, to the law that they administer, and to ready information of what they are doing.

AIMS OF THE CRIMINAL COURTS

3   The Government has identified certain 'overarching' aims of the criminal justice system, including the courts' contribution to it.[1] I have been urged to undertake a similar exercise of my own for the purpose of the Review. I was and remain sceptical of the practical value of such an endeavour in considering what, if any, reforms to recommend in the structure and working of the courts.   The collection of fairly obvious generalities that such definitions normally entail is important as a reminder of the various interests for which provision needs to be made. A checklist of interests is also helpful to the courts when making decisions. But, as the civil courts' experience of 'the overriding objective' of the new Civil Procedure Rules has shown, the weight to be given to the respective interests varies according to the circumstances of the case.

4   However, it is necessary to look beyond bare functional descriptions of the criminal courts, such as: the conviction of the guilty and the acquittal of the innocent;[2] deciding whether the accused is guilty and the appropriate sentence if he is;[3] or "providing a fair trial and just disposal".[4] Once the courts are considered in the context of the criminal justice system as a whole, including the community at large and the various agencies and others involved in the process, it is obvious that their purpose and function are not confined to the forensic practicalities of convicting and sentencing the guilty and acquitting others. So, it is necessary to keep an eye on the over-all purposes of criminal justice.

5   Similar considerations exercised Lord Woolf in formulating the "overriding objective" of the Civil Procedure Rules, namely "of enabling a court to deal with cases justly,"[5] and "so far as practicable:

   (a) ensuring that the parties are on an equal footing;

   (b) saving expense;

   (c) dealing with the case in ways which are proportionate

        (i)   to the amount of money involved;

        (ii) to the importance of the case;

        (iii) to the complexity of the issues; and

        (iv) to the financial position of each party;

   (d) ensuring that it is dealt with expeditiously and fairly; and

---

[1] see *Criminal Justice Strategic Plan 1999 -2002* and *Criminal Justice Business Plan 2000 -2001*

[2] *Report of the Departmental Committee on Jury Service*, Cmnd 2327 (HMSO, 1965), para 13

[3] *Review of the Crown Prosecution Service*, Cmnd 3960 (HMSO, 1998), Ch.7, para 4

[4] a possibility suggested by Professor John Spencer in his capacity as a consultant to the Review

[5] Civil Procedure Rules Part 1

(e) allotting to it an appropriate share of the court's resources, while taking into account the need to allot resources to other cases."

6   Now, formulating such an overriding aim or objective for civil justice must have been difficult enough. It is an even more problematic task for criminal justice. First, there are more than just the courts and the immediate parties to consider; there are a number of criminal justice agencies and other bodies and individuals, such as victims, witnesses and jurors. The prosecutor has a higher burden of proof than a plaintiff in a civil case, and in many criminal cases the accused's liberty and/or reputation is more likely to be at stake. The undertaking and outcome of criminal proceedings are usually of much greater consequence to the public than in civil proceedings. And, as a by-product of the criminal burden and standard of proof, and of an accused's 'right of silence', defendants in criminal cases have certain absolute rights, not enjoyed by their civil counterparts, that may modify their obligation to co-operate in the forensic process. It follows that there is more to identifying the aims of the courts in the criminal justice system than attempting a definition of a just trial and/or a sentencing process simply by balancing the interests of both parties, coupled with some regard to the commitment of public resources and of involved individuals to the task.

7   Second, there is the more fundamental question of the main purpose of the criminal justice system in all its parts. The Government has defined two 'aims' for the system, namely reducing "crime and the fear of crime and their social and economic costs" and dispensing "justice fairly and efficiently and to promote confidence in the law".[6] They are purportedly particularised - but in fact largely repeated - in the form of 'objectives', for many of which there are set somewhat mechanistic performance measures or targets. The second of those aims, which is primarily directed at the courts, has the following objectives:

> "to ensure just processes and just and effective outcomes;
>
> to deal with cases throughout the criminal justice process with appropriate speed;
>
> to meet the needs of victims, witnesses and jurors within the system;
>
> to respect the rights of defendants and to treat them fairly;
>
> to promote confidence in the criminal justice system."

---

[6] see *Criminal Justice System: Strategic Plan 1999-2002*, para 1.3

8   I am content to take those predictable general aims and particularising objectives for the criminal courts as an appropriate starting point for the Review.   The first of the aims, reduction of crime, and part of the second,efficient and effective process, are much as Professor Andrew Ashworth has described the "general justifying aim" of the criminal justice system, namely "crime control" by detecting, convicting and duly sentencing the guilty.[7] It is implicit in that formulation that the system should also acquit those not proved to be guilty - which comes within the Government's second aim.   But it does not follow that the operation of the system or its general aim should be to make it as difficult as possible to convict the guilty or, under the banner of the presumption of innocence, to advance every possible forensic device as an obstacle to conviction.   Equally, as Professor Michael Zander observed in the concluding sentence of his dissent in the Report of the Runciman Royal Commission, "[t]he integrity of the criminal justice system is a higher objective than the conviction of any individual".[8]

9   However, we should not expect too much of the criminal justice system, the courts in particular, as a medium for curing the ills of society.   Courts undoubtedly have deterrent, rehabilitative and reparative roles, but they are all too often the last resort after all other attempts to deter and/or reform have failed.   In their present sentencing role they are a blunt instrument of social repair.   However, with development of new and constructive combinations of punishment and rehabilitation - one form of 'restorative justice' - they may have more of a role, with other agencies, in diverting people from crime before recidivism sets in.

10   Below the general aim or aims of a criminal justice system, familiar and well accepted principles may be identified at various levels of generalisation. They are not so much principles as blinding glimpses of the obvious.   Thus, at the highest level, it could be said that the fundamental principles of a good system are that it should be just and efficient.   To those in a jurisdiction like ours that depends heavily on lay magistrates and juries, could be added a third, lay and local involvement in the administration of criminal justice. Drop to a lower level of generalisation, and several important, but commonplace principles or notions emerge.   Most are gathered together in Article 6 against the back-cloth of our common law tradition of adversariality: the presumption of innocence, the right to silence, legality and due process, right of access to a court, a fair and public hearing and so on.   I mention all of these in various contexts in the Report, but cannot here, by a process of analysis or assignment of priorities, draw on them to provide an over-all approach or answer to the many practical questions posed in the Review. Different priorities apply in different contexts and circumstances.

---

[7] *Concepts of Criminal Justice* [1979] Crim LR 412, at 412
[8] *Royal Commission on Criminal Justice*, Cm 2263 (HMSO, 1993), p 235

STARTING POINTS

11   I gather under this heading a number of fairly obvious features of our system of criminal justice that give rise to important practical issues. I take them as starting points for more detailed discussion in later chapters and, where appropriate, to indicate the main issues and my lines of thought on them.

A right to a fair trial and 'balance'

12   Procedural fairness has always been a feature of our law. Its articulation as such by our recent adoption of Article 6 adds little of substance to the tradition, though it may generate much litigation on its application in individual circumstances. My main concern here is with the notion of 'balance'. In determining the provision of courts, manner of trial and the search for fair, speedy and otherwise efficient procedures, it should be remembered that they are not there just to protect defendants. They also serve the community. And the criminal process is not a game. It is a search for truth according to law, albeit by an adversarial process in which the prosecution must prove guilt to a heavy standard.[9]

13   I do not regard it as within my terms of reference to consider whether, as a generality, the present balance of a criminal trial should be tipped so as to favour one party more than the other, as variously urged by some in the course of the Review. A defendant's right to a fair trial is as near absolute as any notion can be. However, in its application to different circumstances and on a case by case basis, considerations of balance or proportionality inevitably intrude.

14   In 1972 the majority of the Criminal Law Revision Committee, in their Eleventh Report,[10] were sympathetic to the idea of a balance, in the narrow sense of tilting it in favour of the prosecution. For them, a fair trial was one which would "secure as far as possible that the result of the trial [was] the right one" even if that meant modification of procedural rules protecting an accused's right of silence.[11] The Report provoked so much controversy that the Government of the day took no action on it.[12]

15   A few years later, in 1978, the Philips' Royal Commission looked again at the problem of balance, though in a broader sense than had the Criminal Law

---

[9] cf the German inquisitorial system in which the courts are enjoined to find the truth and where there is no provision for a formal plea of guilty, but in which, nevertheless, they have to be sure of guilt before they can convict

[10] *Eleventh Report of the Criminal Law Revision Committee*, Cmnd 4991 (HMSO, 1972)

[11] ibid paras 12, 15 and 16

[12] it was subsequently revived in the Runciman Royal Commission Report and is now to be found in the Criminal Justice and Public Order Act 1994, ss 34-37, enabling the court in certain circumstances to draw adverse inferences from silence

Revision Committee. It described it as its 'central challenge' and a difficult one:

> "1.12. At first sight the notion of a fundamental balance of the kind specified may appear unarguable, almost axiomatic, a matter of common sense, but further consideration of the matter raises a number of difficult, and perhaps, in the last analysis, insoluble questions. Can there be in any strict sense an equation drawn between the individual on one side and society on the other? Is it the balance of some sort of social contract between the individual and society? What are the rights and liberties of the individual which are assumed to provide part of the balance? Who gives and what justifies them? Are they all of equal weight; all equally and totally negotiable or are some natural, absolute, fundamental, above the law, part of the human being's birthright? On the other side of this assumed balance, especially in an increasingly heterogeneous and specialised society, how is the interest of the whole community to be defined with any useful precision? And where does one see, where do the police see, the role of the police being applied; in one or other of the scales, or at the fulcrum, or both? What is clear is that in speaking of a balance between the interests of the community and the rights of the individual issues are being formulated which should be the concern not only of lawyers or police officers but of every citizen."

> 1.20. In the context of an increasing complexity of society and the growing power of the state the individual has found it difficult to organise for his own protection and has got caught in the dilemma of looking to the state for help whilst fearing the misuse of powers that have been given to institutions of the state. The need to define and assert the rights of the individual, to seek a balance, has assumed urgency and significance." [13]

16   The Philips Royal Commission decided to look for and formulate a framework of first principles as a means of measuring the adequacy of the then existing procedures, of proposals to change them and of the likely contribution of the latter to establishing a proper balance.[14]   The first principles - or 'principal standards' that it identified and formulated for each of these enquiries were: "Are they fair? Are they open? Are they workable?"[15]

---

[13] *Report of the Royal Commission on Criminal Procedure*, Cmnd 8092 (HMSO, 1981), paras 1.12 and 1.20

[14] ibid, para 1.35

[15] ibid, para 2.18

Applying those principles to, *inter alia*, the defendant's right to silence, the Commission recommended no change.[16]

17   The Runciman Royal Commission was cautiously receptive to the notion of balance:

> "It may be argued that however practical our recommendations, and however cogent the reasoning behind them, there is a potential conflict between the interests of justice on the one hand and the requirement of fair and reasonable treatment for everyone involved, suspects and defendants included, on the other. We do not seek to maintain that the two are, or will ever be, reconcilable throughout the system in the eyes of all the parties involved in it. But we do believe that the fairer the treatment which all the parties receive at the hands of the system the more likely it is that the jury's verdict ... will be correct .... [T]here are issues on which a balance has to be struck...".[17]

18   Imprecise though the Runciman approach may be, I agree with it, certainly when questions arise as to the form of provision of a system of courts and procedures for administering the criminal justice system. A balance of some sort has to be struck between the community's interest in providing an efficient and economic system for administering justice, bearing in mind also its many other commitments, and the manner of fair trial that it provides for offences of different seriousness. There is also, in appropriate circumstances, a place for such considerations by a court when deciding contentious procedural issues between the prosecution and an accused. It is a reassurance that this seems be of a piece with Strasbourg jurisprudence where, for example, there is an issue between an accused's procedural claim based on his right to a fair trial and disruption of the prosecution or exposure to harm of its witnesses[18] and/or victims.[19]

Lay justice

19   For reasons that I give in Chapters 4 and 5, I accept that resolution of questions of fact going to the issue of guilt should continue in the main to be the responsibility of lay magistrates and juries. For centuries both tribunals of fact have been corner-stones of our system of criminal justice. In their different ways they continue to be practical and public manifestations of the citizen's involvement in the administration of criminal justice and his

---

[16] ibid, Ch.4

[17] *Royal Commission on Criminal Justice*, Chapter 1, para 27

[18] see eg *Doorson v Netherlands* [1996] 22 EHRR 330, EctHR and *Van Mechelan v Netherlands* [1997] 25 EHRR, 647, ECtHR

[19] see eg *Baegen v Netherlands* [application no 16696/90, 27/10/95]; *Z v Finland* [application no 22009/93, 25/2/97]; and *TP v United Kingdom* [application no 28945/95, 10/5/01]

leavening of the power of state institutions. It is useful citizenship and is, or should be, a powerful contributor to public confidence in the system.

20   As to lay magistrates and their role as summary judges, they do not only have centuries of tradition and public acceptance to commend them. They reflect - imperfectly, but with scope for improvement - the mix of the community from which they are drawn. Among their strengths are independence, a range of backgrounds, experience and a common-sense approach to their task. The weight of the submissions and other evidence in the Review is that they do their work conscientiously and well.[20] There are over 30,000 of them, as against about 100 stipendiary magistrates, now called District Judges (Magistrates' Courts). They are, in the main, laymen and laywomen, not professional lawyers, but they receive training and acquire considerable experience of the law that they are regularly called upon to apply. And, although they usually sit as a court of three and tend to be slower than a District Judge, who sits on his own, they account for the vast majority (91%) of summary work, which itself accounts for 95% of all prosecuted crime. Less than 1% of their decisions are the subject of appeal to the Crown Court. Even smaller percentages of their work are the subject of appeals to the High Court by way of case stated or judicial review.

21   All that is simply a summary of my decision taken early in the Review that lay magistrates should continue to exercise their traditional summary jurisdiction. As appears in Chapter 4, I am nevertheless of the view that there is considerable scope for making them, as a body, more representative of the community, nationally and locally, and for improving the method of their appointment, the provision for their training, management structures and working procedures.

22   As to juries, my experience in the Review has been the same as that of the Runciman Royal Commission.[21] There is wide and firm support for jury trial. Few proposed its general abolition. Many vehemently urged its retention in its present form. Some suggested research with a view to determining whether it is as sound a form of trial as many believe. Others were of the view that juries are not the appropriate tribunal for many cases of certain types and levels of seriousness that now come before them.

23   Unlike the Runciman Royal Commission, I do not believe that it is necessary or desirable to amend section 8 of the Contempt of Court Act 1981 to permit research of a more intrusive kind than is already possible. As I indicate in

---

[20] it is interesting to note that in the 1998 British Crime Survey, 61.1% of the public thought that magistrates were out of touch with what ordinary people thought, compared to 80% who thought that the professional judiciary were

[21] *Royal Commission on Criminal Justice*, Chapter 1, para 8

Chapter 5,[22] there is already a wealth of useful jury research throughout the common law world. Much of it is of a kind that would not offend the 1981 Act; and it shows where the strengths and weaknesses of juries lie and the considerable scope for improving their composition and the way in which they work. Those were the major issues under this heading in the Review.

24   In Chapter 5, I have looked at proposals that a defendant should be entitled to waive jury trial in all or certain classes of case presently triable on indictment. I have also considered whether there is a case for removing or qualifying a defendant's present right to trial by jury in certain procedures and types of case, notably: serious fraud or other complex or technical cases, alleged offences by young defendants, offences triable either on indictment or summarily - 'either-way' offences, and fitness to plead.

25   As to the mode of trial of 'either-way' offences - in respect of which the Government twice failed in its parliamentary attempts at reform last year[23] - where a democratic society like ours has devised different forms of trial according to the type and/or seriousness of the crime alleged, it must be for it to draw the line between them, and from time to time to vary it, according to its perception of public interests and the individual's right to a fair trial.[24] The critical questions, which I examine in Chapter 5, are by what criteria should cases be allocated to one or other form of tribunal where legislation permits a choice, and should the court or the accused decide? Other common and civil law countries draw lines between different levels of jurisdiction, but often at a higher level of seriousness than we do. And our system is probably unique in that, in a large range of offences many of them often relatively trivial in nature, the accused, not the court, decides how and where he is to be tried.

Professional judges

26   There were few proposals in the Review for any radical changes in the judicial structure. But there was considerable dissatisfaction with the match, or mis-match, of judges to work, and with the inflexibility of their deployment between different courts and levels of jurisdiction. Many consider that this mis-match and inflexibility causes inefficiency and sometimes injustice. In Chapters 7 and 6 I have considered changes to court structures and to the system of deployment of judges at first instance and on appeal in order to meet these criticisms.

---

[22] paras 76 - 87

[23] Criminal Justice (Mode of Trial) Bills Nos 1 and 2

[24] relatively recent examples of such change were the conversion of the following former 'either-way' into offences triable summarily only: taking a vehicle without consent, common assault and battery, (see Criminal Justice Act 1988, ss 37 and 39) driving whilst unfit to drive through drink or drugs (Road Traffic Offences Act 1988, s 9 and Sched 2 Pt I) and criminal damage to the value of less than £5,000 (see Magistrates' Courts Act 1980, s 22)

Local justice

27   Local justice, like lay justice, is considered by many to be a fundamental principle or requirement of our criminal justice system. It has three aspects. The first is geographical locality. All other things being equal, it is clearly desirable for reasons of convenience that courts should be readily accessible to their local communities. There has been much concern about court closures in rural areas in recent years. Clearly, some courthouses are little used and some could not realistically be improved to the standards now rightly demanded of courts. But decisions on court closure should not be taken without assessment of their implications for all involved. It is not solely or even primarily a matter of the potential savings to the courts and their administration. Second is the locality of those dispensing justice, particularly magistrates and jurors. As the embodiment of local lay justice, it is important that, so far as practicable, they should truly reflect the mix of the community from which they are drawn. Third, there is the question of courts, in their application of the law to the facts, responding to local needs or other circumstances, for example, when there are local surges of particular types of offence or where there is endemic deprivation. However, such locality should be balanced against a national framework for clarity and consistency in the application of the law.

Adversarial process

28   Like the Philips[25] and the Runciman[26] Royal Commissions, I consider that there is no persuasive case for a general move away from our adversarial process. Not only is it the norm throughout the common law world, it is beginning to find favour in a number of civil law jurisdictions which have become disenchanted with their inquisitorial tradition. However, as I discuss in Chapter 10, there are already signs of an inquisitorial approach in some of our pre-trial and public interest immunity procedures. And some have argued for its introduction to the trial process for certain purposes, for example, in the treatment of expert evidence and in cases involving the evidence of very young children, matters that I have considered in Chapter 11.

---

[25] *Report of the Royal Commission on Criminal Procedure*, para 1.8
[26] *Report of the Royal Commission on Criminal Justice*, paras 11-14

Categorisation of offences

29   The division of offences into those triable only summarily by magistrates or a District Judge and those triable only on indictment by a judge and jury is of long standing. Of lesser antiquity is the hybrid category of 'either-way' offences that were introduced in a small way in the mid-nineteenth century and that have grown in fits and starts throughout the twentieth century to the large number they are today. The basic framework of these three categories seems to me to be sound in principle, but to need attention in their use, particularly as to the manner of determining mode of trial in 'either-way' cases. I have, therefore, accepted the three categories of offence and that those triable on indictment only should go to what is now the Crown Court and that those triable summarily only should remain in what is now the magistrates' courts. As to the wide category of 'either-way' offences, I have not sought to resolve the mode of trial issue by suggesting transfers from one category to another at the margins - though individual candidates could be found. In Chapters 5 and 7 I have looked instead for alternative and appropriate ways of trying some of those cases and, also, for a new system for determining how they should be tried.

Complexity

30   The strongest impression that I have formed of the criminal justice system in the course of the Review is of the complexities in every corner of it. Their consequence is much damage to justice, efficiency and effectiveness of the system and to the public's confidence in it. The central thrust of this Report has been to find ways of removing or reducing these complexities and the damage they do. The 'system', a legacy of centuries of piecemeal change, is a mix of autonomous national and local bodies attempting to collaborate and consult with each other through a network of committees at different levels. There is no over-all direction; there are no over-all lines of management or accountability; there is, instead, co-ordination of variable quality, and cross-reporting. In Chapter 8, I consider the introduction of a single line of national direction and local management of the criminal justice system as a whole, headed by a national Criminal Justice Board supported by local Boards. For their part, the courts are presently split into two quite separate structures of the Crown Court and magistrates' courts, separately administered and financed, each with distinct practices and procedures. In Chapter 7, I consider the creation of a new unified Criminal Court made up of three Divisions and supported by a single administration and, so far as practicable, using common practices and procedures. In Chapters 9, 10, 11 and 12, I consider what can be done to simplify court procedures in preparation for and at trial and on appeal, including, in Chapter 11, changes to some basic rules of the law of

evidence. The criminal law as a whole suffers from centuries of haphazard statutory and common law accretion, a process that has accelerated dramatically in recent years. It is all immensely complicated for lawyers and laymen alike, and urgently in need of codification, as I mention at the end of this chapter and in many other parts of the Report.

Public confidence

31   Public confidence is an elusive concept, first in identifying it as an attitude of the community at large, and second in evaluating how well informed it is. By its very nature, the criminal justice system is bound to engender a significant level of dissatisfaction from those, like convicted and sentenced offenders, who feel that it is has treated them unjustly, or those, like victims, witnesses, and jurors who believe that it has treated them with indifference or insensitivity. More generally, the system falls between the views of many who consider that it is not tough enough in catching, convicting and sentencing criminals and of many others who maintain that it fails to have sufficient regard for the rights of the individual and for those, including some members of ethnic minorities, who come from deprived backgrounds or who are otherwise vulnerable. Not only are people's attitudes to the criminal justice system conditioned by their own different experiences of it, they often result from their ignorance of the system and of the nature and effect of courts' decisions. This is all too apparent from the results of attempts, through polls, surveys and the like, to gauge the levels of confidence of a broad cross-section of the community. And there is the tendency in much of the media to misunderstand and to misreport what happens in court. Although the courts and criminal justice agencies have become increasingly aware of the need to raise their level of performance and to inform the public better than they have done, there is more to do.

32   Public confidence is thus, and is likely to remain, an imprecise tool for determining how well a criminal justice system is performing and what needs to be done to improve it. Public confidence is not so much an aim of a good criminal justice system; but a consequence of it. The aim should be for those responsible to inform themselves in a more thorough and measured way than they do now of what changes are required and, in making them, adequately to explain them to the public. That is a very general proposition, easy to articulate and hard to achieve. But I make it here more as a caution against attempting insufficiently informed reforms in response to perceptions by some of injustice or discrimination and against treating such perceptions as proxies for a low level of public confidence.

Ethnic disadvantages

33   Much of what I have said about public confidence is of particular importance
under this heading. In recent years, and given special impetus by Sir William
Macpherson's *Report of the Stephen Lawrence Inquiry*,[27] there has been
growing concern that members of ethnic minority communities experience
discrimination within the criminal justice system. The way in which data on
race and criminal justice is currently collected is so unsatisfactory and the
issues are so complex that it is difficult to determine whether the concern is
well-founded. There is evidence, however, that members of ethnic minority
communities are under-represented in various ways in the courts and criminal
justice agencies and bodies of various sorts. For the reasons I gave in the last
paragraph, it would be a mistake to attempt to skew the system or the criminal
justice process in response to perceived weaknesses. But the perceptions
should be thoroughly tested and, if well-founded, remedied. As I say later in
the Report,[28] the first step should be to establish a system for comprehensive
and accurate collation of data about minority ethnic representation in the
system and relative outcomes of each stage of its process. Once such
information is available the criminal justice agencies would be in a far better
position than they are to work with minority ethnic organisations and others to
eliminate discrimination and counter any fears that prove to be unfounded.
There is now an urgency about this. Professor Roger Hood set alarm bells
ringing as long ago as 1992.[29] The Runciman Royal Commission in 1993
urged thorough monitoring in connection with various racial issues brought to
its attention.[30] But little seems to have been done. Part of the problem, no
doubt, is the primitive state of information technology for the criminal justice
system as a whole and among its various agencies, another area in which I
make a call for urgent action in various contexts in the Report.

Politics

34   It would be naïve to suggest that politics should be removed from the forces
driving change in the criminal justice system. As for any other field of public
concern, politicians have a legitimate interest in the formation of criminal
justice policy and in legislative and other means of implementing it.
However, the criminal justice system and the public's confidence in it are
damaged if, as has happened all too often in recent years, insufficiently
considered legislative reforms are hurried through in seeming response to
political pressures or for quick political advantage. I take it as a legitimate
starting point that there should be some mechanism of objective and informed

---

[27] *Report of the Stephen Lawrence Inquiry*, Cmnd 4262-1 (HMSO, February 1999)

[28] Chapter 8, para 66

[29] R Hood, *Race and Sentencing: A Study in the Crown Court* (Oxford, 1992)

[30] *Report of the Royal Commission on Criminal Justice,* Chapter 1, para 26

assessment between the rawness of political enthusiasms of the moment and the transformation of their products into law. More is needed than the present unofficial, often perfunctory and late consultation with the higher judiciary, coupled with the absence of any consultation for the purpose with the Criminal Justice Consultative Council. In Chapter 8, I consider a new and more effective consultative mechanism in the form of a Criminal Justice Council alongside what should, in consequence, be a more timely and well used line of informal consultation with the Lord Chief Justice and other higher judiciary. The Council's function, unlike that of the Law Commission, which is to undertake specific law reform projects, would be to keep the criminal justice system under review and to examine and initiate proposals for reform.

CODIFICATION

35   I take the opportunity early in the Report to join the swelling chorus for codification of the criminal law, a basic tool for understanding and application of the law commonplace in many civil and common law jurisdictions. As Lord Bingham of Cornhill has recently illustrated in his plea, *A Criminal Code: Must We Wait For Ever?*,[31] the chorus has been swelling for a long time. It began in the early nineteenth century, and was the subject of many authoritative reports and parliamentary attempts until the late part of the century and revived again in 1965 with the establishment of the Law Commission. The Commission, working through a distinguished team of lawyers, began work on the production of a code, publishing the first version in 1985 and a revision in 1989. In its Report containing the revision, it summarised the need for it in the following terms:

> "The position of the common law in criminal matters, and in particular the interface between common law and statutory provisions, undoubtedly contributes to making the law obscure and difficult to understand for everyone concerned in the administration of justice, whether a newly appointed assistant recorder or magistrates' clerk. Obscurity and mystification may in turn lead to inefficiency: the cost and length of trials may be increased because the law has to be extracted and clarified, and there is greater scope for appeals on mis-directions on points of law. Moreover, if the law is not perceived by triers of fact to be clear and fair, there is a risk they will return incorrect or perverse verdicts through misunderstanding or as deliberate disregard of what they are advised the law is. Finally, the criminal law is a particularly public and visible part of the law. It is important that its

---

[31] originally in a speech delivered at a dinner for HM Judges at the Mansion House in London on 22nd July 1998 and now published in his collection of essays and speeches, *The Business of Judging* (OUP, 2000) pp 295-297

authority and legitimacy should not be undermined by perceptions that it is intelligible only to experts."[32]

36   The Law Commission, the judiciary at all levels, distinguished academics, practitioners and many others with experience of the problems and needs of the criminal justice system have since continued to press for this reform, but to no avail. The nearest we get to it is some consolidation of statutes from time to time when the law in a particular area has become so dispersed that it has become unmanageable, but without attention to its equally inconvenient and unstructured overlay of case law. A recent example is the Powers of Criminal Courts Act 2000, on which the ink was barely dry before it was subject to amendment by other statutes. In a codified system, the law – both statutory and case law and practice – is, where necessary, reformed as well as restated, and the code itself is amended on a regular basis to keep it up to date, a task that electronic technology could aid dramatically. I am pleased to see that the Government has also recently indicated its support for a core criminal code.[33] It should consist of four parts:

- **A Criminal Offences Code** – The Law Commission has already done much of the groundwork for this in a series of Reports on Legislating the Criminal Code, starting with its 1989 draft.[34] It should be given the responsibility, and the necessary resources, to produce the Code and subsequently to keep it under regular review.

- **Code of Procedure** - In Chapter 10 I consider the need for replacement of the separate practices and procedures of magistrates' courts and the Crown Court with a single procedural code or, if my recommendations for a new unified Criminal Court are accepted, for a code for the three Divisions of that Court. As I recommend in Chapter 10, the responsibility for producing and subsequently maintaining the Code should vest in a new statutory Criminal Procedure Rules Committee working under the general oversight of the new Criminal Justice Council. Like the Civil Procedure Rules, it should be enshrined in primary legislation with a clear statement of principles and detailed in subordinate legislation enabling ready amendment to keep it up to date.

- **A Code of Criminal Evidence** – In Chapter 11 I recommend that there should be a wide-ranging and principled reform of the law of criminal evidence, and have suggested that it should include consideration of a general move away from many rules of inadmissibility to trusting courts, judges and lay fact finders alike, to give relevant evidence the weight that it deserves. Such a review would lay the foundation for a Code of Criminal Evidence, for the production and maintenance of which, in due course, a standing body should be appointed to work under the oversight of the Criminal Justice Council.

---

[32] Law Comm Report No 177

[33] *Criminal Justice: The Way Ahead*, Cmnd 5074, (HMSO, February 2001), para 3.57

[34] Law Comm Report No 177

- **A Sentencing Code** – As I mention briefly in Chapter 11, codification of our law and practice of sentencing is urgently needed, despite the recent consolidation exercise and with or without implementation of the significant reforms of sentencing proposed in the recent Report of the Halliday Sentencing Review, *Making Punishments Work*.[35] Again, this should be the responsibility of a standing body working under the oversight of the Criminal Justice Council.

> **Accordingly, I recommend that, under the general oversight of the new Criminal Justice Council and with the involvement and support as necessary of the Law Commission, A Code of Criminal Law should be produced and maintained in four sections:**
>
> - **criminal offences;**
> - **criminal procedure;**
> - **criminal evidence; and**
> - **sentencing.**

Postscript

37   In the treatment of various subjects and in making recommendations in the body of the Report I have taken the liberty, for convenience of expression, of appearing to assume that some of my recommendations for structural reform will be adopted, for example, for a new Criminal Justice Board and Criminal Justice Council and a unified Criminal Court and its Divisions. Whenever I have done so, I have tried to make clear whether other individual reforms are equally applicable to present structures or, with adaptation depend on the proposed new structures. Also, and solely for simplicity of expression, I have in general confined pronouns to the masculine throughout, and mostly used the word 'magistrates' when referring to 'lay magistrates' in order to acknowledge the different nomenclature now that stipendiary magistrates have become District Judges (Magistrates' Courts).

---

[35] *Report of the Review of the Sentencing Framework for England and Wales,* (Home Office, July 2001)

CHAPTER 2

SUMMARY AND RECOMMENDATIONS

1. In this chapter, I summarise and set out my recommendations. In the summary I take a different order from that of the main body of the Report. I start with the recommendation for codification in Chapter 1 and continue with the structure of the criminal justice system over-all and that of the criminal courts and their composition, and then with the way in which cases progress through them. I follow the summary with the recommendations in the order made and with references to the paragraphs and pages in the text to which they relate .

Introduction (Chapter 1 – pages 7-22, rec 1)

2. The criminal law should be codified under the general oversight of a new **Criminal Justice Council** and by or with the support as necessary of the Law Commission. There should be codes of offences, procedure, evidence and sentencing **(paras 35-36, rec 1).** See also: as to a code of criminal procedure, **Chapter 10 paras 271-280, recs 228-234);** as to a code of criminal evidence, **Chapter 11, paras 76-77,);** and as to a sentencing code, **Chapter 11, para 198, and Chapter 12, paras 110-111).**

The Criminal Justice System (Chapter 8 – pages 315-336, recs 121-139)

3. A national **Criminal Justice Board** should replace all the existing national planning and 'operational' bodies, including the Strategic Planning Group, and the Trial Issues Group. The new Board should be the means by which the criminal justice departments and agencies provide over-all direction of the criminal justice system **(paras 37-66, recs 121-122)**. It should have an independent chairman and include senior departmental representatives and chief executives of the main criminal justice agencies (including the Youth Justice

Board) and a small number of non-executive members **(paras 67-72, recs 123-125)**. At local level, **Local Criminal Justice Boards** should be responsible for giving effect to the national Board's directions and objectives and for management of the criminal justice system in their areas. Both the national and local Boards should be supported by a centrally managed secretariat and should consult regularly with the judiciary **(paras 73-77, recs 126-129)**. The national Board should be responsible for introducing an integrated technology system for the whole of the criminal justice system based upon a common language and common electronic case files, the implementation and maintenance of which should be the task of a **Criminal Case Management Agency** accountable to the Board. **(paras 92-114, recs 137-139)**.

4. A **Criminal Justice Council,** chaired by the Lord Chief Justice or senior Lord Justice of Appeal, should be established to replace existing advisory and consultative bodies, including the Criminal Justice Consultative Council and the Area Strategy Committees. It should have a statutory power and duty to keep the criminal justice system under review, to advise the Government on all proposed reforms, to make proposals for reform and to exercise general oversight of codification of the criminal law. The Council should be supported by a properly resourced secretariat and research staff **(paras 78-88, recs 130-135)**.

A unified Criminal Court (Chapter 7 – pages 269-314, recs 83-120)

5. The Crown Court and magistrates' courts should be replaced by a unified Criminal Court consisting of three Divisions: the Crown Division, constituted as the Crown Court now is, to exercise jurisdiction over all indictable-only matters and the more serious 'either-way' offences allocated to it; the District Division, constituted by a judge, normally a District Judge or Recorder, and at least two magistrates, to exercise jurisdiction over a mid range of 'either-way' matters of sufficient seriousness to merit up to two years' custody; and the Magistrates' Division, constituted by a District Judge or magistrates, as magistrates' courts now are, to exercise their present jurisdiction over all summary matters and the less serious 'either-way' cases allocated to them **(paras 2-35, recs 83-87)**. The courts, that is those of the Magistrates' Division, would allocate all 'either-way' cases according to the seriousness of the alleged offence and the circumstances of the defendant, looking at the possible outcome of the case at its worst from the point of view of the defendant and bearing in mind the jurisdiction of each division. In the event of a dispute as to venue, a District Judge would determine the matter after hearing representations from the prosecution and the defendant. The defendant would have no right of election to be tried in any division **(paras 36-40, recs 88-95)**. (In the event of the present court structure continuing, the defendant should lose his present elective right to trial by jury in 'either-way' cases; see paragraph 10 below.)

6. Whether or not the Crown Court and magistrates' courts are replaced with a unified Criminal Court, there should be a single centrally funded executive

agency as part of the Lord Chancellor's Department responsible for the administration of all courts, civil, criminal and family (save for the Appellate Committee of the House of Lords), replacing the present Court Service and the Magistrates' Courts' Committees. For the foreseeable future, circuit boundaries and administrations should remain broadly as they are and the courts should be locally managed within the circuits and the 42 criminal justice areas **(paras 41-73, recs 96-103)**. Justices' clerks and legal advisers responsible to them should continue to be responsible for the legal advice provided to magistrates **(para 74, rec 104)** see also **Chapter 4 – Magistrates paras 50-58, recs 6-7)**.

Magistrates (Chapter 4 – pages 94-134, recs 2-15)

7. Magistrates and District Judges should continue to exercise their established summary jurisdiction and the work should continue to be allocated between them much as at present **(paras 1-49, recs 2-5)**. If my recommendation for the establishment of a new unified Criminal Court with a District Division is adopted, they should also sit together in that division exercising its higher jurisdiction. I do not recommend any further extension of justices' clerks' case management jurisdiction **(paras 50-58, rec 7)**. Steps should be taken to provide benches of magistrates that more broadly reflect the communities they serve. **(paras 59-86, recs 8-9)**. In order to strengthen the training of magistrates, the Judicial Studies Board should be made responsible, and be adequately resourced, for devising and securing the content and manner of their training **(paras 91-100, recs 11-15)**.

Juries (Chapter 5 – pages 135-225, recs 16-60)

8. Jurors should be more widely representative than they are of the national and local communities from which they are drawn. Qualification for jury service should remain the same, save that entitlement to, rather than actual, entry on an electoral role should be a criterion. Potential jurors should be identified from a combination of a number of public registers and lists **(paras 21-24, recs 17-18)**. While those with criminal convictions and mental disorder should continue to be disqualified from service, no one in future should be ineligible for or excusable as of right from it. Any claimed inability to serve should be a matter for discretionary deferral or excusal **(paras 27-40, recs 20-24)**. Provision should be made to enable ethnic minority representation on juries where race is likely to be relevant to an important issue in the case **(paras 52-62 rec 25)**.

9. The law should not be amended to permit more intrusive research than is already possible into the workings of juries, though in appropriate cases trial judges and/or the Court of Appeal should be entitled to examine alleged improprieties in the jury room **(paras 76-98, recs 26-29)**. The law should be declared, by

statute if need be, that juries have no right to acquit defendants in defiance of the law or in disregard of the evidence **(paras 99-107 rec 30)**.

10. The defendant should no longer have an elective right to trial by judge and jury in 'either-way' cases. The allocation should be the responsibility of the magistrates' court alone and exercisable where there is an issue as to venue by a District Judge. The procedures of committal for trial and for sentence in 'either-way' cases should be abolished. Under my recommendation for a unified Criminal Court with three divisions, matters too serious for the Magistrates' Division would go direct either to the District or Crown Division depending on their seriousness In the meantime 'either-way' cases for the Crown Court should be "sent" there in the same way as indictable-only cases **(paras 119-172, recs 32-36)**. Trial by judge and jury should remain the main form of trial of the more serious offences triable on indictment, that is, those that would go to the Crown Division, subject to four exceptions. First, defendants in the Crown Court or, if my recommendation for a unified Court with three divisions is accepted, in the Crown and District Divisions, should be entitled with the court's consent to opt for trial by judge alone **(paras 110-118, rec 31)**. Second, in serious and complex frauds the nominated trial judge should have the power to direct trial by himself and two lay members drawn from a panel established by the Lord Chancellor for the purpose (or, if the defendant requests, by himself alone) **(paras 173-206, recs 37-47)**. Third, a youth court, constituted by a judge of an appropriate level and at least two experienced youth panel magistrates, should be given jurisdiction to hear all grave cases against young defendants unless the charges are inseparably linked to those against adults **(paras 207-211, recs 48-50)**. Fourth, legislation should be introduced to require a judge, not a jury, to determine the issue of fitness to plead. **(paras 212-213, rec 51)**.

The Judiciary (Chapter 6 – pages 226-268, recs 61-82)

11. The current hierarchy of judges and their jurisdictions should continue, subject to my recommendations for the establishment of a District Division of a new unified Criminal Court and extension of the powers of District Judges and magistrates when sitting in it **(paras 1-18)**. Systems of judicial management and deployment should be strengthened and also made more flexible to enable a better match of High Court and Circuit Judges to criminal cases, proper regard also being given to the arrangements for civil and family justice. In particular, there should be a significant shift in heavy work from High Court Judges to the Circuit Bench, coupled with greater flexibility in the system for allocating work between them. Save in the case of Circuit Presiding Judges, the present rigid circuiteering pattern of High Court Judges should be replaced by one in which they travel out to hear only the most serious of cases **(paras 19-56, recs 63-70)**. In implementing the recent recommendations for reforms in the system of appointing judges, the Lord Chancellor's Department should exercise vigilance to root out any indirect discrimination, hurry forward the substitution of assessment exercises for short interviews and establish and publish a clear policy

for the appointment of disabled persons to judicial office **(paras 65-88, recs 76-78)**. There should be a strengthening in the training provided to judges, appropriately enlarging the Judicial Studies Board's role for the purpose **(paras 89-97, rec 79)**. There should be a system of appraisal for all part-time judges, and consideration should be given to the appraisal of full-time judges **(paras 98-104, recs 80-82)**.

Decriminalisation and alternatives to conventional trial (Chapter 9 – pages 367-394, recs 140-151)

12. I have found little scope or justification for decriminalisation of conduct that Parliament has made subject to penal sanctions **(paras 1-6)**. There should, however, be greater use of a system of fixed penalty notices subject to a right of challenge in court, for example for television licence evasion and the existing provisions for road traffic offences **(paras 7-25, recs 140-142)**. There is no compelling case at present for the creation of any specialist courts, in particular, drugs or domestic violence courts **(paras 26-40*)*. Consideration should be given to the wider use of conditional cautioning or 'caution-plus' alongside existing and future restorative justice schemes, for which a national strategy should be devised **(paras 41-47 and 58-69, recs 143-144 and 150)**. Once the Financial Services Authority has assumed full responsibility for supervision in the financial services field, consideration should be given to transferring appropriate financial and market infringements from the criminal justice process to the Authority's regulatory and disciplinary control. Consideration should also be given in this field for combining parallel criminal and regulatory proceedings **(paras 48-57, recs 145-149)**. Preparatory work should be undertaken with a view to removal of all civil debt enforcement from courts exercising a criminal jurisdiction **(paras 70-77, rec 151)**.

Preparing for trial (Chapter10 – pages 395-513, recs 152-235)

13. The key to better preparation for, and efficient and effective disposal of, criminal cases is early identification of the issues. Four essentials are: strong and independent prosecutors; efficient and properly paid defence lawyers; ready access by defence lawyers to their clients in custody; and a modern communications system **(paras 1-34, recs 152-153)**. All public prosecutions should take the form of a charge, issued without reference to the courts but for which the prosecutor in all but minor, routine or urgent cases, would have initial responsibility. It should remain the basis of the case against a defendant regardless of the court which ultimately deals with his case, thus replacing the present mix of charges, summonses and indictments **(paras 35-63, recs 154-170)**. A graduated scheme of sentencing discounts should be introduced so that the earlier the plea of guilty the higher the discount for it. This should be

coupled with a system of advance indication of sentence for a defendant considering pleading guilty **(paras 91-114, recs 186-193)**.

14. The scheme of mutual disclosure established by the Criminal Procedure and Investigations Act 1996 should remain, but subject to the following reforms: its expression in a single and simply expressed instrument; a single and simple test of materiality for both stages of prosecution disclosure; automatic prosecution disclosure of certain documents; removal from the police to the prosecutor of such responsibility as the police have for identifying all potentially disclosable material; and encouragement, through professional conduct rules and otherwise, of the provision of adequate defence statements **(paras 115-184, recs 194-205)**. There should be a new statutory scheme for third party disclosure **(paras 185-190, rec 206)** and for instruction by the court of special independent counsel in public interest immunity cases where the court considers prosecution applications in the absence of the defendant **(paras 191-197, rec 207)**.

15. In the preparation for trial in all criminal courts, there should be a move away from plea and directions hearings and other forms of pre-trial hearings to cooperation between the parties according to standard time-tables, wherever necessary, seeking written directions from the court. In the Crown and District Divisions and, where necessary, in the Magistrates' Division, there should then be a written or electronic 'pre-trial assessment' by the court of the parties' readiness for trial. Only if the court or the parties are unable to resolve all matters in this way should there be a pre-trial hearing before or at the stage of the pre-trial assessment. The courts should have a general power to give binding directions and rulings either in writing or at pre-trial hearings **(paras 198-234, recs 208-221)**. In the Crown and District Divisions and, where necessary, in the Magistrates' Division, following the pre-trial assessment and in good time before hearing, the parties should prepare, for the approval of the judge and use by him, them, and the jury in the hearing, a written case and issues summary setting out in brief the substances of charge(s) and the issues to be resolved by the court **(para 235; see also Chapter 11, paras 15-24, recs 235-236)**.

The Trial: procedures and evidence (Chapter 11 – pages 514-610, recs 236-300)

16. In trials by judge and jury, the judge, by reference to the case and issues summary, copies of which should be provided to the jury, should give them a fuller introduction to the case than is now conventional **(paras 14-24, recs 235-236)**. The trial should broadly take the same form as at present, though with greater use of electronic aids in appropriate cases. The judge should sum up and direct the jury, making reference as appropriate to the case and issues summary. So far as possible, he should 'filter out' the law and fashion factual questions to

the issues and the law as he knows it to be. Where he considers it appropriate, he should require the jury publicly to answer each of the questions and to declare a verdict in accordance with those answers **(paras 25-55, recs 237-250***)***.

17. In trials by judge and magistrates in the District Division, the judge should be the sole judge of law, but he and the magistrates should together be the judges of fact, each having an equal vote. The order of proceedings would be broadly the same as in the Crown Division. The judge should rule on matters of law, procedure and inadmissibility of evidence in the absence of the magistrates where it would be potentially unfair to the defendant to do so in their presence. The judge should not sum up the case to the magistrates, but should retire with them to consider the court's decision, which he would give and publicly reason as a judgment of the court. The judge should be solely responsible for sentence **(paras 57-61, rec 251)**.

18. There should be a comprehensive review of the law of criminal evidence to identify and establish over-all and coherent principles and to make it an efficient and simple agent for securing justice. Subject to such review, I consider that the law should, in general, move away from technical rules of inadmissibility to trusting judicial and lay fact finders to give relevant evidence the weight it deserves. In particular, consideration should be given to the reform of the rules as to refreshing memory, the use of witness statements, hearsay, unfair evidence, previous misconduct of the defendant, similar fact evidence and the evidence of children **(paras 76-128, recs 254-261)**. There should be reforms to strengthen the quality and objectivity of expert evidence and improve the manner of its presentation both from the point of view of the court and experts, following in some respects reforms made in the civil sphere by the Civil Procedure Rules **(paras 129-151, recs 262-275)**. Urgent steps should be taken to increase the numbers and strengthen the quality of interpreters serving the criminal courts and to improve their working conditions **(paras 155-162, recs 276-286)**. There are a number of ways in which the facilities and procedures of the courts should or could be modernised and better serve the public **(paras 163-196, recs 287-295)**. The criminal courts should be equipped with an on-line sentencing information system **(paras 200-211, recs 296-299)**.

Appeals (Chapter 12 – pages 611-658, recs 301-328)

19. There should be the same tests for appeal against conviction and sentence respectively at all levels of appeal, namely those applicable for appeal to the Court of Appeal **(paras 5-13, and 45-46, recs 300-301)**. There should be a single line of appeal from the Magistrates' Division (Magistrates' Courts) and above to the Court of Appeal in all criminal matters. This would involve: 1) abolition of appeal from magistrates' courts to the Crown Court by way of rehearing and its replacement by an appeal to the Crown Division (Crown Court) constituted by a judge alone; and 2) abolition of appeal from magistrates' courts and/or the Crown Court to the High Court by way of a case stated or claim for

judicial review and their replacement by appeal to the Court of Appeal under its general appellate jurisdiction enlarged if and to the extent necessary **(paras 14-44, recs 302-307)**.

20. I support the general thrust of the Law Commission's recommendations for the introduction of statutory exceptions to the double jeopardy rule, save that a prosecutor's right of appeal against acquittal should not be limited to cases of murder and allied offences, but should extend to other grave offences punishable with life or long terms of imprisonment **(paras 47-65, recs 308-309)**. There should be provision for appeal by the defence or the prosecution against a special verdict of a jury which on its terms is perverse; see para 16 above **(paras 66-67, rec 310)**.

21. The Court of Appeal should be reconstituted and its procedures should be improved to enable it to deal more efficiently with, on the one hand appeals involving matters of general public importance or of particular complexity and, on the other, with 'straightforward' appeals **(paras 73-101, recs 311-321)**. The law should be amended: to widen the remit of the Sentencing Advisory Panel to include general principles of sentencing, regardless of the category of offence; and to enable the Court of Appeal to issue guidelines without having to tie them to a specific appeal before it **(paras 108-111, recs 324-325)**.

RECOMMENDATIONS

CHAPTER ONE   INTRODUCTION

Codification *(paras 35 – 36, pages 20 - 22)*

1. A Code of criminal law should be produced and maintained in four sections:

   - criminal offences;

   - criminal procedure;

   - criminal evidence; and

   - sentencing.

CHAPTER FOUR   MAGISTRATES

Introduction *(paras 1 – 14, pages 94 - 99)*

2. Magistrates and District Judges should continue to exercise summary jurisdiction.

Present working patterns *(para 18, pages 100 - 101)*

3. Whilst magistrates should continue to be appointed to one commission area, there should be a ready mechanism for enabling them, when required, to sit in adjoining areas.

The extent of summary jurisdiction *(para 20, pages 101 - 102)*

4. There should be no general change in the level of summary jurisdiction as it is presently defined, of District Judges or magistrates; though the matter may need review in the light of the Halliday recommendations for the introduction of a new sentencing framework, including combined custody and community sentence orders.

Deployment and allocation of work *(paras 21 – 49, pages 102 - 114)*

5. In the exercise of their summary jurisdiction:

   5.1 District Judges and magistrates should not routinely sit as mixed tribunals to deal with the general range or any particular type of case or form of proceeding, though there may be training and local 'cultural' advantages in their doing so from time to time depending on their respective availability and case loads;

   5.2 subject to changing workloads resulting from implementation of any of my recommendations or otherwise, there should be no significant change in the balance of numbers of District Judges and magistrates, or in the relative volumes or nature of summary work assigned to each of them; and

   5.3 summary work should continue to be allocated between District Judges and magistrates in accordance with the recommendations of the Venne Committee, namely that each, normally sitting separately, should be available to deal with the whole range, but that District Judges should concentrate on case allocation and management, cases of legal or factual complexity, cases of priority, such as those involving young offenders or offences of a sexual nature, and long cases.

Justices' Clerks *(paras 50 – 58, pages 114 - 119)*

6. District Judges should normally sit without a legal adviser.

7. There should be no extension of justices' clerks' case management jurisdiction.

Composition of the bench

Selection and appointment of magistrates (paras 80 – 86, pages 126 - 129)

8. Steps should be taken to provide benches of magistrates that reflect more broadly than at present the communities they serve by:

   8.1 reviewing the number, role and support given to them, including, in the event of the establishment of a unified Criminal Court, the present division of responsibility for them between the Lord Chancellor's Department and the Duchy of Lancaster;

   8.2 passing responsibility for determining the number of magistrates required for each commission area from local Advisory Committees to court staff in consultation with the chairman of each bench, the justices' clerks and, in the event of the establishment of a unified Criminal Court, also the Resident Judge;

   8.3 reviewing the community relations and educational initiatives of benches with a view better to inform the public of their work and to attract more suitable candidates for appointment;

8.4   in support of the local Advisory Committees, establishing a properly resourced National Recruitment Strategy aimed, not only at candidates for the magistracy, but also at their employers;

8.5   equipping local Advisory Committees with the information to enable them to submit for consideration for appointment, candidates that will produce and maintain benches broadly reflective of the communities they serve, including the establishment and maintenance of national and local data-bases of information on the make-up of the local community and on the composition of the local magistracy;

8.6   instituting a review of the ways in which the role and terms of service of a magistrate might be made more attractive and manageable to a wider range of the community than is presently the case; and

8.7   persisting with the current search for occupational and/or social groupings as a substitute for political affiliations as a measure of local balance.

9.   The Lord Chancellor should continue with – but keep under careful review – his present policy of not normally appointing certain persons who are close to the criminal justice system or who, by the nature of their occupation, could not commit themselves to sitting regularly, or whose character or association would make them undesirable for appointment.

District Judges (paras 87 – 90, pages 129 - 131)

10.   The Lord Chancellor should be more ready to take the initiative to assign a District Judge to an area where, having consulted as appropriate, he is of the view that local justice in the area requires it.

Training (paras 91 – 100, pages 131 - 134)

11.   The Judicial Studies Board should be made responsible, and be adequately resourced, for devising and securing the content and manner of training of all magistrates.

12.   Such training should, in the main, be provided at local level through trainers, ideally justices' clerks and/or legal advisers, appropriately trained for the purpose by the Board.

13.   District Judges should also be involved in the training of magistrates in the area or at the court centre at which they are normally based.

14.   The Magistrates' National Training Initiative scheme should be refined in order to provide a less complex, weighted set of competences for magistrates, supported by clear national standards.

15.   The Judicial Studies Board should establish systems to ensure that appraisal of magistrates takes place in a timely and effective manner across the country and that training programmes take account of the training needs identified during that process.

CHAPTER FIVE   JURIES

Composition of the jury

Size of the jury (paras 17 – 20, pages 142 - 143)

16. A system should be introduced for enabling judges in long cases, where they consider it appropriate, to swear alternate or reserve jurors to meet the contingency of a jury otherwise being reduced in number by discharge for illness or any other reason of necessity.

Qualification for jury service (paras 21 – 24, pages 143 - 145)

17. There should be no change in the present statutory criteria for qualification for jury service, save as to registration, as distinct from entitlement to registration, on an electoral roll.

18. The law should be amended to substitute for the condition of registration on an electoral roll, inclusion in such a roll and/or on any one or more of a number of other specified publicly maintained lists or directories, but excluding anyone listed who, on investigation at the summons stage, is found not to be entitled to registration as an elector.

Enforcement of jury service (paras 25 – 26, pages 145 - 146)

19. There should be rigorous and well publicised enforcement of the obligation to undertake jury service when required, and consideration should be given to doing so by way of a system of fixed penalties subject to a right of appeal to the magistrates.

Ineligibility (paras 27 – 34, pages 146 -149)

20. Everyone should be eligible for jury service, save for the mentally ill, and the law should be amended accordingly.

21. There should be no change to the categories of those disqualified from jury service.

Excusals as of right and discretionary excusal (paras 35 – 40, pages 149 152)

22. Save for those who have recently undertaken, or have been excused by a court from, jury service, no-one should be excusable from jury service as of right, only on showing good reason for excusal.

23. The Central Summoning Bureau or the court, in examining a claim for discretionary excusal, should consider its power of deferral first.

24. The Bureau should treat all subsequent applications for deferral and all applications for excusal against clear criteria identified in the jury summons.

Random selection

Ethnic minority representation on juries (paras 52 – 62, pages 156 - 159)

25. A scheme should be devised, along the lines that I have outlined in Chapter 5, paragraphs 60 and 61, for cases in which the court considers that race is likely to be relevant to an issue of importance in the case, for the selection of a jury consisting of, say, up to three people from any ethnic minority group.

Verdicts

Jury research (paras 76 – 87, pages 164 - 168)

26. There should be no amendment of section 8 of the Contempt of Court Act 1981 to enable research into individual juries' deliberations.

27. Careful consideration should be given to existing research material throughout the common law world on jury trial in criminal cases, with a view to identifying and responding appropriately to all *available* information about how juries arrive at their verdicts.

28. If and to the extent that such research material is insufficient, consideration should be given to jury research of a general nature that does not violate the 1981 Act.

The unreasoned verdict (paras 88 – 98, pages 168 - 173)

29. Section 8 of the Contempt of Court Act 1981 should be amended to permit, where appropriate, enquiry by the trial judge and/or the Court of Appeal (Criminal Division) into alleged impropriety by a jury, whether in the course of its deliberations or otherwise.

Perverse verdicts (paras 99 – 108, pages 173 - 176)

30. The law should be declared, by statute, if need be, that juries have no right to acquit defendants in defiance of the law or in disregard of the evidence, and that judges and advocates should conduct criminal cases accordingly.

Trial of cases on indictment without a jury

Defendant's option for trial by judge alone (paras 110 – 118, pages 177 - 181)

31. Defendants, with the consent of the court, after hearing representations from both sides, should be able to opt for trial by judge alone in all cases tried on indictment (whether, as now, in the Crown Court or, if my recommendations in Chapter 7 for a new unified Criminal Court are adopted, in the Crown or District Divisions).

32.   In all 'either-way' cases, magistrates' courts, not defendants, should determine venue after representation from the parties.

33.   In the event of a dispute on the issue, a District Judge should decide.

34.   The defence and the prosecution should have a right of appeal on paper from any mode of trial decision on which they were at issue to a Circuit Judge nominated for the purpose, and provision should be made for the speedy hearing of such appeals.

35.   The procedure of committal of 'either-way' cases to the Crown Court for trial should be abolished and, pending the introduction of a system of allocation as part of my recommendations in Chapter 7 for a new unified Criminal Court, such cases should be "sent" to the Crown Court in the same way as indictable-only cases.

36.   The procedure of committal for sentence should be abolished.

Fraud and other complex cases (paras 173 – 206, pages 200 - 214)

37.   As an alternative to trial by judge and jury in serious and complex fraud cases, the nominated trial judge should be empowered to direct trial by himself sitting with lay members or, where the defendant has opted for trial by judge alone, by himself alone.

38.   The category of cases to which such a direction might apply should, in the first instance, be frauds of seriousness or complexity within sections 4 and 7 of the Criminal Justice Act 1987.

39.   The overriding criterion for directing trial without jury should be the interests of justice.

40.   Either party should have a right of appeal against such decision to the Court of Appeal (Criminal Division).

41.   Judges trying such cases, by whatever form of procedure, should be specially nominated for the purpose as now, and provided with a thorough, structured and continuing training for it.

42.   There should be a panel of experts, established and maintained by the Lord Chancellor in consultation with professional and other bodies, from which lay members may be selected for trials.

43.   The nominated trial judge should select the lay members after affording the parties an opportunity to make written representations as to their suitability.

44.   Lay members should be paid appropriately for their service.

45.   In a court consisting of a judge and lay members, the judge should be the sole judge of law, procedure, admissibility of evidence and as to sentence; as to conviction, all three should be the judges of fact.

46.   The decision of a court so constituted should wherever possible be unanimous, but a majority of any two could suffice for a conviction.

47. The judge should give the court's decision by a public and fully reasoned judgment.

Young defendants *(paras 207 – 211, pages 214 - 217)*

48. All cases involving young defendants who are presently committed to the Crown Court for trial or for sentence should in future be put before the youth court consisting, as appropriate, of a High Court Judge, Circuit Judge or Recorder sitting with at least two experienced magistrates and exercising the full jurisdiction of the present Crown Court for this purpose.

49. The only possible exception should be those cases in which the young defendant is charged jointly with an adult and it is considered necessary in the interests of justice for them to be tried together.

50. The youth court so constituted should be entitled, save where it considers that public interest demands otherwise, to hear such cases in private, as in the youth court exercising its present jurisdiction.

Fitness to plead *(paras 212 – 213, pages 217 - 218)*

51. Legislation should be introduced to require a judge, not a jury, to determine the issue of fitness to plead.

Information for and treatment of jurors

Information (paras 217 – 220, pages 219 - 221)

52. The essential parts of the jury summons and explanatory documents issued by the Central Summoning Bureau should be expressed in several languages, and over-all, the documentation should be more informative and couched in a more informal and friendly tone than at present.

53. The Court Service should review the adequacy of the information courts provide to potential jurors against the best provided by other jurisdictions.

Length and frequency of service (paras 221 – 224, pages 221 - 223)

54. There should be an urgent review of the machinery, as between the Central Summoning Bureau and the courts, for summoning jurors who may be called upon to serve on long case.

55. There should be an examination and piloting of options for shortening the length of jury service by introducing as an aim a one day or one trial system or a variation of it.

56. Consideration should be given to lengthening the cycle over which it is possible to claim excusal by reason of previous jury service.

Facilities (para 225, page 223)

57. The Court Service should press on with its present programme to improve court facilities for jurors and jurors in waiting, including those who are disabled.

58. As a matter of urgency, it should also institute a programme of provision at all courts of adequate working facilities and other means to enable jurors in waiting to conduct their own affairs.

Compensation (para 226, page 224)

59. There should be a review of the amounts of allowances payable to jurors for their attendance at court.

60. Consideration should be given to an additional allowance to cover the cost to potential jurors who, but for it, could justifiably claim excusal because of caring responsibilities.

CHAPTER SIX   THE JUDICIARY

The judicial hierarchy

Recorders (paras 14 – 16, pages 231 - 232)

61. It should be a condition of a Recorder's appointment to sit for a minimum of three weeks a year in one continuous block, unless for exceptional reasons a Presiding Judge permits him to sit in more than one block.

62. The Judicial Group in the Lord Chancellor's Department should, in consultation with the Presiding Judges, liaise closely with the Court Service to ensure that a minimum of three weeks' annual sitting is provided for each Recorder.

Matching judges to cases

'Ticketing' (paras 20 – 25, pages 234 - 237)

63. Most of the rigidities of the present 'ticketing' system should be removed and replaced by the conferment on Resident Judges wide responsibility, subject to general oversight of the Presiding Judges, for allocation of judicial work at their court centres, but coupled with:

   63.1 regular and systematic appraisal enabling Resident Judges and Presiding Judges to determine the experience and interests of the judges; and

   63.2 the undertaking by judges of such training by the Judicial Studies Board as may be required as a pre-condition for the trial of particular categories of work.

Circuit listing *(paras 26 – 43, pages 237 - 243)*

64. Consideration should be given to reducing the formal legal vacation periods for High Court Judges sitting in the Crown Court, in particular, to confining the summer vacation to the month of August.

65. This should be achieved by greater staggering of the existing sitting commitments of the High Court Bench, not by increasing them.

66. The systems of appointment and assignment of judges should be reviewed with a view to achieving a more efficient system than now obtains to ensure a planned and prompt succession of Resident Judges and appropriately experienced judges at court centres and, for this purpose, the Presiding Judges, Resident Judges, and Circuit Administrators should be consulted regularly.

67. The Lord Chancellor's Department should agree targets with the Presiding Judges within which vacancies for Resident, Circuit and District Judges should be filled after it has received notification of projected or actual vacancy.

Better matching of judges to cases *(paras 44 – 56, pages 243 - 249)*

68. There should be a formal and significant shift in the balance of heavy circuit work from High Court Judges to the more experienced Circuit Judges, coupled with greater flexibility in the system of allocating work between them, along the following lines:

   68.1 all work within the jurisdiction of the Crown Court should be triable by a Circuit Judge unless, on referral to a Presiding Judge, he specially reserves it for trial by a High Court Judge;

   68.2 the listing officer should draw to the attention of the Resident Judge any case which in accordance with criteria set by the Lord Chief Justice may be appropriate for reservation to a High Court Judge, for the Resident Judge, if he agrees, to refer it to one of the Presiding Judges for his decision; and

   68.3 the overriding criterion for reservation for trial by a High Court Judge should be whether "the case is one of special complexity and/or seriousness and/or public importance requiring trial by a High Court Judge".

69. The formal 'tiering' of court centres for the trial of certain classes of cases should be abolished and replaced by a more flexible system, overseen by the Presiding Judges, for the assignment of cases, adapted to the needs of each circuit and the work, and having regard to the physical constraints and convenience of location of different courts.

70. Save for the Presiding Judges, the present regular pattern of circuiteering by High Court Judges should be replaced by one under which the Presiding Judges decide, in consultation with their Circuit Administrators, where and when cases specifically reserved to High Court Judges should be tried.

Judicial administration *(paras 57 – 59, pages 249 - 250)*

71. Adequate time should be given to:

   71.1 judges to enable them to manage and prepare cases assigned to them; and

71.2   judges with additional administrative responsibilities to enable them to fulfil those responsibilities.

72.   In each case suitable provision should be made in secretarial, administrative or clerical help, as may be appropriate, to meet those needs.

Judges' lodgings *(paras 60 – 64, pages 250 - 252)*

73.   Future use of judges' lodgings should depend on the future volume and pattern of distribution of High Court Judge work on each circuit, not the other way round.

74.   In assessing the future volume and pattern of circuit High Court Judge work, allowance should also be made for present and projected needs of civil and family work and the development of intermittent provincial administrative law and appellate jurisdictions.

75.   If my recommendations are adopted for confining High Court Judge work on circuit to the gravest cases and for greater flexibility as to where and when they should be tried:

75.1   lodgings that are reasonable value for money, taking into account among other things their convenience to major court centres and the number of judges they normally accommodate and for how long, should be retained or obtained; and

75.2   in other cases consideration should be given to suitable alternative accommodation appropriate to length of sitting and type of case[s], for example, hotels, guest houses of the Wolsey Lodge variety and rented and serviced accommodation.

Composition of the judiciary

Appointment to judicial office (paras 68 – 87, pages 254 - 262)

76.   The risk of indirect discrimination in those cases where the candidates for judicial appointment may not have had much exposure in the consultation process, notably women, ethnic minorities and solicitors is the most constantly raised and anxious concern of those who feel that the appointments system is unfair to them.   It is not enough to wait for the professions to present the Lord Chancellor's Department with suitably 'visible' as well as qualified candidates for appointment.   He should vigorously pursue his declared policy of consulting as widely as possible in all cases.

77.   If the assessment centre pilot proposed by the Lord Chancellor proves to be successful, consideration should be given to extending its use to other full and part-time judicial appointment procedures.

Disability (para 88, pages 262 - 263)

78.   The Lord Chancellor's Department should establish and publish clear guidelines on the appointment of disabled persons to judicial office.

Training and appraisal

Training (paras 89 – 97, pages 263 - 266)

79.   The Judicial Studies Board should be adequately resourced to meet the increasing training needs of the judiciary, including those in respect of special jurisdictions, case management, information technology and judicial administration.

Appraisal (paras 98 – 104, pages 266 - 268)

80.   An appraisal scheme should be introduced for all part-time judicial post-holders, and reinforced by a system of regular self-appraisal.

81.   The assessments produced should be available to those advising the Lord Chancellor on full-time judicial appointments.

82.   Consideration should be given, following wide consultation among the judiciary and others, to a system of appraisal for full-time judges; the results of such assessments should, however, only exceptionally be made available to anyone other than the Presiding Judges or the relevant Head of Division.

CHAPTER SEVEN   A UNIFIED CRIMINAL COURT

A unified Criminal Court *(paras 2 – 35, pages 270 - 281)*

83.   A unified Criminal Court should be established.

84.   There should be three levels of jurisdiction within the unified Criminal Court consisting of: the Crown Division to exercise jurisdiction over all indictable-only matters and such 'either-way' cases as are allocated to it; the District Division to exercise jurisdiction over such 'either-way' matters as are allocated to it; and the Magistrates' Division to exercise jurisdiction over all summary-only matters and such 'either-way' cases as are allocated to it.

85.   The Crown and Magistrates' Divisions should be constituted as are the Crown Court and magistrates' courts respectively, and the District Division should consist of a judge, in the main a District Judge, and at least two experienced magistrates (or if a defendant with the consent of the court so opts, of a judge alone).

86.   The District Division's jurisdiction over 'either-way' offences should be limited to those within a likely maximum sentence in the circumstances of the case viewed at its worst (as distinct from the legal maximum for a case or cases of that category) of, say, two years custody, a maximum financial penalty to be determined and/or a maximum of community, or combination of custody and community, sentences to be determined in the light of future reforms of the sentencing framework.

87.   The District Division, sitting as a youth court, should also try grave cases against young defendants presently dealt with in the Crown Court; see recommendation 48.

The allocation of cases *(paras 36 – 40, pages 281 - 283)*

88.   All cases should have an allocation hearing in the Magistrates' Division at which pleas should be taken.

89.   All cases triable only summarily should remain in the Magistrates' Division and all cases triable only on indictment should be sent to the Crown Division.

90.   The court should allocate all 'either-way' cases according to the seriousness of the alleged offence and the circumstances of the defendant in accordance with statutory and broadly drawn criteria, looking at the case at its worst from the point of view of the defendant and bearing in mind the jurisdiction of each division.

91.   Where there is no dispute or uncertainty as to venue, magistrates should allocate the case; otherwise a District Judge should do so after hearing representations on the matter from both parties.

92.   The Government should ensure, as a matter of urgency, routine provision, through an integrated system of information technology or otherwise, of complete and accurate information of a defendant's criminal record at all allocation hearings.

93.   Where there are linked charges and/or defendants, all should normally be allocated to the division with jurisdiction to hear the most serious of the charges.

94.   The defence and the prosecution should have a right of appeal on paper from a contested allocation decision to a Circuit Judge nominated for the purpose, and provision should be made for speedy hearing of such appeals.

95.   The defence and the prosecution should be able, up to a specified point before trial, to seek re-allocation in the light of any material change in the circumstances of the alleged offence(s) and/or of the defendant between allocation and trial.

The circuits *(paras 41 – 49, pages 283 - 287)*

96.   For the foreseeable future circuit boundaries and administrations should remain broadly as they are.

97.   Each circuit should continue to have Presiding Judges, Chancery Supervisory and Family Liaison Judges and a Circuit Administrator undertaking their present respective functions, so that the Circuit Administrator continues to act as the focal point of contact for them.

98.   Whatever changes are contemplated for the administrative organisation of the circuits, a decision should first be made whether to replace the present dual system of courts with a unified Criminal Court paying close attention to the

needs of the civil and family jurisdictions outside London as well as to those of crime.

99. There should be a review from time to time of the appropriateness of the South Eastern Circuit remaining one circuit, taking into account, among other things, its size and the special needs of Greater London.

A new management structure *(paras 50 – 73, pages 287 - 295)*

100. A single centrally funded executive agency, as part of Lord Chancellor's Department, should be responsible for the administration of all courts, civil, criminal and family (save for the Appellate Committee of the House of Lords), replacing the Court Service and Magistrates' Courts Committees.

101. The agency should be headed by a national board and chief executive.

102. Within each circuit the criminal courts should, if consistent with the efficient and effective operation of civil and family courts, be organised managerially on the basis of the 42 criminal justice areas.

103. Implementation of national policy and management at local level for all three jurisdictions should be the responsibility of local managers working in close liaison with local judges and magistrates, much as the Circuit Administrators and Presiding Judges, Chancery Supervisory and Family Liaison Judges do at circuit level.

The future role of the justices' clerk (para 74, pages 295 - 295)

104. In a unified Criminal Court:

104.1 justices' clerks should continue to be responsible for the legal advice provided to magistrates;

104.2 arrangements should be made to ensure that, in the absence of the justices' clerk, magistrates at each courthouse have ready access to a senior legal adviser; and

104.3 justices' clerks should not normally exercise administrative responsibilities unrelated to their role as legal adviser to the magistrates.

Judicial management *(paras 75 – 83, pages 296 - 300)*

105. In a unified Criminal Court:

105.1 Resident Judges should be responsible, under the oversight of the Presiding Judges, for judicial management of court centres;

105.2 in relation to the District Bench and magistracy, these responsibilities should include oversight of: listing; membership of panels; case allocation; training and development; and appraisal;

105.3 Resident Judges should be provided with the necessary time out of court and degree of administrative and other support to carry out these additional responsibilities;

105.4 there should be consequential reviews of the number and location of Resident Judges, and also of their remuneration; and

105.5 the future organisation and structure of the District Bench should be reviewed in the light of these changes.

Court accommodation *(paras 84 – 90, pages 300 - 304)*

106. If my recommendations in Chapter 8 for a national Criminal Justice Board and local Criminal Justice Boards are accepted, decisions as to the provision and closure of court centres should become the responsibility of local Boards, subject to oversight and guidance of the national Board.

107. Decisions should be made in the interests of all involved in the criminal justice process in their areas, and with the benefit of a cost/benefit exercise taking the public interest in its widest sense into account.

108. There should be a review of all accommodation of the courts and criminal justice agencies to enable a joint assessment of the most efficient use for the system as a whole of available accommodation and planning for future needs.

109. In the planning and provision of court accommodation, proper allowance should be made for the fact that a just and efficient criminal justice system does not require all courtrooms to be in use full-time.

110. In the planning and provision of court accommodation, a significant tolerance should be allowed for the high volatility of demands on court time and the uncertainties of future criminal justice policy initiatives (that is, "an adequate tolerance over assumed full capacity").

111. A new Criminal Court Design Guide should be prepared as a standard to which, over time, court buildings should conform.

Information technology *(paras 91 – 102, pages 304 - 308)*

112. A single information technology system should be developed for the unified Criminal Court, combining the best design elements of all the systems currently under development in the magistrates' courts and Crown Court and taking into account corresponding developments in the civil and family jurisdictions.

113. The management of the implementation of information technology for a unified Criminal Court should be under the supervision of a Board upon which the judiciary are represented, and should be undertaken in close consultation with the Judicial Technology Group.

114. Planning and implementation of procedural reforms should go hand in hand with development and introduction of the necessary supporting information technology.

Security *(paras 103 – 116, pages 309 - 314)*

115. The Lord Chancellor should, as a matter of urgency, take direct responsibility for and control of security of courts of all levels and jurisdictions.

116. Those invested with a duty of providing security should have the same powers in all criminal courts.

117. Consideration should be given to requiring the police to resume provision of security in all criminal courts, or to the establishment of a uniformed Sheriff Officer Service which would be fully trained, have police powers and would operate under the general oversight of the local judiciary.

118. There should be a review of the necessary provision, in terms of accommodation, technology and otherwise, to protect vulnerable witnesses and others at court, and to enable the former where appropriate and necessary to give their evidence by video-link away from the court.

119. In the event of my recommendations in Chapter 8 being adopted, the extent of and financial responsibility for security provided in the Criminal Court should become a joint criminal justice responsibility exercised by the Criminal Justice Board on behalf of Ministers.

Inspection *(para 117, page 314)*

120. If, in accordance with my recommendations, a unified Criminal Court and single supporting administrative agency are established, there should be created an independent Inspectorate of that agency, which should report to the Lord Chancellor.

CHAPTER EIGHT   THE CRIMINAL JUSTICE SYSTEM

Managing criminal justice *(paras 43 – 77, pages 330 - 346)*

121. A Criminal Justice Board should replace the Strategic Planning Group, the national Trials Issues Group and its sub-groups, and take over such responsibilities of the Criminal Justice Consultative Council as may be operational.

122. The Criminal Justice Board should be responsible for over-all direction of the criminal justice system, with a remit including, but not limited to:

- planning and setting criminal justice system objectives;

- budgeting and the allocation of funds;

- securing the national and local achievement of its objectives;

- the development and implementation of an integrated system of information technology;

- research and development; and

- combating inequality and discrimination throughout the criminal justice system.

123. The Board should be chaired by an independent chairman and its membership should include senior civil servants from the three main criminal justice departments and the Treasury, the Chairman of the Youth Justice Board, Chief Officers of the Criminal Case Management Agency, the unified Criminal Court, Police, Prison and Probation Services and a small number of non-executive members.

124. The Board should not include a judge, but should consult regularly with the Lord Chief Justice and other senior judiciary.

125. The Board should be supported by a secretariat and a national administrative structure accountable to it and be responsible for developing a system of information technology for the whole criminal justice system.

126. Local Criminal Justice Boards should replace the Area Strategy Committees, local TIGs, Chief Officer Groups and, where they exist, informally constituted local Criminal Justice Boards, and should draw on their memberships.

127. Local Criminal Justice Boards should be responsible for giving effect at local level to the national Criminal Justice Board's directions and objectives and for management of the criminal justice system in their areas.

128. Membership of the local Boards should include: local managers of the Criminal Court, the Prison Service and the National Health Service; the local Chief Constable; the local Chief Crown Prosecutor; the local Chief Probation Officer; representatives from the Youth Offenders Team, Victim Support, possibly representatives of the local Bar and solicitors and at least two non-executive members.

129. Each local Board should be provided with a dedicated and properly resourced secretariat accountable to the national secretariat, be provided with a joint local budget and should select its own chairman.

Advising on criminal justice *(paras 78 – 88, pages 346 - 351)*

130. The Criminal Justice Consultative Committee should be replaced with a Criminal Justice Council with a statutory power and duty, and suitably equipped:

- to keep the criminal justice system under review;

- to advise the Government on the form and manner of implementation of all proposed criminal justice reforms and to make proposals to it for reform;

- to provide general oversight of the programme and structures for introduction and maintenance of codification of substantive criminal law, procedure, evidence and sentencing that I recommend in Chapter 1;

- to advise the Government on the framing and implementation of a communication and education strategy for the criminal justice system; and

- for any of those purposes, to consult and/or commission programmes of research.

131. Before initiating key proposals for reform of the criminal justice system, the Government should be statutorily obliged to refer them to the Council for advice and to take account of any proposals or advice tendered by it in response to such reference or of its own accord.

132. The Council should be chaired by the Lord Chief Justice or a senior Lord Justice of Appeal and composed of judges of all levels, magistrates, criminal practitioners,representatives of the key agencies and organisations involved in the criminal justice process and one or more distinguished legal academics specialising in the field (none of whom should be members of the Criminal Justice Board).

133. The Council should be provided with a properly resourced secretariat and research staff.

134. Such of the Criminal Justice Consultative Council's functions as relate to the development and improvement of inter-agency co-ordination, through the Area Strategy Committees and otherwise, of national policies and objectives should become the responsibility of the Criminal Justice Board and its administrative support structure.

135. The Area Strategy Committees should cease to exist.

Joint inspection *(paras 89 – 91, pages 351 - 352)*

136. A Joint Inspection Unit should be formally established under the collective control of the Criminal Justice Chief Inspectors and be given sufficient resources to instigate and co-ordinate a programme of cross-agency inspection.

Information technology *(paras 92 – 114, pages 352 - 366)*

137. The Criminal Justice Board should discontinue the IBIS project of linking up the six main information technology systems in the criminal justice system, and should instead, within a set timescale, produce an implementation plan for an integrated information technology system for the whole of the criminal justice system based upon a common language and common electronic case files.

138. The implementation of an integrated system of information technology should be organised in six projects, to run either in parallel or sequentially, namely:

- case tracking;

- management information;

- unification of data;

- extending the categories of user;

- case management; and

- unification of enabling technologies.

139. A Criminal Case Management Agency should be established, to be accountable to the Criminal Justice Board for managing the implementation

of the integrated system and, when implemented, managing those elements of the system that require central management, namely:

- production of system protocols and quality assurance of system data;

- management and monitoring of case progression;

- data standards for system management information;

- standards and protocols for access by victims, witnesses, defendants and their representatives;

- storage and maintenance of data;

- data security and control of access to data; and

- case management at the system level.

CHAPTER NINE	DECRIMINALISATION AND ALTERNATIVES TO CONVENTIONAL TRIAL

Summary prosecutions

Television licence evasion (paras 10 – 13, pages 369 - 371)

140. The use of a television without a licence should remain a criminal offence, but should be dealt with in the first instance by a fixed penalty notice discounted for prompt purchase of a licence and payment of penalty, and subject to the defendant's right to dispute guilt in court.

Other summary matters (20 – 25, pages 371 - 375)

141. Fixed penalty notices should be used in respect of all offences provided for in the Road Traffic Offenders Act 1988, Part III and Schedule 3, unless there are special circumstances requiring the offender to attend court.

142. There should be a systematic review leading to similar fixed penalty and/or notice-to-correct schemes for a wider range of infringements that are presently the subject of criminal prosecution.

Alternative procedures

'Caution-plus' (paras 41 – 47, pages 380 - 381)

143. Consideration should be given to the introduction of a conditional cautioning scheme over a wide range of minor offences, enabling the prosecutor with the consent of the offender and, where appropriate, with the approval of the court:

- to caution him subject to his compliance with specified conditions; and

- to bring the conditionally cautioned offender before the court in the event of his failure to comply with the conditions.

144. In considering the introduction of such a scheme, regard should be had to its place alongside existing provisions for avoiding or modifying the criminal process and future developments in the form of 'restorative justice', with a view to over-all rationalisation into a single scheme.

Regulatory enforcement (paras 48 – 51, pages 383 - 384)

145. Once the Financial Services Authority has assumed full responsibility for supervision in the financial services field, consideration should be given to transferring appropriate financial and market infringements from the criminal justice process to its regulatory and disciplinary control.

Parallel proceedings (paras 52 – 55, pages 384 - 386)

146. Consideration should be given, for appropriate cases of parallel proceedings, to combining the criminal justice and regulatory processes, with a judge as the common president, and with lay members or expert assessors for the second and regulatory part.

147. In cases of fraud and other financial offences courts should, wherever possible and appropriate, exercise their existing powers of a regulatory nature as part of their sentencing disposal.

148. Consideration should be given, in appropriate offences, to enlarging or extending the courts' conventional sentencing powers in this respect.

149. In the exercise of such powers courts should be assisted by counsel on behalf of the parties, properly instructed for the purpose.

Restorative justice *(paras 58 – 69, pages 387 - 391)*

150. A national strategy should be developed and implemented to ensure consistent, appropriate and effective use of restorative justice techniques across England and Wales.

Enforcement of civil debts *(paras 70 – 77, pages 392 - 394)*

151. Preparatory work should be undertaken with a view to the removal, in due course, of all civil debt enforcement from courts exercising a criminal jurisdiction.

CHAPTER TEN   PREPARING FOR TRIAL

Essentials

A strong and independent prosecutor (para 12, page 399)

152. The Crown Prosecution Service should be given greater legal powers, in particular the power to determine the initial charge, and sufficient resources to

enable it to take full and effective control of cases from the charge or pre-charge stage, as appropriate.

Efficient and properly paid defence lawyers (paras 13 – 27, pages 400 - 404)

153.   Urgent consideration should be given to changing the structure of public funding of defence fees in the criminal courts so as properly to reward and encourage adequate and timely preparation of cases for disposal on pleas of guilty or by trial, rather than discourage such preparation as it perversely does at present.

Identifying the issues

The charge (paras 35 – 45, pages 408 - 413)

154.   The Crown Prosecution Service should determine the charge in all but minor, routine offences or where, because of the circumstances, there is a need for a holding charge before seeking the advice of the Service.

155.   In minor, routine cases in which the police charge without first having sought the advice of the Service, they should apply the same evidential test as that governing the Service in the Code for Crown Prosecutors.

156.   Where the police have preferred a holding charge, and in other than minor, routine offences, a prosecutor should review and, if necessary, reformulate the charge at the earliest possible opportunity.

157.   'Minor' or 'routine' offences for this purpose should be identified in the Criminal Procedure Code that I have recommended or in other primary or subsidiary legislation.

Private prosecutions (paras 46 – 50, pages 413 - 414)

158.   The right of private prosecution should continue, subject to the power of the Director of Public Prosecutions, on learning of a private prosecution, to take it over and discontinue it.

159.   Any court before which a private prosecution is initiated should be under a duty forthwith to notify the Director of it in writing.

160.   The Director, in deciding whether to discontinue a private prosecution that he has taken over, should apply the public interest test as well as the evidential test set out in the Code for Crown Prosecutors.

Consent to the charge (paras 51 – 52, pages 415 - 416)

161.   The Law Commission's recommendation to remove the requirement for the Attorney General's or Director of Public Prosecution's consent to prosecution should be adopted, save in those categories of case where its retention clearly protects the public interest.

Mechanics of charging (paras 53 – 63, pages 416 - 422)

162. All public prosecutions should take the form of a charge, issued without reference to the courts, which should remain the basis of the accusation against the defendant throughout all stages of the case, irrespective of the level of court in which it is tried.

163. The charge may be oral or in writing, a written copy or original, as the case may be, being served manually or by postal service.

164. In either case, under arrangements with the court's administration, the charge should specify the date of first attendance at court on pain of arrest on warrant.

165. The present procedure for application for a warrant, by swearing an oath as to service of process, in summary offences should be abolished and replaced by paper application considered and determined in open court.

166. The same regime for commencing proceedings should apply to private prosecutions, save that: 1) the charge should only be administered in writing; 2) it should be subject to the prior permission of the court; 3) the permission should be endorsed on the charge sheet by an officer of the court; and 4) the court, before listing the matter, should notify the Director of Public Prosecutions.

167. The voluntary bill of indictment should be abolished and, to the extent necessary under new procedures of allocation of work in a unified Criminal Court, safeguards should be introduced to secure the interests of justice by Criminal Procedure Rules.

168. The form of charge should be common to summary and indictable offences.

169. The prosecution should be entitled to amend the charge up to the pre-trial assessment date (or in a summary trial without such an assessment, up to a date to be specified), but thereafter only with the permission of the trial court.

170. The procedure for issue of warrants should be simplified.

Dropping the prosecution *(paras 64 – 68, pages 422 - 424)*

171. The law should be amended to provide a form of procedure common to all courts to enable a prosecutor, without the consent of the defendant or the approval of the court, to discontinue proceedings at any stage before close of the prosecution case on trial.

172. In the event of the prosecution discontinuing at any time before pre-trial assessment or, where there is no pre-trial assessment, before a stage to be specified, the prosecution should be entitled to reinstate the prosecution, subject to the court's power to stay it as an abuse of process.

173. In the event of the prosecution discontinuing after that stage, the defendant should be entitled to an acquittal, save where the court for good reason permits the prosecution to 'lie on the file'.

174. There should be common provision for all courts, subject to their approval and the agreement of the parties, to give formal effect to such discontinuance and, where appropriate, acquittal in the absence of the parties.

Bail *(paras 69 – 82, pages 424 - 431)*

175. Magistrates and judges in all courts should take more time to consider matters of bail.

176. Listing practices should reflect the necessity to devote due time to bail applications and allow the flexibility required for all parties to gather sufficient information for the court to make an appropriate decision.

177. Courts, the police, prosecutors and defence representatives should be provided with better information for the task than they are at present, in particular, complete and up to date information of the defendant's record held on the Police National Computer, relevant probation or other social service records, if any, verified information about home living conditions and employment, if any, and sufficient information about the alleged offence and its relationship, if any, to his record so as to indicate whether there is a pattern of offending.

178. Courts and all relevant agencies should be equipped with a common system of information technology, as recommended in Chapter 8, to facilitate the ready availability to all who need it of the above information.

179. There should be appropriate training for magistrates and judges in the making of bail decisions, with Article 5 ECHR and risk assessment particularly in mind, as the Law Commission has proposed.

180. All courts should be provided with an efficient bail information and support scheme.

181. Bail notices should be couched in plain English, printed and given to the defendant as a formal court order when the bail decision is made, so that he understands exactly what is required of him and appreciates the seriousness of the grant of bail and of any attached conditions.

182. All courts should be diligent in adopting the Law Commission's proposals for the recording of bail decisions in such a way as to indicate clearly how they have been reached.

Appeals against bail decisions (paras 83 – 90, pages 431 - 434)

183. The right of application to a High Court Judge for bail after determination by any criminal court exercising its original or appellate jurisdiction should be removed, and there should be substituted therefor a right of appeal from the District Division or Crown Division (Crown Court) on a point of law only.

184. Defendants should have a right of appeal against conditional grants of bail in the Magistrates' Division (magistrates' courts) to the Crown Division (Crown Court) in respect of conditions imposed as to their residence away from home and/or to the provision of a surety or sureties or the giving of security.

185. The prosecution should have a right of appeal to the Crown Division against the grant of bail by the Magistrates' Division (magistrates' courts) in respect

of all offences that would, on conviction, be punishable by a custodial, or partly custodial sentence.

Advance indication of sentence *(paras 91 – 114, pages 434 - 444)*

186. There should be introduced, by way of a judicial sentencing guideline for later incorporation in a Sentencing Code, a system of sentencing discounts graduated so that the earlier the tender of plea of guilty the higher the discount for it, coupled with a system of advance indication of sentence for a defendant considering pleading guilty.

187. On the request of a defendant, through his advocate, the judge should be entitled formally to indicate the maximum sentence in the event of a plea of guilty at that stage and the possible sentence on conviction following a trial.

188. The request to the judge and all related subsequent proceedings should be in court, in the presence of the prosecution, the defendant and his advisers and a court reporter, but otherwise in private, and should be fully recorded.

189. The judge should enquire, by canvassing the matter with both advocates, as to the mental competence and emotional state of the defendant and as to whether he might be under any pressure falsely to admit guilt.

190. The prosecution and defence should be equipped to put before the judge all relevant information about the offence(s) and the defendant, including any pre-sentence or other reports and any victim impact statement, to enable the judge to give an indication.

191. The judge should only give an indication if and when he is satisfied that he has sufficient information and if he considers it appropriate to do so.

192. Where, as a result of such an indication, a defendant's advocate indicates to the judge that he wishes to plead guilty, the judge should, by questioning the defendant direct, satisfy himself that the defendant understands the effect of his proposed plea, that it would be true and that it would be voluntary.

193. The judge should be bound by his indication, as should any other judge before whom the defendant may appear for sentence, on the consequent plea of guilty.

Disclosure

Advance disclosure by the prosecution (paras 117 – 120, pages 445 - 447)

194. There should be a single set of statutory rules imposing on the prosecution in all cases a duty to provide its proposed evidence in sufficient time to enable the defence adequately to prepare for trial, the precise timescale to be prescribed by rules.

Disclosure of unused material and defence statement (paras 121 – 184, pages 447 - 474)

195. The Criminal Procedure and Investigations Act 1996 scheme of material disclosure should be retained, in particular, two stages of prosecution

disclosure under which the second stage is informed by and conditional on a defence statement indicating the issues that the defendant proposes to take at trial.

196. The present mix of primary and subsidiary legislation, Code, Guidelines and Instructions should be replaced by a single and simply expressed instrument setting out clearly the duties and rights of all parties involved.

197. There should be the same test of disclosability for both stages of prosecution disclosure providing in substance and, for example, for the disclosure of "material which, in the prosecutor's opinion, might reasonably affect the determination of any issue in the case of which he knows or should reasonably expect" or, more simply but tautologically, "material which in the prosecutor's opinion might weaken the prosecution case or assist that of the defence".

198. In addition, there should be automatic primary disclosure in all or certain types of cases of certain common categories of documents and/or of documents by reference to certain subject matters.

199. The police should retain responsibility for retaining, collating and recording any material gathered or inspected in the course of the investigation; police officers should be better trained for what, in many cases, may be an extensive and difficult exercise regardless of issues of disclosability, and subject, in their exercise of it to statutory guidelines and a rigorous system of 'spot' audits by H.M. Inspectorates of Constabulary and/or of the Crown Prosecution Service.

200. Such responsibility as the police have for identifying and considering all potentially disclosable material should be removed to the prosecutor.

201. The prosecutor should retain ultimate responsibility for the completeness of the material recorded by the police and assume sole responsibility for primary and all subsequent disclosure.

202. The requirements of a defence statement should remain as at present, as should the requirements for particulars where the defence is alibi and/or the defence propose to adduce expert evidence.

203. More effective use of defence statements should be facilitated by the general improvements to the system for preparation for trial that I have recommended, and encouraged through professional conduct rules, training and, in the rare cases where it might be appropriate, discipline, to inculcate in criminal defence practitioners the propriety of and need for compliance with the requirements.

204. There should be a clearly defined timetable for each level of jurisdiction for all stages of mutual disclosure unless the court in any individual case orders otherwise.

205. The Prison Service should introduce national standards for access to due process for remand prisoners that ensure they experience no greater difficulty than bailed defendants in preparing for their trials.

Third party disclosure (paras 185 – 190, pages 474 - 476)

206. There should be consideration of a new statutory scheme for third party disclosure, including its cost implications to all concerned, to operate alongside and more consistently with the general provisions for disclosure of unused material.

Public interest immunity (paras 191 – 197, pages 476 - 479)

207. A scheme should be introduced for instruction by the court of special independent counsel to represent the interests of the defendant in those cases at first instance and on appeal where the court now considers prosecution applications in the absence of the defence in respect of the non-disclosure of sensitive material.

Case management

Case allocation (paras 200 – 202, pages 480 - 481)

208. Under the present system of criminal courts, a single, simple form of procedure for movement of all cases from magistrates' courts to the Crown Court should be substituted for the present mix of procedures of committal, voluntary bill, transfer and sending.

209. If my recommendations for a unified Criminal Court are adopted, a similar, single procedure should govern the movement of all cases from the Magistrates' Division to the District or Crown Divisions.

Pre-trial hearings and pre-trial assessments (paras 204 – 235, pages 482 - 495)

210. In the preparation for trial in all criminal courts, there should be a move away from plea and direction hearings and other forms of pre-trial hearings to co-operation between the parties according to standard or adapted time-tables, wherever necessary seeking written directions from the court.

211. There should be national standard timetables and lists of key actions for preparation for trial in each of the three divisions of the new unified Criminal Court, with suitable variations to meet categories of case of different nature and complexity.

212. The Magistrates' Division, when allocating cases to the Crown or District Divisions and, where appropriate, in summary cases at an early administrative hearing, should issue the parties with the appropriate standard timetable and list, including dates for mutual disclosure and a date within a short period after secondary disclosure for 'pre-trial assessment'.

213. The parties, by agreement or on notice to each other, should be at liberty to seek in writing leave from the trial court to vary the standard timetable.

214. The parties should endeavour to prepare for trial in accordance with the timetable and list of key actions appropriate to the case and to resolve

between themselves any issues of law, procedure or evidence that may shape and/or affect the length of the trial and when it can start.

215. The timetable in each case should set a date for the 'pre-trial assessment', that is, an assessment by the parties and the court as to the state of readiness for trial.

216. By the pre-trial assessment date the parties should complete and send to the trial court a check-list showing progress in preparation and as to readiness for trial, and seeking, if appropriate, written directions.

217. Only if the court or the parties consider it is necessary for the timely and otherwise efficient preparation for, and conduct of, the trial should there be a pre-trial hearing, for example where one or other of the parties cannot comply with the timetable, or where there are unresolved issues affecting the efficient preparation for or conduct of the trial, or when the case is sufficiently serious or complex to require the guidance of the court.

218. Where there is a pre-trial hearing, and the defendant is in custody and consents, he should not be brought to court, but should participate in it to the extent necessary by video-link with the prison in which he is housed.

219. A judge or magistrates conducting an oral pre-trial hearing should be empowered to give binding directions or rulings subject to subsequent variation or discharge if justice requires it.

220. Where a pre-trial hearing is necessitated by one or other or both parties' failure without good cause to comply with the time-table or other directions of the court, or to resolve issues of procedure, law or fact between them, the court should have power:

220.1 to make such order as to payment of a publicly funded defence advocate for his attendance at the hearing as may be appropriate in the circumstances; and/or publicly to reprimand either party's advocate or those instructing them as appropriate; any such public reprimand to be communicated to and taken into account by the professional body of the person reprimanded and, where the person is franchised for publicly funded defence work, by the Legal Services Commission; and/or

220.2 to make such order of costs against one or other or both sides as may be appropriate.

221. All interlocutory court rulings, orders or directions in criminal courts as presently structured or in a new unified Criminal Court should be expressed in writing as a formal document of the court and served forthwith or shortly afterwards on all parties.

Listing and docketing (paras 236 – 238, pages 495 - 496)

222. There should be a move to greater use of fixed trial dates in cases of substance.

223. There should be a corresponding move to early allocation of such cases to a judge for case management and trial.

Information technology *(paras 256 – 261, pages 501 - 504)*

224. The present provision for the use of video-link with prisons in pre-trial hearings in magistrates' courts should be extended to all such hearings in all criminal courts; and as technology develops, consideration should be given to the use of web technologies for them.

Time limits *(paras 262 – 270, pages 504 - 508)*

225. The present maximum custody periods should continue, save that, in the event of abolition of committal proceedings for 'either-way' offences and/or of the establishment of a unified Criminal Court, the periods should be 56 days for cases tried summarily (whether summary only or 'either-way') and 182 for those tried otherwise.

226. Section 22 of the Prosecution of Offences Act 1985 should be amended to enable a court to consider and grant an extension of the custody time limit after its expiry, but only if such power is closely circumscribed, including a provision that the court should only grant an extension where it is satisfied that there is a compelling public interest in doing so.

227. An effective right of appeal should be provided outside the custody time limit period against the refusal of an extension within the period.

A code of criminal procedure *(paras 271 – 280, pages 509 - 513)*

228. The law of criminal procedure should be codified, but in two stages:

   228.1   first, the Law Commission should be requested to draft legislation consolidating existing primary and secondary legislation coupled, possibly, with some codification of the more important and uncontroversial common law rules; and

   228.2   second, a statutory Criminal Procedure Rules Committee should be established to draft a single procedural code for a unified Criminal Court, restating and reforming as necessary statute and common law, custom, judicial practice directions and other guidance.

229. The code, which should be expressed concisely and in simple English and Welsh, should provide, so far as practicable, a common set of rules for all levels of jurisdiction, and different rules only to the extent that they are necessary for different forensic processes.

230. The draft code should be enacted in primary and subsidiary legislation, and the Committee should, thereafter maintain it, proposing amendments where necessary for the Lord Chancellor's approval and initiation of amendment by secondary legislation subject to negative or positive resolution as may be appropriate.

231. In all its activities, the Committee should be under the general oversight of the Criminal Justice Council.

232. The Government should be under a statutory duty to refer to the Committee all proposals for amendment of the law of criminal procedure.

233. The Criminal Procedure Rules Committee should be chaired by the Lord Chief Justice and its membership should include: the Vice-President of the Court of Appeal (Criminal Division), the Senior Presiding Judge, at least two High Court Judges and two Circuit Judges sitting in crime, together with an appropriate number of District Judges, magistrates and justices' clerks, a number of experienced criminal practitioners from both branches of the profession and at least one academic specialising in the field, together with appropriate representatives of voluntary organisations with a direct interest in the work of the criminal courts.

234. The Committee should be supported by a full-time staff of lawyers and administrators experienced in the work of the criminal courts.

CHAPTER ELEVEN THE TRIAL: PROCEDURES AND EVIDENCE

The start of a jury trial (paras 15 – 24, pages 518 - 523)

235. In all cases tried by judge and jury:

235.1 each juror should be provided at the start of the trial with a copy of the charge or charges;

235.2 the judge at the start of the trial should address the jury, introducing them generally to their task as jurors and giving them an objective outline of the case and the questions they are there to decide;

235.3 the judge should supplement his opening address with, and provide a copy to each juror of, a written case and issues summary prepared by the parties' advocates and approved by him;

235.4 The judge, in the course of his introductory address, and the case and issues summary, should identify:

- the nature of the charges;

- *as part of a brief narrative*, the evidence agreed, reflecting the admissions of either side at the appropriate point in the story;

- *also as part of the narrative*, the matters of fact in issue; and

- with no, or minimal, reference to the law, a list of likely questions for their decision.

236. If and to the extent that the issues narrow or widen in the course of the trial, the case and issues summary should be amended and fresh copies provided to the judge and jury.

Time estimates (paras 25 – 26, pages 523 - 524)

237. Advocates should regard it as of the highest importance to attempt accurate estimates of the likely length of their principal witnesses' evidence, including a review of them as the issues become clearer in the course of preparation for trial.

Opening speeches (paras 27 – 28, pages 524 - 525)

238. I endorse the Runciman Royal Commission's recommendation that a defence advocate should be entitled to make a short opening speech to the jury immediately after that of the prosecution advocate, but normally of no more than a few minutes.

Evidence in chief (paras 29 – 33, pages 525 - 527)

239. Screens and projection equipment should be more widely available to enable electronic presentation of evidence in appropriate cases.

The defence case (para 35, page 528)

240. A defence advocate who makes a short opening speech after the prosecution opening should not, thereby, forfeit his right to make an opening speech at the beginning of the defence case.

241. A defence advocate's entitlement to make an opening speech at the start of the defence case should no longer depend on whether he intends to call a witness as to fact other than the defendant.

Taking stock (paras 37 – 39, pages 529 - 531)

242. At the close of evidence and before speeches, the judge and advocates, in the absence of the jury, should finally review the case and issues summary and, if necessary, amend it for the jury.

243. Such a procedure, along with those already established by the Court of Appeal for review of evidential and legal issues at this stage of a trial, should be considered for express inclusion in the Criminal Procedure Code that I have recommended and, in the meantime, by the Lord Chief Justice for a special practice direction.

244. If, and to the extent that, the law and professional codes of conduct do not require a defending, as well as a prosecuting, advocate to seek to correct a judge's error of law or of material fact of which he becomes aware, both the law and the codes should be changed to require it.

Judges' directions on law and summing up (paras 41 – 55, pages 532 - 538)

245. Consideration should be given to including in the Code of Criminal Procedure that I have recommended and, in the meantime in a practice direction of the Lord Chief Justice, a requirement that a judge should use a case and issues summary and any other written or visual aid provided to a jury, as an integral part of his summing-up, referring to the points in them, one by one, as he deals with them orally.

246. Courts should equip judges with, and in cases meriting it they should consider using, other visual aids to their summings-up, such as PowerPoint and evolving forms of presentational soft-ware.

247. So far as possible, the judge should not direct the jury on the law, save by implication in the questions of fact that he puts to them for decision.

248. The judge should continue to remind the jury of the issues and, save in the most simple cases, the evidence relevant to them, and should always give the jury an adequate account of the defence; but he should do it in more summary form than is now common.

249. The judge should devise and put to the jury a series of written factual questions, the answers to which could logically lead only to a verdict of guilty or not guilty; the questions should correspond with those in the updated case and issues summary, supplemented as necessary in a separate written list prepared for the purpose; and each question should be tailored to the law as the judge knows it to be and to the issues and evidence in the case.

250. The judge, where he considers it appropriate, should be permitted to require a jury to answer publicly each of his questions and to declare a verdict in accordance with those answers.

Trial by judge and magistrates in the District Division *(paras 57 – 60, pages 538 - 540)*

251. In the District Division:

251.1 the judge should be the sole judge of law;

251.2 the judge and the magistrates should together be the judges of facts, each having an equal vote;

251.3 the judge should normally conduct any pre-trial hearings on his own;

251.4 the judge should be empowered to make binding pre-trial rulings as would a Crown Division judge;

251.5 the judge should rule on matters of law, procedure and the admissibility of evidence in the absence of the magistrates whenever he considers it would be potentially unfairly prejudicial to the defendant to do so in their presence;

251.6 the same order of speeches and structure of trial should apply as in the Crown Division;

251.7 the judge should not sum up the case to the magistrates, but, after retiring with them to consider the court's decision, should give a publicly reasoned judgment of the court; and

251.8 the judge should be solely responsible for sentence.

Trial in the Magistrates' Division *(paras 62 – 64, page 541)*

252. The structure and procedures of trial in the Magistrates' Division of a new unified Criminal Court should broadly follow those of the present magistrates' courts.

Abbreviated procedures (paras 65 – 67, pages 542 - 543)

253. All prosecuting authorities should use the provisions of section 12 of the Magistrates' Courts Act 1980, as amended, for disposal of cases on pleas of guilty or on proof of guilt in the absence of the defendant.

Evidence

General principles (paras 76 – 78, pages 546 - 547)

254. The English law of criminal evidence should, in general, move away from technical rules of inadmissibility to trusting judicial and lay fact-finders to give relevant evidence the weight it deserves.

Refreshing memory/witness statements (paras 81 – 85, pages 548 - 551)

255. As a first step and/or failing adoption of the following recommendation for use of prior witness statements as evidence, consideration should be given to making the only condition for a witness's use of a written statement for refreshing memory that there is good reason to believe that he would have been significantly better able to recall the events in question when he made or verified it than at the time of giving evidence.

Prior witness statements as evidence (paras 86 – 94, pages 551 - 556)

256. Consideration should be given to amending the law as to admissibility of witness statements so that:

    256.1   where a witness has made a prior statement, in written or recorded form, it should be admissible as evidence of any matter stated in it of which his direct oral evidence in the proceedings would be admissible provided that he authenticates it as his statement;

    256.2   an integral part of the new rule should be that a defendant's previous statement should in principle be admissible whether it supports or damages his case and the fact that it may appear to be self-serving should go only to weight; and

    256.3   the witness should be permitted, where appropriate, to adopt the statement in the witness box as his evidence in chief.

257. There should be consideration in the long term of extending the present provisions for the use of video-recorded evidence to the evidence of all critical witnesses in cases of serious crime, coupled with provision where required of a record and/or transcripts or summaries of such evidence and also of that in cross-examination and re-examination.

Hearsay (paras 95 – 104, pages 556 - 560)

258. There should be further consideration of reform of the rule against hearsay, in particular with a view to making hearsay generally admissible subject to the principle of best evidence, rather than generally inadmissible subject to specified exceptions as proposed by the Law Commission.

259. In this respect, as with evidence in criminal cases generally, there should be a move away from rules of inadmissibility to trusting fact finders to assess the weight of the evidence.

Unfair evidence (paras 105 – 111, pages 560 - 563)

260. As part of the over-all reform of the law of criminal evidence that I have recommended, consideration should be given to rationalising and simplifying the various forms of statutory and common law rules for exclusion of evidence because of its unfairness and that of staying a prosecution for abuse of process on account of improperly obtained evidence.

Previous misconduct of a defendant/Similar fact evidence (paras 112 – 120, pages 563 - 568)

261. There should be consideration of the Law Commission's imminent final report on evidence in criminal proceedings of a defendant's misconduct in the context of a wider review of the law of criminal evidence, having regard, in particular, to the illogicality, ineffectiveness and complexity of any rule, whatever its form, directed to keeping a defendant's previous convictions from lay, but not professional, fact finders.

Expert evidence (paras 129 – 151, pages 571 - 582)

262. Consideration should be given to concentrating in one self-governing professional body within England and Wales the role of setting, or overseeing the setting, of standards and of conduct for forensic scientists of all disciplines, the maintenance of a register of accreditation for them and the regulation of their compliance with its conditions of accreditation.

263. For those purposes, the several existing expert witness bodies providing for all or most forensic science disciplines should consider amalgamation with, or concentration of their resources in, the Council for the Registration of Forensic Practitioners.

264. The new Criminal Procedure Rules that I recommend should contain a rule in the same or similar terms to that in Part 35.3 of the Civil Procedure Rules that an expert witness's overriding duty is to the court.

265. Any witness statement or report prepared by an expert witness for the assistance of the court should contain at its head a signed declaration to that effect.

266. Criminal courts' power to control the admission of experts' evidence should be formalised in the new Criminal Procedure Rules that I have recommended, and put on a similar footing to that for the Civil Courts as set out in the Civil Procedure Rules, Part 35, 1 and 4, namely by imposing upon them a duty, and

declaring their power, to restrict expert evidence to that which is reasonably required to resolve any issue of importance in the proceedings.

267. Judges and magistrates should rigorously apply the test governing that power and duty, and the Court of Appeal should support them.

268. In publicly funded defence cases, where a judge or magistrates' court has directed that it would be justifiable to call a defence expert, that direction should constitute authorisation for the expenditure of public money on an expert at a specified rate.

269. Where there is an issue on a matter of importance on which expert evidence is required, the court should not have a power to appoint or select an expert, whether or not it excludes either party from calling its own expert evidence.

270. Where there is no issue, or one in which the parties are content that the matter should be resolved by a single expert, they should be encouraged to deal with it in that way, agreeing his report or a summary of it as part of the evidence in the case.

271. The prosecution and defence should normally arrange for their experts to discuss and jointly to identify at the earliest possible stage before the trial those issues on which they agree and those on which they do not agree, and to prepare a joint statement for use in evidence indicating the measure of their agreement and a summary of the reasons for their disagreement.

272. Failing such arrangement, the court should have power to direct such a discussion and identification of issues and preparation of a joint statement for use in evidence and to make any consequential directions as may be appropriate in each case.

273. Close attention should be given in any further and general review of the rule against hearsay to the increasing reliance of forensic science laboratories and of many experts in certain disciplines on electronic recording, analysis and transmission of data.

274. There should be greater use by legal practitioners of video-conferencing and other developing new technology for communicating and conferring with experts in preparation for trial.

275. The law and the provision of national facilities should be developed to enable experts to give evidence by video-link or other new technologies in appropriate cases.

Interpreters *(paras 155 – 162, pages 584 - 587)*

276. The Government should continue to encourage the concentration in the two national Registers as appropriate of the role of oversight of national training, accreditation and monitoring of the performance of interpreters, with a view to providing an adequate national and local coverage of suitably qualified interpreters.

277. Training and accreditation of all interpreters should include coverage of the basics of criminal investigation and court procedures, and should provide for changing and different geographic demands for linguists.

278. The Government should consider central funding of further education establishments to equip them, where necessary, to provide courses in lesser known languages for the Diploma in Public Service Interpreting.

279. The Government should undertake a national publicity campaign in further education establishments and other colleges in support of the two national Registers.

280. There should be a review of the levels of payment to interpreters with a view to encouraging more and the best qualified to undertake this work and to establishing a national scale of pay.

281. Interpreters should be provided with facilities appropriate to an officer of the court when attending court to provide their services.

282. The standard check-list for agreement or directions leading to the pre-trial assessment should require all parties to indicate to the court in good time before the trial date the need for an interpreter, identifying the party or witness for whom he is required and the language.

283. The check list should also require the parties to agree or, failing agreement, to seek the court's directions for making available to the interpreter in good time before trial, any documents likely to assist him in his task at court.

284. An engaged interpreter should be entitled to apply direct to the Court for such access.

285. In all cases where an interpreter is provided with or given access to such documents, it should be in circumstances under which he undertakes to preserve their confidentiality until trial or otherwise in conditions of security directed by the court.

286. Standards of best practice in the design of new court buildings should be developed and equipment adapted in existing courtrooms for the provision of adequate accommodation and facilities to interpreters.

Information about the court *(paras 163 – 168, pages 588 - 590)*

287. Early progress should be made to equip each court centre or group of court centres, as appropriate, with:

287.1 its own website containing information of cases listed for future hearing and their fixed or estimated hearing dates, daily listings of cases and information as to their progress; and general information about the court centre, travel to it and local facilities; and

287.2 an automated telephone information system giving like information.

288. Early progress should also be made to equip each court centre with:

288.1 electronic bulletin boards indicating the progress of cases listed each day; and

288.2 diagrams of the layout of courtrooms in waiting areas and corresponding signs inside each courtroom.

Sitting times *(paras 169 – 178, pages 590 - 593)*

289. There should be thorough examination of the need for and the costs/benefits of extending court working hours, including the use of evening, night and weekend courts, whether as a general provision or for areas with a concentration of serious and/or minor crime.

290. Out-of-hours provision should be made for administrative assistance to court users through the medium of help-desks, the telephone and electronic means for obtaining advice or information, paying fines, obtaining forms etc.

Court dress *(paras 179 – 184, pages 594 - 595)*

291. The Higher Judiciary, in consultation with all levels of the judiciary, the legal professions and any other appropriate bodies, should consider and advise the Lord Chancellor on what, if any, formal court dress judges, barristers and solicitors should wear in future in the Supreme Court of Justice and the County Court.

Forms of address *(paras 185 – 187, page 596)*

292. The Higher Judiciary, in consultation with all levels of the judiciary, the magistracy, the legal professions and any other appropriate bodies, should consider and advise the Lord Chancellor on future forms of address in all courts.

Court language *(paras 188 – 189, page 597)*

293. A Criminal Procedure Rules Committee should examine all court procedures, forms and terms with a view simplifying their language and content.

Oaths and affirmations *(paras 190 – 196, pages 598 - 600)*

294. The witness's oath and affirmation should be replaced by a solemn promise to tell the truth.

295. The juror's oath and affirmation should be replaced with a promise in the following or similar form: "I promise to try the defendant and to decide on the evidence whether he is guilty or not".

Sentencing *(paras 197 – 226, pages 600 - 610)*

296. There should be early establishment of an online sentencing information service for all full- and part-time judges. The system should include:

  296.1   a statistical record of sentences imposed in the criminal courts at all levels, analysed according to key case features;

  296.2   a statement of sentencing principles and the text of judgments in key cases via an online sentencing textbook; and

  296.3   online and up-to-date information about the availability of sentencing and related facilities.

297. The sentencing information system should be available online to members of the public and the media and should be designed with their needs also in mind.

298. Consideration should be given to charging the Judicial Studies Board with the responsibility for establishing and administering a sentencing information system, resourcing it sufficiently for the purpose.

299. I support the recommendation in the Halliday Sentencing Review Report for the creation of a sentence review jurisdiction for the criminal courts, provided that resource and practical difficulties can be overcome.

CHAPTER TWELVE   APPEALS

The appellate tests *(paras 5 – 11, pages 612 - 615)*

300. There should be the same tests for appeal against conviction and sentence respectively at all levels of appeal below the Appellate Committee of the House of Lords, namely those applicable to the Court of Appeal.

301. Consideration should be given to amendment of the statutory test of unsafety as the ground for quashing a conviction so as to clarify whether and to what extent it is to apply to convictions that would be regarded as safe in the ordinary sense, but that follow want of due process before or during trial.

Appeals from magistrates' courts *(paras 14 – 35, pages 616 - 623)*

302. A defendant's right of appeal against conviction and/or sentence in the magistrates' court to the Crown Court by way of re-hearing should be abolished.

303. It should be replaced by a right of appeal to the Crown Division (Crown Court), with leave from that court, on the same grounds that would support appeal from the Crown Division (Crown Court), sitting in its original capacity, to the Court of Appeal.

304. The constitution of the Crown Division (Crown Court) for this purpose should be a judge sitting alone who, depending on the nature and importance of the appeal, could be a High Court Judge, Circuit Judge or Recorder.

305. There should be no right of appeal from the Magistrates' Division (magistrates' courts) to the High Court by an appeal by way of case stated or by a claim for judicial review.

Appeals from the Crown Court to the Court of Appeal *(paras 36 – 44, pages 623 - 627)*

306. Where it is sought to challenge the decision of the Crown Division (Crown Court) sitting in its appellate capacity:

    306.1   there should be no right of challenge to the High Court by appeal by way of case stated or by claim for judicial review;

306.2　instead, appeal should lie to the Court of Appeal under its general appellate jurisdiction enlarged, if and as necessary, to cover matters presently provided by the remedies of appeal by way of case stated or claim of judicial review – and for which the Court should be suitably constituted; and

306.3　all such appeals should be subject to the permission of the Court of Appeal, which it should only give in a case involving an important point of principle or practice or where there is some other compelling reason for the Court to hear it.

307.　Where it is sought to challenge the decision of the Crown Division (Crown Court) as a court of first instance or of the District Division:

307.1　there should be no right of challenge to the High Court by appeal by way of case stated or by claim for judicial review; and

307.2　instead, appeal should lie only to the Court of Appeal under its general appellate jurisdiction enlarged, if and as necessary, to cover matters presently provided by the remedies of appeal by way of case stated or of claim for judicial review - and for which the Court should be suitably constituted.

Prosecution rights of appeal *(paras 47 – 65, pages 627 - 636)*

308.　Whilst I support the general thrust of the Law Commission's recommendation for the introduction of statutory exceptions to the double jeopardy rule, I recommend that:

308.1　the exceptions should not be limited to murder and allied offences, but should extend to other grave offences punishable with life and/or long terms of imprisonment as Parliament might specify; and

308.2　there should be no reopening of an investigation of a case following an acquittal without the Director of Public Prosecution's prior, personal consent and recommendation as to which police force should conduct it.

309.　I also support the general thrust of the Law Commission's recommendations for:

309.1　extending the present preparatory bearing regime to include appealable rulings on potentially terminating matters such as severance, joinder, quashing the indictment or staying the prosecution as an abuse of process;

309.2　giving the prosecution a right of appeal against an acquittal in certain cases arising from a terminating ruling during the trial up to the close of the prosecution case; and

309.3　giving the prosecution a right of appeal against an acquittal arising from a ruling of no case to answer under the first limb of the rule in *R. v. Galbraith.*

Appeals against perverse verdicts *(paras 66 – 67, pages 636 - 637)*

310. Where any special verdict of a jury reveals on its terms that it is perverse:

   310.1   if the verdict is guilty, the defence should have a right of appeal to the Court of Appeal, subject to the usual leave procedure, on the ground that the perversity renders the conviction unsafe; and

   310.2   if the verdict is not guilty, the prosecution should have a right of appeal to the Court of Appeal, also subject to leave, on the ground that the perversity indicates that the verdict is probably untrue or unfair and such as to merit a re-trial.

Procedure on appeals to the Court of Appeal *(paras 73 – 101, pages 639 - 651)*

311. Single judges of the Court of Appeal should be allowed time to consider and determine written applications for leave to appeal against conviction or sentence in chambers as part of their regular sitting plan.

312. A single judge of the Court of Appeal should be empowered, when considering applications for leave to appeal, to give procedural directions for the hearing of the application or of the appeal that need not trouble the Full Court, subject to a right on the part of the applicant or the prosecution, as the case may be, to renew the application to the Full Court.

313. Consideration should be given to combining, or more closely associating in content and time, appellants' grounds of appeal and skeleton arguments, and to making appropriate adjustments to time limits for their filing and service.

Reorganisation and reconstitution of the Court of Appeal *(paras 87 – 94, pages 644 - 647)*

314. The Court of Appeal should be variously constituted according to the nature, legal importance and complexity of its work:

   314.1   in cases where there is a point of law of general public importance or of particular complexity or public interest, including sentencing cases calling for guidelines or involving some other point of general principle or very long custodial sentences, the Court should consist of the Lord Chief Justice or the Vice-President or a Lord Justice and two High Court Judges;

   314.2   in straightforward appeals against conviction, or in respect of short sentences where the law and procedures are clear and the only issue is whether the trial judge has correctly followed them, or where the issue turns on his treatment of the facts, the Court should consist of two High Court Judges or one High Court Judge and one Circuit Judge; and

   314.3   consideration should be given to introducing a system under which, in cases of exceptional legal importance and complexity, a distinguished academic could either be appointed *ad hoc* to act as a judge of the

Court or be invited to submit a written brief to the Court on the point(s) in issue.

315.   A single judge of the Court should be responsible for allocation of appeals to the Full Court as variously constituted under these recommendations, subject to review by the Full Court before or during the hearing of the appeal.

Practice and procedure *(paras 95 – 101, pages 648 - 651)*

316.   The Court, however it is constituted, should 'slow down' - its judges should be allowed more time for preparation and judgment writing as part of their sitting plan, and appeal hearings should be less rushed so as to allow advocates adequate time to deploy their arguments and judges to consider them.

317.   The Lord Chief Justice should consider issuing a Practice Direction for the better conduct by the parties of their preparation for hearing, including provision for pre-appeal directions hearings in complex cases, the form and contents of appeal bundles and advance notification to the Court of last minute changes likely to affect the content or duration of the appeal.

318.   Criminal practitioners should provide a standard of service to the Court of the same level as is presently required of their counterparts in the Court of Appeal (Civil Division) and they should be paid properly for it.

319.   In conviction appeals the Court should support trial judges' robust case management and control of the trial, so long as it has not prejudiced the fairness of the trial over-all and thereby put the safety of the conviction at risk.

320.   In sentence appeals the Court should be vigilant not to 'tinker' with the sentence of the court below, but only to intervene where it is wrong in principle, that is, of the wrong sort or far too long in the circumstances.

321.   The Crown Prosecution Service should consider on a case by case basis whether to appear on the hearing of an appeal against sentence so as to be able to assist the Court, if required, on matters of fact, including the effect on any victim, or of law.

Criminal Cases Review Commission *(paras 102 – 107, pages 651 - 653)*

322.   Section 23A of the Criminal Appeal Act 1968 should be amended to extend the Court of Appeal's power to direct the Criminal Cases Review Commission to investigate and report on a matter on appeal, to a matter in an application for leave to appeal.

323.   On any reference by the Commission to the Court of Appeal or the Crown Court of a conviction or sentence, those courts should apply the law in force at the time of conviction or sentence as the case may be.

Sentencing Advisory Panel *(paras 108 – 111, pages 653 - 655)*

324.   The law should be amended to widen the remit of the Sentencing Advisory Panel to include general principles of sentencing, in particular as to the courts'

use of the various sentencing options available to them regardless of the category of offence.

325. The law should be amended, to enable the Court of Appeal to work more closely with and respond more speedily to the Panel's advice, by empowering it to issue guidelines without having to tie them to a specific appeal before it.

Appeals to the House of Lords *(paras 112 – 117, pages 655 - 658)*

326. Consideration should be given to introducing a system under which, in cases of exceptional legal importance and complexity, a distinguished academic could be invited to assist an Appellate Committee, say, by the submission of a written brief, with copies to the parties, on the point(s) at issue.

327. On points of law of general public importance, where there are conflicting decisions of the Court of Appeal or the law on them is otherwise in such an unsatisfactory state that only the House of Lords can resolve it, consideration should be given to introducing a form of 'leap-frog' appeal from the Crown Division (Crown Court) to the House of Lords, similar to that provided for civil appeals by Part II of the Administration of Justice Act 1969.

328. Section 34(2) of the Criminal Appeal Act 1968 should be amended to empower the House of Lords and Court of Appeal, as the case may be, to extend the time within which a prosecutor may apply for leave to appeal, as it does in the case of a defendant.

CHAPTER 3

THE CRIMINAL COURTS AND THEIR MANAGEMENT

INTRODUCTION

1   Many readers of this Report will be familiar with the system of criminal justice in England and Wales, others less so. For the latter, I hope the following brief outline will be of help. The former can, if they wish, move straight to the next chapter, though there are some aspects of the management of magistrates' courts and that of the Crown Court that may be new, even to them.

2   There are two levels of criminal courts, magistrates' courts and the Crown Court. About 95%[1] of all prosecuted cases start and finish in the magistrates' courts. These are prosecutions for the less serious – 'summary' - offences, some of which carry a penalty of up to 6 months' imprisonment. Magistrates also have jurisdiction in certain civil, family and child care matters and, for the present, also licensing matters. Barristers and solicitors exercise the main rights of audience in magistrates' courts. The remainder of the criminal work,

---

[1] this may be an under-estimate because annual criminal statistics understate their significance; see Dr Penny Darbyshire, *An Essay on the Importance and Neglect of the Magistracy* [1997] Crim LR 627, pp 628-9

the more serious – 'indictable' - cases are sent to the Crown Court for trial by a judge and jury or for sentence by a judge.[2]

3   Magistrates' courts' powers to commit cases for trial in the Crown Court are the vestiges of the old grand juries' function of examining and, where they considered there was sufficient evidence, committing indictable cases for trial by judge and jury. I say 'vestiges' because, since 1987[3] serious frauds and, since 1991,[4] sexual offences and offences involving violence or cruelty to children may be 'transferred', and since 15th January 2001,[5] all offences triable only on indictment must be 'sent', direct to the Crown Court. Only 'either-way' cases,[6] - offences that are triable summarily or on indictment - are still committed for trial and then, in the main, by a paper process and without consideration of the evidence. Magistrates' courts may deal summarily, but only with the consent of the defence, with 'either-way' offences. However, in the event of their deciding, in a matter that has proceeded before them summarily, that their sentencing power is insufficient, they must commit the offender to the Crown Court for sentence.

4   Lay magistrates or Justices of the Peace have an ancient history, dating from the late 12th century when Richard I commissioned certain knights to preserve the peace in unruly areas. They were responsible to the King for ensuring that the law was upheld and were known as Keepers of the Peace.[7] They first acquired the title of Justices of the Peace in 1361,[8] by which time they had authority to arrest suspects, investigate alleged crimes and punish offenders. For centuries they also had local administrative responsibilities. But in the 19th century, except for liquor and gaming licensing, these passed to local authorities; and their policing role passed to local police forces. They are appointed by the Lord Chancellor from all walks of life; few are lawyers. When sitting they rely for legal advice on a legal adviser, who is, or is responsible to, a justices' clerk.

5   Lay magistrates, sitting part-time and normally in benches of three, account for about 91% of all summary criminal cases ; they also deal with some civil cases, in the main family and licensing matters. There are about 30,400 of them and, typically, they serve for between 10 and 20 years. They are unpaid, receiving only a modest allowance for financial loss and subsistence. They are required to sit for a minimum of 26 half-day court sittings each year, but on average sit 40 or more times a year. In addition, they spend the equivalent

---

[2] a comparison between workloads in terms of trials showed that in 1995 "over four times as many trials took place in magistrates' courts as in the Crown Court"; Penny Darbyshire, ibid p 629

[3] Criminal Justice Act 1987, ss 4 and 5

[4] Criminal Justice Act 1991, s 53

[5] Crime and Disorder Act 1998, ss 51 and 52

[6] unless related to an indictable-only offence 'sent'" for trial; see 1998 Act s 51(11)

[7] in 1327, by a statute of Edward III, there were assigned in every county "good men and lawful . to keep the peace"

[8] by virtue of the Statute of Westminster of that year

of about a week a year on training and other magisterial activities. They are 'lightly', but reasonably well, trained for their increasingly demanding work. They have only a local jurisdiction, that is, for the Commission area to which they are appointed, and they have no national judicial 'champion' in the form of, say, a Chief Magistrate. But, as I describe below, they organise such matters as deployment and sittings thought their local benches and justices' clerk, and their general administration through the medium of magistrates' courts committees.

6   District Judges (Magistrates' Courts) - until recently known as stipendiary magistrates - sitting singly and full-time, deal with the remaining 9% of the criminal work of the magistrates' courts. They are legally qualified, either as barristers or solicitors of at least seven years' standing, but nevertheless they too have the assistance in court of a legal adviser. They rarely sit with magistrates. There are about 105 of them,[9] supported by about 150 Deputy District Judges who sit part-time. About 50 of the full time appointees sit in London and 50 in the Provinces. They are headed by a Senior District Judge (Chief Magistrate), who sits in Bow Street. The current annual employment costs of a full-time appointee are about £90,000.[10]

7   Stipendiary magistrates stem from the mid-eighteenth century when they were introduced in London largely to replace the corrupt Middlesex Justices of the Peace. In the early 19th century they were also appointed to some of the other large metropolitan areas to complement, not to replace, the lay bench. In what became Inner London, stipendiaries did all the work in their own court-houses, lay magistrates sitting in separate courthouses dealing only with trivial matters. In 1964, as a result of the Administration of Justice Act of that year, they began to share some jurisdictions and court-houses. The pattern in the provinces was quite different. There, the two normally shared jurisdictions and court-houses, but with the strengthening of the lay benches, there was a gradual falling off in numbers of stipendiaries.[11] In the last 20 years or so provincial stipendiaries began to increase again. As academic commentators from the Centre for Criminal Justice Studies at the University of Leeds have recently pointed out,[12] there were three reasons for that: first, they were needed to meet the increasing workload and difficulties in many areas in recruiting lay magistrates; second, there was heightened political concern about court efficiency and delays; and third, in 1973 legislation[13] introduced for the first time a power to appoint acting stipendiaries for up to

---

[9] the present statutory limit is 106

[10] the figures in this paragraph and elsewhere in this report on the subject of magistrates are taken from Rod Morgan and Neil Russell, *The Judiciary in the Magistrates' Courts*, RDS Occasional Paper No 66 (Home Office, December 2000)

[11] *Stipendiary Magistrates and Lay Justices* (1946) 9 MLR 1; Report of the Interdepartmental Committee on Magistrates in London, Cmnd 1606, 1962 - the "Aarvold Committee"; and Sir Thomas Skyrme, *History of the Justices of the Peace*, Barry Rose, Chichester, 1991

[12] *The Development of the Professional Magistracy in England and Wales*, Peter Seagoe, Clive Walker and David Wall, [2000] Crim LR 631, pp 633-4

[13] Administration of Justice Act 1973, s 2(7)

three months at a time. As the Leeds University commentators and Rod Morgan and Neil Russell[14] have also noted, the growth over-all of stipendiaries has been modest and proportionate to that of lay magistrates, though there has been a rapid increase in the number of provincial appointments in the last decade - from 16 to over 50.

8   As a result of the Access to Justice Act 1999,[15] London and provincial District Judges (Magistrates' Courts) have become a unified body. The Lord Chancellor, in announcing the change, said that its purpose was to provide greater flexibility in their allocation to fluctuations in workloads throughout the country for District Judges and "to complement and work alongside" lay magistrates. Each District Judge, although assigned to a specific area, has a national jurisdiction enabling him to sit elsewhere when needed. Acting stipendiaries have now become Deputy District Judges (Magistrates' Courts), without statutory limitation of the period for which they may be appointed, as a precursor to substantive appointment. Although District Judges are assigned to a particular centre or Magistrates' Courts Committee area, they may be required to sit anywhere as the work demands. It is unusual[16] for them to be involved in the management of the courts in which they sit, save for those in London where they have a formal role in the management structure.

9   District Judges and lay magistrates have exactly the same jurisdiction, enabling them to try summary offences carrying a maximum penalty of 6 months' imprisonment or, in certain cases of more than one offence, of up to 12 months' imprisonment.[17] District Judges undertake the same range of criminal and civil work as magistrates, though they are often assigned cases that are longer, more complex and/or sensitive, frequently the 'either-way' cases.

10   The Crown Court, which was created by the Courts Act 1971, replaced the old system of Quarter Sessions and Assizes swept away in the Beeching reforms.[18] It is a single Court, which sits at centres throughout England and Wales. Every case in the court is presided over by a judge who, when trying the issue of guilt, sits with a jury of 12 randomly selected lay people. When dealing only with sentence the judge sits on his own, and when hearing appeals against conviction from a magistrates' court, which are by way of rehearing, he sits with two lay magistrates. Many judges who sit in the Crown Court also exercise, as judges of the High Court or county court, a

---

[14] *The Judiciary in the Magistrates' Courts*, p 3, para 1.2

[15] by amendment of the Justices of the Peace Act 1997, s10; and see the LCD Consultation Paper *Creation of a Unified Stipendiary Bench*, 1998

[16] some have been elected to Magistrates' Courts' Committees

[17] when sitting in a Youth Panel, both can impose a Detention and Training Order. These orders can be made for a maximum period of operation of 2 years, but only half of the time may be served in custody

[18] see Report of *The Royal Commission on Assizes and Quarter Sessions 1966 -1969*, chaired by Lord Beeching, Cmnd 4153

civil and/or family jurisdiction, often moving from one jurisdiction to another as their daily list requires.

11   There are 78 permanent and 15 satellite Crown Court centres throughout the country,[19] designated as first, second and third tier, reflecting the seriousness of the offences normally triable there.   These centres are spread among six judicial circuits, having their origin in the centuries old system of judges travelling around the country to administer criminal and civil justice.[20]   An important feature of the circuit system introduced by Lord Beeching, and formalised by statute,[21] is that of the Presiding Judges.   Their role today, and the reasons for it, are much as he intended them when, in 1969, he recommended their creation:

> "256. ... it is our intention that the administrative officers, to whom we refer later, shall exercise firm managerial control over all matters affecting the smooth running of the courts other than those which have a direct bearing upon the discharge of judicial functions. This being so, we consider it very necessary, on constitutional grounds, to provide a visible and effective safeguarding of the position of the judges serving the Circuits by assigning to each Circuit a senior member of the judiciary who will have a general responsibility for that Circuit and a particular responsibility for all matters affecting the judiciary serving there."[22]

12   Judges of the Crown Court consist of those High Court Judges who visit the more important centres regularly on circuit and, in much greater numbers, Circuit Judges and Recorders (part-time judges) who are, in the main, attached to particular centres.   However, they all have jurisdiction to sit anywhere in the country if asked to do so. There are just over 100 High Court Judges, nearly 600 Circuit Judges and about 1,400 Recorders.   Practising barristers at present exercise the main right of audience in the Crown Court. But recent statutory provision has allowed for the appearance there of greater numbers of practising solicitors than before and also for barristers and solicitors in employment, including Crown prosecutors.[23]

13   All judges of the Crown Court are headed by the Lord Chief Justice of England and Wales who is responsible, in consultation with the Lord Chancellor, for their deployment and allocation of judicial work, and for advice on judicial appointments.   In exercising these responsibilities, he acts largely through the Senior Presiding Judge for England and Wales, the

---

[19] including the Central Criminal Court in the City of London

[20] Midland, North Eastern, Northern, South Eastern, Wales and Chester and Western

[21] Courts and Legal Services Act 1990, s 72

[22] Beeching Report, paras 256-259

[23] Courts and Legal Services Act 1990, s 31A inserted as from 31 July 2000 by Access to Justice Act 1999, s 37

Presiding Judges of each of the six judicial circuits and the Resident Judges[24] of the major court centres within each circuit. Save for those constitutionally important responsibilities and their involvement in a consultative capacity in various bodies concerned with the administration of justice, the judges have no formal role in the management of their courts.

14   Appeals against conviction and sentence lie from magistrates' courts to the Crown Court by way of rehearing, and from the Crown Court to the Court of Appeal (Criminal Division). The Court of Appeal normally sits in the Royal Courts of Justice in London, but in recent years has occasionally sat for short periods on circuit. In London it sits in several constitutions or panels of judges. Each constitution normally consists of three, one Appeal Court Judge drawn from a list of 19 who regularly sit in that Division, sitting with two High Court Judges or with one High Court Judge and one experienced Circuit Judge. Appeals require leave, either from the trial or sentencing judge, or from the Court of Appeal itself, most commonly acting through a single High Court Judge.

15   More limited forms of appeal, on points of law or jurisdiction or matters of procedure, also lie from magistrates' courts and the Crown Court to the High Court, sitting mostly in London but occasionally on circuit, by way of case stated or judicial review.

16   The final court of appeal for England and Wales, though not for Scotland in criminal matters,[25] is the Appellate Committee of the House of Lords. It consists of twelve Lords of Appeal in Ordinary who normally sit in panels of five. Appeals lie to the Appellate Committee only on points of law of general public importance and with leave of the Court of Appeal or of the Committee.

MAGISTRATES' COURTS

Management

17   As I have said, unlike professional judges at any level[26], magistrates are responsible for the administrative management of their own courts, though subject to increasing oversight by the Lord Chancellor's Department. Since 1949, they have done so through local magistrates' courts committees

---

[24] ie the senior Circuit Judge at each centre appointed to oversee its criminal work

[25] where the Scottish Inner House sitting in Edinburgh is the final court of appeal, save for devolution issues, where appeal lies to the Judicial Committee of the Privy Council

[26] save for District Judges in London; see para 20 below

('MCCs') - in effect, local management boards - responsible for the "efficient and effective administration" of their courts.[27] These now number 42 and correspond to the 42 criminal justice system areas established for England and Wales.[28] The MCCs are composed in the main of magistrates, but act through a justices' chief executive and his staff. Their role is purely administrative.

18   An MCC may have more than one 'bench' of magistrates within its area, each with its own chairman. His responsibilities are informal, but various and heavy. They include: chairing meetings of the bench and of its sub-committees; regular consultation with the justices' clerk on such matters as sitting rotas and court listing; election of members of the bench to various positions; liaison with the MCC and the various criminal justice agencies; the application of various guide-lines and bench policies; review of sentencing statistics as against national patterns; general encouragement of good practice; pastoral matters; attendance at meetings of various local criminal justice bodies; and maintenance of good public and media relations. The justices'clerk, who in many MCC areas is now responsible for more than one bench, has dual roles, not always readily distinguishable, of principal legal adviser to the magistrates and of responsibility for administrative and staff matters to his 'line-manager', the MCC's justices' chief executive.

19   The current annual cost of administration of the magistrates' courts is about £330 million. Local authorities, as 'the paying authorities', provide the courthouses and ancillary accommodation and, initially, all the funding for MCCs in their respective areas. The Lord Chancellor's Department repays 80% of revenue expenditure which, since 1992, has been subject to a cash limited grant, leaving the local authorities' obligation at 20%. Despite this obligation of local authorities, MCCs have little accountability to them. And local politicians or council officers have little direct involvement in the business of the courts other than as serving magistrates or in connection with local authority prosecutions, so it does not often figure highly in their priorities.[29] The authorities have no right to representation on the MCCs or say in their spending plans, save by inefficient and sometimes confrontational statutory procedures. These are particularly troublesome in the case of capital projects where several local authorities may together provide a 6% contribution towards the running costs of an individual PFI/PPP scheme. On one view, one of the authorities may obstruct and delay an MCC's plans with which the other local authorities agree; on another view, it may be expected to contribute to a project outside its area in which it has no interest or which it regards as contrary to its interest.

---

[27] created by the Justices of the Peace Act 1949; see now Justices of the Peace Act 1997, s 31; see also Seagoe, Walker and Wall, p 640

[28] see para 31 below

[29] as distinct from their involvement in local crime prevention, youth offending teams, crime and disorder partnerships etc

20   There are now special financial arrangements for London. On 1st April 2001 a new body, called the Greater London Magistrates' Courts Authority, came into being. It differs from MCCs in a number of important respects: in mandatory inclusion of representatives of local authorities and of the District Judge Bench; in its ownership of property; and in the mechanics of its financing. It consists of magistrates, at least one of whom must be a District Judge, and mayoral and other local authority nominees. Not only does it own its courthouses and associated property, but it also acts as a paying authority in its own right. However, it will receive its revenue funding from two different sources and in the same proportions as the MCCs, namely 80% from the Lord Chancellor's Department and 20% from the Corporation of the City of London and the 32 London Boroughs.

21   I have attempted to describe in a few paragraphs the present highly complex system of administration of magistrates' courts. I find it hard to believe that anyone skilled and experienced in the art of public administration and financing would, if starting afresh, devise it that way today. It is, of course, a product of history and an increasingly tortuous legislative overlay, which the following may in part explain.

Origins

22   Until half way through the 20th century there was a patchwork system throughout the country of about 1,000 county and borough Commissions of the Peace of different sizes. Benches administered summary justice in court-buildings usually provided and maintained by their local authorities. They were largely independent entities who appointed their own justices' clerk, mostly a part-time appointment from among the local solicitors, and contributed to their running costs out of fines and fees that they paid to their local authorities. Local authorities found themselves making up increasing deficits in the cost of running their local courts. Under somewhat loose oversight of the Home Office, each court was administered by its own bench of magistrates and in their own way, with their justices' clerk doubling as legal adviser and court administrator.[30]

23   In 1944 a Departmental Committee on justices' clerks chaired by Lord Roche recommended[31] the establishment of MCCs to administer petty sessional areas based on administrative counties and large boroughs. In keeping with the long and close involvement of magistrates in local public administration alongside their judicial duties, the Committee was content to leave the

---

[30] see the Report of the Le Vay *Efficiency Scrutiny of Magistrates' Courts* (HMSO, 1989), Vol 1, para 2

[31] Report, Cmnd 6507, HMSO, para 231

membership of MCCs and responsibility for their administration to magistrates themselves.

24   The Justices of the Peace Act 1949 implemented that recommendation, creating MCCs for each administrative county and for certain non-county boroughs. The Committees were made up of magistrates chosen from each commission area together with one or two ex officio members.

25   The main functions of MCCs, under the continuing general administrative oversight of the Home Office, were administrative. They were to propose, where appropriate, for order by the Home Secretary, the division of their areas into petty sessional divisions, to appoint one or more justices' clerks for their area and to provide courses of instruction to magistrates. Each petty sessional division was to have a bench chairman chosen by its magistrates in secret ballot. The local authority(ies) within whose area each MCC was located was (were) to be responsible for the court accommodation and all the expenses of transacting the business of the court, the nature of that provision to be determined by the MCC in consultation with the authority(ies). All fines and fees were to be paid to the Home Office. The Home Office in turn was to make a grant to the local authority(ies) within each MCC area of an amount representing the proceeds of certain fines, plus twothirds of the difference between them and actual expenditure. In practice the grant represented about 80% of the total cost, leaving the local authority(ies) to fund the balance of 20%. The Criminal Justice Act 1972 formalised that funding ratio.

26   A key principle of the 1949 Act was that magistrates' courts should operate on a local basis with a large degree of autonomy. However, as Julian Le Vay, who, in 1989, conducted an *Efficiency Scrutiny of the Magistrates' Courts* on the instruction of the Home Secretary, commented, neither the Roche Report nor the 1949 Act dealt with management in any modern sense:

> "The Act left the justices' clerk with responsibility for day to day running of courts and court offices, but did not make clear to whom he was answerable (if at all), now that he was appointed by a body separate from the bench he served. Nor was central Government given any say in the level or use of resources it was committed to provide." [32]

27   In the 1960s and early 1970s the Bar Council, Law Society, Magistrates' Association and Justices' Clerks' Society proposed centralisation of the management of magistrates' courts with a view to achieving greater efficiency, training and use of accommodation. The county councils opposed the proposal, arguing that it was against the trend of devolution. The Home

---

[32] Le Vay Report, para 2.3

Secretary of the time also resisted it on the ground, amongst others, that it would transform justices' clerks and their staff into a central government service.

28   As a side note in this short history, I should mention again Lord Beeching's inquiry in the late 1960s into the administration of Assizes and Quarter Sessions, another layer of justice countrywide steeped in antiquity, complexity and some amateurism. He recommended the abolition of both those jurisdictions and their replacement with a single, nationally administered court.[33] If his terms of reference had included magistrates' courts, it is inconceivable that he would not have included their even more complex administration in the same or some similar national reorganisation.[34] That appears to have been the initial instinct of the Government in the late 1960s. With the encouragement, amongst others, of the Justices' Clerks' Society, it considered amalgamating magistrates' courts and their management into a new national courts structure like that proposed for the Crown Court. However, it did not pursue it.[35] In 1976 the Layfield Committee recommended that funding for MCCs should be centralised, but its recommendations were not adopted.[36]

29   By 1989 when Le Vay was conducting his efficiency scrutiny of the magistrates' courts, the cost of administering them was about £200 million. Most of it was met from central funds, but with limited central supervision. He observed in his report that "it would be difficult to think of any arrangements less likely to deliver value for money", and added:

> "The arrangements for managing magistrates' courts and their resources retain the local, part-time, almost amateur flavour of an earlier age. The arrangements have never been systematically appraised, and have not adapted to take account of the enormous increase since 1949 in the volume of business and the number of permanent staff, or the fact that central Government now foots most of the bill".[37]

His principal recommendation was that administration of magistrates' courts should be "run as a national service, funded entirely by the Government - but with maximum delegation of managerial responsibility and control of resources to the local level", a proposal rejected, seemingly, on the grounds of expense. He also made a number of other recommendations for improvements of the system, many of which found more favour.

---

[33] Report of the *Review of Assizes and Quarter Sessions*, chapter IV
[34] ibid, see eg para 155
[35] Le Vay Report, para. 2.5;
[36] *Local Government Finance: Report of the Committee of Inquiry*, Cmnd 6453 (HMSO, May 1976), pp 114

30   On 1st April 1992, the Lord Chancellor assumed responsibility for the administration of the magistrates courts. By then the cost of administering them was approaching £300 million.   Le Vay's findings prompted the Government to issue a White Paper in 1992 entitled a *A New Framework for Justice*, which in turn led to changes introduced by the Police and Magistrates'Courts Act 1994.   These included: the amalgamation of MCCs; making them more clearly responsible for the administration of magistrates'courts in their areas and defining their responsibilities; permitting the co-option of two members in place of the former ex officio members; requiring each MCC to appoint a legally qualified chief executive, a justices' chief executive, whose function was to be purely administrative, as distinct from the legal and advisory role of the justices' clerk; giving the Lord Chancellor power to combine MCC areas and to direct MCCs as to their standards of performance; and the establishment of the Magistrates' Court Service Inspectorate.

31   When the present Government came to power it expressed a strong desire to improve the over-all management of the criminal justice system at both national and local level.   It sought to reduce the number of MCC areas, creating larger ones to share boundaries ('co-terminosity') with other criminal justice agencies, and to enable MCCs to determine and vary the structure of their petty sessional areas. It also sought a clearer distinction than had been achieved by the 1994 reforms between the administrative functions of the justices' chief executive and the legal and advisory responsibilities of the justices' clerk.   The chosen areas for co-ordination of management were the 42 police authority areas[38] established by the Local Government Act 1972.   In 1997 there were 105 Magistrates' Courts Committees but, as I have said, these have now been reduced to 42.   There has been similar re-organisation of the Crown Prosecution Service and Probation Service.   And the Prison Service has moved to a 13 area structure which aligns more closely with the 42 area boundaries.

32   The move to sharpen the distinction between the administrative role of the justices' chief executive and the legal and advisory role of the justices' clerk was impeded by a statutory requirement[39] that justices' chief executives could not be appointed unless eligible for appointment as a justices' clerk. This led to many of the posts being filled by former justices' clerks or their legally qualified deputies. The Access to Justice Act 1999 removed that requirement and further defined the functions of justices' chief executives in an attempt to reinforce the distinction.[40]   However, both are employed by the MCCs.   And, although justices' clerks' primary duty is to their bench or benches as legal

---

[37] Le Vay Report, paras 1.5 and 2.7

[38] for this exercise the City of London is included with the Metropolitan Police

[39] initially in the Police and Magistrates' Courts Act 1994 and subsequently incorporated into the Justices of the Peace Act 1997, s 40(5)

[40] Access to Justice Act 1999, ss 87 and 88(1)

advisers and in the organisation and conduct of their court work, they continue, if their MCC so decides, to exercise certain administrative functions on behalf of the justices' chief executive.[41] As I have said, he is their 'line-manager' for that purpose.

Commentary

33 I make recommendations for the future administrative structure of the criminal courts in chapter 7,[42] but discuss here some of the present problems of the system. Nicholas Stephens, the President of the Justices' Clerks Society for 1999-2000, described the legal and administrative divide in the magistrates' courts as creating a "leadership vacuum".[43] Put another way, it is not always clear where the boundary lies between the responsibilities of the bench and of the MCC or to whom the justices' clerk is accountable in his different responsibilities. For example, the divide between 'scheduling' of work - the MCCs' responsibility - and 'listing' of cases and case-management – magistrates' and justices' clerks' responsibility - is not always easy.[44] And an issue that has arisen in at least one MCC area is whether a justices' chief executive could direct a justices' clerk to delegate his powers and to whom he should delegate them.

34 There have been further changes in the roles and responsibilities of MCCs. Members of MCCs are now selected for the contribution they can make to the task of efficient administration of their courts, not as representatives of individual benches. The Lord Chancellor's Department has set targets, in the form of public service agreements, for magistrates' courts, and collects data to establish 'National Performance Indicators' of their efficiency and effectiveness. The 1999 Act also gave the Lord Chancellor greater authority over MCCs, including: an ability to direct them to implement recommendations of the Magistrates' Courts' Service Inspectorate; to issue a code of conduct for MCC members; and the right to dismiss them for non-compliance with it. The Judicial Studies Board has introduced the Magistrates' New Training Initiative (MNTI) to all MCC areas from September 1999. Also, the Narey reforms for reducing delays in the criminal justice system were introduced from November 1999. Reports of the Magistrates' Courts Inspectorate indicate a substantial improvement in MCCs' performance since 1997. Notable achievements, in addition to the sometimes painful Government-driven structural re-organisations of the MCC areas and of court provision within them, are the improvements they have

---

[41] see *A Strategic Steer*, the LCD's response in January 2000 to its September 1998 consultation paper, *The Future Role of the Justices' Clerk*

[42] Ch 7, paras 50 - 73

[43] in an address at the Justices' Clerks' Conference in May 2000

[44] as the Association of Justices' Chief Executives and the Justices' Clerks' Society have pointed out in a joint submission in the Review

made in the service to and treatment of those who use the courts. These include better facilities for witnesses and the disabled, the introduction of complaints procedures, expressing court documents in plain English and the publication of charters concerning quality of service.

35   The MCCs and the courts that they administer are still in a state of transition. Their reduction, from over 100 in 1997 to the present 42, has been accompanied by a steady progression of amalgamations of benches and closures of little-used courts, mainly in rural areas.[45] These amalgamations have been accompanied by a move to confine a number of benches within individual MCC areas to a single justices' clerk. A number of factors have contributed to these developments, the most important being the limits placed by central Government on MCCs' budgets, recognition of the need to provide better facilities for all who have to attend court, and a drive to concentrate work to achieve speedier, more efficient and cost effective justice.

36   These developments have caused, and continue to cause, concern among magistrates and many others about loss of 'local justice'. MCCs are responsible for very large areas, mostly corresponding with counties but some, such as Dyfed-Powys, West Mercia, Devon and Cornwall and Thames Valley, extending over several counties. Within these new areas the courts are already widely spaced, making unreal any notion of 'local justice'. For example, in the Cumbria MCC area six courthouses serve a population of less than 500,000 spread over nearly 2,700 square miles, and the distance between them is up to 50 miles. Similarly, in North Yorkshire, nine magistrates' courts serve a population of 742,000 spread over 3,000 square miles.

37   The members of the MCCs are responsible, through their justices' chief executives and, subject to the Lord Chancellor's Department guidelines and oversight, for administering considerable budgets and any capital or PFI spending plans. For example, the 1999/2000 annual expenditure for the Merseyside and West Midlands MCCs were respectively nearly £10 million and about £17.5 million. Examples of corresponding figures for MCCs at the lower end of the scale are Bedfordshire - about £3.2 million and Warwickshire - about £2.4 million. However, whatever the level of annual expenditure, as the Central Council of Magistrates Courts Committees (CCMCC) has observed, the reality is that MCCs have no budgetary control over their affairs - in the sense that they simply bid each year to the maximum permitted by the Treasury. And the arrangements for their accounting as between themselves and the local authority or authorities in whose area(s) they fall are unsatisfactory. In addition, they are not subject to a satisfactory regime of audit.

---

[45] The Justices of the Peace Act 1997, s 33, imposes a duty on MCCs to keep their petty sessional areas under review and, if directed by the Lord Chancellor, to consider whether any alteration is required and, having done so, to submit to him a draft order for their alteration or a report for not doing so

38 Although MCCs do not have to submit their budgets to the Lord Chancellor's Department for approval and, almost without exception, set budgets that will utilise all the available grant, technically they are still required to 'determine' their expenditure needs. And although the local authorities, as 'paying authorities' are entitled to appeal to the Lord Chancellor against the determination of the budget by the MCC, they see no point in doing so, believing that a budget based on the cash limit will, by its nature, be considered reasonable. Thus, the introduction of the cash limit, though providing an effective cap on MCCs' expenditure, has, paradoxically, reduced the extent to which the paying authorities have any incentive to monitor or challenge their budget-setting processes.

39 The MCCs' accounting arrangements are unsatisfactory because, with the exception of the Greater London Magistrates' Courts Authority (GLMCA),[46] they hold no money or property. This arrangement is particularly cumbrous and productive of delay where an MCC falls within two or more local authority areas. Normally, one of the authorities takes the lead in any dealings with the Lord Chancellor's Department, but there can be disputes about the contribution each authority makes towards the 20% local authority funding. And, more seriously there can be disputes about the principle of MCCs' proposals for capital projects (normally by PFI or PPP[47]) or minor works for which they must make special bids to the Lord Chancellor's Department. Such disputes, if not resolved, may have to be submitted to the Lord Chancellor for his determination. This is a particularly unhappy and inefficient consequence of the combination of MCCs'responsibility to determine their need for court and other accommodation with the local authorities' obligation to provide it.

40 In addition, with the exception of the GLMCA, there is no statutory requirement for audit of MCCs' accounts; and there are only patchy and variable internal audits by the local authorities. Similarly, there is little detailed examination of MCCs' financial affairs by the external auditor appointed by the Audit Commission to scrutinise local government expenditure or by the Lord Chancellor's Department's internal auditors. And, although the Magistrates'Courts Service Inspectorate has indicated that it expects MCCs to institute an appropriate auditing regime, it frequently finds gaps in coverage during inspections.

41 Despite increasing oversight by the Lord Chancellor's Department of MCCs' management of their affairs, there remain considerable differences in the ways

---

[46] established by Access to Justice Act 1999, s 83 which inserted a new s30A in the Justices' of the Peace Act 1997

[47] in the case of PFI or PPP projects the effective cost to local authorities is 6% of the total cost. So far three magistrates' courts projects have commenced, and ten more are in the pipeline. None has been delivered

in which they do things. They are left to devise their own procedures and forms in implementation of legislation and central government policy. As a result, practices vary considerably from one MCC to another, for example, the format of case file sheets and even legal aid application forms. They do not have the same information technology systems to enable the establishment of common data-bases of their work for the setting and monitoring of targets of efficiency, or to facilitate research,[48] or even for the ready communication of information to each other. In addition, each MCC is responsible for training its magistrates, which it pays for out of its own budget. The Magistrates' Committee of the Judicial Studies Board provides much material and some support to the MCCs for this purpose, but each devises and conducts its own training scheme.

42   This lack of administrative consistency, which spills over into court procedures, is to some extent mitigated by the separate efforts of four bodies, the CCMCC, the Magistrates' Association, the Justices' Clerks' Society and the Association of Justices' Chief Executives. However, as to the CCMCC and the Magistrates' Association, their 'constituencies' appear to be different and their relationship, if any, distant - mirroring the distance between those of MCCs who administer large areas and local benches who are primarily concerned with the day to day running of their own courts. The Justices' Clerks' Society and the Association of Chief Executives have a closer and good working relationship, assisted in part by the fact that many current justices chief executives were formerly justices' clerks.

43   The CCMCC represents all the MCCs in England and Wales. It is composed of one magistrate member of each MCC, eight justices' chief executives as associate members and a number of co-opted and observer members from other bodies and associations involved directly and indirectly with magistrates' courts. The Council, which meets four times a year, has a management committee that meets more frequently. The Council concerns itself with anything involving the work of MCCs, including the training of magistrates and issuing of good practice guidance and advice on Lord Chancellor's Department's initiatives. It also responds to proposals for reform or reviews, such as this, affecting them.

44   The Magistrates' Association, which was incorporated by Royal Charter in 1962, is a 30,000 strong body of magistrates, that is, most of the magistrates in England and Wales. It has 59 branches throughout the country. Through its Council and various committees and through the medium of its monthly journal, *The Magistrate*, it provides information and advice to its members. It also contributes to their training and, from time to time, issues guidance on specific matters. Recently, and with the approval of the Lord Chief Justice, it

---

[48] see, for example, *The Judiciary in the Magistrates' Courts*, p 33, para 3.1

has issued sentencing guidelines, which have been well received. The Association also provides representation on, and liaises with, various bodies concerned with the criminal justice system.

45   The Justices' Clerks' Society was founded in 1839 and incorporated in 1909. Its aim is "to provide national cohesion and to harness its members' expertise to develop: the legal framework for magistrates' courts, the science and practice of the law, good practice and effective relationship with others interested in the provision of justice". It comprises all the justices' clerks and the great majority of justices' chief executives in England and Wales. As it said in its first response in the Review, "[b]etween them, they are responsible for providing legal advice and support, including training and development, to every lay justice in the country".

46   The Association of Justices' Chief Executives is constituted to lead the development of the management and administration of the Magistrates'Courts. It comprises all the justices' chief executives in England and Wales and meets at least four times a year. The Association acts as the national forum of justices' chief executives to consider matters affecting their duties, and works closely with the Central Council and the Justices' Clerks' Society in the best interests of the magistrates' courts as a whole.

47   I should add that District Judges, though working in the same courts and exercising the same jurisdiction as the magistrates, have no part in the CCMCC or the Magistrates' Association. That is not just because they have always had their own organisation, now the National Council of Her Majesty's District Judges (Magistrates' Courts). It results from their separateness from magistrates because of their professional status, the manner of their appointment and payment, the fact that they sit alone and that they are not necessarily confined to one MCC area or court. Whilst, in many areas, District Judges and the local benches of magistrates have established good working relationships, there are, unfortunately, some pockets of mutual resentment and distrust. Some benches feel threatened by the arrival of District Judges to share or, as they see it, to take their work. They do not welcome them, they criticize their different working patterns and attitudes and they try to control the work that is given to them. The Runciman Royal Commission noted this unhappy phenomenon over 10 years ago,[49] and I regret that there are still traces of it here and there. Some District Judges, on the other hand, make little effort to involve themselves socially or otherwise with the magistrates and the courts in which they sit, or to assist them in disposing of their lists when necessary. Some appear to be critical of the competence or suitability of magistrates to do their job. This is not the general picture, but it is frequent enough to be of concern for the administration of justice where it

---

[49] The Report of the *Royal Commission on Criminal Justice*, Cmnd 2263 (HMSO, July 1993), Ch 8, para 103

occurs. I am glad to say that the National Council of District Judges, the CCMCC and the Magistrates' Association are all alive to such problems and are taking vigorous steps to overcome them.

THE CROWN COURT

The Judiciary

48 The Lord Chief Justice, in consultation with the Lord Chancellor, is responsible for the deployment of and allocation of work to the judiciary, and for advising the Lord Chancellor on a number of matters of judicial administration and on senior judicial appointments. He has no responsibility, statutory or otherwise, for magistrates or District Judges (Magistrates' Courts). He fulfils his responsibilities by means of practice and other directions, and by general oversight, assisted by the Senior Presiding Judge, Presiding Judges of the circuits and Resident Judges of Crown Court centres. He heads no formal administrative structure. The nearest to it is his chairmanship of a body of senior judges known as the Judges' Council and his chairmanship of a termly meeting of the High Court Judges, a meeting given over, in the main, to their deployment and allocation of work in London and on circuit in the ensuing law term.

49 The Senior Presiding Judge and the Vice-President of the Queen's Bench Division assume much of the responsibility of the Lord Chief Justice for deployment of High Court Judges who try crime. And the Senior Presiding Judge has a wider and demanding delegacy of administrative and pastoral responsibilities for High Court and Circuit Judges sitting on circuit, whether in crime or in civil or family matters. This he exercises, in consultation with the Chief Executive of the Court Service and/or, as appropriate, through the Presiding Judges, Chancery Supervisory or Family Liaison Judges in conjunction with Circuit Administrators. These responsibilities include judicial deployment and allocation of work, court practices generally and at individual court centres.

50 The Senior Presiding Judge has other responsibilities that he exercises independently of administrators, notably advising the Lord Chancellor and the Lord Chief Justice on judicial appointments and authorisations to Circuit Judges to try particular classes of work and to sit in the Court of Appeal, Criminal Division. He spends one day of each working week on his administrative duties and chairs meetings of the Presiding Judges twice every law term. In addition, he usually spends one week of each law term visiting court centres, meeting judges, circuit and court administrative staff and

representatives of various criminal justice agencies. I refer again to his role and those of the Presiding and Resident Judges in connection with the circuit system in Chapters 6[50] and 7[51] below.

The Court Service

51   I have mentioned that many High Court and Circuit Judges deal with civil and family matters as well as crime, often in the same court and sometimes in the course of a mixed daily list. In whatever jurisdiction they sit, their deployment and allocation of work are matters of judicial administration, as I have mentioned. But the administration and management of their courts are the responsibility of the Court Service, an executive agency of the Lord Chancellor's Department established in 1995. That was the scheme intended by Lord Beeching in 1969:

> "… our proposals are consistent with the preservation of all existing safeguards which ensure the independence of the judiciary, and which keep the judicial work of the courts subject to the overriding control of the judges, and we recommend that they be preserved".[52]

52   The Court Service is responsible for the administration and management of criminal justice in the Crown Court as well as for civil and family matters in the county court, the High Court of Justice and in the Court of Appeal, Civil and Criminal Divisions. It is also responsible for certain tribunals and the Probate Service. The administration of the Appellate Committee of the House of Lords is the responsibility of the House.

53   The Court Service Board is responsible for the strategic direction of the Service. It meets monthly and consists of the Chief Executive, a number of Executive Directors, two Circuit Administrators and two non-executive Directors. At present, there is no division for administrative purposes between criminal, civil and family work above the level of the courts themselves. However, the Service has recently made some changes to its internal management structure, and is considering more wide-ranging changes – on which it has reached no final decision – that could involve a separation of those jurisdictional responsibilities at a higher level.

54   The Court Service Board administers the courts through a dispersed regional organisation divided into the six judicial circuits, the Supreme Court Group

---

[50] paras 20 - 21

[51] paras 75 - 83

[52] *Royal Commission on Assizes and Quarter Sessions*, para 170

and the Criminal Appeal Office. From April 2002, the circuits will be divided into 18 court groups, each made up of a number of court centres, each with an appropriate level of administrator. The Circuit Administrator, in the conduct of his circuit-wide responsibilities, consults the Presiding Judges of the circuit on important matters, in the main on deployment of the judiciary and allocation of their work. At the group or court level the managers consult in a similar way on more day to day matters with Resident or other local judges.

55 Only in London are the civil and criminal courts administered separately. The administration of civil business in London, both in the High Court and the county court, is now the responsibility of the Supreme Court Group. All of the London Crown Court centres are administered by one Group Manager and, uniquely, the Criminal Appeal Office is headed by a person combining administrative and judicial roles, the Registrar of Criminal Appeals and Master of the Crown Office.

Commentary

56 I should begin by saying how submissions in the Review have more than confirmed my long experience of the high commitment of Court Service staff, particularly those in the courts and at group level. They have had to bear the main brunt of frequent change and inadequate resources which have characterised the early years of the Service, and they have invariably done so with stoicism, improvisation and cheerfulness. That spirit and the strong bond at local level between them and the judiciary in attempting to provide a fair and efficient justice system are one of the most heartening features of it. In the short life of the Court Service there has been much restlessness within its structure and organisation. And there have been a number of proposals for change, including a management structure review, a pay and grading review and an ill-considered project called *Transforming the Crown Court*. It has also had a number of organisational shortcomings, most of them, no doubt, dictated by policies and directives of the government of the day and short-term funding arrangements, namely:

- setting its own inward-looking 'commercial' targets regardless of their impact on other agencies in the criminal justice system and others exposed to it;

- over-centralisation of its organisation, leaving those whose job it is to manage and work with other agencies at court level with little autonomy or budgetary flexibility;

- short-termism or lack of strategy in planning, particularly in the field of information technology and accommodation needs; and

- failure to consult adequately or in a timely fashion with the judiciary and others in or involved with the criminal justice system about its projects for change, of which the largely unworkable project, *Transforming the Crown Court* was a particularly unfortunate example.

57   However, with the present impetus for all criminal justice agencies to establish common aims and plans and to work more closely together, the Court Service has begun to take a broader look at the way in which it should manage the courts. The extent to which it can succeed in shedding its inward-looking 'commercialism'[53] will depend largely on the vigour with which the Government pursues its goal of a criminal justice system in which all agencies can truly work towards a common end, untrammelled by their separate finances and lines of accountability. The Court Service is not alone among the criminal justice agencies in having to change old habits.

58   As to over-centralisation within the Court Service, local managers still lack the authority and budgetary freedom exercised by their counterparts in other criminal justice agencies. This, coupled with the fact that the organisation of the Court Service within each circuit does not coincide with the 42 area structure adopted by most of the other agencies, including the Police, the Crown Prosecution Service and the Probation Service, leaves them unable to commit the Service to local joint agency initiatives as most other agencies can. However, the Service has now largely realigned its management areas with the ten administrative regions of Government, some of them approximating to the six judicial circuits and others to be established within them. Within those ten regions the Court Service is also considering re-organisation within the circuit boundaries, rather than within the regional boundaries - and, possibly, setting up three separate jurisdictional accounting mechanisms for criminal, civil and family work and two separate administrative mechanisms at court level.

59   As to re-alignment of Court Service management areas, there is obvious sense in making them correspond as closely as possible with those of other criminal justice agencies, but there are three main difficulties.

60   The first is that, as I have said, the courts outside London are not only concerned with criminal justice, but also with civil and family work whose administrative arrangements and needs are not the same.

61   The second is that in some parts of the country the present distribution of courts and the centres of population that they serve are so widely dispersed that re-aligning the management of the courts with the criminal justice areas would be very difficult. Before the most recent re-organisation of group

---

[53] or "silo mentality", as it is known in Whitehall

boundaries, there was concern among some in the Court Service that some group budgets were too small to allow for effective and flexible management of resources. To establish 42 separate budgets for the Crown Court alone would increase, not reduce, this concern. An extreme example is the poorly located and uncoordinated provision of court accommodation in Wales. The overriding principle of the Beeching Commission in determining circuit boundaries was to contain rather than to divide main concentrations of population.[54]. Such a principle would have led to the disappearance of the Wales and Chester Circuit, because it did not

> "have such predominant concentrations of population in limited areas as do most of the other circuits, and its mountainous terrain prevents the development of natural lines of communication between north and south".[55]

However, the Commission retreated from its preferred solution because of the special circumstances for treating the circuit as a single unit and administering it from Cardiff.[56] Today, the circuit has four criminal justice areas. The largest of those, Dyfed Powys, is vast, mountainous and thinly populated. It extends from Haverfordwest, Carmathen and Llanelli in the south west into the whole of central Wales and as far north as Welshpool. It has no permanent Crown Court; its needs are met by three separate Crown Court centres in other criminal justice areas,[57] with only occasional Crown Court sittings within it. As the Presiding Judges for the Wales and Chester Circuit have observed in the Review, there is no need for a permanent Crown Court or any separate management for this huge criminal justice area. Also, Cardiff and Newport operate and are jointly managed, though in different criminal justice areas, a system which works well and in respect of which few, if any, local agencies want change. Conversely, the Crown Court centres in Swansea and Cardiff, the two largest civil and criminal court centres in Wales, though in the same criminal justice area, are managed separately and work well that way. The peculiar problems of Wales have led the Presiding Judges, in consultation with the Magistrates' Courts Committees, to prepare a strategy for consultation on the future location and better use of court and associated accommodation throughout the Principality.

62   The third difficulty in aligning management of the Court Service with the 42 criminal justice areas is that the circuits are an established and integral part of the deployment of judges and of allocation of judicial work in all three jurisdictions throughout the country. Much of their strength in those respects is the single point of contact that they provide at senior level between Presiding Judges and Circuit Administrators. They are also an important and hallowed part of the organisation of the bar in providing a service to the

---

[54] *Royal Commission on Assizes and Quarter Sessions*, para 284

[55] ibid, para 295

[56] ibid, paras 285 and 295-297

[57] namely, Swansea and Merthyr in the South Wales police area and Chester (including Mold) in the Cheshire police area

courts outside London. However, such traditions are not untouchable, particularly as to circuit boundaries. There have been changes in those boundaries in the past to meet the needs of the time and there may be a case for further changes now.

63   As to the Court Service's proposals for financial accounting, the intention is to ensure that expenditure on each of the three jurisdictions is matched by the resources allocated to each. Put another way, the intention is that each jurisdiction should pay for itself and should not subsidise or draw on either of the others. Now, why a public service organisation should fragment itself administratively and financially at the point, as the Service puts it, of 'delivery of services', and according to the nature of the services, is not immediately obvious where so much of the medium of 'delivery' is common or interchangeable. Although the courts and the judges are, in the main, employed in more than one of the three jurisdictions, sometimes, as I have indicated, in the same courtroom and in the course of a mixed list on the same day, it is proposed to separate the administrative and financial systems supporting them. The need for such complicated machinery has, it seems to me, little to do with administrative efficiency. It is to be found in the separate sources of funding that the Treasury has decreed for the three jurisdictions, notwithstanding the shared and overlapping resources devoted daily to their administration and exercise. Any attempt to provide the sort of data collection at court level to enable separate accounting for the costs of each jurisdiction would, even if it were worth it, require considerably more sophisticated information technology than that presently available or planned.

64   As to consultation, there has been some improvement. But there is considerable scope for better and more timely involvement of the judiciary and others, particularly at national level.

ONE SYSTEM OR TWO?

65   Thus, the system of administration of the Crown Court is very different from that of magistrates' courts. It is centralised and, some say, too monolithic and inflexible to meet local needs and the different jurisdictions it has to administer. The MCCs, despite increasing oversight by the Lord Chancellor's Department, are a fragmented and diverse system of local bodies hobbled by difficult financial and managerial mechanisms and with inconsistent practices and procedures. Not only are there great differences between the two systems, there is poor co-operation between them. Those who are likely to have the closest experience of this are the members of the Justices' Clerks' Society who, in their submission in the Review, wrote:

>   "There is little, if any, day to day co-operation between the administration of the Crown Court ... and the

Magistrates'Courts.... The Society would suggest that the enquiry examine whether the time has come to establish a single, integrated courts service with common rules and practices (possibly with a separate, specialist arm for youth justice)".

66   However, both systems are striving to overcome their considerable structural problems; and both, in their present forms, are relatively new and in a state of transition. The question for decision is whether to continue them as separate administrative structures, leaving them to develop their own improvements, with or without structural change, or to consider a single administrative body and, possibly, a unified court, accommodating both levels of jurisdiction.

CHAPTER 4

MAGISTRATES

INTRODUCTION

1   No country in the world relies on lay magistrates as we do, sitting usually in panels of three, to administer the bulk of criminal justice. I have already mentioned that magistrates' courts deal with 95% of all prosecuted crime. Lay magistrates – about 30,400 of them – handle 91% of that work. Our system is also unique in giving exactly the same jurisdiction to a small cadre of about 100 full-time professional judges, now called District Judges (Magistrates' Courts), supported by about 150 part-time Deputies, sitting singly, who deal with the remaining 9%. And, unlike in other countries where both lay and professional judges exercise the same jurisdiction, magistrates and District Judges in England and Wales rarely sit together as a mixed tribunal. It is matter of chance, so far as defendants are concerned, whether a lay or a professional bench deals with them. As one academic commentator of great experience in this field has observed, this major contribution of the magistracy to the criminal justice system has until recently been largely disregarded by the Judiciary, many academics, review bodies, law-makers and others.[1]

2   As I have indicated in Chapter 1, I am confident that magistrates should continue to exercise their established jurisdiction alongside District Judges. I have also given a brief description of the history and current jurisdiction of the magistracy and District Judges in Chapter 3. In this Chapter, I consider the future for their summary jurisdiction and their respective roles in the exercise of it. In doing so, I have had the advantage of submissions from many knowledgeable contributors to the Review, including the Magistrates' Association, the Central Council of Magistrates' Courts' Committees, the Joint Council of Her Majesty's Stipendiary Magistrates,[2] the Justices' Clerks' Society, the Association of Justices' Chief Executives, the Association of Magisterial Officers and many individual magistrates. I have also drawn heavily on two pieces of research published during the currency of the

---

[1] Dr. Penny Darbyshire, *An Essay on the Importance and Neglect of the Magistracy* [1997] Crim LR 627, at 634-640

[2] now the National Council of Her Majesty's District Judges (Magistrates' Courts)

Review. The first is an article by Peter Seago, Clive Walker and David Wall, *The Development of the Professional Magistracy in England and Wales*, published in August 2000.[3] The second is the Report of Professor Rod Morgan and Neil Russell, *The judiciary in the magistrates' courts*, published in December 2000, on their research into the balance of lay and stipendiary magistrates and on the effectiveness of their respective deployment. The latter research, which was commissioned by the Lord Chancellor's Department and the Home Office, was undertaken during the first nine months of 2000 and of this Review. It drew on data collected nationally and locally, but concentrated on ten magistrates' courts in London and the provinces, with and without District Judges. In addition, it sought the views of regular court users of the ten courts and also of the general public through a nationally representative sample of about 1,750 people, and took into account comparative material drawn from European jurisdictions.

3 Morgan and Russell's main findings were that the magistracy is not wholly representative of the community, but that in most respects magistrates' courts, whether constituted by magistrates or District Judges, work well and command general confidence. They concluded that to eliminate or greatly diminish the work of magistrates would not be widely understood or supported.

4 Their findings, in a little more detail, were as follows. District Judges, because of their legal knowledge and experience and because they sit full-time and alone, are significantly faster and otherwise more efficient than magistrates who need to confer with each other and often take the advice of their court clerk. District Judges achieve this edge in speed whilst being more interventionist than magistrates and without loss of judicial fairness, efficiency or general courtesy.[4] When indirect costs, i.e. of premises and administration etc.,[5] are taken into account, they are still moderately more expensive than magistrates.[6] When allowance is made for the savings (unestimated by Morgan and Russell) to other court users from the increased use of District Judges and for lay magistrates 'opportunity costs', i.e. the loss to their employers of their donated time, they would be moderately less expensive.[7] They also found evidence that District Judges are more likely to remand in custody and to sentence more heavily than their lay colleagues.

---

[3] Seago, Walker and Wall, [2000] Crim. Law Review 631

[4] See Morgan and Russell, *The judiciary in the magistrates' courts*, RDS Occasional Paper No 66 (Home Office, 2000), pp ix and 34-43 which suggests that District Judges can deal with 30% more than magistrates of the latter's normal case load;. and Seago, Walker and Wall, who suggest that a District Judge can equal the work of anything between 24 and 32 magistrates in metropolitan and provincial areas respectively; [2000] Crim L R, p 638.

[5] by far the biggest components in the costs of running magistrates' courts; ibid, pp xii and 97

[6] ie costing just over £52 against magistrates' nearly £62 per appearance when indirect costs such as premises and administration staff were brought into the equation; ibid, p xi and p 89

[7] ibid, pp 90-91

5   Morgan and Russell concluded that most court users had confidence in both, but more in District Judges. Those unfamiliar with the system – "the overwhelming majority of the public" – after it had been explained to them, regarded magistrates as more representative of the community. Nevertheless, they thought that the work should be divided equally between them or that the type of tribunal did not matter. As the researchers commented, these and other findings were "not entirely consistent nor ... [were] their implications entirely clear".[8] As uninformed opinion, it seems to me, that even if those thoughts were consistent and their implications clear, they are valueless as an aid to determining the relative strengths of District Judges and lay magistrates.

6   Unsurprisingly, Morgan and Russell felt unable to recommend any change in policy direction. Broadly, they confined themselves to concluding that those familiar with the system, in the main criminal justice practitioners, have greater confidence in District Judges and that the uninformed general public think that panels of magistrates should make the more serious judicial decisions. Their last words, in the light of all these findings and conclusions, were delphic. They suggested that:

> "....the nature and balance of the contribution made by lay and stipendiary magistrates could be altered so as better to satisfy these different considerations without prejudicing the integrity of a system founded on strong traditions and widely supported".[9]

7   On the question of relative cost, my view, contrary to that of the Magistrates' Association,[10] is that Morgan and Russell were correct to take into account the 'opportunity costs' of magistrates to society as a whole in their donation of time to this public service, rather than confining the analysis to one of cost to the criminal justice system. However, their calculations are necessarily somewhat theoretical and speculative and are open to criticism in a number of respects.

8   First, Morgan and Russell concluded that such savings as might be achieved, say, by doubling the numbers of District Judges, would, in any event, be off-set by additional Prison Service costs of over £30 million resulting from their greater tendency than magistrates to remand more accused persons in custody and to impose custodial sentences.[11] Putting aside the question of accuracy of these estimates and the assumptions on which they are made, about which the authors are suitably cautious, there is a point of principle in their putting into

---

[8] ibid, p 117

[9] ibid p

[10] Press Release of 14th December 2000

[11] *The judiciary in the magistrates' courts*, pp xii, 49 - 50 and 92 – 94

the balance increased custodial costs. If there is a difference between District Judges and magistrates in this way when dealing with like cases, one or other must be getting it wrong, just as in the case of the perceived difference between sentencing in the Crown Court and in magistrates' courts in 'either-way' offences.[12] Save as a cynical measure of expediency, it would be wrong to consider whether to change the present sharing of summary jurisdiction on the basis that District Judges are too hard or that magistrates are too soft in their decisions as to custody. As it happens, I believe that District Judges are more likely to follow national practice and sentencing policy guide-lines in this respect than magistrates, with their individual traditions and training, and history of disparate sentencing.

9   Second, there are other more detailed criticisms that can be made of Morgan and Russell's analysis of potential savings on various hypotheses.[13] These include their failure: to allow, when calculating relative costs per session, for the greater complexity of cases heard by District Judges; sufficiently to recognise magistrates' greater call than District Judges on legal support and court overheads; and to give sufficient consideration to the 'knock-on' savings to all other criminal justice agencies resulting from the undoubted efficiency savings that would flow from an increase in the use of District Judges.

10   As to the future, the cost comparison could be significantly affected to the disadvantage of magistrates by implementation of some of the recommendations that I make below for more systematic investment in recruitment of applicants for selection, appointment, training and allowances for loss of earnings etc. And, as Morgan and Russell acknowledge,[14] much of their analysis would be irrelevant, and there would be greater scope for savings than they have identified, if the present courts structure were to be replaced by a unified court in which judges and magistrates could be deployed flexibly according to work needs in busy urban centres.

11   It is enough to note for the purpose of this Report, Morgan and Russell's conclusion that District Judges are more efficient than magistrates, and that, assuming little change in their respective numbers and the present system of summary justice, there may not be much to choose between them as to cost.[15] As they observe, though one District Judge can handle the work presently handled by about 30 magistrates, it would need a significant increase in the use of District Judges to achieve reductions on any scale in administrative staff and courtroom costs.[16]

---

[12] see Chapter 5, paras 161 - 163

[13] drawn to the Review's and their attention by Robert McFarland, a member of the Glidewell Committee

[14] *The judiciary in the magistrates' courts*, p 115

[15] ibid, pp 111-112

[16] ibid, pp xii and 85-86

12 Many magistrates believe that there is a national policy or 'agenda' gradually to enable District Judges and justices' clerks to squeeze them out of the system. I know of no such agenda and no hint of it has appeared in the course of the Review. Nevertheless, it has been a constant theme in the many submissions that I have received from benches and individual magistrates all over the country. It has persisted despite the Lord Chancellor's publicly expressed commitment to the principle of the lay magistracy continuing to play a significant part in our system of justice[17] and my publicly expressed interim view[18] that I was satisfied that there was a sound case for their retention. District Judges too feel uneasy about their precise role in the system of summary justice, believing, with some justification that their greater legal expertise, as well as their speed, could be put to better use than sometimes is the case. This is a long-standing concern. The Runciman Royal Commission, reporting over 10 years ago,[19] noted that stipendiary magistrates were sometimes not always given work that made the best use of their skills and qualifications, and recommended correction. Morgan and Russell neatly sum up the dilemma for policy makers on this issue in the following words:

> "… many lay magistrates are wary of what they see as the asset-stripping consequences of employing stipendiaries. Why, they ask, should they volunteer to give so much of their unpaid time to this public office if they are deprived of the opportunity to hear interesting cases likely to engage their intelligence? By the same token, stipendiary magistrates think it odd if their legal expertise is not exploited by allocating to them the most legally and procedurally demanding cases in which serious decisions must be made".[20]

13 As with juries, magistrates are not wholly reflective of the communities from which they are drawn, but nevertheless they have an important symbolic effect of lay participation in the system which should not be under-valued. Unlike juries, they are volunteers who bring to their work public spirited commitment and ever increasing legal and procedural knowledge and experience. Their vulnerability to case-hardening - in a way that juries are not - is off-set by a number of factors, namely: the relative infrequency of their sittings; the discipline that comes from their training; their sitting in ever changing panels; the advantage of a clerk to advise them on the law; and their obligation to explain their decisions. However, there is scope for improvement, particularly in the manner of their recruitment, so as to achieve a better reflection, nationally and locally, of the community, and in their training, so as to develop fairer, more efficient and more consistent procedures and sentencing patterns.

---

[17] in a speech to the Annual Dinner of Stipendiary Magistrates on 13th April 2000

[18] my third interim report published on the Review's web-site on 14th October 2000

[19] Report of *Royal Commission on Criminal Justice*, Ch 8, para 103.

[20] *The judiciary in the magistrates' courts*, p 31

14 The evidence in the Review as to the value of District Judges in complementing the work of magistrates at a summary level is also of a piece with the findings of the Morgan and Russell Report. There are undoubted advantages in the legal expertise, authority, speed, continuity and consistency that they can bring to the conduct of the longer and more complex cases, to case management and to the increasing sophistication and variety of sentencing options. They are also of value in their speed in dealing efficiently with the long lists of more straightforward work that is the staple diet of magistrates' courts, particularly in large metropolitan centres. Now, too, that magistrates' courts are in the front judicial line for Human Rights challenges,[21] it is important to have the benefit of their legal and judicial skills in that potentially difficult field. In my view, District Judges are too important to the administration of criminal justice at a summary level to consider - as some contributors to the Review have suggested - removing them from it.

Accordingly, I confirm the indication I have already given in my interim reports and recommend that magistrates and District Judges should continue to exercise summary jurisdiction.

Present working patterns

15 District Judges were given national jurisdiction when the Stipendiary Bench was unified by the Access to Justice Act 1999, in order to enable them to deal more flexibly with the work wherever and whenever it arises. The official policy of the Lord Chancellor's Department for them is that they should normally sit in the area to which they have been assigned and should deal with the same range of cases as magistrates. But the Senior District Judge, acting on behalf of the Lord Chancellor, may also direct their deployment anywhere in the country to deal with fluctuations in workload or particularly complex cases.[22]

16 Magistrates, on the other hand, are appointed to and sit only in a particular commission area, though in each area their numbers provide the necessary flexibility. However, whilst I do not advocate that magistrates should normally sit outside or far outside the area to which they have been appointed, I have considered two candidates for improvement in their territorial jurisdiction. First, there should be a ready means of transfer from one bench to another. Until recently this was cumbersome, resulting sometimes in

---

[21] which, so far, have not been as numerous as some expected

[22] see para 275 of the explanatory notes to the Access to Justice Act 1999, s 78; and para 35 of the memorandum on conditions and terms of service of District Judges

magistrates of great experience being lost to, or excluded for some time, from the system. However, there is now developing[23] a simple procedure of 'active transfer', that is, without a break in service, between commission areas. Such procedure, which preserves magistrates' continuity of experience, is becoming the norm for those seeking transfer providing they have the support of the chairman of their transferor bench and acceptable MNTI reports, and there is a suitable[24] vacancy. Second, in the event of there being a new unified Criminal Court, although I would expect magistrates to sit mainly in their local courthouses, there is no reason why their jurisdiction should be restricted to one particular locality when they could be usefully deployed from time to time in adjoining areas, especially for longer cases and if they live in the boundary area spanning them.

17   The terms of District Judges' appointment are that they should sit five days a week. However, there are some local variations, mainly in London, to allow for out of hours on call and emergency duties. And, as always, the unpredictability of lists or the need to give more time to preparation of cases or decisions, may mean that they do not always sit in court every day of the week. Like magistrates, they too have other commitments, including training sessions of the Judicial Studies Board, attending various meetings and assisting with the training of Deputy District Judges and magistrates. Although one or two provincial District Judges are members of MCCs, it is unusual.

18   Magistrates are required, as a minimum, to sit 26 half-days a year, but are normally expected to sit between 35 and 45 and not more than 70 a year. In addition, they are expected to undertake training for their general jurisdiction as 'wingers' and, in time, as chairmen and for any specialist panels, such as youth or family on which they seek to sit. They are also expected to involve themselves in different ways in the affairs of their bench and local community, by attending meetings, sitting on local committees and participating in various activities to educate the public about the work of the courts. These activities include participation in court open days, in presentations to schools and community and employer groups and in mock trial competitions. There have been some suggestions in the Review for relaxation of the Lord Chancellor's sitting constraints, mainly to raise the maximum to beyond 70 sittings a year to allow those who can give more time to it to do so. However, I could not recommend that for two reasons: first, it would be likely to be taken up in large part by the retired or financially independent, swelling the already over-represented older and well-to-do members of the community on the magistracy. Second, to sit regularly for some two days or more a week would not be consonant with the notion of part-time lay justice and would attract perceptions of case-hardening.

---

[23] in anticipation of a proposed amendment to the Lord Chancellor's Directions to take effect in the autumn of this year

[24] bearing in mind that the transferee bench should continue broadly to reflect the community it serves

Accordingly, I recommend that, whilst magistrates should continue to be appointed to one commission area, there should be a ready mechanism for enabling them, when required, to sit in adjoining areas.

FUTURE SHAPE OF SUMMARY JUSTICE

19   There are five main issues. They over-lap, one with another, and must also be considered in the context of the reforms that I recommend for the court system as a whole. They are:

- the extent of summary jurisdiction;

- the deployment of and allocation of work between District Judges and magistrates;

- the role of the justices' clerks;

- the composition of the magistracy; and

- the training of the magistracy.

THE EXTENT OF SUMMARY JURISDICTION

20   There have been some suggestions in the Review for a general increase or decrease in summary jurisdiction, but I can discern no wide or well-based support for a change in the general limit of six month's custody or £5,000 fine now applicable to District Judges and magistrates alike.[25] Whilst magistrates have a generally higher jurisdiction than that given to lay tribunals in other jurisdictions, they are increasingly well-trained for their task and have their legal advisers to assist them, where necessary, on points of law or procedure. A notable feature of their handling of their jurisdiction to date is the very low level of appeal from their decisions.   But, as the division between summary jurisdiction and that of trial on indictment turns on the maximum severity of sentence – currently defined in terms of length of custody or amount of fine – implementation of the recommendations in the recent Sentencing Review, for combined custody and community service orders for up to 12 months[26] could require reconsideration of the dividing line.

---

[25] the one seeming anomaly is the extension of their powers in the Youth Court to make detention and training orders for a maximum two years; see Powers of Criminal Courts (Sentencing) Act 2000, ss100-107

[26] *Making Punishments Work: Report of a Review of the Sentencing Framework for England and Wales* (Home Office May 2001), p iv, para 0.11, recommendations 15-18

I recommend that there should be no general change in the level of summary jurisdiction, as it is presently defined, of District Judges or magistrates, though the matter may need review in the light of the Halliday recommendations for the introduction of a new sentencing framework including combined custody and community sentence orders.

DEPLOYMENT AND ALLOCATION OF WORK

21   According to Morgan and Russell[27] and information provided in the Review, District Judges deal routinely in London and in some other major metropolitan areas with the whole range of summary matters as well as the heavier work. Elsewhere, their caseload, while covering much of the range, is slanted towards the heavier work. As I have said, the Morgan and Russell research indicated that District Judges rarely sit with magistrates. This finding is of a piece with the indications of most District Judges and magistrates in the Review that neither wanted to sit routinely with the other in summary matters. District Judges feel that they do not need the assistance of magistrates. And magistrates do not wish to lose the opportunity of chairing their own courts, though the Magistrates' Association and many individual magistrates have expressed appreciation of the experience to be gained from sitting with District Judges from time to time. However, the indications in the Review are that magistrates, at least, might take a different view - and different considerations would arise - if they were to be given an enhanced jurisdiction sitting with a District Judge in a new unified Criminal Court.

22   The allocation of work between lay and professional magistrates has been the subject of much examination, professional and academic, over the years. Any attempt at a logical and tidy solution to the question is impeded by the way in which summary justice in this country has evolved over the centuries to its present mix of a small number of professional judges exercising singly the same jurisdiction as a large number of lay magistrates sitting in panels. The question is not just of the efficient and effective use of judicial resources, though that is important. There are more fundamental concerns that also bear on it, namely fairness and involvement of the community in decision-making. Those two concerns in turn invite consideration whether there should always be a number of lay fact-finders in a summary criminal tribunal and whether that tribunal, in whatever form, should reflect the local community. The debate as to primacy between lay and professional justice in these matters invariably ranges over a whole range of broad, overlapping and elusive notions claimed to support the former. They include public confidence, lay justice, people's or citizens' justice, 'participative democracy', 'locality' or community justice, magistrates as 'surrogate jurors', judicial independence

---

[27] *The judiciary in the magistrates' courts*, pp 26-31, 99 and 109

and, the right to a 'fair' trial. On the other side, usually prayed in aid as favouring District Judges, are the more tangible qualities of legality, consistency, speed and other efficiency and effectiveness.

23   The debate, whatever notions or concepts are in play, largely consists of the deployment of ideologies to support unsound or out-dated comparisons and rival caricatures. The reality is that District Judges and magistrates today are closer in their social and legal culture than many give them credit for. If the reforms that I recommend in this and other chapters of the Report are implemented, the scope for this arid debate will be further reduced. Nevertheless, out of deference to the many who feel strongly about these considerations and who have made submissions to the Review, I consider each of them below.

24   I should add that, just as it is impossible for outside researchers and reviewers to evaluate the relative 'correctness' of juries' verdicts and magistrates'courts' decisions, so also is it impossible to evaluate the relative justice of the decision-making of District Judges and magistrates, for example, as to perceptions of over-ready conviction or over heavy sentencing by one or the other. Morgan and Russell disclaimed any attempt to assess the appropriateness or justice of their respective decisions or to recommend how better to balance the work of District Judges and magistrates at summary level.[28] They construed their remit as being more concerned with the mechanics of the present court process and how each form of summary tribunal performs, or is perceived to perform. As I have said, they were generally favourable to both.

Quality of hearing

25   As to court manner and general sensitivity to the parties, District Judges and magistrates both came well out of the Morgan and Russell research. There was not much to choose between them in such matters as attentiveness, clarity, courtesy and so on. But they concluded that District Judges had the edge in their control of proceedings, in moving them on and in resisting delaying adjournments, so that the more District Judges the less court appearances there were likely to be over-all. However, as I have indicated, they also found that District Judges are more likely than magistrates to refuse bail, to issue arrest warrants for failure to attend court and to impose immediate custodial sentences.[29]

---

[28] ibid, p 5, para 1.3
[29] ibid, pp ix, x, and 48-50, paras 3.4.2 - 3.4.4

People's justice and public confidence

26   One contributor to the Review[30] has drawn attention to the dichotomy in people's attitudes towards the magistracy, according to whether they are considering the elective right to trial by jury in 'either-way' cases or the relative advantages of lay and professional judges in summary cases. On the former issue magistrates are often portrayed as part of the establishment, being used to deny defendants a basic human right; on the latter they are depicted as the near equivalent of a jury - the peers of people who appear before them, ordinary people with experience of the real world, bringing common sense to bear etc.

27   Some see magistrates as 'surrogate jurors' or as a manifestation of democracy in the administration of criminal justice. A recent example of many contributions over decades to this topic has been that developed during the course of the Review, and published in January 2001, by Professor Andrew Sanders under the auspices of the Institute for Public Policy Research.[31] He takes as his starting point the low level of public confidence in magistrates' courts based largely on the recent British Crime Survey,[32] a MORI poll and focus groups with the public and with offenders. He then argues: that 'participative democracy', along with fairness and efficiency, are the principles by which the summary system should be judged; that trial by judge and jury in the Crown Court is assumed to be 'the best' system and one which commands more public confidence than trial by magistrates; and that, therefore, the aim should be "to make magistrates proceedings more like Crown Court trials".[33] By that route he concludes that a District Judge sitting alone should deal with simple cases, "requiring legal rather than social skills", and that a District Judge should sit with magistrates in all cases where social as well as legal skills are required. In practical terms he proposes that District Judges should sit on their own only when dealing with bail, remands, mode of trial determinations and pleas of guilty and that, in all other cases, they should sit with magistrates, who would need less legal expertise, training and experience and would sit less frequently than now – "more jury-like". He suggests that the greater costs of requiring a mixed tribunal for all trial work would be off-set by the savings in District Judges dealing on their own with long remand and guilty plea lists and the removal of the need for legal advice from justices' clerks or legal advisers.

28   Accordingly, under Professor Sanders' proposals, District Judges, despite their legal knowledge and expertise, would when sitting alone, deal with

---

[30] Robert McFarland

[31] *Community Justice: Modernising The Magistracy In England and Wales*, Andrew Sanders. Criminal Justice Forum, IPPR; p1

[32] Home Office Research Study *Attitudes to Crime and Criminal Justice: Findings from the 1998 British Crime Survey*, (2000) (Joanna Mattinson and Catriona Mirrlees-Black), pp 3-8 and 47-49

[33] *Community Justice*, pp 8 and 9

mainly routine interlocutory work and uncontested cases, and magistrates would be relegated to sitting, and then only infrequently, as 'wingers' with little, if any, training or experience for the work. I believe that such a 'half-way jury system', if introduced, would deprive summary justice of the best features of professional and lay judges sitting separately. It would encumber and slow all its trial procedures and, for that reason and because of the many more District Judge appointments it would require, would be prohibitively expensive.

29   Like many arguments of this sort, it takes as its starting point, public confidence. Morgan and Russell found that those with some knowledge of the system - court practitioners - though generally confident in both District Judges and magistrates, had more confidence in the former.[34] However, their assessment of public opinion, on the strength of their poll of under 2,000 people - nearly 75% of whom did not know, until told, that there were two types of summary judge - was that magistrates reflected the community better and were more likely to sympathise with defendants' circumstances. They were of the view that District Judges were better at making correct judgments of guilt or innocence, considered on balance that single magistrates should deal with motoring offences, and, by a large majority, that panels of magistrates should deal with the more serious questions of guilt or innocence and sending people to prison. To cap it all, most of the respondents thought that the work of magistrates' courts should be divided equally between District Judges and magistrates or that it did not matter which.[35] It is not surprising that Morgan and Russell were, as I have indicated, baffled by the seeming conflicts in some of these expressions of 'public opinion'.

30   The Sanders MORI poll and focus group research, like that of Morgan and Russell, revealed a similar picture of public ignorance of the system:

> "The public know little about how the magistracy works. One third of IPPR's MORI poll did not know that the majority of magistrates are lay people. They also hugely underestimated the proportion of cases heard in the lower courts. The role of the Magistracy is not visible to the public".[36]

31   Despite this dismal picture, the authors of these research projects, and others who set store by what they perceive to be public opinion, rely significantly on public confidence as a factor, or at least something on which a value judgment may be made, as to one or other aspect of the system. Thus, Morgan and Russell, after identifying the level of public ignorance about

---

[34] *The judiciary in the magistrates' courts*, pp x, 59, 62 and 67

[35] ibid, pp x, xi, 69-82, 116

[36] *Community Justice*, p 2

magistrates'courts, observed[37] "[i]t would be a mistake to construe lack of public knowledge with lack of opinion or public indifference" and went on to rely on the uninformed opinions they had identified as among a number of factors to be satisfied in some unspecified way. Similarly, Sanders clearly regards safeguarding and increasing of public confidence as an argument in favour of fashioning the system to meet the largely uninformed view of those whom his researchers had approached as representative of the larger public.

32   As I have said in Chapter 1, it is one thing to rely on uninformed views of the public as a guide to what may be necessary to engender public confidence, and another to rely on such views as an argument for fashioning the system to meet them. Public confidence is not an end in itself; it is or should be an outcome of a fair and efficient system. The proper approach is to make the system fair and efficient and, if public ignorance stands in the way of public confidence, take steps adequately to demonstrate to the public that it is so.

Magistrates as 'surrogate jurors'

33   This argument implicitly includes, or is sometimes expressly coupled with, the notion that, as compared with District Judges, magistrates are less case-hardened and, therefore, approach their task with fresher or more open minds. To regard magistrates as 'surrogate jurors' is a tenuous comparison between trained and largely experienced lay judges sitting as judges of law and fact up to about once a week for, on average, between 10 and 20 years, and those who mostly know little or nothing of the system, and probably only serve as finders of fact for a fortnight or so once or twice in a lifetime. It is also an insecure comparison to the extent that it suggests that jury trial is the ideal model for all criminal trials whatever the level of seriousness. As to fresh and case-hardened minds, Morgan and Russell put magistrates in a continuum for case-hardening closer to professional judges than juries, noting the frequent argument used against them of higher conviction rate in magistrates' courts than in the Crown Court.[38] Such a comparison also ignores the contribution of the respective training and courtroom experience of both District Judges and magistrates to maintaining an objective and judicial approach to their task.

'Participative democracy'

34   As to the argument based on democracy, it is doubtful, even if benches of magistrates were representative of the community, what that quality would

---

[37] *The judiciary in the magistrates' courts*, p 116
[38] ibid, p 9, para 1.4.3

bring to the judicial role if not heavily overlain by the objectivity and skills that should come with courtroom training and experience. Moreover, as Morgan and Russell have observed by reference to other jurisdictions:

> "… there is no straightforward relationship between the degree to which democracy is embedded and lay involvement in judicial decision-making. Many longstanding democracies involve lay persons while others do not. The re-establishment of democracy in a country does not necessarily stimulate the introduction of lay involvement in judicial decision-making, sometimes the reverse occurs, depending on the cultural and political tradition".[39]

And, as they also note,[40] although the lay magistracy are a sign of the active engagement of the citizen in the administration of justice, the distinction between them and District Judges in this and other respects is, in practice, diminishing. Their social position is likely to be much the same, though, if my recommendations for securing a more widely diverse magistracy are adopted, this should change. However, both are, and will continue to be trained for and experienced in their respective roles and familiar with the extensive 'locality' over which they exercise the same jurisdiction.

'Locality' of justice

35   As I have mentioned in Chapter 1, 'locality' of justice is an issue for the criminal justice system as a whole. It is, however, most commonly voiced in relation to the role of magistrates. There is a widely and firmly based instinct that lay and 'local' justice is "a bridge between the public and the court system which might otherwise appear remote".[41] Although magistrates must normally still live in or within 15 miles of their commission area, closures of courts in rural areas have led to some sitting well outside the area in which they live and work. They cannot know or, in any normal sense of the term, be regarded as representative of, the whole locality or community for which they administer justice. District Judges, most of whom will spend all or most of their time in their assigned area, will acquire as much or little 'local' knowledge as magistrates, and many will also live there as part of the broad community. And, like it or not, justice has been and is becoming less geographically localised as larger and better equipped full-time courts replace old, small, inadequate and insecure courthouses in part-time use in rural areas. With the loosening of small community ties resulting from increasing mobility and wider use of information technology, 'locality' of justice, like locality of shops and other community facilities now has a wider connotation.

---

[39] ibid, p xii and pp 100-101

[40] ibid, pp 6-7

[41] Home Affairs Committee Report, *Judicial Appointments (1995-96)*, HC 52-1, para 198 and see Seago, Walker and Wall, *The Development of the Professional Magistracy in England and Wales*, Crim L R [2000], pp 649-651

As Seago, Walker and Wall have commented, touching on the wider question of court structure to which I turn in Chapter 7:

> "The logical next step would be to rationalise further in terms of the provision of judicial administration. In this way, as justice becomes less localised, why should magistrates' courts buildings be distinct from Crown Court buildings? Why should there be a separation of the staff working within them? And most controversial of all, in the absence of any practical need for, as opposed to abstract ideology of, localism, why is there a need for lay justices to reflect local connections?"[42]

36   'Locality' of justice also has its downside in the wide inconsistencies to which it leads between MCC areas and between individual benches in their patterns of decision-making, particularly as to bail and sentencing. Such inconsistencies, often branded by the media and civil rights groups as 'post-code justice', do great damage to public confidence in the system.[43] They result, not in the main from magistrates responding to the prevalence in their areas of particular types of crime or other local community needs. They owe more to the culture of individualism of benches themselves, often inculcated by their justices' clerk and sometimes aggravated by the independence of their MCCs in the training that they provide. The presence and, I hope, increasing involvement of District Judges in the life of magistrates' courts and in magistrates' training, coupled with a greater role for the Judicial Studies Board in the training of both District Judges and their lay colleagues, can only be beneficial in reducing this unfortunate aspect of 'locality' of justice and improving public confidence in magistrates' embodiment of it.

37   Another disadvantage of 'locality' of justice, whether in the form of magistrates or a District Judge, is that the tribunal may, on occasion, know too much about accused persons, whose guilt or sentence they should determine only on the material put before them in court.

A 'fair' trial and the 'hybrid court'

38   There is much to be said for the contention that two or more heads are better than one in determining important questions, such as the issue of guilt or the appropriate sentence, even if the one is a professional judge. Its supporters draw on the wider experience of life that a panel of lay magistrates bring collectively to the task, their independence, the greater chance of their

---

[42] ibid, p 649

[43] see eg *Unequal Before The Law*, Liberty (1992); also a Report by NACRO for the Youth Justice Board, *Factors Associated with Differential Rates of Youth Custodial Sentencing* (September 2000)

collegiate decision being fair because of the inter-action between them and their relative lack of case-hardening. Glanville Williams was an early protagonist of collegiate decision-making both as to guilt and as to sentence because he saw it as a better protection against "the vagaries of the individual".[44]

39   There have from time to time been suggestions that professional judges should not sit on their own to determine the issue of guilt and/or that they should not sentence on their own, especially in both cases where the possible outcome for a defendant is loss of his liberty. In addition to the proposal of Professor Sanders, there have been a number of submissions in the Review to like effect, also praying in aid the Article 6 concept of a fair trial. However, I can see nothing in Article 6 or in any Strasbourg jurisprudence to suggest that trial by a professional judge sitting on his own violates it.[45] Single fact-finders and sentencers are commonplace in Convention countries[46] and in common law jurisdictions with a statutory declaration of rights containing a similar provision, and they have not been singled out for such attack.

40   Like Morgan and Russell, I would tread warily, certainly with the level of cases now dealt with by magistrates' courts and where lay and professional judges sitting separately from each other are well established, before suggesting, on the ground of fairness or otherwise, that either should be routinely submerged in some form of hybrid court. As I have said, the overwhelming evidence in the Review is that they each do a good job in their separate ways. And neither magistrates nor District Judges would welcome such a general transformation and diminution of their respective roles at that level. It would undoubtedly make recruitment of both difficult. And relegating the role of magistrates to untrained, short-term 'jury-like wingers', as in the Sanders model, would have the further disadvantage of producing a tribunal two of whose members would, in the main, be unlikely to make an effective contribution to the process. Different considerations arise, however, when considering the conferment of an enhanced jurisdiction on a mixed tribunal of, say a District Judge and suitably trained magistrates, for certain types of more serious case, a matter with which I deal in Chapter 7.

---

[44] *The Proof of Guilt*, The Hamlyn Lectures, 7th Series (Stevens, 1955) pp 233 and 273-281

[45] see eg *Murray v. U.K.*(1996) 22.EHRR 22

[46] eg in Holland where there are two types of 'first instance' courts. The 'kantongerechten''(magistrates' courts) deal with less serious offences – misdemeanours or contraventions; also appeals against fines imposed by the police for traffic offences. These proceedings are dealt with by a single judge. More serious offences are dealt with by the district courts, where single judges (politierechters, who may sentence up to six months of imprisonment) and chambers of three judges sit. Economic offences are tried by single economic judges or by chambers of three economic judges. In Germany there are four types of 'first instance' courts. A single judge (Einzelrichter) at the District Court (Amtsgericht) has jurisdiction in the less serious criminal offences, including the majority of road traffic offences and may sentence up to two years of imprisonment

Independence

41   As to independence, where it is often suggested magistrates have the edge over District Judges, it is difficult to see why the latter, whose appointment is subject to essentially the same criteria and procedures as other professional judges, should today be regarded as likely to favour the executive at the expense of the citizen. If anything, experience over recent decades has tended to show the reverse at all judicial levels. The implementation as part of our domestic law of the European Convention of Human Rights is likely to accentuate that instinct of independence. Moreover, the scope for District Judges sitting singly to act as 'government placemen', favouring the executive at the expense of the citizen, is likely to be limited. Most of their time is spent, not on cases of general public interest or of sensitivity to central government, but on general lists involving, in the main, pre-trial work, sentencing and run of the mill trials.[47] Seago, Walker and Wall, commenting on their fieldwork supporting that general picture, said:

> "... stipendiary magistrates do not emerge as markedly specialised or compliant judicial figures who are willing to adopt whatever central government desideratum that comes their way. There is also no evidence to date, for example, in regard to sentencing, that stipendiaries have a greater deterrent impact, nor have they been more liberal when policy has so required it. So, an outside observer who believed, however fancifully, that the explicit purpose of the magistrates' courts is 'the maintenance and reproduction of existing forms of structural dominance' or even of 'conveyor belt' justice would find little to choose between the zeal of lay or professional magistrates."[48]

Conclusion as to deployment and allocation of work

42   As I have said, the pace of increase in the number of stipendiary magistrates in proportion to that of lay magistrates has been modest. Their role, despite their recent change of title and status to District Judges, was and is to support and complement the work of magistrates where necessary. Given the current structure and jurisdiction of magistrates' courts, I can see no justification, whether of justice or efficiency, for a move to District Judges and magistrates routinely sitting as mixed tribunals to deal with the general range or any

---

[47] see eg Seago, Walker and Wall, p 637; Morgan and Russell, pp26-29; Sanders and Young, *Criminal Justice* 2nd Edition, 2000, pp 488-489

[48] Seago, Walker and Wall, pp. 637-638

particular type of case or form of proceeding, though there may be training and local 'cultural' advantages in their doing so from time to time depending on their respective availability and caseloads. Nor can I see any basis for recommending any significant change in their respective numbers. The position may be different if my recommendation in Chapter 7 for the creation of a unified Criminal Court with an intermediate tier is adopted. In either case, our strong tradition of lay justice and the availability of a vast body of increasingly trained, experienced volunteer judges are compelling reasons for retaining a sizeable lay magistracy. Even if a move to all or significantly more District Judges were considered desirable and achievable, it would require a major programme of change to reduce and otherwise rationalise the present apparatus of summary justice. A move the other way would throw away the value of professional judges in the fair and efficient disposal of summary work of all levels of importance, and would require thousands of newly recruited magistrates to replace them and to train for the purpose.

43   As to allocation of work between the two forms of tribunal, I consider that it would be a mistake to be too prescriptive. Nevertheless, there are obvious strengths of District Judges of which advantage should be taken in the interests of both justice and efficiency, namely their knowledge of law and procedure, their authority borne of that knowledge and its daily use and, because they normally sit alone, their speed. As Morgan and Russell have observed,

> "It scarcely makes sense for the well-rewarded skills of stipendiaries not to be employed on court business which will benefit most from the application of those skills".[49]

44   In September 1994 the Lord Chancellor, with the agreement of the Lord Chief Justice, established a committee which was charged with identifying more clearly the respective roles of the stipendiary magistracy and the lay bench in the administration of justice in magistrates' courts. The Committee, chaired by Roger Venne of the Lord Chancellor's Department, was composed of metropolitan and provincial stipendiary magistrates, lay magistrates and justices' clerks. The resulting report[50] spoke of the particular strengths and value of stipendiaries to the system in cases involving complex points of law or evidence, some mode of trial decisions, cases involving complex procedural issues, long and/or inter-linked cases, cases involving considerations of public safety, public interest immunity applications and extradition cases. The Committee recommended that, in such cases, there should be a presumption that where a stipendiary was available he should undertake such work.[51] In so recommending, the Committee did not ignore their important contribution to the system, and benefit to all those involved in

---

[49] *The judiciary in the magistrates' courts*, p 109

[50] *The Role of the Stipendiary Magistracy* (the Venne Report) (1996), pp 15-18, para 5.3

[51] The Venne Report, page 14, para 5.3

it, in the speed with which they can dispose of a general list of pre-trial work and pleas of guilty.

45   At first, I baulked at the Venne Committee's use of the word 'presumption' in recommending that, where a stipendiary magistrate was available, he should undertake the heavier work. However, when dealing with cases involving complex points of law or evidence, it made what I consider to be a strong general case for it. It spoke of the increasing legal complexity of work in magistrates' courts "in an evolving system of justice which will always endeavour to refine the requirements of due process". But, importantly, it qualified its recommendation by a reminder of the value to the system of stipendiaries taking a fair share of routine work because of: their speed and its contribution to the efficient administration of justice; a need for exposing them to and giving them experience of every aspect of the work of a magistrates' court; the salutary effect that their customary presence in court in such cases can have on those who habitually prosecute and defend in them; and so as not exclude or give magistrates the impression of excluding them from the more interesting work of the court.[52]

46   I cannot improve on the approach of the Venne Committee. District Judges, while making themselves available to do the whole range of summary work, should concentrate on case allocation and management, cases of legal or factual complexity, cases of priority, such as those involving young offenders or offences of a sexual nature, and long cases that most magistrates could not undertake, at any rate under their present patterns of sitting.

47   The following conclusion of the Venne Committee as to how such a system of allocation can and does work in most places is well supported by many submissions to the Review and by my experience from visits and talking to District Judges, magistrates and justices' clerks all over the country:

> "The balance to be struck is a fine one, but we are satisfied
> from our own visits to magistrates' courts where Stipendiary
> Magistrates sit, that it can be achieved where the Stipendiary,
> the Justices' Clerks and the lay justices are alive to the need
> to achieve such an appropriate balance of work."[53]

48   Who should allocate summary work as between magistrates and District Judges under the present court structure or the new one that I recommend in Chapter 7? Is it a 'scheduling' responsibility of the justices' chief executive (court manager) or, in individual cases at any rate, a listing exercise for the chairman of the bench and the justices' clerk? The view of the Venne

---

[52] The Venne Report, para 5.4
[53] The Venne Report, see p 18, para 5.4

Committee, with which I agree, is that in most cases listing decisions of this sort are for the justices' clerk, who should have regard to its general guidance. Though, as the Committee also observed, there may be some cases in which it would be appropriate for him to consult the District Judge and/or Chairman of the Bench, for example, where there are issues of legal difficulty or local sensitivity. The allocation of the heavier and more interesting work can be contentious. Justices' clerks may find themselves in the middle of a tug of war between District Judges and magistrates, both staking their claim to it. A frequent complaint of magistrates in the Review was that they were losing, or would lose, much of this work to District Judges. I learned of instances where the local Chairman of the Bench heavily influenced what work should be given to the District Judge. Equally, there were accounts of District Judges insisting on being given work that they considered their status merited. As Morgan and Russell indicate,[54] local listing practices or policies of this sort raise questions of accountability or, in plain terms, of knowing who is in charge.

49 Under our present system, where do the Lord Chancellor's Department, the newly created Senior District Judge and the local MCC fit into all this? To whom is the justices' clerk, and for that matter, the District Judge and chairman of the bench, responsible for such decisions? In the Crown Court, listing has always been regarded as a judicial, not an administrative, function in the sense that the judges are the ultimate arbiters of listing practices at their court and of their own lists, albeit in close consultation with administrators. In my view, whether or not the present structure of the courts changes, there is an urgent need to establish lines of accountability and ultimate responsibility for listing and its manner of exercise in summary proceedings. If District Judges and magistrates become judges of a new unified Criminal Court, it seems to me that the immediate responsibility should be with the equivalent of the present justices' clerk after consultation with the District Judge, chairman of the bench and court manager. But, in the event of disagreement the Resident Judge should have the ultimate decision. I make a recommendation to that effect in Chapter 7.[55]

I recommend that in the exercise of their summary jurisdiction:

- **District Judges and magistrates should not routinely sit as mixed tribunals to deal with the general range or any particular type of case or form of proceeding, though there may be training and local 'cultural' advantages in their doing so from time to time**

---

[54] *The judiciary in the magistrates' courts*, pp 27-30 and 109-110

[55] para 81

depending on their respective availability and case loads;

- subject to changing workloads resulting from implementation of any of my recommendations or otherwise, there should be no significant change in the balance of numbers of District Judges and magistrates, or in the relative volumes or nature of summary work assigned to each of them; and

- summary work should continue to be allocated between District Judges and magistrates in accordance with the recommendations of the Venne Committee, namely that each, normally sitting separately, should be available to deal with the whole range, but that District Judges should concentrate on case allocation and management, cases of legal or factual complexity, cases of priority, such as those involving young offenders or offences of a sexual nature, and long cases.

JUSTICES' CLERKS

50   The office of the justices' clerk has developed piecemeal over the centuries. Originating as the personal servant to the local justice of the peace in mediaeval times, its subsequent history is of steady accretion, diversification and professionalism as the business of the summary courts has increased and the law has become more complex. Traditionally, each bench had its own justices' clerk who was normally a solicitor, sometimes a full-time employee but, often in the more rural areas, a part-time appointment from among the local practitioners. The Justices of the Peace Act 1949, in introducing Magistrates' Courts Committees, provided that they should appoint justices' clerks. The trend was then towards full-time posts, with some clerks serving more than one bench. At that stage, most clerks managed all the legal and administrative staff within their petty sessional divisions – collectively known as their 'clerkship'. As a result of recent legislation,[56] Government policy[57] and the current programme of amalgamations of MCCs and benches, their numbers are depleting, their territorial responsibilities widening, their former broad administrative responsibilities diminishing and their legal role concentrating primarily on the provision, mostly through other members of

---

[56] The Police & Magistrates' Courts Act, 1994, brought into existence the role of Justices' Chief Executive. The Justices of the Peace Act 1997, ss 41 and 45, as substituted by the Access to Justice Act 1999, ss 88 and 89, confirm the role of the JCE in being responsible for the efficient and effective administration of the courts within the area of their MCC and the independence of justices' clerks in the exercise of their legal and judicial functions. Section 90 of the Access to Justice Act enabled the transfer of responsibility for administrative functions to JCEs, allowing justices' clerks to concentrate on their key functions as legal adviser to magistrates

[57] *The future role of the Justices' Clerk: A Strategic Steer* (January 2000)

staff, of legal advice to magistrates, together with certain case management functions. The Government has indicated that their core job description should be that of "a professional legal adviser to justices ... rather than based on the model of 'clerkship'",[58] and has transferred most of their statutory administrative and accounting functions to justices' chief executives.[59] However, it remains for MCCs to determine individually how to and to what extent justices' clerks in their area should continue to exercise management responsibility for administrative and accounting matters. Arrangements vary considerably across the country. Justices' clerks only have total independence in respect of their responsibilities for advising magistrates on the law, which includes procedure and practice, and for any function also exercisable by magistrates.[60]

51   The amalgamations have significantly reduced the number of posts of justices' clerk, encouraging some of them to seek appointment as justices'chief executives or appointment as Deputy District Judges as a stage in the process of becoming District Judges. Some MCCs now only have one Justices' Clerk, often responsible for several benches of hundreds of magistrates, spread over a very wide area.[61] For example, the justices' clerk in Lancashire and Dyfed Powys each serves ten benches sitting in 11 and 15 courthouses respectively; in Hampshire and the Isle of Wight the tally is seven benches and ten courthouses. There are considerable benefits to be gained from one person having responsibility for the legal function across a large geographical area; the chances of neighbouring courts making conflicting decisions or adopting different procedures are considerably reduced; and the various criminal justice agencies are able to discuss their needs and concerns with a single individual. However, such broad territorial responsibilities can create tensions between justices' clerks and the benches they serve. Magistrates who have been used to regular contact with their clerk are understandably resistant to organisational changes which place him or her in a geographically distant location overseeing several teams of legal advisers, as court clerks are now known. A number of MCCs have responded to these concerns by identifying senior legal staff to liaise with individual benches. In this way, the justices' clerk can assume responsibility for the consistency and quality of legal advice provided to magistrates across a wide area, whilst at the same time devolving responsibility for day-to-day communication with the bench to a suitably experienced and qualified colleague. In the new unified Criminal Court that I recommend in Chapter 7 the justices' clerk and the legal advisers responsible to him should have essentially the same role and independence, albeit as part of a different court structure.

---

[58] *A Strategic Steer,* pp 3 and 13

[59] Access to Justice Act, s.90 and Sch 13

[60] Access to Justice Act 1999, s 89, substituting a new section 48 of the Justices of the Peace Act 1997

[61] in a diminishing number of instances, he combines the post with that of the Justices' Chief Executive, "though such combination of posts is being phased out"

52 The daily work of advising magistrates in court is the immediate responsibility of legal advisers only some of whom are professionally legally qualified, that is, as barristers or solicitors. Also qualified to act as legal advisers are those who have obtained a Diploma in Magisterial Law, those who have passed a preliminary professional examination coupled with two years experience, or staff of a certain age and experience who hold a certificate of competence.[62] The increasing focus on legal advice and case management, and its delegation in large part to legal advisers, led Government to conclude, as the Roche Committee had recommended over 50 years ago,[63] that all legal advisers should be professionally qualified. It resolved that, from 1st January 1999, all legal advisers would be required to qualify as a barrister or solicitor within 10 years; and it provided funding to MCCs for a training programme in conjunction with joint guidance from representative bodies in the magistrates'courts system.[64] It subsequently excluded from that requirement all court clerks who were 40 or over on 1st January 1999. Following considerable opposition, including legal action from a minority of younger legal advisers who felt that the requirement for them to qualify was unreasonable, the Government agreed to make a further change to the rules exempting all staff in post on 31 December 1998. Since 1 January 1999 it has been a requirement that all *new* appointees are professionally qualified. At the end of March 2001 there were around 1,800 legal advisers in England and Wales, two thirds of whom were professionally qualified. Given the increasingly testing jurisdiction of magistrates, particularly in case management, disclosure, human rights and sentencing, and the introduction of non-lawyers to prosecute in some uncontested cases,[65] it is vital that they should have the support of high quality lawyers with specialist training in their jurisdiction.[66]

53 District Judges, like magistrates, are assisted in court by legal advisers. District Judges value their presence, but rather for the smooth process of the court's work than requiring their legal advice. As Morgan and Russell have observed,[67] there is a question whether they need legally qualified court advisers. While there may be occasions when District Judges would welcome the assistance of a legally qualified clerk with experience of a particular area of work, they should normally be able to cope with the assistance of a member of the court's administrative staff.

---

[62] see the Qualification of Assistants Rules, 1979, as amended by the Justices' Clerks (Qualifications of Assistants) (Amendment) Rules, 2001,.

[63] *Report of the Departmental Committee on Justices' Clerks, 1944*, Cmnd 6507, Chapter VI, see, in particular, paras 117-119 and 126

[64] *Guidance for the Professional Qualification of Legal Advisers,* 3 July 2001

[65] Crime and Disorder Act 1998, s 53

[66] *For the New Lord Chancellor – Some Causes for Concern about Magistrates'*, Dr. Penny Darbyshire, Crim LR at pp 872-4

[67] *The judiciary in the magistrates' courts*, pp. x and 54

I recommend that District Judges should normally sit without a legal adviser.

54   The Lord Chief Justice, on 2nd October 2000, issued a practice direction[68] setting out the responsibilities and powers of justices' clerks and legal advisers, taking into account the provisions of the Human Rights Act 1998 which came into force on the same day. The main responsibilities are: the giving of legal advice to magistrates in and out of court; case management; the reduction of unnecessary delay; assisting unrepresented parties to present their case; and, in enforcement cases, with the agreement of the court, to assist it to discover the facts by impartial questioning of the defaulter. Legal advice includes advice on questions of law and of mixed law and fact, matters of practice and procedure, the range of available sentencing penalties, any other relevant issues and how to structure and formulate decisions. Any legal advice given in the magistrates' retiring room should be provisional and repeated in open court to enable the parties, if they wish, to make submissions on it; following which the advice, in original or varied form should be stated in open court.[69]   The Practice Direction also acknowledges the well established exclusion of the court clerk from participation in magistrates' fact-finding, save by questioning witnesses and/or the parties to clarify the evidence and, if requested, by reminding the magistrates of the evidence, ordinarily in open court.

55   Under the Narey recommendations implemented in the Crime and Disorder Act 1998,[70] some case management powers previously exercisable only by two or more magistrates can now be exercised by a single magistrate. These include 'early administrative hearings' in which a justices' clerk, or a legal adviser whom the former has deputed for the task, has also been given some case management jurisdiction. This includes: the power to remand the accused on bail subject to existing conditions or, with the consent of the parties, to varied conditions (but not to remand him in custody); marking an information as withdrawn or dismissing an information where the prosecution offer no evidence; power to request a pre-sentence and/or medical report; power to remit an offender to another court for sentence; and to give certain directions for the conduct of a trial, namely the timetable of the proceedings, the attendance of the parties, the service of documents, including summaries of legal arguments and the manner in which evidence is to be given. Justices'clerks are specifically excluded from exercising some of the powers available to a single magistrate, including: the imposition of new bail conditions without the consent of the parties, giving an indication of the

---

[68] Practice Direction (Justices: Clerk to Court) 2000, [2000] All ER 895, replacing and revoking Practice Direction (Justices: Clerk To Court) [1981] 1 WLR 1163

[69] this has been recognised as best practice for years, but it had proved difficult to persuade magistrates and legal advisers to change established routines

[70] Crime and Disorder Act 1998, ss 49 and 50

seriousness of an offence for the purpose of a pre-sentence report and remanding in custody for the purpose of a medical report.

56   Benches have varied in the extent to and manner in which a justices' clerk rather than a single magistrate exercises these powers. Courts in two thirds of all MCC areas hold at least some early administrative hearings presided over by a single magistrate or a justices' clerk or legal adviser.[71]   Some sit in the normal way with a bench of magistrates and a clerk, but the clerk deals with the directions and the magistrates deal with matters reserved to them. Some sit in split session, starting with the clerk alone and then bring in the magistrates to deal with anything outside the clerk's jurisdiction. And some sit as they always have, as a full directions court, consisting of a bench of magistrates and the clerk, with the magistrates dealing both with matters reserved to them and otherwise exercisable by the clerk.

57   Detailed evaluation of the relative effectiveness of the different types of early administrative hearings is not yet available. An initial assessment of the Narey pilots [72] provided some evidence that where the hearing was conducted by a clerk, the case took fewer days to complete over-all than where a bench of magistrates or a single lay magistrate dealt with case management. The assessment also noted conflicting views as to the extent of case management powers exercisable by a justices' clerk under these new provisions.

58   As Morgan and Russell have observed,[73] quoting the Narey Report, this is the latest in a long line of extension of powers to justices' clerks previously reserved to magistrates, "thereby arguably blurring the line" between their respective judicial and administrative roles. Justices' clerks have argued for further extension. The majority of them are frustrated by the limitations of their newly acquired jurisdiction. They suggest that they should be empowered to grant or refuse bail, to make mode of trial decisions, to give indications of the seriousness of the offence, to enable them to order a specific sentence report and to rule on matters of law. Similar views were expressed by many others - though not all - of those who commented on the issue in the Review. In my view, whilst the line between judicial and advisory functions has been blurred as I have described, there is no justification, so long as magistrates continue to play the central role that they do in summary justice, for blurring it further. Moveover, in cases of complexity or particular difficulty where robust case management is required, the matter should normally, and wherever practicable, be put before a District Judge. That is what he is there for.

---

[71] *Reducing Delays in the Magistrates' Courts*, D. Brown, Research Findings No. 131, Home Office Research, Development and Statistics Directorate

[72] *Reducing Delays in the Criminal Justice System; evaluation of the pilot schemes* (1999) Ernst and Young

[73] *The judiciary in the magistrates' courts*, p 4, para 1.2

Accordingly, I recommend that there should be no extension of justices' clerks' case management jurisdiction.

COMPOSITION OF THE BENCH

59   The fact that the magistracy is not a true reflection of the population nationally or of communities locally is confirmed by a number of studies, of which the Morgan and Russell research is only the latest.[74] The main problem is in the recruitment and identification of a sufficient and appropriate range of candidates for appointment, not in the criteria for or mechanics of appointment. If the magistracy is both to survive and to earn public confidence as a lay element in the administration of criminal justice, urgent steps must be taken to remove its largely unrepresentative nature.

60   The Morgan and Russell Report, based mainly on their inquiry questionnaires and, to a lesser extent, on out of date and inadequate[75] data provided by the Lord Chancellor's Department, shows that the magistracy is gender balanced, in marked contrast to the overwhelmingly male ranks of professional judges. It is approaching ethnic representativeness of the population at a national level, that is, 2% black, 2% from the Indian sub-continent or Asian origin and 1% other.[76] However, there are substantial local variations and, as the authors say, "more importantly, the fit between local benches and the make-up of the local communities they serve is in several instances wide". This is particularly the case in London where minority ethnic communities are not represented amongst the lay magistracy in anything like the proportion in which they are found within the general population. As to status or class, the magistracy is overwhelmingly drawn from professional and managerial ranks, that is, "disproportionately middle class, and almost certainly financially well-off, compared to the population at large". Finally, a high proportion of it, about two-fifths, is comprised of persons who have retired from full-time employment,[77] which imbalance is exacerbated by their ability to sit more often than those in work.[78] Although the Lord Chancellor requires local benches also to reflect the political affiliation of the community they serve and makes appointments with that in mind, his assessment is based largely on political turnout at the most recent election and cannot practically take into account changes in political affiliation of existing members of local benches

---

[74] ibid, pp. viii and 13-31; see also House of Commons - Home Affairs Committee, Third Report (1996), "Judicial Appointments Procedures, Vol. I, Session 1995-96", p l xi, para. 205; Seago, Walker and Wall, *The Development of the Professional Magistracy in England and Wales*, Crim LR 2000, p 646 and the earlier studies there cited; see also Dr. Penny Darbyshire, *For the New Lord Chancellor - Some Causes for Concern about Magistrates* [1997] Crim LR 861, at 863-868

[75] ie different from those in National Statistics and without reference to the wide range of data provided by the Advisory Committees in their annual reports – inadequacies that the Lord Chancellor's Department is now remedying

[76] in the years 1994-1999/2000 there has been a steady annual improvement in recruitment of members of ethnic minorities from 5% to 8.6% of the total annual recruitment figures; see *Annual Report on Judicial Appointments 1999-2000*, Cmnd 4783, para 5.10

[77] *The judiciary in the magistrates' courts*, p viii and pp 13-17, paras 2.2-1-4

[78] see Dr Penny Darbyshire, *For the New Lord Chancellor...*, at p 865

or of the communities from which they are drawn. Not surprisingly, there are no firm indications of the national or local political balances of magistrates.

61   Morgan and Russell's findings, if representative of the picture country-wide, are worrying insofar as they relate, particularly, to the ethnic and social make-up of benches. The reason for the disproportionate representation in both of those respects, especially in large metropolitan areas with high minority ethnic populations, may be the same. Morgan and Russell have referred to it in relation to social mix:

> "If the duties of lay magistrates are relatively onerous as well as being unpaid, it is not surprising that the composition of benches consists overwhelmingly of persons with the time and personal resources to bear that burden".[79]

62   The Lord Chancellor appoints all magistrates, save for those in the Duchy of Lancaster, on the advice of local Advisory Committees, also appointed by him. In the Duchy, which includes Lancashire, Greater Manchester and Merseyside, the appointments are made by the Chancellor of the Duchy[80] on behalf of The Queen, acting on the advice of similarly constituted local Advisory Committees appointed by her. The criteria for appointment, the composition and manner of working of local Advisory Committees are the same in the two systems. And, since May 2001, the Lord Chancellor's Department trains new members as they do appointees to local Advisory Committees elsewhere. There is thus little, if any, difference in the patterns of appointment between the Duchy and the rest of the country.

63   This anomaly of a 'fourth' criminal justice Minister with no formal role in the system other than to appoint magistrates for this relatively small part of the country is one of the interesting relics of the acquisition by Henry IV in 1399 of the estates and jurisdiction of the Duchy of Lancaster. Consideration has recently been given to removing it. That would no doubt be tidy. But local traditions matter and if, as appears to be the case, this one creates no harmful inconsistencies as between the Duchy and the country as a whole, I can see no reason for changing it so long as the magistrates' courts remain separate from the Crown Court. But, if, as I recommend in Chapter 7, they become part of a unified Criminal Court, there would be little justification or practical sense in preserving the anomaly.

64   Local Advisory Committees are chaired by the Lord Lieutenant or by a Circuit Judge. There are at present 90 Advisory Committees and 117 Sub-Committees in England Wales outside the Duchy of Lancaster, and 17

---

[79] *The judiciary in the magistrates' courts*, p 16, para 2.2.4

[80] the present holder of the office is the Right Hon. Lord MacDonald of Tradeston, CBE, Minister of State for the Cabinet Office

Advisory Committees and 5 Sub-Committees in the Duchy. They are made up, for the most part, of magistrates,[81] but the Lord Chancellor now requires at least a third of the membership to consist of local people who are not magistrates. They have no budget of their own and are supported by a part-time secretary provided either by the local authority or a justices' clerk.

65   The Lord Chancellor appoints members of local Advisory Committees and sub-committees following interview and recommendation by an Advisory Committee Appointments Panel. They are appointed for a term of nine years. The Committees vary in size according to their Commission Areas. In addition to his requirement of a ratio of two thirds magistrates and at least one third non-magistrates,[82] the Lord Chancellor requires each Committee to have at least one supporter of each of the main political parties and at least one who is politically uncommitted. Beyond that, so far as practicable, the composition of each Committee should broadly reflect the political balance of the area that it covers and in the same other respects as required for the appointment of magistrates.[83] All newly appointed Committee members are required to attend a standard training seminar provided and funded by the Lord Chancellor's Department.

66   Although selection procedures for magistrates are laid down in Directions issued by the Lord Chancellor, local Advisory Committees are left to devise their own methods of recruitment of magistrates in their area,[84] including the provision of information to the public and the prompting of applications for appointment. Their proposals are subject to authorisation by the Lord Chancellor's Department and paid for by it. The result, as one commentator has noted,[85] is that there are considerable differences between them in the way they go about it. Often this might be a proper reflection of local conditions. Some leaflet households. Others circulate information to local community organisations. Many rely largely on the network and overlapping memberships of local bodies, with the result that there is an undue draw towards the local 'great and good' - local councillors, members of health authorities and school governing bodies and the like. The Magistrates' Association, through its Magistrates in the Community project, undertakes a wide-range of initiatives aimed at increasing confidence in and knowledge of the magistracy amongst the general public. Although this project clearly produces benefits in respect of the recruitment of magistrates, that is not its primary purpose; it is not, nor does it pretend to be, a national recruitment drive.

---

[81] in order to avoid a perception or the reality that benches select their own members, bench chairmen are not permitted to chair or sit on local Advisory Committees or their sub-committees

[82] on the recommendation of the Public Appointments Unit at 10 Downing Street

[83] see paras 80 - 86 below

[84] *The Lord Chancellor's Directions for Advisory Committees on Justices of the Peace* include suggestions as to the types of promotion and advertising that they can undertake

[85] Dr Penny Darbyshire, *For the New Lord Chancellor – some causes of concern about magistrates*, at 867

67   It is interesting to note the modest level of national resources devoted to encouraging members of the public to serve in this vital area when compared with that, for example, to attracting them to serve in the Territorial Army - £35,000 as against £4.7 million. In March/April 1999 the Lord Chancellor's Department, for the first time, undertook a national publicity campaign at the cost of £1/2 million to raise awareness of the magistracy and to emphasise that ordinary people could apply. This was, however, something of a one-off, the results of which have yet fully to be evaluated.[86] Notwithstanding the need to maintain a strong local focus among magistrates, there seems to me to be a clear need for a stronger sense of national direction in both their recruitment and their training. Looking at the arrangements for recruitment, I am concerned at the low level of financial assistance given to Advisory Committees, the *ad hoc* nature of their secretarial support and the lack of co-ordination between them in determining their policies for appointment.

68   As I mention in more detail below, the Lord Chancellor requires that each bench should broadly reflect the community it serves in terms of gender, ethnic origin, geographical spread, occupation and political affiliation. It is for the Advisory Committees to obtain their own information on the make-up of their local community in each of these respects. They are required to report to the Lord Chancellor's Department the information on which they rely, enabling the latter to assess how successful they have been, and to advise or give directions if necessary, on the social and ethnic make-up of their benches. However, so far as I can tell, the Committees' main sources of information in this respect, if they seek it, are the local authorities. It is unclear to me – and I believe to the Lord Chancellor's Department - what statistics or other information local authorities have of the balance at any time of the make-up of their local community which would assist local Advisory Committees. Without reliable information of this nature, the Committees are not equipped to identify the necessary balances or the sections of the community at whom their recruitment activities should be particularly directed.

69   There are also the deficiencies found by Morgan and Russell in the Lord Chancellor's Department's records of the characteristics of magistrates in post. In particular, the Department should establish and keep up to date information about the composition of the magistracy in terms of gender, age, ethnic, current occupational and other status, using the same classification as that in the national census.[87] Such a move would be a valuable tool for securing a magistracy which is broadly reflective of the community in the

---

[86] The Lord Chancellor's Department in its *Annual Report on Judicial Appointments for 1999-2000*, para 5.11, said that it "was too soon to see whether it [had] had a significant impact in encouraging applications for appointment from a wider cross-section of the community".

[87] I understand that the Lord Chancellor's Department is already developing a database using the national census classification; see its *Annual Report on Judicial Appointments for 1999-2000*, para 5.21

area from which it is drawn and also for ready demonstration of that fact in the event of public perceptions to the contrary.

70   Even if the tools for improvement of the 'geo-demographic' selection process are provided, there is still not a wide enough range of potential appointees from which to choose.[88]   Part of the problem stems from the increasing demands of the workplace.   This is not to say that major employers are unsympathetic to or unappreciative of the magistracy.   On the contrary, the Magistrates' Association has been able to work closely and constructively with a wide range of leading companies, at least at board level.   The problem lies in translating statements of intent given by top management into practical action in local offices, where more junior staff often find it difficult to secure the support of their managers when considering applying to become a magistrate. It has also been suggested that the limited circumstances in which a financial loss allowance can be claimed can be a deterrent to self-employed people, particularly those on a relatively low income.

71   This is a worrying picture, especially given the present imbalances in the make-up of the magistracy.   It is precisely those who work in more junior positions, or who are self-employed, whom it is important to attract to the lay bench in greater numbers.   There are also important benefits to be reaped by organisations, both in terms of the wide range of skills and competences magistrates now acquire through their training, and in the commitment which an employer can demonstrate to the local community through supporting participation by its employees in the criminal justice system.   It is also worth remarking that the increasing variation in working patterns (particularly in the retailing and technology sectors) may present employees with a wider range of possibilities for court sittings, provided that the courts themselves are prepared to be flexible in their listing and rostering arrangements.   In short, I think there is considerable room for improvement on both sides.

72   A number of alternatives have been suggested for securing a more representative magistracy: first, to make the role and terms of service of a magistrate more attractive to and manageable for a wider range of the community than it is at present, while maintaining its 'volunteer' ethos; second, the introduction of a system of short-term conscription akin to that of jury service;[89] third, co-option of citizens "on a rotating basis, each serving, say, a specified number of sittings for one year";[90]   and, fourth, election, perhaps along the lines adopted, in the main, at similar levels in the United States.   Just to list those four main alternatives drives one back to the first. Conscription of the sort suggested would radically change and diminish the respective roles and strengths of District Judges and magistrates - all in the

---

[88] see *The Development of the Professional Magistracy in England and Wales*, p 647

[89] *Community Justice – Modernising the Magistracy in England and Wales*, p 43

[90] *The Development of the Professional Magistracy in England and Wales*, p 647

name of jury trial as the supposed 'gold standard' for all alleged offences, however minor. The co-option system might be more workable than conscription or election, but it would involve considerably more work and costs on administration and training. The notion of election might be a gesture to democracy, but, as experience of its operation in the United States demonstrates only too well, this use of democracy would be less rather than more likely to produce a tribunal reflective of the community as a whole.

73 In my view, the first of the four alternatives is the way ahead, starting with a review of how the role and terms of service of a magistrate might be adapted to attract a wider range of persons than it does at present. This could include development of the present community relations and educational initiatives of benches with a view better to inform the public of their work and to attract more and suitable candidates for appointment. In general, I consider that the review should proceed on the basis of the present average number and length of sittings as a norm, but not as a strait-jacket. There may be scope for magistrates to sit more or less often, for longer or shorter periods at a time and more flexibly, according to their individual circumstances.[91] This might increase the pool of candidates for appointment and ease the task of justices'clerks in finding members of their benches to commit themselves to continuous hearings of cases lasting several days. And if magistrates were given an opportunity to hear more serious and interesting trials in the District Division, as I recommend in Chapter 7, there would be an additional attraction in the role. The fact that these trials would tend to be longer than those currently dealt with in magistrates courts, would make a review of sitting patterns all the more necessary.

74 Also, I believe that, whilst maintaining as far as possible the essentially voluntary nature of the role, consideration should be given to providing greater financial assistance than at present to those who might need it. For this purpose, I support Morgan's and Russell's useful suggestion of occasional surveys of serving magistrates to see how and at what cost they manage to continue to serve.[92] However, as they point out,[93] such an initiative to encourage a more socially representative magistracy would inevitably increase its cost.

75 Any new recruitment strategy, to be effective in attracting magistrates in sufficient numbers, must be directed not only at potential candidates, but also, if they are employed, at their employers and employers' organisations generally. The Lord Chancellor is considering what action he could take to ease the difficulties magistrates are increasingly finding in securing time off

---

[91] e.g. to allow for school half-terms and holidays
[92] *The judiciary in the magistrates' courts*, p 17, para 2.2.4
[93] ibid, p 112

to sit on the bench.[94] One suggestion is for a scheme for accreditation or other public recognition for those employers who adopt best practice standards in this respect. A scheme of this kind has been operating for over two years in Gwent where a 'Justice in the Community Award' is presented to employers nominated by their employees as being particularly supportive and flexible in responding to requests for time off to undertake magisterial duties. Some Advisory Committees have involved local employers in their recruitment drives and in the work their employees undertake in the courts. But they do not all do so and, in any event, the initiatives so far taken suffer from a lack of central co-ordination and support.

76   Also, as part of a general exercise to outlaw ethnic and other discrimination in the system, there should be a standing review, monitoring and correcting any aspect of the circumstances of service as a magistrate that may directly or indirectly discriminate against any section of society that might otherwise produce worthy candidates for the magistracy.

77   As a matter of practical implementation of most of these suggestions, there should be a nationally directed and adequately funded strategy to assist local Advisory Committees in their task of identifying and encouraging a sufficient and broad range of candidates for appointment as magistrates. I understand that the Lord Chancellor's Department is in the process of planning "a more co-ordinated approach throughout England and Wales to the recruitment strategy for the appointment of lay magistrates".[95]   I believe that each Advisory Committee should be provided with a professional and dedicated secretariat, accountable not only to the Committee, but to the Lord Chancellor (and/or the Chancellor of the Duchy) for local implementation of the National Strategy.   Advisory Committees should be able to draw upon expert consultancy support where necessary.

78   As well as determining the community balance of the benches for which they are responsible, local Advisory Committees have the task of determining the numbers of magistrates needed to deal with the caseload of their courts. The Lord Chancellor's direction is that they should consult the MCC, Bench Chairmen and the justices' clerk(s), but they do not always do so. In my view, responsibility for determining the number of magistrates required should pass from Advisory Committees to the court. If a unified Criminal Court is established, I consider that local managers (in consultation with their Resident Judges, Bench Chairmen and justices' clerks) should assume the responsibility.   In doing so, they would also need to take account of requirements for magistrates to sit in the family court and in what remains of

---

[94] *Judicial Appointments Annual Report for 1999-2000*, para 5.23; note the provision in S.50(4)(c) of the Employment Rights Act 1996

[95] see the *Annual Report on Judicial Appointments for 1999-2000*, p.64, paras 5.18 and 5.19 and the Government's recent policy paper, *Criminal Justice: The Way Ahead*, Cmnd 5074, p 64

their other civil jurisdiction. Advisory Committees could then focus on their most essential task, the recruitment of and recommendation of candidates for appointment.

79 While the system for appointment of magistrates must for constitutional reasons be kept independent of the administration of the courts themselves, I believe that any move to a unified Criminal Court should be accompanied by a review of the structure and functions of Advisory Committees, to ensure appropriate geographical divisions of responsibility, improve support, remove responsibility for determining need for magistrates etc. Such examination should also include the continued role of the Duchy of Lancaster.[96]

Selection and appointment of magistrates

80 This section is comparatively short because, as I have said, the main problem is in the recruitment and identification of a sufficient and appropriate range of candidates for appointment, not in the criteria for or mechanics of their appointment.

81 Candidates are interviewed twice by members of the local Advisory Committee. The first interview is general in nature; the second more focused on assessing judicial aptitude. The only legislative restriction on the Lord Chancellor's and Chancellor of the Duchy's powers of appointment is that normally the magistrate should live in or within 15 miles of the commission area to which he is appointed.[97] There are no formal qualifications, exclusions or disqualifications for appointment, as is the case for jurors.

82 Advisory Committees generally make their recommendations to the Lord Chancellor once a year during a given month. In doing so, they consider, in addition to the personal suitability of each candidate, the number of vacancies and, as I have said, the need to ensure that the composition of each bench broadly reflects the community which it serves. As to personal suitability, the Lord Chancellor, in his current notes for guidance to candidates, indicates that:

- the six 'key qualities' for appointment are good character, understanding and communication, social awareness, maturity and sound temperament, sound

---

[96] there is legislative machinery for this, allowing MCCs to submit to the Lord Chancellor proposals for the alteration of any commission area within their boundaries; see s 32A Justices of the Peace Act 1997, inserted by s 74 of the Access to Justice Act 1999

[97] Justices of the Peace Act 1997, ss 5 and 6; special provision is made for the Lord Mayor and Aldermen who are appointed to sit in the City of London (s 6 (1A)) and, more generally, for the Lord Chancellor to dispense with the residence condition elsewhere, if he considers it in the public interest to do so (s 6(2))

judgement and commitment, and reliability. He will not normally appoint anyone under 27 or over 65. Magistrates must retire at 70, which accords with the provisions for jurors who are entitled to sit until the age of 70, but may be excused, if they wish, when aged 65 or over;

- they should have reasonable knowledge of the area to which they seek appointment and, generally, have lived in it for a minimum of a year;

- they should be in sufficient good health to enable them to carry out all the duties of a magistrate;[98]

- though British nationality is not a requirement, they must be willing to take the Oath of Allegiance; (cf. the position of jurors who, under present provisions, are effectively required to be of British nationality);

- he will consider their personal suitability for appointment regardless of ethnic origin, gender, marital status, sexual orientation, political affiliation, religion or, subject to the requirements of the office, disability;[99]

- there are a number of categories of person whom he will not normally appoint (some of which correspond to present categories of ineligibility or excusal as of right for jurors); these include present and past police officers and traffic wardens and their families, others involved in various ways in the criminal justice system, full-time members of the armed forces, persons who, or whose spouse or partner, have previous convictions and/or are undischarged bankrupts.

83   Although the Lord Chancellor requires that each bench should broadly reflect the community it serves, he has not achieved that nationally in respect of occupation (or 'class') or, in respect of various of the criteria, in many localities. Formerly, he also required that benches should be balanced in terms of age. But because of difficulties in achieving some of the other balances, he has suspended that requirement in order to attract a wider choice of candidates.[100] The result, as I have said, is a disproportionately middle class and middle aged bench. If the difficulties in recruitment to which I have referred can be overcome, the Lord Chancellor should, in time, be able to reinstate the age balance requirement.

84   There are two concerns about the criteria for appointment: first that of reflecting the political balance of the community; second, the need for the Lord Chancellor regularly to review the categories of person whom he will not appoint to ensure its consistency with the overriding obligation to provide defendants with a fair trial.

---

[98] as a result of a successful two year experiment with nine visually impaired magistrates, the Lord Chancellor has recently announced that people with visual disabilities who fulfil all the normal criteria for appointment may be considered for appointment

[99] for example, he will not normally appoint members of the Magistrates' Courts Service. If he were to do so, the appointment would be to a different commission area from that in which they work. There could be Article 6 difficulties in perception of bias if they were to sit in their own area.

[100] *Judicial Appointments Annual Report, 1999-2000,* paras 5.14 and 5.22

85 The first is, on the face of it, an unusual criterion for judicial appointments in this country. The question was considered by the Lord Chancellor following a consultation exercise in 1998.[101] He concluded, though reluctantly, that for the time being the requirement for political balance should remain, but that work should continue on searching for a more appropriate measure of social balance, possibly using occupational groupings, either alone or with social groupings based on the National Statistics classification. It seems to me that that is the right approach. I believe that the only basis for the use to date of political balance can have been that it was regarded as a crude proxy for occupational and/or social groupings. Political views, balanced or otherwise, are hardly relevant to the fairness and ability of a tribunal. And, as – true to the intention of a democratic system – political views or preferences change; so may the make-up of a bench or the community from which it is drawn over a period of time regardless of attempts to reflect the latter in the appointments process.

86 As to the second, it seems to me that the long-term and regular commitment of magistrates to the criminal justice process requires a more rigorous approach to the question of bias or perceived bias than in the case of jurors in respect of whom I recommend, in Chapter 5,[102] removal of nearly all categories of ineligibility, including all those that have their root in bias or perceived bias. It is right that there should be differences in this respect between those who can be appointed as magistrates and those eligible to serve as jurors. For example, if a police officer were to serve as a magistrate he would be likely to sit regularly in cases involving police officers from his own force requiring him equally regularly to withdraw. Also, sitting as one of a bench of three with wide judicial responsibilities, he would be more likely to raise a perception or fear of effective bias than he would engender as one of a jury of 12 with a narrower, though important, role. As a further example, and in the event of the creation of a unified Criminal Court,[103] court staff should not sit as magistrates, at least not in the criminal justice area in which they are so employed.

> **I recommend that steps should be taken to provide benches of magistrates that reflect more broadly than at present the communities they serve by:**
>
> - **reviewing the number, role and support given to them, including, in the event of the establishment of a unified Criminal Court, the present division of responsibility for them between the Lord Chancellor's Department and the Duchy of Lancaster;**

---

[101] *Political Balance in the Lay Magistracy*, LCD (1998), para 7
[102] paras 27 - 34
[103] see Chapter 7, paras 50 - 73

- passing responsibility for determining the number of magistrates required for each commission area from local Advisory Committees to court staff in consultation with the Chairman of each Bench, the justices' clerks and, in the event of the establishment of a unified Criminal Court, also the Resident Judge;

- reviewing the community relations and educational initiatives of benches with a view better to inform the public of their work and to attract more suitable candidates for appointment;

- in support of the local Advisory Committees, establishing a properly resourced National Recruitment Strategy aimed, not only at candidates for the magistracy, but also at their employers;

- equipping local Advisory Committees with the information to enable them to submit for consideration for appointment, candidates that will produce and maintain benches broadly reflective of the communities they serve, including the establishment and maintenance of national and local data-bases of information on the make-up of the local community and on the composition of the local magistracy;

- instituting a review of the ways in which the role and terms of service of a magistrate might be made more attractive and manageable to a wider range of the community than is presently the case; and

- persisting with the current search for occupational and/or social groupings as a substitute for political affiliations as a measure of local balance.

I also recommend that the Lord Chancellor should continue with – but keep under careful review – his present policy of not normally appointing certain persons who are close to the criminal justice system or who, by the nature of their occupation, could not commit themselves to sitting regularly, or whose character or association would make them undesirable for appointment.

District Judges

87 Although stipendiary magistrates are now called District Judges, it is convenient to deal here with their selection and appointment to sit alongside lay magistrates in magistrates' courts. As I have already noted in Chapter 3, only barristers or solicitors of at least seven years' standing may be appointed

as District Judges. There are more solicitors than barristers on the District Bench and about a quarter of all of them were formerly justices' clerks. Appointments are based solely on merit and regardless of ethnic origin, gender, marital status, sexual orientation, political affiliation, religion or disability, except where the disability prevents the fulfilment of the physical requirements of the office. District Judges tend to be mostly male (about 84%), white (about 98%) and middle-aged (more than 50% aged 45-54), though in the main they are younger than magistrates.[104] The Lord Chancellor appoints them in annual open competition, first, to sit part-time as a Deputy District Judge. After selection they attend an induction course provided by the Judicial Studies Board and are each then assigned to a District Judge as pupil master. The same procedure applies, after they have undertaken about 40 sitting days or two years' service, to full-time appointment of District Judges. They are then assigned to a particular MCC area.

88   District Judges sitting in the magistrates' courts, unlike their counterparts in the county court, are paid out of the Consolidated Fund. Their salaries and other employment costs are about £90,000 a year. They are not, therefore, a burden on the MCC in whose area they sit and, the MCC's revenue grant is not adjusted to take account of the savings in magistrates' allowances etc. or in sitting time that they bring. Some District Judges also sit as Recorders in the Crown Court, normally for about three weeks a year, and the appointment is emerging as the first step on a judicial rung that may lead to permanent appointment as a Circuit Judge and, possibly, beyond.

89   Outside London, assignment of a District Judge is normally at the request of an MCC; it is not the Lord Chancellor's policy to foist a new or replace a retiring full-time appointment on an unwilling MCC. However, he may encourage it, perhaps prompted by a recommendation from the Magistrates Courts' Service Inspectorate, where he considers it appropriate.[105] He makes the appointment in consultation with the Senior District Judge. Unhappily, there have been instances when local benches have, by their opposition, successfully delayed the appointment of a stipendiary to their area when such an appointment was sorely needed. In my view, such parochialism demeans the otherwise worthy contribution that magistrates make to the running of the criminal justice system, and it should no longer hold sway. If, as I have recommended, the Government's policy is to continue with magistrates and District Judges sitting in roughly their present proportions and sharing the work between them much as they do now, the cause of such opposition should diminish. And if, as I recommend in Chapter 7, magistrates join with District Judges in exercising an enhanced jurisdiction in an intermediate tier of a unified Criminal Court, there will be even less cause for it.

---

[104] *The judiciary in the magistrates' courts*, pp viii and 24, para 2.7

[105] see LCD Consultation Paper, *Unification of the Stipendiary Bench*, (1998) p 7, para 26

90   In my view, the decision whether to appoint a District Judge should no longer turn primarily on, or be impeded by, the views of magistrates, whether expressed through their local bench or the MCC. I share the view of the Runciman Royal Commission that there should be a more systematic approach to the role of professional judges in the summary system to make the best use of their special skills and qualifications,[106] and this applies to their appointment as well as to their deployment. In my view, the Lord Chancellor should take the initiative rather more than he has been minded to do in the past, after consulting the local bench or benches, acting through their chairman or chairmen, the justices' clerk and all relevant local criminal justice interests. If my recommendations for a unified Criminal Court are adopted, these should include the Presiding Judges, the Resident Judge and the local group or court manager.

> **I recommend that the Lord Chancellor should be more ready to take the initiative to assign a District Judge to an area where, having consulted as appropriate, he is of the view that local justice in the area requires it.**

Training

91   Each MCC has a statutory duty to establish and administer schemes providing for training courses for magistrates in its area.[107] The Lord Chancellor requires the training to satisfy standards set by the Judicial Studies Board. These are, in practice: the Magistrates' New Training Initiative (MNTI), a 'competence'-based training and appraisal scheme that it established in 1999; occasional national guidance on specific matters for local provision, for example, the recent project on implementation of the Human Rights Act 1998; advice and residential national training courses for chairmen of benches when they are elected; and the establishment and maintenance of a database on its web-site of approved training materials produced by MCCs and others.

92   All that sounds better than it is. MNTI was the product of extensive consultation with magistrates and justices' clerks and is an improvement on what went before. But the scheme has been much criticised for its complexity; for example, there are 104 different 'competences' even for those who sit only as 'a winger' in the adult courts. And, some two years after the scheme's introduction, no national standards have been set in respect of these competences. The first priority was to arrange for the mentoring and appraisal of new magistrates, and MCCs by now should be ensuring that all magistrates are appraised against the relevant competences at least once every

---

[106] Report of *Royal Commission on Criminal Justice*, Ch 8, para 103 and recommendation 255
[107] Justices of the Peace Act 1997, s 64

three years. Although the Judicial Studies Board is not systematically monitoring the coverage and effectiveness of MNTI nationally, it is clear that a number of MCCs are not meeting this requirement. The Board has recently published an evaluation of MNTI,[108] in which it concluded that its basic concepts and principles were sound, but that there was too great a variation in the manner of its implementation. It recommended the introduction of national performance standards, the weighting of competences and simplification of documents.

93   The problem of lack of consistency extends beyond the core training provided under the MNTI framework. Some MCCs do not distribute the Judicial Studies Board's material to individual magistrates. And some have produced their own training material, which they do not always copy to the Board. With the exception of the Human Rights Act programme, all training for magistrates has been essentially voluntary, and has been criticised by those making submissions to the Review as haphazard and lacking in structure.

94   Even if those defects can be overcome, the system of MCCs training their magistrates under the loose oversight of the Judicial Studies Board, sometimes using its training materials and sometimes not, is deficient. The Board has a trivial budget for the purpose: £175,000 out of a total of over £5 million. That pays for the equivalent of only two full-time professional staff, very limited external consultancy support and the production and provision of a limited range of guidance and training material of various sorts. And it lacks the means to ensure that MCCs use its training materials to best effect or, in some cases, at all. It can only advise the Lord Chancellor to make alternative training arrangements for, and withdraw funding from, an MCC that chooses to ignore its guidance. The Board has not, so far, taken such a drastic and potentially counter-productive a step.

95   The Magistrates' Association does a great deal to make up for the patchy nature and lack of consistency in training provided by some MCCs. It has a Training Unit which, with the assistance of an annual grant of £130,000 provided by the Judicial Studies Board, issues guidance and provides training on specific matters from time to time. Three recent examples are its 'Can We Get On Please' training pack to assist court chairmen in taking more control over the progress of cases, its Sentencing Guidelines (issued with the approval of the Lord Chancellor and the Lord Chief Justice) and a training programme for mentors.

96   The lack of consistency in the training of magistrates from one MCC area to another is a source of legitimate concern, particularly in its contribution to wide variations in the effectiveness of case management and in sentencing

---

[108] *Magistrates' New Training Initiative: Evaluation of Implementation, Final Report,* (December 2000) pp 4-5

patterns. Although responsiveness to local circumstances, particularly in sentencing, is one of the strengths of the magistracy, they should not receive varying accounts of what the law requires or differing criteria for the exercise of their discretion. In my view, there is an urgent need for clearer and simpler national standards in the training of magistrates and for more consistency in and monitoring of its provision than are now the case.

97   The establishment of a unified Criminal Court would, of itself, require a new training structure. MCCs would cease to exist and, in addition to training magistrates for their summary jurisdiction, it would be necessary to provide joint training of District Judges and some magistrates for sitting as 'mixed tribunals' in the District Division. I believe that the Judicial Studies Board should be given a strengthened responsibility for formulating and overseeing the content and manner of training of all magistrates whilst, in the main, retaining locality of its provision. It would not be realistic or fair to magistrates, other than bench chairmen, to require them to travel long distances to attend residential training courses, as in the case of the professional judiciary. If more consistency in the provision of training and, consequently, in the handling of cases between different areas is to be achieved, it will require a significant increase in resources to prepare national training materials, to select and train local trainers and to ensure the use everywhere of the same materials.

98   This is also a field in which District Judges, with their professional skills and their own more generous training by the Judicial Studies Board,[109] could be further developed to advantage both as local trainers and in occasional sittings where appropriate with magistrates.[110] A beneficial by-product of such participation of District Judges in the broader life of magistrates' courts would be the removal of the 'wall' that exists between them and magistrates in many areas. However, the mainstay of local training of magistrates should, in my view, continue to be the justices' clerks (in whatever their manifestation, depending on the court structure). They have unrivalled knowledge of the practices and procedures of the jurisdiction and of the forensic needs of magistrates of all levels of experience.

99   I should not leave this subject without mentioning the potential of information technology to facilitate greater use of distance learning through CD-ROMs and website based courses and sources of the sort the Board is already providing for the professional Judiciary.[111]

---

[109] one day's national training a year provided by the Judicial Studies Board

[110] as many already do; see *The Development of the Professional Magistracy in England and Wales*, p 641; cf. the training provided by Liaison (Circuit) Judges; see protocol *Guidance for Liaison Judges* (1995) HHJ Francis Allen

[111] for example, as part of the Board's recent training in preparation for implementation of the Human Rights Act 1998

100 All this would call for a significant increase in resources for the Judicial Studies Board to enable it to devise and ensure consistent provision, in the main at a local level, of training for magistrates. I realise that this would be a significant extension of the Board's responsibilities, but with its excellent record of training of professional judges and, more selectively, of magistrates, it is well fitted for it.

Accordingly, I recommend that:

- **the Judicial Studies Board should be made responsible, and be adequately resourced, for devising and securing the content and manner of training of all magistrates;**

- **such training should, in the main, be provided at local level through trainers, ideally justices' clerks and/or legal advisers, appropriately trained for the purpose by the Board;**

- **District Judges should also be involved in the training of magistrates in the area or at the court centre at which they are normally based;**

- **the MNTI scheme should be refined in order to provide a less complex, weighted set of competences for magistrates, supported by clear national standards; and**

- **the Judicial Studies Board should establish systems to ensure that appraisal of magistrates takes place in a timely and effective manner across the country and that training programmes take account of the training needs identified during that process.**

CHAPTER 5

JURIES

INTRODUCTION

1   The jury is often described as 'the jewel in the Crown' or 'the corner-stone' of the British criminal justice system. It is a hallowed institution which, because of its ancient origin and involvement of 12 randomly selected lay people in the criminal process, commands much public confidence. In the van of such confidence are the judges and legal practitioners who, when asked, invariably say that, in general, juries 'get it right'. For most it is also an important incident of citizenship; De Tocqueville memorably described it as "a peerless teacher of citizenship". However, support for it is not universal, not least among those who have been jurors. And there are many, in particular leading academic lawyers, who express reservations because we do not, and are not permitted by law[1] to, know how individual juries reach their verdicts. It is also well to keep in mind how rarely juries are used in the criminal trial process given the enormous importance with which they are invested by the public, politicians and legal professions. Only about 1% of criminal cases in England and Wales culminate in trial by jury.[2]

2   I take as my starting point that any change to the system of trial by jury requires a compelling case. I should say 'further' change, because it has evolved to its present form over many centuries, responding where necessary to the circumstances and demands of the time on the criminal justice system as a whole. 19th and 20th century examples of such change are the innovation in 1855 of a statutory system that grew over the next 150 years or so into the present wide category of 'either-way' cases, the introduction in 1967 of majority verdicts, the widening in 1972 of general eligibility for jury service

---

[1] Contempt of Court Act 1981, s 8

[2] see Appendix IV to the Report

135

from certain landowners to all on the electoral roll, the conversion in the 1980s of certain offences previously triable on indictment to summary only offences, and the abolition in 1988 of the right of peremptory challenge.

3   The Royal Commission on Capital Punishment, reporting in 1953, said that it had been "struck by the almost unanimous tributes paid by the judges and other experienced witnesses to the reliability and common sense of British juries".[3]   The Morris Committee on Jury Service, in 1965[4] observed that, although the merits of jury trial and the types of cases that should be heard by a jury were outside its terms of reference, it thought it right to record that the evidence before it showed "in general an acceptance of the desirability of maintaining the jury system in criminal cases".   And the Runciman Royal Commission in 1993 said much the same, though it urged research into the way in which juries worked, principally, it would seem, with a view to improve the system of jury trial rather than to consider whether it should continue:

> "Juries are not specifically mentioned in our terms of reference. This may seem an anomaly since convictions of the innocent *[sic]* and acquittals of the guilty *[sic]* in serious cases are always jury decisions. But we are conscious that the jury system is widely and firmly believed to be one of the cornerstones of our system of justice. We have received no evidence which would lead us to argue that an alternative method of arriving at a verdict in criminal trials would make the risk of a mistake significantly less". [5]

4   We talk of 'trial by jury', but it is more accurately described as 'trial by judge and jury'. It is a partnership in which the two have separate and overlapping contributions to the final outcome. The judge tells the jury what the law is and how it bears on the issues in the case; and they apply their new-found understanding of the law to their consideration of those issues. As to the facts, whilst the jury have primary responsibility for finding them, the judge has much to do with that too.[6] He may be called upon to rule whether there is evidence on which they could find the accused guilty; he may warn them to take particular care before acting on certain evidence; he may direct them about circumstantial evidence and whether, on the evidence before them, they can draw certain inferences from it; and he notes and sums up the evidence for them to assist their deliberations. The resultant verdict is, therefore, a product of a 'partnership' between judge and jury.

---

[3] Cmnd 8932, 1953, p 202, cited by Glanville Williams, *The Proof of Guilt*: The Hamlyn Lectures, 7th Series (Stevens, 1995) p 214

[4] *Report of the Departmental Committee on Jury Service*, (The Morris Report) Cmnd 2627 (HMSO, 1965), paras 3 and 6

[5] *Report of the Royal Commission on Criminal Justice*, Chapter 1, para 8

[6] more than in most United States jurisdictions; but, unlike many of their judges, he has no power to set aside verdicts with which he does not agree or which he regards as perverse

5   Many of the rules of criminal procedure and evidence that still dominate jury trial stem from its long evolution from trial by ordeal to its present form, and until 1965 against a back-drop of capital and other severe penalties for a wide range of offences. They also derive from judges' lack of confidence in the competence of juries for their task, despite their tradition of eulogy of the jury system. Hence also their elaborate directions on the law, emphatic cautions and often laborious rehearsal of the evidence before permitting jurors to consider their verdict. Dr Glanville Williams, one of the greatest English academic criminal lawyers of the last century, observed,[7] citing Mr Justice Swallow in Sir Alan Herbert's hilarious tale, *Uncommon Law*, that such assistance should be deemed necessary is an acknowledgement of the peculiar difficulties of an amateur tribunal:

> "Gentlemen of the jury, the facts of this distressing and important case have already been put before you some four or five times, twice by prosecuting counsel, twice by counsel for the defence, and once at least by each of the various witnesses who have been heard; but so low is my opinion of your understanding that I think it necessary, in the simplest language, to tell you the facts again".

6   The only qualification required for jury service in England and Wales, apart from age and ordinary residence in this country, is entry on the electoral roll. The nature of this record results in under-representation of those in their early 20s, ethnic minorities and the more mobile sections of the community, such as those living in rented accommodation. Similarly, the many categories of ineligibility and scope for excusal as of right or for good reason mean that those in a wide range of demanding occupations are less likely to undertake jury service than the general population. Applications for excusal are most frequently received in long and complex cases where a range of experience and intellect is most needed. In New York[8] and many other States of the USA source records for jury service have been expanded, all or most of the exemptions from jury trial have been swept away, and excusals have largely become deferrals. The result is that nearly everyone does jury service as an acknowledged civic duty, including judges, lawyers, policemen, doctors and clergymen.

THE 'RIGHT' TO TRIAL BY JUDGE AND JURY

7   In England and Wales there is no constitutional or indeed any form of general right to trial by judge and jury, only a general obligation to submit to it in indictable cases. It is often claimed that Magna Carta, traditionally regarded

---

[7] *The proof of guilt*, pp.237-8
[8] this development was pioneered in New York as a result of *The Jury Project*, a report of 31st March 1994 commissioned by the Chief Judge of the State of New York, Judith Kaye

as the foundation of our liberties, established such a right. The claim is incorrect. Certainly, Magna Carta is no basis for jury trial as we know it today. First, such right as it may have indicated seems to have had an earlier origin in the inquisition of the Carolingian Kings, adopted and imported into this country by the Normans.[9] Second, as legal historians have pointed out,[10] its reference to a free man's right to the lawful judgment of his 'peers' did not refer to trial by jury. Third, it did not protect everybody in the rigid class system of the time - it was not a truly democratic reform. Fourth, as Lord, then Sir Patrick, Devlin noted in his Hamlyn Lectures in 1956 entitled *Trial By Jury*,[11] it began as "something different". The form of trial to which it referred originated from an earlier reform of Henry II replacing trial by ordeal of fire or water. His jury consisted of 12 persons in the neighbourhood, witnesses, who swore to the truth of what they knew. It was not until much later that they emerged as a body of strangers to the case whose task was to decide it rationally upon evidence put before them. And, fifth and in any event, Magna Carta's statement of an accused's right was to one of two alternatives, either "by the lawful judgment of his peers or by the law of the land".[12]

8   Quite independently of Magna Carta, there is no legal basis for regarding the claimed 'right' to jury trial as a constitutional entitlement, that is an entrenched right overriding all other legal instruments, as in the United States for offences carrying more than six months imprisonment [13] or under the Canadian Charter of Rights and Freedoms for offences punishable by five years imprisonment or more,[14] or as a right at all. Nor has it become a right as a result of the incorporation into our law of the European Convention of Human Rights' Article 6 concept of a fair trial. On the contrary, there are suggestions that in some respects it may contravene that provision.[15] Originally, the accused had no choice but to be tried by jury in all indictable cases; he still has no choice in indictable only cases. It was only when, in 1855, Parliament began to permit him to opt for summary trial of certain offences which had formerly been triable only on indictment, that he acquired an elective right to jury trial in what developed over the next 150 years into a wide range of 'either-way' offences. And, as I have already noted, Parliament has made a number of changes in recent years modifying or removing the right in certain of those offences. The right is claimed "only for a fluctuating class of crimes of intermediate gravity".[16]

---

[9] per Maitland, quoted by Holdsworth, *A History of English Law*, 3rd ed., p312, quoted in turn in the Morris Report, para 7; and see generally paras 6-11

[10] Forsyth, *History of Trial by Jury*, 1852, at 108; Holdsworth, *A History of English Law, Vol 1, 1903,* W R Cornish, *The Jury,* 1968 at p 12

[11] 8th Series, 1956, at pp 5 and 67

[12] Clause 39

[13] see the 6th amendment to Article III of the US Constitution enshrining it as right in Federal and State jurisdictions for all offences not deemed to be 'petty'

[14] Chapter 11(B)

[15] see below, paras 88 - 98

[16] Andrew Ashworth, The Criminal Process: An Evaluation Study, 2nd ed. (OUP, 1998), pp 255-262

9   Nevertheless, the institution of the jury has for long been a powerful symbol in our criminal justice system. In the 18th century Blackstone described it in a famous passage as 'the palladium' or 'the grand bulwark' of the Englishman's liberties.[17] Sir Patrick Devlin in 1956, spoke of it as "a little parliament" and the "lamp that shows that freedom lives".[18] But, save possibly for the so-called 'dispensing power' of the jury, it is doubtful whether those metaphors are apt as main or practical justifications for the institution. Random selection - to the extent that it has ever existed, given our history of restricted qualification for and exclusions and rights of excusal from jury service - is not to be equated with democracy. The jury does not represent or reflect the community as a whole, save in the broad sense of enabling some citizens to participate in the trial process. Over the last two or more centuries judges have been more instrumental than juries in declaring and protecting the rights of citizens. Sadly, juries did not prevent the miscarriages of justice uncovered in the late 1980s and early 1990s arising, in the main, from falsification or concealment of evidence that so shook public confidence and gave rise to the appointment of the Runciman Royal Commission some ten years ago. And, from the earliest times many offences have not been triable by jury; today, as I have said, it is a response to only 1% of all prosecuted crime.

10   However, the jury retains its aura – one of involvement of the community in the administration of justice. For many this counts for more than its efficiency as a fact-finding tribunal, as many distinguished academic lawyers have, sometimes wryly, observed.[19] Baroness Kennedy of the Shaws is one of the many who have recently and eloquently articulated this basis for it:

> "… jury tradition is not only about the right of the citizen to elect trial but also about the juror's duty of citizenship. It gives people an important role as jurors - as stakeholders - in the criminal justice system. Seeing the courts in action and participating in that process maintains public trust and confidence in the law".[20]

---

[17] Commentaries, IV (1776) p 347; see also 349; see also Stephen, History of the Criminal Law. I, p 566

[18] *Trial By Jury*, The Hamlyn Lectures, 8th Series, 1956, p 164, also quoting, at 165, Blackstone's celebrated passage in his Commentaries, at IV, pp 349-350, inaccurately founding trial by jury as it became on the 39th clause of Magna Carta

[19] see eg Baldwin and McConville, *Jury Trials*, 1979 at p 1; Penny Darbyshire *The Lamp That Shows That Freedom Lives: Is It Worth The Candle?*, [1991] Crim. L.R. 740, at pp 740-1; Sir Louis Blom-Cooper, QC in *Article 6 and Modes of Criminal Trial* [2001] EHRLR, pp 1-19

[20] Criminal Justice (Mode of Trial) (No. 2) Bill, House of Lords, 28 September 2000, Hansard, HL, col 995

COMPOSITION OF THE JURY

11 Despite all the reforms of the latter half of the last century, juries in England and Wales mostly still do not reflect the broad range of skills and experience or ethnic diversity of the communities from which they are drawn. Jury service may be an important incident of citizenship, but many in this country do not qualify for this civic privilege and duty. And many who do qualify, do not regard it as a privilege and do their best to avoid it. If the jury is to fulfil its valued role of giving the community a say in the administration of justice, it should reflect the community better than it does.

12 About a quarter of a million people are summoned for jury service every year. A recent Home Office research project[21] suggests that only about a third of them are available to do it. It shows that, in a sample of 50,000 people summoned for jury service in June and July 1999, only one-third was available for service, about half of whom were allowed to defer their service until a later date. Of the remaining two-thirds, 13% were ineligible, disqualified or excused as of right, 15% either failed to attend on the day or their summonses were returned as 'undelivered' and 38% were excused.

13 The variety of mechanisms and broad scope for avoidance of jury service illustrated by these figures suggest that public perception of it as a civic duty is far from universal. And it is unfair to those who do their jury service, not least because, as a result of others' avoidance of it, they may be required to serve more frequently and for longer than would otherwise be necessary. Most of the exclusions or scope for excusal from jury service deprive juries of the experience and skills of a wide range of professional and otherwise successful and busy people. They create the impression, voiced by many contributors to the Review, that jury service is only for those not important or clever enough to get out of it.

14 In my view, no-one should be automatically ineligible or excusable from jury service simply because he or she is a member of a certain profession or holds a particular office or job. Where the demands of the office or job are such as to make jury service difficult for him over the period covered by the jury summons, he should be subject to the same regime as the self-employed or ordinary wage earners or others for whom jury service is also costly and burdensome, that is, discretionary excusal or deferral. There is nothing new about this proposition in other common law jurisdictions. It was pioneered in New York in the mid-1990s and has been widely adopted throughout the USA. If and to the extent that it may be thought to bear heavily on persons with demanding and responsible jobs, it should be remembered that the wider

---

[21] *Jury Excusal and Deferral, Research Findings No. 102*, Home Office Research Development and Statistics Directorate

the pool from which jurors may be drawn the less frequently each of them will be required for jury service and, on average, the shorter the time they will have to give to it.

15   Before continuing, I pause to say a word about the New York Jury Projectinitiated in 1993 by Judith S Kaye, the Chief Judge of the State of New York. One of its three objectives was the attainment of jury pools that were "truly representative of the community". At that time, the New York State's Judiciary Law,[22] in accordance with the United States Supreme Court's oft stated constitutional guarantee, declared its policy to be that all litigants were entitled to trial by a jury drawn from a "fair cross section of the community". It had long before established source lists for jurors in addition to voter registration rolls but, as in this country, there were many occupational exclusions and exceptions.   As a result of the Project Panel's recommendations, the maximum age limit of 70 was abolished and those above that age were left to seek excusal on the ground of physical or mental incapacity or serious inconvenience, all statutory occupational exclusions and exemptions were abolished, the scope for excusal was reduced to non-permanent excusal for incapacity by reason of mental or physical ill-health or undue hardship, and those summoned for service were permitted one deferral as of right to a date specified by the potential juror.

16   In England and Wales, until earlier this year, each court (other than those in London) had its own arrangements for summoning jurors. A Central Juror Summoning Bureau has now been established to administer the juror summoning process for the whole of the country. It is designed to overcome the deficiencies of the former system, principally in securing a better match in numbers of jurors summoned to the workload of each court, in providing better communication with potential jurors and accommodation of their needs, and in bringing greater consistency to the treatment of their applications for excusal or deferral. It has developed a computer system to select potential jurors at random from the electoral roll and to generate summonses and letters confirming dates for service. Such a national body should be well placed to introduce and develop some of the reforms I recommend below. I have in mind, in particular, the combination of a number of directories and lists, entry on which would assist in identifying persons qualified for jury service, and better communication systems as to jurors' qualification for and ability to undertake jury service. As to the latter, I understand that, as a first step, the Bureau has established an electronic link with the police criminal records system to enable automatic checks on any previous convictions of potential jurors.

---

[22] NY Jud.L 500

The size of the jury

17   We take for granted that a criminal jury should consist of twelve people. This is a matter of tradition rather than logic.[23] There have been some - not many - proposals for change, mostly for a reduction in size to achieve economies and to reduce the general burden of jury service. Though those matters are relevant, they are not, in my view, of sufficient weight or merit to justify changing an institution that draws much of its public support from the number of decision makers that it brings to the task of determining guilt. Traditions of jury size vary from country to country, both in common law as well as civil law jurisdictions. For example, in Scotland, the number is 15.

18   There is, however, some support and precedent for the swearing of alternate or reserve jurors in case the number falls below the minimum of nine by reason of illness or other necessity, a particular hazard in long cases. Whilst this would involve extra expense in jury allowances and additional jury accommodation, the over-all savings in long cases, in both financial and in human terms, of aborted trials and re-trials could be worth it. To meet the possibility of lack of commitment to the case by alternate jurors, they and the primary jurors could be sworn and treated in exactly the same way throughout the trial. In that way neither they nor anyone else would know that they were in reserve until the time for deliberation. Alternatively, there could be a ballot at that time to determine who is to form the final jury. I acknowledge that a practical obstacle to such provision is the present size of jury boxes in courts all over the country, but enlargement would only be necessary in those courts large enough and customarily used for long and heavy trials. Such a system and provision are well and widely established in the USA, and is also to be found in some Commonwealth jurisdictions.

19   The Roskill Fraud Trials Committee was lukewarm about such an insurance provision for long cases; it was not opposed to it in principle, but not satisfied that the problem was sufficiently serious to warrant doing anything about it.[24] Enquiries made by the Court Service in 1998 disclosed no instance when a trial had had to be aborted because the number of the jury fell below nine. However, in one case, a fraud trial of some ten months' duration, the jury were reduced to nine during the course of their deliberations, which must have caused much anxiety to all concerned, including the remaining jurors. Jury trial in long and complex cases is a fragile and highly expensive exercise. It is also an ordeal to which all involved should not be subject a second time for want of a quorate jury.

---

[23] Sir Patrick Devlin, in his Hamlyn Lectures, at pp 8-9 said that "many romantic explanations" had been offered for the figure and, somewhat flippantly, compared it with the old currency of twelve pennies to the shilling exhibiting an early English abhorrence of the decimal system

[24] Report, para 7. 41

20   Although I later recommend a system of trial without jury in long and complex frauds,[25] I consider that a system of alternate or reserve jurors could have value in some other very long cases here. It would also have the advantage of maintaining a jury of 12 while continuing to provide for majority verdicts.[26] If such a system were introduced, judges would have to be vigilant to maintain the stringent criterion of 'necessity' for the discharge of jurors during the trial. There are indications in the USA of jurors being more prone to seek discharge in circumstances short of necessity because they know that there are jurors in reserve. I do not suggest that alternate jurors should be sworn in every long case, but that the judge should consider it at the pre-trial stage.

I recommend the introduction of a system enabling judges in long cases, where they consider it appropriate, to swear alternate or reserve jurors to meet the contingency of a jury otherwise being reduced in number by discharge for illness or any other reason of necessity.

Qualification for jury service

21   Until 1972[27] there was a statutorily imposed property qualification for jury service. Sir Patrick Devlin in 1956[28] reckoned that it excluded the majority of the adult population. As a result of the recommendations of the Morris Committee in 1965,[29] which eventually gave rise to the Juries Act 1974, that has gone. The only qualifications now are an age of at least 18 and not more than 70, to have been ordinarily resident in this country for a period of at least five years since the age of 13 and registration as a parliamentary or local government elector.[30] There have been a few submissions in the Review as to the age limit and residence qualification, but I see no compelling case for change in either of them. The requirement of entry on the electoral register is, however, an important candidate for change on grounds of principle and practicality. The overriding principle of selection from that register and, later in the process, from the panels and part panels drawn from it for each court, is that of random selection. Randomness is not an end in itself. It does not necessarily improve the quality of the decision-making. Its value is that it is considered to be the best, albeit a rough and ready way, of empanelling a jury that is likely to be collegiately independent and to reflect the community at large.

---

[25] see paras 173 - 206

[26] Juries Act, ss 16 and 17

[27] abolished by the Criminal Justice Act 1972, s 25(1); see now Juries Act 1974, s 1

[28] *Trial by Jury*, paras. 60-64

[29] ibid, paras 60-64

[30] Juries Act 1974, s 1

22 As I have said, there are many who, by statute, are ineligible to serve on a jury or who are entitled to excusal as of right, and some who are disqualified. There is also provision for discretionary excusal and for discharge of jury summonses because of disability. But quite apart from all of those exclusionary mechanisms, there is a fundamental weakness in dependence on entry on the electoral register as one of the main criteria of eligibility for jury service. Home Office research[31] shows that in 1999 about 8% of those eligible for registration according to the 1991 Census and Electoral register were not registered. There are a number of reasons for that. Until earlier this year, the electoral register was simply a 'snapshot' of names and addresses in October of each year, and so rapidly became out of date. Although, the introduction of 'rolling' registration will improve the situation, people who live in insecure accommodation or who move relatively frequently will continue to be under-represented on the register. Comparisons with the census indicate that those aged 20 to 24, ethnic minorities and those living in rental accommodation are the most under-represented on the electoral roll.

23 It is plain that we should do what USA Federal and State jurisdictions and a number of Commonwealth countries have done for some time – supplement and/or cross-check the electoral roll by reference to other sources, for example the Driver and Vehicle Licensing Authority, the Department for Work and Pensions, the Inland Revenue and telephone directories. This would require a merging and constant updating of records from the various sources, but, with modern computer technology, it can be done. One complication of widening the net in that way is that it would include non-Commonwealth citizens who, save for citizens of the Republic of Ireland, are not entitled to vote or, therefore, to entry on the electoral roll. However, this could be dealt with, as it is in the United States, by resolving the issue of qualification at the summons stage.

24 Such a reform would be an important contributor to juries becoming a better reflection of the community from which they are drawn and would encourage the perception of jury service as a universal civic duty. And, by significantly increasing the jury pool, it would have the practical benefit of reducing both the frequency with which people are required for jury service and the length of it.

I recommend:

- **no change in the present statutory criteria for qualification for jury service, save as to registration,**

---

[31] see footnote 21

as distinct from entitlement to registration, on an electoral roll; and

- **amendment of the law to substitute for the condition of registration on an electoral roll, inclusion in such a roll and/or on any one or more of a number of other specified publicly maintained lists or directories, but excluding anyone listed who, on investigation at the summons stage, is found not to be entitled to registration as an elector.**

Enforcement of jury service

25   The Home Office Research to which I have referred indicates that about 15% of summoned jurors fail to attend court on the day or have their summonses returned as 'undelivered'. Failure to attend court in response to a jury summons is punishable summarily by a fine of up to £1,000 or as a contempt of court.[32] But there is little attempt at enforcement. Those who do not respond to a summons are sent a further letter and their names are passed to the court. The courts rarely follow up those who, they know, have not responded to the summons or those who have indicated that they would attend, but have failed to do so. Even when recalcitrant potential jurors are brought before the court, judges are reluctant to impose any significant punishment. Some courts occasionally list a number of such acts of defiance for hearing on the same day with a view to giving publicity to their enforcement proceedings, but the publicity is too limited, patchy and sporadic to do much good. The result of all this is that it has become widely known that a jury summons may be ignored with impunity.

26   Something must be done to bring home to the public that jury service is a public duty, that they must do it unless ineligible or excused and that they will be punished if they do not. It can be done, as is shown by what has been achieved in New York and elsewhere in the United States, where very few now escape jury service. At the same time, it would be wasteful of court time to clutter up lists with the original penal proceedings for which the law now provides. I suggest that a better course would be to examine the practicalities of introducing a system of fixed penalties subject to a right of appeal to magistrates.[33] If introduced it should be accompanied by regular publicity of the sort that currently highlights action taken against those using a television without a licence.

---

[32] 1974 Act, s 20

[33] cf the automatic fine system in New York

I recommend that there should be rigorous and well publicised enforcement of the obligation to undertake jury service when required and that consideration should be given to doing so by way of a system of fixed penalties subject to a right of appeal to the magistrates.

Ineligibility

27   There are many categories of person whom the 1974 Act makes ineligible for service. They include: present and past members of the judiciary at all levels, including justices of the peace; all those concerned with the day to day administration of the legal system or any court; others from a whole range of professions and occupations concerned with the administration of justice, including present or past barristers, solicitors, legal executives, police, prison and probation officers; and also clergymen, the mentally ill[34] and any person on bail in criminal proceedings.[35]   There is also provision in the Act for disqualification of persons with a criminal record who have received particular types of sentence.[36]

28   As to those who practise law or are concerned with the business of the courts and otherwise with administration of the law and justice, the Morris Committee had recommended before the 1974 Act that they should continue to be excluded from jury service. It was not of that view because such persons would readily deduce from what was and was not said in the proceedings whether the defendant had a criminal record. The Committee acknowledged that many without formal legal training knew enough about the workings of the courts to make a shrewd guess about that. But it considered that such persons' specialist knowledge and the prestige attached to their occupations would enable them unduly to influence their fellow jurors. For that reason,[37] it recommended a considerable widening of the categories of exclusion (to which the 1974 Act gave effect); and the Runciman Royal Commission, reporting in 1993, recommended no change.[38]

29   The most commonly voiced objection to removing the ineligibility of all or most of those connected with the courts and the wider administration of justice is the one not relied on by the Morris Committee – that they would be able to deduce from the lack of reference to a defendant's good character, that he has previous convictions. In my view, such concern is unreal for the

---

[34] 1974 Act, Sch I, Pt I

[35] Criminal Justice and Public Order Act 1994, s 40

[36] Sch1, Pt.2

[37] The Morris Report, paras 103-115

[38] save as to the excusal of clergymen and members of religious orders; *Royal Commission on Criminal Justice*, Ch 8, para 57

reason given by the Morris Committee. It is widely known that a defendant is generally entitled to keep quiet in court about his past if it is bad and to make much of it is good. Any juror who has served before will know that, and any juror who sits for the first time will soon become aware of it if he does not already know. The second main objection - the one relied upon by the Morris Committee - that such persons, by reason of their status or position could unduly influence their fellow jurymen, is unlikely today. People no longer defer to professionals or those holding particular office in the way they used to do. Experience in the USA where, in a number of States, judges, lawyers and others holding positions in the criminal justice system have sat as jurors, is that their fellow jurors have not allowed them to dominate their deliberations.[39] A number of them have also commented on how diffident they would have felt about trying to do so since, despite their familiarity with court procedures, they found the role of a juror much more difficult than they had expected.

30   There is also the anxiety voiced by some that those closely connected with the criminal justice system, for example, a policeman or a prosecutor, would not approach the case with the same openness of mind as someone unconnected with the legal system. I do not know why the undoubted risk of prejudice of that sort should be any greater than in the case of many others who are not excluded from juries and who are trusted to put aside any prejudices they may have. Take, for example shopkeepers or house-owners who may have been burgled, or car owners whose cars may have been vandalised, many government and other employees concerned in one way or another with public welfare and people with strong views on various controversial issues, such as legalisation of drugs or euthanasia. I acknowledge that there may be Article 6 considerations in this. But it would be for the judge in each case to satisfy himself that the potential juror in question was not likely to engender any reasonable suspicion or apprehension of bias so as to distinguish him from other members of the public who would normally be expected to have an interest in upholding the law. Provided that the judge was so satisfied, the over-all fairness of the tribunal and of the trial should not be at risk.[40]

31   As I have said, I consider that there is a strong case for removal of all the categories of ineligibility based on occupation. My one reservation has been as to judges. I say that, not because I consider that they are too grand for the task or that their work is so important that they could not be spared for it. On the contrary, I consider that it would be good for them and the system of jury trial if they could experience at first hand what jurors have to put up with. In particular, it would surely help them see how well or badly they and all those concerned in the process assist jurors in their task. And I have been heartened

---

[39] note the greater scope for challenging jurors in USA and the strong warnings as to impartiality etc that American judges give potential jurors before the challenge process

[40] see eg *Pullar v United Kingdom* (1996) 22 EHRR 391, which stated that jury trial was not unfair where an employee of a key prosecution witness was a member of the jury

by the knowledge that judges have sat on juries or been potential jurors in the USA.[41] A number have spoken warmly of the experience. They include Judith S Kaye, the Chief Judge of the State of New York, Shirley Abrahamson, Chief Justice of the Wisconsin Supreme Court and Justice Breyer, of the Supreme Court of the USA who gave an account at the American Bar Association Meeting in London in July 2000 of his jury service.

32   There are two main reasons why I have hesitated over the notion of judges as jurors. First, some observers of and participants in the scene might regard the innovation as little more than a gesture, or as one New York columnist described it in its early days there, "a foolish experiment in injudicious pseudo-egalitarianism". But, if it is well meant and, as I believe, capable of contributing both to the work of individual juries and to improvement of the jury system as a whole, it should be considered. A more practical difficulty is that potential judge/jurors may often know or be known to the trial judge or advocates or others involved in the trial. This could be regarded as compromising their independence and/or, dependent on their seniority or personality, as inhibiting the judge or advocates in their conduct of the case. However, such problems could be dealt with as and when they arise by discretionary excusal rather than a blanket ineligibility by reason of their occupation. They would be in no different position in that respect from all others concerned with the administration of justice if my recommendation for the general removal of ineligibility is adopted. For those reasons, I have come to the conclusion that it would be wrong to single out the judges for special treatment in this respect.

33   As to the ineligibility of clergymen, the 1974 Act reflected the Morris Committee's recommendation for no change because of the possible embarrassment to them flowing from their pastoral role and compassionate instincts.[42] However, there are many others in the community with similar roles and instincts. Like the Runciman Royal Commission[43] I consider that there is no justification for excluding them from jury service unless they find it incompatible with their tenets or beliefs. Provision has since been made for the excusal as of right of "a practising member of a religious society or order the tenets of which are incompatible with jury service",[44] but I am not sure that that is quite what the Commission intended.[45] It seems to me that this would be more appropriately dealt with by way of discretionary excusal rather than an entitlement by reference simply to claim membership of a religious body.

---

[41] eg in Colorado, Connecticut, Illinois, District of Columbia, New York and Wisconsin

[42] The Morris Report, para 118-121

[43] *Royal Commission on Criminal Justice*, Ch 8, para 57

[44] Juries Act 1974, Sch 1 Pt. III, implementing the Runciman Royal Commission's recommendation

[45] *Royal Commission on Criminal Justice*, Ch 8, para 57 and recommendation 217

34 Thus, in my view, there is a strong case for removing all the present categories of ineligibility based upon occupation, that is, those in Groups A – the Judiciary, B – others concerned with the administration of justice and C – the clergy, in Part I of Schedule 1 to the 1974 Act. Any difficulty or embarrassment that the holding of any such office may pose in a particular case can be dealt with under the courts' discretionary power of excusal. As to the categories of disqualification for those with a criminal record who have received particular types of sentence, as set out in Part II of Schedule 1 to the Act, I see no reason for change. Until recently there was very little check that persons summoned met the requirements for jury service, in particular, as to whether they had previous convictions. However, that has now changed with the establishment by the Central Summoning Bureau of an electronic link with the Police National Computer, which enables an automatic check on each person summoned.

Accordingly, I recommend that:

- **everyone should be eligible for jury service, save for the mentally ill, and the law should be amended accordingly; and**

- **there should be no change to the categories of those disqualified from jury service.**

Excusals as of right and discretionary excusal

35 In addition to persons who within specified periods have previously served on a jury or who have been excused by a court from doing so,[46] a large range of persons are entitled to excusal from sitting on a jury if they claim it. They include persons over 65 and members of certain religious bodies to whom I have referred and two groups of persons who, by reason of their public duties or medical responsibilities, might find it difficult to undertake jury service. The first group includes, Peers and Peeresses, Members of Parliament and full-time members of the armed forces. The second consists of medical practitioners, dentists, nurses, midwives, veterinary practitioners and pharmaceutical chemists.[47] The two groups reflect the reasoning and recommendations of the Morris Committee that excusal as of right should be granted to an occupation where it is in the public interest because of the special and personal duties to the State that it involves or because of the

---

[46] Juries Act 1974, s 8

[47] ibid, Sch I, Pt. III

special and personal responsibilities of its individual members for the immediate relief of pain and suffering.[48]

36   Excusal as of right of those over 65 is relatively new, having been introduced by a statutory amendment in 1988.[49] But it seems to me that the increasing number and better health of persons over that age justify treating them as other potential jurors under the qualifying limit of 70, namely, fit to serve unless they can show that they are so physically or mentally unfit as not to be able to act effectively as jurors. No doubt, claims by persons over 65 on that account would be sympathetically considered.

37   As to the main two categories of persons excusable as of right, I consider that there may be a good reason for excusing them where it is vital that they are available to perform their important duties over the period covered by the summons. But I see no reason why that should entitle them to excusal as of right simply by virtue of their position. As the Morris Committee acknowledged,[50] it is extremely difficult to draw a line between those whose work is and is not so crucial that it would be against the public interest to compel them to serve as jurors. Invidious choices of that sort can be avoided, and the jury strengthened, by replacing excusal of right in such cases with discretionary excusal or deferral.

38   The remaining category of excusal as of right is that of persons who have served on a jury or who have attended to serve on a jury within two years before the service of the summons or who are within a period of excusal granted by the court.[51] If my recommendations as to the composition of juries are adopted, many more jurors should become available for service than at present, with a consequent reduction in the need to expose them as often to selection for jury service. With that in mind, once patterns of jury usage for each court catchment area have emerged and the Central Summoning Bureau has developed more sophisticated computer controls, consideration could be given to permitting local increases in the period of excusal of right under this head. Such a proposal, it seems to me, would be more flexible and fair to those who wish to do jury service than another suggestion made in the Review. It was for the creation of three jury qualification lists, one for those who have never served on a jury, a second for those who have served once, and a third for those who have served more than once, and for random selection from the first list until it was exhausted, then from the second and then the third.

---

[48] The Morris Report, para 148
[49] Criminal Justice Act 1988, s 119(2)
[50] The Morris Report, para. 147
[51] Juries Act 1974, s 8

39   As to discretionary excusal or deferral, an officer of the court may excuse or defer the attendance of a person summoned for jury service if he is satisfied that there is good reason for doing so. There is a right of appeal to the court in the event of refusal.[52] The present scope for excusal accounts, as I have indicated, for 38% of those currently summoned for jury service who are able to avoid it. It is taken up in the main by those who are self-employed or in full-time employment who can make out a case for economic or other hardship for themselves or others if they have to give up their work for even a short period, and also by parents who are unable to make alternative arrangements for the care of their children. If, as I recommend, the main categories of ineligibility and all of excusal as of right are abolished, there will be more work for officials and judges in deciding whether to grant discretionary excusals or deferrals in such cases when sought. The claims will be at least as pressing as many claims for discretionary excusal already are. But they should be tested carefully according to the individual circumstances of each claim, otherwise there could be a reversion to the present widespread excusal of such persons by reason only of their positions or occupations. I hope that much of the present pressure to avoid jury service may go if, in accordance with these and other of my recommendations, people are asked to do it less often, for shorter periods, with more consideration for their personal commitments and under better conditions than now.

40   Where a claim for excusal appears to be well founded, the Central Summoning Bureau officers should aim to deal with it by way of deferral rather than excusal. I am much attracted by the regime successfully introduced in New York and many other USA courts of requiring the claimant to offer and make arrangements to do his jury service at some alternative time suitable to him or her. In certain counties in New York State, for example, an automated telephone system enables jurors to 'postpone' their first summons for up to six months, usually to a specific date of their choice. Subsequent applications for deferral should be considered against clear, published criteria and, if granted, for a specific period, with scope for an extended period where appropriate. Only if a request for deferral is not practicable or reasonable should the Bureau normally refuse it or consider its power of excusal.[53]

I recommend that:

- **save for those who have recently undertaken, or have been excused by a court from, jury service, no-one should be excusable from jury service as of right, only on showing good reason for excusal;**

---

[52] ibid, ss 9 and 9A

[53] the present jury summons states: "You will only be excused if the jury summoning officer is satisfied that it will not be reasonable to expect you to do jury service during the next year."

- **the Central Summoning Bureau or the court, in examining a claim for discretionary excusal, should consider its power of deferral first; and**

- **the Bureau should treat all subsequent applications for deferral and all applications for excusal against clear criteria identified in the jury summons.**

Discharge of jury summons on account of disability or incapacity

41   The court has power to discharge a jury summons if it considers that the person, on account of disability[54] or "insufficient understanding of English"[55] will not be able to act effectively as a juror.[56]

42   In both cases this power of discharge is quite distinct from that of excusal for good reason. As to disability, amendment of the law in 1994[57] effectively established a presumption that people with disabilities attending court in response to a summons can serve on juries. In a case of doubt the judge should only discharge the summons if he is "of the opinion that the person will not, on account of his disability, be capable of acting effectively as a juror". This is of a piece with the strong move in this country and civilised countries everywhere to accommodate and, as far as possible, positively to include people with disabilities in all society's activities. The European Convention on Human Rights speaks of the right of each individual to pursue a dignified and fulfilling life, and Article 14 of it, as interpreted by the Strasbourg Court, prohibits discrimination against people with disabilities. The Disability Discrimination Act 1995 is our opening legislative contribution to that movement.

43   As the Bar Council Disability Committee have observed, in a powerful submission in the Review, the concept of disabled persons sitting on juries is wholly consistent with the principle of random selection from all members of society. Enabling them to do so is not just a question of evaluating their disability and relating it to the task, but also of providing, where reasonably practicable, the facilities and/or assistance to them to undertake it. This includes fairly predictable needs, such as access for people with mobility difficulties to and, as necessary, throughout the court-building, space for jurors in wheelchairs in or near the jury box, special lavatories and suitable equipment for people with visual impairments. The Court Service has been

---

[54] 1974 Act, s 9B

[55] 1974 Act, s 10

[56] the Morris Committee had recommended that persons with physical difficulties, such as blindness or deafness, rendering them incapable of jury service should be ineligible; paras 123-127

[57] Criminal Justice and Public Order Act 1994, s 41, introducing s 9B of the 1974 Act.

alive to these basic needs for some years. All courts have been audited against the standards implied by the Disability Discrimination Act 1995 and a schedule of works has been compiled that should ensure compliance with those standards by October 2004. Priority will be given to works to the main court centres for each circuit.

44   There are, however, additional problems for the profoundly deaf since, if they are to contribute effectively to the verdict, they will require the assistance of an interpreter in the jury room before and during the jury's deliberations. Judges to date have ruled that if a person was so deaf that he could not participate in the jury's deliberations without an interpreter, he should be discharged as incapable of acting effectively as a juror, because the presence of a 13th party in the jury room would be an incurable irregularity.[58]

45   In recent years a number of organisations concerned with disability generally and the deaf in particular have pressed for amendment of the law to permit a deaf person to act as a juror with the assistance of a sign language interpreter or lip speaker. The Bar Council Disability Committee suggest that anxieties about an interpreter intruding on the privacy of the jury room would be met if he were required to undertake to communicate with the disabled person and the other jurors only as an interpreter and not to divulge the jurors' deliberations to any third person.

46   There is understandable caution about the prospect of such a 13th person in the jury room. But accredited interpreters work to agreed professional standards that should preclude any attempt to intrude on or breach the confidence of juries' deliberations. In April 2000 the Lord Chancellor indicated that he could see no objection to deaf people serving as jurors. The Government has committed itself to a general review of support in court and in the jury room to jurors with disabilities and to those who cannot speak English. The Home Office was to issue a consultation paper on the matter towards the end of 2000, but has yet to do so. In the circumstances, it would be premature to attempt any specific recommendation. But, in principle, I consider that all reasonable arrangements, coupled with suitable safeguards, should be provided to enable people with disabilities to sit as jurors with third party assistance. I say this, not because there is a general right, as distinct from duty, to undertake jury service or under any anti-discrimination legislation,[59] but because such inclusiveness is a mark of a modern, civilised, society.

---

[58] see *Goby v Wetherill* [1915] 2KB 674; *R v McNeil* [1967] Crim LR 540, CACD; *Re Osman* [1996] 1 Cr App R 126 (Sir Lawrence Verney, the Reorder of London)

[59] although the courts are 'providers of services' under section 19 of the Disability Discrimination Act 1995, selection as a juror is not a service provided by them, as distinct from the services they should provide to jurors once selected

47   In the United States a policy of automatic exclusion of blind or deaf persons from jury service would violate the Federal Anti-Discrimination legislation.[60] The experience of the American Courts where deaf people have sat on juries is that they have not been a hindrance. On the contrary, the need for juries to work at their pace, although lengthening the deliberations somewhat, has tended to make them more structured, with the advantage, if nothing else, of only one person talking at a time.

48   Regardless, of the outcome on that particular issue, I consider that more needs to be done than at present to inform all people with disabilities summoned for jury service that they will be considered for it, if they wish. I know that the Central Summoning Bureau is alert to identify and, in liaison with the courts, to meet these needs. But I think it could do more by way of positive encouragement. Given the Home Office's current review of the whole subject, I consider that, apart from a general exhortation to make proper provision at all Crown Court centres for people with disabilities to serve as jurors, it would be wrong for me to attempt any specific recommendation in advance of the Home Office's completion of its review.

Discharge of jury summons because of incapacity to understand English

49   As to command of and literacy in English, the Morris Committee considered and rejected a number of proposals variously calling for educational, intelligence or literacy tests as a requirement for inclusion on the list for jury service.[61] However, it recommended that no-one should be qualified to serve on a jury who found it difficult to read, write, speak or understand English. The Roskill Committee doubted whether the formula in the 1974 Act of "insufficient understanding of English" sufficiently met those recommendations as to literacy. Whilst the Committee noted a judicial readiness to excuse jurors who acknowledged a difficulty in reading and writing in cases involving documentary evidence, it regarded it as no guarantee of excluding them in such cases. It was of the view that, either by amendment of the statutory formula or by leaving it to those responsible for the administration of the courts, it should be ensured that only literate persons should serve as jurors in fraud cases.[62]

50   To impose literacy as a qualification for jury service would exclude a significant section of the community who, despite that inability, have much to

---

[60] see eg *People v Caldwell* 603 N.Y.S. 2d. 713 (NY Crim. Ct, 1993) *and Galloway v Superior Court of District of Columbia* 816 F Supp 12 D.D C 1993; see also 57 Albany L Rev 289, 296-305
[61] The Morris Report, paras 76-80
[62] The Fraud Trials Committee Report (HMSO, 1986), paras 7.9 -7.11

contribute to the broad range of experience and common-sense that is required in a jury. However, in my view, it is becoming increasingly necessary for jurors to have a reasonable command of written English. Even in the simplest case, there are usually exhibited documents that they must be capable of understanding. If, as I recommend, there is a move to more use of visual aids in court, to written summaries of the issues and of admitted facts and to more wide-spread use of written directions, the need will become greater. I have sympathy with the Roskill Committee's concern that there should be a means of ensuring that illiterate persons do not sit as jurors in fraud trials or any case that involves critical documentary evidence. It would be difficult to entrust the matter to the Central Summoning Bureau to sort out by way of discretionary excusal at the summoning stage. It would not be known then whether the illiterate person summoned would be required to sit as a juror in a case with critical documentary evidence. And to leave it to discreet enquiries by court staff when organising panels of jurors for particular cases is both chancy and offends the principle of randomness. The present system of leaving the judge as the final filter during the process of jury selection is probably the best that can be achieved. By then the nature of the case for trial and its likely demands on the literacy of potential jurors can be assessed. The judge should give the panel of potential jurors an ample and tactfully expressed warning of what they are in for, and offer them a formula that would enable them to seek excusal without embarrassment. As a very last resort, there is always the option for the prosecution to 'stand by' a potential juror who clearly has difficulty, when being sworn, in reading the oath.

RANDOM SELECTION

The principle

51   I have mentioned the principle of random selection and how its application to the process of selecting names from the electoral register is skewed by the latter's incompleteness, tending to exclude many from the poorer and more mobile sections of society, including ethnic minorities. The principle is further damaged by the removal from the pool of a large swathe of those who are presently ineligible or excused as of right or for good reason. If and when those distortions are reduced by enlarging the sources for jury qualification, removing the main categories of ineligibility and of excusal as of right and introducing a scheme of flexible deferral, there should be a significant improvement in the quality of juries and a general reduction in the burden of jury service. But juries will still not include many of the less fortunate in society who, for one reason or another, would not be found on any list from which potential jurors could be drawn. Not only does randomness not equal representativeness, but it can result in juries in individual cases being grossly unrepresentative. This is not ideal, but I share the Runciman Royal Commission's reluctance to interfere with the general principle of random

selection.[63] There are, however, two candidates for some modification - ethnic and linguistic.

Ethnic minority representation on juries

52   The Crown Court study undertaken during 1992 on behalf of the Runciman Royal Commission[64] indicated that, nationally, ethnic minority communities were not seriously under-represented on juries. There has been no comprehensive monitoring since then of the national or local ethnic make-up of juries and, in the absence of a similar national study, I cannot, therefore, say that the position remains the same. A fundamental problem is that ethnic minorities are among the highest categories of persons who, though entitled to serve on juries, do not qualify because they are not registered as electors. Recent Home Office research[65] indicates that about 24% of black, 15% from the Indian sub-continent and 24% of other ethnic minorities are not registered. A limited and relatively unscientific survey undertaken for the Review in Liverpool, Nottingham and Durham in August and September last year showed a noticeable lack of ethnic mix in jury trials at all three centres.

53   The Court of Appeal in 1989 held that a judge has no power to influence the composition of the jury by directing that a multi-racial jury be empanelled or by the use of his power of discretionary discharge, or by directing that the panel should be drawn from another jury catchment area. The Runciman Royal Commission agreed with that as a general proposition. But it recommended that, in exceptional cases with "a racial dimension" involving an ethnic minority defendant or victim, the judge could, if persuaded that one or other reasonably believed there would not be a fair trial from an all-white jury, direct the selection of a jury consisting of up to three people from ethnic minority groups. It also recommended that in an appropriate case he should be able to direct that one or more of the three jurors should be drawn from the same ethnic minority as the defendant or the victim. It suggested that either variation could be achieved by the jury bailiff continuing to draw names randomly selected from the panel available at court until the three requisite persons were drawn.[66] The Government of the day did not adopt the recommendation because it considered it offended the principle of random selection from a cross-section of the population as a whole.

54   The Law Society, the Race Relations Committee of the Bar Council, The Commission for Racial Equality and others have sought to revive the

---

[63] *Royal Commission on Criminal Justice*, Chapter 8, para 62

[64] *The Royal Commission on Criminal Justice, Research Study No 19*, Professor Michael Zander and Paul Henderson (1993)

[65] *Research Findings No 102*, (Home Office Research, Development and Statistics Directorate, 1999)

[66] *Royal Commission on Criminal Justice*, Chapter 8, paras 63 and 64

Runciman Royal Commission recommendations. They have suggested two further alternatives. The first, also mentioned by the Commission, was that the judge could direct transfer of the case to a court centre in another locality where the ethnic mix would give a better chance of drawing a multi-racial jury. The second was that, in order to create a better chance of ethnic minority representation on a jury, the panel from which it is drawn could be amalgamated with that from another court area or drawn from that other panel.

55 As to the Runciman Royal Commission's proposal, the arguments against it are the familiar one of principle - the importance of random selection - and practicality, the difficulty of early identification of cases calling for a multi-racial jury so as to provide panels with sufficient members of ethnic minorities to ensure the availability of at least three of them for selection in such cases. The suggestion of moving cases to another court centre, initially appealed to me as a pragmatic solution to an otherwise difficult question. There would be no legal obstacle to it[67] and little practical difficulty (save for those who might have to travel longer distances to court). But, on reflection, it smacks of forum shopping and could cause grave upset, say when the victim and the defendant are of different ethnicity and/or are at odds as to where the matter should be tried. The suggestion of drawing potential jurors, or amalgamating panels with those, from areas of higher ethnic minority populations would be equally unacceptable for similar reasons, and would be inefficient.

56 Dr. Penny Darbyshire's analysis for the Review of jury research[68] indicates, unsurprisingly, that the race of jurors can affect the verdict in cases where either the defendant or the victim or witnesses on one side or another are of a different race from those on the jury. This is of some significance when put against the 1995 British Crime Survey's figure for that year of nearly 400,000 crimes in England and Wales considered by the victim to be racially motivated. Where there is evidence of racial bias on the part of jurors, it is clearly capable of affecting the fairness of the trial. So, is the principle of random selection a sufficient answer to the problem when considered against the following factors: the emergence of a large number of racially aggravated offences coupled with recent statutory recognition of them;[69] the relatively recent loss of the right of peremptory challenge; the inability to challenge for cause without a prima facie case of its existence; and the newly applicable Article 6 principle of 'objective impartiality', namely a requirement of sufficient guarantees to exclude any objectively justified or legitimate doubts

---

[67] see Supreme Court Act 1981, s76

[68] see Appendix V to the Report

[69] see eg Crime and Disorder Act 1998, s 28 and Powers of Criminal Courts (Sentencing) Act 2000, s 153.

as to the impartiality of the tribunal?[70] Dr Darbyshire, in her analysis, posed a similar question:

> "For over five centuries, until 1870, members of minorities such as Jews, Germans and Italians had the right to be tried by a jury comprised half of foreigners. It was called the jury 'de mediate linguae'. This right was abolished on the ground that "no foreigner need fear for a fair trial in England". Given the trial data, reported cases and research findings, can we in England and Wales believe this to be true now?"

57   I have found this a difficult question both on the principle of randomness and on the practicalities of change.

58   However, randomness is not an end in itself. It is, so far, the best means we have, absent some system of investigation or examination of potential jurors as in the United States, of trying to secure an impartial and fair jury. A move towards the Runciman Royal Commission's proposals would be a danger to that aim if it were to amount to special pleading, that is to say, for representation on a jury of those from the same background or sympathetic to the defendant or victim. That would clearly be unacceptable. But, as a means of widening the range of backgrounds and experience on the jury in appropriate cases, it could be a positive aid to over-all fairness in cases of particular ethnic sensitivity.

59   That still leaves the question: what makes race so special in the sense that any changes of the sort proposed should not also be made for other special interest groups? The answer may be as follows. Our randomly selected and uninvestigated juries are clearly at risk of one or more of their number bringing prejudice of one sort or another to their task. Such prejudice is usually invisible, and we are content to assume that it will be overcome or cancelled by differing views of the other members. But membership of a particular racial group is usually visible, and, as Dr Darbyshire's research and other studies suggest, white juries are, or are perceived to be, less fair to black than to white people. It is this quality of visible difference and the prejudice that it may engender that singles out race for different treatment from other special interest groups in the courtroom. In my view, that is not a problem that can be solved by a North American style jury examination, which would not, in any event, be well supported in this country for all the obvious practical reasons as well as serious reservations about its efficacy.

60   What then is to be done about the potential for racial prejudice in all-white juries in our system? I believe that the practical problems, in devising a

---

[70] see *Gregory v UK*, 25 EHRR 577, ECHR; and cf *Incal v Turkey*, 29 EHRR 449, ECHR, and *Sander v UK*, Case 34129/96 [2000] Crim L R 767

procedure, in appropriate cases, to ensure a wider racial mix and to balance any competing interests of defendant and complainant, are not insurmountable. The Central Summoning Bureau could ask potential jurors to state their ethnic origins, a question asked in the census. If they don't want to say, they need not do so. The parties could be required to indicate early in their preparation for the pre-trial assessment[71] whether race is likely to be a relevant issue and, if so, whether steps should be taken to attempt to secure some ethnic minority representation on the jury. This could be done by the empanelment of a larger number of jurors than normal from which the jury for the case is to be selected, some of whom would be identified by their juror cards as from ethnic minorities. It may be necessary to allow a longer period of notice in such cases than the standard summons period of eight weeks ahead. The first nine selected would be called to serve and, if they did not include a minimum of – say three – ethnic minority jurors, the remainder would be stood down until the minimum was reached. My recommendations for widening the pool of potential jurors so as to include better ethnic minority representation country-wide, if adopted, should go some way to assist in securing sufficient ethnic minority members of court panels to make such a scheme feasible.

61   As to the suggested difficulty where the defendant and the complainant are of different ethnic origin, the judge's ruling would be for a racially diverse jury in the form that I have suggested, not that it should contain representatives of the particular ethnic background on either side. Any question as to who would qualify as an ethnic minority for this purpose should be an implementation issue to be resolved in consultation with the Commission for Racial Equality and other relevant groups.

62   I do not suggest a parallel process for magistrates' courts constituted by a bench of lay magistrates. Apart from my recommendations directed to secure a lay magistracy more reflective of the local communities it serves, their semi-professionalism, coupled with their sharing of their jurisdiction with professional judges, would make it unnecessary and, on a case by case basis, wholly impracticable.

> **Accordingly, I recommend that a scheme should be devised, along the lines that I have outlined, for cases in which the court considers that race is likely to be relevant to an issue of importance in the case, for the selection of a jury consisting of, say, up to three people from any ethnic minority group.**

---

[71] see Chapter 10, paras 221 - 228

Linguistic composition of juries - Wales[72]

63   There are particular problems about the composition of juries in Wales. They are not new. They concern the Welsh language, looked at from the perspective of jurors whose only or main language is English, or the English language, for jurors whose only or main language is Welsh or who simply prefer to have the evidence in their own language. Over the last 10 to 15 years there has been a renaissance of the Welsh language. It is still very much a 'minority' language, but about half million - about 20% - of those in Wales now speak it. Their numbers are increasing and there will clearly be greater use of it in public life, including in the courts. However, the distribution of Welsh speakers throughout the Principality is not even. In some areas, in particular, the north west, the majority speak it. In others, for example the south east, only a minority do; but even within that area it is variable. According to the 1991 census results, the percentage of those three years old and over able to speak Welsh in the then counties was: Gwent 2.4%; South Glamorgan 6.5%; Mid Glamorgan 8.5%; and West Glamorgan 15%.[73]

64   The Welsh Language Act 1993 requires that in the administration of justice in Wales and Monmouthshire, both languages are to be treated on a basis of equality, and provides that in any legal proceeding any party, witness or other person may speak in Welsh if he wishes to do so. Where Welsh is spoken and not everyone in the case speaks it, simultaneous professional interpretation is provided. Practice Directions require that cases in which Welsh may be used should, wherever practicable, be listed before a Welsh speaking judge and in a court with simultaneous translation facilities. However, because of the system of random selection of jurors, there is no mechanism to ensure that all or, indeed, any of a jury's members are bilingual, thus requiring simultaneous translation in almost all cases where Welsh is used.

65   Mr Justice Roderick Evans, when the Resident Judge of Cardiff, suggested in a paper prepared for the Review that a witness, including a defendant, who has to give evidence to a jury through an interpreter is at a disadvantage, and so are the jury in their assessment of him and of what he says. He suggested that the only way to overcome those disadvantages is by introducing some mechanism to ensure bilingual juries in all Crown Court trials where Welsh is spoken. He went further and maintained that the underlying principle of the 1993 Act requires it to accommodate Welsh-only speakers by amendment of section 10 of the Juries Act 1974 which requires the discharge of any potential juror with insufficient understanding of English to act as a juror.

> "The present inability to select a jury whose members are
> bilingual is inconsistent with the principle that English and

---

[72] I am particularly indebted to Lord Justice Pill, Mr Justice Thomas and Mr Justice Roderick Evans for much of my treatment of this topic

[73] the Welsh Household Interview Survey showed a small increase on these figures, *Digest of Welsh Local Area Statistics, 2001*

Welsh should be treated on a basis of equality, militates against the exercise of the right to use Welsh in court, draws an inappropriate distinction between citizens who choose to use Welsh rather than English and has the potential to work injustice."

66   In 1973, Lord Justice Edmund Davies, as he then was, in a report to the Lord Chancellor of an informal study on the use of Welsh in courts in Wales,[74] concluded that selecting bilingual juries would offend against the principle of random selection. I understand that Welshmen may differ about that. But assuming that it is so, Mr Justice Roderick Evans questioned:

"whether adherence to a tenet of English law developed in a monolingual England is a good reason for perpetuating an injustice in an officially bilingual Wales."

67   Mr. Justice Thomas, a Presiding Judge of the Wales and Chester Circuit, and Mr Justice Roderick Evans, drawing on the experience of the Canadian Federal Courts and the Provincial Court of New Brunswick in the use of both French and English, urge the introduction of a system of bilingual juries in Wales in any case in which the Welsh language is likely to be used and in which a bilingual judge would be required to preside. They do not identify who should determine that, or by what criteria. They suggest that a jury panel of bilingual speakers should be drawn from those identified as such on a new register or that a bilingual jury should be selected in court from a panel summoned as now. The latter procedure, which is that in use in Canada, would be lengthy and expensive since it would involve bringing to court much larger panels than now to ensure a jury of 12 bilingual speakers. There would still have to be provision for simultaneous interpretation of the evidence of those witnesses who wish to give their evidence in English, as happens in Canada in French language trials.[75] But that is a feature of any trial in England and Wales where witnesses are unable or unwilling for good reason to give their evidence in English. All this would require amendment of the Juries Act 1974 to put English and Welsh on an equal footing, in particular in the provision enabling discharge of a potential juror on the ground of insufficient understanding of English, rather than Welsh, to be an effective juror.

68   However, there are others of great experience in the administration of criminal justice in Wales who, while acknowledging the importance of removing any inhibition on speaking Welsh in court in the Principality, take a different view. In a submission to the Review, Lord Justice Pill, a former

[74] see Hansard, HL, 12 June 1973, cols 534R to 537L for a summary of Lord Justice Edmund Davies' recommendations, referred to in a statement by the Lord Chancellor, Lord Hailsham of St Marylebone
[75] in Canada the preferred method is phrase by phrase consecutive interpretation, which is lengthier and tends to interrupt the flow of evidence

161

Presiding Judge of the Wales and Chester Circuit, has expressed a number of concerns about the proposal.

69   As to the principle of random selection, Lord Justice Pill has pointed out that, to require bilingual juries in every case in which the Welsh language is likely to be used, would clearly violate it in its exclusion of 75% or 80% of the Principality's population (increasing to over 90% in the heavily populated south east) from the privilege, as well as the civic duty, of jury service. That privilege – cherished by the supporters of the jury system – was also of concern to Lord Justice Edmund Davies. He stated in his Report:

> "… while jury service is often regarded merely as a duty, it is in fact one of the important privileges of citizenship. To take steps to ensure that 75% of the population of the Principality should be debarred from jury service in a particular case on the sole ground that they cannot understand Welsh would involve a radical departure from that random formation of the jury panel which Blackstone described as a 'palladium' of our liberties".

70   As to the suggestion that the principle of random selection is a tenet of English law no longer applicable in a bilingual Wales, Lord Justice Pill has observed, "[t]here is nothing particularly English about it", it is of general application throughout the common law world and "[d]eparture from it, whether on linguistic or other grounds, inevitably amounts to a fundamental attack upon it":

> "Quite apart from the privileges of citizenship, there is a potential for injustice in excluding from the pool from which the jury is selected 90% of the defendant's peers. Moreover, in South East Wales ability to speak Welsh rightly has important social and cultural associations and a defendant may be deprived of a trial by a jury including members of that monoglot majority with which he has most in common."

71   There are other difficulties in the proposal to which Lord Justice Pill has also referred. They include the important and difficult questions of who should determine in any case whether there should be a bilingual jury and by reference to what criteria, and how to identify potential jurors with sufficient knowledge of Welsh for the subtleties and rigours of a criminal trial.

72   As a non Welshman, I approach this debate with timidity. My view, for what it is worth, is that the proposal of a power to order bilingual juries in particular cases is worthy of further consideration - but not by me. It should be developed and examined, with appropriate consultation, in Wales. The aims should be: to secure a solution that would encourage the greater use of the Welsh language whilst recognising the balance of English and Welsh

speakers in the Principality and the importance of maintaining the privilege and civic duty of jury service for the population as a whole; to preserve, so far as possible, the principle of random selection; to provide an efficient procedure for jury selection; and, most important of all, to ensure that each defendant has a fair trial. Among the matters that will require detailed attention are: the criteria for exercise of the power of directing bilingual juries; who should exercise it and how; how it should be administered so as to secure efficiency and sensitivity to the interests of all concerned; and, in the light of what emerges, whether any, and if so, what amendment is necessary to section 10 of the 1974 Act.

Jury challenge

73   The right of jury challenge is very limited in England and Wales in comparison with that in the United States of America. There is no longer a right to peremptory challenge. It was abolished in 1988,[76] no doubt in the light of the Roskill Committee's Report. The Committee saw it as an erosion of the principle of random selection and, in its general use, an abuse that was on the way to bringing the whole jury system into public disrepute. It recommended its abolition in fraud cases, making plain that, had it been within its terms of reference, it would have recommended its general abolition.[77]   The prosecution still has the right to 'stand by' a juror, notwithstanding a similar recommendation by the Roskill Committee, again because it eroded the principle of random selection. However, its use is now tightly restricted by guidelines issued by the Attorney General in 1988.[78] Challenge for cause also remains, but the burden of proof is on the person who seeks to make it. And before it can be explored by examination of a potential juror there must be some factual foundation for it. The Roskill Committee, before recommending the removal of the peremptory challenge, considered whether there would be pressure to extend the challenge for cause in the form common in the United States. It forecast correctly that English and Welsh judges would stand firm against any such attempts at fishing challenges.

74   There have been very few proposals in the Review for change as to jury challenge and much support for resisting any move to the United States system. I make no recommendations for change either by restoring the right to peremptory challenge or by opening the present limited challenge for cause procedure to permit fishing examination of jurors. The latter would bring with it a considerable threat to the principle of random selection and much expense and prolongation of criminal proceedings. I add that the lack of

---

[76] Criminal Justice Act 1988, s 118(1)
[77] *The Fraud Trials Committee Report*, paras 7.37-7.38
[78] 88 Cr App R 123

opportunity here to investigate the possibility of bias in individual jurors has to be put alongside our provision for majority verdicts (which are unknown or unusual in the USA), which prevents individuals thwarting the otherwise general consensus of the jury.

VERDICTS

Unanimous and majority verdicts

75 The verdict of an English or Welsh jury in a criminal case should normally be unanimous. But since 1967[79] majority verdicts are permitted, of at least ten when there are 11 or 12 jurors and of at least nine when the jury has been reduced to ten. The system has worked well over the years. Its strength is that it requires an overwhelming majority[80] and yet prevents the odd crank or possibly biased juror insisting on a disagreement and thereby frustrating the process. The Review has produced little support for change either in the levels of the required majorities or for reversion to unanimity in all cases or for any form of intermediate verdict, such as that of 'not proven' in use in Scotland.

Jury research

76 There are two possible and overlapping purposes of jury research. The first would be to determine whether juries, in their present form, should continue as fact finders in serious cases. The second would be to learn whether there are better ways of enabling them to do their job. Dr Glanville Williams has said that if one proceeds by the light of reason, there are formidable arguments against the jury system.[81] It is a randomly picked and legally untrained body of men and women trying to cope with inconvenience, discomfort and artificialities of a criminal trial. On the other hand, as he acknowledged, drawing on two of Stephen's three claimed advantages of jury trial, juries' verdicts are, in the main, accepted more readily than those of judges and they bring ordinary citizens into the administration of justice.[82] Implicit in both of those advantages is a widespread public acceptance that a number of heads are better than one and that, in the case of most serious crime, they trump any conceivable alternative. Certainly, very few contributors to the Review have suggested that I should recommend the general abolition of trial by jury and leave the entirety of the criminal process

---

[79] Criminal Justice Act 1967, s 13; see now Juries Act 1974, s 17

[80] cf the Scottish criminal jury of 15, where a simple majority of 8 to 7 will suffice for guilt

[81] *The Proof of Guilt: A Study of the English Criminal Trial.*, pp 207-214;

[82] Stephen, *History of the Criminal Law, I*, pp 566; the third was that the jury relieves the judge of part of the responsibility of his office

to professional judges.[83] And many of those who are agnostic about juries and/or favour their reform, urge some research first into the way in which they work. I have some sympathy with 'the need to know' argument.

77 Despite many advances in the last few decades in administrative arrangements for, and forensic assistance to, jurors, once they are in the jury box we still subject them to archaic and artificial procedures that impede them in their task. They are given very little objective or conveniently summarised guidance at the start of a trial as to the issues they are there to decide and as to what evidence is and is not agreed. They are expected to have prodigious powers of concentration and memory both as to the, mostly oral, evidence and the advocates' submissions. And, at the end of the trial, the judge orally gives them complex directions on the law and a summarised regurgitation of the evidence, much of which must become a blur for many of them by the time they are considering their verdict. In the more complex or serious cases judges increasingly provide them with a brief written list or summary of the questions they have to decide, but that is about as far as it goes.

78 Some might say, given the way juries have to work, it is just as well that we do not know how they reach their verdicts, in particular, whether they are loyal to their oaths or affirmations "to give a true verdict according to the evidence". It was for long undeclared law that jurors should not tell and no-one should ask them what went on in the jury room. This mutual constraint became formalised, in very wide terms, in section 8 of the Contempt of Court Act 1981, which also made breach of it a contempt of court.[84]

79 The main evils that would flow from disclosure of jurors' deliberations seem to be that publicity might engender doubt in the validity of their verdicts and/or might deter them from expressing their views frankly for fear of exposure to intimidation or acts of revenge from disgruntled parties. The latter is understandable, but should the ban be so wide as to prevent legitimate and discreetly conducted research? Is the view of Lord Hewart CJ expressed in 1922[85] defendable today, namely that the value of a jury's verdict lies only in its unanimity, not in the process by which they arrived at it? As Dr Glanville Williams has said, it suggests that "the real reason for keeping the jury's deliberations secret is to preserve confidence in a system which more intimate knowledge might destroy."[86]

80 If jurors in a significant number of cases are not returning verdicts on the evidence and are influenced by other considerations, should we find out about

---

[83] as has always been the case in Holland, save for a short period during the French Revolution
[84] Contempt of Court Act 1981, s 8
[85] *R v Armstrong* [1922] 2 KB 555, at 568; see also *Ellis v Deheer* [1922] 2 KB 113, per Bankes LJ at 118
[86] *The Proof of Guilt: A Study of the English Criminal Trial*, p 205

it? Should section 8 of the 1981 Act be amended to permit legitimate research (and, while we are about it, to enable the Court of Appeal, Criminal Division, to examine conduct in the jury room the subject of appeal)?[87] Or is public confidence in juries' oracular verdicts so precious to our legal system that we should not put it at risk? Many fear that the very undertaking of intrusive research - that is, into how individual juries reach their decisions - could damage public confidence by sewing doubt as to the integrity of verdicts. That is important, not only for those verdicts that might be vulnerable to challenge, but also to those, guilty and not guilty alike, which examination might eventually show to have been justified. The process, which might take some years, could result in a clean bill of health for juries, but would it justify the possible damage done in the meantime?

81   On the other hand, such research might show that all is not well and that changes are needed. That would be worthwhile, subject to three considerations. First, still assuming the sort of research for which amendment of the 1981 Act would be necessary, it would be essential to find an effective machinery for it. Jurors under observation, or speaking after verdict of how they reached it, may not give an accurate picture, respectively, of how an unobserved jury would have behaved or of how they did behave. Shadow juries must be suspect too because they are not subject to the same responsibility or stresses of the true jury. Second, there would be no point in such research unless we could be reasonably sure of devising a significantly better system, either without a jury or to ensure that jurors can and do their job properly. Third, the outcome of intrusive research might be inconclusive, no more than that juries are infinitely variable in their make-up and in their responses to the individual circumstances of each case and to the competence and personalities of those involved, including the judge and the advocates.

82   As to the validity of jury trial in principle, I am much of the same view as previous review bodies and the vast majority of those who have made submissions on the point to the Review. I share their instinct to accept the jury system unless and until it is found so wanting that we should seek to replace it with some other mode of trial. I would go further in accepting the powerfully symbolic effect of the jury as a means of enabling citizens to participate in the trial process and the public confidence that, rightly or wrongly, it engenders in the system. However, I also agree with the Runciman Royal Commission that some research could be of value. For the reasons I have given, I have grave doubt whether intrusive research of the sort requiring amendment of the 1981 Act would be wise, or that it would produce any definitive answer or one that would enable us with confidence to substitute some other system.

---

[87] see eg *R v Thompson* [1962] 1 All E R 65; and *R. v Young* [1995] 2 Cr App R 379

83   As to improvement of the jury system, there is already a wealth of well-documented research throughout the common law world. Most of it is of a non-intrusive kind that would not require amendment of the 1981 Act. Dr Penny Darbyshire of the Kingston Law School has undertaken for the Review an analysis of the major pieces of research in the twentieth century. I have listed them in Appendix V, just to indicate the volume and breadth of the material available. Much of this research has been, and is now being, put to good use in improving trial by judge and jury in the various jurisdictions where it has been undertaken.

84   In all or most common law jurisdictions the law prevents observation of or listening to a jury's deliberations and considerably restricts what jurors can be asked afterwards.[88]   Research has, in the main, taken one of three forms: interviews of jurors before and/or after their deliberations; comparison of their verdicts with those of other participants in the trial, including the judge and the advocates; and use of shadow or mock juries either present at the trial or in viewing re-enactments or video-films of the trial.[89]

85   Most of the research has been in the United States of America,[90] which has a different form of jury trial from ours. For that reason, it should be approached with care. But it has much to teach us, in particular, as to the composition and treatment of juries and as to how courts should assist them in their task.[91] I have already mentioned the pioneering work of the 1994 New York Jury Project, which has been influential in jury reform throughout the United States, and much of which is relevant to our system. There has also been a great deal of valuable research in Commonwealth countries, one of the most recent and impressive of which is a study of a sample of trials for a Review by the Law Commission of New Zealand of Juries in Criminal Trials.[92]   The study consisted of questioning jurors before trial as to their knowledge, if any, of the case, observing the trial, interviewing the trial judge and questioning jurors after verdict on the adequacy and clarity of pre-trial information, their reactions to the trial process, their understanding of the law, their decision-making process, the nature of and basis for their verdict and the impact of pre-trial and trial publicity.[93]   As I have said, and as the authors of the New Zealand study have acknowledged,[94] its value depends on the accuracy and

---

[88] Dr Darbyshire's analysis for the Review indicates that there was some intrusive research in Kansas but that it was very quickly outlawed in most of the States of the USA

[89] see Cornish, *The Jury*, 1970

[90] starting in the late 50s and early 60s (no apostrophes), in particular, the Chicago Jury Project which, as Dr Darbyshire has indicated, resulted in over 70 publications, the most famous and quoted of which was *The American Jury* by Kalven & Zeisel (1966) Boston, Little, Brown & Co

[91] see, in particular, the pioneering *The Jury Project*, a report commissioned by the Chief Judge Judith Kaye of the State of New York

[92] see Preliminary Paper 37, Vols. 1 and 2, November 1999; and Report 69, "Juries in Criminal Trials", February 2001, Wellington, New Zealand, Chapter 14

[93] ibid Vol. 2, para 1.6

[94] ibid Vol. 2, paras 1.12-1.16

honesty of jurors in recounting their reasoning processes and/or on the possible effect on their behaviour of the knowledge that it was taking place.

86   In framing my recommendation on the treatment of jurors in this chapter and on procedure in jury trials in Chapter 11, I have drawn heavily on Dr Darbyshire's analysis of existing research, on the wealth of material I have been provided by other common law jurisdictions and on the many authoritative submissions in the Review on the subject. To the extent that further research of the non-intrusive New York or New Zealand variety may be necessary for our system of trial by judge and jury, I would commend it.

87   What I have in mind is an enquiry of jurors and others for their general views on the conditions and manner of their service and on the assistance that they are given by court staff, the judge and advocates. Work of this nature, if carefully conducted, should not require amendment of the law or damage public confidence in the jury system pending attempts to improve it. Those who have read Trevor Grove's entertaining and revealing account of his service on a jury, *The Juryman's Tale*, or have looked at research elsewhere will have some idea of the possibilities.

> **I recommend:**
>
> - **no amendment of section 8 of the Contempt of Court Act 1981 to enable research into individual juries' deliberations;**
>
> - **careful consideration of existing research material throughout the common law world on jury trial in criminal cases with a view to identifying and responding appropriately to all *available* information about how juries arrive at their verdicts; and**
>
> - **if and to the extent that such research material is insufficient, consideration of jury research of a general nature that does not violate the 1981 Act.**

The unreasoned verdict

88   The jury is unique among decision-makers in the English criminal trial process in not having to explain its decision. There is a question whether its oracular verdict satisfies Article 6 of the European Convention of Human Rights in its requirement of a reasoned decision. The Strasbourg Court has not, so far, had to consider the point directly,[95] but the English courts may

---

[95] but see the discussion on *Condron v UK* [2000] 31 EHRR1, para 95 below

well have to do so soon. Those who are sanguine about a finding of compliance rely on the argument that the English judge's public directions of law and summing-up of the evidence stand proxy for the jury's reasons. But such an argument depends upon an assumption that they follow and understand his directions on the law and reach their verdict in accordance with the evidence, applying to their findings of fact those directions. Such an argument would be flawed if it included the proposition that, for the purpose of acquittal, though not for conviction, juries are free to do as they like and without explanation. It appears likely that the argument will be tested. If it were to fail and, jurors were required publicly to reason their verdicts, perhaps by answering a short series of questions, as some civil juries do, the courts could not stand powerless in the face of overtly perverse acquittals any more than of perverse verdicts of guilty.

89   Independently of Article 6, it is a function of due process in the common law that a professional judge[96] when determining issues of law or fact should normally give reasons for his decision. A reasoned judgment tells the parties why they have won or lost; it is more likely to be soundly based on the evidence than an unreasoned one;[97] and, by its openness is more likely to engender public confidence in the decision-making system.[98] Until recently no such general duty applied to other decision-makers, including lay magistrates and many administrative tribunals and, of course, juries. However, the general trend has been towards the giving of reasons by decision-makers. In recent years lay magistrates have increasingly been expected to explain their findings, in addition to their long-standing obligation to do so on appeal from their decision by way of case stated to the High Court. But the precise impact of Article 6 on this trend and the continuing exception of the jury verdict is uncertain. The Judicial Committee of the Privy Council have suggested the need for some general appraisal in the light of its provisions.[99]

90   Before considering the possible effect of Article 6, it is important to note that there is no absolute test in English law for the adequacy of reasons. The degree of detail depends, in general, on the nature of the case and the issues in it. In certain types of case it is necessary for the courts, not only to identify the evidence they have accepted or rejected, but also why they have done so. In others it may be sufficient simply to record the acceptance or rejection of evidence without explanation.

---

[96] in recent years stipendiary magistrates have increasingly given reasons for their decisions, despite the absence of any formally expressed legal duty to do so

[97] see *Flannery v Halifax Estate Agencies Ltd. (trading as Colleys Professional Services)* [2000] 1 WLR 377, per Henry LJ at 381G

[98] PM Craig, *The common law, reasons and administrative justice* [1994] Cambridge Law Journal, 283

[99] *Stefan v GMC* [1999] 1 WLR 1293, at 1300 G-1301D

91   What is, what should be, the future for the English jury's unreasoned verdict, given the Article 6 requirement of a fair trial that there should be a public pronouncement - a publicly reasoned - decision in criminal cases? It is said that the English draftsmen of the provision some 50 years ago did not intend it to apply to jury verdicts. Presumably, they felt that it could be assumed that juries would loyally abide by the directions of law and decide issues of fact in the light of them and according to the evidence.

92   For a number of reasons, I incline to the view of a number of eminent British commentators that the Strasbourg Court, in taking account of the way in which our system of jury trial works as a whole, would not consider our juries' unreasoned verdicts to breach Article 6.[100] First, the Strasbourg case law is not precise about the content of reasons required to satisfy the fair trial test. The Court has said that it varies according to the nature of the decision and the circumstances of each case,[101] though it has identified as an important requirement a sufficiency of reasoning to enable the decision to be reviewed by a higher court.[102] Second, as Professor John Spencer has commented in the Review, the Strasbourg case law "is not particularly exacting". As well as allowing for different national traditions, the Court has stressed in a number of cases that the general duty to give reasons does not require a detailed answer to every question. Third, the case law does not suggest that courts must identify the pieces of evidence that they have accepted and why. Fourth, the Court has expressly ruled that the publicly unreasoned determination of a Danish jury was not contrary to the Convention.[103] And, fifth, in considering whether there has been a fair trial, the Court looks at the trial and any appeal together. In England the Court of Appeal (Criminal Division) has some, albeit limited, ability to quash a conviction if it considers that it was contrary to the evidence,[104] but the absence of reasoned decisions limits its ability to remedy unfairness which may have resulted from a defect in, or misunderstanding of, a judge's summing-up.

93   As to the Strasbourg Court's respect for individual national traditions, the Review's Cambridge conference with European Judges and Jurists[105] illustrated the variety of modes of trial that it has to accommodate. Just as some member countries have no jury or other lay involvement in their criminal process,[106] others have very different jury systems, both in their composition and in the way in which they function. Unsurprisingly, there is

---

[100] Professor Spencer in his advice to the Review; Harris, O'Boyle and Warbrick, *The Law of the European Convention on Human Rights* (1995) p 215

[101] see eg *Van De Herk v Netherlands* (1994) 18 EHRR 481, para.61; *Ruiz Torija v Spain* (1994) 19 EHRR 553, para 29; and *Hiro Balani v. Spain* (1995) 19 EHRR 566, para. 27

[102] *Hadjianastassiou v Greece* (1992) 16 EHRR 219

[103] *Saric v Denmark*, application number 31913/96 (decision on 2/2/1999)

[104] but see *Condron v UK* (2000) 31 EHRR 1, at para 46 where the Court commented that jury verdicts in England "are not accompanied by reasons which are amenable to review on appeal".

[105] see Foreword, para 13

[106] e.g. Holland

no general continental consensus as to what is meant by the reasoning, 'motivation', of a judicial decision. In France, for example, it can mean, depending on the context, no more than an identification of the legal principles by reference to which the court has reached its decision on the facts.

94   However, many contributors to the Review have suggested that the system may not, as a matter of English law, withstand a challenge, that the unreasoned jury verdict violates Article 6. And a number of members of the Bar have indicated at Review seminars that they intend to make such a challenge. There is some encouragement for it in the Strasbourg Court's decision in *Murray v UK*[107] where it held that inferences from silence in a Diplock court complied with Article 6 because the judge fully and openly reasoned his decision. Some have inferred that the absence of the opportunity for such reasoning by a jury would lead to a different result.

95   However, the *Murray* judgment does not say that it is *only* by way of a reasoned judgment that such an inference can be justified or that a verdict following a proper direction on the law and summing-up of the material evidence on the issue is not a reasoned verdict.[108] That this is so is indicated by the Strasbourg Court's recent decision in *Condron v UK,*[109] another adverse inference from silence case, but this time before a jury where the complaint was of the inadequacy of the judge's direction to them on the point.[110] The Court, taking *Murray* as the starting point, but noting that jury trial was different, said that "the fact that the issue of the applicant[s]' silence was left to a jury cannot of itself be incompatible with the requirement of a fair trial".[111] Such reasoning suggests that the Court is amenable to accepting the jury's verdict as the final word in a judgment of which the summing-up furnishes the overt reasoning process. The Commission, however, has considered the related but different point whether a Belgian jury's answers 'yes' or 'no' to each of a series of questions put to them by the judge satisfied Article 6. It held that they did since they formed "a framework for the jury's verdict",[112] a mechanism to which I return in Chapter 11 when considering judges' directions to juries.

96   There are a number of reasons why the English courts may be more determinative than the Strasbourg Court on the effect in England and Wales of Article 6 on our unreasoned jury verdict. I believe that their approach should not simply be to shield us from possible criticism in Strasbourg, but to

---

[107] (1996) 22 EHRR 29

[108] I am indebted to Lord Justice Sedley for the analysis in this paragraph

[109] *Condron v United Kingdom* (2000) 31 EHRR1

[110] at para 46

[111] at para 57

[112] Application 15957/90; DR 72, p 195

ensure that our criminal process, however long established and cherished, meets our own present requirements of a fair trial. Over the last two or three decades we have demanded much more of all in the criminal justice process than we previously found acceptable, particularly in the formulation of judicial reasons and in the volume and sophistication of judicial directions to the jury. Yet the jury, in the way in which it is expected to do its job, has barely changed at all. There is also the broader point made by Sir Louis Blom-Cooper, QC,[113] that a publicly unaccountable jury is a 'curiosity' in today's democratic society.

97   Whilst it is certainly arguable that a judge's direction, coupled with a jury's verdict, amounts to a reasoned judicial decision, it falls short of what English law expects from a court composed only of a judge who is required to give one. Unlike the judge, a jury do not have to identify the evidence that they have accepted or rejected or, where there is more than one route to conviction, which route they have taken. These features can cause difficulty where there are a number of ingredients in the offence alleged, and various pieces of evidence that may constitute them, or different routes by which a jury can arrive at their verdict, for there is no means of ensuring or knowing that they were unanimous in the way they reached it. This is a common problem in complex fraud and other cases where the prosecution case is of a course of conduct, but it also arises frequently in more straightforward cases. The way in which the, often, many and complex alternatives are put to juries must be very difficult for them, untrained as many of them are for such close analysis. It is fertile ground for error and injustice that are, in the main, undetectable by way of appeal. The dilemma for the trial judge in directing juries in such cases, and for an appellate court in examining the validity of jury verdicts in them, has given rise to a plethora of conflicting and otherwise unsatisfactory jurisprudence.[114] In my view, the time has come for the trial judge in each case to give the jury a series of written factual questions, tailored to the law as he knows it to be and to the issues and evidence in the case. The answers to these questions should logically lead only to a verdict of guilty or not guilty. I discuss this again in more detail, and make a recommendation on it, in Chapter 11. I go on to recommend that, where the judge considers it appropriate, he should be permitted to require a jury to answer publicly each of his questions.

98   There is also the wider problem of the secrecy of the jury's deliberations insofar as it prevents any effective enquiry by the Court of Appeal into possible misconduct in the jury room. The jurisprudence of the Court, in its laudable attempt to overcome the unduly restrictive prohibition in section 8 of the 1981 Act, is logically hard to justify. It will not enquire into what jurors

---

[113] (2001) EHRLR, p 5

[114] see *R v Brown (K.)* (1984) 79 Cr App R 115, CA; and the many differing applications of it over the years set out in *Archbold, Criminal Pleading, Evidence and Practice, 2001*, paras. 4-391-393; and for a recent and helpful discussion of the difficulties in such cases, see per Otton LJ, giving the judgment of the Court in *R v Boreman* [2000] 1 All E.R. 307, CA

have done or said in the course of their deliberations in the jury room, but it will do if they are elsewhere, say while in a hotel overnight.[115] In my view, the effective bar that section 8 puts on an appellate court inquiring into and remedying possible bias or other impropriety in the course of a jury's deliberations is indefensible and capable of causing serious injustice. Recent Strasbourg case law suggests that, for those reasons, it is also highly vulnerable under Article 6.[116] If, as I shall recommend, Parliament should amend section 8 to permit the Court of Appeal to investigate such matters, it is hard to see why the scope of its investigation should not also extend to allegations of impropriety of reasoning or lack of any reasoning, for example, that some jurors ignored or slept through the deliberations or that the jury decided one way or other on some irrational prejudice or whim, deliberately ignoring the evidence. In making the recommendation I should record that I have considered and rejected a suggestion made by a number of contributors to the Review that the trial judge should retire with the jury to 'police' them in their deliberations. Such a proposition is alien to our criminal process and would, if anything, be more vulnerable to the open reasoning requirements of Article 6 than our present system.

> **I recommend that section 8 of the Contempt of Court Act 1981 should be amended to permit, where appropriate, enquiry by the trial judge and/or the Court of Appeal (Criminal Division) into alleged impropriety by a jury, whether in the course of its deliberations or otherwise.**

Perverse verdicts

99   There are many, in particular the Bar, who fervently support what they regard as the right of the jury to ignore their duty to return a verdict according to the evidence and to acquit where they disapprove of the law or of the prosecution in seeking to enforce it. Lord Devlin attributed this notion to a later misapplication or hardening of the Magna Carta provision to which I have referred. Nevertheless, he saw it as a protection against laws that the ordinary man might regard as "harsh and oppressive" and an insurance "that the criminal law will conform to the ordinary man's idea of what is fair and just".[117] EP Thompson, expressed a similar view in a memorable passage in 1980:

> "The English common law rests upon a bargain between the
> Law and the People. The jury box is where people come into
> the court; the judge watches them and the jury watches back.
> A jury is the place where the bargain is struck. The jury

---

[115] see eg *R v Young* (S) [1995] 2 Cr App R 379, CA

[116] See *Remli v France* (1996) 22 EHRR 253 and *Sander v UK* [2000] Crim LR.767 but cf *Gregory v UK* (1998) EHRR 577

[117] *Trial by Jury*, p 160

attends in judgment, not only upon the accused, but also upon the justice and humanity of the law...." [118]

100   The *Clive Ponting*, and *Randle* and *Pottle* cases and, more recently, a number of acquittals in cases of alleged criminal damage by anti-war and environmental campaigners cases may be modern examples of juries exercising such 'dispensing' ability. But not all perverse verdicts have the attractive notion of a 'blow for freedom' that many attach to them. There are other prejudices in the jury room that may lead to perverse acquittals, for example, in sexual offences where the issue is consent or in cases of serious violence where a lesser verdict than that clearly merited on the evidence may be returned. There may also be perverse convictions based, for example, on irrelevant factors or irrational argument which, because of their undetectability, are not capable of being corrected on appeal.

101   However, although juries may have the ability to dispense with or nullify the law, they have no right to do so. Indeed, it is contrary to their oath or affirmation "faithfully [to] try the defendant and give a true verdict according to the evidence". But, at present there is no procedural means of stopping them exercising their ability to return what in law may be a perverse verdict of not guilty[119] or, to the extent that it is undetectably perverse, of guilty.

102   Dr Glanville Williams has pointed out that, though juries had long had this ability, there was no evidence of their wide use of it:

> "Most of the great pronouncements on constitutional liberty, from the eighteenth century onwards, have been the work of judges, either sitting in appellate courts or giving directions to juries. The assumption that political liberty at the present day depends upon the institution of the jury ... is in truth merely folklore.
>
> The notion that an English jury will, as anything like a regular matter, take the law into its own hands and acquit in defiance of the judge's direction upon the law rests on a misapprehension of its function. The English jury is a trier of fact only ....
>
> A lawyer, if he is true to his calling, must have some reservations about any instance whereby jurymen gain applause by disregarding their oath to give a true verdict

---

[118] *Writing by Candlelight*

[119] see Sir Patrick Devlin, *Trial by Jury*, pp 84 and 90-91, citing Sankey LC in *Woolmington v DPP* [1935] AC 462, at 480, and Lord Mansfield CJ and Willes J in *R v Shipley* (1764) 4 Doug 171, at 176 and 178 respectively; and see Holmes J, giving the judgment for the majority of the US Supreme Court in *Horning v District of Columbia* I 254 US 135, at 138 (1920): "The jury has the power to bring in a verdict in the teeth of both law and facts"

according to the evidence. If we really wish juries to give untrue verdicts, why do we require them to be sworn?" [120]

103   Other distinguished jurists have spoken in similar vein. Mr Justice Holmes, writing in 1897, spoke of "growing disbelief in the jury as an instrument for the discovery of truth" and described its use as "to let a little popular prejudice into the administration of law - (in violation of their oath)".[121] Hermann Mannheim, a leading criminologist of the last century, was more forthright, opining that jury trial had in modern times replaced the tyranny of the judge by that of the juror:

> " ... flagrant mistakes, in particular unjustifiable verdicts of 'not guilty', are bound to occur only too often. The layman may be inclined to regard this as one of the chief advantages of the system that it can act as an unofficial pardoning agency. However, if this is the idea it should be clearly expressed, instead of being disguised as justice". [122]

104   Despite the illogicality of this 'dispensing' ability of juries, I can understand why there is such an emotional attachment to it. It has been an accepted feature of our jury system for a long time and is seen as a useful long-stop against oppression by the State and as an agent, on occasion, of law reform. And illogicality is not necessarily an obstacle to the retention of deeply entrenched institutions, especially where, as here, there may be infrequent recourse to them. There is the further point that under our present procedures the courts cannot prevent juries from acquitting perversely; as yet their verdicts are unreasoned and there is no appeal against an acquittal.

105   However, I regard the ability of jurors to acquit, and it also follows, convict,[123] in defiance of the law and in disregard of their oaths, as more than illogicality. It is a blatant affront to the legal process and the main purpose of the criminal justice system - the control of crime - of which they are so important a part. With respect to Lord Devlin, I think it unreal to regard the random selection, not election, of 12 jurors from one small area as an exercise in democracy, 'a little parliament', to set against the national will. Their role is to find the facts and, applying the law to those facts, to determine guilt or no. They are not there to substitute their view of the propriety of the law for that of Parliament or its enforcement for that of its appointed Executive, still less on what may be irrational, secret and unchallengeable grounds. Moreover, I do not see why this form of lay justice, responsible for only about 1% of criminal cases, should be distinguished in this way from the lay justice administered by

---

[120] *The proof of guilt*, p 197, and see generally at pp 195-200

[121] Holmes-Pollock Letters, Vol I, p 74, Belknap Press, Harvard

[122] *Criminal Justice and Social Reconstruction*, p 246, Kegan Paul, Trench, Trubner & Co Ltd, [1946]; see also Sir Louis Blom Cooper, QC, *Article 6 and Modes of Criminal Trial*, pp 1-19

[123] see Baldwin and McConville, *Jury Trials*, at 128

magistrates who, like their professional colleagues, are accountable for any perversity revealed on appeal by way of case stated.

106 Finally, the ability of juries to ignore their oaths by entering perverse and publicly unreasoned verdicts of acquittal, or guilty, is vulnerable to Article 6 and our own independent move towards reasoned judgments. If, as I have mentioned and consider again in Chapter 11, judges were able to require juries to give reasoned verdicts, the scope for perverse verdicts, one way or the other, could be significantly and justly reduced by opening them up to appeal, a matter that I consider in Chapter 12.

107 In the meantime, I consider that the law should be declared, by statute if need be, that juries have no right to acquit in defiance of the law or in disregard of the evidence. I consider also that judges and practitioners in their conduct of criminal cases should acknowledge that truth and not invoke the ability of a jury to defy the law or breach their oath in that way.

I recommend that the law should be declared, by statute if need be, that juries have no right to acquit defendants in defiance of the law or in disregard of the evidence, and that judges and advocates should conduct criminal cases accordingly.

108 If that is too great a shock to the system, then should the law– and the juror's oath - be more honest in their form and application? Should we provide juries with an express power of dispensation or nullification, instead of just letting them get away with it,[124] and should jurors undertake to give a verdict according to the evidence or their conscience? In at least two States in the United States, Indiana[125] and Maryland,[126] their respective Constitutions come close to it in conferring upon the jury the right to determine the law and the facts. To appreciate the full impact of such a step, one has only to consider the sort of direction that it would require judges to give to juries, namely that they need not convict if they disagree with the law or with the decision to prosecute. Just articulating the direction brings home the enormityof such a possible clarification of the law, but as one distinguished academic has asked,[127] "what other way is there for an honest system to behave?"

---

[124] for a useful discussion of the arguments in favour of an express power of nullification, see MDA Freeman, *Why Not a Jury Nullification Statute Here Too?*, (1981) 131 New Law Journal 304, referring to the Indiana and Maryland Statutes

[125] Indiana Code Title 35, Art 37, Ch 2, s 2(5)

[126] Maryland State Constitution, Declaration of Rights, Art 23

[127] Professor Edward Griew, *Summing Up the Law,* [1989] Crim LR 768, at 779-780

TRIAL OF CASES ON INDICTMENT WITHOUT A JURY

109 I have considered a number of proposals affecting the trial of cases presently triable by judge and jury. In doing so, I have, as I have already said, taken as given the distinction between what are presently known as indictable offences (offences triable by judge and jury), and summary offences (offences triable in the magistrates' court by a District Judge or magistrates). I have also accepted the need for continuance of a broad group of hybrid or 'either-way' offences (offences that may be tried on indictment or summarily). The following are the main proposals for change:

- Defendant's option for trial by judge alone - to enable the defendant to opt for trial by judge alone, 'jury-waiver' or 'bench trial' as it is known in the United States and Canada;

- 'Either-way' offences - in cases triable either on indictment or summarily – to empower the court, instead of the defendant, to decide where and how he is to be tried;

- Fraud and other complex cases – in serious and complex fraud cases - to enable the court to provide for their determination without a jury;

- Young defendants – in cases against young defendants - to extend the existing provision for trial without jury; and

- Fitness to plead – to amend the law to require a judge, instead of a jury, to determine the issue of fitness to plead.

Defendant's option for trial by judge alone

110 The Runciman Royal Commission did not mention 'jury waiver' in its Report, that is, permitting defendants, with the consent of the court after hearing from both sides, to opt for trial by judge alone. Although it has not figured prominently in contributions to the Review, I have been struck by its widespread use in other common law jurisdictions modelled on our system of trial by judge and jury. Its popularity lies, in part in its provision of a simpler, speedier and cheaper procedure than trial by jury, and in part in what trial by judge and jury can never provide, a fully reasoned decision. It is widely used in the United States and also, in various forms in Canada, New Zealand and a number of Australian States.

111 In the United States, where all defendants charged with an offence carrying more than 6 months' imprisonment have a constitutional right to trial by jury, most jurisdictions, including the federal courts, permit them to waive jury trial with the agreement of the court and prosecutor. It is estimated, on patchy and imperfect data, that in 1988, expressed as percentages of the total numbers of felony trials in different states, non-jury trials accounted for between 2% to

over 70% and that in 1993 14% of all serious federal cases were tried without a jury.[128]

112 Different jurisdictions and local cultures may have provided their own imperatives for this form of trial. For example, the well-developed systems of plea bargaining in United States have encouraged its use where no bargain is achievable and the parties are content that a judge should be left to determine the issue of guilt and assess the seriousness of the case and the appropriate sentence – sometimes called the slow plea of guilty".[129] But in the United States and in the Commonwealth jurisdictions I have mentioned there are a number of other reasons for defendants opting for such a mode of trial over a wide range of offences. These include:

- those who believe themselves to be innocent of the offence charged, often in serious and factually or legally complex cases, and who are anxious that the tribunal will be able to understand their case;

- defendants with 'technical' defences who wish a verdict to be accompanied by appealable reasoning or who, in any event, want a fully reasoned decision;

- defendants who are charged with offences that attract particular public opprobrium, such as sexual and/or particularly brutal violence, or from minorities or sects who may consider a judge to be a more objective tribunal than a jury;

- where there has been much publicity adverse to the defence;

- defendants in cases turning on alleged confessions or identification, where judges tend to be more rigorous in the exclusion of alleged confession than when trying cases with a jury, and in the rejection of evidence of purported identification than juries tend to be; and

- lower tier professional judges, for example, the Provincial Judge in Canada, are local and well-known to practitioners who can judge their ability or otherwise to try cases on their own both competently and fairly.

113 The Diplock Courts in Northern Ireland and their counterparts south of the border are nearby examples of how trial by judge alone can work and earn a fair degree of public acceptance, albeit as a necessary measure to overcome the threat of intimidation of juries in the trial of terrorists.[130] The Diplock Courts stem from the recommendations of the "Commission on Legal Procedures to Deal with Terrorist Activities" under the chairmanship of Lord Diplock which, in 1972, recommended the abandonment of trial by judge and jury for serious terrorist crimes.[131] The Northern Ireland (Emergency

---

[128] *Rethinking Adversariness in Nonjury Criminal Trials*, Doran, Jackson and Seigel, American Journal of Criminal Law, (1995) Vol 23, 1, at pp 8-11

[129] in particular, in Philadelphia ; see *Is Plea Bargaining Inevitable*, Stephen J Shulhofer, 97 Harvard L R. 1037

[130] see Jackson and Doran, *Judge without Jury: Diplock Trials in the Adversary System*, 1995, Clarendon Press

[131] Cmnd 5185

Provisions) Act 1973[132] introduced a system of 'scheduled' - terrorist - offences in respect of which the court may direct trial by judge without jury. With some amendments the system has operated now for nearly 30 years and, despite the public commitment to return to trial by judge and jury in all cases,[133] looks likely to continue at least until the emergency is lifted.[134] I say 'at least' because Professors John Jackson and Sean Doran, in their seminal study in 1995, *Judge without Jury,*[135] have presented a strong case for optional trial without jury to become a permanent part of the criminal justice system, not just a temporary and necessary response to terrorist intimidation.

114   I am not concerned with the reason for suspension of jury trial in certain cases in Northern Ireland, but as to how the system operates with a judge alone. There are two important ways in which it provides safeguards not found in the unreasoned, and, therefore, not readily appealable, verdict of the jury. The first is that the trial judge, if he convicts, is required, to give a reasoned judgment identifying the principles of law that he has applied and his findings on the evidence leading to conviction. If he acquits he also normally provides such a judgment. The second is that the person convicted has an absolute right of appeal to the Northern Ireland Court of Appeal against both conviction and sentence. There is a further important feature, namely that the trial process, so far as it can, follows the normal rules of procedure and evidence in a jury trial.[136]

115   Whilst the quality of justice dispensed by the Diplock judges has not been without criticism, Doran and Jackson, have noted that its non-partisan focus has been more on their handling of the law than on their findings on the evidence.[137] There is also the phenomenon similar to that noted in North American jurisdictions that judges tend to be more rigorous in the exclusion of alleged confession statements than when trying cases with a jury and in the rejection of evidence of purported identification than juries seem to be from what some gather from their verdicts.

116   In my view, there is a strong case for the introduction of a system permitting defendants to opt for trial by judge alone, both in cases in the Crown Court and in those which, if my recommendations in Chapter 7 are adopted, would be tried in the District Division. It is for consideration whether it should apply to all indictable offences as it has done in Canada since 1985,[138] or

---

[132] see now the Northern Ireland (Emergency Provisions) Act 1996, in particular, ss 10 and 11

[133] see *Review of the Criminal Justice System in Northern Ireland,* March 2000, HMSO, para 7.3

[134] see now the Terrorism Act 2000 which, by section 75, preserves the trial by judge alone for scheduled offences in Northern Ireland

[135] (Clarenden Press, 1995); see also *The Judicial Role in Criminal Proceedings,* a collection of essays edited by Jackson and Doran (Hart Publishing, 2000)

[136] though the Northern Ireland Office has recently recommended some changes in the rules of evidence before Diplock Courts

[137] see footnote 130

[138] Canadian Criminal Code, RSC 1985, C-46, ss 473, 476

exclude the most serious as in New Zealand where offences carrying a maximum of 14 years imprisonment or a mandatory life term are excluded.[139] It seems to me that the interest of the public[140] as well as that of the defendant would be better protected by letting the judge decide on a case by case basis whether to accede to a defendant's option for trial without jury rather than by imposing some general statutory limit on offences to which the option could apply. The judge should decide only after hearing representations from both sides; I would not go further and make the defendant's option subject to the consent of the prosecution as in most United States jurisdictions, including the Federal Courts, or even for the most serious offences, as in Canada. By the same token, as in New Zealand,[141] the judge should be entitled to override the defendant's wish for trial by judge alone if he (the judge) considers that the public interest requires a jury, for example, in cases of certain offences against the State or public order.

117   In short, trial by judge alone, if defendants wish it, has a potential for providing a simpler, more efficient, fairer and more open form of procedure than is now available in many jury trials, with the added advantage of a fully reasoned judgment. I should add that under such a system, in the event of a conviction by a jury where the defendant has not opted for trial without jury, I can see no basis for any Article 6 challenge that he might wish to make based on the lack of public reasoning in the jury's verdict.

118   There are, no doubt, all sorts of practical questions that would require careful attention if such a system were adopted. One of them is the time at which the defendant should exercise the option, so as to prevent 'judge-shopping'. In Western Australia, for example, he is required to opt before allocation of the trial judge.[142] In the system that I have in mind for trial of indictable offences,[143] whether for trial in the Crown or District Divisions of a new unified Criminal Court, this should be early in the preparation for trial, by the pre-trial assessment at the latest. Procedures would have to be introduced to ensure that defendants are fully advised beforehand of the significance of opting for trial by judge alone. They should also be allowed a short period after doing so within which they could change their minds, as in Canada.[144] There is also the problem of co-defendants opting for different modes of trial. There are at least three possible solutions: first, the New Zealand solution, that all must opt for trial by judge alone before the judge can consider it; second, the judge can deal with it on a defendant by defendant basis, ordering separate trials as necessary; and third, give the judge a general discretion after

---

[139] Crimes Act 1961, ss 361 A-C and 361B(5); and see generally the New Zealand Law Commission's Report 69, *Juries in Criminal Trials*, Wellington, NZ February 2001, paras 58-71

[140] see *Brown v R* (1986) 160 CLR 171, cited in Doran & Jackson, *The Case for Jury Waiver* [1997] Crim LR 155, at 164

[141] though the New Zealand courts generally assume that the defence is the best judge of the interests of justice as far as the accused is concerned; see *R v Narain* [1988] INZLR 580, at 589

[142] Western Australia Criminal Code, s651A

[143] see Chapter 10, paras 198 - 235

[144] Canadian Criminal Code

hearing representations from all the parties. The principled and practical answer, it seems to me, is most likely to be the New Zealand rule, all or none, unless independently of the question of choice of forum, there is a good case for separate trials. This is all part of the topic of allocation of cases to the appropriate level of court, to which I return in Chapter 7.[145]

> **I recommend that defendants, with the consent of the court after hearing representations from both sides, should be able to opt for trial by judge alone in all cases now tried on indictment (whether as now, in the Crown Court or, if my recommendations in Chapter 7 for a new unified Criminal Court are adopted, in the Crown or District Divisions).**

'Either-way' offences

119   One of the major issues in the Review has been the trial of 'either-way' cases, those triable either by a judge and jury or summarily. There are two competing and strongly held views. The first is that too many trivial cases not meriting trial by judge and jury are taking up the resources of the Crown Court when they could be tried more speedily and economically, and just as fairly in the magistrates' courts. The second is that trial by judge and jury is the fairest, if not the only fair, form of trial in our system of criminal justice and that no inroads should be made on defendants' present right to it; some have even suggested that it should be extended to all criminal offences carrying a custodial sentence, however short. This conflict has given rise to a number of questions:

- whether the 'either-way' regime should be replaced by one in which all or some offences presently subject to it are dealt with by one form of process, whether by judge and jury or by magistrates sitting summarily with enhanced jurisdiction[146] or in a new intermediate jurisdiction consisting, say, of a District Judge sitting on his own or with magistrates;

- whether, if the present system is to continue, it should be modified by re-classifying some of the present 'either-way' offences as indictable only or as summary offences;

- whether, in addition or as an alternative to re-classification by offence, there could be re-classification of some offences according to their seriousness, say, by reference to the value of property stolen or damaged;[147] and

---

[145] paras 36 - 40
[146] say, as in the case of the youth court
[147] as has recently been done in relation to a few offences; see below, paras 127 and 132

- whether the present system should be modified so as to make the courts, not defendants, the arbiters of how they shall be tried, that is, to remove defendants' right to opt for trial by judge and jury in 'either-way' cases.

120   The main focus of the debate has been the last of these issues. It is plain that trial by judge and jury cannot reasonably be extended to all offences however trivial, even though conviction of some summary offences could, according to an accused's circumstances, be very damaging to his reputation or livelihood.[148] Some system of allocation must be made according to, among other matters, the seriousness of the offence. And in many of them, for example, theft, handling, obtaining by deception, various forms of assault, the range of seriousness is great. The need for a system of allocation remains and is distinct from the introduction of an intermediate tier of jurisdiction in the form of a District Division of a new unified Criminal Court that I recommend in Chapter 7. As to re-classification in whatever form, the historical emergence of the present category of either way offences shows it can be done,[149] and there might be scope for some reconsideration of the present list. But it would still be a rough and ready division that would not provide a definitive solution to the main debate on a case by case basis for those offences remaining on the list. In my view, both principle and practicality dictate that the fourth issue, who should decide how these either way cases are tried, is the critical one for determination.

121   There are three possibilities: the prosecution, as in a few common law jurisdictions, including Scotland and Canada; the court, as in most common law jurisdictions; or the accused, as in England and Wales - possibly, the only common law jurisdiction to accord him that privilege.

122   Few, if any, have suggested in the Review that the Crown Prosecution Service should determine the matter. Any analogy with the Scottish system would be misleading, given its great differences from ours. There, neither the court nor the defendant has any say in the matter The prosecutor, as "the master of the instance", decides on the mode and venue of trial (save in cases of very serious offences such as murder or rape which must go to the High Court or minor offences which are reserved for the Sheriff Court). The judge of the lower court is a professional judge, a sheriff whose custodial sentencing jurisdiction in summary matters is normally limited to 3 months; and who has no power, on summary conviction of a defendant, to commit him to a higher court for sentence. The Crown Prosecution Service, by contrast, lacks the authority of the Procurator Fiscal, both legally, historically and popularly; it shares its decisions as to prosecution with local police forces, its function being essentially one of review of charges initially preferred by them. The

---

[148] eg assault on a police officer, keeping a brothel, cruelty to animals, cruelty to or neglect of children, driving when unfit to drive through drink, unauthorised taking of a vehicle

[149] see paras 123 – 132 below

question is, therefore, whether the court should decide the matter on an objective basis or the accused should continue to be permitted to do so on a subjective basis.

The history of 'either-way' offences

123 Contrary to popular belief, including that of a number of distinguished legal practitioners who have contributed to the debate, until 1855 there was no right to claim trial by jury.[150] Before then there were just two categories of offence for this purpose, those triable on indictment and those triable summarily. The accused had no choice in the matter. The Administration of Justice Act of that year, the long title of which was "An Act for diminishing expense and delay in the administration of criminal justice in certain cases", began the process of blurring the line between the two. It permitted magistrates to try simple larcenies. In the Summary Jurisdiction Act 1879 provision was made for summary trial of a range of indictable petty larcenies and like offences if the court thought it expedient to do so "having regard to the character and antecedents of the person charged, the nature of the offence, and all the circumstances of the case", and if the accused consented.[151]

124 There were further considerable increases in the categories of indictable offences that might be tried summarily. The Criminal Justice Act 1925 so provided in a wide range of offences, for example, serious offences of larceny, offences against the person, including inflicting bodily harm, certain forgery offences and indecent assault on a person under 16. It followed the 1879 Act in including in the mode of trial criteria the circumstances of both the offence and of the accused:

> "... the character and antecedents of the accused, the nature of the offence, the absence of circumstances which would render the offence one of a grave or serious character and all the other circumstances of the case (including the adequacy of the punishment which a court of summary jurisdiction has power to inflict) ..."[152]

125 And subsequent statutes over the next forty or so years added more categories, including non dwelling house burglary and related offences, certain offences of forgery and indecent assault in 1962,[153] gross indecency between men in 1967[154] and dwelling house burglary other than where entry was obtained by

---

[150] save for children under the age of 16 charged with simple larceny; see Further Extension of Summary Jurisdiction in Cases of Larceny Act 1850, s 2

[151] s 12 and Sch. 1

[152] s 24

[153] Criminal Justice Administration Act 1962

[154] Sexual Offences Act 1967

force or deception in 1968.[155] Thus, there was a progressive growth throughout the last century of the number of indictable offences for which the option of summary trial was provided and, consequently, a corresponding statutory increase in the defendant's elective right to trial by jury in such cases.

126 The 1879 Act had also given the accused a right to claim jury trial in summary offences other than assault punishable with more than 3 months imprisonment.[156] And other statutes made certain offences triable either summarily or on indictment, some carrying a right to trial by jury and some not.

127 This muddle of various forms of hybrid offences persisted until the 1970s when the Home Secretary and Lord Chancellor appointed Lord Justice James to chair an Interdepartmental Committee on the Distribution of Criminal Business between the Crown Court and the magistrates courts. The Committee reported in 1975,[157] recommending that the unstructured legislative mix, largely directed to granting or extending summary jurisdiction to magistrates, should be replaced with the threefold classification of offences as summary, indictable and triable 'either-way' - now found in the magistrates'Courts Act 1980.[158] It also recommended a reduction in the number of Crown Court cases by re-classification of various 'trivial' offences as triable only summarily and certain indictable only offences as triable either way. The James Report in this respect was much criticised as an attack on civil liberties. Nevertheless, it led to some further changes, for example, some public order offences and criminal damage to a value of less that £200 became summary only offences. Petty dishonesty, however, remained triable either way. Later, the Criminal Justice Act 1988 downgraded a further three 'either-way' offences to summary only, namely common assault, taking a vehicle without consent and driving whilst disqualified, and raised the summary only level of value for criminal damage to £2,000.[159]

The present law

128 The 1980 Act, as amended, lists about 30 species of 'either-way' offences, comprising about 700 individual crimes, ranging from public nuisance, a number of offences of violence, including threats to kill and inflicting grievous bodily harm, unlawful sexual intercourse with a girl under 16,

---

[155] Theft Act 1968
[156] s 17
[157] Cmnd 6323
[158] s 17 and Sched I
[159] the effect of which, as Professor Ashworth noted, was to reduce the Crown Court workload by about 6%; *The Criminal Process: An Evaluation Study*, p.259; see Criminal Statistics for England and Wales (1989), para 6.12

indecent assault, theft, handling and related offences, most burglaries and, thefts, certain frauds and forgery offences, violent disorder and affray, arson not endangering life and causing death by aggravated vehicle-taking. Even where, under the procedure that I outline in the next paragraph, an accused is tried and convicted summarily, the magistrates still have power to commit him for sentence to the Crown Court if then of the view that the proper sentence for it is beyond their powers.[160] Those are 6 months' custody and/or a fine of £5,000 for a single offence or 12 months for concurrent or consecutive sentences for two or more 'either-way' offences.[161]

129 Charges of 'either-way' offences must first be brought before the magistrates. In summary, the accused may elect trial on indictment and, if he does, they are bound to commit him for trial to the Crown Court. However, the legislative scheme is a little more complicated than that. Since the introduction of the plea before venue procedure in October 1997,[162] the defendant is first asked whether he intends to plead guilty. If he so indicates, he has no right to elect trial in the Crown Court, but the magistrates may still commit him there for sentence if they consider their sentencing powers inadequate. In considering those powers they are required to take into account as a mitigating factor that he has pleaded guilty at that early stage.[163]

130 If the defendant does not indicate a plea of guilty, magistrates must first consider, after hearing representations from both sides, whether they or the Crown Court should try the accused. In doing so, the Act gives them a broad discretion as to what is relevant. They are required to have regard to: [164]

> "...the nature of the case; whether the circumstances make
> the offence one of serious character; whether the punishment
> which a magistrates' court would have power to inflict for it
> is adequate; and any other circumstances which appear to the
> court to make it more suitable for the offence to be fixed in
> one way rather than the other".

131 National Mode of Trial Guidelines originally issued by Lord Lane, Chief Justice, in 1990[165] indicated that the defendant's antecedents and personal mitigating circumstances were irrelevant to the decision. But the current (1995) version of those Guidelines for some unexplained reason, has removed the prohibition on taking account of previous convictions and personal

---

[160] originally in section 38 of the 1988 Act; now in section 3 of the Powers of Criminal Courts (Sentencing) Act 2000

[161] ie for one 'either-way' offence and one summary the maximum aggregate would be 6 months; see generally the 1980 Act, ss 31 and 133

[162] Criminal Procedure and Investigations Act 1996, s 49

[163] Powers of Criminal Courts (Sentencing) Act 2000, s 152, reflecting prior judicial practice; see *R v Rafferty* [1999] 1 Cr App R 235, CA

[164] s 1999(3)

[165] (1991) 92 Cr App R 142

mitigation.[166] They now advise magistrates to assume that the prosecution version of the facts is correct, to consider committal for trial in cases involving complex questions of fact or difficult questions of law, and to consider their powers to commit for sentence if information emerges in the hearing leading them to conclude that they are inadequate. However, the practice is still to keep a defendant's criminal record, if he has one, from the magistrates at this stage. In the event of their learning of previous convictions and deciding, with his consent, on a summary trial, the matter would be listed before another bench.

132 If the magistrates decide that the alleged offence is more suitable for trial on indictment, the defendant has no further say in the matter and they then proceed to consider it as examining justices with a view to committal for trial.[167] If they decide that summary trial appears to be more suitable, they must inform the defendant, tell him that he has the option of summary trial or trial by jury and warn him that, even if he does consent to summary trial and is convicted, they may still commit him to the Crown Court for sentence.[168] Thus, it is only at that stage and in respect of those cases that the magistrates do not consider warrant trial by jury that the right of election arises. There are also two 'either-way' offences, criminal damage and aggravated vehicle-taking, where, if the damage caused does not exceed £5,000, the matter must be tried summarily.[169]

Proposals for reform

133 As the James Committee noted,[170] the English system is unusual in allowing a defendant to choose his court of trial for certain offences. The Committee also observed that, although it was not possible to gauge the views of the public,[171] the defendant's right of election had strong support from legal practitioners and organisations expressing a wider interest in the criminal justice system. The same is true today. The support is based principally on what has been variously described as a constitutional or fundamental right of the citizen to trial by jury. The other view, which is held by many judges and those closely involved in the administration of the criminal justice system, is that defendants' exercise of their right to elect trial by jury, for whatever reasons, brings to the Crown Court relatively minor cases that do not belong there. The result, it is claimed, is unjustifiable expense to the public, because trial in the Crown Court is much more expensive than before magistrates, and

---

[166] see Ashworth, *The Criminal Process: An Evaluation Study*, 260; the current edition of Blackstone, para D 37, and see S White *The Antecedents of the Mode of Trial Guidelines [1996] Crim LR 471*
[167] s 21
[168] ss 19 and 20
[169] s 22 and Sched 2, as amended by the Criminal Justice and Public Order Act 1994
[170] Report, para 60
[171] Report, para. 61

delay in the trial of other and more serious cases properly there. Like the James Committee, I have been unable to gauge from my Review what the public at large think about the issue.

134   It is instructive to see how the James Committee and the Runciman Royal Commission grappled with the question of who should decide where this intermediate class of cases should be tried, and why the former considered that the defendant should have the last word and the latter recommended that that the court should have it.

135   The James Committee, while acknowledging "weighty support" for the proposal that the magistrates' court should take the decision, rejected it because: first, the difficulty it saw in devising criteria and their consistent application; second, it was unlikely to be acceptable to a wide section of the public; third, it would engender hostility of defendants towards magistrates; fourth, the proposed mode of trial procedure, including an appellate process, would be a potential cause of delay; fifth, most defendants who elected trial by jury did so because they thought they would get a fairer trial; and sixth, that, for the system to work at all, magistrates determining mode of trial would have to know whether the defendant was of good or bad character, which would be discriminatory.[172] As Lord Ackner observed in the second reading of the Mode of Trial (No. 2) Bill in the House of Lords,[173] those considerations encapsulate the main arguments of the opponents of the Mode of Trial Bills 25 years later.

136   However, there have been some changes since the James Committee's consideration of the matter.   First, the statutory scheme subsequently introduced, and now found in the 1980 Act and in the National Mode of Trial Guidelines, establish detailed criteria and guidance for magistrates' courts throughout the country. Second, the Committee, like the Review, was faced with two competing lobbies, but it is plain from its Report that, despite being unable to assess the weight of public opinion on the matter, it was strongly influenced by the importance that defendants attached to their right. On that somewhat one-sided basis it concluded that there was a risk of loss of public confidence in the system if so 'highly prized' a right were to be removed. Third as to the embarrassment for magistrates trying summarily a case in which they had refused a request for jury trial, I do not understand the problem.   I cannot see why magistrates would be placed in an invidious position because defendants object generally to their courts, or to a magistrate personally unless there is a reasonable case making it undesirable for him or her to adjudicate in the case.   Fourth, as to delay from multiplicity of procedures, all the procedures mentioned, save appeal, are a feature of the

---

system now found in the 1980 Act. And, fifth, as to 'two-tier' justice, from 1855, until at least 1980[174] both as a statutory requirement and as a matter of practicality, a defendant's character, good or bad, was a relevant consideration in magistrates' decisions whether to commit a defendant for trial by jury, regardless of his wish for summary trial.

137   By the early 1990s when the Runciman Royal Commission was at work, over 35,000 defendants elected jury trial - about 37% of all the 'either-way' cases then committed to the Crown Court. The Commission, assisted by research commissioned by the Home Office [175] found that those electing jury trial had one or more of three main objectives: first, a wish to put off trial with a view to securing in the meantime the advantages of a more liberal prison regime which would count towards a sentence if convicted and imprisoned; second, a well-founded belief that there was better chance of acquittal in the Crown Court than before magistrates; and third, a mistaken belief that, if convicted, the sentence would be lighter.[176]   Of those three the most prominent in the debate was the belief that there was a better chance of acquittal before a jury. However, the Commission noted, in mistaken reliance on the Home Office research, that most of those who elected trial eventually pleaded guilty in the Crown Court - 70% to all charges and a further 13% to some charges. I say 'mistaken' reliance on that research because, as Professor Lee Bridges of Warwick University has pointed out,[177] the sample upon which it was based did not include those who elected trial in the Crown Court and were eventually acquitted.

138   The Runciman Royal Commission recommended the removal of the defendant's entitlement to insist on jury trial in 'either-way' cases, though retaining his right to make representations on the matter. It did so as a matter of principle:

> "…We do not think that defendants should be able to choose their court of trial solely on the basis that they think that they will get a fairer hearing at one level than the other…Nor in our view should defendants be entitled to choose the mode of trial which they think will offer them a better chance of acquittal any more than they should be able to choose the judge who they think will give them the most lenient sentence".

As to loss of reputation, the Commission regarded it as relevant, though often only to alleged first offenders, and as only one of the factors to be taken into account.

---

[174] see para 123 above

[175] Carol Hedderman and David Moxon, *Magistrates Court or Crown Court? Mode of Trial Decisions and Sentencing*, Home Office Research Study No. 125, (HMSO 1992)

[176] *Royal Commission on Criminal Justice*, Ch 6, paras 6 - 8

[177] in *Limiting the right to jury trial – half truths and false assumptions*, a paper submitted to the Review in February 2000, p 2

139   The Runciman Royal Commission's proposed solution was that, where both sides agreed on summary trial, the magistrates should try it, and similarly, where both sides agreed on trial by jury, it should go to the Crown Court. When there was a dispute, it said that the magistrates should determine the venue, having regard to the existing statutory criteria and, in addition, such matters as the defendant's reputation and record, the gravity of the offence, the complexity of the case and its likely effect on the defendant. The result, the Commission expected, would be fewer mode of trial hearings and fewer cases going to the Crown Court, allowing it to concentrate on more serious cases.[178]

140   There was much hostile reaction to these recommendations, based mainly on the belief that they represented a threat to a constitutional right to trial by jury. In the result, the Government of the day took no action on the matter. However, there continued to be much discontent from many involved in the criminal justice process about the perceived waste of public time and money on comparatively trivial 'either-way' cases in the Crown Court, and also about the consequent delays to other more serious work awaiting trial there. In 1997 Martin Narey, a senior Home Office civil servant, looked at the issue again as part of his Review of Delay in the Criminal Justice System. His view was similar to that of the Runciman Royal Commission, though more robust. It was that magistrates, not a defendant, should decide his court of trial, albeit after hearing representations from both sides. He differed from the Runciman Commission over its recommendation that magistrates should be bound by any agreement between the parties:

> "A large majority of defendants electing trial plead guilty at the Crown Court. A substantial proportion of elections are little more than an expensive manipulation of the criminal justice system and are not concerned with any wish to establish innocence in front of a jury. Those defendants who have a valid reason for electing, such as the potential damage to their reputation, should be able to make their case to magistrates who should be free to commit the case to the Crown Court. But the automatic defendant veto on the magistrates' decision on mode of trial should be removed".[179]

141   The present Government, supported by the then Lord Chief Justice, Lord Bingham of Cornhill, the former Master of the Rolls, Lord Donaldson of Lymington, almost all the High Court Judges who try crime, the Magistrates' Association and the Police, accepted the broad thrust of the Runciman and Narey recommendations that courts, not defendants, should decide where all 'either-way' cases should be tried.[180] In November 1999, just

---

[178] *Royal Commission on Criminal Justice,* Chapter 6, paras 13 and 14

[179] *Review of Delay in the Criminal Justice System*, Chapter 1, p 2 and Chapter 8, p 33

[180] see Hansard, 20th January 2000, p 1256, col 1

before establishing this Review, the Government introduced in the House of Lords the first of two unsuccessful legislative attempts to remove the defendant's ability to elect trial in the Crown Court, the Criminal Justice (Mode of Trial) Bill. In the explanatory notes to the Bill, it estimated its likely financial effects as an annual reduction of about 12,000 Crown Court trials producing a net yearly saving of £105 million. By this time, probably as a result of the introduction of the plea before venue system in 1997 and the courts' increased use of their long established practice of reflecting such early pleas of guilty in their sentences,[181] the annual number of those electing trial in the Crown Court had reduced from about 35,000 at the time of the Runciman Royal Commission to about 18,500.

142   The Government's proposal was that magistrates should determine mode of trial (subject to a right of appeal to the Crown Court) in the light of representations from both sides and of a number of familiar, if not all previously so explicitly identified, considerations. These were the nature and seriousness of the case, their powers of punishment, the effect of conviction and sentence on the defendant's livelihood and reputation and on any other relevant circumstances. It did not specifically include in this list consideration of a defendant's record, as previous Acts had done, for example, the 1879 and 1925 Acts. But it appears from the explanatory notes to the Bill that its draftsman envisaged that previous convictions would be relevant to the issue of a defendant's livelihood and reputation by way of rebuttal or explanation of anything that he might say about that. The only new thing about those two criteria was their express mention, for they had been implicit in the various formulations since at least 1879 of matters for magistrates to consider when determining, *inter alia*, the adequacy of their sentencing powers in the event of conviction.

143   The Bill and its successor were hotly opposed by the majority of legal practitioners undertaking criminal work,[182] major civil liberties organisations[183] and ethnic minority groups.[184] The express mention of a defendant's livelihood and reputation was a particular target for criticism in the House of Lords as creating 'two-tier justice', the argument being that it would lead to magistrates' courts discriminating against the poor or unemployed and in favour of defendants with higher economic or social status. The Bill had two other features that were to add to the controversy. First, it contained no proposal to abolish magistrates' power to commit defendants for sentence in 'either-way' cases after trying and convicting them summarily. It was argued that if defendants know they are at risk of ending up in the Crown Court anyway, it is likely to discourage a significant number

---

[181] see also Criminal Justice and Public Order Act 1994, s 48(1) and (2); now in Powers of Criminal Courts (Sentencing) Act 2000, s 152(1) and (2)

[182] including the General Council of the Bar, the Law Society, the Black Lawyers' Association, the Legal Action Group

[183] including JUSTICE, Liberty and NACRO

[184] including the Commission for Racial Equality

of them from consenting to summary trial. Second, the Government, whilst disclaiming any great reliance on the £105 million savings that it claimed would result from its proposed reform, nevertheless engendered much debate about them. It transpired that the Government attributed about two thirds — (then about £66m) of the estimated savings to lower custodial costs because, it claimed, magistrates tend to sentence less heavily than the Crown Court for like offences.[185]

144   The Bill failed in the House of Lords, largely on the central and vehement argument of its opponents that it would remove a long established and fundamental right of the citizen to trial by jury, but also on the complaint that it would create a 'two-tier' system of justice, unfairly favouring those of good position and reputation and, therefore, with much to lose, over others without those advantages. There was also much criticism of the proposed retention of magistrates' right to commit for sentence and considerable questioning of the claimed cost savings.

145   Undaunted by that defeat, the Government, in February 2000, introduced, this time in the House of Commons, a further and modified version of the Bill, the Criminal Justice (Mode of Trial) (No. 2) Bill. There were four main changes.

146   The first was that, in an attempt to meet the criticism of 'two-tier' justice, the Government, not only removed the formerly proposed criteria of the defendant's livelihood and reputation, but it also expressly excluded a discretion to consider any of his circumstances.[186] It did so by substituting for the various criteria in the first Bill "the nature of the case""any of the circumstances of the offence (but not of the accused) which appears to the court to be relevant" and whether, having regard to those circumstances, "the punishment which a magistrates' court would have power to impose for the offence would be adequate". The second difference was that the new Bill did not speak of the seriousness of the offence, as both the first Bill had done and the 1980 Act does, only of its "circumstances". The third was that it removed the mention of any other relevant circumstances, also present in the first Bill and the 1980 Act. And the fourth was that it introduced a new requirement that magistrates should give reasons for their decision. In short, the proposal, despite the welcome newcomer requiring reasons, was for a drastic reduction in the discretionary powers of magistrates in making mode of trial decisions, not only in comparison with the current statutory criteria but also with those introduced over 120 years before in the 1879 Act.

---

[185] the claim, which was based on a Home Office model of costs and flows developed in collaboration with the Lord Chancellor's Department and the CPS, was that those who elected trial were three times more likely to receive a custodial sentence than before magistrates and that Crown Court custodial sentences were two and half times as long as those imposed by magistrates

[186] thus, departing from the Runciman Commission's recommendation; see para 138 - 139 above

147   As before, the Government continued to rely, though with less emphasis, on the savings in custody costs that it claimed would result from more lenient sentencing in magistrates' courts than in the Crown Court. It also increased from 12,000 to 14,000, its estimate of the number of cases with which magistrates would deal instead of the Crown Court, presumably because of the narrower mode of trial criteria now proposed As a result, it increased its total claim of savings from £105 million to £128 million and the custody savings component from £66 million to £84 million. It also emphasised, as it had done from the outset, the savings in other resources, principally Crown Court time, that would flow from enactment of its proposals.

148   This Bill was the subject of even more vociferous opposition, both in and outside Parliament. By dint only of a three line whip and the guillotine in the House of Commons, it made its way to the House of Lords, who again defeated it. Its opponents, and many of the first Bill's supporters, regarded it as even more flawed than the first in its specific exclusion from the mode of trial criteria of any of a defendant's personal circumstances. Some argued that, paradoxically, it would achieve the reverse of the first Bill that good reputation and bad character alike, depending on the circumstances, could be relevant to the mode of trial decision. Whereas, it was argued, the provisions of the first Bill would have been likely to discriminate in favour of those with an apparently good character, these could operate unfairly against those with a previous good or bad character, as neither was permitted to be a relevant consideration for magistrates in deciding whether, on summary conviction, their powers of sentencing powers would be adequate. The result, they maintained, would have been to deprive trial by judge and jury to many of those who, whether by election or not, are now committed to the Crown Court for trial. The reality, as Professor Lee Bridges has commented, would have been a dilemma for all concerned.[187]

149   Again, undaunted by the Parliamentary reverse, the Government indicated that it would include the same or similar proposals in its future programme of legislation for introduction in the House of Commons and that it intended, if necessary, to use the Parliament Act 1911 to secure its enactment. However, such a Bill does not figure in the Government's present legislative programme.

Current committals to the Crown Court

150   Before turning to what I regard as the real issues in the Mode of Trial debate, I pause to attempt to put them in context. I say 'attempt' because there is a disturbing lack of current, comprehensive or well-based data bearing on the

---

[187] in *Jury Trial - a Challenge to Parliament*, p 3, a further paper submitted to the Review in March 2000

issue, a fruitful ground in itself for academic criticism.[188] I set out in Appendix IV to the Report the basic workload figures available to me during the Review. These indicate that 'either-way' cases are approximately one quarter of the total workload of the criminal courts and that around 11% of 'either-way' cases are committed to the Crown Court for trial. The Crown Prosecution Service estimates that about 30% of committals for trial take place are elective. 55% of defendants convicted by the Crown Court after committal for trial receive sentences which are within the powers of the magistrates' courts.

151   Under the present statutory regime, it is not surprising that magistrates commit for trial many cases that they can try themselves. They are required under the Mode of Trial Guidelines to assume that the prosecution version of the facts is correct. They tend to be cautious as to the adequacy of their sentencing powers, and are more likely to be so where they may suspect but do not know that the defendant has a bad record. There are thus, as the Runciman Royal Commission observed,[189] already considerable inroads on the need for defendants to exercise their right of election and the contribution of that right to the Crown Court load.

152   There are a number of reasons why defendants opt for trial and, in the case of each, there is much dispute on inadequate statistics as to how important it is. I list the main reasons without attempting to express a view on the conflicting claims as to their relative importance.

153   Some defendants believe that they have a better chance of acquittal before a jury than before magistrates. This may be because they think Crown Court procedures and juries to be more favourable to the defence than magistrates. There are suggestions based on disputed statistics, that such belief is well-founded, namely that magistrates convict more readily than juries, or because juries are more gullible or sympathetic to them than magistrates would be. Why this should be so, it is difficult to understand unless, as a generality, magistrates are to be regarded as case-hardened and cynical in their work, in which case they should not be entrusted with summary cases either. Professor Michael Zander undertook for the Review a study of the minimum percentage required by magistrates and others involved in the criminal justice system of the standard of proof of sureness in criminal trials. Of those sampled, it showed that three quarters of both the general public sample and the magistrates' sample indicated that they would need to be at least 90% sure before convicting. His conclusion was that "most people, whatever their role

---

[188] see, in particular, the many powerful criticisms of Professor Lee Bridges of Warwick University, of the Government's various figures in support of the savings it claims would result from its proposals, set out in various papers, including those referred to in footnotes 177 and 187 above

[189] Chapter 6, paras 4-19

and experience, take the business of convicting very seriously", a view well supported in the case of magistrates by most contributors to the Review.

154   Defendants may hope that the prosecution will weaken with time or not proceed, say as the result of prosecution witnesses changing their mind or, for one reason or another, failing to attend the trial to give evidence. This is a particular and well-known hazard of Crown Court trials in certain areas, for example, in Liverpool and Manchester.

155   Some elect trial because they believe that they have been over-charged and that there is a better chance of pleading guilty to fewer or lesser charges after the Crown Prosecution Service have reviewed the indictment and the strength of its case in the Crown Court. There has undoubtedly been a good deal of overcharging leading to defendants electing to go to the Crown Court when otherwise they might have consented to summary trial. This is in part due to the difficulties that the Crown Prosecution Service has undergone in its first ten years, identified in, and now being remedied, as a result of, the Glidewell Report.

156   There are other factors. Some defendants, particularly those with bad records, elect trial in the Crown Court because they believe that the magistrates, if they convict them, are likely to commit them to the Crown Court for sentence in any event.[190] The availability of paper committal proceedings in which the prosecution case need not be tested encourages delay in defence preparation that election can accommodate. The structure of the present legal aid system perversely encourages such delay.[191] Until recently, defendants have had an incentive to elect trial in the Crown Court because of the better procedures that it provided for advance disclosure of the prosecution case and of any un-used material. However, this disparity has now been eroded by recent guidelines on prosecution disclosure issued by the Attorney General.[192] Some defendants, in the exercise of their undoubted legal right to elect trial in the Crown Court, abuse the system in order to delay the trial or a plea of guilty, either to remain on bail or, where they are remanded in custody, in order to secure for as long as possible a more liberal prison regime than would otherwise have been permitted. While there will always be some who, for short-sighted reasons, want to put off the evil day, the sentence discount for early pleas made possible under the plea before venue system is likely to continue to reduce their number.[193]

---

[190] see Home Office Research commissioned for the Runciman Commission
[191] see Chapter 10 paras 13 - 27
[192] November 2000
[193] there seem to be no national standards of privilege granted to remand prisoners; the nature and extent of them vary from prison to prison.

157   The debate in which parliamentarians, many of them experienced criminal practitioners, distinguished academics and persons from all walks of life, have engaged over the last year or so has been mired by a number of features.

158   First, many of those opposing the legislative proposals relied on over-emotive and legally and historically mistaken arguments exaggerating the status, longevity and extent of a defendant's elective right to trial by jury. Second, the form of the proposals distracted attention from the central issue of principle, namely who should decide where and how a defendant is to be tried. The express introduction of potential damage to livelihood and reputation to the mode of trial criteria in the first Bill followed by their exclusion, as part of any of the defendant's circumstances, in the second Bill was, to say the least, maladroit.

159   Third, the Government's claims of the financial and other savings its proposals would bring in the main lacked principle and in their entirety were highly speculative. They fell into two main categories. The first was savings in unnecessary cost and delay involved in committal and preparation for Crown Court trials which often resulted in sentences that the magistrates could have imposed. Second, there were the savings in the additional cost of custodial and other sentences that the Government claimed would otherwise have resulted from heavier sentencing by Crown Court judges than magistrates for like offences.

160   As to savings in remand time by avoiding unnecessary committals for trial, the Home Office claimed, in reliance on national figures for 1999, that, on average, it took three months longer for the Crown Court than magistrates'courts to deal with 'either-way' contested cases and that further improvements in the latter's performance were expected as a result of the Narey proposals which came into force in November 2000. Professor Lee Bridges has suggested[194] various inaccuracies and incorrect conclusions drawn by the Home Office as to likely savings in remand custody time. In particular, he has pointed out that getting rid of elective cases in the Crown Court would not make much of a dent in the remand costs resulting from late pleas of guilty because most of them come from the much higher proportion of non-elective cases that go there.

161   As to the claimed savings in custody costs, the Home Office relied on ten year old Home Office research before the Runciman Royal Commission that Crown Court Judges sentence far more heavily than magistrates in like

---

[194] in his paper submitted in the Review

cases.[195]   Professor Bridges has also criticised this research as flawed in a number of important respects because of its authors' misunderstanding, or unfamiliarity with the workings of, the criminal justice system, and also because of the considerable reduction in numbers and proportion of 'either-way defendants who now elect trial in the Crown Court.

162   There may be some differential in sentencing levels between the Crown Court and magistrates' courts for like offences committed by similar defendants in similar circumstances; that certainly seems to be the impression of many legal practitioners. But the extent of it today, in the absence of recent and well-based research must be speculative. In any event, I doubt whether the claimed savings of some £84m in additional custody costs is more than marginal when compared with the custody costs of all those convicted by the Crown Court for 'either-way' offences.

163   But, whatever the scope for debate about such matters, there is a fundamental flaw in the Government's reliance on arguments, well founded or not, that magistrates sentence less heavily than the Crown Court in like cases.   The premise of the argument is that one or other part of the criminal justice system is not working properly; either Crown Court judges are sentencing too heavily or magistrates' courts are sentencing too leniently. The financial implications of this premise may be weakened by the suggestions of others that Crown Court juries are acquitting when they should convict and/or that magistrates are convicting when they should acquit. But whichever it is, the Government, in its abortive legislative attempts, clearly saw some advantage in what it perceived to be the cheaper option. The proper and principled approach would have been to investigate the extent, if any, of the claimed or assumed disparities in conviction and sentencing and to devise proposals to remove them rather than attempt to 're-arrange' the system to take advantage of them.

164   Fourth, the Government's proposals and various estimates of the likely effect of them were also flawed because they were advanced without regard to possibilities for wider reform, many known to be under consideration in this Review. Most important of these is the fundamental view urged by many, and which I recommend in Chapter 10, that all cases should start and finish in the same court (subject to appeal). Its application in this context would be the removal of committals for trial in 'either-way' cases, (as has now been done in indictable-only cases,) and abolition of committal for sentence in those tried summarily, replacing them with a procedure of initial allocation to the court that will both try and, if it convicts, sentence.   Abolition of the committal for trial procedure would improve justice by reducing over-charging and shortening remand times, also saving money, including remand costs. Abolition of committal for sentence would remove the reason why

---

[195] Carol Hedderman and David Moxon, *Magistrates Court or Crown Court? Mode of Trial Decisions and Sentencing*, Home Office Research Study No. 125, (HMSO 1992)

many defendants presently elect trial in the Crown Court, namely because they feel that is where they will be sent for sentence in any event.

165   Other candidates for reform which affect the debate are: the sitting patterns of magistrates; making summary justice less summary by enabling them to examine cases more thoroughly, for example through better disclosure provisions; and possible reform of a perversely structured legal aid system that favours delay in getting to grips with a case.

Conclusions

166   In my view, a court, not a defendant, should decide how he is to be tried. For the following reasons, I agree with the main thrust of the Runciman and Narey recommendations to that effect. First, as I have said, "the right to trial by jury", upon which opponents of the Government's proposals stand, is not some ancient, constitutional, fundamental or even broad right of the citizen to jury trial. It began in the 19th century as an elective right to avoid the obligation of trial by jury in a limited number of indictable cases. It was a right to avoid, by consenting to summary trial in those cases, all the panoply, delay, risk of unjust conviction and heavy penalties that then went with trial on indictment. The development has to be seen in the context of the harsher criminal law and justice process of the day, in which most crimes were indictable and subject to severe punishment and in which the trial process provided very few of the protections currently afforded to defendants.

167   Second, in drawing a line between the two forms of trial the public has a legitimate interest in the financial and human cost of the criminal justice system and how best to apply its finite resources and with justice to all. It is a policy decision, according to the nature and seriousness of the offence, and in the light of the public interest, how different offences should be tried. Even if it can be said that those at risk of being sentenced to more than the maximum set by Parliament for magistrates courts are entitled to the 'fairest' form of trial, [196] there is still the question of where and how should Parliament draw the line. Some cases by their very nature justify the facilities and more searching pre-trial and trial procedures than magistrates' courts can provide. Others do not. Similarly, it is implicit in a scheme of 'either-way' offences – whoever has the ultimate say as to venue – that, depending on the seriousness and other circumstances of the case, some cases do not merit the more elaborate, costly and time-taking procedures of the Crown Court.   But

---

[196] eg Professor Lee Bridges in *Modernising Criminal Justice - Reform without Principle*, a talk given at the Bar Millenium Conference, London, 14th October 2000, p 10

permitting the law or courts to decide where defendants are to be tried would not, in itself, deprive defendants of a fair trial.[197]

168 As to defendant's perceptions that juries acquit more readily than magistrates, even if that is so, it does not mean that juries' verdicts are 'correct' and decisions of magistrates are not. Nor, in itself, is it a sound reason for enabling defendants to opt for jury trial whenever they want. There are all sorts of reasons why, if it is the case, that juries may be more inclined to acquit. Just as it is said that magistrates may be case-hardened, so juries may be more gullible because they are new to the process. Their respective tasks are likely to be affected by the seriousness of the type and circumstances, and the degree of *mens rea*, of the offences with which they respectively deal. Before any firm conclusions on this issue[198] could be drawn there would need to be much more comprehensive and thorough research, with appropriately weighted comparisons according to offences and their circumstances than there has been so far.

169 I accept that perceptions matter if there is to be public confidence in the criminal justice system. But that works both ways. Many involved in or exposed to the criminal process consider that valuable time and resources of the Crown Court are being wasted on cases more suitable for trial by a District Judge or magistrates. Ethnic and other minorities, rightly or wrongly,[199] perceive themselves to have a better chance of acquittal in the Crown Court than before magistrates, because of initial overcharging[200] and/or because they believe magistrates to be case-hardened and unsympathetic to them.[201] Young men also feel that juries, with their different social mix and age range, are more likely to understand and empathise with them. But, in my view, the proper response to such perceptions, if they can be justified, is to remedy any unfairness in the magistrates' courts, not to skew the system by providing a right to avoid them on the basis that they are unfair. As Professor Ashworth and others have urged, the focus should be to remedy any deficiencies in magistrates' justice through their selection, training and courtroom procedures, not in abandoning them for the Crown Court.[202] Public confidence in the system should be regarded as an outcome, not as a goal of a good criminal justice system. That, I take to be the thrust of the Macpherson Report in its identification of the need of every part of the criminal justice

---

[197] see Dr Penny Darbyshire, *The lamp that shows that freedom lives – is it worth the candle?*, [1991] Crim LR 740, at 741

[198] Ashworth, *The Criminal Process: An Evaluation Study*, pp 256-6

[199] as to which there is dispute on the statistics; see, eg, Roger Hood, *Race and Sentencing* (Oxford, Claredon Press, 1992) and the Home Office 1999 publication under section 95 of the Criminal Justice Act 1991, *Statistics on Race and the Criminal Justice System*

[200] see McConville, Sanders and Leng, *The Case for the Prosecution*, (Routledge, 1991); and Phillips and Brown, *Entry into the criminal justice system: a survey of police arrests and their outcome*, Home Office Research Study No 185, (1998)

[201] see eg *Ethnic Minority Defendants and the Right to Elect Jury Trial*, an examination by Lee Bridges, Satnam Choongh and Mike McConville of limited sample data from an Economic and Social Research Council study of decision making of ethnic minority defendants in the criminal justice system, prepared at the request of the Commission for Racial Equality

[202] *The Criminal Process: An Evaluation Study*, p.262; and see also Dr Penny Darbyshire *For the new Lord Chancellor – some causes for concern about magistrates* [1997] Crim L R 861-869

system to examine its policies and practices to assess whether their outcomes create or sustain patterns of discrimination.[203]

170   Third, I regard it as a matter of principle that the decision where a defendant should be tried is one for a court, not for the defendant. This is a decision in which the public as well as the accused have an interest, and the decision should be an objective one, bearing both in mind, not a subjective choice of the defendant based solely on his own self-interest. I respectfully adopt the following proposition of Lord Hardie, then the Lord Advocate, in the Committee stage of the first Mode of Trial Bill in the House of Lords:

> "...in determining the appropriate forum for trial, an objective assessment founded on relevant and specified criteria would appear to be more just and equitable than one dependent on the subjective views and considerations of an accused. The objective approach balances the interests of the accused against the interests of society in general and victims and witnesses in particular.
>
> What is essential in any system is that the various interests are balanced; that society's interests, as represented by victims and witnesses, are balanced against the interests of the accused. But what must be ensured is that the accused is protected from the effect of arbitrary decisions. Who better to perform such task than an independent judiciary?"[204]

171   Accepting, as I do, the need for continuance of the broad division between indictable and summary offences and for an overlapping category of 'either-way', medium range, offences between the two, I consider that a magistrates' court, not an accused, should decide which mode of trial is suitable for his case. However, given my recommendations in Chapter 7 for the replacement of the present dual system of courts with a unified Criminal Court consisting of three levels of jurisdiction, I consider that, where there is an issue between the parties as to venue, a District Judge should be entrusted with the decision; otherwise lay magistrates could deal with it. Both sides should have a right of appeal from the mode of trial decision to the Crown Court. It should be brisk and on paper and dealt with by a small panel of experienced Crown Court judges at each court centre, possibly nominated for the purpose. Though an appeal may add some cost and a day or two's delay, it is valuable in two respects. First, it is a safeguard, particularly in border-line cases. Second, it should improve the quality and consistency of District Judges' decisions. I return in more detail to the system of allocation in Chapter 7 when describing the new court structure that I have in mind.

---

[203] para.45.24; see also para. 46.27
[204] Hansard, HL, 20 January 2000, col 1285

172   Such a change, if accompanied by other reforms that I propose elsewhere in this Report, should provide a more just, expeditious and otherwise efficient criminal justice system. It should not significantly increase the potential number of proceedings or consign defendants to longer delays in disposal of their cases in any level of jurisdiction, as the critics of the Mode of Trial Bills claimed they would have done. It should achieve savings in the system over-all and remove any need to continue the speculative and arid debate on the accuracy, adequacy and interpretation of statistics that the narrow focus of the Mode of Trial Bills engendered.

> **I recommend that:**
>
> - **in all 'either-way' cases magistrates' courts, not defendants, should determine venue after representation from the parties;**
>
> - **in the event of a dispute on the issue, a District Judge should decide;**
>
> - **the defence and the prosecution should have a right of appeal on paper from any mode of trial decision on which they were at issue to a Circuit Judge nominated for the purpose, and provision should be made for the speedy hearing of such appeals;**
>
> - **the procedure of committal of 'either-way' cases to the Crown Court for trial should be abolished and, pending the introduction of a system of allocation as part of my recommendations in Chapter 7 for a new unified Criminal Court, such cases should be 'sent' to the Crown Court in the same way as indictable-only cases; and**
>
> - **the procedure of committal for sentence should be abolished.**

Fraud and other complex cases

The issues and the options

173   There has long been concern about the special problems posed for trial by jury in cases of serious and complex fraud. In recent years the increasing sophistication and complications of commercial and international fraud have

added to that concern. There are well-founded anxieties about possible injustice in the difficulties they pose for juries in understanding them and the enormous financial and other demands that jury trial imposes on the system and on all involved in it. This is not just a matter of expense and toil flowing from the use of procedures peculiar to jury trial in such difficult cases. The remorseless increase in the length of such trials over recent years has become a severe intrusion on jurors' working and private lives.[205] It cannot be good for them or for justice.

174   At present the problem is compounded by the unrepresentative nature of juries, particularly in serious fraud and other complex cases. Judges are reluctant to require busy working people to prejudice their livelihoods or their employers' businesses by taking them from their work, frequently for months at a time. The Bar Council, while opposing any move away from jury trial in such cases, has acknowledged in its submission in the Review that it is difficult to find a juries for them which are a true cross-section of society. If, as I have recommended, steps are taken to ensure that juries generally are more representative of the broad range of skills and experience of the community, the hardships that such cases impose on many jurors would be greater.

175   Long serious fraud and other complex cases, or their prospect, are also often too much for defendants. As the Serious Fraud Office has commented in a paper submitted in the Review, ill health, or claimed ill health, is a particularly troublesome cause of substantial delay and, often severance. Such delay, when added to the already long incubation periods for these cases can then lead to applications to stay the proceedings for abuse of process.

176   In 1983 Lord Roskill was appointed to chair a Fraud Trials Committee to consider how more justly, expeditiously and economically these cases could be conducted. In 1986 the Committee reported, recommending a number of procedural changes in the trial of serious and complex fraud, many of which were implemented the following year in the Criminal Justice Act 1987.[206] These included the establishment of the Serious Fraud Office and procedural and evidential reforms. In addition, a new regulatory framework, including the introduction of the Financial Services Tribunal, was introduced by the Financial Services Act 1986.

177   The majority of the Roskill Committee also recommended the replacement of juries for trials of serious and complex fraud by a Fraud Trials Tribunal

---

[205] cf the comments of the New Zealand Law Commission on this aspect in its Report 69, *Juries in Criminal Trials*, February 2001, para 93, and its recommendation on p 54 that in all, save 'high tier' offences a judge should be empowered to order trial by judge alone in cases likely to exceed 30 days
[206] *Fraud Trials Committee Report*, Chairman, Lord Roskill, PC, (HMSO, 1986)

consisting of a judge and a small number of specially qualified lay members.[207] It was the most widely supported proposal of those who gave evidence to the Committee, the other three being special juries, trial by judge alone and trial by a panel of judges. One of its members, Walter Merricks,[208] in a powerfully reasoned dissenting note, argued that there was no firm basis for removing the established right to jury trial in such cases. He said that, in the absence of general research into the workings of juries, the way forward was to simplify and otherwise improve trial procedures.

178   Mr. Merricks' dissent on this point was strongly taken up by the Criminal Bar, and the Government of the day put to one side the majority's proposal. It did so in part to see how far the recommended procedural changes would go in remedying the problems of handling these cases. But a number of ensuing high profile trials drew attention to continuing problems of manageability caused by their complexity and length. In more than one case that reached the Court of Appeal, the Court commented that such problems put at risk the fairness of trial, imposed great personal burdens on all those involved and made great demands on limited and expensive resources.

179   In 1993 the Runciman Royal Commission, whilst implicitly acknowledging the continuing problems, felt unable to make recommendations on the matter without the benefit of jury research which, it considered, was barred by section 8 of the Contempt of Court Act 1981.[209]

180   Since then, the debate has rumbled on, prompting the Home Office, in February 1998,[210] to issue a consultation document setting out four possible alternatives to jury trial in serious and complex fraud cases. These were special juries, a judge or judges alone or sitting with expert assessors, a 'Roskill' style tribunal and a single judge sitting with a jury on key issues for decision.

181   The arguments for and against the present form of jury trial in cases of serious and complex fraud have been canvassed many times. Arguments for, include:

- jury trial is a hallowed democratic institution and a citizen's right in all serious cases which necessarily include serious and complex frauds;

- the random nature of selection of juries ensures their fairness and independence;

---

[207] paras 8.47-8.51

[208] Solicitor, then Secretary, Professional and Public Relations Committee of the Law Society

[209] *Royal Commission on Criminal Justice*, Chapter 8, paras 76-81

[210] *Juries in Serious Fraud Trials*, February 1998

- mostly the question is one of dishonesty, which is essentially a matter for a jury who, by reason of their number and mix, are as well as, or better equipped than, a smaller tribunal, however professional, to assess the reliability and credibility of witnesses;

- there is no evidence, for example in the form of jury research, that juries cannot cope with long and complex cases or that their decisions in them are contrary to the evidence; on the contrary, most judges and legal practitioners' assessment, based on their trial experience, is that their verdicts are in the main 'correct'; and

- there is an openness and public intelligibility in the parties having to accommodate the jury's newness to the subject matter by presenting their respective cases in a simple and easily digestible form, and that there is scope for improvements in such presentation.

Arguments against, include:

- if jurors are truly to be regarded as the defendant's peers, they should be experienced in the professional or commercial discipline in which the alleged offence occurred;

- although the issue of dishonesty is essentially a matter for a jury, the volume and complexities of the issues and the evidence, especially in specialist market frauds, may be too difficult for them to understand or analyse so as to enable them to determine whether there has been dishonesty;

- the length of such trials, sometimes of several months, is an unreasonable intrusion on jurors' personal and, where they are in employment, working lives, going way beyond the conventional requirement for such duty of about two weeks' service;

- that has the effect of making juries even less representative of the community than they are already, since the court excuses many who would otherwise be able and willing to make short-term arrangements to do their civic duty;

- such long trials are also a great personal strain and burden on everyone else involved, not least the defendant, the victim and witnesses;

- judges, with their legal and forensic experience, and/or specialist assessors would be better equipped to deal justly and more expeditiously with such cases;

- that would also have the benefit of greater openness, since there would then be a publicly reasoned and appealable decision instead of the present inscrutable and largely unappealable verdict of the jury; and

- the length of jury trials in fraud cases is very costly to the public and also, because of limited judicial and court resources, unduly delays the efficient disposal of other cases waiting for trial.

182   I have considered these conflicting arguments with care. Like the Roskill Committee, I have concluded that those for replacing trial by judge and jury with some other form of tribunal in serious and complex fraud cases are the more persuasive. Indeed, they have become more pressing since the Committee reported, given the ever lengthening and complexity of fraud trials and their increasingly specialised nature and international ramifications. Moreover, the main basis for not implementing the Roskill Committee's recommendation for a Fraud Trials Tribunal, the hope that the procedural and evidential reforms in the 1987 Act would significantly reduce the problems of jury trial, has not been realised.

183   If I had to pick two of the most compelling factors in favour of reform, I would settle on the burdensome length and increasing speciality and complexity of these cases, with which jurors, largely or wholly strangers to the subject matter, are expected to cope. Both put justice at risk. The Director of the Serious Fraud Office has recently said that the average length of a serious fraud prosecuted by it is six months, which would come largely before a jury of "the unemployed or unemployable".[211] I have considered the thoughtful submissions of the Criminal Bar Association, the Law Society, the Fraud Advisory Panel and some others that further improvements in the conduct and presentation of the issues and evidence in fraud trials could ease those difficulties.[212] But, as the Criminal Bar Association has acknowledged in putting them forward, they are "no more than scratching the surface" on the general issue of the use of juries in such trials. The fact is that many fraud and other cases, by reason of their length, complexity and speciality, now demand much more of the traditional English jury than it is equipped to provide. The point that juries have not kept pace with modern requirements of the criminal justice system in this respect has been made in a number of recent writings and submissions to the Review.

184   I am firmly of the view that we should wait no longer before introducing a more just and efficient form of trial in serious and complex fraud cases. The main candidates are those considered by the Roskill Committee, namely: special juries, trial by judge alone, trial by a panel of judges and trial by a tribunal of a judge and lay members. As I have said, the Committee opted for a 'Fraud Trials Tribunal', which they recommended should consist of a High Court or Circuit Judge and two lay members drawn from a panel of persons with general expertise in business and experience of complex transactions.[213]

---

[211] The Times, 5th March 2001

[212] ie proposals similar to those advanced by the Fraud Advisory Panel in October 1998 in response to the Home Office February 1998 Consultation Document (see para. [181] above), all or most of which I adopt in my recommendations in Chapter 11 for the conduct of jury trials generally

[213] paras 8.53-74

Special juries

185   This proposal would revive for a special category of criminal case an institution that was abolished in criminal and most civil cases in 1949,[214] and had been little used in crime for several decades before that. Although originally 'special' in the sense of being composed of persons with special qualifications, it had become by the early 19th century a jury with special social or property qualifications. If the institution were to be revived for fraud and, possibly, other complex cases, the first question would be the nature of the qualifications required for selection as a potential special juror. Presumably, in the context of fraud, they would need to include wide experience of business and finance. In other contexts, they could involve familiarity with medical and/or other scientific disciplines. But, as the Roskill Committee pointed out in rejecting this option,[215] it would be difficult to empanel a jury, even from such a restricted category, who would collegiately have the degree of specialist knowledge or expertise which, by definition, they would be required to have for the particular subject matter in each case. And, even if suitably qualified juries, maybe smaller than 12, could be found, it would be unreasonable to expect them to serve the length of time that many such fraud trials now take.

Judge alone

186   The Roskill Committee, whilst acknowledging that trial by judge alone is feasible in complex cases and that it would be the most economic way of dealing with them, was of the view that it would be burdensome to judges:

> "… we think it would be desirable to avoid placing a judge in this position if, as we believe, there is a more suitable alternative. We should add that very few of those who submitted evidence to us supported the proposal that a judge alone should try complex frauds".[216]

187   It is difficult to understand why the Roskill Committee felt this way. It is a role to which judges are well accustomed in their civil jurisdiction,

---

[214] Juries Act 1949 s 18
[215] para 8.44
[216] para 8.46

particularly in commercial and chancery cases where they have to determine allegations of fraud and when the outcome of their findings, though not immediately causing loss of liberty, may be as or more catastrophic for the victim or fraudsman. It is true that the civil burden of proof is less than that in crime,[217] but that is an argument in favour, rather than against, reform in criminal cases. The criminal test of sureness of guilt is far less intellectually testing for the judge than the more finely balanced civil test of preponderance of probability.

188   Even when judges are sitting in crime they frequently have to make findings and reach value judgments on matters of fact that are critical to the outcome of the case. For example, they may have to rule on applications to stay the prosecution for abuse of process, or on the fairness of evidence on the question of its admissibility or, at the close of the prosecution case, on the sufficiency of evidence for it to continue. There is also long experience of judges as fact finders in terrorist cases in the Diplock Courts in Northern Ireland, and their counterparts in Republic of Ireland. When talking of the burden for judges of acting as fact finders in criminal cases, I do not believe the Roskill Committee can have had in mind the preparation of written judgments. The detailed directions of law and summary of the issues and evidence that such cases require are, or should be, a ready framework for judgment. It is only a short step, and one that should not cause any or any significant delay, for judges to turn them into reasoned judgments. Many judges who have made submissions to, or expressed views in, the Review have said that they would find their task in long and complex cases less burdensome without a jury. It is true that many also say that they enjoy the present luxury of not having to decide the issue of fact for themselves. But loss of luxury is one thing; treating its loss as a sufficient burden to hold back in appropriate cases from fixing on a more just and efficient system of trial is another.

Panel of judges

189   There has been little or no support for this option. I would not recommend it for the practical reasons identified by the Roskill Committee.[218] It would strain valuable and limited judicial resources. And to introduce a panel of judges would merely increase judicial expertise without, in the main, providing the specialist knowledge and experience required of fact-finders in such cases.

---

[217] though the more serious the allegation the more cogent must be the evidence to overcome the unlikelihood of what is alleged and thus to prove it; see per Ungoed-Thomas J in *In re Dellow's Will Trusts* [1964] 1 WLR 451, at 455, cited with approval by Lord Nicholls in *In re H (Minors)* [1996] AC 563, at 586D-G
[218] para 8.47

190   The Roskill Committee favoured this model of a judge sitting with lay members[219] drawn from a panel of persons experienced in the world of business and finance. As I have said, it was the option most widely supported by those who gave evidence to the Committee. It envisaged that the judge would, in the main, sit and rule on his own on matters of law, procedure and the admissibility of evidence. On matters of fact he and each of the lay members would have the same vote; their decision could be by a majority, but the judge would give a single reasoned judgment of the tribunal.[220]

191   In my view, there is much to be said for a proposal of this sort. However, I share the ambivalence of many contributors to the Review who have looked for an alternative to jury trial, as to whether it should be trial by judge alone or sitting with lay members drawn from a panel of persons with financial expertise. The Serious Fraud Office,[221] the Crown Prosecution Service, the police, including the Association of Chief Police Officers, and a number of departmental investigation and prosecution bodies[222] favoured some sort of combined tribunal. The Serious Fraud Office has cautioned, however, that lay members selected for any particular trial should be drawn from a different discipline from that in issue, otherwise they might assume the role of untested expert witnesses. This caution seems to run counter to the Roskill Committee's intention that lay members should be selected for their specialist knowledge of the business or financial activity the subject matter of the case, not simply for their general business and financial experience.[223] In my view, the caution is well-founded. There could be difficulties where lay members' views are possibly conditioned by their own out of date or narrow experience, or by a 'bee in their bonnet' about the norms of professional conduct in the area of speciality in issue. In such circumstances, it is doubtful what proper role they could perform in assisting a judge to assess conflicting expert evidence in the case. That is not to say that specialists in the particular discipline or market concerned should never be part of the tribunal, simply to note the need to avoid too close a connection where working practices and norms are likely to be an issue as distinct from an understanding of the system and mechanics of the alleged fraud.

192   My first instinct had been to recommend that the court could direct trial by judge and jury or by judge and lay members or by judge alone, as he considered appropriate. However, after considerable thought, I consider that

---

[219] as distinct from assessors

[220] paras 8.50-51; cf Crown Court when sitting as an appeal court from a magistrates' court

[221] in its response of 27th May 1998 to the Home Office Consultation Document; the Director has recently suggested that it should be judge and 'expert assessors', The Times, 5th March 2001

[222] including the National Crime Squad, National Investigations Service (Customs and Excise) National Criminal Intelligence Service, the Department of Trade and Industry; Customs and Excise and Inland Revenue

[223] see para 8.50, and cf para 8.61

the need for reform would be best met by a combination of enabling the court to direct trial by judge and jury or by judge and lay members. It seems to me that if a defendant in such cases is deprived against his wish of trial by jury, he should be entitled, if he wishes, to trial by a tribunal comprised in part of persons with appropriate business and financial experience. However, it should also be open for a defendant to opt, with the court's consent, to trial by judge alone under the general provisions for doing so that I have recommended.

193   The first step would be to allocate the case to a judge, whether a High Court Judge or Circuit Judge, with experience of trying serious and complex fraud. He should decide, after hearing representations from both sides, whether it should be heard with a jury or by himself and lay members or, if the defendant has opted for trial by judge alone, by himself. If he decides on trial with lay members, he should determine, again after hearing representations from both sides, from what, if any, speciality(ies) they should be drawn.[224] Consistently with my recommendations on mode of trial decisions in either-way and jury "waiver" cases, I do not suggest that an agreement of the parties as to any of these modes of trial should bind the judge, but such agreement would no doubt be an important factor for him in reaching his decision.

194   Where the judge has a choice between directing trial by himself and lay members or, at the defendant's option, of trial by himself alone, one factor that may influence the decision is the extent to which the case requires some knowledge of a specialist market or other commercial discipline. Another may be whether the issue is likely to turn on a factual understanding and analysis of the evidence or on conflicting contentions on professional or commercial norms and, if so, whether expert evidence is to be called. There may be other considerations depending on the individual circumstances of the case. All these mode of trial decisions should, in my view, be subject to a right of speedy appeal by either side to the Court of Appeal (Criminal Division).

195   The lynch-pin of all three potential forms of trial in serious and complex frauds is the judge. It is vital that he or she is of a high level of judicial competence with a good knowledge and experience of commercial and financial matters. At present there are 51 Circuit Judges nominated to try cases that meet current criteria for 'serious frauds'.[225] Those criteria are broadly those which meet the Serious Fraud Office's definition of seriousness and complexity for it to undertake the prosecution, to which I refer in more detail below.[226] In addition, particularly 'heavy' cases of serious and complex

---

[224] cf the recommendation of George Staple, CB, QC, the former Director of the SFO, that a judge alone should try long and complex trials and that a special juries should be brought in for specialised cases
[225] agreed by the Senior Presiding Judge, the SFO, the CPS and other prosecuting agencies
[226] see para.201 below

fraud with a high degree of public interest, are tried by High Court Judges, usually drawn from the Commercial Court and nominated on a case by case basis by the Lord Chief Justice.

196   As to procedure at the trial, I envisage something similar to that of the District Court Division of the new unified Criminal Court that I recommend[227] in Chapter 7. I would expect the judge normally to sit on his own in pre-trial hearings and when ruling on law and such matters as the admissibility of evidence. However, as the Roskill Committee noted,[228] the lay members could be of assistance in discussions as to the manner in which certain evidence could most helpfully be presented. I also agree with the Roskill Committee[229] that the judge and lay members should retire to consider their decision without any prior public direction from the judge on the law, and that, once they have reached their decision, he should express it in a publicly and fully reasoned judgment of the court. The judge should be the sole judge of law, but on matters of fact, each would have an equal vote, and, as the Roskill Committee recommended, a majority of any two could suffice for conviction.[230] As to sentence, this should be left entirely to the judge, since the lay members are not selected for any expertise in that field. Appeal should lie to the Court of Appeal (Criminal Division), against conviction and/or sentence on the same basis as appeals after conviction by a jury.

197   I have given anxious consideration to a number of other practical considerations that should be borne in mind by those responsible for deciding whether and how to undertake such a radical reform.

Allocation

198   Many of the anxieties about jury trial in serious and complex fraud cases are applicable to the whole range of cases that fall to be tried by judge and jury; they are simply more pronounced in fraud cases. For example, in trials for murder or other violence there are frequently difficult medical or other scientific issues where jurors are expected to follow and evaluate competing expert evidence. The Home Office, in its 1998 Consultation Document, drew attention to this aspect of the problem.[231] Mr. Merricks, in his note of dissent to the Roskill Committee's Report, argued that, before starting to chop away at jury trial in particular types of cases, it would be wise to evaluate the performance of juries across the whole range of their work in order to see

---

[227] see Chapters 7, paras 21 - 35 and 11, paras 57 - 58

[228] para 8.67

[229] para 8.68

[230] para 8.69

[231] para 2.35

whether jurors in fraud cases understand more or less than jurors in other types of cases.[232] But, as I have said, there is already a wealth of research work on juries throughout the common law world.[233] The preponderance of it, in its emphasis on the need to simplify their task, only underlines what is already obvious, the more complicated the issue the more difficult is for them. As I have noted in summarising the arguments in favour of reform, whilst the central issue in many fraud cases may be one of dishonesty, an ability to understand and analyse conflicting highly complex and/or technical evidence is vital for their determination of that issue. Often there is no need for any value judgment as to the dishonesty of the defendant, for example, where the only issue is whether he is factually responsible for, or a party to, whatever conduct is alleged, and where analysis of the evidence one way or another effectively determines the issue of dishonesty. In many cases of complexity, for example, cases where the issue turns on medical or other scientific evidence, the issue is not one of dishonesty at all, or even of assessment of the reliability or credibility of witnesses or the defendant. It is simply one that requires a jury to understand and to evaluate conflicting expert views.

199   Lord Roskill intended that his proposed Fraud Trials Tribunal should be limited to a relatively small number of complex frauds, the focus in his suggested guidelines,[234] being on 'City' frauds. If, as I have suggested in the preceding paragraph, the need for reform is not confined to fraud cases, but should apply to any case of complexity, what should the criteria be? Some might argue that, even with the loosest of guidelines, it will be difficult to justify, generally or on a case by case basis, putting one defendant in charge of a jury and another in front of some other form of tribunal when, the difference between them is not as to complexity but as to the type of offence.

200   One course would be to adopt similar criteria to those for determination whether there should be trial by jury in civil proceedings for fraud, libel, slander, malicious prosecution or false imprisonment. Such cases are to be tried with a jury "unless the court is of the opinion that the trial requires prolonged examination of documents or accounts or any scientific or local investigation which cannot conveniently be made with a jury".[235] On the question whether the matter can 'conveniently' be heard with a jury, the civil courts have four criteria: first, the physical problem of handling the documentation; second, prolongation of the trial, since jury trial takes much longer than with judge alone; third, expense, since jury trial is much more expensive, both as a result of prolongation and its very nature; and fourth, and the most important, the jury may not understand the case.[236] There is no way of knowing whether a jury has misunderstood the issues and/or the evidence

---

[232] p 194, para C17

[233] see Appendix II

[234] para 8.55 and Annex

[235] Supreme Court Act 1981, s 69

[236] *Beta Construction Ltd. v Channel 4 TV Ltd.*[1990] 1 WLR 1042, per Stuart-Smith LJ at 1049B

since the trial judge or the Court of Appeal has little or no means of discovering that. Even if, as I recommend in Chapter 11, juries in criminal cases might be asked to answer specific questions on certain issues, as happens in civil jury trials, jury misunderstandings may still be difficult to unearth. By contrast, in trial by judge alone or with lay members, he would be required to give a fully reasoned judgment, and mistakes, if any, are open to full scrutiny on appeal.

201 A simpler, but more limited, solution would be to confine the option for dispensing with juries to cases prosecuted by the Serious Fraud Office and like cases prosecuted by other government prosecuting departments. These are cases that satisfy criteria of the sort presently justifying 'transfer' and/or call for a preparatory hearing under sections 4 and 7 respectively of the Criminal Justice Act 1987, namely frauds of great "seriousness or complexity".[237] The Home Office, in its 1998 Consultation Document,[238] favoured such criteria, estimating that they would produce a total of 80-85 cases a year potentially suitable for trial without jury. That estimate is considerably higher than the number of references accepted annually by the Serious Fraud Office, exercising its own stringent criteria for that purpose.[239] In 1999/2000 it accepted about 30 new references and completed 8 trials.[240] As Parliament has already provided a rigorous procedure for this relatively small category of cases, it seems to me that it would be a good starting point for identifying prosecutions in which a judge could order trial by judge and lay members or, in the event of the defendant's option for trial by judge alone, the latter.

202 I say 'starting point', despite a strong logical case for, at the same time, extending the reform to other serious and complex cases. There is something to be said for establishing and developing these new procedures first on a limited and readily identifiable category of cases where there is urgent need for a more just and efficient process. If the reform is a success then consideration can be given to extending it in the light of the experience gained.

203 Whatever the breadth of the allocation criteria adopted, I consider that the overriding criterion in each case should be expressed as "the interests of justice", which itself should include factors of the sort applicable to the

---

[237] see also, more generally, cases of complexity or length under ss 29-31 and 34 of the Criminal Procedure and Investigations Act 1996

[238] paras.3.3-3.7

[239] including: a value of at least £1 million; likely attraction of national publicity and widespread public concern; requiring a highly specialised knowledge, for example of financial markets and their practices; a significant international dimension; and requiring a combination of legal and accountancy skills; see SFO Annual Report 1999/2000, p 3

[240] in the year April 1999 to April 2000 the SFO worked on a total of 95 cases (excluding appeals); by the year end it had 81 continuing cases with an aggregate value of alleged sums at risk of £1.38 billion; eight trials were concluded within the year, involving 12 defendants of whom 11 were convicted and one acquitted. See SFO Annual Report 1999/2000 p 21

present mode of trial decision in civil cases. They are, in this context, that the case requires an ability to understand a specialised financial discipline, consideration of complex and voluminous evidence, including prolonged consideration of accounts and/or other documents, and which is likely to take a long time.

The allocation decision

204 Then there is the question who should make the mode of trial decision. The Roskill Committee recommended that it should be a High Court judge other than the nominated trial judge, after hearing representations from both sides.[241] The Home Office, in its 1998 Consultation Document,[242] proposed that the decision should be taken by the nominated trial judge before or at the preparatory hearing (or, as it may become under my recommendations in Chapter 10,[243] the pre-trial hearing). In my view, the nominated trial judge, whether High Court Judge or Circuit Judge, should be best placed for the decision. He will be required to master the essentials of the case at an early stage to prepare himself for the pre-trial assessment[244] and hearing(s). In doing so, he can equip himself to form a view on the mode of trial that provisionally he considers it will require. He will have the papers, which may already be voluminous; he will have to give the parties an opportunity to make representations on the matter. To impose such a time-consuming task on a judge who will not try the case would, in my view, be an unnecessary and potentially inconvenient duplication of work. And, if my recommendation for a right of appeal is adopted, the decision will be subject to review by the Court of Appeal, (Criminal Division).

205 The nominated 'Serious Fraud Judges' and Commercial Judges of the High Court are, by definition, men and women of great knowledge and experience in this class of work. But their skills, in the main, have only been acquired incrementally by exposure in the course of their practice as advocates and of their judicial career to fraud cases of various levels of seriousness and complexity. The Judicial Studies Board has attempted over the years to provide some training for judges in this field. But it has been sporadic and of a very limited nature, in the main, restricted to single day conferences or as one of many topics in short residential seminars every three or four years. I share the view of the Fraud Advisory Panel[245] that there is an urgent need for more extensive, structured and continuing training of judges for this task. Such training should include, where necessary, familiarising them with

---

[241] paras 8.55 and 8.59
[242] paras 3.15-3.17
[243] paras 204 - 220
[244] see Chapter 10, paras 221 - 228
[245] see paras 15.1-2 of the Panel's response of October 1998 to the Lord Chancellor's consultation in that year on pre-trial procedures on serious fraud cases

information technology, including computer transcription of proceedings, basic accounting and company documents, financial systems of markets prone to fraud, financial practices commonly encountered in serious fraud cases, forensic handling of such cases and the preparation and form of summings-up or judgments in them. There is a correspondingly urgent need for the establishment of formal criteria for nomination to and retention on the panel of judges doing such work. There may also be a case for providing serious fraud judges with additional facilities, according to their workload generally or on a case by case basis, for example, specialised information technology and suitably qualified judicial assistants.

206　As to the panel from which lay members might be drawn, I envisage the sort of arrangements proposed by the Roskill Committee.[246] These could include the establishment and maintenance by the Lord Chancellor, in consultation with professional and other bodies, of a panel of persons drawn from various specialities. In order to secure and retain persons of high quality for the task, they should be paid appropriately; the Roskill Committee suggested a daily rate equivalent to that of a Circuit Judge, which seems to me a reasonable level for the purpose. The nominated trial judge should select the lay members, after affording the parties an opportunity to make written representations as to their suitability.

I recommend that:

- **as an alternative to trial by judge and jury in serious and complex fraud cases, the nominated trial judge should be empowered to direct trial by himself sitting with lay members or, where the defendant has opted for trial by judge alone, by himself alone;**

- **the category of cases to which such a direction might apply should, in the first instance, be frauds of seriousness or complexity within sections 4 and 7 of the Criminal Justice Act 1987;**

- **the overriding criterion for directing trial without jury should be the interests of justice;**

- **either party should have a right of appeal against such decision to the Court of Appeal, (Criminal Division);**

- **judges trying such cases, by whatever form of procedure, should be specially nominated for the purpose as now, and provided with a thorough, structured and continuing training for it;**

---

[246] paras 8.61-65

- there should be a panel of experts, established and maintained by the Lord Chancellor in consultation with professional and other bodies, from which lay members may be selected for trials;

- the nominated trial judge should select the lay members after affording the parties an opportunity to make written representations as to their suitability;

- lay members should be paid appropriately for their service;

- in a court consisting of a judge and lay members, the judge should be the sole judge of law, procedure, admissibility of evidence and as to sentence; as to conviction, all three should be the judges of fact;

- the decision of a court so constituted should wherever possible be unanimous, but a majority of any two could suffice for a conviction; and

- the judge should give the court's decision by a public and fully reasoned judgment.

Young defendants

207   Young defendants, that is, those under 18 charged with an indictable offence other than murder must be tried summarily unless the offence is one of certain grave crimes for which they may be sentenced to detention for a long period, or where they are charged with a person of 18 or over and magistrates consider it necessary in the interests of justice that all should be tried together.[247] Young defendants, therefore, have no right of election for jury trial. A significant number of young defendants do, however, end up in the Crown Court. In 1999 4718 were committed there for trial and 851 were committed for sentence.[248]

208   There are strong arguments that, even for grave crimes, a different form of tribunal should be provided. The younger the young defendant, the stronger the case for it, and the more it overlaps with arguments for raising the criminal age of liability in England and Wales above the age of 10. The judgment of the Strasbourg Court in *T and V v UK*,[249] raised a number of issues about the inappropriateness of the public, formal and otherwise intimidating procedure of a Crown Court trial for young children charged with the sort of offences that take them there. In the light of that judgment, Lord Bingham, the then Lord Chief Justice, issued a practice direction in February

---

[247] Magistrates' Courts Act 1980, s 24, and Powers of Criminal Courts (Sentencing) Act 2000, s 91
[248] the figures for 2000 are, apparently, not yet available
[249] (1999) 30 EHRR 121

214

2000 designed to reduce the scope for avoidable intimidation, humiliation or distress to young defendants on trial in the Crown Court.[250] Whilst that practice direction contained valuable guidance for minimising many of those features, there is still the question whether the Crown Court is appropriate either for the trial or sentencing of young defendants. Most other European and Commonwealth countries have separate adult and youth criminal justice systems, and there appears to be wide agreement here that they should be treated differently from adults in this respect. Many contributors to the Review have urged that they should not be tried in the Crown Court or before a jury, whatever the seriousness of the charge. In my view, there is a strong case for removal of all such cases to the youth court. As Professor Andrew Ashworth has observed,[251] their seriousness could be appropriately marked in that court, where necessary, by constituting it with a judge and magistrates. In the more flexible three tiered court structure that I recommend in Chapter 7, the District Division could provide such a tribunal presided over by a judge, from High Court to Recorder level, appropriate to the seriousness and importance of the case. Lord Warner, the Chairman of the Youth Justice Board, has supported the use of such a tribunal in the more serious juvenile cases.

209   There are two other factors. The first is a matter of judicial training and experience of cases involving young defendants. District Judges and magistrates who sit in youth courts receive specialist training. Judges who try young defendants in the cases that reach the Crown Court are usually the more senior and experienced, many of them also having received special training and authorisation to sit in County Court and High Court cases involving children. It is strange, therefore, that trials of grave cases against young defendants should be consigned to a random selection of jurors all or most of whom will be unfamiliar, not only with the court and their role in it, but also with the trial and evidence of young persons. No doubt they bring to the task their own knowledge and experience of young people; as do magistrates and judges, but that in itself is not considered a sufficient qualification for the latter in these cases.

210   The second factor - and it is a priority in young offender cases - is the particular need for speed and efficiency in bringing them to trial and sentence. It is an important aim of the Youth Justice Board, which is charged by the Government with the task of reducing the average time between arrest and sentence of persistent young offenders. Although these only account for a proportion of young defendants who appear before the courts, average waiting times give a good indication of how speedily each of the two court systems deal with young offenders. In May 2001, for example, the national average

[250] [2000] 1 Cr App R 483
[251] in a commentary on *T & V v UK* in [2000] Crim LR, at 188

from arrest to sentence was 73 days.[252] In the Crown Court, where 40% of all youth cases involve persistent young offenders, the average time from arrest to sentence was 197 days as against 66 days in the Youth Court.[253]

211 I consider, therefore, that young defendants charged with murder or other grave offences that may merit a sentence of greater severity than is presently available to the youth court should no longer be tried by judge and jury in the Crown Court or be committed there for sentence. Instead, they should go to a youth court consisting, as appropriate, of a High Court Judge, Circuit Judge or Recorder sitting with at least two experienced youth panel magistrates and exercising the full jurisdiction of the present Crown Court for this purpose. Under the structure of the new unified Criminal Court that I propose in Chapter 7, the youth court, so constituted, could be regarded as part of the District Division. Notwithstanding the public notoriety that such cases now attract through intense media coverage, I consider that the court proceedings should normally be entitled to the same privacy as those in the present youth court. The only exception to this course should be for those young defendants who are presently brought before the Crown Court only because they are charged jointly with a person who has attained the age of 18 and it is considered necessary in the interests of justice that they should be tried together. In that event, Lord Bingham's practice direction should be observed. And, in the event of the adult co-defendant pleading guilty in the Crown Court there should be power to remit the case against the young defendant to the youth court.

Accordingly, I recommend that:

- **all cases involving young defendants who are presently committed to the Crown Court for trial or for sentence should in future be put before the youth court consisting, as appropriate, of a High Court Judge, Circuit Judge or Recorder sitting with at least two experienced magistrates and exercising the full jurisdiction of the present Crown Court for this purpose;**

- **the only possible exception should be those cases in which the young defendant is charged jointly with an adult and it is considered necessary in the interests of justice for them to be tried together; and**

- **the youth court so constituted should be entitled, save where it considers that public interest demands**

---

[252] *Lord Chancellor's Department Statistical Bulletin No. 8/2001*, August 2001

[253] in the first six months of 1999, 11% of all persistent young offenders were sentenced in the Crown Court, taking an average of 206 days from arrest to sentence

**otherwise, to hear such cases in private, as in the
youth court exercising its present jurisdiction.**

Fitness to plead

212   There is a strong case for transferring from the jury to the judge determination of the issue of fitness to plead. By statute[254] the issue must presently be determined by a jury either on arraignment or, if the court so decides, at any time during the trial until the opening of the defence, and only on the written or oral evidence of two registered medical practitioners at least one of whom is approved for the purpose. The question for the jury is whether the defendant is under such a disability that, apart from the statute, "it would constitute a bar to his being tried". If they do so find, a jury then has to determine whether he did the act or made the omission charged against him as the offence. If the verdict of unfitness to plead is returned on the arraignment, a second jury must be empanelled to try this secondary factual issue; if it is returned in the course of the trial, the jury trying him also determines this issue. The test of disability upon which the courts rely is still to be found in the early 19th century case of *R v Pritchard*.[255] It is broadly whether the defendant has sufficient intellect to instruct his advocate, to plead to the indictment, to follow and understand the evidence and to give evidence. If the defence raises the issue, the defendant has to prove it on a balance of probabilities; if the prosecution raises it, it must prove it to the criminal standard.

213   In the majority of cases the jury's role on the issue of unfitness to plead is little more than a formality because there is usually no dispute between the prosecution and the defence that the defendant is unfit to plead.[256] However, the procedure is still cumbrous, especially when the issue is raised, as it mostly is, on the arraignment, because it can then require the empanelling of two juries. More importantly, it is difficult to see what a jury can bring to the determination of the issue that a judge cannot. He decides similar questions determinative of whether there should be a trial, for example, whether a defendant is physically or mentally fit to stand or continue trial in applications to stay the prosecution or for discharge of the defendant. The consequences of a finding of unfitness to plead are now much more flexible than they were,[257] ranging from a hospital order with restrictions to an absolute discharge; and the judge is entrusted with the often very difficult task of what to do with the defendant, with the assistance of medical evidence. In my view, he, not the

---

[254] Criminal Procedure (Insanity) Act 1964, as amended by the Criminal Procedure (Insanity and Unfitness to Plead) Act 1991
[255] (1836) 7 C & 303
[256] R D Mackay and Gerry Kearns, *An Upturn in Unfitness to Plead? Disability in Relation to the Trial under the 1991 Act* [2000] Crim L R 532, at 536
[257] as a result of the 1991 Act's amendments; see fn 254 above

jury, should determine the issue of fitness to plead at whatever stage it is raised, leaving, where it arises, the jury to determine whether the defendant did the act or made the omission charged.

I recommend that legislation should be introduced to require a judge, not a jury, to determine the issue of fitness to plead.

INFORMATION FOR AND TREATMENT OF JURORS

214   It is vital for the criminal justice system and public confidence in it that everyone qualified for jury service does it with a good will and regards it as time well spent. Jurors who are unhappy with their lot may lack the will or the ability to do their job properly; and, as the largest section of the public closely exposed to the workings of the Crown Court, they are likely to make poor ambassadors for it. For many it is a new, exciting and rewarding experience. But for some, it can be intimidating and frustrating; they may find it physically, intellectually or socially arduous; for others, it can also be emotionally disturbing. And, for all, it is an interruption of the normal rhythm of their lives, causing variously inconvenience, disruption of their family and/or working routines and financial loss. Potential jurors should be adequately informed of what jury service involves and of the court and local facilities available to enable them perform it and to keep an eye on of their own affairs the while. At court the processes of selection and of serving on a jury should be as short, efficiently conducted and as considerate to them as possible, make the best use of their time and minimise the financial and other costs that service may cause them. And, after jury service is over, they should know, not only that their service is appreciated, but also that they will not be required to repeat it, unless they wish, for a long time.

215   A Court Service survey undertaken in early 2000 of juror satisfaction as to information, facilities and treatment indicated that 95% of jurors who had served as jurors or who had merely attended court were either "satisfied" or "very satisfied" by the court's over-all treatment of them.[258] However, the level of satisfaction of court facilities, looked at individually was lower, 82%; and nearly half of those who expressed dissatisfaction underlined their view with specific comments.

216   I find these reported levels of jurors' satisfaction with their service surprising. It has been a repeated refrain from former jurors in their contributions to the Review, and in the jury research collated by Dr Penny Darbyshire, how

---

[258] Court Service *Juror Survey 2000*; based on a 48% response rate out of 3926

unsatisfactory many jurors find the experience. I share her view that the complaints are too common to be dismissed as merely anecdotal. They include:

- inconvenience and hardship as a result of the short notice given (eight weeks);

- boredom and irritation with endless waiting at court without being selected to serve on a jury;

- inadequate facilities in jury assembly and waiting rooms;

- inadequacy of jury boxes and other facilities in court;

- officious and/or inconsiderate treatment by court staff;

- lack of objective information at the start of the case about the essential issues and the law applicable to them;

- artificial and repetitious trial procedures and the frequent interruption of them for discussions between the judge and advocates on matters of law;

- insufficient use of visual and written aids both by the parties and the judge; and

- lengthy and arduous trials, with too long or inconsiderately structured working days.

Information

217   Recommendations of the Morris Committee and the Runciman Royal Commission have led to considerable improvements in information provided to those summoned for jury service. They are told about qualifications for and exclusions from service, the trial process, their role and responsibilities and brief details of the court's location and facilities. On their first day at court they are given an introductory briefing by a bailiff and shown a video. All of this is good and the Court Service, in recent years, has introduced a number of thoughtful additions to the information provided. However, there is room for further improvement.

218   First, the jury summons, when summarising the bases of qualification for jury service, should do so in a number of languages so as to inform recipients of the need for a good understanding of English and the need to inform the Central Summoning Bureau at an early stage if there is thought to be any difficulty about that. Second, the summons should deal rather more fully than it does at present with the possibility of deferral instead of excusal. Subject to the precise form of change that might be made to the present system, potential jurors could be invited to suggest dates for their service - whether as an original proposal or as an alternative to those mentioned in the summons - within a period, say, of six months, after receipt of it. As to excusal, the form should set out clearly the criteria and how to apply for excusal, doing so in a

more informal and friendly way than the present summons, whilst making clear that the criteria will be rigorously applied. To accommodate those who may be dischargeable on account of physical disability, but who may yet wish to do jury service, the form should indicate in outline what support facilities the courts can provide. My general impression of the present summons is that it is a bleak and somewhat off-putting document for persons whom it is hoped to encourage to do their jury service.

219   There is also much more information that the courts should give potential jurors once they have received the lists from the Central Summoning Bureau. In my view, it is important to do this in writing and well before the start of jury service so that the potential jurors can take time to see what it involves and what, if any, arrangements to make with regard to their work, families, pets and any other commitments that may be affected. As I have mentioned, courts provide an introductory video on the first day that potential jurors report for service and supplement it with instructions from the jury bailiff. Nevertheless, the strangeness of the surroundings, domestic and other distractions of the first day and, often lateness or reporting to the wrong court, result in much of it not being taken in or missed.

220   If and to the extent that courts do not already do it, I consider that each court should produce a booklet or briefing pack expressed, as the New Zealand Law Commission has emphasised,[259] in an informal and friendly tone. It should start, as is the practice in many other common law jurisdictions, with a short account of the nature and importance of jury service and a warm appreciation of the task about to be undertaken. This part of the booklet or pack could be in the form of a personal communication from the Resident Judge of the court. The information could also usefully include: an explanation of the process of random selection from the qualifying list(s); the likely length of service; the arrangements for and on first reporting for duty; plans of the location of the court and of the layout of the court-building; an account of its facilities for enabling them to manage their own affairs while waiting to serve on a jury, for example, desks, telephone and fax machines and e-mail points; bleepers, on-call telephone arrangements etc.; arrangements for smokers; what to wear; some account of the process of forming sub-panels at court and selection from them to serve on a jury; confidentiality; security; the likely routine, or lack of it, of each day; what types of case they may hear; facilities for eating and shopping, car-parking, public transport to court and any other essential services (e.g. medical or social security) and telephone numbers; jurors' compensation for financial loss and expenses; and the penalty for not attending. Consideration should also be given to outlining some guidance on certain matters on which jurors are frequently unsure when sitting for the first time, including note-taking, asking questions, selection of the foreman and the

---

[259] Preliminary Paper 37, Vol 1, Pt Two, para 17; see also Report 69, *Juries in Criminal Trials*, Wellington, New Zealand, Chapter 9

deliberation process and, if required, the availability of counselling after sitting on particularly distressing cases. I know that much of this information is briefly touched on in the documentation accompanying the jury summons, but it also would come well from the court itself when potential jurors are beginning to focus more clearly on their jury service. Additionally, all of this information could be included on the court's internet website.

I recommend that:

- **the essential parts of the jury summons and explanatory documents issued by the Central Summoning Bureau should be expressed in several languages, and, over-all, the documentation should be more informative and couched in a more informal and friendly tone than at present; and**

- **the Court Service should review the adequacy of information courts provide to potential jurors against the best provided by other jurisdictions.**

Length and frequency of service

221   As the authors of the New York Jury Project[260] have said and the New York courts have demonstrated, the best way to reduce the burden of jury service is to minimise its length and frequency. In England and Wales the Central Summoning Bureau now issues all jury summonses according to the requirements notified to it by each court centre. The summonses give eight weeks' notice of the first date on which recipients are required to attend court for service. Claims of ineligibility, excusal as of right, discharge because of incapacity and requests for discretionary excusal or deferral are dealt with by the Bureau's staff and, where appropriate, referred to the court for the matter to be put before a judge. The normal period of jury service is two weeks. Where there are long trials, the period may be much longer, sometimes for several months, but the Bureau's summons gives no specific warning to recipients that they may be required to sit on a long case. Before the Bureau took over this task, each court was responsible for it, and some used to prepare for a long trial by enclosing a letter with the summons asking whether the recipient would be available for a longer period than normally required. However, it was feared that such enquiries tended to informal pre-selection of juries for such cases and, therefore, breached the principle of random selection. Under the new system such enquiries are conducted for the first time in court when the jury is being selected. The result of all this is that, when a long trial is scheduled to start, courts need a far larger pool of potential jurors available for the process of jury selection than are eventually

---

[260] *The Jury Project*, p 23

required for service. Some people may have to wait several days before being selected for any trial, short or long; some may not be selected at all, partly because of the necessary surplus but also because a significant number of defendants plead guilty on the day of trial resulting in fewer trials than expected. The result is costly to the courts, wasteful of jurors' and potential jurors' time and gives the system a bad name.

222   Although such uncertainties are an inevitable part of any criminal justice system, subject, as it is, to the human factor, more can be done to reduce their effect on potential jurors and juries. In my view, there is an urgent need to review the machinery, as between the Bureau and the courts, for summoning jurors who may be called upon, when attending at court, to serve on long cases. This will be particularly important if my recommendations are accepted for primacy to be given to deferral rather than excusal, for introducing a system in which potential jurors may proffer dates for their service within a set period and a move to fixed lists.[261]

223   There should also be an examination of ways and means of shortening, where possible, the present norm of two weeks' service and of lengthening the present two year cycle of entitlement to excusal from it. The New York Project is an example of what can be done. Its authors recorded that in 1994 many of the counties in the State had achieved jury terms of one week or less and that those who had served were disqualified from further service for four years except in certified 'juror shortage' counties. They recommended that the State should aim for a 'one trial or one day' system, under which jurors would be treated as having done their jury duty after only one day unless selected for a jury trial on that day, in which event they would complete it at the end of the trial. This scheme had been pioneered in Houston, Texas in about 1970. As the Project authors observed, it enables more people to serve with less inconvenience to themselves, produces fewer requests for postponement and makes it easier for courts to justify enforcement proceedings. However, I should add that it is not achievable everywhere, not even in New York State.

224   It is plain that a move towards such a system would involve major changes in the present practice of the Central Summoning Bureau and of the courts. The major change would be that courts would no longer have the security of the availability of a panel of jurors for two weeks, but would have to bespeak panels for shorter periods, which it is said would increase the numbers of those attending unnecessarily. The Court Service also points out that courts now make every effort to release potential jurors on days of their service when it is clear that they will not be needed, with instructions to telephone the court to check whether and when they are next required. Despite the

---

[261] as to the last, see Chapter 10,paras 237

complications for the Court Service of introducing a more flexible system than we now have, I believe the prizes it could bring in making better use of jurors' time, shortening the burden of their service, reducing the requests for deferrals and excusals and gaining their goodwill are worthy of consideration. In my view, the one day or one trial system or variations on it should be explored, and consideration given to testing it in local pilot projects.

I recommend :

- **urgent review of the machinery, as between the Central Summoning Bureau and the courts, for summoning jurors who may be called upon to serve on a long case;**

- **examination and piloting of options for shortening the length of jury service by introducing as an aim a 'one day or one trial' system or a variation of it; and**

- **consideration of lengthening the cycle over which it is possible to claim excusal by reason of previous jury service.**

Facilities

225   I know from my visits to Crown Court centres in the course of the Review, and earlier as Senior Presiding Judge, that the Court Service and its staff have made special efforts in recent years to improve the facilities for and working conditions of jurors. Court-buildings vary considerably in size, design and age and, for those reasons, there is often a practical limit to what can be done. There are a number of predictable priorities, for most of which there is reasonable provision throughout the country. Though in some of the older and more remote court-buildings they are seriously lacking. Those priorities include adequate eating and comfortable waiting facilities, readily accessible lavatories, provision for the disabled, a separate area for smokers, comfortable and roomy jury boxes, writing materials and a good even working temperature in the courtrooms. But the biggest and most urgent area for further improvement is in the provision of facilities to enable jurors in waiting to keep an eye on their own affairs and/or work, for example, quiet working areas, readily accessible and sufficient telephones, a fax machine, desks or carrels equipped with points for lap-top computers and e-mail, bleepers to enable them to leave the court-building to do necessary shopping and return at short notice when called.

I recommend that:

- **the Court Service should press on with its present programme to improve court facilities for jurors and**

jurors in waiting, including those who are disabled; and

- **as a matter of urgency, it should also institute a programme of provision at all courts of adequate working facilities and other means to enable jurors in waiting to conduct their own affairs.**

Compensation

226   Jurors are entitled to payment of compensation for financial loss, including loss of earnings and subsistence for the period of their service. The current levels of maximum compensation are £51.68 per day for the first 10 full court days and £103.39 per day thereafter, plus small sums of daily subsistence. This is less favourable than similar daily compensation throughout to employed and self-employed lay magistrates of £65.18 and £83.56 respectively. These maxima are relatively low and the payments may well not approach the full loss to a significant number of jurors or their employers, particularly on long trials. The present limits may also lead many potential jurors to claim excusal when they would not otherwise do so. For example, 20% of current excusals are to those - in the main, women - who care for young children or the elderly. In my view, there should be a general review of the allowances available to jurors with a view to securing adequate compensation for the losses they incur. I should add that, if implementation of this recommendation were to result in a significant increase in the daily amounts payable to jurors, it could be offset, at least in part, by achievable reductions in their waiting time at court.

> **I recommend:**
>
> - **a review of the amounts of allowances payable to jurors for their attendance at court; and**
>
> - **consideration of an additional allowance to cover the cost to potential jurors who, but for it, could justifiably claim excusal because of caring responsibilities.**

Appreciation

227   Most judges thank juries warmly at the end of a trial, mentioning the importance of the public duty they have performed and expressing appreciation of their hard work and patience etc. In some other jurisdictions, particularly in the USA, the courts express their appreciation in a more tangible and lasting way, for example, by providing them with certificates of

their service, mementoes of the court and letters of thanks signed by the trial judge. Some courts even arrange thank you parties. Whilst I do not suggest that we should go all the American way on this, a signed, albeit standard, letter from the trial judge would be a suitable and pleasing way of recording in more permanent form what may be a memorable and unique experience for many.

CHAPTER 6

THE JUDICIARY

INTRODUCTION

"A major cause of difficulty is the limited availability of High Court judge time, intensified by the inflexibility and inefficiency of the Assize system. As a result, continuous loading of the judges is given the first priority and time and convenience of other people concerned with the business of the courts is at a discount. We are faced with the highly unsatisfactory situation that, while judges are fully employed and even over-burdened, accused persons, litigants, witnesses, jurors, counsel, solicitors, prison officers, police officers and probation officers are kicking their heels in the corridors of the courts waiting for their cases to come on, and many return to do the same thing on more than one occasion."[1]

1   But for the reference to the Assize system, that lament in the Beeching Report over 30 years ago is typical of the many complaints about the operation of the criminal justice system today. One of the greatest ills of the system is its lack of flexibility in the matching of judges, courts and cases. This manifests itself in the over rigid divide between magistrates' courts and the Crown Court, in the types of cases that High Court Judges, Circuit Judges and Recorders can try in the Crown Court and as to where and when they can try them. The result in all three jurisdictions, crime, civil and family, can be injustice, delay, waste of public and private time and money, and a great deal of frustration all round. There are also difficulties in projecting workloads and how many judges of what level will be needed to deal with them. Under-estimation of both or either, failure because of Treasury constraints to budget sufficiently for either, or inability, because of undue rigidity in the appointments process, to time new appointments to meet workloads all add to the problem.

---

[1] *Report of the Royal Commission on Assizes and Quarter Sessions*, Cmnd 4153 (HMSO, 1969) para 67

2   At one time, a judge, like the jury, was expected to come to a case without any prior knowledge of the evidence to be adduced, or the legal points that were likely to arise. Nearly all the work that judges did, they did on the bench in court. Now, an increasing amount of their time is spent outside the courtroom in case management and preparing for each day's work in court. In addition, a considerable number of judges have increasingly important and onerous management responsibilities. The Resident Judge at each Crown Court centre takes over-all responsibility for the listing of cases, and for the supervision and co-ordination of disposal of business by both full- and part-time judges. Liaison Judges provide the current link between the judiciary in the Crown Court and the magistracy. At the apex of the system, the Presiding Judges have ultimate accountability for the judicial administration of their circuits, for providing judicial leadership, and for providing a link between the judiciary and the two branches of the legal profession.

3   As I have said in Chapter 4, I do not suggest any change in the division between the summary jurisdiction of magistrates and the jurisdiction of judges sitting in what is now the Crown Court. As to the division and overlap of criminal jurisdiction in the Crown Court, between High Court Judges on the one hand and Circuit Judges and Recorders on the other, I start by acknowledging the special position of High Court Judges and the need to retain it. The need for two levels of criminal and civil jurisdiction above the summary jurisdiction of magistrates has long been recognised. It is a common feature of civilised common law jurisdictions all over the world. It has the value of reserving to a small number of senior judges issues of law and fact of particular difficulty and matters of general public importance, including the protection of the liberty and the rights of the subject against the State.

4   However, in the exercise of criminal jurisdiction, there is a strong case for leaving more of the work now undertaken by High Court Judges to the Circuit Bench. Such a consideration necessarily requires an examination of the centuries' old tradition of High Court Judges 'going on circuit' - visiting on a regular basis the main court centres all over the country. I say straightaway that I am firmly of the view that the circuit system should continue, a view supported by the overwhelming majority of those who have made submissions about it in the Review. It is still a powerful symbol and practical means of bringing justice at the highest level to people all over the country - one form of 'locality' of justice. It is also a valuable means, through the mutual exchange of information and ideas between visiting High Court Judges and local judges of spreading best practice and encouraging national consistency in the administration of justice. As the Council of Circuit Judges have observed in their submission in the Review, it has advantages to both levels of judge. It keeps High Court Judges in touch with what is going on at 'the sharp end' of the criminal justice system. And, because High Court Judges trying crime sit, when in London, in the Court of Appeal (Criminal

Division), it keeps the Circuit Bench up to date with current developments and national good practice.

THE JUDICIAL HIERARCHY

A career judiciary?

5   We used to take pride, rightly or wrongly, in not having a career judiciary. Judicial appointment was and still is to a large extent regarded as an honourable culmination to a successful career as a practising barrister or solicitor. The transition from practitioner to judge was made at or about 50, often without any apprenticeship, other than that of a lifetime's experience as an advocate, or of any special training. Unlike most European civil law jurisdictions, ours was not a 'career judiciary', save for the occasional promotion from the county court Bench to the High Court and, of course from the High Court to the Court of Appeal and beyond.

6   Part-time appointments as Recorders of Quarter Sessions and, to a lesser extent as Chairmen or Deputy Chairmen of County Quarter Sessions, were a means for criminal practitioners who practised on circuit to get the feel of the job and to impress or otherwise as potential full-time judges. At a higher level, distinguished silks might be tried out once or twice as Commissioners of Assize before consideration for appointment to the High Court Bench. But none of those part-time appointments was a pre-condition of full-time appointment and there were relatively few of them.

7   The position changed with introduction of the Beeching reforms in the early 1970s. The comparatively few part-time Quarter Session appointments were transformed into many more Crown Court Recorderships. The new Recorders were committed to sit for only four weeks a year and the fledgling Judicial Studies Board began to provide some rudimentary training for them. As the flow of criminal justice legislation and the complexities and volume of the work increased, so did the training provided by the Board. And, by 1996, when open competition was introduced for all judicial offices below the High Court Bench, the Lord Chancellor's Department decided that, in the main, the only route to full-time appointment was via a number of years' successful sitting as a part-time judge, usually as a Recorder and sitting at least in part in crime.[2] Thus, high flying commercial practitioners - potential Lords of Appeal in Ordinary via the Queen's Bench and Court of Appeal - like

---

[2] not a statutory requirement, see Courts and Legal Services Act 1990, s 70

criminal and other civil practitioners all had to undergo this probationary period as part-time criminal judges in the Crown Court.

8   Over the same period, more and more work traditionally reserved to High Court Judges was 'released' to Circuit Judges and to a small number of senior Recorders through a system of general and special authorisations. Over the last five or six years, experienced Circuit Judges have also been invited to sit on a regular basis in the Court of Appeal (Criminal Division). These developments have led to greater movement than previously between the Circuit Bench and the High Court Bench. In the last ten years 16 stipendiary magistrates, now known as District Judges, have moved to the Circuit Bench, and 14 Circuit Judges have been promoted to the High Court Bench, one of whom was a former solicitor. So, gradually, some semblance of a career judiciary is emerging. Its further growth is still greatly constrained by the traditional route to it of a successful career as an advocate, but even that is now no longer a necessary pre-requisite of full-time appointment.

High Court Judges

9   High Court Judges, on appointment, must have had either a ten year right of audience in relation to all proceedings in the High Court, or to have been a Circuit Judge for at least two years.[3] There are now 106 High Court Judges, whose annual salary is £132,603. 71 are Queen's Bench Judges, of whom 12 sit in the Commercial List and 23 in the Administrative Court.[4] Most Queen's Bench Judges normally spend half of each law term on circuit and half in London.[5] On circuit they try serious crime and civil cases, but mostly crime. In London their time is split, usually between hearing appeals in the Court of Appeal (Criminal Division) and sitting in civil or administrative matters. There are 17 High Court Judges assigned to the Chancery Division. They sit mostly in London, but two of them also sit frequently on circuit.[6] The 17 High Court Judges assigned to the Family Division also sit mostly in London, but frequently go out on circuit for short periods as the work demands.

10   As one contributor to the Review has observed, proper use of Queen's Bench Judges is fundamental to the efficient working of the senior judiciary and of the various jurisdictions in which they sit.[7] They constitute about two-thirds of all High Court Judges and they play a crucial role in civil and public law proceedings as well as criminal matters. The Bowman Committee, which has

---

[3] Courts and Legal Services Act 1990, s 71
[4] until recently known as the Crown Office List
[5] those who sit in the Commercial List normally only go out on circuit for one half term a year
[6] Chancery Supervising Judges
[7] The Right Hon Lord Justice Keene

recently undertaken a review of administrative law work, envisages a substantial increase in it and, thus, an increase in the work of the Queen's Bench Judges sitting in the Administrative Court.[8] This is due largely to the ever increasing calls on its jurisdiction in judicial review, now given further impetus by the advent to our domestic law of Human Rights and recent changes to immigration and asylum law and practice. These developments are likely to require a greater focus of High Court Judges' time on matters of public and constitutional importance and less on some of the traditional work that they now share with Circuit Judges when sitting in crime. The High Court Bench is thus a job that requires and should attract appointees of the highest quality, a comparatively small number of judges at the apex of our hierarchy of trial judges, also exercising the vital jurisdiction of judicial review and participating in a major way in criminal appeals.

11   The question, therefore, is not whether significantly to increase the number of High Court Judges or to do away with the distinction between them and Circuit Judges. It is how better to allocate work between them in the interests of appropriate use of judicial resources, of providing an efficient and considerate service to all involved or interested in the criminal process and of attracting suitable candidates for all levels of appointment.

Circuit Judges

12   On appointment, Circuit Judges must have had a ten year right of audience in the Crown or county courts or to have been a Recorder, or to have held a full-time post, such as a member of an administrative tribunal or a District Judge.[9] There are now about 570 Circuit Judges, whose annual salary is £99,420. They are normally appointed to hear both criminal and civil cases, though some exercise specialist civil or criminal jurisdictions. They are supported by part-time judges, Recorders, each of whom normally sits for between three and six weeks a year, with a broadly similar jurisdiction to that of Circuit Judges but generally dealing with less complex and difficult matters. Both Circuit Judges and Recorders are assigned on appointment to one of the six circuits. They may exercise jurisdiction at any court centre in the country, but normally sit at one centre or in one group of courts on their assigned circuit. At each court centre one of the Circuit Judges is appointed by the Lord Chancellor to act as the Resident Judge, that is to undertake responsibility, under the oversight of the Presiding Judges, for management of the judicial work at the centre and as a point of liaison with the court manager. The appointments, which are for four years and may be renewed, carry no extra pay. In the largest centres, these responsibilities are undertaken by judges designated as Senior Circuit Judges, who are appointed under a different

[8] Sir Jeffrey Bowman, *Review of the Crown Office List* (LCD, 12 April 2000)
[9] Courts and Legal Services Act 1990, s 71

system and are paid more than a Circuit Judge, to reflect the considerable administrative and judicial burden that the posts involve.

13 As I have mentioned, the criminal jurisdiction of Circuit Judges has increased markedly since they emerged from their pre-Beeching Quarter Sessions origins, that they now try the bulk of all cases in the Crown Court (82% in 2000) ranging from murder to shop-lifting.[10] As I have also mentioned, some are authorised by the Lord Chancellor to sit in the Court of Appeal (Criminal Division) at the request of the Lord Chief Justice. Many also sit from time to time as Deputy High Court Judges in civil and/or family business.[11]

Recorders

14 England and Wales is almost unique in its extensive reliance on part-time judges, Recorders, in the exercise of criminal and civil jurisdiction in its higher courts. Practitioners are eligible for appointment as a Recorder if they have had a right of audience in the Crown or county courts for ten years or more. There are now nearly 1,400 of them and, in 2000 they dealt with 14% of trials in the Crown Court. For many years until recently, appointment was initially made as an Assistant Recorder for up to three years. At the end of that period, or earlier if the appointee was a Queen's Counsel, and if all went well, he could expect appointment as a full Recorder, again for three years and renewable thereafter every three years. In November 1999, the High Court of Justiciary in Scotland held that Scottish temporary sheriffs were insufficiently independent of the Executive for the purpose of Article 6 of the European Convention of Human Rights because of the insufficiency of their security of tenure.[12] As a result, the Lord Chancellor appointed all existing Assistant Recorders as Recorders and now makes all new appointments to a full Recordership. Appointment is through open competition, the initial period of appointment is normally for not less than five years and is normally renewable automatically. This is part of a general change in the terms of service of all part-time judicial office-holders in England and Wales.

15 On appointment, Recorders are entitled to a minimum of 15 days' sitting a year, and may sit up to a maximum of 30 days each year. If possible, at least ten days' sitting should be in one continuous period. Compliance with these requirements is important for two main reasons. First, if the probationary period as a Recorder is to give them the experience they need and to enable them to demonstrate their ability to cope with the work, they must sit for the minimum periods required and on a reasonably regular basis throughout the

---

[10] *Judicial Statistics Annual Report 2000* (LCD, Cm 5223)

[11] known as 'Section 9 Judges', after the provision made for them by section 9 of the Supreme Court Act 1981

[12] *Starrs & Chalmers v Procurator Fiscal, Linlithgow* [2000] HRLR 191

whole period of their appointment. Second, unless they commit themselves to continuous sittings of at least two weeks at a time, it is difficult to list work before them efficiently. Even two weeks makes for difficulties in listing, because in the second week even a short case of, say two or three days, cannot be started if there is a risk of not completing it by the end of the week.

16   Ideally, Recorders should commit themselves to a single period of three or more weeks' sitting and keep to it. But the demands of practice often drive them to offering two weeks or less and sometimes having to cancel at short notice. Also, Court Service budgetary constraints at local level have from time to time resulted in courts not being able to provide Recorders with sufficient sittings to enable them to meet their commitments. The result then is often a poor service both ways. If, as the Lord Chancellor intends, "Recordership is a potential step on the ladder to appointment to the Circuit Bench" and is intended to continue as an integral part of the criminal justice system, some changes need to be made. Now that the minimum sitting commitment is for only three weeks a year, I consider that it should be a condition of appointment and renewal that, save in exceptional circumstances and with the permission of a Presiding Judge, Recorders should meet their commitment in a single continuous sitting. Booking sittings well in advance and planning court commitments, including the fixing of trial dates with the booking in mind, should be the aim, even if not always achievable due to the uncertainties of listing. Equally, the Court Service should organise sittings for Recorders to enable them to meet their sitting commitments in this way. If, as I recommend in Chapter 7, the present dual system of courts is replaced by a unified Criminal Court with three Divisions, it may be that work could be found for Recorders in the middle District Division jurisdiction, as well as at the Crown Division level.

I recommend that:

- **it should be a condition of a Recorder's appointment to sit for a minimum of three weeks a year in one continuous block, unless for exceptional reasons a Presiding Judge permits him to sit in more than one block; and**

- **the Judicial Group in the Lord Chancellor's Department should, in consultation with the Presiding Judges, liaise closely with the Court Service to ensure that a minimum of three weeks' annual sitting is provided for each Recorder.**

District Judges

17   For convenience, I repeat briefly here some of the information that I gave about District Judges in Chapter 4 in the context of their exercise of magisterial jurisdiction. There are about 100 District Judges (Magistrates' Courts) who are paid about £80,000 per year from the Consolidated Fund; they are supported by about 150 Deputies, who sit part-time. District Judges are appointed by The Queen on the recommendation of the Lord Chancellor. They are full-time members of the judiciary and deal with a broad range of business that comes before the magistrates' courts, but in particular may be expected to hear the lengthier and more complex criminal matters coming before those courts. The qualification for appointment is to be a barrister or solicitor of at least seven years' standing. There are rather more solicitors than barristers, and about one quarter of District Judges were formerly justices' clerks. Although they have national jurisdiction, they are appointed to a particular MCC area.

Deputy District Judges

18   Finally, I should mention the 150 or so Deputy District Judges. Deputy District Judges are assigned to panels in MCC areas where there is a full-time District Judge. Although they are part-time members of the judiciary, they undertake the full range of business which normally falls to their full-time colleagues. In addition, a full-time District Judge will act as pupil master for each part-timer, periodically observing them in court and providing reports on their progress.

MATCHING JUDGES TO CASES[13]

Levels of jurisdiction in the Crown Court

19   There are effectively four levels of Crown Court judge and four classifications of offence according to their seriousness.[14] First, there are the High Court

---

[13] since District Judges have, at present, the same jurisdiction as panels of magistrates, I have dealt with this topic in their case in Chapter 4 rather than here

[14] *Practice Direction (Crown Court: Allocation of Business)* (No. 4), 12 February 2001

Judges who can deal with any case within the jurisdiction of the Crown Court, but who, in theory, try the most serious and difficult cases, for example, treason and murder (class 1) and manslaughter and rape (class 2). Second, there are 'ticketed' Circuit Judges. These are judges of experience who are variously authorised to try certain Class 1 and 2 cases, mainly murder and rape,[15] and also, by reason of its special difficulty and complexity, serious fraud (mainly class 3). Many Circuit Judges now have an authorisation of one or more sorts and the bulk of murders and rapes and other serious sexual offences are now tried by authorised 'murder' and 'rape' judges. Third, there are the Circuit Judges who, whether 'ticketed' or not, try the main range of work in classes 3 and 4, some of which, for example, drug trafficking, armed robberies and frauds of various sorts are of great seriousness and difficulty. Fourth, there are Recorders who, depending on their experience and ability, may try work of various levels of seriousness, including rape (class 2) and offences in classes 3[16] and 4, but usually the less serious and, because they only sit for a week or so at a time, the shorter cases.

'Ticketing'

20   There are a number of 'vertical' constraints on, and mechanisms for, matching judges to cases. As I have said, experienced Circuit Judges can be authorised, or 'ticketed', to deal with a range of cases normally reserved for High Court Judges. Thus, currently 26 out of about 570 Circuit Judges have been authorised by the Lord Chancellor to sit in the Court of Appeal (Criminal Division), if requested by the Lord Chief Justice to do so.[17] Each sits usually for one three week period a year in a constitution with a Lord Justice and a High Court Judge. About 50 Circuit Judges have been approved by the Lord Chief Justice to try murder cases specifically released to them by a Presiding Judge. There are about 25 Circuit Judges, not approved to try murder, but approved to try attempted murder, to whom the Presiding Judges may release specific cases. And, there are about 340 Circuit Judges who have been approved by the Senior Presiding Judge to try rape or other serious sexual offences if released to them by a Presiding Judge. On a more informal basis Resident Judges may be consulted by their listing officer about assigning certain types of case or cases to suitably experienced Circuit Judges or Recorders sitting at their court centres.

---

[15] it is now a pre-condition of a rape authorisation that the judge should attend two days' special training by the Judicial Studies Board. These courses are run twice a year, generally in July and November

[16] as a result of the recent abolition of the office of Assistant Recorder, Recorders may now only try cases in class 3 if they have attended a Judicial Studies Board Continuation Seminar, which is normally two or three years after their appointment, and if they have been authorised to do so by a Presiding Judge; see *Practice Direction (Crown Court: Allocation Of Business)* (No. 4), 12th February 2001

[17] Supreme Court Act 1981, s 9(1)

Circuit judge authorisations

Total number of circuit judges: 577
Judges with no ticket: 178
Figures accurate to November 2000

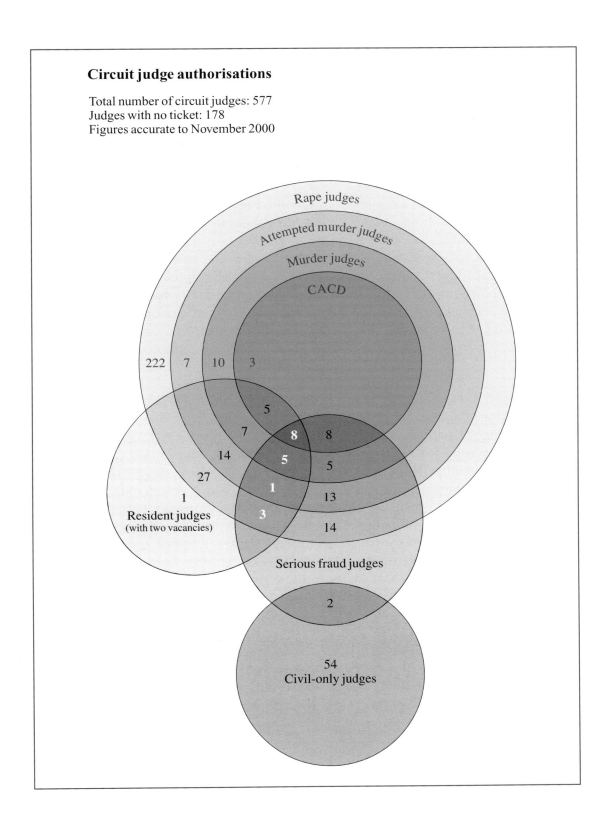

21 As this summary demonstrates, these processes variously involve the Lord Chancellor, the Lord Chief Justice, the Senior Presiding Judge, the Presiding Judges, the Resident Judge of each court centre and, of course, his listing officer who has to match his lists according to the availability of suitably authorised judges.

22 Below the level of authorisations to sit in the Court of Appeal the system has a number of serious defects. First, it is unduly bureaucratic and rigid. It is bureaucratic in the work required in compilation and maintenance of up to date lists nationally and for each court, and in the burden that it imposes on Resident Judges and Presiding Judges in its operation on a case by case basis. Its rigidity impedes efficient listing. In the constantly moving scene of last minute changes of plea and adjournments for one reason or other, listing officers are required, among all the other pressures on their time and decisions, to keep an eye on which judge is formally authorised to try what.

23 Second, the system is, in any event, a somewhat rough and ready means of marking aptitude for or experience in a particular field of work or in the handling of particular cases. At present, authorisations are given primarily, not as a badge or recognition or of advancement, but to relieve High Court Judges from having to try certain cases of a particular class or category where there are too many for them to try. Thus, there may be many Circuit Judges at court centres all over the county who are not authorised to try rape or other serious sexual offences or serious fraud, not because they are not up to it, but because their centres already have a sufficient number of authorisations and there is other work for them to do. Others may not want to try such work regularly, whatever their ability to do so, and thus do not seek it. And, over the years, the aptitude and application of judges to try work for which they have been particularly authorised may dull. Or, as was discovered a few years ago when the list of 'serious fraud' judges was reviewed, some, for one reason or another, may not have tried for years work for which they are authorised. For those reasons, I suggest that those who, like the Bar Council, suggest developing the system into a formal hierarchy and promotional ladder, perhaps reflected in differing salary scales, are mistaken.

24 Third, for the reasons given in the last paragraph, many individual Circuit Judges regard the system as invidious. Authorisations are awarded on the recommendation of the Presiding Judges, and I know that some Circuit Judges have concerns about how candidates are identified. This concern is heightened by the fact that, although they are encouraged to let their Presiding Judges know if they are interested in trying certain kinds of work, there is no formal system by which they can 'apply' for a ticket. Unless kept within reasonable limits, this system would, in my view, endanger the morale of the Circuit Bench as a whole. Certainly, the formalisation of a hierarchy would

increase the Circuit Judges' general dislike of it and engender more resentment among those whom it did not favour. Any sharpening and/or multiplication of distinctions would, in addition, aggravate the present bureaucracy of and inflexibility in the present system. And, to tie salary scales to a hierarchy of authorisations would be administratively complex and, when ability or application fades, difficult to adjust.

25   What is needed is less complexity and a more flexible system, coupled with a requirement of such judicial training as may be necessary as a pre-condition for undertaking particular categories of work. There should also be some form of regular and systematic appraisal, in which the Resident Judge, in periodic consultation with the Presiding Judges, could assume more responsibility for general and particular allocation of judges to cases at his court centre.

> **I recommend that:**
>
> - **most of the rigidities of the present 'ticketing' system should be removed and replaced by the conferment on Resident Judges wide responsibility, subject to general oversight of the Presiding Judges, for allocation of judicial work at their court centres, but coupled with:**
>
>   - **regular and systematic appraisal enabling Resident Judges and Presiding Judges to determine the experience and interests of the judges; and**
>
>   - **the undertaking by judges of such training by the Judicial Studies Board as may be required as a pre-condition for the trial of particular categories of work.**

Circuit Listing

26   There are also 'horizontal' constraints in the competing jurisdictions for judges' time and as to the courts in which certain offences may be tried.

27   First, there is always a tension between circuits and between circuits and London in their respective claims on High Court Judge time. In London, High Court Judges sit 'on circuit' at the Central Criminal Court. They also sit in civil matters in the Queen's Bench Division, including the Commercial List and in the Administrative Court, in criminal appeals in the Court of Appeal

(Criminal Division) and preside over tribunals. In the regular bidding process for High Court Judges the Vice-President of the Queen's Bench Division[18] has to assess the competing claims of circuits and of London, the aim always being to put the scarce resource of High Court Judges where they are most needed.

28   Second, there is tension in the demands of two or more jurisdictions to which the criminal listing officer must have regard when matching judges to his lists. Some Circuit Judges, depending on the court centre or group of courts in which they regularly sit, sit in crime for only part of the time. Many of them also sit in civil or family matters or both, each of which jurisdictions has its own scheme of 'ticketing'. For example, those who also exercise a family jurisdiction and are authorised to deal with public law care issues are often authorised and much in demand to try rape cases.

29   Third, territorial restrictions are inevitable, given the variety in sizes, facilities and levels of security of different court centres. A case with many defendants, or demanding an especially spacious and/or well equipped and/or secure court, has to be tried at a particular court centre that can provide for it.

30   Fourth, there are the troublesome restrictions that flow from the divide between High Court work and Circuit Judge work and their different working patterns. As I have said, High Court Judges 'go on circuit', that is they follow a pattern of visiting certain courts for short periods. Circuit Judges don't 'go on circuit'; they are assigned on appointment to one of the six circuits and work there, usually full-time in the same court or group of courts, and normally live nearby.

31   The legal year for High Court Judges runs from the beginning of October to the end of July, with, in addition, vacation courts sitting in London and on circuit over the Christmas, Easter and Summer breaks. For practical purposes, the formal legal year is split into three terms and, in turn, into six half-terms of about six weeks each.[19] Routinely, at any one time, about 40% of the Queen's Bench Judges who try crime are on circuit and the other 60% remain in London. Thus, most Queen's Bench Judges go out three times a year or, if they also do vacation duty on circuit, four times a year. At the half-term, those out on circuit return to London and those in London go out. The number of High Court Judges assigned to each circuit and the frequency and length of their visits to individual court centres depends on both the criminal and civil workload. But each circuit has a fairly regular pattern, which may be of a number of judges sitting at one busy centre for the whole six week period, or of one or more visiting a less busy centre for two to three weeks

---

[18] currently Lord Justice Kennedy

[19] technically, there are four terms, Autumn, Winter, Spring and Summer, but the last two run from Easter to the end of July

every other half term, or a single judge visiting up to three court-centres for about two weeks at a time. While on circuit, High Court Judges are accommodated in what are known as judges' lodgings, to which I return.[20]

32 A further constraint arises from the 'tiering' of court centres to classes of offences. Not only do cases have to be listed before the right level or suitably authorised judge, certain of them can only be tried in certain court centres. Thus, all class 1 and some class 2 cases (other than rape, sexual intercourse or incest with a girl under 13 or an inchoate offence under those categories, which can also be tried at third tier centres specified for the purpose by the Presiding Judges) must be tried at a court centre at which a High Court Judge regularly sits. This is usually restricted to those court centres where there are judges' lodgings. However, some lodgings serve two centres,[21] and Presiding Judges in certain instances arrange for judges to sit at court centres within about an hour's travel from lodgings. All other cases should be listed for trial at the most convenient location.

33 So, in the case of High Court Judges, the court listing officer's task of matching the right judge to the right case is the more difficult because, not only must he fit his listing of it into the pattern of circuiteering, he also has to list it early enough during the judge's six weeks' (or shorter) stay to ensure that he can finish it before he returns to London (or moves to another circuit centre). There are, of course, exceptions to these constraints in special cases, but the six weeks' strait-jacket is the norm. The result is to distort the system in a number of ways that are unjust and upsetting to defendants, witnesses, victims and others involved in the process, and costly and damaging to public confidence.

34 First, there are long delays in the listing of serious cases; it is not unusual for defendants in murder cases for trial by a High Court Judge to have to wait for over a year. These delays not only affect criminal cases, but heavy civil matters too. Because of the infrequency or shortness of a High Court Judge's visits, one or other party may be forced into an unsatisfactory settlement. Or the case may be moved, at great inconvenience to the parties, to another circuit centre or to London. Or they may be faced with a Deputy High Court Judge in a high profile or legally difficult case that they had been led to believe deserved 'a proper High Court Judge'. Or the matter may simply be adjourned at the last moment because the judge cannot reach it before he leaves, because of the priority he is required to give to his criminal list.

35 Second, because of the shortness of each High Court Judge's circuit visit, and in some centres because of its infrequency, it may not be possible to find work

---

[20] paras 60 - 64

[21] eg those for Newcastle and Teesside, Maidstone, Canterbury and Medway and St Albans and Luton

that is both 'heavy' enough to justify the visit and short enough for him to complete in the time. Complex and lengthy cases meriting trial by a High Court Judge, but which are likely to last, or are at risk of lasting, more than six weeks, cannot normally be put before him. Or his list may collapse at the last moment as a result of late changes of plea to guilty. He may be left with some 'proper', that is, unreleaseable High Court Judge work, but also with some cases which, though technically 'High Court Judge work' would otherwise have been released to suitably authorised Circuit Judges. He may also end up trying lesser and short cases in classes 3 and 4, normally triable by a Circuit Judge or Recorder, just to fill in some time. Meanwhile, the Resident Judge or another Circuit Judge may be sitting next door trying the really heavy and lengthy work that, but for the six week constraint, the Presiding Judges might otherwise have not released.

36   If there is some unexpected short break in a High Court Judge's list it is often good for him and for young local advocates to have some exposure to each other in 'run of the mill' cases. But where, for want of suitable work, he is diverted to lesser matters for any length of time, it is a waste of scarce judicial resources. Information provided by the Court Service in the course of the Review indicated that, taking an average for all six circuits over the year April 1999 to March 2000, over 25% of High Court Judge time sitting in crime was spent in hearing cases properly triable by Circuit Judges.

37   Third, there are the so-called judicial vacations, namely three weeks at Christmas, two weeks at Easter, one week at Whitsun and the two months of July and August in the summer. I say 'so-called' judicial vacations for a number of reasons. First, because these are High Court vacation periods, Circuit Judges do not enjoy the same formal breaks in their work; they are required to sit for a minimum of 210 days a year against the High Court Judges' commitment of 189 days a year. Second, there are sittings by High Court Judges on circuit and in the Court of Appeal in London throughout much of the vacation periods. Thus, although the end of each law term marks an administrative break point in the sense that judges stop sitting wherever they are, the break may be to take a holiday or it may be to undertake vacation duty elsewhere, say four weeks on circuit in September or two weeks in the Court of Appeal over Easter. Second, both High Court and Circuit Judges, who mostly sit in court five days a week, have only the early mornings before and evenings after court and weekends in which to prepare for cases, summings-up and to write reserved judgments. For High Court Judges in particular, the first few days, or sometimes weeks, of vacation are necessary judgment writing time; without it they would never catch up.

38   However, the main point in this context is the break at the end of the law term and the start of the vacation period, or vice versa, which interrupts the continuity of listing and the options open to a listing officer when trying to allocate cases, particularly to a High Court Judge. The Beeching Commission

recommended a progressive shortening of High Court Judges' summer vacation period of two months to something nearer a month, but to be achieved by a staggering of holidays rather than a reduction in holiday entitlement without recompense.[22] I consider that that recommendation should be looked at again, particularly with a view, formally as well as practically, to marking the end of a two months' shut-down of High Court Judge work in many Crown Court centres in the Summer.

39 I recognise that it is more difficult to list cases for trial over the vacation periods than it is in the conventional law terms. Even if judges and court staff are on duty, one or more of the parties or their representatives or witnesses may be unavailable because they have booked a holiday. It only needs one critical participant in a case to be away to hinder its listing for trial. Depending on the outcome of my recommendations below[23] for more sparing use of High Court Judges on circuit, it could lead to a modest increase over-all in circuit demands on them and possibly court staff. However, it seems to me that to curtail the summer legal vacation period to one month in August could help to speed the flow of work once September is recognised as a normal working month for all involved in the criminal process. I should note that, even in August, the Crown Court deals with about 70% of its usual monthly workload, and magistrates' courts, in the main, sit at the same rate as for the rest of the year. It would be a useful discipline in maintaining the momentum of case preparation and management. It would be more in line with the working patterns of most public and private sector organisations. And, it would help to correct a popular misconception about the present work pattern and load of the higher judiciary.

I recommend that:

- **consideration be given to reducing the formal legal vacation periods for High Court Judges sitting in the Crown Court, in particular, to confining the summer vacation to the month of August; and**

- **this should be achieved by greater staggering of the existing sitting commitments of the High Court Bench, not by increasing them.**

40 Fourth, the system for appointment of Circuit Judges is such that there may be long delays before vacancies are filled by judges suitably authorised to try work of the range undertaken by their predecessors. There is an annual cycle of appointments starting in April with a public advertisement, followed by short-listing for interviews, which take place between September and December. This is followed by the submission of names to the Lord

---

[22] Report of *Royal Commission on Assizes and Quarter Sessions* para 424

[23] paras 44 - 56

Chancellor at about the beginning of February and his personal approval and appointment later that month. This inflexible and lengthy regime can result in courts going for months without sufficient judges authorised to try rape and other serious sexual offences. This in turn can result in long delays, or diversion of the Resident Judge or other senior judges at the centre from other serious work, or transfer of cases to another and less convenient court. Whilst the Lord Chancellor's Department, in consultation with the Presiding Judges, does the best it can in its existing appointments process to anticipate further needs, there is a limit to which it can provide for the various and unexpected contingencies. A system that takes over a year from advertisement to appointment is far too long.

41   Sir Leonard Peach, in his recent *Scrutiny of the Appointments Processes of Judges and Queen's Counsel*, expressed concern about the length of the process and recommended that "consideration should be given to establishing a (very much more) swift procedure for assessing the merits of individual applications".[24] However, this was one of the few of his recommendations that the Lord Chancellor did not accept. He was of the view that, as appointments to most judicial posts are already made following a time-limited competition, he did not see how the process could be shortened appreciably.[25] Perhaps the Lord Chancellor's Department could, as a start, investigate how other senior professional or administrative appointments are made in the public sector and in large organisations in the private sector. I should add that the problem is not confined to new appointments requiring advertisement and open competition; it also affects informal, but critical appointments, for which the Lord Chancellor has personal responsibility, such as that of Resident Judge.

42   With all these obstacles to efficient matching of judges to cases, it is a tribute to them and to administrators of all levels that the Crown Court manages as well as it does in the despatch of its heavy work-load. In all of this, the listing officer is in the front-line. In many large metropolitan court centres he or she may have as many or more than 20 criminal and civil courts to keep occupied with High Court Judges, Circuit Judges and Recorders, - all with their different sitting patterns and some moving from crime to civil or family according to dictates of the work. In that constantly changing scene the listing officer is expected to have regard to the interests and/or availability of the parties, their representatives and others involved in each case, including, importantly, witnesses and victims. Apart from nerves of steel and sensitivity to a wide range of, often conflicting, interests, he needs the support and guidance of the Resident Judge. Most Resident Judges, who have a wide range of administrative responsibilities in addition to sitting full-time as judges, play a critical role in overseeing this daily challenge. Unfortunately,

---

[24] Lord Chancellor's Department, December 1999, recommendation 21

[25] *Judicial Appointments Annual Report 1999-2000* , Cmnd 4783, (LCD, October 2000), para 2.12

many now are also called upon to sit in other courts from time to time; and, as I have indicated, there may be long delays between the retirement of a Resident Judge and the appointment of his successor. Although the Presiding Judges may designate another judge who sits regularly at the centre to exercise the responsibility, lack of continuity in such general oversight is another impediment to the efficient allocation of judicial resources and listing of work.

43 There are similar problems of delays in replacing a judge at a court centre who has retired or moved elsewhere, with another similarly authorised to do certain classes of work. For example, in the case of a vacancy for a judge to try rape or other serious sexual offences, this may necessitate a wait of several months for the next Judicial Studies Board serious sexual offences training course, attendance at which is a pre-requisite of authorisation to try such work. The Judicial Appointments Group are alive to these problems and have begun to consult the circuits more closely on their judicial needs; however, it is hampered by the ponderous and rigid appointments cycle to which I have referred. If my recommendations below for a more flexible system of allocation of work are adopted, it may be that the vacancy problem could become less acute, but something needs to be done to speed up the appointments system and make it more flexible.

> **I recommend that:**
>
> - **the systems of appointment and assignment of judges should be reviewed with a view to achieving a more efficient system than now obtains to ensure a planned and prompt succession of Resident Judges and appropriately experienced judges at court centres and that, for this purpose, the Presiding Judges, Resident Judges, and Circuit Administrators should be consulted regularly; and**
>
> - **the Lord Chancellor's Department should agree targets with the Presiding Judges within which vacancies for Resident, Circuit and District Judges (Magistrates' Courts) should be filled, after it has received notification of a projected or actual vacancy.**

BETTER MATCHING OF JUDGES TO CASES

44 One suggestion is that High Court Judges, like Circuit Judges, should sit permanently or for a period of several years on circuit, say two or three of them assigned to one or more of the major circuit towns. Given the predominance of criminal work at major court centres outside London, this is

close to a suggestion that only those with considerable experience of criminal work should sit as High Court Judges in crime. Whilst criminal law and procedure are now highly technical, and experience of them of a considerable advantage to a new judge on circuit, most of the contributors to the Review who have considered the suggestion are against it; and so am I. Under the present system, even the most rarefied commercial practitioner will usually have had some years of experience of sitting in crime as a Recorder before full-time appointment. It would create a two tier system of Queen's Bench Judges: those sitting and trying mainly crime on circuit and those dealing with the whole range of High Court work, criminal and civil, including, the commercial list, judicial review, and appellate work, in London. In that respect it would be out of key with the pattern of work for some Chancery, and all Family, High Court Judges who sit both on circuit and in London. It would discourage many of the highest quality candidates from applying for appointment to the Queen's Bench Division, not only because of the permanent location and limited nature of the work, but also because it could require them to uproot their home and family either at the beginning or end of their tenure or both. It would deprive both the High Court Bench and the Circuit Bench of the exchange of information and ideas, so important an aid to maintaining high standards and consistency in the administration of the system as a whole.[26] And it would blur the distinction between the High Court and Circuit Benches.

45   Another and similar proposal is to build on the present system in which the Queen's Bench Judges who sit in the commercial list go on circuit only once a year instead of three times like all the others. Under this proposal, potential appointees would be sounded out as to whether they preferred circuit work - mostly crime - or the wider range of criminal and civil work in London. If the former, they would be allocated to a list of judges who would spend most of their time on circuit; if the latter, they would spend all or most of their time in London concentrating on their own speciality or doing the wide range of High Court Judge work available there. Whilst this might go some way towards relaxing some of the present constraints on listing, the improvement would be minimal because it would not increase the availability of High Court Judges on circuit; there would simply be fewer, visiting court centres more often. It would also suffer from most of the same evils as the last suggestion, namely: the creation of a two tier system of High Court Judges; it would narrow the mutual exchange of information between the High Court Bench and Circuit Bench countrywide, since the circuiteering High Court Judges' main experience would be provincial; and, again it would blur the distinction between the circuiteering High Court Judges and Circuit Judges.

---

[26] a feature of the system warmly supported by the Beeching Commission; see Report of *Royal Commission on Assizes and Quarter Sessions*, paras 69, 104 and 152

46   A third suggestion is that High Court Judge visits, as part of a regular circuit pattern, should be concentrated on fewer and larger court centres, in the main those requiring two or more High Court Judges sitting at a time. There would be undoubted advantages in the greater efficiency resulting from flexibility of listing that such concentration of judges and work suitable for them would provide. However, even at major centres at which three or four High Court Judges regularly sit under the present circuit regime, there is much waste or inappropriate use of High Court Judge time resulting from late changes in the list for various good or bad reasons, aggravated often by the constraints imposed on their deployment by the rigidity of their six week sitting pattern. And any gain in the efficiency of use of High Court Judges resulting from their concentration at a few major centres would be off-set by the loss of 'locality' of the justice they provide and the inconvenience and expense to all others involved in cases brought in from a long distance. After all, the whole point of the circuit system in its inception and in its continuance is to bring justice at the highest level to where it is needed.

47   A fourth solution, sometimes suggested in conjunction with the last, is to move away from the present regime of sending judges out for blocks of six weeks at a time to try cases that, often, but for their presence, local Circuit Judges could and would try. Under this proposal, High Court Judges would go out on circuit only to try those cases that really demand their attention and, in the main, only for so long as it takes to deal with them. The pattern of working of the judges of the Family Division of the High Court provides a model, as does the allocation of High Court Judges for the trial of specific cases at the Central Criminal Court.

48   Family Division Judges work at the apex of a three tier system of family justice, the High Court, the county court and magistrates' courts. They deal only with the most serious and sensitive cases. For each circuit one of them acts as the Family Division Liaison Judge, a role approximating in the family jurisdiction to that of the Presiding Judges for criminal and civil work. Like the Queen's Bench judges they go on circuit from London. In some instances they go for fixed periods, usually for three or four weeks at a time, to the larger court centres, and in others they leave London only for cases which merit their attention and which are allocated to them by the Liaison Judge. Then they return to sit in the Family Division in London. They too stay in judges' lodgings when on circuit, but usually for much shorter periods than the Queen's Bench Division judges.

49   Prior to the Beeching reforms, the Central Criminal Court - the Old Bailey - was in effect the Assize Court for criminal cases for the Greater London area and the Quarter Sessions for the City of London.[27] Now, it is one of the

---

[27] Report of *Royal Commission on Assizes and Quarter Sessions*, para 39

Crown Court centres for Greater London. It is headed by two judges appointed by the Queen, following a joint recruitment exercise by the Corporation of London and the Lord Chancellor's Department, namely the Recorder of London and the Common Serjeant, who have the status of Senior Circuit Judges. They are supported by an additional 13 Senior Circuit Judges. All the Old Bailey judges are authorised to try murder, undertaking much work that outside London would be reserved to High Court Judges. Even so, as I have said, High Court Judges 'go on circuit' to the court, usually two or three at a time, to try the most serious cases by its standards.[28]

50   The loosening of the system of 'ticketing' that I have recommended would allow a formal and significant shift in the balance of heavy circuit work from High Court Judges to the more experienced Circuit Judges all over the country. It could follow a similar pattern to that established at the Central Criminal Court, though not necessarily involving any or any significant increase countrywide in the number of designated Senior Circuit Judges.

51   In my view, we should face reality by treating all the work within the jurisdiction of the Crown Court as triable by Circuit Judges unless, on referral to the Presiding Judges, they specifically reserve it for trial by a High Court Judge. It should be the responsibility of the listing officer to draw to the attention of the Resident Judge any case which, in accordance with criteria set by the Lord Chief Justice, may be appropriate for reservation to a High Court Judge. For this purpose, the listing officer should prepare a short assessment, enclosing where available a prosecution summary of the case, for the Resident Judge's consideration. If the Resident Judge agrees, it would then be for him to send the assessment and summary with any comments of his own to one of the Presiding Judges for his decision.[29]

52   Consideration would have to be given to the overriding criterion for reservation. It could be something like "where the case is one of special complexity and/or seriousness and/or public importance requiring trial by a High Court Judge", and include factors of the sort already listed in the Lord Chief Justice's current practice direction.[30] Such a criterion and factors would not apply to many murder or rape cases that many experienced Circuit Judges are competent to try, but which presently require the Presiding Judges to release on a case by case basis. Conversely, they could apply to certain serious and high profile armed robberies and large scale drugs distribution cases, to which Presiding Judges might not now normally be required to give separate consideration because they are class 3 cases.

---

[28] the South Eastern Circuit Presiding Judges have recently asked the London Crown Court Listing Co-ordinator to review the deployment of High Court Judges in London

[29] this is already a common-place procedure at many large court centres for consolidation of 'High Court Judge cases' for release to the Circuit Bench

[30] see paras 19 – 25 and footnote 15 above

53 Similarly, I consider that the formal 'tiering' of Crown Court centres should go, especially if, as I recommend in Chapter 7, many 'either-way' cases presently tried in the Crown Court would go to the District Division and all cases triable only on indictment would start in the Crown Division of a unified Criminal Court. The Presiding Judges, in consultation with their Circuit Administrators, should be able to decide who sits where and for what case or cases. Subject to the physical constraints and convenience of location of different courts, if a case needs a particular judge, then he will either move to it or it to him, according to the circumstances.

54 In my view also, the present termly regime of six weeks on circuit and six weeks in London should end. Save in the case of the Presiding Judges, the present regular pattern of circuiteering by High Court Judges should be replaced by one under which the Presiding Judges decide, in consultation with their Circuit Administrators, where and when cases specifically reserved to High Court Judges should be tried. It would mean that particularly serious and high profile cases likely to run for six weeks or more could be put before them more readily than the present system permits, and that they could tailor their visits for shorter cases, whether effective as trials or pleas of guilty. The only exception should be that the Presiding Judges, each of whom holds office for four years, should continue their regular pattern of visiting and sitting at the major court centres on their respective Circuits. That would have two main benefits. First it would counter parochialism and enable them to continue their valuable circuit administrative and 'pastoral' responsibilities, as envisaged by the Beeching Commission in recommending their creation:

> "We propose that they shall, alternately, spend substantial periods in their Circuit so that they may, between them, provide the continuous presence of a judge knowledgeable about the affairs of the Circuit and about the Circuit judges serving there. They will be responsible for a general oversight of the administration and, in particular, for the location and well-being of the judges in the Circuit".[31]

55 Second, they would from time to time deal with the less serious cases as the vagaries of the list dictate, thus ensuring what one contributor to the Review[32] has well described as cross-pollination of the circuits with good practice as it develops at the heart of the administration of justice in London. They would also continue the valuable mutual exchange of information and ideas with the local judiciary, Bar and solicitors which is so valuable a part of the present system.

---

[31] Report of *Royal Commission on Assizes and Quarter Sessions*, para 176(f); see also paras 256-265, especially 265
[32] The Hon Mr Justice David Steel

56   Apart from making proper use of High Court Judges on circuit and increasing their general availability in London, such a scheme would secure a better match of judge to case, would make the system more flexible and provide a better service to all involved in it. And, as an important by-product, it would do much to encourage high quality candidates for the High Court Bench who, presently, might be discouraged from accepting appointment by the prospect of spending half their working year away from home on circuit. Most potential appointees are now in their late 40s or early 50s, many have a spouse who has her or his own career, some still have a young family. The days are gone when aged judges shut up their home and proceeded on circuit with their wives for the duration.

I recommend that:

- **there should be a formal and significant shift in the balance of heavy circuit work from High Court Judges to the more experienced Circuit Judges, coupled with greater flexibility in the system of allocating work between them, along the following lines:**

  - **all work within the jurisdiction of the Crown Court should be triable by a Circuit Judge unless, on referral to a Presiding Judge, he specially reserves it for trial by a High Court Judge;**

  - **the listing officer should draw to the attention of the Resident Judge any case which, in accordance with criteria set by the Lord Chief Justice may be appropriate for reservation to a High Court Judge, for the Resident Judge, if he agrees, to refer it to one of the Presiding Judges for his decision; and**

  - **the overriding criterion for reservation for trial by a High Court Judge should be whether "the case is one of special complexity and/or seriousness and/or public importance requiring trial by a High Court Judge";**

- **the formal 'tiering' of court centres for the trial of certain classes of cases should be abolished and replaced by a more flexible system, overseen by the Presiding Judges, for the assignment of cases, adapted to the needs of each circuit and the work, and having regard to the physical constraints and convenience of location of different courts; and**

- **save for the Presiding Judges, the present regular pattern of circuiteering by High Court Judges should be replaced by one under which the Presiding Judges decide, in consultation with their Circuit**

Administrators, where and when cases specifically reserved to High Court Judges should be tried.

JUDICIAL ADMINISTRATION

57 A common feature of the working life of the High Court and Circuit Benches has been a dramatic increase in the volume and complexity of their judicial work and in their involvement in the administration of the courts in which they sit and/or for which they are responsible. This has been accompanied by an increasing awareness of the importance of the role of judges in case management if the system is to work justly and efficiently. In the civil jurisdiction this change of judicial culture, including recognition of work done outside, as well as in, court and of their need for more administrative support, now has the formal imprimatur of Lord Woolf's reforms and is bearing fruit. In the criminal jurisdiction it has taken the form of years of national refinement, with local variants of plea and directions hearings, but generally with insufficient time for judicial preparation and patchy administrative assistance. If the recommendations that I make in this Chapter as to judicial deployment and in Chapter 10 as to preparation for trial are accepted, these out of court responsibilities will increase.

58 Notwithstanding these developments and the reasons for them, there is still a public perception, so well described by the Beeching Royal Commission in the passage from its Report at the head of this Chapter, that courts' working patterns are for the benefit of the judges. And, until recently, the Court Service, long after judges and most others involved in the work of the courts had realised its absurdity, clung to the notion that efficiency equals keeping the judge busy in court all day every day whatever the cost to others. The Court Service and the Treasury have now begun to acknowledge that what may be cost-efficient for the Court Service may not be efficient for the criminal justice system as a whole or to all those who are exposed to its workings. I refer to this question more generally in Chapter 8. I mention it here in the context of Circuit Judges, and in particular, Resident Judges. Despite the increasing complexity of their judicial work and the case management demands made on all of them, little concession is made to the time they need out of court to prepare efficiently for what they do in court. In the case of Resident Judges, who undertake considerable and time-taking administrative responsibilities for no extra pay and, often, with little or no adequate secretarial support, the hindrance to the effective discharge of their daily judicial work and court-wide administrative responsibilities is more serious.

59 I hope and believe that change may be on the way. My proposals should ultimately offer more flexibility in listing cases, and should make available

more time for judges' preparatory and administrative work, but they will also increase their work. There is no reason, for example, why a judge, whose murder trial 'goes short' or collapses on its first day, should not spend time preparing future cases or in dealing with outstanding administration, rather than trying a number of much less serious matters simply to keep him on the bench. The Court Service should, in my view, be more open to opportunities such as this and, in any event, ensure that judges are given adequate time to prepare and manage cases assigned to them, and for Resident Judges to undertake their wider administrative responsibilities. The latter should also be given adequate secretarial or administrative support for the purpose.

I recommend that adequate time should be given to:

- **judges to enable them to manage and prepare cases assigned to them;**

- **judges with additional administrative responsibilities to enable them to fulfil those responsibilities; and**

- **in each case to make suitable provision in secretarial, administrative or clerical help, as may be appropriate, to meet those needs.**

JUDGES' LODGINGS

60   Judges' lodgings are a frequent butt of media and other criticism, which depicts them as the provision of lavish living for judges at the taxpayers' expense. They come in all shapes and sizes, though most are houses of substance that need staff to run them. The Lord Chancellor's Department owns some, rents some and also at court centres that High Court Judges visit infrequently and, for short periods, hires some. In some instances they may be more expensive than suitable hotel accommodation, in others less so, depending on the extent of their use and the particular financial arrangements for each lodging. Their advantages to the system as a whole is that they provide a home and working environment for judges and their clerks who are presently required to spend half their working life away from home. They also provide necessary privacy and security for them and their, often, highly sensitive working papers. The Court Service has recently conducted a study of judges' lodgings and, in November 2000, reported on it to the Lord Chancellor. The report has not yet been made public.

61   The comfort and privacy of lodgings are regarded by some as the quid pro quo of requiring High Court Judges to commit themselves regularly to stretches of six weeks or more away from home. But if the commitment were for less frequent and, often, shorter circuit visits, then, depending on the nature of the case(s) to be tried and the length of stay, I believe that many

High Court Judges sitting outside the major court centres would be content with a good hotel. It would mean that on such, mainly short, visits the judge would not have the benefit of lodgings for fostering and maintaining professional and social links with the community. These links consist, in the main, of the High Sheriff, Circuit Judges, the local bar and solicitors and others involved in the work of the courts. However, as is already the case, the Presiding Judges, who each visit their circuit three times a year, would stay mostly in lodgings at the major court centres and continue to encourage these valuable links there and elsewhere on the circuit. In addition, they and other visiting High Court Judges would continue the present almost universal practice of lunching each day with the Circuit Judges at court, thus ensuring the continuance of mutual exchange of views and experience so important a feature of the circuit system.

62   However, there are other considerations. Whilst the traditional pattern of circuiteering may have had its day, the flexible arrangements that I propose would result in High Court Judges trying more lengthy major cases than is now the case. Also, there are developments that may perpetuate or even increase the need for suitable judicial accommodation in some of the main provincial court centres. As I have mentioned, civil litigants on circuit are poorly served by the High Court Bench, their cases often not listed or put out of the list at a late stage because of the priority given to the criminal list. The removal of inappropriate criminal work from High Court Judges' lists may enable them to give greater attention to their civil responsibilities. And, from time to time, the Court of Appeal both in its Criminal and Civil Divisions now sits outside London, as do judges of the Administrative Court, particularly in Wales and on the Northern and North Eastern Circuits. Some Chancery judges, like Family judges, also go on circuit, as the work demands. The provincial exercise of all such jurisdictions could and should increase as a further manifestation of local justice. This not only takes proper account of the convenience of all concerned in the matters before the court. It may often be cheaper to the system as a whole where the costs of bringing batches of cases to London would exceed the costs of taking judges to the cases.

63   Security is sometimes relied on as an obstacle to substituting a hotel for lodgings. But modern hotels can provide adequate security if required. Advocates and businessmen use hotels even when engaged in sensitive cases and negotiations. And High Court Judges on circuit in Northern Ireland and Scotland and throughout the Commonwealth seem to manage well enough with hotels. As to expense, in larger court centres where lodgings accommodate more than one judge for any length of time, putting them up in hotels would no doubt be more expensive. But there would be beneficial savings in some of the smaller centres where lodgings are used only infrequently and for short periods.

64 It is important that the future of judges' lodgings should not dominate the debate about the future of the circuit system; their future use, and the extent of it, should be determined by it. If my recommendation for confining High Court Judges to trying the gravest criminal offences, whether long or short, on circuit is accepted, there should be an assessment of its likely effect on the existing distribution of work and corresponding need for accommodation on each circuit, whether in the form of judges' lodgings or otherwise. Such assessment should also take into account the likely demands of the circuits for judges of the Chancery and Family Divisions and the development of an intermittent provincial appellate and administrative law jurisdiction to which I have referred.

I recommend that:

- **future use of judges' lodgings should depend on the future volume and pattern of distribution of High Court Judge work on each circuit, not the other way round;**

- **in assessing the future volume and pattern of circuit High Court Judge work, allowance should also be made for present and projected needs of civil and family work and the development of intermittent provincial administrative law and appellate jurisdictions;**

- **if my recommendations are adopted for confining High Court Judge work on circuit to the gravest cases and for greater flexibility as to where and when they should be tried:**

  - **lodgings that are reasonable value for money, taking into account among other things their convenience to major court centres and the number of judges they normally accommodate and for how long, should be retained or obtained; and**

  - **in other cases consideration should be given to suitable alternative accommodation appropriate to length of sitting and type of case[s], for example, hotels, guest houses of the Wolsey Lodge variety and rented and serviced accommodation.**

COMPOSITION OF THE JUDICIARY

Introduction

65   I have considered the systems for and appointment of magistrates and selection of jurors because they (the systems) go to their quality as decision-makers. The professional judiciary come to appointment as trained and experienced barristers or solicitors, mostly with a solid background of work in the courts. There have for a long time been clearer direction and purpose in the arrangements for their appointment than for the selection of their lay counterparts. And Sir Leonard Peach, at the request of the Lord Chancellor, has recently reviewed and reported on the procedures for making judicial appointments.[33] His valuable recommendations for reform are in the course of implementation and, with the exception of a few untied ends, there is not much that I can usefully add to them.

66   The primary criterion for appointment of professional judges is merit. Nevertheless, it is clearly desirable that all sections of society should feel that they have a stake in the administration of justice whether through lay or professional judges. Some contributors to the Review have alleged incompetence and/or unfairness on the part of individual judges or levels of judiciary, or in relation to their ability to try particular types of work. However, the overwhelming impression I have from those who have made submissions or participated in seminars and discussions around the country is of reasonable satisfaction with the quality of the professional judiciary, but of concern that it does not sufficiently reflect the diverse elements of our society. The complaint that it is largely white, male, middle-class and middle aged is borne out by the figures. Taking the span from Lords of Appeal in Ordinary to Deputy District Judges, about 98% are white, about 87% are male[34] and I have no doubt that they are mostly middle-class and middle-aged.

67   There are a number of fairly obvious reasons for this imbalance, as Sir Leonard's and other recent reports[35] have demonstrated. The criteria for

---

[33] *An Independent Scrutiny of the Appointment Processes of Judges and Queen's Counsel in England and Wales*, (LCD, December 1999)

[34] see *Judicial Appointments Annual Report for 1999-2000*, Cm 4783, (The Stationery Office, 2000), p 88

[35] notably a *Report of a Joint Working Party on Equal Opportunities in Judicial Appointments and Silk* submitted to the Lord Chancellor in September 1999. The Working Party consisted of the Bar Council, the Law Society, the African, Caribbean and Asian Lawyers' Group, The Society of Asian Lawyers, the Society of Black Lawyers, the Association of Women Barristers and the Association of Women Solicitors

appointment are predicated on the (historically correct) assumption that the appointees are the most well-known and well regarded of professional advocates. Consequently, solicitors are, inevitably, less visibly qualified. This is coupled with difficulties in meeting the Lord Chancellor's requirement of initial service as a part-time judge, and a perception on the part of some that the appointments process operates unfairly. Even within the Bar, women and ethnic minorities have difficulties establishing a professional profile of the sort ensuring recognition of achievement enabling them to qualify for appointment. There is a consequent disinclination to apply for it, thereby leading to an even more diminished pool of qualified candidates. The Lord Chancellor's response to those reports, accepting all or most of their recommendations, shows that he is alive to the problems, not least the composition of the professions from which judges are drawn, and to the urgency of doing something about them. An account of his plans and progress can be seen in his Department's Annual Report on Judicial Appointments for 1999-2000.[36]

Appointment to judicial office

68 I should give a brief account about the general principles and mechanics of selection for appointment and refer to Sir Leonard Peach's main recommendations for change, some of which have already been implemented and others are in the process of it. As I have said, there are also some untied ends with which I should deal. The first is the continuing relatively low representation of women, members of ethnic minority communities and solicitors. The second is the weight presently given to the performance in a short interview of candidates for judicial appointments and in respect of whom a wealth of other information is available. The third is the failure sufficiently to tailor appointments to needs, to which I have in part already referred.[37]

69 The Lord Chancellor has a pivotal role in the appointment of all professional and part-time judiciary in England and Wales. His general principles for professional appointments are that: he makes them strictly on merit, regardless of the gender, ethnic origin, professional and other diversities of those he considers for appointment; he does not regard experience of advocacy as an essential requirement for appointment; he normally regards part-time service as a pre-condition of full-time appointment; and he gives significant weight to the views of the professional legal community as to suitability for appointment. As to mechanics, there have been a large number of changes over the last few years and, as a result of Sir Leonard's Report, more are now being made.

---

[36] at pp 18 - 25
[37] paras 40 - 43 above

70   An anomaly in the obligation to sit part-time as a pre-condition for consideration for a full-time post is that part-time judicial appointments are, at least in relation to crime, available only to those in private practice or who are employed in the private sector. The policy of successive Lord Chancellors has been that it is not appropriate for those who are employed by central government to exercise judicial functions in cases to which the State itself is a party. This policy was considered by Sir Iain Glidewell who recommended reconsideration, not least because it denied the possibility of judicial appointment to employees of the Crown Prosecution Service.[38] The Joint Working Party on Equal Opportunities in Judicial Appointments and Silk also recommended "that the ban on the appointment of lawyers serving in the Government Legal Service and Crown Prosecution Service should be removed".[39]

71   There are clearly issues of perception to be considered here (as Sir Iain Glidewell noted), together with the requirement for criminal trials to be conducted by an independent and impartial tribunal required by Article 6 of the European Convention of Human Rights. Movement between the professions of prosecutor and judge is, however, a feature of a number of continental jurisdictions.[40] And staff from the office of the DPP of Northern Ireland have been appointed direct to the Bench within our own jurisdiction. And nowadays, much as some may regret it, many criminal practitioners, both barristers and solicitors, specialise either in prosecution or defence work and are nevertheless considered eligible for part-time judicial appointments, I see no reason why Crown Prosecution Service and other prosecuting authorities employees should not be treated in the same way.

72   As to the most senior appointments, namely the Law Lords, the Lord Chief Justice and other Heads of Division and the Lords Justices of Appeal, the Lord Chancellor advises the Prime Minister, who is responsible for making recommendations to the Queen. As to High Court Judges, Circuit Judges, Recorders and District Judges, the Queen appoints on the Lord Chancellor's recommendation.

73   In the case of High Court Judges the Lord Chancellor has recently begun to advertise the appointments, though he has reserved the right to approach persons who have not applied in response to the advertisements. As Sir Leonard Peach has noted, it is argued that, as "at this level … the candidates are well known with proven records, there are no interviews".[41] The Lord Chancellor decides whom to appoint after taking into account the record of

---

[38] *The Review of the Crown Prosecution Service* Cm3960 (HMSO, June 1998) p 179

[39] *Report of the Joint Working Party on Equal Opportunities in Judicial Appointments and Silk*, recommendation 5

[40] Italy and Germany, for example

[41] the Peach Report p 11

general consultations - soundings - on each candidate over the years and the views, given in a meeting, of the Lord Chief Justice and other Heads of Division, the Senior Presiding Judge, the Vice-President of the Queen's Bench Division and the Vice-President of the Court of Appeal (Criminal Division).

74   In the case of Circuit Judges and Recorders, the Lord Chancellor makes the appointment through a system of annual open competitions based on projections of requirements for the following year and his published criteria for appointment. As to Circuit Judges he at present normally considers applications from Recorders of at least two years' standing who are aged between 45 and 60 or from District Judges of three years' standing. As to applicants for Recordership, they are normally expected to be in active practice or already hold another full-time judicial office; and appointment is for at least five years and, subject to age limits, normally automatically renewable at the end of that period.

75   In the case of Senior Circuit Judges, Circuit Judges, Recorders and District Judges appointments, the Lord Chancellor invites applications for appointment by advertisement. For all of those categories, - a panel, consisting of a senior member of the Lord Chancellor's Department (who acts as chairman), a judge of an appropriate level or a Recorder of some seniority and a lay member, [42] short-lists applicants for interview after taking account of: the information provided by them; a record of assessments of the candidate in extensive and systematic annual consultations over many years of judges and others of standing who know his or her worth - described by critics of the system as 'secret soundings'; views of any consultees nominated by the candidate as familiar with his or her work; and the views of the Presiding Judges. Interviews, usually lasting about three quarters of an hour, are conducted by a similarly constituted panel. On the strength of their assessment of each candidate based on all the material available at the short-listing stage, his or her performance in interview and any further views of the Presiding Judges, the panel presents the Lord Chancellor with a list of those whom, in order of priority, it considers as 'highly suitable' or 'suitable' for appointment. Because each of the appointments to be made results from a separate competition and because of the difficulty in making accurate predictions of the judicial manpower required, some of those considered suitable for appointment may be put on a 'reserve list' for possible appointment should a vacancy occur within the ensuing year. If no such unexpected vacancy occurs within the year, those on the reserve list must re-apply in the next annual competition. [43]

---

[42] currently selected from membership of the local Advisory Committee responsible for recommending appointments to the magistracy; though the Lord Chancellor has been considering other additional sources

76   Resident Judges, who, as I have said, are responsible for management of the judicial work at the Crown Court Centre for which there is no Senior Circuit Judge appointment, are appointed under a different regime. The Lord Chancellor appoints them for an initial period of four years on the recommendation of the Senior Presiding Judge and Presiding Judges of the circuit. He may and does renew such appointments, usually only once unless there are exceptional circumstances. When a vacancy arises, all the Circuit Judges on the circuit are invited to consider applying for it.

77   Sir Leonard Peach, in a letter submitting his report, said:

> "… My overall impression of the Department's work is one of thoroughness, competence and professionalism. It has embraced the many changes of process introduced in recent years and demonstrates a willingness and enthusiasm to pursue further improvements. My assessment is that the procedures and their execution are as good as any which I have seen in the Public Sector".

He included in this tribute the system of annual consultations, the continuance of which he recommended. As he rightly recognised, they are of great value in identifying a broad consensus over a period of time on the suitability of a candidate for judicial appointment. The Lord Chancellor's Department, in its Annual Report on Judicial Appointments for 1999-2000, also rightly challenged the description of the system as one of 'secret soundings':

> "… the consultation system is not one of soundings nor is it secret. The consultations are extensive and systematic. Candidates are generally told which judges and members of the profession will be consulted and are asked to name people who can assess their suitability. Consultees must assess each candidate's suitability against the criteria for appointment … They are asked to be objective in their assessments and to provide written evidence to support those assessments. All comments not based on that approach are disregarded. …"[44]

78   The source of the information is not divulged to applicants, because it is given in confidence, as happens with other appointments processes in the public and private sector. Only in that way can the system ensure full and frank views on the candidates. If a consultee alleges professional misconduct, it is disclosed to the candidate to give him or her an opportunity to respond. And such allegations are not taken into account if they are discriminatory in nature, or

---

[43] the rationale for this is the maintenance of the 'purity' or separateness of each year's competition but, as Sir Leonard Peach has argued on page 36 of his Report, the numbers of appointments and competitions are now so great that its proportionality is questionable

[44] *Annual Report 1999-2000*, para 1.10

non-specific, or hearsay without identifying the source, or if the consultee refuses to allow the allegation to be communicated to the candidate. And, unlike other such processes, the Lord Chancellor's Department has a system of reporting back to disappointed applicants about the assessments given on a non-attributable basis, a system that Sir Leonard described as 'impressive'. As Sir Leonard and the Government have acknowledged, the validity of the consultation system depends, not only on the quality and accuracy of the information provided, but also whether there is enough of it in those cases where, for reasons other than merit, the candidate has had insufficient exposure to consultees.

79   Sir Leonard's recommendations included:[45]

- bringing the system of appointment of Deputy High Court Judges, from whom many of the candidates for full-time appointments are drawn, into line with that of Recorders and other part-time appointments, namely inviting applications, consultation, short-listing and interviewing along the established lines;

- piloting a one day 'assessment centre' type selection procedure as a possible substitution for the present interview;

- testing and, if appropriate, commissioning a psychometric and competences test and, after appointment, introducing an annual self-appraisal scheme;

- in the procedure for making full-time appointments, making full use of the material resulting from a self-appraisal system for part-time judges;

- a restructure of the application form to provide more self-appraisal and, so, more information to short-listing and interview panels;

- redesign of the consultation forms to improve the value of the opinions they contain;

- more emphasis on nominated consultees (not less than three nor more than six), particularly in the case of those applicants who may not be sufficiently well known to generate much information in the general consultation, for example, women who have had a break in their career to bring up young children and/or who, for domestic reasons, have concentrated on a paper work practice rather than advocacy, ethnic minorities or solicitors;

- the appointment of a Commissioner for Judicial Appointments and a number of Deputies to participate as lay members in the short-listing and interview panels and to oversee and advise generally on the working of the system;[46]

- allowing applicants who have been assessed as suitable for appointment and placed on a 'reserve list', to remain on it for two years or automatically listing them for interview in the next annual competition;

---

[45] the Peach Report, pp 45-48

[46] with the exception of the Lord Chief Justice and the Lords of Appeal in Ordinary

- greater speed and flexibility in the making of appointments, including possible compression of the period of sitting as a part-time judge - for example, through concentrated blocks of sittings - and by raising the normal upper age limits for full-time appointment; and

- in order to promote equal opportunity, to introduce greater flexibility in the criteria for appointment and in working patterns and terms of service.

80   The award of silk is seen by many as a stepping stone to the bench. However, as Sir Leonard observed, the qualities required for each, though overlapping, are not identical and achievement of silk should not depend on or be confused with potential for the judiciary.[47] He made a number of recommendations for improvement of the information provided by general and nominated consultees and the contents of the application form similar to his recommendations for improvement of judicial appointments.[48]

81   The Lord Chancellor accepted most of Sir Leonard's recommendations[49] and also most of those in the Report of the Joint Working Party on Equal Opportunities in Judicial Appointments and Silk,[50] which Sir Leonard had also discussed in his Report. As I have said, an account of developments is set out in the Lord Chancellor's Department's Annual Report on Judicial Appointments for 1999-2000.[51] Most importantly, the Queen has now appointed Sir Colin Campbell as the "First Commissioner for Judicial Appointments". His role, and that of his Deputies, is not to decide on appointments to be made. It is independently to conduct a continuing audit of judicial appointments procedures and to advise the Lord Chancellor on any aspect of them that he chooses. In publicly announcing Sir Colin's appointment, the Lord Chancellor said:

> "The First Commissioner and the Deputy Commissioners will be able to investigate every appointment, every piece of paper, every assessment, every opinion and they will also have the right to attend interviews for judicial appointments and meetings at which the most senior appointments are discussed."[52]

82   It remains to be seen whether this grafting of an auditing and general advisory function onto the Lord Chancellor's system of exercising his wide powers of judicial and other legal appointments will satisfy those who think it should be

---

[47] the Peach Report, pp 39-40

[48] ibid., pp 40-44

[49] he did not accept the recommendation that the Commissioner or one of his Deputies should participate as a lay member in the short listing and interview panels. They only attend the meetings of such panels as auditors. Nor did he accept the recommendations questioning whether part-time service was essential, or whether an applicant's earnings were relevant, or the strong recommendation for speeding up the process of appointment

[50] see para 67 above

[51] *Annual Report 1999-2000*, Ch 2

[52] LCD Press Notice 103-01, 15th March 2001

taken out of his hands altogether. There is a widely held and growing view that, as in many other jurisdictions, appointment should be made by a minister on the recommendation of an independent commission consisting variously of judges, lawyers, academics, lay people and members of the executive and legislature, using modern methods of selection. As Lord Steyn[53] has observed, the advent of Human Rights to our domestic law has given that cause a further impetus in that judges at all levels will be called upon to make decisions with a higher 'political' content than previously.

83   Whoever is responsible for appointing judges, the present system of regular and wide consultation is of immense value in assessing the worth of candidates and should be retained. As I have indicated, its strength lies in its coverage of a long period of a candidate's career and of the wide range of consultees that it normally includes, as well as the views of his or her circuit's Presiding Judges. There is thus no chance of an effective black ball, however influential the person responsible for it may be, if it differs from the general consensus of assessment. Provided that the method of consultation and the criteria employed are fair, and that the assessments given are sufficiently informative, they are likely to produce a more reliable picture of a candidate for appointment than many conventional procedures for the appointment of senior personnel elsewhere in the public or private sector.

'Untied ends'

84   The first of my 'untied ends', which Sir Leonard recognised in recommending improvements in the other sources of information, is the risk of indirect discrimination in those cases where the candidates may not have had much exposure to the consultees, notably women, ethnic minorities and solicitors. As I have said, the Lord Chancellor has adopted most of his recommendations and of those of the Joint Working Party. He has also encouraged the legal professions to assist with these concerns and has instructed his Department's Judicial Group to consult as widely as possible in the case of all applicants.[54] It is unfortunate and a serious hindrance to those endeavours that the Law Society, in its submission to Sir Leonard Peach's Scrutiny, announced its withdrawal from the process and persists in that stance.

> **I recommend the utmost vigilance in not letting this iron grow cold, for it is the most constantly raised and anxious concern of those who feel that the appointments system is unfair to them.   It is not enough to wait for the**

---

[53] speaking at the Annual Conference of the Bar of England and Wales in October 1999

[54] in 1998 the Lord Chancellor's Department established a team of its officials to concentrate on equal opportunity issues and to encourage applications at events organised by various diversity groups; *Judicial Appointments Annual Report 1999-2000*, para 1.32

professions to present the Lord Chancellor's Department with suitably 'visible' as well as qualified candidates for appointment.

85   My second concern is as to the process of combining - weighting of - the information provided by the candidate, the views of the general and nominated consultees most of whom have seen the candidate at work, and the assessment by three strangers of his or her performance in a short interview. There are instances, of which the Presiding Judges have spoken, of startling differences between peer assessment of a candidate's performance over many years and the impression he appears to have given in interview, and also between widely differing assessments of different panels interviewing the same applicant in two consecutive rounds.

86   Although Sir Leonard spoke highly of the interview process, I believe that the weight to be given to it alongside the information provided by consultees was also of concern to him. As he observed, a limitation of all interviews is that they are necessarily restricted in time, and exploration of some skills and qualities is correspondingly limited.[55] It was for that reason that he recommended other improvements, some of which I have summarised, in the information to be provided to interviewing panels before putting their recommendations to the Lord Chancellor.[56] Possibly the two most important of these are: first, the creation of the post of First Commissioner for Judicial Appointments, who should be able to pick up any startling imbalance between a candidate's proven record of suitability and a contrary assessment in interview; and second, if it proves in pilot to be successful, the substitution of a one day 'assessment' for the conventional three quarters of an hour interview. The Lord Chancellor announced on 5 April 2001[57] that he is intending to pilot 'assessment centres' and has now appointed a firm of recruitment consultants to assist with the development of the first arrangements. The aim is that the 2002-2003 Deputy District Judge competition should be used as an assessment centre pilot.

I recommend that, if the assessment centre pilot proves to be successful, consideration should be given to extending its use to other full and part-time judicial appointments.

87   My third main concern is in part a repeat of my earlier criticism of the slowness of the appointment process[58] and of the lack of tailoring of appointments to needs. As the Presiding Judges have commented in their

---

[55] the Peach Report, p 17
[56] ibid p 20
[57] LCD Press Notice 139-01
[58] see paras 40 – 43 above

submission in the Review, if a judge of experience in a particular jurisdiction is needed to fill a vacancy, it is not helpful to appoint a judge with other experience, even if he or she did better than others in the most recent round of applications, or a judge who does not live in or near enough to be accessible to the area in which the vacancy has occurred. There are also problems when an appointment is required at short notice to meet an emergency, yet the best candidate may not have applied in the last round and it may be too long to await the next. I know that the Lord Chancellor's Department is alive to these difficulties and is considering how best to overcome them. Nevertheless, I consider it worth emphasising that speedy removal of these basic faults should do much for efficiency of listing and, hence, the service provided by the courts to all court users; and it should be relatively inexpensive. As the Presiding Judges have also observed, this requires input from them as well as the Lord Chancellor's Department. Their proposals, with which I agree and are, in summary, covered by my recommendations 66 – 67,[59]are that:

- in formulating bids for Circuit Judge appointments, Circuit Administrators, in consultation with the Presiding Judges should identify any particular needs that cannot be met from the existing judges on the circuit;

- in the event of unexpected vacancies requiring appointees of particular expertise or experience, consideration should be give to ad hoc consultation and assessment, the evaluation of candidates together with those considered but not appointed in the previous round; and

- in the case of both Circuit Judge and Recorder appointments, the results of the consultation and the assessment should be provided to the Presiding Judges for their comment on Circuit needs before any recommendation is put to the Lord Chancellor.

Disability

88   The Government's present policy is to encourage suitably qualified people to apply for judicial appointment, although they will not be appointed if for reasons of ill health or disability they cannot properly carry out the duties of judicial office. Candidates will not be appointed to a full-time post unless medical examination shows there is the prospect of them "providing a realistic return on the investment made in their training and appointment". Sir Leonard recommended that informal guidelines used by the Lord Chancellor's Department on this subject should be made public, but this has yet to happen. I warmly support Sir Leonard's recommendation that a disabled person's inability to demonstrate that his or her period in office will be of the maximum or stipulated duration should not block appointment or promotion and that appropriate arrangements in such cases should be made for early

---

[59] see para 43

retirement or loss of office necessitated by disability.[60] I also take the view that, if they do not already exist, formal guidelines should be developed and published, setting out the Department's clear policy on the appointment of disabled persons.

I recommend that the Lord Chancellor's Department should establish and publish clear guidelines on the appointment of disabled persons to judicial office.

TRAINING AND APPRAISAL

Training

89 Training for full and part-time professional judges in England and Wales is the responsibility of the judges themselves, acting through the Judicial Studies Board, a non-departmental public body established in 1979[61] and funded by the Lord Chancellor's Department.[62] The Board is chaired by a Judge of the Court of Appeal, currently Lord Justice Waller, and each of its main committees is chaired by a High Court Judge, thus reflecting the important constitutional principle[63] that the judiciary should control and manage its own training. The Criminal Committee of the Board, currently chaired by Lord Justice Kay, trains all judges who sit in the Crown Court, and its Magisterial Committee, currently chaired by Mrs Justice Hallett, oversees the training of District Judges. The work of the Board has grown enormously since the early 1980s. In the last financial year, it spent nearly £5m in judicial training, excluding the cost of its own accommodation and of other centrally provided services.[64]

90 The scheme of appointment and training of judges who are to try criminal cases is that on appointment to part-time office, either as Recorders or as Deputy District Judges, they must attend a residential induction course before they begin to sit. Thereafter, they are required to attend a residential continuation seminar periodically throughout their judicial career. The content of the courses is continuously reviewed and developed in response to changes in law and procedure, and in society.[65]

---

[60] the Peach Report, p 35

[61] following a report by Lord Justice Bridge, as he then was

[62] under a "Memorandum of Understanding" it enjoys "a level of autonomy in its financial affairs … consistent with its independence in assessing the need for, and providing, judicial training"

[63] *Starrs & Chalmers v Procurator Fiscal, Linlithgow* [2000] HRLR 191

[64] *Judicial Studies Board Annual Report for 1999-2000*, p 2

[65] ibid, Annual Strategy, Annex 1

91   For Recorders, the induction course lasts five days and consists typically of a mix of instruction on trial management, evidence, procedure, directions and summing-up to juries, sentencing, discussion of practical problems in small groups and an extended mock trial exercise. Fundamental issues, such as equality of treatment and human rights are the subject of individual treatment as well as being woven into the practical exercises. Considerable preparation is required for the course, in particular, the group work, which can be demanding for those whose professional practice has not been mainly in criminal work. For Deputy District Judges the course lasts four days, with sessions on communication skills in a courtroom context and replicating those elements on the Recorders' course which are not specific to jury trial. To bridge the gap between the induction course and the continuation seminars the Board runs annual 'Recorder Criminal Conferences' for those with between one year and eighteen months' experience of sitting in the Crown Court.

92   Residential, four day continuation seminars are organised on three year cycles for Recorders, Circuit Judges and High Court Judges to inform them of developments in criminal law and procedure and to enable them to discuss sentencing and other practical issues. District Judges and Deputy District Judges also receive continuation training annually by means of a two-day seminar, though this programme is currently under review by the Board. In addition, the Board organises seminars on specific matters such as the conduct of trials of rape and other serious sexual offences (twice yearly) and of serious fraud (biannually),[66] and supports annual sentencing seminars organised by the Presiding Judges of the circuits.

93   In comparison with other jurisdictions the training of our professional judiciary may seem modest. For example, we do not have a centrally staffed and administered national judicial training college or institution as found in many civil and common law jurisdictions.[67]   This is partly because of the small size of our professional judiciary, less than 3,000 compared with, for example, over 30,000 in Germany. It is also partly because, unlike in continental jurisdictions, our judges are appointed from the ranks of experienced legal practitioners who, in the main, come to the bench with a good knowledge of the law and procedure they are to administer. As I have indicated, the Board provides most of its training in short residential courses in hotels and conference centres around the country, a system which, so far, has had the advantages of flexibility and good value for money. There have been suggestions that it should be developed into a body more closely resembling a Judicial Training College, with its own premises capable of accommodating its administration, teaching and residential course requirements. With increasing demands made on the Board, some of which

---

[66] for all judges who are newly authorised to hear such cases; see para 20 above

[67] eg the Ecole Nationale de la Magistrature in France, the Escuela Judiciale in Spain, the Australian Institute of Judical Administration and the Federal Judicial Centre in Washington, DC, USA

would flow from implementation of various of my recommendations, this is an option that may become more efficient than the present system, and is one that should be kept under review.

94   Another possibility would be to combine in a single body responsibility for judicial training with other aspects of judicial policy. There are a number of Commonwealth precedents for this. For example, Canada has a Judicial Council with the broad statutory remit to promote efficiency and uniformity, and to improve the quality of judicial services in its Superior Courts and Tax Court. This remit includes, continuing judicial education, the handling of complaints against Federal Judges, developing consensus among Council members on issues involving the administration of justice and judicial salaries and benefits.[68] New South Wales has a Judicial Commission with a similarly broad statutory role of contributing to the enhancement of the quality of justice by providing professional support services to judicial officers and the courts. Its functions include continuing judicial education, assistance towards consistency in sentencing, complaints against judicial officers and advising the Attorney General on such matters as it thinks appropriate.[69]

95   These examples illustrate the contrast between the Judicial Studies Board's present minimalist, but effective, training function and the possibility of it making a much greater contribution to the role of the judiciary in the administration of justice. Lord Woolf, the Lord Chief Justice, has recently urged such an extension of the Judicial Studies Board's functions to include that of a properly resourced 'think tank' to consider a range of issues including the desired qualities of judges, the manner and terms of their appointment, their deployment, career development and management, the support they require and their role in promoting mediation.[70]

96   Whilst such a proposal is on the fringe of my terms of reference, I would not miss this opportunity of supporting it. But even without such extension of the Board's role, it is plain that its training responsibilities will continue to increase. My recommendations for a move away from a rigid system of authorising or 'ticketing' judges for the trial of specific offences towards a more flexible one based on judicial experience and training will require a sharper focus to the Board's work in fields such as serious sexual offences, serious fraud and possibly drug offences and those involving young offenders. There is also certain to be a continuing and increasing demand for training in information technology. The Board has already adopted a new strategy for training in that field, involving a regular assessment of and response to judicial training needs. There will obviously be a considerable demand for such judicial training if the recommendations I make in Chapters 8, 10 and 11

---

[68] Canadian Judicial Council: *Annual Report 1999/2000*

[69] Judicial Commission of New South Wales: *Annual Report 1999/2000*

[70] *"The Needs of a 21st Century Judge"*, a speech given to the Judicial Studies Board on 22nd March 2001

for the increased use of information technology in the management of cases, and at trial, are accepted.

97   There is also an increasing need for the training of judges in management skills. There are two aspects to this. First, there is the process of case management itself, where the court will need to take an increasingly robust attitude to the way in which criminal cases are prepared for trial. If my recommendations in Chapters 5 and 7 for allocation of either-way cases are adopted, there will need to be an extensive programme of training of District Judges in their new responsibilities in that respect. Also Presiding and Resident Judges will have to acquire a broader range of judicial management skills if they are to undertake the additional responsibilities that I recommend in this Chapter and Chapter 7.

I recommend that:

- **the Judicial Studies Board should be adequately resourced to meet the increasing training needs of the judiciary, including those in respect of special jurisdictions, case management, information technology and judicial administration.**

Appraisal

98   A trial judge's job is a solitary one. The only judge he sees or hears in action is himself. Such authoritative reassurance or criticism he may receive of his performance is limited to transcripts from the Court of Appeal long after the event. The frequency of those transcripts or the outcome of appeals are no sure indicator that he is doing a good job on a daily basis. Few appeals or unsuccessful appeals from his rulings of his summings up or sentences may indicate little more than that he is over-cautious to the point of undue deference to the defence case out of a desire not to fall foul of the Court of Appeal. Regular exposure to the gaze of the Court of Appeal could mean that he is getting it wrong too often or that he is a judge of sturdy independence making difficult decisions on which there are often two views. Informal enquiries by the judge himself as to how he is doing, or reliance on the views of court clerks, advocates, ushers and others are demeaning and inadequate substitutes for systematic appraisal.

99   Appraisal of work performance is a feature of most public and major private employments. Appraisal for those at the Bar consists largely in the approbation or disapprobation of instructing solicitors and hence on the size and quality of their practice. Most solicitors, though subject to similar client discipline, have developed and are well used to appraisal schemes. Yet there

is no provision for appraisal of members of either profession once they become judges. The Runciman Royal Commission in 1993 recommended the introduction of an effective formal system of performance appraisal,[71] a recommendation that the Government of the day did not accept.

100 Some argue that to introduce a system of appraisal for judges would be a threat to their independence. But I do not see why judges should be inhibited in how they go about their job by some form of objective and knowledgeable assessment of that sort. Magistrates, who have equally powerful claims to judicial independence, have now adopted a national system of appraisal. The District Judges (Civil) on the Wales and Chester Circuit pioneered a system for their Deputies which was so successful that Sir Leonard Peach recommended its extension nationally, and the Lord Chancellor appears to have accepted that recommendation.[72] It is already a feature of their counterparts in the criminal jurisdiction, (and for part-time tribunal members in the Appeal Service). As His Honour Judge John Samuels QC observed in his contribution to the Review, if there are to be closer links between the magistracy, the District Bench and the senior judiciary - as I now recommend in Chapter 7 - it would be anomalous to stop the progress of appraisal below the level of the Circuit Bench. But even without such development, there is, in my view, much to be said for extending some form of appraisal higher up the judicial ladder.

101 What form, or forms, should appraisal of Recorders and full-time judiciary take? There are obvious differences between the needs of the two. In the case of Recorders, particularly those newly appointed, its main purpose should be to enable them better to equip themselves for full-time appointment through observation of, and discussion about, their work in court: As to full-time judges, it should serve as a means of correcting foibles or bad habits that they have consciously or unconsciously developed over the years, alerting them to other and better ways of doing their job and also, importantly, as a medium for development of their judicial career.

102 Any scheme should command the support of the judges, not compromise their independence or distract them from their work. And it should not jeopardise their careers, save in exceptional circumstances and then only on the intervention (in the case of the Circuit Bench) of a Presiding Judge in consultation with the Senior Presiding Judge. The form or mechanics of appraisal would require detailed consideration and consultation among the judiciary and others.

---

[71] Report of *The Royal Commission on Criminal Justice*, paras 98 and 99, and recommendation 251
[72] *Judicial Appointments Annual Report 1999-2000*, para 1.35

103   Appraisal of full-time judges could, perhaps, be conducted by a group of three appraisers, not all of whom need be judges or retired judges, but at least one of whom should be or have been a judge of at least the same seniority as the person being appraised. The appraisers would observe him, with his knowledge, in court and in chambers, as if they were court users but sitting in the public benches. They might in an appropriate case or cases be given access to his court papers. At the conclusion of their observations they would reach and formulate joint provisional views, perhaps using a standard format, though in simpler form than presently provided for the magistracy.[73] They would review their provisional views with the judge in an informal way, taking into account his response.

104   The extent to which the appraisers should communicate their conclusions to the higher judiciary or the Lord Chancellor is a matter of some sensitivity and requires careful consideration. It may be that in the case of District or Circuit Judges, they should go to the Presiding Judges, and in the case of High Court Judges to the appropriate Head of Division. Only in the event of some particular problem requiring attention would they communicate further, say, in the case of a Circuit Judge, to his Resident Judge or, exceptionally to the Lord Chancellor through one of his senior officials. This or some similar scheme would require considerable time and money to develop.[74] But it would, in my view, be of considerable benefit, not only in enabling judges to improve the way in which they do their job, but also to bolster public confidence in their professionalism and competence.

I recommend:

- **the introduction of an appraisal scheme for all part-time judicial post-holders, and its reinforcement by a system of regular self-appraisal;**

- **the assessments produced should be available to those advising the Lord Chancellor on full-time judicial appointments; and**

- **consideration, following wide consultation among the judiciary and others, of a system of appraisal for full-time judges; the results of such assessments should, however, only exceptionally be made available to anyone other than the Presiding Judges or the relevant Head of Division.**

---

[73] Chapter 4, paras 90 - 91

[74] I am indebted to Judge Samuels for much of the content of this suggested framework

CHAPTER 7

A UNIFIED CRIMINAL COURT

'PRINCIPLES'

1   In considering the structure of our criminal courts and looking to see how it could be improved, I have accumulated a number of general propositions. I hesitate to call them 'principles'. Like most such generalisations, they are blinding glimpses of the obvious; but here they are:

- although different cases may call for different tribunals, practices and procedures, each should be capable of providing a fair hearing and of securing a just outcome;

- the nature of the tribunal to which a case is allocated and its procedures should be proportionate in form, time and cost to the seriousness and/or complexity of the alleged offence and the severity of the potential sentence;

- the allocation decision should be taken by a court;

- practices and procedures should be simple and, as far as practicable, the same for all tribunals;

- after allocation, all cases should start and finish at the same level, subject to an appeal;

- concerns about the quality of justice in one level of court should not be a basis for allocation of cases to another and higher level if they are not sufficiently serious and/or difficult to warrant its practices and procedures; no system of justice should be structured or operated on the basis that part of it is not working properly; it should be made to work properly at all levels;

- the structure of the courts should be such as to contribute to the efficient working of the criminal justice system as a whole;

- the administration of criminal justice should be organised in such a way as to achieve justice, efficiency and economies in the shared and flexible use of accommodation, judiciary, administrative staff and other resources; and

- the courts should treat all of those involved in or exposed to their procedures with consideration.

A UNIFIED CRIMINAL COURT

2   The Review has demonstrated a strong and widely supported case for unifying the Crown Court and magistrates' courts into one criminal court with, so far as practicable, the same practices and procedures and a common administration.[1]   As I have explained in Chapter 3, the differences in practices, procedures, management and funding of the two systems and their respective administrative cultures are inefficient and harmfully divisive. They also contribute to the fractured nature of the criminal justice system as a whole, aggravating its present difficulties in providing a fair and efficient criminal process for all. In my view:

- there should be a single criminal court accommodating all levels of jurisdiction; and

- it should be supported by a single and nationally funded administrative structure, but one providing significant local autonomy and accountability.

3   As recent research projects have demonstrated,[2] many of the public do not know that there are two criminal court systems or appreciate the difference between them. The media tend to concentrate on cases in the Crown Court, where only a small fraction of all prosecuted cases, albeit the most serious, are heard by a professional judge and jury. Many do not know that panels of lay magistrates or a single District Judge hear the vast majority of criminal cases. For many, a court is a court and they do not know what to expect when first exposed to it or why, after a case has seemingly started, they may be required to attend another with a different tribunal and different procedures. Others, particularly in large metropolitan areas, think of magistrates' courts as 'Police Courts'. It would be an important start to improving public confidence in the system to create a simpler structure and process – a single court with as many common characteristics and procedures as practicable in which cases could start and finish at the same level.

4   If my recommendations for greater jurisdictional flexibility in the allocation of cases to levels of tribunal and for a single and simpler code of procedure for most criminal process are adopted, a unified court and administration would be the best medium for ensuring a fair, efficient and effective criminal process. Some have argued for unification of the two administrations whilst leaving the court systems separate. However, I see little point in that. If, as I

---

[1] among its supporters are the Justices' Clerks Society, the Association of Chief Police Officers, the Crown Prosecution Service, members of the judiciary and the Bar
[2] see Chapter 4, paras 2, 5 and 26 - 32

believe, there is a strong case for unifying the administration and, so far as possible, the procedures of magistrates' courts and the Crown Court, it is a short step to unifying the court itself.

5   I have in mind a single criminal court, which might be called simply the Criminal Court, in which professional judges and lay magistrates would sit, at their different levels, all as judges of the same court. I emphasise that I do not mean by this a concentration of all courts in present Crown Court centres, regardless of the needs of the communities served by the present two systems. No doubt, there may be centres for which a long term court building programme might suitably provide a combined court building or co-located court buildings, but there will be many instances in which separate centres or buildings will continue in the main to provide separately for different levels of offences. But they would all be part of the same court and, depending on the available accommodation, location and facilities, would be available for use at any jurisdictional level as the need arises. Thus, such a reform should not involve any reduction otherwise than is presently under way in the 'locality' of lay or professional justice, or in a concentration of work in fewer court centres than would, in any event, be required. On the contrary, as I explain below, my proposals are likely to preserve some magistrates' court centres that might otherwise be closed. The important thing is for the structure to continue to provide at the appropriate level and where it is needed a strong lay element reflective of the community it serves. As the Magistrates Courts' Service Inspectorate has observed,[3] in some ways the present trend is towards an increase in the local character of criminal justice in the closer working of local agencies within the same areas and the introduction of Crime and Disorder Partnerships. To which I would add the prospect of using information technology to bring the courts and the agencies working with them into closer contact with those who become involved in the criminal justice process.

6   The replacement of the present dual system of administration with a single organisation need not involve the creation of a national monolithic and rigid administrative structure. Whilst Magistrates' Courts Committees would disappear, magistrates would not - only the confusion of their judicial role with that of administrators introduced by the Justices of the Peace Act 1949 – a confusion not thrust on judges sitting in the Crown Court. Local control and accountability could be preserved at summary level and introduced at indictable level through the medium of professional managers with more autonomy than now enjoyed by Court Service local managers, but within a national framework.

---

[3] in its Annual Report for 1998/99, at p v; see also its 1999-2000 Report, in which, at p 8, it states that there are many courthouses at which it will never be possible – or only at prohibitive cost – to provide the range of facilities for custody, professional users and disabled people that are expected nowadays

7   If, as I recommend below,[4] a third, intermediate tier of jurisdiction of a mix of professional and lay judges is introduced, it would be vital to set it in a single court structure consisting also of the other two tiers and supported by the same administration. In addition, it would fit and benefit from the system of judicial management provided by the Presiding Judges and Resident Judges.

8   The establishment of a single court for all criminal cases would not, I believe, prejudice or affect the administration of civil and family justice. Judges or magistrates exercising more than one of those jurisdictions in the same or different courts could continue to be deployed between them. Thus, judges, when exercising their civil and family jurisdiction would sit, as now, as judges of the High Court or county court, and magistrates would continue to exercise their family jurisdiction.

9   The establishment of a unified Criminal Court would bring some feeling of unity of function and purpose between judges in the Crown Court and magistrates, and encourage and facilitate more consistency in their respective approaches to trial and sentencing.

10   There is also the unsatisfactory feature that magistrates, unlike judges, have no formal support structure at a national level, no judicial 'champion' to whom they can turn for general support and guidance. At a local level they have their bench chairmen and justices' clerks[5] and, more broadly, they have the invaluable guidance and assistance of the Magistrates' Association. But District Judges can turn to their Senior District Judge and Circuit Judges all have the support of the hierarchy of the local Resident or Senior Circuit Judge, the Presiding Judges, the Senior Presiding Judge and, ultimately, the Lord Chief Justice. In my view, the present large and widely perceived gap between lay magistrates and the Crown Court should be removed by bringing all members of the judiciary, whether lay or professional, within the responsibility of the local Resident Judge and the judicial hierarchy of which he is part. Such incorporation in the general judicial 'college' would, in any event, be a practical necessity if, as I recommend, a third, intermediate, tier of jurisdiction is created in which magistrates would sit with judges as part of a mixed tribunal.

11   There are many other aspects of the current system that could be improved through the introduction of a unified Criminal Court. I shall refer to many of them as the Report progresses, but mention three of them here for convenience.

---

[4] see paras 21- 35
[5] and informal advice and guidance of the local liaison judge

12   First, the fact that cases have to commence in the magistrates' court before being sent or committed to the Crown Court for trial or sentence means that there are unnecessary delays inherent in our current system. The Narey changes have clearly helped to reduce the delays in indictable-only cases, but little has been done to address 'either-way' cases. A unified Criminal Court would enable the appropriate court to take control of a case at the earliest opportunity, thus keeping delays to a minimum.

13   Second, we generate unnecessary confusion in our current system by allowing the separate courts to operate under different procedural codes, even though they are dealing with a continuum of criminal work. Although this is not dependant on the introduction of a unified court, the adoption of a single criminal code would be a more straightforward, and therefore speedier, exercise if the judiciary, professional and lay, and the administration of the courts were all part of the same structure.

14   Third, the separate administrations of the Crown and magistrates' courts mean that there is no electronic sharing of information between the two. This results in duplication of work, can contribute to delays in hearing cases, and increases the risk of error. Again, a unified Criminal Court is not a necessary precursor to the introduction of a common information technology system, or, indeed, one that could be shared with the other criminal justice agencies, but a single administration serving all levels of criminal jurisdiction should help to speed the implementation process. I return to this in more detail towards the end of this chapter.

15   There are a number of arguments against the establishment of a unified Criminal Court. One, made mostly by magistrates, is that it would be a 'judge dominated' system and would "thereby remove appropriate tensions between the professional and lay judiciary at their different levels, particularly when one is an appellate tribunal of the other".[6] But different jurisdictional levels, including a route of appeal within the same court structure are common-place in various of our jurisdictions. And there is no reason why lay magistrates, any more than judges, should be insulated from the oversight and guidance of judiciary at the next level up. In the criminal jurisdiction Circuit Judges already preside in appeals, by way of rehearing from magistrates, they share the jurisdiction of the Crown Court with High Court Judges who frequently, as members of the Court of Appeal (Criminal Division), hear appeals in cases over which they have presided, and the most experienced Circuit Judges also sit in that court. And District Judges (particularly in London) are well used to a formal system of judicial management, albeit one organised nationally rather than locally.

JURISDICTION

16 A number of authoritative reviewers of and commentators on the criminal justice system have queried from time to time the artificiality of our rigid courts structure, with a view to substituting a more flexible and suitable matching of judges to caseloads and individual cases across jurisdictional boundaries. The Beeching Commission contrasted the convention of artificial tiering of cases and judges with the reality of a gradation of the two; it noted the frequency of changes in jurisdiction; and it pointed out the subjectivity of the notion of seriousness of an alleged offence, especially when unqualified by its difficulty, urging a more flexible system for allocating cases based on both those factors.[7]

17 While the Beeching Reforms went some way to relaxing jurisdictional boundaries, the rigid line between summary trial and trial by judge and jury still remains. The seriousness of many 'either-way' offences can vary considerably according to their nature and circumstance. The present choice is limited to a summary trial, which may be a panel of lay magistrates or a single professional judge with no lay element, and the full panoply of trial in the Crown Court by a judge and jury of twelve. Many, mostly 'either-way', cases now dealt with in Crown Court are not sufficiently serious or difficult to warrant the use of what is a relatively slow, cumbersome and expensive process.[8] Some indication of the relative seriousness of the Crown Court's case-load can be seen from the following figures. 54% of all adult custodial sentences are of six months or less. The Crown Court accounted for about 25% of those and, in addition, imposed nearly 26,000 non-custodial sentences. If the latter were treated as six months or less, the Crown Court might be said to account for a much higher percentage of cases that need not have left the magistrates' courts. 14% end up with a sentence of between six and 12 months, of which most are imposed in the Crown Court, and 15% between 12 months and 24 months.[9] There is thus a readily discernible tendency of the Crown Court to give much the same sentence that magistrates could have done or not to give a significantly heavier sentence below a threshold of about 12 months.

18 In those cases that remain in the magistrates' courts, some may be essentially 'jury' issues where a panel of magistrates might be thought by some to be more appropriate. Some may be legally or factually complex where a District Judge would often be the preferred tribunal. Some may fall into both categories where a mix of a judge and magistrates would be ideal. At present,

---

[6] the Central Council of Magistrates' Courts Committees' submission in the Review

[7] Report of *Review of Assizes and Quarter Sessions*, paras 134–139; see also Dr Penny Darbyshire *The lamp that shows that freedom lives – is it worth the candle?*, [1991] Crim LR 740, at 741; Morgan and Russell, *The judiciary in the magistrates' courts*, p 119, para 8.6

[8] see Chapter 5, paras 157 - 172

[9] *Criminal Statistics England and Wales 1999*, Cmnd 5001, (Home Office, December 2000)

despite best efforts to list cases appropriately in accordance with the Venne recommendations,[10] the small number of District Judges makes it difficult always to allocate cases to the more appropriate form of tribunal. And even then, the choice is limited to a professional judge or magistrates, never or rarely a mix of both.

19   Thus, there are two ways in which the sharp divide between the summary trial and trial on indictment will continue to result in the trial of a significant number of cases at a level and by a process that are not appropriate for them.

20   As I have noted in Chapter 6, a judicial system should be designed and run so as to give maximum flexibility in the matching of judges to cases. However, like judicial discretion, it requires some guidelines or outer limits if chaos is to be avoided. Whatever new courts structure may be contemplated, the Review has not thrown up any significant argument for the abolition of trial by judge and jury for the more serious cases or of trial by professional judges sitting on their own or magistrates in the vast majority of less important cases. Nor has there been any convincing suggestion for a radical re-definition of the boundary between indictable and summary offences. I take as my starting point, therefore, a continuation of the basic boundary line between the two forms of trial according to the two broad categories of offences presently described as indictable and summary offences. The question is whether, for many cases around the borderline, a mixed tribunal would be a more appropriate and acceptable forum than consigning them to one or other of the present two very different forms of proceeding.

A MIDDLE TIER OF JURISDICTION

21   There has been much support in the Review for a tier of jurisdiction between that of magistrates' courts and the Crown Court to be exercised by a tribunal consisting of a professional judge and two lay magistrates. There is also a widespread view that our system does not make optimum use of the skills of the District Bench. 'Mixed' tribunals are commonplace in many civil law jurisdictions and account for a good deal of cases of medium seriousness, though the roles of the lay members vary considerably.[11] They are less common in common law jurisdictions, where the trend has increasingly been to rely on professional judges.[12]

---

[10] see Chapter 4, paras 44 – 47

[11] eg Austria, France, Finland, Germany, and Sweden

[12] see *Toward a Unified Criminal Court* (Law Reform Commission of Canada Working Paper 59, 1989)

22   I recognise that there is a limit to which one can import models from other jurisdictions, whether civil law or common law, because their legal institutions and practices are the products of their own national traditions and constitutional frameworks. However, there are some comparisons close at hand. First, as Morgan and Russell point out,[13] some District Judges occasionally sit with lay magistrates in family and youth courts and they always do so in Northern Ireland.[14] In Scotland there have been multi-disciplinary children's panels for some time, and they have recently been introduced in England and Wales for juveniles appearing in court for the first time and pleading guilty.[15] And there is, of course, the Crown Court which, when sitting as a court of appeal by way of rehearing from magistrates' courts - that is, essentially as a first instance hearing - consists of a judge and two or more magistrates.

23   The main rationale for mixed tribunals is that they combine the advantages of the legal knowledge and experience of the professional judge with community representation in the form of lay magistrates, and as Professor Andrew Sanders has noted,[16] there is evidence to suggest that a degree of collectivity in decision-making can improve its quality. What distinguishes England and Wales from the many civil jurisdictions in which mixed tribunals are well established, and also from the models suggested by Professor Sanders, is the existence of the magistracy, with its wide experience of hearing cases carrying a custodial penalty of up to six months. I believe that these skills could be put to good use as part of a tribunal of fact in cases of medium seriousness. The use of magistrates in this way should also increase the locality of justice, since such a mixed tribunal could sit in existing magistrates' courthouses, as well as in existing Crown Court centres, and in that way contribute to the preservation of some presently under-used magistrates' courts that might otherwise disappear.

24   One contrary view is that such a system would not work because the presiding judge would tend to dominate the magistrates sitting with him. I do not see why that should be so. Magistrates already sit in the Crown Court on appeals from magistrates' courts in which they can and do out-vote the judge, as their predecessors did for many years in Quarter Sessions. Accounts vary as to the influence they have on the decisions. Much depends on personalities and relative experience. As I have said, they have the advantage over many of their counterparts in mixed tribunals in civil jurisdictions in that they are well trained and often of considerable experience. Their recent introduction to structured decision-making as part of the move to reasoned decisions should strengthen their competence and their confidence in this respect.

---

[13] *The judiciary in the magistrates' courts*, pp 107-108, para 7.4.5

[14] *ibid*, p 103

[15] see the provision for mandatory and discretionary referral of young offenders the Powers of Criminal Courts (Sentencing) Act 2000, Part III

[16] *Community Justice: Modernising the Magistracy in England and Wales* (IPPR 2001) p 29

25   Another argument against introducing such a mixed tribunal is that it would be difficult to find sufficient magistrates to sit in such courts, because few would be willing to commit themselves to the longer trials, possibly lasting for several days, that some of them could involve. I do not see this as an insuperable problem and nor do the Magistrates' Association in their submissions in the Review. There are many magistrates who, for one reason or other, are not restricted by their employment or other commitments to sitting for half a day a week and who might well relish the opportunity to sit on longer and more substantial cases. And, as I mentioned in Chapter 4,[17] there is a strong case for introducing greater flexibility into magistrates' sitting patterns, for example, to enable and encourage block sittings and to enable some to sit more than they do at present.

26   In my view, it is time for a further step along the Beeching road towards greater flexibility in matching cases around the borderline between the present two tiers of jurisdiction to the right level and form of tribunal. There should be a third tier for the middle-range of cases that do not warrant the cumbersome and expensive fact-finding exercise of trial by judge and jury, but which are sufficiently serious or difficult, or their outcome is of such consequence to the public or defendant, to merit a combination of professional and lay judges, but working together in a simpler way. Cases eligible for such a jurisdiction could be those where, in the opinion of the court, the defendant could face a sentence of imprisonment of up to, say, two years or a substantial financial or other punishment of an amount or severity to be determined. In the main, these would fall within the present categories of 'either-way' cases. For the purposes of this Report, I have called the three tiers of the unified Criminal Court the Magistrates' Division, the District Division and the Crown Division.

27   How should the jurisdiction of the District Division be defined? The logical approach, it seems to me, would be to confine it to 'either-way' cases, subject to general sentencing maxima turning on the seriousness of the circumstances of the case or cases charged as distinct from the legal maxima for a case or cases of that category. I do not include complexity because, as between a judge and jury and a judge and two experienced magistrates, the critical common factor is the judge, and it is doubtful what advantages juries have over experienced magistrates as the lay element in cases of complexity. Mostly, but not always, seriousness of a case would be measured by the likely sentence it could attract looking at the case at its worst, which would require consideration both as to the circumstances of the offence as well as of the defendant, including any previous convictions.

---

[17] Chapter 4, para 73

28   Under our present sentencing options, general maxima for this purpose could be two years' custody and a significantly higher financial penalty than those marking out the limits for summary jurisdiction of six months or £5,000 respectively. I have suggested a maximum level of custodial jurisdiction of about two years given the large number of cases with outcomes not only well within that limit but also within that of the summary jurisdiction which currently reach the Crown Court. To allow such a bracket of sentencing at cases near the margin would enable them to be tried at a level and in a manner more appropriate to their individual seriousness. However, how and where to draw the line in the future will shortly need wider consideration in the light of the Government's proposal in its recent policy paper, *The Way Ahead*,[18] and the recommendations of the Halliday Report on Sentencing[19] for focusing more on the offender and introducing a range of mixed custodial and community sentences. If anything, such widening of sentencing options would provide an even stronger reason for the added flexibility that the new jurisdiction could bring.

29   Trial by such a 'mixed' tribunal would have a number of the characteristics and safeguards provided by trial in the Crown Court. A professional judge would make all the rulings and orders at the pre-trial stage, conduct any necessary case management and rule on bail. In the trial itself, the professional judge would also deal with all questions of law, procedure and evidence, hearing arguments on them and making rulings, where necessary in the absence of the magistrates.

30   For all other purposes, however, the mixed bench would constitute a single tribunal. It would hear all the evidence together and, at the close of the trial, the judge and magistrates would retire together to consider the question of guilt or innocence. Clearly the judge would take the leading role in guiding the discussion in areas in which the law, or the application of the law to the facts, is in any way uncertain. But he would not need to give magistrates the sort of elaborate directions Crown Court judges give to juries, since they come to the task with the benefit of their experience and training in structured decision taking in the magistrates' court. Trials in the District Division should thus be considerably shorter than trial by judge and jury, since the magistrate members would be familiar with the practices, procedures and language of the court, together with much of the day-to-day law required. At the close of their deliberations, the judge and magistrates would make their decision, by majority if necessary, each having an equal vote. On their return to the courtroom, the judge would give the reasoned decision of the court.

---

[18] *Criminal Justice: The Way Ahead*, paras 2.61-2.75

[19] *Making Punishments Work – Report of a Review of the Sentencing Framework for England and Wales* (Home Office, July 2001), recommendations 15-22

31   As in the Crown Court, the task of passing sentence would be reserved to the judge. There are important questions of competence and experience to consider here. Sentencing in cases of the level of seriousness which would be considered by the District Division would be a different exercise from that at the summary level under the existing sentencing framework. And the division may become more complicated if the recommendations of the Halliday Sentencing Review Report are implemented. It is also relevant that Parliament has recently taken away the jurisdiction of magistrates to contribute to decisions on cases committed to the Crown Court for sentence, and reserved these instead to the professional judiciary.[20] However, this is partly also a matter of practicality, as many of the cases coming before the District Division would have to be adjourned for reports after conviction. It would often be difficult to reconstitute the same panel for the purpose of passing sentence.

32   The judge in the District Division would normally be a District Judge, but depending on the case and circumstances, it could be a judge of any level, from High Court Judge to Recorder. For example, a particular case or block of cases, perhaps involving young children or complex legal issues, or a grave case against young defendants presently beyond the jurisdiction of the youth court, could be assigned to a court presided over by a High Court Judge or by a Circuit Judge experienced in such work. Recorders could spend much of their time sitting in the new jurisdiction, to the advantage of the system and to them. As to the magistrates assigned to sit in it, they would need to be experienced so as to hold their own with the judge and, as I have mentioned, they would probably need to be able to give more time for continuous sittings than is now normally required in summary proceedings. Some system of selection would have to be devised to ensure a sufficient panel of experienced, available and, so far as possible, broadly representative magistrates for the task. In paragraph 81 below, I recommend that this function should be exercised under the ultimate control and oversight of the local Resident Judge.

33   To those who fear for the jury system, I would say that the history of the criminal law has been one of constant jurisdictional changes of boundary according to the needs and developments of the time, and it is necessarily a matter of policy for the government of the day to determine where the line needs to be drawn. The introduction of an intermediate tier, as I propose it, is not so much a re-drawing of a line, but of spanning two systems of trial with one that draws on the strengths of both and allocates cases between all three according to the individual circumstances of the offence and offender. It recognises the line, but also gives effect to the Beeching Commission point[21] about the unreality and rigidity of jurisdictional demarcations in individual cases. And, in the allocation system that I propose - in which a District Judge

---

[20] Access to Justice Act 1999, s 79

[21] Report of *Review of Assizes and Quarter Sessions*, para 137

would determine disputed issues of venue subject to appeal[22] - it provides an objective way of matching cases to the appropriate tribunal.

34   The creation of a unified Criminal Court would necessitate the assimilation of the current magistrates' courts and Crown Court procedural rules, new rules governing the conduct of trials in the new District Division, and also as to the allocation of cases. I recommend the way in which these tasks should be approached, when discussing a new Code of Criminal Procedure in Chapter 10.

35   If my recommendation for the introduction of an intermediate tier, when coupled with a power in the court of allocating cases to it, does not find favour, I urge its introduction on the basis that a defendant may, with the consent of the court, opt for it, either by a mixed tribunal or by judge alone in either-way cases in which the court would otherwise determine that he should be tried by judge and jury. For many of the reasons that I consider defendants might opt for trial by judge alone in the Crown Court,[23] so I believe that many defendants might wish to take advantage of it by opting for one or other form of trial in the District Division. Such an option would be of particular value in particularly complex and/or lengthy cases and in high profile and/or otherwise emotive cases which have attracted much publicity.

Accordingly, I recommend:

- **the establishment of a unified Criminal Court;**

- **the establishment of three levels of jurisdiction within the unified Criminal Court consisting of: the Crown Division to exercise jurisdiction over all indictable-only matters and such 'either-way' cases as are allocated to it; the District Division to exercise jurisdiction over such 'either-way' matters as are allocated to it; and the Magistrates' Division to exercise jurisdiction over all summary-only matters and such 'either-way' cases as are allocated to it;**

- **the Crown and Magistrates' Divisions should be constituted as are the Crown Court and magistrates' courts respectively, and the District Division should consist of a judge, in the main a District Judge and at least two experienced magistrates (or if a defendant with the consent of the court so opts, of a judge alone);**

- **the District Division's jurisdiction over 'either-way' offences should be limited to those within a likely**

---

[22] paras 36 – 40 below

[23] see Chapter 5, paras 110 - 118

maximum sentence in the circumstances of the case viewed at its worst (as distinct from the legal maximum for a case or cases of that category) of, say, two years custody, a maximum financial penalty to be determined and/or a maximum of community, or combination of custody and community, sentences to be determined in the light of future reforms of the sentencing framework; and

- the District Division, sitting as a youth court, should also try grave cases against young defendants presently dealt with in the Crown Court.

THE ALLOCATION OF CASES

36   The criteria and procedure for allocation of either-way cases between the District Division and the Crown Division should be broadly the same as that between the Magistrates' Division and the other two Divisions, save only that it is governed by a higher jurisdictional boundary and, for the reasons I have given, complexity need not be a consideration.

37   Thus, the criteria should be broadly drawn according to the seriousness of the alleged offence, mostly, but not always, judged by the severity of the potential sentence. As to the potential sentence, the allocation should be based on the prosecution case at its highest, taking into account also the alleged offender's criminal history, if any.   If there is a real possibility that the appropriate sentence on conviction would exceed six months custody but not, say two years, the matter should be allocated to the District Division. If there is a real possibility that the appropriate sentence would exceed two years custody, or any other maxima, then it should go to the Crown Division. However, even if it is considered that the sentence in any individual case would not exceed the relevant limit, it could still be allocated to a higher level by means of its seriousness whatever the likely sentence.

38   As all indictable-only cases would automatically be sent to the Crown Division and all summary-only cases would remain in the Magistrates' Division, an allocation procedure would only be necessary, as now, in 'either-way' cases. The decision should be made in the light of the defendant's plea, taken at that stage. In the majority of cases the question of venue would be likely to be undisputed and could be dealt with by magistrates. Where there is an issue or uncertainty about venue, I consider, as I have said in Chapter 5, that the matter should be put before a District Judge. He could then hear both parties and inform himself of all the relevant circumstances of the offence and of the defendant, including his criminal record, if any. He would then allocate the case, looking at the possible outcome at its worst from the defendant's

point of view. I should add that the efficiency of the procedure would depend on accurate information of the defendant's criminal record, if any. At present, the police are poorly equipped to provide this information; the Chairman of the Magistrates' Association has recently commented that antecedents presented to magistrates can be three to four months out of date.[24] Early implementation of the integrated information technology system that I recommend in Chapter 8 should overcome the problem.

39 Where a defendant faces a number of linked charges, some of which would merit allocation to a higher level of jurisdiction than others, all, so far as practicable, should normally be allocated to the higher level. Similarly, where co-defendants are facing a number of charges triable at different levels, the trial and sentencing of all of them should be allocated to the level appropriate for the most serious. Of course, if the more serious matter is later dropped, the linked cases could then revert to the appropriate Division for their disposal. The present statutory provisions covering such matters are a muddle[25] and will need a radical revision to enable courts at higher levels to exercise jurisdiction over all matters at and below their levels.

40 The defence and the prosecution should have a right of appeal on paper from a contested allocation decision to a Circuit Judge nominated for the purpose, and provision should be made for speedy hearing of such appeals. Quite separately from such right of appeal, both defence and prosecution should be able to seek re-opening of the matter, if the circumstances of the case or of the defendants change before trial. In that event, application should be made to the Division to which the case has been allocated, at any time in the Crown and District Divisions up to and including the completion of the pre-trial assessment and, in the Magistrates' Division to a date before the trial to be specified.

I recommend that:

- **all cases should have an allocation hearing in the Magistrates' Division at which pleas should be taken;**

- **all cases triable only summarily should remain in the Magistrates' Division and all cases triable only on indictment should be sent to the Crown Division;**

- **the court should allocate all 'either-way' cases according to the seriousness of the alleged offence and the circumstances of the defendant in accordance with statutory and broadly drawn criteria, looking at the case at its worst from the point of view of the**

---

[24] *Improving Sentence Information*, The Magistrate, Summer 2001, p208

[25] principally the Criminal Justice Act 1988, ss 40 and 41 and the Magistrates' Courts Act 1980, s 20

defendant and bearing in mind the jurisdiction of each Division;

- where there is no dispute or uncertainty as to venue, magistrates should allocate the case; otherwise a District Judge should do so after hearing representations on the matter from both parties;

- the Government should ensure, as a matter of urgency, routine provision, through an integrated system of information technology or otherwise, of complete and accurate information of a defendant's criminal record at all allocation hearings;

- where there are linked charges and/or defendants, all should normally be allocated to the Division with jurisdiction to hear the most serious of the charges;

- the defence and the prosecution should have a right of appeal on paper from a contested allocation decision to a Circuit Judge nominated for the purpose, and provision should be made for speedy hearing of such appeals; and

- the defence and the prosecution should be able, up to a specified point before trial, to seek re-allocation in the light of any material change in the circumstances of the alleged offence(s) and/or of the defendant between allocation and trial.

THE CIRCUITS

41   As I have said, the circuits had their origin in itinerant judges, their key officials and members of the Bar setting out from London at regular intervals to tour different regions of the country. Over the centuries these circuits varied from time to time, but they continued to be based, until the Beeching reforms, on groupings of counties, most of the Assizes being held at each county town.[26]   Those reforms made great improvements, notably in providing a better match of judges to cases and caseloads. For the lower tier of indictable work, they substituted for the periodic sittings of Quarter Sessions, a permanent Crown Court in which full-time Circuit Judges sat at fewer court centres. They also concentrated High Court circuit sittings in Crown Court centres where they were most needed - mainly at major centres of population - and for longer and more regular periods.

---

[26] Courts Act 1971

42	The Beeching reforms left largely untouched the traditional circuit boundaries. The new administration, though no longer itinerant, organised itself on a regional basis corresponding with them. When the Court Service was formed in 1995 to assume responsibility for, *inter alia*, the administration of the High Court, the Crown Court and the county courts, it continued the same circuit structure. And the Bar, though becoming more locally based, continued to organise itself on a circuit basis. Thus, each circuit has its Presiding Judges responsible for judicial administration and associated 'pastoral' responsibilities for Bench and Bar on the circuit. Each circuit has a Circuit Administrator responsible, in consultation with the Presiding Judges, for the administration of all the courts within the circuit. Each circuit has a Bar Association taking its name, headed by a 'Circuit Leader', which provides a professional and social focus for its members. The Leader is also an important point of contact with the Presiding Judges and the Circuit Administrator on such matters as appointments to silk and the bench and the administration of justice generally on the circuit. I should mention that solicitors, who have an increasingly important role to play in the efficient operation of the Crown Court, both in their preparation of cases and as advocates, have no corresponding circuit organisations.

43	However, Judges, Circuit Administrators and their staff and the Bar are not the only people concerned with the administration of justice, particularly of criminal justice. As I have mentioned in Chapter 3, there are ten Government regions, each with a Regional Director, representing central Government, developing its policies in the regions and encouraging regional integration in the work of the various Government departments. Within those ten Government regions are grouped the 42 criminal justice areas on which the Police, the Crown Prosecution Service, the Probation Service and the MCCs are based and with which the Lord Chancellor has decided the circuits should largely correspond.[27]

44	Whatever the future structure of the criminal courts, it makes sense for the circuits to correspond broadly with the territorial organisation of most of the criminal justice agencies. It is for consideration whether, as presently organised judicially and administratively, they can achieve that. Before looking at that question in a little more detail, I should say that the strong ties of tradition and affection that bind the Judges and the Bar together in defending the circuit system should not hinder change if it is necessary and beneficial to the administration of justice as a whole. The system is not for their benefit; they are there to serve it. In any event, the long history of Assizes and circuiteering has seen many territorial and administrative changes, before and since the Beeching reforms.[28] At the time of the

---

[27] some concessions being made to the Wales and Chester and Western Circuits

[28] see eg *Aspects of the Legal Profession in the late Fifteenth and Early Sixteenth Centuries*, E W Ives (University of London PhD thesis, 1955); Clarke's *New Law List* (1787) showing six English and four Welsh circuits; and an Order in Council of 5

Beeching Report there were seven circuits, the old Oxford Circuit only merging with the old Midland Circuit to form the Midland and Oxford Circuit in 1972. The dwindling band of Oxford circuiteers have had to come to terms, successively, with losing Berkshire to the South Eastern Circuit, part of Gloucestershire to the Western Circuit and, most recently, Oxfordshire to the South Eastern Circuit. If my recommendations for a unified Criminal Court are adopted, consideration may have to be given to further change, especially as the Presiding Judges would become ultimately responsible for over 30,000 magistrates.

45 There have been suggestions of a need to align the administration of the courts and of the circuits with the ten Government regional groupings of the 42 areas. The Northern Circuit is the only one that contains only one region, though not all of it, namely North West minus Cheshire. The Wales and Chester Circuit and the Western Circuit each broadly corresponds with one region, namely, Wales and South West respectively. The former includes Cheshire from the North West Region[29] and the latter includes Hampshire which is part of the South East Region. I understand that the Lord Chancellor proposes no change in the administration of those circuits to align them with the regional boundaries. That leaves the other three circuits, the Midland and the North Eastern accounting for two regions each and the South Eastern Circuit, accounting for three. As I understand it, the Lord Chancellor is of the view that there is no case for dividing the Midland or the North Eastern Circuit administrations to align them with the regional divisions, but is concerned about the size of the South Eastern Circuit independently of the regional structure.

46 As to all six circuits the questions are: 1) whether they and the circuit administrations should remain as they are, broadly aligned with the 42 area boundaries; 2) whether the circuits should remain broadly as they are, but with a regional Court Service manager or managers, based on the Government region pattern, replacing the present Circuit Administrator and Group Manager structure; or 3) whether the present six circuits should be replaced by ten corresponding to the regional groupings. In the case of the South Eastern Circuit, as I have said, there are concerns, regardless of the Government regional structure, that it is too large and should be broken up into smaller circuits.

47 I have already referred to one of the difficulties of a change of the administration of criminal justice to a structure based on regional groupings; it does not take account of the mix of civil and family work undertaken by the High Court and Circuit Bench at main court centres throughout the country.

February 1876, reducing the number of eight circuits to seven, including an amalgamation of the Home and Norfolk Circuits to the South Eastern

[29] the Wales and Chester Circuit's problems are 'internal' rather than associated with its boundaries; see Ch 3, para 61

And the Presiding Judges also see a problem in any attempt to combine the existing circuit pattern with more than one regional manager for each circuit. It is the loss of the Circuit Administrator as a single point of contact for them in dealing with the already arduous and time-consuming business of administering judicial business on the circuit. They reject the counter-suggestion that one of the regional managers could take the lead for both or all on each circuit. In their view, it would be administratively cumbrous since the selected manager would not have authority to deal with many matters requiring speedy decision, often on the telephone, without reference back to his colleagues. And, it would place him in an invidious position in cases of possible conflict as to the allocation of limited resources between his and another region for which he was deputed to speak. As to the alternative that the present six circuits could be broken up into ten to correspond with the regional groupings, they consider that it would be judicially and administratively inefficient and increase rather than reduce the present rigidity in the deployment of judges.

48   In my view, for all those reasons, the first option – maintenance of present circuit boundaries and administrations, broadly aligned to the 42 areas – would be the best course for the time being. A decision should first be made whether to replace the existing dual system of courts with a unified Criminal Court, with all the increased responsibilities that that could bring to the Presiding Judges and court administrators. There is also the problem of ensuring that, in any system introduced to replace the present, suitable arrangements are made for civil and family jurisdictions who, though sharing their judiciary, administrators and courts with the criminal justice system, have needs of their own.

49   The South Eastern Circuit is undoubtedly a special problem by virtue of its size and number of judges and courts and heavy concentration of work in the London area. It includes the whole of East Anglia, Greater London (including much of the newly enlarged Supreme Court Group), Thames Valley,[30] Buckinghamshire and Berkshire to the west and Surrey, Sussex and Kent to the south and south east. It accounts for 268 of the country's 570 Circuit Judges and has over 220 criminal courtrooms. It is a vast and burdensome responsibility for its Presiding Judges and for its Circuit Administrator. There are three options. The first, which has just taken place,[31] is to leave the circuit and circuit administration broadly as it is, but increase the number of Presiding Judges to three, with the intention that one of them, at any one time, should take the major responsibility for Crown Court centres in Greater London. The second is to divide the circuit into three to correspond with the three Government regions, namely Eastern, Greater London and South East. The third is to divide it into two, Greater London and the rest. There is much

---

[30]   from 1 April 2001

[31]   Mr Justice Bell has been appointed as the third Presiding Judge for the South Eastern Circuit, with effect from 30 June 2001

to be said for the last, so as to treat London separately. Criminal and civil work there are already dealt with in separate Crown and county court centres. The civil courts, which formerly fell within one of two separately administered groups, the Supreme Court and the London county courts, have, from 1 April 2001, become the responsibility of one court group. However, given the recent appointment of a third Presiding Judge to the circuit to enable one of the Presiders to concentrate on the Crown Courts in Greater London, I think that the first of the options should at least be given a trial.

I recommend that:

- **for the foreseeable future circuit boundaries and administrations should remain broadly as they are;**

- **each circuit should continue to have Presiding Judges, Chancery Supervising and Family Liaison Judges and a Circuit Administrator undertaking their present respective functions, so that the Circuit Administrator continues to act as the focal point of contact for them;**

- **whatever changes are contemplated for the administrative organisation of the circuits, a decision should first be made whether to replace the present dual system of courts with a unified Criminal Court, paying close attention to the needs of the civil and family jurisdictions outside London as well as to those of crime; and**

- **there should be a review from time to time of the appropriateness of the South Eastern Circuit remaining one circuit, taking into account, among other things, its size and the special needs of Greater London.**

A NEW MANAGEMENT STRUCTURE

50   Much of the debate about the management structure of the courts has had as its premise the continuance of the present system of two separate criminal court structures, the Crown Court and the magistrates' courts. As I have described in Chapter 3, their respective forms of management through the Court Service and the Magistrates' Courts Committees are unsatisfactory in themselves and also in the divide between them. There are strong arguments for unifying the two systems whether or not the court structures they serve are unified. They become overwhelming if unification of the two court structures is contemplated, especially if it includes the introduction of an intermediate tier of jurisdiction.

51   As I have already detailed in Chapter 3, the administration of magistrates'
     courts is now organised on the basis of the 42 criminal justice areas, and the
     Court Service has recently re-organised its boundaries to ensure that no group
     or circuit boundary crosses through a criminal justice area. [32] However, local
     Court Service managers have comparatively little budgetary or other
     independence, which inhibits the efficiency of their contribution to the
     handling of the continuum of work shared with magistrates' courts. On the
     other hand, Magistrates' Courts Committees, though subject to increasingly
     close oversight by the Lord Chancellor's Department, have considerable
     independence.   This results in inconsistency among themselves in
     implementation of national policy, in court practices and procedures and,
     indirectly, in local sentencing levels. Their funding system – 80% provided
     by national and 20% by local government - is cumbrous and inefficient, and
     their dependence on local authorities for their court and other accommodation
     can obstruct orderly planning and fail to make the optimum use of court
     space. There is little feeling of unity of purpose in the performance of the two
     administrative systems.

52   Many have urged the replacement of the Court Service and the Magistrates'
     Courts Committees with a single administrative structure. Some have argued
     that the two court systems should continue to be separately administered, but
     each in the form of local management based on the 42 areas operating within
     a national framework for the criminal justice system as a whole. The Central
     Council of Magistrates' Courts Committees is a strong proponent of this
     solution and of continuing the committees in all but name. It suggests that
     magistrates, selected for their managerial and other expertise, should continue
     to have the main responsibility, with their justices' chief executive, for the
     administration of their courts, but possibly supplemented by few non-
     magistrates from the local community, acting together as a local management
     authority on the model of the Greater London Magistrates' Courts Authority.
     The Central Council accepts that the current system of financing can be
     frustrating and that there is a need to 'clarify' it, but nevertheless urges
     retention of the 80/20 funding arrangement, particularly for revenue
     expenditure under the cash limit formula.[33] However, it recommends a review
     of the present grant allocation formula, permitting Magistrates' Courts
     Committees to bid for additional 100% revenue expenditure or capital monies
     direct from the Lord Chancellor's Department and to own and manage their
     own estate.

53   Some, including the Central Council, have expressed the view that, at the very
     least, Magistrates' Courts Committees, having undergone much change, most
     recently in their amalgamation and reduction in numbers to match the 42
     criminal justice areas, should be given time to settle down and prove

---

[32] with the exception of Welshpool on the Wales and Chester Circuit

[33] see Chapter 3, paras 19 - 20

themselves. There have been similar suggestions in respect of the Court Service, so as to enable it to develop its administrative structures to meet the modern needs of the Crown Court. It is a relatively new agency, which has also undergone considerable change in its short life.

54   The Magistrates' Courts Service Inspectorate, in its 1998-1999 Annual Report, expressed the view that it was too early to say whether the present system should give way to a centralised, national system. It commented:

> "On the whole the MCC structure seems still to work well. It has shown itself capable of reform, and of increasing efficiency and effectiveness. The challenge is to help MCCs to strengthen their membership and improve their procedures to meet the new requirements." [34]

55   In the Inspectorate's 1999-2000 Report, it appeared to be of the same view, noting that the Committees were making steady progress despite recent changes and uncertainties and that there had been an improvement in over-all efficiency throughout the Service.[35]

56   However, the Inspectorate has a much narrower remit than this Review, in particular as to the administration of the criminal courts system as a whole. And, as to the magistrates' courts, I note that the Inspectorate's 1999-2000 Report confirms the continuance of the difficulties in the legal and administrative divide in the Magistrates' Courts Service to which I referred in Chapters 3 and 4:

> "Unfortunately, in some parts of the Service, this distinction has led to unhelpful tension between the legal and administrative staff. Inspectors have seen MCCs where there is a reluctance to take responsibility for some issues which fall between the two, and others where there is physical segregation of legal and administrative staff. There are many areas of an MCC's work in which both legal and administrative inputs are required – the listing of cases is an obvious example. It is essential that the distinction of roles is balanced by a recognition of the importance of both sides of the MCC's staff working together as a team." [36]

57   In my view, the deficiencies in the individual systems that I have identified and the lack of commonality in their structures and working are so fundamental that little is to be gained by waiting for them to settle into their respective new roles. To do so would not overcome the unnecessary,

---

[34] *Annual Report of Her Majesty's Chief Inspector of the Magistrates' Courts Service 1998-1999*, p v

[35] *Annual Report of Her Majesty's Chief Inspector of the Magistrates' Courts Service 1999-2000*, p 6

[36] ibid, p 8

inefficient and often wasteful divide between the two systems as they are, and would certainly frustrate the establishment of a unified Criminal Court. Although simplification of funding and property management for Magistrates' Courts Committees or their successors might be achievable, it would not cure the problems of duplication of effort and of inconsistency that arise from each Committee alighting in isolation on different solutions to similar problems and devising different forms and procedures to implement national policies, a constant irritant to legal practitioners working in more than one Magistrates' Courts Committee area.

58   The separation of administrative responsibilities, particularly in the case of the Court Service, is an added complication to the already complex relationship with the various local criminal justice agencies which, through one or other medium, are responsible for trying to make the system work at local level. It is clearly desirable that, in the new 42 area structure, there should be a representative of all of the criminal courts in each area, with budgetary authority to commit them to a single, efficient and effective system of working with the other agencies.

59   There is also the question of investment in and use of common information technology. Perpetuation of the present dual system of administration would in the short to medium term encourage unnecessary and wasteful duplication of expenditure between Magistrates' Courts Committees or their successors and the Court Service in the phased development of a common information technology system for the criminal justice system.[37]   In addition, the continuance of and vesting of funds in local administrative bodies for the magistrates' courts could complicate and delay its development.

60   The present divided system leads to much waste of court and other accommodation.   There is some sharing between the Crown Court and magistrates' courts.   But it is complicated by different ownerships, funding and timing arrangements and Treasury Guidelines affecting the Court Service on the disposal of un-used and under-used property.   It usually involves the passing of public money from one public agency to another, the general scheme being that the occupying agency should reimburse the owning agency for its occupation.   It depends on the willingness of the agency with spare courtroom capacity to make it available to the other, and on the willingness of the other to spend money to use it.[38]   Many magistrates' courts are under-used and some Crown Court centres, from time to time, have insufficient courtrooms to list the work they have. The Lord Chancellor's Department has been working recently to reduce the over-capacity in the magistrates' courts;

---

[37] see Chapter 8, paras 92 - 111

[38] in January 2001 the Lord Chancellor's Department issued guidance in the form of *Principles for the Joint Usage of Magistrates' Courts and Court Service's Buildings*, the overriding principle of which is that "financial arrangements are to be directed at reimbursing the party in occupation for the costs that the other party's occupation causes".

and, through closer working with other courts and tribunals, more efficient use is now being made of the estate in many areas. However, a unified court with a single budget would be better placed to deal flexibly, at short notice, if need be, and without concerns about budgetary boundaries, with allocating work between courts whatever their customary use. In that way, the system could deal more sensitively with venue in terms of jurisdiction, location, physical access, facilities for child witnesses, secure custody areas, number of defendants, media interest etc.

61   A unified administration should also bring various other economies of scale and scope for an appropriate level of specialisation in support functions such as personnel, finance, office accommodation, information technology and management and staff training.

62   I am, therefore, driven back to the conclusions of the Beeching Commission in 1969 and Le Vay in his 1989 Scrutiny, writing of the future administration respectively of the Crown Court and magistrates' courts, but in terms applicable to both. The Beeching Commission stated:

> "We consider that the administration of justice should be recognised for what it has largely become, namely a central Government responsibility, and that it should be financed directly, by the Exchequer, instead of indirectly, as much of it is at present...." [39]

63   And Le Vay concluded that:

> "the requirement is for a centrally-funded and centrally-run service which:
>
> - ensures that overall policy responsibility for administration of the courts rests clearly with the Government;
>
> - but shields magistrates from an excessive degree of Government influence in judicial policy;
>
> - and allows the service to be so far as possible, locally managed, with managers having the control over (and responsibility for) resource use which is needed to achieve optimum performance". [40]

64   If a unified administration is the answer, what form should it take? Again, it seems to me that Le Vay's interpretation and modification of the Beeching

---

[39] Report of *Review of Assizes and Quarter Sessions*, para 307

[40] *Efficiency Scrutiny of the magistrates' courts*, para 8.2, and see generally paras 7.15 – 8.13

Commission's approach suggests an answer[41] – an executive agency providing a national service, but with maximum delegation of managerial responsibility and control of resources to an accountable local manager working in close liaison with the professional and lay judiciary. Such a system would provide much needed efficiency and flexibility in the use of judges, accommodation, staff and other resources for the two tier system that we have and, even more so, for the three tier system that I recommend. Subject to what I say below, it should be able to do the same for the three jurisdictions, civil, family and crime at all levels. It would fit reasonably well with the circuit system and the structure of judicial oversight and management provided by the Presiding and Resident Judges. As a nationally directed, but locally managed, service, it would be more effective than the present fragmented systems. And it would provide greater flexibility and, I believe, would be quicker and cheaper to achieve than the alternatives.

65   It would follow that there is no sensible reason why local authorities should continue to fund 20% of the magistrates' part of the system, or to provide or manage its accommodation and other facilities. As I have said, the funding that they are presently required to provide gives them little or no control or influence over the way in which summary justice is provided within their areas, and most have little feeling of involvement in its provision. The new unified Criminal Court should be 100% funded by central government.

66   But for one aspect, such a structure would also suit the administrative requirements of the civil and family jurisdictions, often presided over by the same judges or magistrates using the same courts. In general terms, it seems to me that it could only be beneficial for all three jurisdictions if they were managed by one administrative structure. It would encourage readier sharing of court and other accommodation and of speedier allocation of work to the right levels. And it should bring with it other the advantages of a single administrative system. One of these is flexibility in the deployment and sharing of resources, particularly important in the court system which suffers from high volatility over short periods in the relative workloads of the three jurisdictions for which it has to provide. However, a complication is the Government's resolve, now partly achieved, to organise the administrations of the criminal courts and the criminal justice agencies on the 42 areas basis. As I have said, the Court Service remains a notable exception and there may be sound administrative and geographical reasons for it or any new body undertaking responsibility for the courts over-all to remain so. An additional factor is the Government's policy decision to operate separate systems of funding and accounting for each of the three jurisdictions.

---

[41] ibid, paras 7.15 – 7.24

67   One alternative would be to introduce local and largely autonomous court agencies or boards on the lines of the Magistrates' Courts Committees, but each responsible for both levels of criminal jurisdiction. The only rationale for such a course could be to maintain a degree of locality in the management of the courts. Now, I can see an argument for locality in the lay membership, and in the siting, of courts themselves, but not for managers in the sense of their reflecting the local community. Nor can I see a case for extending to all the criminal courts the confusion of judicial and management functions embodied in Magistrates' Courts Committees. I do not see how it could work efficiently alongside the civil and family jurisdictions with which it would have to share judicial, accommodation and staff resources - unless it is to be suggested that they too should be governed by the same local bodies.

68   In family work for instance, the High Court, county court and magistrates' courts, for the most part, exercise the same jurisdiction and are, in all but name, a Family Court in which the work is allocated to different levels according to certain criteria. Yet they too have, as between the magistrates' court on the one hand and the county courts and High Court on the other, different administrations, with problems of discontinuity, inconsistency and delay in allocation of work between them similar to those I have described in the criminal courts. At the magistrates' courts level, they also suffer from inconsistencies in priorities and practices between Magistrates' Courts Committees similar to those in the administration of their criminal jurisdiction.

69   The second main alternative would be to create two new national agencies, one to administer the whole range of criminal jurisdiction and the other to combine responsibility for the civil and family work of all courts. In my view, such a course would be a highly expensive way of introducing an unnecessary and highly inefficient divide at national and local level in the running of three jurisdictions which require a single over-all direction and maximum flexibility in the use of their shared resources.

70   Whatever form a unified administrative structure is to take, I am of the view that it should be seen as a fresh start. If, for example, the decision is for a national agency with maximum delegation to local managers, it should not be seen as a modified and enlarged Court Service taking over the Magistrates' Courts Committees. One of the important factors in determining the organisational structure would be the sheer scale of the responsibilities it would be undertaking when compared, say, to those of the Court Service. It would add 435 magistrates' courts and their 95% of all criminal cases to its 78 Crown Court centres and their small, in percentage terms, balance of criminal work.

71   In my view, there should be one administrative agency, as part of the Lord Chancellor's Department, responsible for the three criminal jurisdictions at all levels, save for the House of Lords. The responsibilities of the Magistrates' Courts Committees and the Court Service should be transferred to this new agency, which should also be responsible for the whole court system. I have already recommended in this Chapter that, for the moment at least, there should continue to be six Circuit Administrators responsible for all of the courts on their circuit. Below circuit level, there should be a structure dedicated to the administration of the unified criminal court and, possibly, separate and similar structures for the administration of the civil and family jurisdictions.

72   In order to meet the concerns I have discussed, a unified Criminal Court should, if possible, be organized managerially on the 42 area basis. The amalgamation of the present separate systems should make such areas financially viable with large enough budgets to enable flexible management of resources in a way that the Court Service, so far, has not been able to achieve. The precise administrative and geographical relationship between the structures of all three jurisdictions is beyond the scope of this Review. However, as I have said more than once, it is vital that the relationship, at local, as well as at national level is given careful attention. It is at local level that the judiciary, day to day management, support facilities and accommodation have, in the main, to be shared between them. And it is at local level, the way the Court Service is seemingly headed, that budgetary divides and controls will have to be erected to keep the three jurisdictions financially separate. I caution against any move to organising a new criminal court system on a strictly 42 area basis until a satisfactory scheme for management of the whole justice system has been devised.

73   It would, therefore, be for others to determine the most practical way to link administratively and geographically the three Criminal Court Divisions that I propose and the civil and family courts. I have assumed that each magistrates' court (including its youth court) should be joined with the Crown Court to which it sends cases, and with which, as parts of a unified Criminal Court, it would provide District Judges and experienced magistrates to sit in the new District Division. Of course, workload and local accommodation could influence how this would work in practice. The question of London, where all class 1, 2 and 3 cases within the Greater London area are sent to the Central Criminal Court, would also need to be considered separately. It would follow that the present Court Service would disappear, or be reconstituted for a wider role, along with the local administrative and court staffs of the magistrates' courts. Magistrates' Courts Committees would cease to exist and so, in their present manifestation, would justices' chief executives. However, the latter would, I am sure, become much sought after for senior administrative roles of comparable or greater responsibility in the new national agency. Justices' clerks and legal advisers in the magistrates'

courts would retain their distinctive advisory role, but exercise it in the Magistrates' Division of the new Criminal Court.

I recommend that:

- **a single centrally funded executive agency, as part of the Lord Chancellor's Department, should be responsible for the administration of all courts, civil, criminal and family (save for the Appellate Committee of the House of Lords), replacing the Court Service and Magistrates' Courts Committees;**

- **the agency should be headed by a national board and chief executive;**

- **within each circuit the criminal courts should, if consistent with the efficient and effective operation of civil and family courts, be organized managerially on the basis of the 42 criminal justice areas; and**

- **implementation of national policy and management at local level for all three jurisdictions should be the responsibility of local managers working in close liaison with local judges and magistrates, much as the Circuit Administrators and Presiding Judges, Chancery Supervising and Family Liaison Judges do at circuit level.**

The future role of the justices' clerk

74   I discussed in Chapter 4 variations in the role and geographical coverage of justices' clerks. The creation of a unified Criminal Court would provide an opportunity to clarify their responsibilities in order to ensure that the primary focus is on their role as professional legal adviser to the justices. This would require them to have management responsibility for all legal advisers within the area and, therefore, to play a part within the wider structure of the criminal court. However, priority should be given to ensuring that there are direct and effective lines of communication between justices' clerks and their benches and that magistrates have ready access to good quality and authoritative legal advice.

I recommend that, in a unified court:

- **justices' clerks should continue to be responsible for the legal advice provided to magistrates;**

- **arrangements should be made to ensure that, in the absence of the justices' clerk, magistrates at each**

courthouse have ready access to a senior legal adviser; and

- **justices' clerks should not normally exercise administrative responsibilities unrelated to their role as legal adviser to the magistrates.**

JUDICIAL MANAGEMENT

Introduction

75   As I have said,[42] judges in England and Wales - in contrast to judges in many other common law jurisdictions - have no formal role in the management of their courts.   However, an increasingly important system of judicial management (ie the management of judges by judges) has nevertheless grown up since the passing of the Courts Act 1971 under the oversight of the Senior Presiding Judge and Presiding Judges of the circuits.[43]

76   In the Crown Court, the fulcrum of the system is the Resident Judge.[44] His responsibilities cover:

- allocation of work - including the implementation of directions from the Lord Chief Justice and Presiding Judges, and judicial oversight of the listing of cases;

- judicial performance - including leadership of the local full and part-time judiciary, promoting consistency of approach and nomination of judges for authorisations and training;

- court performance – including regular review of cases which are delayed and initiatives to reduce the number of cracked and ineffective trials; and

- communication – promoting regular communication with the other relevant agencies, chairing the Court User Committee and, in appropriate cases, the Area Strategy Committee.

77   In practice, the time required by these responsibilities varies considerably. Some of the tasks involved, particularly in relation to allocation and court performance, are in any event undertaken by court staff under the Resident Judge's judicial supervision. This is also a field in which the advance of information technology, and in particular the provision to all full-time judges

---

[42] Chapter 3 para 13

[43] who were given statutory recognition in the Courts and Legal Service Act 1990, s 72

[44] similar responsibilities are exercised in relation to Civil Law by Designated Civil Judges

of computers with access to the internet,[45] has further eased the administrative burden. But it is of real constitutional importance that these functions are ultimately under the control and oversight of the judiciary rather than the executive, and that there is an ultimate line of accountability through Resident Judges to the Presiding Judges for the way they are exercised.

78   In the magistrates' courts, however, there is no equivalent of the Resident Judge. Each petty sessions area has a bench comprising all the magistrates who sit in that area, which has wide responsibilities for the administration of justice at summary level, including the election of magistrates to sit on youth and other panels. In practice, most of these responsibilities are delegated either to a bench training and development committee, which is responsible for providing training to magistrates under the MNTI scheme, or to the officers elected at the bench annual general meeting, in particular, the chairman of the bench. Arrangements vary, but the bench chairman will typically be the main link between the magistracy and the justices' chief executive and justices' clerks, and will take a key role in decisions relating to rostering arrangements, composition of panels, and questions of conduct or discipline. The bench chairman would also normally act as the main contact point where there is a statutory requirement for the bench to be consulted, for example over proposals for court closures. In addition, one of the Circuit Judges at each Crown Court centre will be nominated as liaison judge, responsible for providing the institutional link and channel of communication between the judiciary and magistracy.

79   Different again are arrangements for the District Bench. Outside London, few District Judges have any formal link with their local bench or MCC (and many have no link at all). Nor do District Judges normally have any regular contact with the Resident Judge or other judges sitting in the Crown Court, unless they (the District Judges) are Recorders. Indeed, until recently, stipendiary magistrates (as they then were) sitting in courts outside of London were not subject to any form of judicial management at all. Now there is a Senior District Judge (Chief Magistrate), who has over-all responsibility for the deployment of the full- and part-time District Bench countrywide and takes a leading role in appointment, training and 'pastoral' issues.

80   Whether or not my recommendation for a unified Criminal Court is adopted, I believe that it would provide a helpful collegiality to the judges of the criminal courts, professional and lay, to be brought under the responsibility and to have the support of the Presiding Judges. In a unified court it would, I believe, be essential to put all questions of judicial administration within a circuit under the oversight of the Presiding Judges. This would enable them to gain a wide perspective of the performance of all Divisions of the Criminal Court, the manner and speed in which cases were disposed of, and the effectiveness of its links with the other relevant agencies. It would enable

---

[45] see below, para 97

them to exercise a more effective role when being consulted, by those within and outside the courts system, on questions that would affect its working at every level.

81   Within each court centre, the key figure would be the Resident Judge. Resident Judges would retain their current responsibilities for the existing work of the Crown Court, but would also assume oversight of the following functions in relation to the work of District Judges and magistrates:

- Listing – it is a well established principle in the Crown Court that the listing of cases, while generally carried out by administrative staff, is undertaken under judicial supervision and with judicial authority. This approach should, in my view, be applied throughout a unified Criminal Court, so that whoever in future undertakes the listing of cases at whatever level would be ultimately accountable for it to the Resident Judge.

- Panels – as I have mentioned, the membership of the youth and other panels is at present decided by election at the annual general meeting of each bench. While I have no doubt that the decisions reached are, in the main, perfectly satisfactory, it does not seem to me that this method of selection provides an adequate institutional link between the jurisdictions magistrates exercise and their acquisition of competences under MNTI. I therefore believe that members of panels dealing with criminal jurisdiction should be appointed by the Resident Judge on the advice of the bench chairman, who would no doubt consult with his fellow magistrates as he considers appropriate. This would include the membership of panels of suitably experienced magistrates eligible to sit with professional judges trying more serious cases in the District Division. An equivalent mechanism could be adopted for membership of family panels.

- Case allocation – a consequence of the recommendation I have made in Chapter 6 for the abolition of most forms of judicial 'ticket' is that Resident Judges would become much more closely involved in the allocation of complex or sensitive cases to individual judges in the Crown Division. This responsibility would extend also to oversight in the District Division of a system of assignment of judicial chairmen in accordance with national guidelines and, in the Magistrates' Division, of allocation of work between the magistracy and District Judges in accordance with the Venne criteria.[46]

- Training and development – Resident Judges would also take an interest in the training of full- and part-time judges, in order to assist them in their case allocation function.

- Appraisal – In the event of acceptance of my recommendation in Chapter 6 for the extension of performance appraisal to judges and Recorders, Resident Judges would acquire an additional role in this sensitive area in relation to Circuit Judges, Recorders, and full- and part-time District Judges. They should also assume general oversight of the appraisal arrangements for

---

[46] see Chapter 4 paras 44 - 47

magistrates, providing clear judicial leadership and also a means of resolving any disputes that might arise.

82   I have already recommended in Chapter 6 that Resident Judges need more time and administrative support to enable them to carry out their existing responsibilities alongside their court work. It is plain from what I have just said that, within a unified Criminal Court, those responsibilities would increase and so would their need for time and adequate support. I believe that as the court is being established there should be a review of their number and location and also of their remuneration.

83   As to the magistracy, the local bench should remain the key group for liaison with the judiciary and court staff. Bench chairmen should continue to provide the principal channel of communication between the Resident Judge, the court administration and magistrates, as well as retaining significant leadership responsibilities of their own. For many, the change should be one of form rather than substance. Similarly, I see a continuing and important role for the Magistrates' Association in the national support and representation of the magistracy. However, I am not so sanguine about the future of the office of Senior District Judge (Chief Magistrate).[47] There is no national equivalent for any other tier of the judiciary below the High Court Bench: there is no Chief Circuit Judge, nor a Chief District Judge on the Civil side, nor Chief (lay) Magistrate. I also believe that the existence of a national chain of judicial authority for one cadre of judges would, in a unified court, cut across the local line of accountability to the Resident Judge upon which much would depend. As to liaison judges, I would expect them to continue in their valuable role of maintaining contact with, and training of, the magistracy, though possibly working more closely with, or deputising for Resident Judges in these respects.

I recommend that in a unified Criminal Court:

- **Resident Judges should be responsible, under the oversight of the Presiding Judges, for judicial management of court centres;**

- **in relation to the District Bench and magistracy, these responsibilities should include oversight of: listing; membership of panels; case allocation; training and development; and appraisal;**

- **Resident Judges should be provided with the necessary time out of court and degree of administrative and other support to carry out these additional responsibilities;**

---

[47] created by the Access to Justice Act 1999, s 78

- there should be consequential reviews of the number and location of Resident Judges, and also of their remuneration; and

- the future organisation and structure of the District Bench should be reviewed in the light of these changes.

COURT ACCOMMODATION

84 Different cases, even when they fall within the same levels of jurisdiction, may require different court accommodation and supporting facilities. If a unified Criminal Court is introduced, it should be possible ultimately for cases to be heard in court buildings or at court centres with sufficiently varied accommodation to provide, where needed, for all types of case – from the Magistrates' Division to the Court of Appeal. This should not be seen as a threat to local justice. When and where such accommodation is provided, it would allow for more, rather than fewer, cases to be heard locally. Where the range of work at many court centres does not, and would not, justify so generous a provision, a more modest standard of accommodation should be retained or provided, even if, for the time being, it would fall short of what is now regarded as ideal court design. I am uneasy about continuation of the current trend to concentrate work at fewer and more widely spaced court centres. The rationale for this trend is that many court buildings, particularly in rural areas, are under-used, old, small, in bad condition and incapable of providing adequate facilities, for example, for witnesses, disabled persons and young persons. But it seems to me that there must come a time when a balance has to be drawn between, on the one hand, cost and the provision of modern court facilities, and, on the other, a sense of local justice which the presence of a court and reasonable accessibility to it gives.

85 As to the cost of running a court under consideration for closure, it is the financial cost to the Lord Chancellor's Department, not the financial and wider costs to the criminal justice system as a whole in the area, which seems to dominate the decision. And the decision is that of the Lord Chancellor, not of all the Departments and agencies responsible for criminal process in the area, notwithstanding that it affects their budgets and the pockets of other court users too. In the case of closure of a Crown Court centre, which, unlike that of county court and magistrates' court buildings, has not occurred for some years, he would decide after local consultation with interested bodies and parties. In the case of closure of a magistrates' court, the decision is notionally that of the Magistrates' Courts Committee, but they are so bound by his guidelines as to usage, available modern facilities, accommodation for

prisoners[48] and budgetary restrictions that, effectively, closures are driven by his Department. They too are required to consult before submitting a draft order for closure to the Lord Chancellor, but only with the relevant local authority(ies) and the magistrates for the area. Some, but not all, consult more widely. The Lord Chancellor only intervenes personally in the event of an appeal by local authorities from a Committee's decision as to closure.[49]

86   In the replacement of old and inadequate court buildings with adequate court accommodation and modern facilities, the Lord Chancellor can direct Magistrates' Courts Committees to meet specified standards of performance, including proper provision for the disabled. The question is not just one of the cost to the Lord Chancellor's Department of meeting such standards in an existing or replacement court building relative to the use of the building for court purposes. That is, of course, an important factor, but there are the other costs to the system too. Closure of existing courts can result in magistrates and court users, official, professional and otherwise, having to travel great distances at great cost to them in money, time and convenience. In mid-Wales, Devon and Cornwall and Cumbria, for example, current closures can result in 30 or 40 miles travelling distance to and from court, often without a choice of convenient public transport. In my view, whatever the future court structure, the Lord Chancellor should not have the monopoly of making decisions that can so affect the way in which criminal justice is provided, or not provided, locally. These are decisions which, if my recommendation in Chapter 8 is accepted, should be taken by local Criminal Justice Boards, subject to oversight and guidance of the national Criminal Justice Board, in the light of the interests of all involved in the criminal, civil and family justice process in their areas, and with the benefit of some sort of cost/benefit exercise taking the public interest in its widest sense into account.

87   The Lord Chancellor's Department is undertaking an audit of all its property with a view to securing the best use of its available accommodation and to disposing of what may be surplus to its requirements. In my view, this is far too narrow an exercise. There should be a much broader examination of the availability of, and need for, accommodation throughout the criminal, civil and family justice systems generally, with a view to sharing and/or flexibility of user where appropriate. For example, looking just at the criminal justice process, the Probation Service, the Crown Prosecution Service, the Criminal Defence Service as it develops and video-link conferencing facilities for defence advocates and their clients in custody could, with advantage to all, be based in or close to major court centres. If such omnibus provision is made in the same building or neighbouring buildings for all those most closely

---

[48] these guidelines are in turn informed by Magistrates' Courts Committees' National Performance Indicators and Standards as to facilities set by the Magistrates' Courts Inspectorate
[49] the Justices of the Peace Act 1997, ss 56(1) and 56(3); in 1999 there were nine appeals, one of which the Lord Chancellor allowed; in 2000 there were 11 appeals, one of which he allowed; and, so far in 2001, there have been 12 appeals, none of which he has allowed

involved in the criminal justice process, I see no danger to the respective independence of the courts or of the various agencies. The advantages of joint planning and sharing of expense in the provision and maintenance of such accommodation and its supporting facilities are obvious.

88 In assessing, as part of such broader exercise, likely court accommodation needs, regard should be had to two factors not conspicuously present in the Court Service's or Magistrates' Courts Committees' planning to date. The first is that the courts and the judges or magistrates are there to serve the criminal justice system, not to receive preferential treatment from all agencies, bodies and individuals using or exposed to it. As I have said in Chapter 6, it should no longer be a tenet of court administration that, regardless of the convenience of others, courtrooms should be in full-time use and that on no account should judges or magistrates be kept waiting. For many years now that has been a Court Service management imperative rather than a judicial edict. Judges have more than enough to do in preparation for their work in court and in case management behind the scenes to feel that their dignity is slighted if they are not on show in court. Second, in the planning of courtroom accommodation, a significant tolerance should be provided to allow for the high volatility of demands on court time and uncertainties of future criminal justice policy initiatives, patterns of offending and priorities in the prosecution of offences.

89 Rationalising and providing modern court accommodation are long-term exercises. The introduction of a unified Criminal Court should assist this rationalisation, not only in terms of efficient use of resources, but also in preserving and strengthening 'locality' of justice. Much of the District Division work could, with advantage, be undertaken in many presently under-used magistrates' courthouses, reducing the trend of closure of magistrates' courts towards ever larger and more distantly spaced Crown Court and magistrates' courts centres. Within limits, there may be some scope for varying the standards of provision according to the size and use of the court centre. However, the adequacy and condition of court buildings and their supporting facilities are a practical contribution to the quality of justice provided and to the public face of the criminal justice system. Inadequate and run-down accommodation engenders inefficiency, low morale and is unlikely to earn public confidence. Some basic aims should be formulated and gathered together in the form of a new Criminal Court Design Guide to provide standards to which courts should, over time, be made to conform. It should also be possible to design more flexible courtrooms, which should be capable of being used for hearings in each Division of the unified Criminal Court.

90 I shall not attempt to prescribe a list of standards, but there are a number of obvious issues that I know the Lord Chancellor's Department has well in mind:

- separate waiting areas for prosecution and defence witnesses;

- accommodation for witness and victim support;

- access and supporting aids for disabled persons;

- separate access, where required, for young persons, jurors, vulnerable witnesses and defendants in custody; and

- an information system at court and - through the medium of telephonic and information technology - away from it as to the listing and progress of cases, witness requirement etc.

I recommend that:

- **if my recommendations in Chapter 8 for a national Criminal Justice Board and local Criminal Justice Boards are accepted, decisions as to the provision and closure of court centres should become the responsibility of local Boards, subject to oversight and guidance of the national Board;**

- **decisions should be made in the interests of all involved in the criminal justice process in their areas, and with the benefit of a cost/benefit exercise taking the public interest in its widest sense into account;**

- **there should be a review of all accommodation of the courts and criminal justice agencies to enable a joint assessment of the most efficient use for the system as a whole of available accommodation and planning for future needs;**

- **in the planning and provision of court accommodation, proper allowance should be made for the fact that a just and efficient criminal justice system does not require all courtrooms to be in use full-time;**

- **in the planning and provision of court accommodation, a significant tolerance should be allowed for the high volatility of demands on court time and the uncertainties of future criminal justice policy initiatives (that is, "an adequate tolerance over assumed full capacity"); and**

- **a new Criminal Court Design Guide should be prepared as a standard to which, over time, court buildings should conform.**

INFORMATION TECHNOLOGY

91   The establishment of a unified Criminal Court would require integration of a range of functions and processes which have developed separately in the magistrates' courts and the Crown Court. One of these is information technology. If a unified Criminal Court is to function efficiently and effectively in its own right, and also as part of the wider criminal justice system, it will need a system of information technology apt for the role.

92   At present, the two court structures have separate information systems and technical infrastructures. In magistrates' courts, the Lord Chancellor's Department has, since 1998, been progressively introducing LIBRA,[50] a computer-based case-management system providing standard office automation and dedicated information technology support for key processes. The present contract with its suppliers runs until 2013. The development and implementation of the new software applications has recently run into difficulties and, as a result, has fallen behind schedule. But, the hope is that, when installed, LIBRA will enable magistrates' courts to transfer information to and from the main criminal justice agencies via a secure web-site. It is also intended to provide a nationwide network infrastructure for external e-mail for all staff, courtroom computing, with on-line access during hearings, and a data store for policy evaluation and information on performance.

93   The Crown Court system – CREST – is more limited in scope. It enables court staff to create electronic case files. But it does not allow them to share them with the main criminal justice agencies, nor to draw much local management information from them. However, the Court Service, as part of its modernisation of the Crown Court (the 'Crown Court Programme'), is developing a new information technology system (CREDO), designed to introduce some sharing of use by all the main criminal justice agencies and to provide hearing information to the public. Other parts of the Programme under development are digital audio recording, electronic presentation of evidence, courtroom technology and improvements in case management. Computerised jury summoning (the JUROR system) has already been implemented. A 'Pathfinder Court' has recently been established in the Crown Court at Kingston-upon-Thames for testing and illustrating the working of the various parts of the Programme. And, over the next year various of them will be piloted in about one quarter of Crown Court centres.

94   Clearly, there is a good deal of work under way in both jurisdictions and there are a number of significant advances in prospect. In particular, one of the projects demonstrated at a recent open day at the Kingston-upon-Thames

---

[50] *Lord Chancellor's Department's Annual Report 2000/2001*, Cmnd 5107 , (The Stationery Office), p 30

Pathfinder Court was a computerised listing system that would enable staff to communicate from courtroom terminals, via the listing office, real time progress and listing information to parties, criminal justice agencies and others involved in its proceedings. This is complemented within the court-building with monitor screens in the public areas displaying information about the progress of each court's work. If, as I hope, such facilities become standard in all or most criminal courtrooms in the country, it would not only make for a much more efficient criminal process, but a more considerate and helpful one to all involved in it, in the provision of timely information and notice and in the reduction in waiting times. There are also the obvious benefits which result from electronic transmission of data: 75% of endorsements of driving licenses are currently transmitted direct from magistrates' courts to the DVLA via magnetic tape or electronic data input.

95   All that is good news, but there remains the wasteful duplication of the LIBRA and CREDO projects, quite apart from their joint and individual shortcomings as part of a general system of information technology for the criminal justice system as a whole. I do not believe that efficiency is best served by the development of two entirely separate systems of information technology in support of the management of criminal cases. If my recommendation for a unified Criminal Court is adopted, the duality of approach would be unsustainable. In Chapter 8 I consider the ways in which an integrated system of information technology, based on the internet could be developed to serve the whole criminal justice system. But, again, even without such a development, there is, in my view, a clear and urgent need for integrating case management support systems for all levels of criminal jurisdiction.

96   In the criminal justice system as a whole, information technology systems should not be developed in isolation from the various agencies or the other bodies, the judiciary and the professions who will, directly or indirectly, use them. There have been a number of initiatives to encourage a more integrated approach, sometimes overlapping, sometimes with the various agencies envisaging different levels of integration and, often, faltering. Since 1985 the Information Technology and the Courts Committee (ITAC), chaired by Lord Saville of Newdgate, has provided a forum for a wide range of participants to exchange views and news about their respective investments and plans. Its membership includes representatives of a number of Government departments and agencies and of the Bar Council and Law Society. Although, it has no executive authority, it has been an important contributor to better identification of common future needs and collaboration in the development of individual systems. The inclusion of professional legal practitioners in its membership is important since, with the increasing use of information technology in the pre-trial and trial processes of the courts, they will have an important interest in, and contribution to make to, the development and use of an integrated system. ITAC is, and should continue to be, a good forum for this.

97   A more recent judicially centred variant of ITAC (and with some overlap in membership) is the Judicial Technology Group, established in 1997, also chaired by Lord Saville and consisting of judges from all tiers of the judiciary, the Director of Studies of the Judicial Studies Board and senior officials of the Court Service. It does not, but in my view, should, include representatives of the District Judges and the magistracy. Its main purpose is to identify judicial information technology needs to enable the Court Service to determine the future of its information technology support for the judiciary. In this, thanks to the persistence of, among others, Lord Justice Brooke, great advances have been made. Through the Judicial Technology Project, over 1,000 judges have been provided with computers and access to the internet. And in April 2001 the Lord Chief Justice announced Lord Justice Brooke's appointment as 'Judge in Charge of Modernisation', his remit being to ensure that the needs of judges are fully taken into account when any decisions are taken which may affect the way we administer justice in our courts. As such, he will represent the judiciary on the Crown Court Programme Board, as he already does on the Civil Courts Programme Board, and lead the judiciary on a new Judicial Technology Project Board, one of the tasks of which will be to develop a strategy for judicial use of information technology over the next ten years.

98   In my view, whatever body and programme emerges for development of a wider system of information technology to serve the whole of the criminal justice system, the judiciary, legal practitioners and others involved in the criminal justice process should be closely involved in its development. The court based initiatives that I have mentioned here are a useful starting point for such involvement and should be continued, whatever the outcome of my recommendations for a unified Criminal Court and administration.

99   As I have mentioned earlier in the Report, information technology is not just a way of doing more quickly and otherwise more efficiently what we do now; it is also a way of changing to advantage the way we do it. It is important to be alert to this potential in the field of criminal procedure which, despite its great changes in the last two and a half centuries, still has a mould which too readily shapes and restricts thoughts for improvement. Unfortunately, there are likely to be few criminal lawyers proficient in information technology systems design and even fewer systems designers with a good working knowledge of criminal law and procedure. Something needs to be done to combine these skills. One of the biggest disappointments to the judiciary has been that civil courts still lack the basic information technology that Lord Woolf envisaged as necessary support for them in the implementation of his civil justice reforms.[51] The problem was in part the inability of the Court Service to commit itself to the long-term capital funding and planning that

[51] *Access to Justice*, Final Report, p 284

such technology required, and partly the separate development of the Civil Procedure Rules themselves and of the system of information technology required to support them. Lord Woolf's reforms are still dogged by the Lord Chancellor's Department's and Court Service's under-estimation of the considerable investment and work required to develop and introduce the necessary supporting systems. These errors should not be repeated in the development and planning of procedural reforms for criminal justice. Planning and implementation of the reforms should go hand in hand with development and introduction of the necessary supporting information technology.

100 It is important to keep in mind in the field of information technology, just as in that of reform of the criminal courts, the needs of the civil and family jurisdictions and the sharing of judicial and other resources between all three jurisdictions. There are likely to be overlaps and gaps between my recommendations and the current proposals of the Court Service to modernise the civil courts.[52] There should, however, be differences between the system that would support a unified Criminal Court and those that would support the civil and family jurisdictions, not only because of the obvious differences in processes, but also because of the wider network of criminal justice bodies and agencies of which the courts are part. I believe that an information technology support system for a unified Criminal Court could connect with those for civil and family law, but should remain distinct from them. Apart from anything else, transfer of personal information between different databases could threaten individuals' rights to privacy.[53] Nevertheless, the Lord Chancellor's Department should identify the extent to which the common and different needs and uses could be accommodated within a single system and those that could not. In the internet solution that I propose in Chapter 8 for the criminal justice system as a whole, it should be possible to devise common technology and a common infrastructure for the various court jurisdictions, but which would enable separate processing of data and information.

101 The Judicial Working Group convened to consider the Court Service Consultation Paper of January 2001, *Modernising the Civil Courts*, has expressed the view that the achievement of further improvements in the civil and family jurisdictions will demand an electronic case record, comprising an electronic case file, an electronic diary and an electronic case management system. Allowing for all the obvious differences between the civil and criminal jurisdictions, there are clearly some common needs for which provision should be made in developing information technology support for them all, as the Judicial Working Group noted:

---

[52] *Lord Chancellor's Department's Annual Report 2000/2001* p 29 and, in particular, the Court Service consultation paper *Modernising the Civil Courts*, issued in January 2001
[53] see Walker *Criminal Justice Processes and the Internet* in Akdeniz, Waler and Wall (eds): *The, Internet, Law and Society* (Longman, 2000) p203

"Although criminal business is outside our terms of reference, we emphasise that in our view such common information systems must also extend to criminal business. The civil and family justice systems do not exist in a vacuum....

The practical advantage of sharing the cost of system development and IT equipment across the whole justice system is obvious. The planning, piloting and implementation of electronic systems for civil, family and criminal business should be co-ordinated from the outset". [54]

102   The Court Service has responded to this sentiment by establishing a single Board, including in its membership Lord Justice Brooke, to oversee the court modernisation programmes for the criminal, civil and family courts.   The Court Service has allocated a total of £165m to the three programmes over the next three years.   I welcome this start in planning and development, with high level judicial involvement, of what may be common components, not only of information technology for all courts, but for one to serve the criminal justice system as a whole.

I recommend that:

- **a single information technology system should be developed for the unified Criminal Court, combining the best design elements of all the systems currently under development in the magistrates' courts and Crown Court and taking into account corresponding developments in the civil and family jurisdictions;**

- **the management of the implementation of information technology for a unified Criminal Court should be under the supervision of a Board upon which the judiciary are represented, and should be undertaken in close consultation with the Judicial Technology Group; and**

- **planning and implementation of procedural reforms should go hand in hand with development and introduction of the necessary supporting information technology.**

---

[54] *Modernising the Civil Courts, Report of the Judicial Working Group*, (The Court Service, May 2001)

SECURITY

103   One of the most serious examples of the tendency of criminal justice agencies
to plan and provide for themselves regardless of the needs of the criminal
justice system as a whole is in the field of security. In recent years Chief
Constables, with their eyes on their own budgetary commitments, have
gradually withdrawn their uniformed officers from court duty, taking the view
that it is for the courts to provide their own security. In particular cases where
there is a known risk of danger the police will provide security as necessary,[55]
but generally not otherwise.

104   In Crown and combined court centres, police officers at court have, in the
main, been replaced by security guards provided under contract,[56] just as
prison officers have been replaced by contracted court escorts. Court security
budgets are controlled centrally and there is regular assessment by the Court
Service of the number of guards required at each court centre. Normally,
even at the larger court centres, they are limited to duty at the main court
entrance where they are equipped with security arches, hand held searching
wands and CCTV cameras. Although their duties include patrolling the
building, they do very little of that in normal court hours.

105   In magistrates' courts, it is for the Magistrates' Courts Committees to
determine what, if any, security is provided in their courts. The only
involvement of the Lord Chancellor's Department in their security is in the
establishment of a Court Security Task Group, who have recently
recommended that the Lord Chancellor should not exercise his statutory
power[57] to fix and direct their compliance with standards of performance.
Instead the Group has issued guidance[58] to Magistrates' Courts Committees
which includes recommendations for assessing the risk of violent incidents,
for the employment of court security officers and for close co-ordination on
matters of security with the criminal justice agencies. It also contains
elaborate guidance as to the system for reporting incidents of violence, for

---

[55] eg in the deployment, with the consent of the Senior Presiding Judge, of armed police officers in court buildings for
particular cases where armed or otherwise violent conduct is feared

[56] however, Chief Constables have recently agreed with Resident Judges as to their respective court centres' individual police
security requirements. There is now an agreed protocol for police security and liaison at each centre

[57] under Justices' of the Peace Act 1997, s 31

[58] 19 October 2000; the LCD also issued in February 2001 a *Protocol For Health and Safety and Fire Precautions In Custody
Areas* drawing the attention of court staff and court escort contractors to their obligations under the Health and Safety at Work
Act 1974 and associated regulations, including a reminder to the latter of their duty to protect their own staff from harm by
withdrawing them, if necessary

reporting to Ministers and "as supporting information when considering bids for funding".

106   Although many Magistrates' Courts Committees employ security officers at their courts, many do not. Most do not make provision for search on entry for metal objects. Where there are no security officers the courts rely on the availability of police, usually on call from a nearby police station, if there is one, or on officers who happen to be attending court.

107   The main function of security officers, where they are provided, is to deter violence or threats of violence in the court building, though they are not responsible for security of the dock areas, which falls to the prison escort contractors. But as a deterrence or as an effective response to violence when it occurs, they are no substitute for a visible, uniformed and suitably equipped police presence in the public parts of the court and, from time to time and where necessary, in the courtrooms themselves. Court security officers lack the powers, training and evident authority of uniformed policemen. Curiously, they have less powers in the Crown Court than in magistrates' courts. In the Crown Court they have no powers to search, eject, control or restrain persons in the court building. In magistrates' courts they have powers of search and of exclusion or removal of any person who refuses to permit it, and of exclusion, removal or restraint in order to maintain order in the courthouse. But they cannot require the removal of clothing other than an outer coat, jacket or gloves,[59] or forcibly search or arrest anyone causing trouble inside the building. Their powers are limited to the use of reasonable force only in the exclusion or removal of a person from the building. As I understand it, the original reason for security guards having so little power in the Crown Court was because there used to be a significant police presence in court buildings to enforce security where required. The removal of police officers from Crown Court buildings has changed the position and left a potentially dangerous gap in security. The Court Service is now considering whether the security guards should have the same powers in all courts as they have in the magistrates' courts. But even if that were to be taken forward, it would still fall far short of what many consider is necessary for the provision of adequate security in the courts as a whole.

108   An equal or greater threat to the administration of justice is the intimidation of witnesses outside court and before they are due to give evidence. Many judges, The Council of Circuit Judges and the Director of Public Prosecutions have expressed concern about such intimidation. There have been accounts in the submissions in the Review of potential witnesses being reluctant to give statements to police; failure of witnesses to attend court to give evidence or of their 'forgetting', when in the witness box, critical parts of their expected

---

[59] Criminal Justice Act 1991, s 77(2)

evidence. The last is an increasing problem, and particularly prevalent in areas of serious crime, such as South Wales and Merseyside. In the latter, it is said to be responsible for more than 50% of judge ordered acquittals, against a national average of 25%. There are clear limits to what can be done to deter or prevent such, mainly covert, intimidation, but a strong and highly visible police presence in and about the court would be of some encouragement and possible help to would-be witnesses who are in fear.

109   The present security position is, therefore, an unsatisfactory mix in the Crown Court of police and contracted security guards, the latter statutorily, contractually and in terms of training, limited in the effectiveness of security that they can provide. Whether even that level of security is available in magistrates' courts depends on individual Magistrates' Courts Committees; in many cases it is not, and they are also less likely to be equipped with electronic searching devices and CCTV cameras. The over-all picture is disturbing. But, most of all, the lack of a police presence and the reassurance and sense of order that it brings, have been the subject of many expressions of concern by the judiciary and magistracy in recent years. It was a recurrent theme in submissions in the Review. Notably, the Director of Public Prosecutions and his staff expressed the view that the absence of police as a security presence in the courts, is "very detrimental". They spoke of open attempts by defendants' supporters to intimidate prosecutors and magistrates on the hearing of bail applications and in other proceedings. The recent release by two armed men of defendants from Slough Magistrates' Court and the unchecked and serious assault on Her Honour Judge Goddard QC at the Central Criminal Court have shown how vulnerable our courts and those who work in them have become.

110   The problem has been obvious for years to anyone involved in the day to day business of the courts and has been well and truly communicated by the Presiding Judges and others to those with the ability to do something about it. I understand that the Lord Chancellor, spurred by the attack on Judge Goddard, is now considering action. I have not been told what he has in mind, but I make the following five main suggestions.

111   First, as a matter of urgency the Lord Chancellor should take direct responsibility for and control of the provision of security at summary level, not leave it to guidance and indications of what he expects Magistrates' Courts Committees to do if they are willing to spend the money. If my recommendation for the establishment of a unified Criminal Court and court administration are adopted, that should follow, but it should not wait until then. If my recommendations in Chapter 8 for greater direction of the criminal justice system as a whole are adopted, the responsibility should pass to the Criminal Justice Board to exercise on behalf of all the criminal justice Ministers.

112   Second, the level of security, in the sense of the statutory powers of those providing it, should be the same for all levels of jurisdiction, certainly not less in the higher jurisdiction than in the lower, as is now the case. This would require primary legislation.

113   Third, serious consideration should be given to returning to uniformed police officers the main responsibility for providing a visible and effective security presence in the criminal courts.[60] This could largely be provided in two ways. First, on a rota basis, officers attending court from time to time as witnesses or otherwise in connection with cases listed for hearing, could routinely patrol the court building instead of sitting in the police room. They could be contacted by tannoy or bleeper when required to give evidence. This suggestion has been made many times, but in general has had a poor response from the police. One of the reasons for that, I believe, stems from the natural concern of police officers to concentrate on the evidence they are about to give and not be distracted by other matters. This in turn is a result of the absurd practice, to which I refer in Chapter 11, of confining police officers in the witness box to aides-memoire in the form of notes made at or shortly after the events in question, yet permitting them unrestricted access to their witness statements until immediately before they enter the witness box to give evidence. The result is that officers huddle in the police room at court, reading and re-reading their notes and their witness statements so as to consign to memory what they are shortly about to say in evidence. If they were allowed to do in the witness box what they are now permitted to do shortly before going into it, the giving of evidence would be less a test of short term memory, and their time waiting at court could be better spent. Second, court corridors could be included on the beat of locally based police officers.

114   An alternative would be to introduce a uniformed Sheriff Officer Service which, unlike present contracted court security officers, would be fully trained and have police powers. They could be based in court buildings and act under the general oversight of the court manager. Such a system operates in British Columbia and is regarded as a success. The sheriff officers combine four roles: jury bailiff, bailiff, security guard and prison escort. They also have limited powers of arrest. The Court Service is currently looking at the feasibility of introducing a similar scheme here. Such a system might be better suited to serve all three jurisdictions. County courts, including their judges are particularly vulnerable. I believe that, unless they are family or care centres, they are not provided with security officers. Sheriff's officers might take over all criminal and civil enforcement, including the role of the civil bailiff.

---

[60] different provision may be acceptable in civil and family courts

115   Fourth, there are other aids to better security the purpose of which is to restrict the scope for intimidation of and violence to witnesses and others within the court building. These include: separate access and accommodation (including separate smoking accommodation) for prosecution and defence witnesses; special access and provision for vulnerable witnesses; court design, including secure docks and electronic door locks where necessary;[61] use of screens or other shielding devices in court; where appropriate, control of public galleries; more efficient staggering of witnesses to minimise the time they have to spend at court; where appropriate and necessary, the giving of evidence by video-link from outside the court building or courtroom; the placing of notices in the public parts of the court building that intimidation is a serious offence and will be prosecuted; routine follow-up by the police of witnesses who have not attended; and vigorous prosecution of any attempted or successful intimidation.

116   Fifth, if ever there was a candidate for a criminal justice - rather than a single agency - budget, it is court security. There is no reason why the courts or - if police officers are to resume responsibility - police forces should carry the sole or main responsibility for this task. It should be regarded and treated, in budgetary and planning terms, as a joint responsibility of the Court Service and all the criminal justice agencies.

I recommend that:

- **the Lord Chancellor should, as a matter of urgency, take direct responsibility for and control of security of courts of all levels and jurisdictions;**

- **those invested with a duty of providing security should have the same powers in all criminal courts;**

- **consideration should be given to requiring the police to resume the provision of security in all criminal courts, or to the establishment of a uniformed Sheriff Officer Service which would be fully trained, have police powers and would operate under the general oversight of the local judiciary;**

- **there should be a review of the necessary provision, in terms of accommodation, technology and otherwise, to protect vulnerable witnesses and others at court, and to enable the former where appropriate and**

---

[61] in the Crown Court only five courtrooms in the country have a secure dock. A pilot scheme of docks fortified with a toughened glass screen has recently been piloted in eight further court centres. In the magistrates' courts there are 55 secure docks and the Lord Chancellor's Department has recently introduced a programme to equip a number of magistrates' courts with more where magistrates' courts' committees are prepared to bid for funds for the purpose

necessary to give their evidence by video-link away from the court; and

- in the event of my recommendations in Chapter 8 being adopted, the extent of and financial responsibility for security provided in the Criminal Court should become a joint criminal justice responsibility exercised by the Criminal Justice Board on behalf of Ministers.

INSPECTION

117 HM Magistrates' Courts Service Inspectorate has done much to improve the performance of Magistrates' Courts Committees in their administration and management of magistrates' courts. There is no equivalent body for the Court Service. If a unified Criminal Court with a single administration for courts of all jurisdiction and levels is established in accordance with my recommendation, it would be sensible to extend the system of inspection to the administration of all the courts. The first step would be to establish targets and performance indicators along with those for the criminal justice system as a whole[62] against which to measure performance. It should report to the Lord Chancellor.

I recommend that:

- if in accordance with my recommendations a unified Criminal Court and single supporting administrative agency are established, there should be created an independent Inspectorate of that agency, which should report to the Lord Chancellor.

---

[62] see Chapter 8, paras 89 - 91

CHAPTER 8

THE CRIMINAL
JUSTICE SYSTEM

'A DIVIDED MINISTRY OF JUSTICE'

1   The word 'system' in the expression 'criminal justice system' is misleading.
     There is no 'system' worthy of the name, only a criminal justice process to
     which a number of different Government departments and agencies and others
     make separate and sometimes conflicting contributions.

2   England and Wales have what some have called 'a Divided Ministry of
     Justice'. There are three main Government departments - those of the Lord
     Chancellor, the Home Secretary and the Attorney General - variously
     responsible for two different criminal court structures and a number of
     national and local criminal justice agencies.[1] There are also the powerful
     influences on matters of policy and expenditure of the Prime Minister,
     assisted by his Policy Unit at Number 10 Downing Street, and of the
     Treasury.   Other Government Ministries have departments with
     responsibilities for criminal policy and legislation and for the prosecution of
     offences within their remit, notably the Commissioners of Inland Revenue and
     of Customs and Excise, the Department of Trade and Industry, the
     Department for Work and Pensions, and the Department for Environment,
     Food and Rural Affairs. There are also others involved, notably the Youth
     Justice Board,[2] the newly created Criminal Defence Service and Victim
     Support,[3] local authorities all over the country and many categories of
     individuals professionally or occupationally involved on a day to day basis in
     the criminal justice process, including legal practitioners and expert witnesses.
     The allocation of responsibilities between departments is somewhat
     unsystematic, but reflects certain underlying principles, including the
     independence of the judiciary and the separation of police from prosecutors.
     As the Public Accounts Committee has put it: "The criminal justice process

---

[1] note also the responsibility of the Chancellor of the Duchy of Lancaster for the appointment of magistrates within the Duchy

[2] established in September 1998

[3] a national charitable organisation subsidised by government

... crosses and re-crosses organisational boundaries".[4] In what follows I concentrate on the three main criminal justice departments and the main criminal justice agencies.

3   The Lord Chancellor is responsible for magistrates' courts and the Crown Court and, through the Legal Services Commission, a statutory non-departmental public body funded by his department, for the provision of defence legal aid in those courts. As I have said, he exercises his responsibility for magistrates' courts through general oversight and financial control of the Magistrates' Courts Committees. He appoints magistrates and, through the Judicial Studies Board, guides and assist the Magistrates' Courts Committees in their training. He sets performance targets, issues guidelines and directives, and monitors their performance. As I have also said, he exercises his responsibility for the Crown Court in a different way, through the medium of the Court Service. He advises the Queen on the appointment of the professional judiciary, many of whom sit in the Crown Court. In consultation with the Lord Chief Justice and the Presiding Judges, he is responsible for disciplining them when necessary. And, through the Judicial Studies Board, he trains them. He is also responsible for substantive civil and family (though not criminal) law, for court procedure and (through the Law Commission) for law reform. Of the current £12.8 billion annual budget for the criminal justice system, his department accounts for £1.6 billion.

4   The Home Secretary is the nearest we have to a Minister of Justice in the field of criminal law. He is responsible for the formulation of policy and initiation of criminal justice primary and secondary legislation, research projects and the collation of statistics. He oversees the 42 Police Authorities (though they have considerable individual autonomy), the Forensic Science Service, the National Probation Service,[5] the Prison Service, the Prison Escort and Custody Service, the Criminal Injuries Compensation Scheme and central funding of Victim Support. His department takes £10.8bn of the over-all £12.8bn criminal justice budget.

5   The Attorney General has a general oversight of prosecutions and direct responsibility for the Crown Prosecution Service and the Serious Fraud Office, though these are managed by their Directors who are fully independent in the decisions they take with regard to the conduct of prosecutions. Between them, they have a budget of £0.35bn.

6   Funds are allocated to the various criminal justice services on a departmental basis. Each department submits an annual bid, which it negotiates and settles with the Treasury, and distributes its allocation among its agencies. In 2000,

---

[4] Report of the Committee of Public Accounts, *Criminal Justice: Working Together*, 26th June 2000

[5] as it is now called; see Criminal Justice and Courts Services Act 2000

for the first time, the three Ministers prepared a joint submission to the Treasury for the spending review (SR2000). The Permanent Secretary of each department is its Accounting Officer and, as such, is personally responsible and answerable to the Public Accounts Committee of the House of Commons for the propriety of his Department's expenditure. In 2000, again for the first time, the Permanent Secretaries of the Lord Chancellor's Department and Home Office, and the Director of Public Prosecutions jointly defended their conduct of and expenditure on the criminal justice system.

7   Over the last three years the three departments have taken significant steps towards some joint management of the system. In 1999 they jointly devised and published a three year strategic plan to 2002 and a business plan for 1999-2000. They have since issued joint business plans for 2000-2001 and 2001-2002 and a joint report on progress for 1999-2001. Notwithstanding these significant advances in working more closely together, at the time of writing the departments remain individually responsible for their own services, they separately submit and negotiate their annual bids for funding and, save for pooling about 1% of their joint resources,[6] they continue to hold their own purse strings.

8   In parallel with these changes, the Government has established the 42 criminal justice areas, based on the geographical areas of police forces. The Crown Prosecution Service, the Probation Service and Magistrates' Courts Committees are now similarly organised and Prison Service and Court Service boundaries, though not coterminous, no longer cut across the criminal justice areas.

9   Each of the departments and of the various agencies has aims, policies and budgets broadly directed to the common end of reducing crime and the fair and efficient administration of criminal justice, but which, in their application, often conflict. These operational conflicts are inter-departmental and inter-agency, but they also occur within different managerial or geographical divisions of the same department or agency. They are, no doubt, the stuff of any large organisation or group of organisations, different parts of which endeavour to contribute in their own ways to a common end. Human nature is such that departmental loyalties engender sectional interests and, sometimes, mutual distrust. But where they arise in the administration of criminal justice, sharpened by firm budgetary and spending constraints, they can cause much harm – including injustice, distress, expense and inconvenience to defendants, witnesses, victims, jurors, legal practitioners and others involved in the process - and much inefficiency and wastefulness in the 'system' as a whole. Legal practitioners, whether for the prosecution or defence, have a critical role in all this; they can contribute to, as well as suffer from, such inefficiencies.

---

[6] see para 23 below

Sadly, many submissions to the Review have illustrated the level of division between the main players in the criminal justice process, each focusing on the failures of the others and mostly making little acknowledgement of their own.

10   Since many of those facing criminal prosecution are guilty and seek to escape conviction or serious sentence, there are, realistically, limits to the co-operation that can be expected from them in the efficient running of the process. That is also true of those who are innocent and who, for one reason or another, distrust the police or the prosecution or the courts themselves. However, despite the ability of a dishonest, feckless or distrustful defendant to throw a spanner in the works, the overwhelming weight of submissions and other material put before the Review shows that the machinery of criminal justice is not working as well or as fairly and sensitively as it could, and that something needs to be done about it.[7] It has also been well documented in the reports of a number of the reviews to which I have referred in the Foreword[8] and in many other internal reviews and studies, the more recent of which are listed in Appendix III. The need has become more acute over recent years with ever increasing complexity of law and procedures, more work and higher public expectations fuelled in part by the entry of human rights into our system of law. The same is true throughout the common law world, from which I have gathered many reports of reviews such as this. The search, which I believe to be vital for a just and efficient system - one that will command public confidence - is for better case management in the widest sense of that expression.

11   It is at local level, where the criminal justice system is at work, that the administrative complexities and muddle of responsibilities have their most practical and visible effect. It is marked by a proliferation of inter-agency bodies with overlapping and, often, ill-defined functions. This multiplicity and confusion of roles have been widely criticised in the submissions in the Review and by those attending its regional seminars. For example, in Suffolk, as recently noted by the Strategic Planning Group, there are 34 different consultative, advisory or other collaborative bodies, often with overlapping terms of reference and/or involving very similar memberships. Such a conglomeration encourages a culture in which dialogue becomes a substitute for action. And where local agencies take the initiative in negotiating protocols setting out what each of them may expect from each other, the task is formidable. An example mentioned by the Public Accounts Committee in its 2000 Report[9] is that of Nottinghamshire and Derbyshire, where 12 different agencies had adopted a protocol containing 82 agreements involving 249 services that various criminal justice agencies were supplying to others.

---

[7] there are some notable dissenters; see eg Professor Michael Zander, *What On Earth Is Lord Justice Auld Supposed To Do?* 2000 Crim LR 419, echoing his similar objections to Lord Woolf's Civil Justice Reforms; see also his Note of Dissent to the Runciman *Royal Commission on Criminal Justice*, pp 223-233;

[8] para 17

[9] *Criminal Justice: Working Together*, paras 7 and 8

12   None of this is news to all those responsible for the administration of the criminal justice process or to those variously engaged in it.   As I have said, the three main criminal justice departments have made considerable efforts in recent years to work better together, both in establishing common aims and in seeking to implement them. I shall mention the more important of them shortly.   But, sadly, this 'working together', or 'joined-up government' as it is called, is not achieving results commensurate with all the enthusiasm and effort put into it.   There is little over-all planning or direction, as distinct from pooling ideas, plans and schemes for co-ordination.   There are a multiplicity of inter-departmental and inter-agency bodies at national and local levels. Mostly they have no authority or operational function.   Sometimes they are uncertain of their role and/or of their relationship one with another.   Often they have overlapping memberships and terms of reference, and spend much time reporting to each other on the same or similar issues.   In addition, some members of these bodies, particularly at local level, have no authority to commit those whom they represent to whatever collective recommendations or decisions that might otherwise be made.

13   Paradoxically, the problems are often compounded by the many recent and current initiatives to improve the level of co-operation between the various departments and agencies.   As Appendix III illustrates, there are pilot studies, working parties, steering groups and reviews all over the place.   Sometimes they are conducted by one department or agency; sometimes they are joint ventures; and sometimes there is overlap between two projects.   In some instances, as I have seen in the course of this Review, one department or agency may not even be aware of the other's connected activity, a phenomenon not unknown even as between the Lord Chancellor's Department and its executive agency, the Court Service.

14   The whole edifice is structurally inefficient, ineffective and wasteful - and the working of the criminal courts is but a part, though a focal part, of it.   The basic problem lies in the shared, but also divided, responsibilities of the three Government departments for the system.   Each, necessarily, must guard its constitutional independence and, in respect of some of its responsibilities, its function from the others, and have regard to its separate financial accountability to the Treasury and to Parliament.   The Public Accounts Committee, in its 2000 Report, observed:

>   "The most common constraints to effective local inter-agency liaison include conflicting objectives and priorities, which can prevent agreement."

>   "Independence of the various players in the criminal justice system is fundamental to justice.   It is also entirely compatible with them taking joint responsibility for

achieving value for money from the substantial resources spent on criminal justice. Current performance in progressing criminal cases is not satisfactory and needs to be improved through more concerted joint monitoring and management of performance across the criminal justice system."[10]

15   The limitations of my terms of reference do not include a possible re-ordering of the great Offices of State or re-distribution of certain of their individual responsibilities. I make only two observations. The first is that, in my view, the present division of responsibilities contributes significantly to the present inefficiencies and wastefulness in the criminal justice process. The second is that the way we do it is, as in so many other matters of public administration, largely a product of historical evolution. It does not have to be this way. It is axiomatic that over-all political accountability for investigation, prosecution and adjudication should remain separate. But beneath that level there needs to be a mechanism for securing some central direction and joint management of the achievement of shared objectives.

'WORKING TOGETHER'

16   Apart from the judiciary, there are three main hierarchies and/or groupings of inter-departmental and/or inter-agency bodies concerned with the administration of criminal justice. For the purpose of identification I shall call them 'Strategic', 'Operational' and 'Consultative', though none of them truly justifies its name. For the purpose of bringing home the complexity, overlap of responsibilities and the absence of any single clear line of direction and accountability in the system, I set out in more detail than might otherwise be necessary the structure and relationship of the three categories.

17   Before doing so, I should mention the judiciary but – as academics might put it – only to exclude them from consideration as part of the main administrative structure. Apart from the Lord Chancellor, in his combined role of the Head of the Judiciary and Minister responsible for the courts system, the judges' administrative role, outside issues of their deployment, allocation of work and general working arrangements, is indirect, consultative and persuasive. In this respect they are unlike many of their brethren in other common law jurisdictions in the Commonwealth and in the USA, who often have a significant formal role in the administration of their courts.

---

[10] ibid, paras 7 and 3

18   Whilst the Lord Chief Justice, other Heads of Division,[11] and other senior judges, including the Senior Presiding Judge, have regular meetings with the Lord Chancellor to discuss matters primarily concerning the courts and the judiciary, they have no direct involvement in the planning or management of the criminal justice system as a whole. The nearest that the Lord Chief Justice has to any such involvement is when he is consulted from time to time by Ministers, usually the Home Secretary, on proposals for new criminal justice legislation. When this occurs, he in turn takes the views of a small body of senior judges and the Registrar of the Court of Appeal (Criminal Division). The Senior Presiding Judge has considerable involvement with national heads and local representatives of the various criminal justice agencies, but it is of an informal, ad hoc, though influential, nature. It is directed mostly at practical ways of improving co-operation between the courts and the agencies. Presiding Judges and Resident Judges have similar relationships with representatives of the various agencies at, respectively, circuit and court centre levels.

Strategic

19   The Ministerial group, which meets periodically, is chaired by the Home Secretary and includes the Lord Chancellor and the Attorney General. As I have said, in April 1999 the Group approved and published the first Strategic and Business Plans for the Criminal Justice System in England and Wales.[12] They set out the aims for the system as a whole, to which I have referred in Chapter 1 - in brief, the reduction of crime and the fair and efficient administration of justice. The Plans included 'objectives', 'performance measures and targets', and proposed 'efficiency' measures. The Ministerial Group also announced their agreement of a policy to align the geographical boundaries of the different criminal justice agencies, including Magistrates' Courts Committee areas and those of the Crown Court, and services within the existing 42 police areas into criminal justice areas. The three departments and/or agencies for which they are responsible have their own formulations of broadly similar and complementary aims and objectives, but often with different and conflicting performance measures and targets.

20   The authors of the 1999 Strategic and Business Plans regarded them as the first "real attempt ... to manage the system as a whole" and as "the start of a developing process".[13] As I have said, in 2000 the three Ministers, for the first time, prepared a joint submission to the Treasury for the spending review (SR2000) outlining their plans for 2001 to 2004. Also, following SR2000, the three departments issued a joint Criminal Justice System Public Service

---

[11] the Master of the Rolls, the Vice-Chancellor and the President of the Family Division

[12] as part of SR 2000, the Government-wide Cross Departmental "cross-cutting" exercise; see para 6 above

[13] paras. 2.2.4 and 6.1.1

Agreement, which is intended to encourage working together and consideration of joint priorities.

21   There is also what is called 'the Grade 1 Trilateral', which consists of the Permanent Secretaries of the three departments. They and their officials meet quarterly. They have no formal terms of reference. I understand that in September 1999 they sought to 'refocus' their meetings with a view to providing some strategic supervision, resolution of problems between departments and presentation to Ministers of policy choices. I have not been able to assess the effectiveness of this group, since its work has been disrupted in the course of the Review by the illness of one of its members. But, so far as I can tell, it makes little, if any, 'strategic' or other contribution to the planning or running of the system; it does not advise or even report to Ministers; and it does not communicate Ministers' views to anybody. In short, I have not been able to discover what, if any, useful role this group performs in the over-all direction of the criminal justice system.

22   The Ministerial Group and the Grade 1 Trilateral are supported by the 'Strategic Planning Group (SPG), which is composed of the Criminal Policy Directors and senior Finance Officers of the three departments, other senior officials, including a representative of the Treasury, a member of the Prime Minister's Policy Unit and a policy adviser to the Home Secretary. It meets about every six weeks and until very recently was chaired by the Criminal Policy Director of the Lord Chancellor's Department. Its terms of reference are:

> "to carry out joint strategic planning and performance management of the criminal justice system as a whole on behalf of the Ministerial and Permanent Secretary Steering Groups[14]. In particular:
>
> to prepare strategic and business plans which best deliver Ministers' objectives within agreed resources;
>
> to monitor and report upon the performance of the criminal justice system as a whole and recommend any corrective action necessary;
>
> to ensure the principles of the new criminal justice policy development are followed; and
>
> to ensure the recommendations of the Cross-Departmental Report are taken forward."

As this wording suggests, and as I have already indicated, the SPG does not decide; it recommends - and the ultimate deciders are the Ministerial Group, seemingly acting without any intermediate advice or recommendation from

---

[14] ie the Ministerial Group and the Grade 1 Trilateral, respectively

the Grade 1 Trilateral. It has no part in the departments', now jointly submitted, bids for funding. Subject to a small experiment to which I refer in the next paragraph, it has no responsibility for allocation of funds throughout the system. And, it has no structural relationship with any of the various local collaborative bodies at national or local level; nor has it any counterparts for the implementation of its strategic planning at local level.

23   A novel feature is the recent creation of a 'strategic reserve' drawn from the over-all criminal justice system budget for disbursement by the SPG on projects that would benefit the whole system, but only if all three Ministers agree. The initial allocation for this purpose is £525m, to be spread over the three years 2000-2002. In fact, the allocation has been reduced to about £400m as a result of the need to find additional resources for the Crown Prosecution Service, the courts and Probation Services to deal with extra work expected to result from a recent provision of additional funds for the recruitment of 9,000 more police officers. That leaves an average yearly sum of about £133 million available for joint disbursement against an average annual budget for the criminal justice system as a whole of £12.8 billion[15] planned for the three years 2000 - 2002. As a joint planning and spending initiative, it is a welcome but tiny start. In the context of expenditure on the criminal justice system as a whole, it is difficult to see how the Ministerial Group on the recommendation of the SPG could realistically claim to be able to put this small joint allocation, which is in any event, limited to a three year period, to any significant 'strategic' purpose.

24   The SPG prepares bids to Ministers for use of the small unallocated reserve. It is supported by:

- an inter-departmental and inter-agency body responsible for developing co-ordination of the various criminal justice agencies' information technology systems, the Board of Integrating Business and Information Systems (IBIS);

- 'champions' for some of the cross-cutting criminal justice system objectives, each of whom reports regularly to it and is supported by a project team; and

- the Criminal Justice Joint Planning Unit (CJJPU), staffed and funded from the departments, which acts as a secretariat, produces plans for the criminal justice system and co-ordinates the activities of part of the consultative hierarchy, the Criminal Justice Area Strategy Committees.

25   Professor Sue Richards, an authoritative observer of and contributor to governmental thinking on the management of the criminal justice system, has recently completed a review of the joint planning and management arrangements.[16] In it, she said that the diagnosis of many who contributed to

---

[15] exclusive of the salaries of the judiciary, including District Judges (Magistrates' Courts)

[16] *Review of the CJS Joint Planning and Management Arrangements*, 8th May 2000

her review was that the SPG "is not strategic and it does not plan".[17] She identified the following "serious weaknesses":[18]

> "... SPG does not provide strategic leadership for the CJS; ... its link into the performance of local CJS agencies (whose 'joined-up' performance is the key to achieving the aims and objectives set out by ministers) is too indirect to be effective; consequently, the management information currently available on the performance of the CJS at national and local level (as opposed to its constituent parts) is poorly developed...."

She described the Government's Strategic Plan as "a compilation of what different parts within the three departments are doing in support of their aims and objectives, rather than the instrument which drives the activity".[19] The Government, no doubt mindful of such criticisms and of the direction of my Review, appears to accept a need to strengthen the SPG.[20]

Operational

26   The National Trial Issues Group (TIG), which was established in 1995[21] was until recently chaired by the Chairwoman of the SPG. It includes senior civil servants and officers drawn from all the main criminal justice departments and agencies and others involved in the system, including the Recorder of London, the Chairman of the Magistrates' Association, an MCC representative, the Chief Executive of the Youth Justice Board, the Police and the Secretaries of the Criminal Bar Association and Criminal Law Committee of the Law Society. It meets monthly.

27   TIG is not an operational arm of the SPG and does not report to it. As I have said, the two bodies have no structural relationship. Like the SPG, it is a creature of the three departments and its role is essentially as their joint planning and co-ordinating agent. Its responsibilities, which it exercises through sub-groups, pilot studies, instructions and guidance, are:

> "to plan and co-ordinate measures to dispense justice fairly and efficiently at a national level by: ensuring just processes and just and effective outcomes, dealing with cases ... with appropriate speed, meeting the needs of victims, witnesses and jurors ... and respecting the rights of defendants and treating them fairly".

---

[17] ibid, para 13

[18] ibid, paras IV and 14

[19] ibid, para 12

[20] *Criminal Justice: The Way Ahead*, CM 5074, (Home Office, February 2001), para 3.230

[21] as successor to the Working Group on Pre-Trial Issues

28   TIG is supported by six specialist sub-groups, each chaired by a member of TIG, and also by local Trial Issues Groups (local TIGs) based on the 42 criminal justice areas. The breadth of TIG's work is well indicated by listing its sub-groups: the Case Management Working Group, the Joint Performance Management Strategy Group, the Manual of Guidance (guidelines on case files) Editorial Board, Tackling Youth Justice Delays, Reducing Delays Sub-Group and the Bail Issues Sub-Group.[22] Each sub-group is chaired by a senior official and consists in the main of relevant departmental or agency representatives and, in a few instances, a Circuit Judge or a magistrate.

29   The core membership of local TIGs, each of which is usually chaired by a senior Crown Prosecutor, includes representatives of all the local criminal justice system agencies and, in two instances, a Circuit Judge. Their prime purpose is to agree action within their areas to ensure that trials are conducted efficiently and in a timely manner. Their terms of reference also reflect the Government's 'overarching' aims for the criminal justice system, requiring them within their areas to assist the system to achieve a number of objectives. These include: "ensuring just process and just and effective outcomes", "meeting the needs of victims, witnesses and jurors", "piloting new initiatives referred by TIG or agreed locally", "considering local criminal justice operational issues, including those referred to it by other groups locally", "keeping TIG and the local Area Strategy Committee informed of its work" and "identifying and sharing best practice".

Consultative

30   Assuming that the reader is still with me, I pass on to the consultative category. The Criminal Justice Consultative Council (CJCC) and its Area Committees were established in 1992, following Lord Woolf's Report into the 1990 Prison Disturbances,[23] with the object of fostering better communication between the main criminal justice agencies.[24]   In the course of his inquiry Lord Woolf had been struck by the insular approach of the various agencies in the way they planned and organised their separate but closely inter-related parts in the criminal justice process. The CJCC's terms of reference[25] are:

> "to promote co-operation within the criminal justice system
> so as to reduce crime and the fear of crime and thereby
> increase confidence in the rule of law" and "to advise

---

[22] two working groups of the now disbanded Witness Care Sub-Group, the Vulnerable or Intimidated Witness Team and the Interpreters Working Group, will continue to report to TIG for their lifespans

[23] *Prison Disturbances*, Cmnd 1456, (HMSO, April 1990

[24] announced in the White Paper, *Custody, Care and Justice: The Way Ahead for the Prison Service in England and Wales*, Cmnd 1647, (HMSO, September 1991)

[25] revised in April 2000 to reflect the new "overarching" aims for the criminal justice system.

government from time to time on matters of practical application in the criminal justice system".

The CJCC has no structural relationship with the SPG or TIG and no managerial role. Its main work consists of considering and advising on reports and other information about the criminal justice system, arranging special conferences, general oversight of the Area Committees and identifying the national implications of their work. It has recently described its role as:

> "to facilitate discussions and agree action across the criminal justice system. It provides a forum for senior officers of the criminal justice agencies (including Government Departments) and senior figures of the legal system to address issues of mutual interest and resolve problems through an agreed agenda". [26]

31   The CJCC's inaugural Chairman was Lord Justice Rose, who was succeeded in October 2000 by Lord Justice Kay. Its membership includes very senior civil servants from the three departments and the various agencies, a Senior Circuit Judge, a District Judge (Magistrates' Courts), the Director of Public Prosecutions, a Chief Constable, a barrister, a solicitor, a magistrate, a justices' chief executive and others involved in various capacities in the criminal justice system.   As its origin and name indicate, its function was intended to be consultative and advisory. It has succeeded in the prime task envisaged for it by Lord Woolf – getting the departments and agencies and all those involved institutionally or professionally in the criminal justice process to talk to each other. It has also made a significant contribution to long-term thinking and understanding of many important criminal justice projects.[27] However, it is not routinely consulted by Governments on their thoughts or proposals for reform of the system. Nor has the Council any standing responsibility, or staff or facilities, to monitor and recommend improvements on its own initiative. And, save for special conferences, it meets only four times a year for two hours at a time. Its coverage is necessarily patchy and its attention to practicalities limited. As its annual summaries of activities indicate, most of its time in meetings is given over to presentations on various topics, leaving only a short time for discussion and occasioning little follow-up.

32   The Area Committees largely replicate at local level the membership of the CJCC. Each is chaired by a local Circuit Judge, usually the Resident Judge of a main court centre. The membership consists, or should consist, of chief officers of the various local criminal justice and other agencies, including the Circuit Administrator, Court Service Group Manager, the MCC's Chairman

---

[26] *Criminal Justice Consultative Council: Summary of Activities 1999-2000*, Annex A to Part 1

[27] see most recently, the report of its Race Sub-Group, chaired by District Judge Davinder Lachhar, of July 2000

or Justices' Chief Executive, the Chief Executive of the Local Authority, the Chief Constable, the Chief Probation Officer, the Chief Crown Prosecutor, and a number of others including a barrister, solicitor, member of the Youth Offenders Team and a local representative of the Witness Service or Victim Support.

33 The Committees are based on the 42 criminal justice areas. They have part-time secretarial assistance from the Court Service. When the CJCC was established in 1992, their role was to take forward its programme of work at local level. However, it was increasingly felt that they did not have a sufficiently clearly defined role. And, in April 2000, they were reconstituted as Area Criminal Justice Strategy Committees with model terms of reference requiring them to promote co-operation between agencies in support of the Government's over-arching aims of the criminal justice system, but to do so in a more interventionist way than their predecessors, the role of which was predominantly consultative. Thus, for example, they are now required to "develop the criminal justice strategy for the area, involving all criminal justice agencies", so as to "secure high level commitment to the strategy", to "ensure that national criminal justice policies are implemented locally"and to "refer initiatives on operational issues to the local TIG".

34 Although the Area Strategy Committees have had only a short time in which to identify and establish the practicality of their new remit of more direct intervention, many of them do not know quite how to go about it. It is also fair to say that some of the judicial chairmen are more effective in this role than others. The CJCC has recently issued a 'template' of guidance on the subject. Their task is complicated by their limited secretarial support and the fact that, even if they tried to do so, they could not act as a collective decision-making body. They have no joint executive authority to enforce or budget to fund any decisions they might make, since some of their key members have no authority to commit the agencies or bodies that they represent to any joint project. These include, importantly, local representatives of the Court Service, who have less autonomy than many of their counterparts from the other agencies, and the legal practitioner members who have no authority at all to commit their professional brethren to any common venture.

35 In recent years, frustration at the Committees' lack of effective executive role has in a number of areas led to Chief Officers sending their deputies to the meetings in their stead and has prompted them to form local Chief Officers' Groups at which they can make collective decisions and pool their authority and resources to implement them. In some areas they have gone further and formed what they have called local 'Criminal Justice Boards'.

36   Below the level of Area Strategy Committees there are also well-established inter-agency and disciplinary bodies to assist the day to day working of the courts. The most important of these are the Crown Court and Magistrates' Courts User Groups, the former usually chaired by the Resident Judge. They are particularly valuable bodies, capable of ready and practical improvement of the system at local level. It is notable that the Comptroller and Auditor General, in his National Audit Report of 1999, *Criminal Justice: Working Together*, found that "much of the practical cross-agency liaison in support of performance improvement" was carried out by such Groups.[28] There are also over 350 Crime and Disorder Reduction Partnerships, bringing together representatives of the criminal justice system with those of local authorities to plan local strategies and actions to reduce crime in their areas. The areas for which these Partnerships are responsible do not coincide with the criminal justice areas or, in consequence, with those of the Area Strategy Committees. Usually there are several within one criminal justice area and, they can also straddle two areas. However, their responsibilities extend beyond the criminal justice process.

NOT WORKING TOGETHER

The structures

37   As I hope I have now made plain, there is no formal link between the SPG, TIG and CJCC and their respective structures, though the recent past Chairwoman of SPG and TIG, the Head of Policy Group of the Lord Chancellor's Department, is also an ex officio member of the CJCC. The SPG has no operational arm, nationally[29] or locally, save through the individual departments who, in turn, are responsible for their representatives on TIG. And there are few signs of either the CJCC or TIG treating the latter as the former's operational arm. At local level the terms of reference of the new Area Strategy Committees, including that of referring initiatives on operational issues to the local TIGs, suggest that the latter are, in part, to be regarded as the operational arm of the Committees. But it seems that the idea has yet to catch on with the Committees.

38   The CJCC has a quasi-administrative relationship with the Area Strategy Committees, providing them with general guidance and in encouraging them to foster good practices and co-operation among the various local agencies. It is certainly not an effective agency for translating national plans and the

---

[28] *Lord Chancellor's Department, Crown Prosecution Service, Home Office: Criminal Justice: Working Together*, National Audit Office, HC 29 1999/2000 (1 December 1999)
[29] other than CJJPU in its generally supporting and secretarial role

means to implement them into local action. For example, it does not set or recommend national or local codes or targets of performance or how to monitor them, or indeed state whether any such codes or targets should be established at all. And the Area Committees, although expected to encourage the achievement of criminal justice system targets, are not required to report to the SPG or the CJCC on their progress to that end, only on their general activities. If, as appears to be widely accepted, some such common objectives are desirable, subject to necessary variation to suit local circumstances, it is unsatisfactory to leave to Area Strategy Committees what, if any, objectives they should set for themselves and, if they had the staff to do it, how they should monitor performance against them. As I have said, the Committees are generally uncertain about their newly acquired local 'strategic' role. And, if it were to become a major and effective part of their working, I could foresee potential conflicts for their judicial chairmen when administrative efficiency confronts judicial independence in securing justice generally and in individual cases.

39   In many respects the work of the CJCC and Area Strategy Committees overlaps with that of TIG and the local TIGs, and, as I have said, they often share some of the same personnel. Moreover, relationships between the CJCC and the Area Strategy Committees on the one hand, and TIG and the local TIGs on the other, are uncertain, in particular as to which system is driving the other. In my view, this replication of responsibilities and work at national and local level is inefficient, wasteful, often ineffective and confusing. A large number of contributors to the Review, including those involved in one or both systems at both levels, have characterised their meetings as largely 'talking shops'. My own examination of their work as part of the Review suggests that there is some truth in that description.

40   Thus, there is much in the way of attempted joint planning and co-ordination, but little or no clear line of over-all 'direction' or accountability in the criminal justice system. Part of the problem lies in the ill-defined relationship between, and functions of, the main three co-ordinating structures and the considerable overlap between them. Part lies in the lack of any over-all planning framework or timetable by reference to which planners at all levels and parts of the system can work. In summary there is no effective joint planning process; there is no significant joint budget; there are three separate joint bodies at national level; to the extent that the SPG has any directing or managerial roles, they are not mirrored at local level; and each local agency is individually accountable to its parent at national level, the nature of that relationship ranging from direct management to degrees of local autonomy. But, most of all, the problem lies in the focus on co-ordination rather than direction and management. If the Government truly intends "to manage the

system as a whole", as the authors of its 1999-2000 Strategic Plan have suggested,[30] it should get on and do it.

41   Some argue that the present tri-partite system of strategic, operational and consultative bodies should continue and that the recent changes - in particular, the new Criminal Justice System Strategic and Business Plans, their oversight and implementation by the SPG and the new more 'pro-active' Area Strategy Committees - should be given time to establish and prove themselves. Others have urged that the system is inherently flawed and that consideration should be given to merging the strategic and operational systems to provide a single and clear line of 'direction', if not of management, for the criminal justice system as a whole. However, Professor Sue Richards has spoken for both sides of the divide in saying that *something* more needs to be done to provide a better system:[31]

> "What was once seen as a major and radical step - CJS aims and objectives and a strategic plan - has now been put in place and it is important to take the next steps towards delivering the promised outcomes. Views will vary as to whether that involves improving the way the current system operates or changing the system. But the next step must be taken, whether bigger or smaller."

42   There are questions as to the form that a national 'directing' body might take. For example, should it be an amalgam of the present SPG and TIG and their respective structures? Or should a differently named CJCC, or a body similarly composed and strengthened for the purpose, undertake the role, subject to Ministerial oversight? Whatever directive or 'managerial' solution might be adopted, many argue the need to retain a national consultative and advisory body along the lines of the CJCC, but untrammelled by quasi-administrative responsibility for local bodies, as a source of authoritative, principled and practical advice.[32]

MANAGING CRIMINAL JUSTICE

A Criminal Justice Board

43   For all the reasons I have given, I consider that there should be a move to central joint direction and local joint management. The present medley of bodies with their ill-defined and overlapping roles and uncertain relationships

---

[30] see footnote 12 above

[31] *Review of the Criminal Justice System Joint Planning and Management Arrangements*, para 43

[32] cf. the Civil Justice Council established by the Civil Procedure Act 1997, s 6

should be replaced with a single line of direction and management, coupled with a separate and an appropriately used consultative system. As to the former, a single national body should plan and direct, rather than merely respond to and co-ordinate individual agencies' plans, as is now the case. It should have only such hierarchy nationally and locally as is necessary to inform it and to execute its directions. In particular, I see no need for separate 'strategic' and 'operational' structures. The overriding aim should be to relieve administrators from repetitive and wasteful meetings and give them more time to get on with their jobs. As to consultation, the Criminal Justice Consultative Council should be replaced by a more effective advisory body with a statutory remit.

44 Democratic accountability requires that ultimate responsibility for the setting of objectives and priorities and over-all allocation and expenditure of resources should remain with Ministers. Budgetary responsibilities are assumed to flow from political control and are subsumed within the broader topic of ministerial responsibility - finances follow departmental responsibilities. But the particular fragmentation of responsibilities for the criminal justice system between several Ministries and the wide acceptance that some of their functions should remain separate and independent of each other are perceived as an impediment to more joint management as distinct from greater co-operation. There is also the close financial control of the Treasury, which effectively gives it a decisive say in policy decisions and planning capabilities, and of the efficiency or otherwise with which adopted policies are implemented. The difficulty is in maintaining safeguards for the independence of different agencies and the interests of all involved in the criminal justice system. There is an innate tension between the functions of different agencies which cannot always appropriately be guided or over-ridden by broad aims such as those devised by the Government for the criminal justice system. As experienced academic commentators in this field have observed, it may be a necessary feature of such a system to maintain a degree of separation and checks and balances in the management of the various agencies and what is expected of each of them.[33] There is the further point that defendants and their lawyers, mostly publicly funded – and now the Criminal Defence Service – are also part of the 'system'. They too have important roles to play in its efficient operation as well as vital sectional interests in what it can do for them.

45 A belief that these difficulties should and could be overcome is encouraged by the Cabinet Office's Performance and Innovation Unit's acknowledgement in its January 2000 Report, *Wiring it up*, of the need to use more cross-cutting budgets and pooling of resources. Early in the Report it classified the disadvantages of the present system of government accounting:

---

[33] Raine and Wilson, *Managing Criminal Justice*, p 63

"Current structures and ways of working inhibit cross-cutting activity. 1.1. Current Whitehall structures and associated ways of working are highly effective in delivering many of the Government's key policies and priorities, but they can also inhibit the tackling of problems and issues which cross departmental boundaries. There are a number of reasons for this:

- there is a tendency to take a provider-centred perspective rather than that of the service user; ....

- budgets and organisational structures are arranged around vertical functional lines ... rather than horizontal, cross-cutting problems and issues; ....

- systems of accountability (eg audit) and the way risk is handled can militate against innovative cross-cutting working ...".[34]

Later, in a chapter devoted to the possibilities of greater flexible funding and its possible forms, it said:

"9.1 Much is said about the perception that there are major barriers to cross-cutting working in the way that budgets are allocated; the conditions that are attached to them; and the accountability structures associated with responsibility for seeing that money is spent wisely and for the purpose for which it was allocated. In practice, there is little evidence of insurmountable barriers; practical solutions can usually be found to get round most problems if there is a good enough reason for doing so, though this may involve a considerable amount of time and effort....

9.3 It is clearly important to maintain budget accountability while avoiding unintended or undesirable consequences. There are now few rules which prevent money being switched between departments .... The main barrier to the funding of cross-departmental policies – particularly between Spending Reviews – is different views about relative priorities; specifically, differing views about the relative priority of cross-cutting issues in relation to purely departmental objectives.

9.4 The key question is how to create the right sort of incentives for departments to spend money on programmes which are not their core business but which are central to the Government's over-all aims and objectives".[35]

---

[34] p 6
[35] ibid, pp 47 - 48

46   In my view – constitutional change or no – the apparent constraints of ministerial accountability and independence of certain functions one from another should not prevent Ministers, if they have the will, to devolve their authority into one body below ministerial level responsible to them for planning, funding and over-all direction of the criminal justice system. Such a national body, which could be called the **Criminal Justice Board**, should replace the existing Strategic Planning Group, Trials Issues Group and also assume such operational responsibilities as the Criminal Justice Consultative Council currently has. It should be the means by which the departments and core agencies provide over-all direction of the criminal justice system. It should be replicated at a local level by **local Criminal Justice Boards**, undertaking much and more of the work that is already undertaken by local TIGs, Area Strategy Committees and informal bodies of chief officers frustrated with the inadequacy of the present formal system.[36] It follows from my proposals that the present mix of 'strategic', 'operational' and 'consultative' structures would disappear, including the following bodies: the SPG, TIG and its sub-groups, the local TIGs, the CJCC and its Area Strategy Committees, Chief Officer Groups and, where they exist informal 'Criminal Justice Boards'. Consideration might also be given to disbanding the Grade 1 Trilateral of the Permanent Secretaries of the three departments unless it can be found something useful to do.

Planning

47   A key responsibility for a national Criminal Justice Board would be the preparation of plans for the criminal justice system for ministerial endorsement. It is a matter for consideration whether the present system of rolling three year strategic and one year business plans,[37] often containing the same or similar bland generalisations and reports on work in hand, are satisfactory planning tools and whether the former are, in any event, for too short a period to be truly strategic, for example in the planning of information technology.[38] The process would have to be underpinned by a more systematic analysis of, and dialogue about, the individual objectives and targets of each department and agency than has occurred hitherto. At present, these are contained in Public Service Agreements negotiated individually by each department with the Treasury, which are then aggregated together into a plan for the system as a whole. This is the wrong way round. The Criminal Justice Board should, after due consultation with the Treasury, produce a plan for the system as a whole, from which each agency would then derive its plan.

48   Another defect is that the annual joint business plan for the criminal justice system has never been produced at a sufficiently early stage to inform or

---

[36] see para 39 above

[37] see eg *Criminal Justice System: Strategic Plan 1999-2002* (1999) and *Business Plan 2001-2002* (February 2001)

[38] see paras 92 - 114 below

influence each agency's preparation of its financial or business plan. For example, the 2001/2002 business plan was published on 26 February 2001, only one month before the commencement of the period to which it related, and far too late to make any difference to the plans of the individual agencies who would be responsible for achieving results on the ground. If the Criminal Justice Board is to provide strategic direction to the system as a whole, then it must ensure the system business plan is available in draft form by the end of October, and published at the latest by the end of November. This would give departments and agencies sufficient time to ensure that the system-wide targets were realistic, and that their own plans would contribute to their attainment, while still allowing the Board scope to adjust targets in the light of up to date information about performance. In short, the planning time-table should be structured so that national plans can inform local ones, as well as the other way round.[39]

49   In addition to the problem of timing, a recent review of performance indicators across the criminal justice system,[40] showed that the existing collection of objectives is over-complex and lacks coherence. It has recommended the establishment of a smaller set of clearly defined joint targets to which departments and agencies should fit their performance indicators. If this work operates as a spur to action rather than a substitute for it, I agree. And I welcome the Government's recent commitment to ensuring that performance objectives do not clash.[41] With all this in mind, an early task for the Criminal Justice Board should be to set, and to manage performance against, a consistent and practical framework of system-wide objectives looking at least five years ahead.

Budgeting

50   Once the plans have been set, the question arises whether the new Board should have a substantial operational budget. There are three possible options:

* to give the new Board both budgetary and management responsibility for all those areas of the system in which the agencies are required to act jointly or collectively in the achievement of targets and objectives;

* to give it a central role in spending reviews by advising both Ministers and the Treasury on the achievement of joint objectives, preparing and submitting a joint criminal justice system budget and to assume direct management for local Criminal Justice Boards, leaving to individual departments their own

---

[39] a point made by contributors to a "Criminal Justice System Planning Event" organised by SPG on 11th December 2000

[40] *Inter-Departmental Review of Performance Indicators Across the Criminal Justice System,* (Criminal Justice Joint Planning Unit, February 2001)

[41] *The Way Ahead,* para 3.227

budgets (except for an element held centrally by the Criminal Justice Board), and operational management; and

- as proposed in *The Way Ahead*,[42] to increase only marginally the central funds available to a strengthened SPG, renamed the 'Strategic Planning Board', to invest on improvements for the system as a whole.

51　As to the first option, I believe that the possibility of a single budget for the criminal justice system has yet to be thoroughly examined. It was apparently considered, but rejected, in the 1998 Comprehensive Spending Review, partly on political grounds, partly because of concerns about the departments' unpreparedness for such radical change and partly because of doubt as to whether it was necessary for the policy of closer collaboration that they were then contemplating. As the Performance and Innovation Unit, in its January 2000 Report noted, there are examples in Sweden, Hong Kong and New Zealand of how it might be done.[43] The general scheme of all of them is a policy co-ordinating structure, with substantial budgetary responsibilities, straddling departmental boundaries.

52　If such an examination were now to take place, it could include consideration of another rigidity in the present structure which impedes a more flexible approach to the problem, that of the separate responsibilities of police authorities and chief constables for local policing policies, priorities and decisions as to application of their individual funds. With such a fragmented police system, police budgets, unlike those of other criminal justice agencies, seemingly cannot be regarded as central government funding available, in part, for pooling to the advantage of the criminal justice system as a whole. Any move in that direction would, no doubt, call for a fundamental reconsideration of the relationship between central government and local policing. Maybe now is the time for it. Whilst the police must retain their separate and independent investigative function – just as prosecutors and the courts have their own distinctive roles in the criminal process – such separateness or independence does not seem to me to depend on local autonomy.

53　The pooling of criminal justice budgets would require, in the case of each department and agency, an exercise in demarcation between, on the one hand, activities and funds allocated to them that contribute to the planning and operation of the system as a whole and, on the other, those on which it is essential to preserve its independence of decision and action. In short, such a scheme would require substantial 'ring-fencing' of each of the criminal justice departments' funds for 'systems' functions.

---

[42] *The Way Ahead*, p 101, paras 3.230 and 3.231
[43] *Wiring It Up*, pp 19 - 24, paras 4.10 - 4.13

54   However, the boundary would not always be easy to draw and some administrative safety valves would have to be devised to overcome possible conflicts of interest or responsibility at national or local levels. That being so, a better course might be to focus more upon planning and monitoring the way in which resources are consumed and targets achieved, rather than upon creation of a pooled budget for its own sake. That was a concern of the Performance and Innovation Unit. In its January 2000 Report it advocated the need for greater flexibility of budgetary arrangements and said:

> "Pooled budgets are ... neither necessary nor sufficient to ensure effective collaborative working. It is important not to think they are a panacea or the solution in most cases. Pooling a budget may just create a different more troublesome boundary in a different place. What is important is that there is a flexibility in the way that funds can be used and a clear, shared responsibility for delivering the outcomes ...".[44]

55   I recognise the force of that point and its obvious attraction to the departments in their present course of 'flexible funding' of the system. However, it is conditioned by two assumptions that themselves need reconsideration. The first is that collaboration rather than over-all direction and local management is the best way to plan and operate a criminal justice system of the size and complexity of ours. The second is a seeming reluctance to explore the possibilities for devising a more flexible system than presently available for accommodating 'boundary' problems of that sort. 'Targets', 'objectives' and 'performance indicators', when spread between a variety of departments and agencies, have 'boundary' problems too.

56   The task of managing an annual expenditure of £12billion across five major agencies and a plethora of smaller ones, each assailed by competing pressures and interest groups with their own cultures and ways of working, might prove too much, particularly as work starts from such a low base. There might also be a risk, in the allocation of funds under a shared budget, for the most powerful or more powerful departments to increase their power and pursue their own priorities at others' expense. These are real difficulties, but if departments put aside any sectional interests and strive for a solution, they may be surmountable by the introduction of suitable constitutional safeguards. The working of the mechanisms for allocation of the present small joint reserve may suggest what forms they might take. In any event, I believe the option is worthy of serious consideration.

57   As to the second option, a central advisory role and management structure, with clear lines of accountability to a single body at the top would be

---

[44] ibid, p 49, paras 9, 8

required. That would probably be best achieved by vesting as much authority in a Criminal Justice Board as is consistent with the constitutional autonomy of the departments and agencies involved, but stopping short of giving it day to day accountability for the use of resources. Under such a scheme the Board, subject to ministerial agreement, would plan and be responsible for implementation of its plans through the medium of individual departments and agencies at appropriate levels. Ministers would remain jointly accountable to Parliament for the Board's performance. The Board, again subject to ministerial agreement, would participate in the annual bidding process by preparing and submitting a joint criminal justice system budget, but the budget would be administered on its behalf by the departments and agencies. Under this option, and if the concerns about the planning cycle that I have set out above are met, each department and agency would be responsible for translating over-all criminal justice system objectives and targets into achievable internal objectives and targets. Agencies and local managers would work to departmental objectives and performance targets derived from the criminal justice system plan. The Board would operate through a national and local administrative structure and through local Criminal Justice Boards[45] in securing implementation of its plans.

58   Whilst not awarding the Board complete financial control of the criminal justice system, such a regime would give it responsibility for planning and setting performance targets across the full range of criminal justice activities. This would meet the need for a simpler, more broadly based and potentially more effective line of over-all 'direction' at national and local levels, without the added complication of managing the resources for the whole system. The individual departments and agencies would retain their own budgets, although the new Board would take a formal role in periodic reviews of spending through advising Ministers and the Treasury on the achievement of joint objectives. Under this option, there would also be a strong argument for increasing substantially the pool of money held centrally in the strategic reserve for undertaking major system-wide projects.

59   The third option, the least radical of all, is the Government's proposal for "manag[ing] the system as a whole"[46] by strengthening the Strategic Planning Group, renaming it the Strategic Planning Board and concentrating on up to three national priorities each year. That could be the way to do it, though the critical question is what sort of strengthening, apart from introducing more senior personnel, it has it in mind. From the rubric in its 'Way Ahead' policy paper under which it treats the subject, "Partnership and effective, joined up delivery", and the following suggestion, the answer appears to be 'not much':

> "This Board could make sure the annual planning process
> took account of practitioners' views and was scheduled to

---

[45] see paras 73 – 77 below
[46] *The Way Ahead*, paras 3.230 and 3.231

give local managers time to make local plans and deploy resources.

Under this model, Ministers, on the advice of SPB - might set a maximum of three national priorities each year. Local areas would then account to the SPB for the delivery of these targets. Learning from experience elsewhere in local government and the public services, it would be important to develop effective incentives for improved performance, where appropriate, by for example rewarding success with additional funding or greater management flexibility".

60   This option seems to me to fall a long way short of what is required. Although the Government talks of 'strengthening' the SPG through enhancing its role in the annual planning process, it is still unwilling to give the body any operational means of securing the various departments' and agencies' compliance with its instructions. Its weakness in such a role is well illustrated by the lack of effective control it has so far exerted over the IBIS project,[47] the Board of which is formally a sub-group of the SPG, but from whom it does not receive regular reports, and whose substantial programme of activities has rarely figured in its agendas or minutes during this Review. For a Strategic Planning Board of the sort the Government appears to have in mind effectively to ensure 'direction' as well as devise 'strategy', it would need authority to manage and monitor respective allocations including, as necessary, the power to re-allocate funds in response to changing priorities.

61   A curious feature of this option is the proposal for Ministers to set a maximum of three national priorities each year, upon which the attention of the Strategic Planning Board and its local network would concentrate. I acknowledge, by way of example, that much has been achieved over recent months by agencies working together to achieve the Government's stated target for reducing the time taken to process persistent young offenders. But the Government's proposal would, in my view, be likely to narrow the focus of the central body to the three priorities, and then only for a year at a time, thus denying it and Ministers the ability to take a strategic and long-term view of the criminal justice system as a whole. Ministers could well from time to time identify specific priorities for co-ordinated effort across several of the agencies and charge a central body with their achievement. But to elevate such tasks into the major function of a central co-ordinating body confuses target setting in specific areas with directions and management of the system as a whole.

---

[47] see para 95 below

62   In my view, the Strategic Planning Group's make-up, its terms of reference,[48] its lack of involvement in the bidding process for funds for the criminal justice system, its seeming inability to initiate over-all planning for the short or long term as distinct from respond to individual departments' and agencies plans, its lack of authority to manage as distinct from seek agreement, and its lack of any structural relationship with the hierarchy above, below and alongside it, all make it an inappropriate vehicle for the task. What is needed is a new body, which is not simply strategic. It is a body that should plan, bid for and allocate funds, direct and through a single administrative structure below it, manage those activities of the criminal justice system on which its justice, efficiency and effectiveness depend. Option three would, in my view, fall considerably short of this aim and I doubt whether option two would come close to it in practical terms. However, perhaps the best course would be to start by establishing a Criminal Justice Board with the remit I describe in option two and seriously examine for the longer term the first option, of the establishment of a system-wide budget for it to devise and administer.

63   Whichever system is chosen in relation to the future direction and management of the criminal justice system, there are three further areas in which greater central direction of the system is required.

Information technology

64   I urge below a different approach to the development of integrated information technology in the criminal justice system, going well beyond the IBIS project of independent, but linked, systems. This new approach, if adopted, would in its turn require a new project management infrastructure. As I have said, the IBIS Project Board functions as a sub-group of the Strategic Planning Group. I consider that this responsibility should be transferred to a central **Criminal Case Management Agency** responsible for the development of a fully integrated information technology system for the criminal justice system.[49] If ever there was an area that called for effective long-term strategic direction, funding and implementation by a single body, this is it.

---

[48] see para 22 above

[49] see para 112 below

Research and development

65   There is a striking disparity between the annual expenditure of the three main
      criminal justice Ministries upon research. The Home Office has for many
      years employed a dedicated research team that commissions projects from
      outside academics and undertakes statistical and computer modelling of the
      likely effects of policy proposals. The annual cost of such research projects in
      the field of criminal justice is over £25m. In contrast, the total annual
      research budget for the Lord Chancellor's Department is less than £700,000.
      In my view, there is an obvious case for centralising research projects that
      affect the system as a whole and for making a Criminal Justice Board
      responsible for it. Such a system would make more sense than the present
      uncoordinated and sometimes overlapping research projects undertaken by
      different departments and agencies.[50]

Equality and diversity

66   A number of studies have provided disturbing evidence of unequal or
      discriminatory treatment within individual criminal justice agencies, most
      recently Sir William MacPherson's finding of institutional racism within the
      Metropolitan Police.[51] A significant barrier to eliminating such conduct is
      difficulty in determining how minorities are treated across the whole of the
      system – or even within individual agencies.[52] Not only is there no way of
      tracking individual cases between agencies, but in many cases different
      definitions or recording systems make it impossible for such data to be
      combined in any useful way. An important and urgent task for a national
      body, such as the Criminal Justice Board I have recommended, would be to
      establish a system for assessing the impact of all aspects of the criminal
      justice system on potentially disadvantaged groups, and be prepared to set –
      and to monitor - challenging targets where present policies or practices are
      shown to have a discriminatory effect. The first step – which is at last under
      way – is to ensure that all the criminal justice agencies adopt the 16 point
      categorisation system used in the 2001 census.

---

[50] see Appendix 3 to the Report

[51] *The Stephen Lawrence Inquiry*, Cmnd 4262 – I, (The Stationery Office, February 1999)

POSSIBLE MANAGEMENT STRUCTURE

Membership of Criminal Justice Board

67   The Strategic Planning Group comprises only senior civil servants from within the main criminal justice Ministries, the Treasury, a member of the Downing Street Policy Unit and Home Office policy adviser. Save for the inclusion of Government policy advisers, I consider that the membership of the new Criminal Justice Board should be similar. But I suggest that it should also include the Chairman of the Youth Justice Board, Chief Executives or officers of the various court and criminal justice agencies, a senior representative of the police and the Director of the Criminal Case Management Agency.[53]   I also recommend that it should contain a small number of non-executive members with experience of high level management of large and complex organisations outside the criminal justice system.

68   I have considered whether the judiciary should be represented on such a body. On the one hand, it might be thought desirable that judges should participate in the joint management of the system and contribute to discussions of objectives, priorities and resources. Judges have shown, through their chairmanship both of the CJCC and the Area Strategy Committees, and membership of TIG and some of its sub-groups that they can contribute to the collaborative working of the various agencies, including the courts, without compromising their independence. Some might argue for giving a senior judge – possibly the Senior Presiding Judge – a seat on a Criminal Justice Board.

69   On the other hand, the role of the Board would be different from that of the TIG or CJCC structures. The Board would have a direct and visible role in formulating and advising Ministers on objectives for the criminal justice system and for planning, budgeting for, directing and, through its administrative supporting structure, managing their attainment. It would be constitutionally wrong and potentially damaging to the independence and integrity of the judiciary for a judge, however senior, to be involved in administrative activity of that sort. In my view, while there should be an open and clear line of communication and consultation between Ministers and the Board on the one hand and the Lord Chief Justice and other senior judiciary on the other, the judiciary should not be members of or represented on the Board.

---

[52] Morgan and Russell, *The Judiciary in the Magistrates' Courts*, p 112

[53] see paras 112 below

Chairmanship

70   As I have said, the chair of the Strategic Planning Group has been taken by one of the senior civil servants as an adjunct of his or her existing role. This is a familiar enough pattern for an inter-departmental body in Whitehall, especially where, as in the case of the Group, it meets only infrequently and for short periods. But the role that I envisage for the Criminal Justice Board is significantly greater and more onerous than that undertaken by the Strategic Planning Group. In my view, for that reason and to avoid potential conflicts of interest, it would require a dedicated and independent chairman who could concentrate on and give continuity and momentum to the direction and management of the criminal justice system.

National administrative support for the Board

71   The new Board would need to be properly supported by a secretariat and an adequately funded administrative structure accountable to it. Its precise nature and membership would be for others to determine, having regard to the nature and extent of the Board's responsibilities. I pause only to express concern at the sort of scheme the Government, in its recent *The Way Ahead* proposals, put forward for "a strengthened" Strategic Planning Group's "strong, clear two-way communication and accountability between the centre and local areas".[54] Such a scheme would be "facilitated by the creation of a Performance and Innovation Directorate" led by a 'Director of Criminal Justice Performance', responsible for: commissioning modelling, research and management information, liaising with the inspectorates, offering expert advice to improve local delivery; and supporting long term strategic thinking and benchmarking. The Government also proposed that the new Directorate should itself be supported by a Practitioners' Panel to offer a 'frontline voice' to policy makers at the centre. To confine the Group to a strategic function of identifying a few national priorities each year[55] and then graft onto it such a mechanism is neither one thing nor the other. Such an approach seems to me to be unwieldy and bureaucratic. What is needed is a central body responsible for the planning, direction and operation of the criminal justice system and with the tools to do it, not some body without such powers engaging in more liaison, information exchange and monitoring. All the functions mentioned for the Government's proposed Directorate, to the extent that they are necessary, would be better included in the remit of a wider administrative structure under the new Board.

---

[54] *The Way Ahead*, para 3.234 et seq.

[55] see para 59 – 60 above

72   It seems to me that TIG and its sub-groups, suitably adapted to accommodate and implement the wide-ranging responsibilities of a new Criminal Justice Board, could provide the basis for an administrative structure accountable to it. Since its establishment in 1995, TIG has drawn in a wide range of those outside central government and the main agencies, and has brought a sharply practical focus to bear upon the problems with which it has been concerned. It has notable achievements, not least in demonstrating the improvements which can be made in the service provided to witnesses if all the agencies work together towards a specific common objective.

Local Criminal Justice Boards

73   The achievement of a greater sense of national direction and management of the criminal justice system would be a considerable step forward. Also needed are the means effectively to turn national plans and directives into reality at ground level. This is one aspect of the present system on which contributors to the Review have been particularly critical and in respect of which clarification and simplification of roles and lines of accountability are urgently needed. Under the umbrella of the Criminal Justice Board and its supporting national administrative structure there would still remain a need for local bodies of some sort to give effect to national planning and directives and manage the system at local level.

74   However, something needs to be done about the present range and proliferation of bodies at local level, as those within the system clearly acknowledge.[56] I have mentioned the emergence of local Chief Officers' Groups and, more recently, of local informal 'Criminal Justice Boards' or 'Criminal Justice Management Boards' as a symptom of frustration by local chief officers with the ineffectiveness of Area Strategy Committees as a mechanism for local joint planning or management. Those initiatives have been widely adopted and appear to be working well. Their development is not only a reflection of the administrative weakness of the Area Strategy Committees; it has accentuated it because of the tendency of many local agencies to send their deputy chief officers instead of their chief officers to the Committees' meetings. I should add, however, that these bodies have not set out to compete with the existing Area Strategy Committees and local TIGs, but to do what they cannot do and also generally to support their work.

---

[56] *2000 Spending Review: Cross-Cutting Study of The Criminal Justice System, Report to Ministers*, Criminal Justice Joint Planning Unit, (May 2000), paras. 48 and 76.

75 Most recently the chief officers of the statutory criminal justice agencies in London have recommended a London Criminal Justice Board.[57] It would consist of the chief officers of the core statutory criminal justice agencies and its function would be to co-ordinate strategies and operations of those agencies in London with a view to achieving the Government's aims for the criminal justice system.

76 Such a formula has a number of authoritative supporters. For example, the Central Council of Magistrates' Courts Committees has said that it viewed with "some scepticism" the ability of the present non-statutory national and local bodies to implement the Government's plans. It suggested the establishment of criminal justice system boards consisting of key decision makers from the six core statutory agencies, together with some lay representation, who would govern and influence the criminal justice system locally within a set of national objectives, and who would be accountable to a national Director-General with powers of direction. In my view, the obvious and pragmatic approach would be to disband the present mix of overlapping operational roles at local level of Area Strategy Committees, local TIGs, Chief Officer Groups and informal 'Criminal Justice Boards', take the best from them and combine them into a single statutory board, known as a **Local Criminal Justice Board**. Each Board should be provided with a dedicated and properly resourced secretariat accountable to the national secretariat. As it would have a significantly greater executive role that that of the present Area Strategy Committee, it would be as inappropriate for a judge to be a member of it as it would for the judiciary to be represented on the national Board.

77 I see no need to be prescriptive about the membership of the local Criminal Justice Boards, as there may be different needs in different areas. However, as a minimum, the following should all be represented on each of the 42 Boards: the local managers of the Criminal Court, the Probation Service, the Prison Service and the National Health Service; the local Chief Constable; the local Chief Crown Prosecutor; representatives from the Youth Offenders Team, Victim Support, possibly, representatives of the local Bar and solicitors and at least two non-executive members. Where the Bar and local solicitors are not represented on the Board, adequate arrangements should be made for regular consultation with them. Each Board should elect its own chairman.

I recommend that:

- **a Criminal Justice Board should replace the Strategic Planning Group, the national Trials Issues Group and its sub-groups, and take over such responsibilities of**

---

[57] see Final Report of *The Taking London Forward* Task Group (June 2000)

the Criminal Justice Consultative Council as may be operational;

- the Criminal Justice Board should be responsible for over-all direction of the criminal justice system, with a remit including, but not limited to:

    1. planning and setting criminal justice system objectives;

    2. budgeting and the allocation of funds;

    3. securing the national and local achievement of its objectives;

    4. the development and implementation of an integrated system of information technology;

    5. research and development; and

    6. combating inequality and discrimination throughout the criminal justice system;

- the Board should be chaired by an independent chairman and its membership should include senior civil servants from the three main criminal justice departments and the Treasury, the Chairman of the Youth Justice Board, Chief Officers of the Criminal Case Management Agency, the unified Criminal Court, Police, Prison and Probation Services, and a small number of non-executive members;

- the Board should not include a judge, but should consult regularly with the Lord Chief Justice and other senior judiciary;

- the Board should be supported by a secretariat and a national administrative structure accountable to it and be responsible for developing a system of information technology for the whole criminal justice system;

- local Criminal Justice Boards should replace the Area Strategy Committees, local TIGs, Chief Officer Groups and, where they exist informally constituted local 'Criminal Justice Boards', and should draw on their memberships;

- local Criminal Justice Boards should be responsible for giving effect at local level to the national Criminal Justice Board's directions and objectives and for management of the criminal justice system in their areas;

- membership of the local Boards should include: local managers of the Criminal Court, the Prison Service

and the National Health Service; the local Chief Constable; the local Chief Crown Prosecutor; the local Chief Probation Officer; representatives from the Youth Offenders Team, Victim Support, possibly representatives of the local Bar and solicitors and at least two non-executive members; and

- **each local Board should be provided with a dedicated and properly resourced secretariat accountable to the national secretariat, be provided with a joint local budget and should select its own chairman.**

ADVISING ON CRIMINAL JUSTICE

A Criminal Justice Council

78   Since its creation in 1992 the CJCC has been a pioneer in bringing the agencies within the criminal justice system together. But as Lord Woolf has recently said,[58] it has sometimes had to struggle with its role. This was inevitable given its mix of tasks as an advisory body and managerial forum providing leadership or central direction to the Area Committees. It and TIG both came into being in the early 1990s in response to a growing perception that there was a need for greater co-operation between the various agencies and organisations involved in the administration of criminal justice. As now constituted, the CJCC is an inter-agency group bringing together top level representatives from across the criminal justice system, with a broad remit to improve co-ordination. Although there is no formal link between it and TIG, the former being primarily advisory and the latter closer to operational, there is considerable overlap between their structures and functions.[59] As I have said, the inevitable consequences are duplication of effort and muddled lines of accountability.

79   One aspect of this confusion is that the CJCC, like the Area Strategy Committees which report to it, has begun to assume, or is expected to assume, more of an executive, as well as a consultative, role in developing and securing criminal justice strategy nationally and locally.[60] As such, their role is growing ever closer to that of TIG and its local TIGs. If my recommendations for the establishment of a Criminal Justice Board and supporting administrative structure are adopted, there is no place for such a

---

[58] speech to the Prison Reform Trust, 31 January 2001

[59] see Criminal Justice Consultative Council and the Trials Issues Group: Joint message from Lord Justice Rose and Joan MacNaughton (June 2000)

[60] see paras 30 – 36 above

mix and overlap of executive and consultative functions in the system. There is, however, an urgent need for a strengthened consultative structure at national level. The CJCC, as it is presently organised, is ill-equipped to undertake the wide-ranging and comprehensive consultative and advisory role that government needs and should ask for in its stewardship of our criminal justice system.

80   The limitations of the current system are highlighted by the Government's policy paper *Criminal Justice: The Way Ahead*. This document was stated by its authors to have three purposes: reviewing the current performance of the criminal justice system and drawing conclusions; setting out work in hand and for the future to prevent and address offending; and setting out work in hand and possible future developments to modernise the criminal justice system.[61] Given such an agenda, many might have expected the Government to have made full use of the CJCC in preparing its proposals, for example by turning to it to assist in identifying the key issues and in framing a response to them which was proportionate, realistic and achievable. But, the Government did not consult the Council, apart from a brief presentation to it shortly before publication.[62]

81   It is little wonder that the recent history of the reform of our criminal law and procedure has been characterised by yearly or twice-yearly short-term measures seemingly aimed more at reassuring the media than as properly considered stages of development of criminal justice policy. It provides a telling illustration of the need for a standing advisory body with a statutory power and duty to keep the working of the criminal justice system under review - capable of initiating proposals for change and to which the Government should be obliged to refer key issues for advice. Such a move would be of a piece with the view expressed by the Performance and Innovation Unit, in its January 2000 Report, of the need to consult more thoroughly and widely on the working of the system.[63] In my view, the CJCC should be re-composed under the chairmanship of the Lord Chief Justice or a senior Lord Justice of Appeal, and re-named the **Criminal Justice Council**. It should be composed of judges of all levels, magistrates, criminal practitioners, representatives of the key agencies and organisations involved in the criminal justice process and one or more distinguished legal academics specialising in the field, none of whom should be members of the Criminal Justice Board. Its functions should include the following:

- to keep the criminal justice system under review;

- to advise the Government on the form and manner of implementation of all proposed criminal justice reforms and to make proposals to it for reform;

---

[61] *The Way Ahead*, p 16
[62] a *Medium Term Overview of the Criminal Justice System* on 19th January at the Imperial War Museum
[63] *Wiring It Up*, p 7, para 1.6

- to provide general oversight of the programme and structures for introduction and maintenance of codification of substantive criminal law, procedure, evidence and sentencing that I recommend in Chapter 1;

- to advise the Government on the framing and implementation of a communication and education strategy for the criminal justice system; and

- for any of those purposes, to consult and/or commission programmes of research.

82   A model exists in the form of the Civil Justice Council,[64] which is chaired by the Master of the Rolls and includes judges, lawyers, Lord Chancellor's Department staff and others, and operates through a number of sub-committees. Its functions are to keep the civil justice system under review, to consider how to make it more accessible, fair and efficient, to advise the Lord Chancellor and the judiciary on its development, to refer proposals for changes to the Lord Chancellor and the Civil Procedure Rules Committee[65] and to make proposals for research. The needs of the criminal justice system are different from and more complex than those in the civil sphere, not least in the number of Government departments and agencies required to make it work and in the wide range of interests for which it provides. With suitable adaptations, it seems to me that such a body to keep the criminal justice system under review in a comprehensive, structured and measured way is long overdue. The range of bodies and interests involved in the criminal justice process whose experience should be tapped, either by representation on such a body or through its consultative role is such that its role, will be, if anything, more demanding.

83   The central role that I foresee for the Council would be as a standing advisory body on the criminal justice system which the Government is statutorily required to consult on all major legislative or other changes that it proposes for the criminal law and/or the criminal justice system, and which would itself initiate proposals for reform. These would be its twin and major roles in keeping the criminal justice system under review.

Codification

84   A key role for the Criminal Justice Council would be to lead the programme of codification of the criminal law in the four parts that I have recommended in Chapter 1. As to the Criminal Offences Code, it should liaise closely with the Law Commission as to how the work which has already been done in this area can be further developed and completed. The Council would also have

---

[64] created by the Civil Procedure Act 1997, s 6
[65] created by the Civil Procedure Act 1997, s 2

an important role to play in advising the Government on future law reform. Similarly, the Council should oversee the work of the other committees that I have recommended in Chapters 10 and 11 to codify the rules of criminal procedure, the law of evidence and sentencing law and procedure.

Communication and education

85 I have referred more than once to public ignorance of the workings of the criminal justice system. At local level, many of the criminal justice agencies and others, including MCCs, the Magistrates' Association and Crown Court centres, have taken commendable initiatives through court open days, mock trials, visits to schools and other events to increase public understanding of their work. A good example of this is provided by the guidance the Magistrates' Association provides through the Magistrates in the Community Programme.[66] Also, from August 2002, schools will have a statutory responsibility to teach programmes of study for citizenship as part of the national curriculum.[67] These are welcome moves, and the Criminal Justice Council should encourage and involve itself in those aims. In particular, the Council should be well placed to advise on a programme of public information and education about the criminal justice system.

86 The role that I propose for the Council is thus far wider than that of the Criminal Justice Consultative Council and would impose a significant workload on its members. If it is to be an authoritative and effective means of keeping the criminal justice system under review and of providing timely advice on it to the Government, it will need strong research and secretarial support.

Local consultation

87 The substitution of a Criminal Justice Council for the Criminal Justice Consultative Council would leave the question of what to do with the latter's satellites, the present Area Strategy Committees. Such consultative role as they have is, in practice, as limited as their new 'strategic' function is unclear. Though there are some notable examples of achievement on both fronts, they too have been characterised by many with experience of them as little more than talking shops. If, as I have recommended, the national and local TIGs become, either in their present or some suitably adapted form, part of an administrative structure reporting to the new Criminal Justice Board, there is little point in retaining the Area Strategy Committees for their recently

---

[66] MIC Guide (Magistrates' Association 2000)

[67] Citizenship: Key stages 3 and 4 (Department for Education and Employment/Qualifications and Curriculum Agency – 1999)

acquired and nebulous executive role of ensuring implementation of national policies and developing local ones. As I have said, to the extent that such a role is identifiable in practice, it is remarkably close to that of the local TIGs,[68] and also to those of the local Chief Officer Groups and informal Criminal Justice Boards. Accordingly, under the scheme I envisage, the Area Strategy Committees would pass their embryo local strategic management functions to the new local Criminal Justice Boards.

88   The strengthening of the consultative function at a national level should remove the need for institutional consultative activity at area level, which is not, as I have said, a prime activity of the present Area Committees. Such local consultation as the Criminal Justice Council would need to undertake could, it seems to me, be organised by its members individually through their own hierarchies. As to consultation by local bodies, the local Criminal Justice Boards should be well equipped, by virtue of their membership, to express informed views on local initiatives. And there are already various local sources from whom they or other bodies can seek views informally, in particular, the local judiciary and magistracy, representatives of the legal professions and court user groups. The highly regarded Court User Groups, which include consultative functions at court centre level, should, of course, continue with their valuable work.

I recommend that:

- **the Criminal Justice Consultative Committee should be replaced with a Criminal Justice Council with a statutory power and duty, and suitably equipped:**

  - **to keep the criminal justice system under review;**

  - **to advise the Government on the form and manner of implementation of all proposed criminal justice reforms and to make proposals to it for reform;**

  - **to provide general oversight of the programme and structures for introduction and maintenance of codification of substantive criminal law, procedure, evidence and sentencing that I recommend in Chapter 1;**

  - **to advise the Government on the framing and implementation of a communication and education strategy for the criminal justice system; and**

  - **for any of those purposes, to consult and/or commission programmes of research;**

---

[68] see para 79 above

- before initiating key proposals for reform of the criminal justice system, the Government should be statutorily obliged to refer them to the Council for advice and to take account of any proposals or advice tendered by it in response to such reference or of its own accord;

- the Council should be chaired by the Lord Chief Justice or a senior Lord Justice of Appeal and composed of judges of all levels, magistrates, criminal practitioners, representatives of the key agencies and organisations involved in the criminal justice process and one or more distinguished legal academics specialising in the field (none of whom should be members of the Criminal Justice Board);

- the Council should be provided with a properly resourced secretariat and research staff;

- such of the Criminal Justice Consultative Council's functions as relate to the development and improvement of inter-agency co-ordination of national policies and objectives should become the responsibility of the Criminal Justice Board and its administrative support structure; and

- the Area Strategy Committees should cease to exist.

JOINT INSPECTION

89   There are currently six inspectorates operating within the criminal justice system: the Crown Prosecution Service Inspectorate; HM Inspectorate of Constabulary, HM Inspectorate of Prisons, HM Inspectorate of Probation, HM Magistrates Courts Service Inspectorate and the Social Services Inspectorate. If my recommendation in chapter 7[69] is implemented, the Magistrates' Courts Service Inspectorate should be superseded by an independent inspectorate for the unified Criminal Court.

90   The Criminal Justice Ministers, in their 1998 Comprehensive Spending Review,[70] identified the need for better-integrated inspection across the criminal justice system. Amongst the areas they identified for improvement was the need for machinery to examine the relationships between the criminal justice agencies and to assess the effect of individual initiatives on the system as a whole. Although work has been done towards setting up such machinery,

---

[69] see para 117

[70] *Cross Departmental Review of the Criminal Justice System: Comprehensive Spending Review 1998*

progress has been slow, and joint working is still carried out on an ad hoc and relatively unstructured basis. A limited number of joint thematic reviews[71] have been undertaken, and often an inspection team organised by one of the inspectorates includes an inspector from another organisation. But these arrangements fall far short of meeting the need for a properly integrated inspection regime across the whole criminal justice system.

91 An option of bringing the existing individual inspectorates together to create a single system-wide inspectorate would be unwieldy, would detract from the specialist work that they undertake and could undermine the important independent positions which have been established (sometimes with difficulty) by individual Chief Inspectors. Instead, they have been working towards the establishment of a Joint Inspection Unit which would instigate and co-ordinate a programme of cross-agency inspections and thematic reviews. It is disappointing that their attempts to secure resources for this unit have so far met with limited success (the proposal did not, for example feature in *The Way Ahead*, which argued for "more co-ordination" of inspection programmes without apparently proposing any additional resources for it).[72] Some form of co-ordinating body is planned and may have been introduced by the time this report is published, but I consider that this work should be placed on a more formal and established footing. The need for a structured programme of joint inspection activity will become all the more acute if a Criminal Justice Board of the nature and with the functions I have suggested is introduced. To maintain its independence, the body should be under the collective control of the Criminal Justice Chief Inspectors and should report direct to Ministers. However, it would have to work closely with the new Board to ensure that the joint inspections have due regard to over-all criminal justice system objectives and priorities.

I recommend that a Joint Inspection Unit should be formally established under the collective control of the Criminal Justice Chief Inspectors and be given sufficient resources to instigate and co-ordinate a programme of cross-agency inspection.

---

[71] *Lifers* (HMIP, HMI Prisons), *How long Youth Cases take* (HMIC, MCSI, CPSI) and *Casework Information Needs across the Criminal Justice System* (CPSI, HMIC, MCSI, HMI Prisons, HMIP, SSI)

[72] *The Way Ahead*, para 3.233

INFORMATION TECHNOLOGY

Introduction

92   The present structural complexities and inefficiencies of the various inter-departmental and inter-agency bodies are not the only impediments to a better over-all direction and management of the system.   Lack of common information technology is another and more fundamental problem.   Each of the main criminal justice agencies has introduced, or is about to introduce, a system designed for its own needs,[73] and with varying or no ability to communicate direct its electronically stored information to other agencies that need it.

93   The criminal justice system is a document and labour intensive operation, most of whose administrative and management systems were developed at a time when the workload of the courts and lawyers was far smaller than today. Many of the systems are crude, paper-based, oriented towards the process of administration and not the community, and not all are able to cope with the increasing demands placed upon them.   This causes high staffing costs, inefficiencies, error, delay, dissatisfaction and poor reputation.   But the criminal justice system can instead be viewed as an information system - a network of millions of individual pieces of data, linked and related to each other in thousands of different and ever changing ways.   Modern information and communications technology could transform the ways in which each agency undertakes its separate function in the speed, reliability and efficiency with which data are processed and also in the manner of management of a prosecution from charge to disposal.   There are also the benefits that would accrue to the system as a whole in the integration of its information infrastructure.

94   That parts of the system are still, in the first decade of the twenty-first century, effectively relying upon manual systems to support some of their key

---

[73] Police: "NSPIS", Custody and Case Preparation (in progress); CPS: "Connect 42", provision of personal computers and an e-mail facility to lawyers and caseworkers (in progress), "Compass", a case management system (contract yet to be awarded); Magistrates' Courts: "LIBRA", (still partly in pilot and yet to be installed nation-wide); Crown Court: "CREDO" (yet to be introduced); National Probation Service: "CRAMS" (yet be introduced) and " Copernicus" (yet to be introduced); Prison Service: "Quantum" (about to be installed)

tasks is a public disgrace. With over 25 million people in the world currently on e-mail, it is remarkable that one still cannot reliably expect to send an e-mail direct to a justices' clerk, to a Crown prosecutor or to a prison governor. It is one of the areas in which those contributing to the Review have been most critical. As the Public Accounts Committee recently noted.[74]

> "Information technology in the criminal justice system is being developed from a very low base. Basic details required by all parties are generally input separately by each agency, which is likely to lead to duplication, error and delay. And there is a lack of comprehensive basic data, for example on the time taken to get cases to court. The systems currently being developed must resolve, not perpetuate, these anomalies."

95   All this is not to ignore governmental attempts to co-ordinate the planning and implementation of information technology throughout the criminal justice system. Since 1999 IBIS,[75] the inter-agency body that I have mentioned, has had the main[76] responsibility for that task. Based in the Home Office, its declared aims have been to identify what needs to be done to develop and implement 'interfaces' between the various systems, to provide "a basis for identifying opportunities" for harmonisation and processes to support automation of the interfaces, and to provide a "framework" for development and implementation of projects. IBIS has, to its credit, largely achieved its aim of introducing major public/private partnerships in each of the existing agencies, and in a form that enables them to communicate electronically. On the other hand, no-one could reasonably claim that it has achieved much in introducing order into the system, shackled as it is with those vague and modest aims and the disparate systems within its remit. In October 1999 it produced a medium-term strategic plan for the ensuing five or so years, to integrate information systems and to improve 'business' processes among the various agencies.[77] But that is largely based on what the individual agencies had already planned for their own systems. It is now engaged on an examination of the longer-term information needs of the criminal justice system and how satisfying them might require changes in the way in which it works. Most recently, the Government has commissioned both a high level technical review of the best means of joining the systems together and a 'Gateway' review of the IBIS project as a whole, and has earmarked £8 million for the programme of work that may result.[78]

---

[74] *Criminal Justice: Working Together*, para 4 (vii)

[75] a sub-group of the SPG since 1999

[76] see also "PITO", a project to improve links between police information technology systems and those of the CPS and magistrates' courts

[77] *Medium Term Strategic Plan for Information Systems in the Criminal Justice System*, (Home Office, October 1999)

[78] *The Way Ahead*, para 3.266

96   It is commonly said that organisations should get their structures right first before planning their information technology and that the latter is no cure for an inefficient structure. But, as I have said, information technology has a potential, not only to improve existing structures and their working, but also to re-shape them to advantage. It is clear that such technology is capable of playing an increasing part in the shaping and operation of the criminal justice system. If it is to do so efficiently and to the best advantage, it too will need more central planning and direction than has been attempted up to now.

97   There are two formidable obstacles to improvement. First, the processes that make up the system are unconnected. Each agency maintains its own case files, though many of the items of information that they contain are, or should be, identical. As a case passes from one procedural stage to the next, data are copied (manually or electronically) from the records of one agency and passed on to the next. There is no single body monitoring or assuring the quality or consistency of the transfer, let alone managing the over-all progression of the case from charge to disposal. On the contrary, the way work flows through the system is dictated largely by the structure of each department and agency.

98   Second, within the field of criminal justice there are, or are about to be, six quite separate national information technology systems - Police, Prosecution, Magistrates' Courts, Crown Court, Probation and Prisons. Each is at a different stage of development, involves a different partner and/or supplier and management regime, is the subject of a different financial and contractual arrangement and has a different planning cycle. The picture is one of separate and different technology, data and management – six information technology infrastructures and applications systems supporting one criminal justice system.

99   There are severe limitations to such a fragmented system. Clearly, it involves much replication of effort. Data passing through it will be subject to constant change, either through the action of one of the agencies (e.g. the defendant is re-arrested on fresh charge) or because of an external event (e.g. a witness changes address). Such a change will typically come to the notice of only one of the agencies, who must then ensure it is effectively communicated to all of the others who need to know. Each of the other agencies needs a separate verification procedure and a means of ensuring verified changes are effected to its own file in a timely manner. At best the system is inefficient and wasteful. At worst it leads to the key agencies holding inconsistent information.

100   Looking at the criminal justice system as a whole, the constraints imposed are, if anything, worse. The progress of a case can be monitored only within each agency, and only by that agency for as long as it has it. Responsibilities for case management are dispersed, creating obvious discontinuities at the

point of transfer, and for buck passing when things go wrong. And there is no possibility of aggregating information about defendants, victims, outcomes or anything else across the system as a whole, because each agency uses its own definitions of the contents of its files.

101   The information technology system within each agency consists of six basic elements. Before I continue, it may help for me to define the terms I use to describe them:

- User interface is the part of the system which appears before the user on the screen and so controls the way in which information is entered and retrieved. Those needing electronic access to case information will include, not only each agency, but defendants and their representatives, victims, witnesses, and others involved or interested in the information;

- Enabling technologies are the hard-ware and soft-ware systems which enable the entry and retrieval of information – the 'plumbing', essential but so far as possible, invisible to the user;

- Data are the basic units of information – for example about crimes, defendants, victims, charges, outcomes, and release dates;

- Communications are the means by which data are transmitted around the system, and to those within and outside it;

- Case management, in this context, is the means by which each agency handles the individual cases for which it is responsible and the administration of the over-all caseload of each agency. In the criminal justice system this will typically involve, not only exchanging information in order to track and prompt the progress of a case, but also performing quality and data sufficiency tests; and

- Management information relates, not only to the current state of any particular case or cases, but more significantly to information about the progress of cases, including volumes, time-scales and compliance with specified success factors. The criminal courts are particularly weak in this area, as recently noted by Morgan and Russell.[79]

102   Figure 1 shows how each agency may be represented in terms of this categorisation. And figure 2 extends this to represent the whole of the criminal justice system.

---

[79] *The Judiciary in the Magistrates' Courts*, p 113

Fig 1

Model of one major system of today

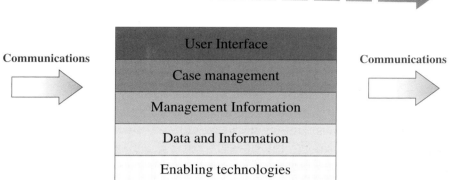

Communications

User Interface

Case management

Management Information

Data and Information

Enabling technologies

Communications

Underpinned by specialist human skills and knowledge

Fig 2

How the systems operate today

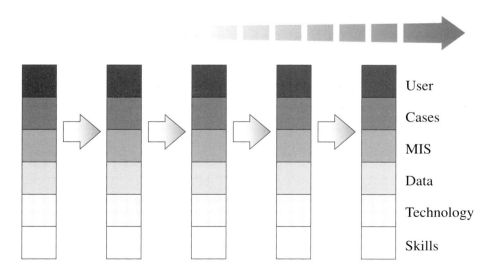

User

Cases

MIS

Data

Technology

Skills

A unified system

102   As can be seen from the above, each of the six existing agencies has, over time, developed its own technological solutions to its own problems. But the fundamental question is whether the system is best served by having six separate ICT systems. For the reasons I have given, it is not. If one were starting from scratch the approach would be to develop one system, not half a dozen. However, in the current state of technology, there is no theoretical or practical reason why all these elements should not, over time, be unified into one system. The various agencies could continue to rely on their existing systems and developing interfaces. On the outside, there would be little change, since the enabling technologies would remain largely hidden from the user. Most of the transformation could be accomplished through modifications to the enabling technologies and by using internet applications to allow users to operate a common body of data.

The electronic case file

103   The fundamental principle of a unified system would be the sharing of data in an electronic file, rather than passing it between agencies. Once created, such a file should contain and record all documents and information about each particular case and be able to flow quickly and cheaply through the entire criminal justice system. Once one part of the system had finished its work on the case, the file would be accessible in electronic form to the next part – as an accurate, complete and up-to-date record, ready for attention by the next set of professionals. Each agency would use the shared file in its own work, updating it to reflect the changes initiated by others and amending it to reflect changes it initiated, or of which it became aware. Each piece of information would need to be entered only once. A prototype of such an approach has recently been piloted on the Wales and Chester Circuit and has clearly demonstrated its benefits in easing and speeding communication and in reducing reduction duplication of paperwork.[80] In due course, provision could also be made for witnesses and members of the public to have internet access to such parts of the file necessary to inform them about the progress of and programme for cases. And defendants and their lawyers would be able to receive material to which they are entitled, and send information required of them under the pre-trial case management regime.

---

[80] *Dyfed Powys IT Project: Progress Report,* (Wales and Chester Circuit, July 2001)

A common language

104 In order to achieve a system of common electronic case files, the criminal justice agencies need first to agree a definition of the smallest unit of data from which they can be constructed. In simple terms, there is no point in providing linked technology if its users cannot understand each other's language. This is a highly complex task and one that TIG, the SPG and IBIS have been examining for some time. The difficulty is that one incident can give rise to a number of charges against a number of defendants, each of whom may already be involved, or may subsequently become involved, in other proceedings. The task is to find the lowest common denominator that will enable agencies to break down an existing set of charges and/or defendants into a smaller subject. As the Public Accounts Committee, in its 2000 Report has noted:

> "Ambitions for closer joint working are being hampered by a lack of consistent definitions, such as what constitutes a criminal case. Investment in information technology will only be effective if the criminal justice agencies can agree to record data in a consistent way, and they should give high priority to completing this task."[81]

In my view, the identification of a common definition for the lowest unit of data in the criminal justice system should be one of the first tasks for the Criminal Justice Board acting through and on the advice of the Criminal Case Management Agency, the establishment of which I also recommend.[82]

A system-wide approach

105 The introduction of new technology enables improvement of a service, but often also changes its nature and that of the system it serves. Such changes are already under way in Victoria,[83] Ontario[84] and in various States in the USA.[85] I have already referred to the possibilities for victims and witnesses, potential jurors and others involved in the criminal process to use the internet to communicate information, for example, about their availability or needs, and to obtain information about the progress of cases. This has potential for speeding and otherwise improving pre-trial case management by enabling the prosecution and defence to use the same electronic file for communication between themselves and with the court – in a 'virtual' court hearing where appropriate. I say more about this in Chapter 11.

---

[81] *Criminal Justice: Working Together*, para 4(iii)

[82] see para 112 below

[83] see *Technology and the Law*, Report of the Victorian Law Reform Committee (May 1999)

[84] progress is summarised at www.integratedjustice.gov.on.ca

[85] see, for example, www.integration.search.org

106   The achievement of such benefits would be expensive. It would require a substantial long-term investment in basic hardware and software and in training and other adjustment costs as each organisation moves to the new technology. And before these stages are reached, there would need to be a fundamental reappraisal of the core functions and responsibilities of each of the agencies within the system, taking account of the full potential for change that a common information base would make possible. The result might be that the system over-all would benefit from one or more agencies undertaking work that goes well beyond their own operational priorities.

Data quality

107   One vital area in which the need for system priorities to take precedence over individual agency targets is data entry and initiation. Whatever solution is found to the problem of the common language, it would be likely to require all police forces to record data about incidents, suspects, victims and witnesses in a new and standardised form designed for the needs of other agencies as well as for their own requirements. This could involve the collection of data, the relevance of which might not be apparent on initial investigation. Another example lies in the field of criminal record information, the quality of which has been a running sore in the system for more than a decade. The system of case allocation that I recommend in Chapter 7 will not work properly unless accurate antecedent information is available to the courts at the first hearing of the case. Another key priority for the Criminal Justice Board before new systems are implemented should be the establishment of agreed protocols for entry and standards of data.

Data security

108   A system of shared data based on a single case file raises issues of security. Much of the information held by criminal justice agencies is highly confidential. Details of offences, injuries suffered or witnesses' circumstances are often intensely personal. Some categories of evidence, particularly that gathered in relation to organised or international crime, is given in strict confidence, and its unauthorised disclosure would put at risk those who provided it. Information about individuals' criminal records should not be accessible except by those with a right to see it. Current methods of data handling allow each agency carefully to limit the range and classes of data passed to other agencies, and tightly to control the way it is then handled; but this could be achieved through one security system as well as with six. I mention all this, not because it is a technical impediment to the creation and use of a single case file, since access can be controlled, but to emphasise the

need for investment in suitable security technology and, thereafter, in continuing assessment of its adequacy. This would be another of the responsibilities of the Criminal Justice Board, acting through and on the advice of the Criminal Case Management Agency.

Constituents of the project

109   It would be a matter for Ministers, as advised by the Criminal Justice Board, to decide upon the programme for introducing an integrated system based upon a common case file. An early question would be how to make the transition from the existing six systems to one. This would require reconsideration of the individual long-term contracts each agency has with its information technology partner and/or provider. In my view, it should also prompt a re-evaluation of whether funding by way of a public/private partnership scheme offers the most effective or reliable way to establish and manage a unified system.

110   These questions are essentially ones of implementation, and therefore outside the ambit of this Report. However, it may be helpful if I set out the separate stages and elements of an integrated system as I see them. Each one of these would, in my view, form an individual phase within a progressive – not a 'big bang' - move to a unified system of information technology. Each would bring its own benefits. It would be for the Criminal Justice Board to determine whether the projects could proceed in parallel or sequentially and, if the latter, in what order. Among the factors it would have to bear in mind are the cost, the capacity of the system to cope with change and, given the variable record of central Government in introducing and managing large scale information technology schemes, the quality of project management expertise available. But I am satisfied that this approach would be a feasible way of introducing a unified system and that it would offer significant benefits to all those who use it.

● Case tracking - An initial stage would involve the introduction of a basic level of case management through the tracking of cases throughout the criminal justice system, and in setting and monitoring progression targets both at a system level and within each agency. The benefits which can accrue through setting targets for case progression have been illustrated by the work undertaken for cases involving persistent young offenders.[86]

● Management information - A second project would involve the production of system-wide management information. This would go wider than the data derived from case progression management, since it would involve the monitoring of aggregate outcomes – at each stage – for categories of offence

---

[86] see *Persistent Young Offenders: Best Practice*, (The Court Service June 2001)

and for categories of individual. Integrated quality and diversity monitoring would be a key aspect of this project.

- Unification of data - The fundamental building block of an integrated system would be unification of the basic data of which the system would be composed. Once the problem of the common language is resolved (and no progress would be possible under this heading until it has been), the project would fall into two phases: conversion of the data into the new standard; and merging the data into the new common case files. Successful completion of this stage would enable data to be shared between agencies, not passed from one to another.

- New categories of user - As I have suggested, an additional and important benefit of an integrated system would be that involved or interested persons outside the agencies (including members of the public and the news media) could send and receive information about cases over the internet. Thus, it should be available as part of the case-management process by defence lawyers and others, such as victims and witnesses to communicate relevant information about themselves or to enquire about the progress of cases.[87]

- Case management - Once the above four phases were complete, the progress of cases and individuals through the system could be more efficiently controlled and monitored against defined quality standards over-all and for each agency involved. The Criminal Justice Board would have to determine how this could be done without compromising the operational independence of each agency. Figure 3 illustrates how it might work

- Unified enabling technologies - The final phase is optional. As I have said, most of the benefits of an integrated system could be achieved using existing user interfaces to gain access to a virtually unified case file via the internet. But, once all the previous five projects had been completed, it would be for consideration whether a unification of enabling technologies into a single criminal justice system of information technology would then be a desirable, and achievable, end. Figure 4 adds this final stage to the scheme shown in Figure 3.

A Criminal Case Management Agency

111   An essential feature of the integrated system I have described is that, once the problem of the common language is solved, there could be a staged transfer of data using web technologies, while allowing each agency to retain a necessary degree of control over its own processes and interfaces. The Criminal Justice Board should assume responsibility for this programme and, thereafter, the management, integrity and security of the data in order to ensure accessibility

---

[87] this is one of the targets of the Government's White Paper, *Modernising Government*, Cm 4310, (March 1999)

Fig 3

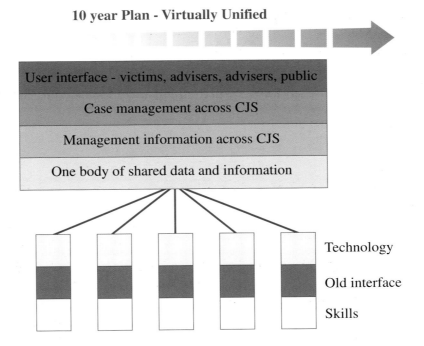

10 year Plan - Virtually Unified

User interface - victims, advisers, advisers, public
Case management across CJS
Management information across CJS
One body of shared data and information

Technology

Old interface

Skills

Fig 4

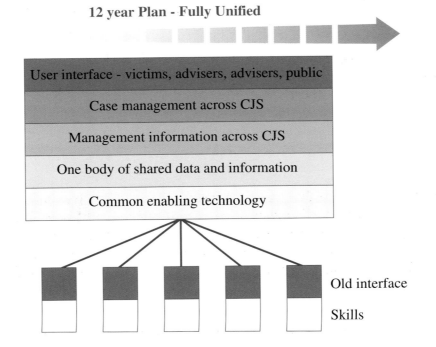

12 year Plan - Fully Unified

User interface - victims, advisers, advisers, public
Case management across CJS
Management information across CJS
One body of shared data and information
Common enabling technology

Old interface

Skills

to all users of accurate, timely and relevant information. I believe that a special agency should be established under the aegis of the Board to:

- draw up a project plan and secure the necessary finance for it;
- manage its implementation; and
- progressively assume responsibility for managing those elements of the system that are to be centrally managed.

I therefore propose that a central Criminal Case Management Agency should be established for these purposes in place of IBIS, with a full-time Chief

Executive who would be a member of the Criminal Justice Board, and directly answerable to it.

Implementation plan

112   The implementation of an integrated information technology system across the whole of the criminal justice system would have profound implications for all those working within it. Issues of working methods, functions and security would have to be faced at a time in which procedural and structural reform would also be consuming significant management and operational resources. The difficulties are well expressed by a paper resulting from the collaborative reappraisal of the Information Systems and Sharing (IS&S) programme in Northern Ireland:

> "The IS&S programme...is ambitious. It is seeking at one go to join together all the Criminal Justice Organisations to share information in a common form. The complexity of each task makes it very difficult to make meaningful progress. Each Criminal Justice Organisation is at a different stage of IS development, with the strategic direction for use of information systems within each organisation emerging or already set. There are no common criminal justice community security standards and no easy method to achieve a joined up CJS using a common infrastructure."[88]

---

[88] Northern Ireland Court Service, 1999

113   The solution that the authors of the Northern Ireland collaborative reappraisal recommend is for a feasibility study to be established, bringing together all those people with the operational experience to develop processes so that the system can be developed and simulated in a setting that presents minimum risk to any of the participating organisations. I believe that such an approach should also feature in the design of an integrated information technology system for our larger and more complex criminal justice system. A feasibility study of some kind would be prudent, provided that it does not become an excuse for further delay. Its establishment and the production of a costed implementation plan within a set time-scale should be among the first tasks of the Criminal Justice Board.

I recommend that:

- **the Criminal Justice Board should discontinue the IBIS project of linking up the six main information technology systems in the criminal justice system, and should instead, within a set timescale, produce an implementation plan for an integrated information technology system for the whole of the criminal justice system based upon a common language and common electronic case files;**

- **the implementation of such an integrated system should be organised in six projects, to run either in parallel or sequentially, namely:**

  1. **case tracking;**

  2. **management information;**

  3. **unification of data;**

  4. **extending the categories of user;**

  5. **case management; and**

  6. **unification of enabling technologies;**

- **a Criminal Case Management Agency should be established, to be accountable to the Criminal Justice Board for managing the implementation of the integrated system and, when implemented, managing those elements of the system that require central management, namely:production of system protocols and quality assurance of system data;**

  1. **management and monitoring of case progression;**

  2. **data standards for system management information;**

  3. **standards and protocols for access by victims, witnesses, defendants and their representatives;**

4. **storage and maintenance of data;**

5. **data security and control of access to data; and**

6. **case management at the system level.**

CHAPTER 9

DECRIMINALISATION AND ALTERNATIVES TO CONVENTIONAL TRIAL

INTRODUCTION

1   Our criminal courts deal with cases that vary enormously in nature, seriousness and complexity. In this Chapter, I gather together and respond to suggestions that particular categories of case should be handled in new ways, suggestions ranging from the removal of certain matters from the criminal arena – 'decriminalisation' – to the creation of separate specialist courts.

2   As to decriminalisation, the criminal courts, particularly magistrates' courts, deal with much work which, though important as a means of securing efficient public administration, is concerned with conduct that is on the borderline of criminality and/or is of relatively slight culpability. In addition, society's view of what justifies criminal proceedings changes from time to time. In considering this issue, I have kept in mind that, however trivial the breach of public duty in question, the potential of criminal proceedings to enforce it may be the only effective means of doing so against some. On the other hand, it is wrong to stigmatise conduct as criminal simply as a means of enforcing a public duty when an average right-thinking person would not so regard it.

3   As to separate specialist courts, the first question is what, if any, significant advantages in justice and efficiency they might bring to their speciality over that which a properly resourced general criminal court could provide. The second and overlapping question in each suggested case is whether the likely use would justify the cost of creating and maintaining a separate, dedicated tribunal with a specialist jurisdiction.

4   I take the following as my starting points:

- criminal courts should not be concerned with infractions that are administrative or civil in nature, save only and to the extent that efficient public administration cannot be secured in any other way;

- there is value in providing for resolution outside the courtroom so far as is consistent with justice, the public interest and efficient public administration; and

- potential savings within the criminal justice system arising from decriminalisation or the modification of criminal proceedings should be measured against the likely cost and disturbance to the public, to enforcing bodies and to those against whom they are proceeding of any alternative means of enforcement.

5   I have received a number of suggestions for removal of work from the criminal courts. The most frequent concerned council tax cases and prosecutions for television licence and vehicle excise duty evasion. I have explored the options for dealing with these three categories of case in some detail with a view to recommending changes that might have more general application. In the event, I found less scope for wholescale decriminalisation than I had at first hoped.

6   Before continuing, I should distinguish between the two categories of case represented by those examples. Television licence and vehicle excise duty offences are criminal matters giving rise to standard summary proceedings. I discuss these offences in particular, and summary offences in general, in the next section of this chapter. Council tax cases are an example of magistrates' courts proceedings being used to recover civil debts. I consider the appropriateness of such a civil jurisdiction being retained within the criminal courts in the final section of the chapter. I also look at possibilities for specialist courts and alternative responses to criminal behaviour such as conditional cautioning, regulatory enforcement and the wider subject of restorative justice.

SUMMARY PROSECUTIONS

7   Where it is argued that existing offences should no longer be the subject of magistrates' court proceedings, there are three main options for change. The first is a fixed penalty scheme with provision for challenge or appeal to the criminal courts. The second is the same procedure but administered by and subject to the adjudication of an independent body. The third is full decriminalisation where the enforcement of any debts is left to the civil courts.

8   There are precedents for the first two options. The Road Traffic Offenders Act 1988 makes provision for the imposition of fixed penalties in a large number of minor vehicle-related offences.[1] A formal notice of offence is served on an alleged offender or left on the vehicle. Offenders have a specified time in which to pay a financial penalty or to request a hearing before magistrates. If they do neither, an increased penalty becomes payable and is registered as a fine for enforcement by the magistrates' court. The retention of a right to a court hearing ensures compliance with Article 6. The collection of fixed penalties in each area is the responsibility of the local Magistrates' Courts Committee. Thus, fixed penalty schemes do not remove cases from the criminal jurisdictions, but significantly reduce the work involved in processing them. In 1998, for example, over 3.4 million fixed penalty notices were issued in England and Wales, of which 78% resulted in payment, 14% were registered as fines and less than 1% were referred for court proceedings.

9   An example of an independent adjudication body can be found in London where local authorities' parking attendants issue notices requiring payment of a fixed financial penalty within a set period.[2] The penalty is discounted if paid promptly. Penalty charge notices may be challenged, in the first instance to the issuing authority, and then by an oral or written appeal to a parking adjudicator. Over 4 million notices were issued in London in 1999/2000, of which less than 1% were appealed. The penalty is enforceable in the civil courts.

Television licence evasion

10 As I have indicated, many submissions in the Review highlighted television licence offences as matters suitable for removal from the criminal courts. The licence fee is a standard hypothecated tax on access to television in its entirety (not just on BBC channels). The Government decides what proportion of the licence fee income should go to the BBC, and currently the BBC receives it all. The BBC collects the fees on behalf of the Government and decides on enforcement and prosecution policies. These policies are based on the Code for Crown Prosecutors issued by the Director of Public Prosecutions and, therefore, take into account public interest considerations such as whether alleged offenders are in genuine financial hardship or otherwise vulnerable. The BBC devolves responsibility for prosecution to a contractor (currently Consignia Customer Management Ltd). The level of over-all collection is high, currently approaching 95% of television users in known households.

---

[1] Part III and Sch 3

[2] Scheme 73 set up under the Road Traffic Act 1991, Part II

11   Using a television without a licence is an offence of strict liability, carrying a maximum penalty of a level 3 fine (£1,000). There is no custodial penalty in the first instance; imprisonment is only possible (ultimately) as a response to non-payment of the fine. Liability is rarely disputed. During the financial year 2000/2001, around 160,000 prosecutions were undertaken. All cases are listed for a hearing, although the vast majority are then be dealt with as written pleas of guilty. It is the perception of many that this is an inappropriate use for criminal proceedings and a great waste of magistrates' courts' time. An unsatisfactory feature is the inconsistency in magistrates' sentencing throughout the country; fines are generally well below the permitted maximum, but the normal amount imposed (in the absence of any information about means) can vary from £30 to £300 according to locality.

12   Full decriminalisation of TV licence enforcement is not a straightforward option. Such an approach would mean that people would no longer risk a penalty as a consequence of using a television without a licence. Instead, detection would result only in the threat of County Court proceedings to recover the cost of the licence. There would, therefore, be no practical incentive to purchase a licence ahead of contact from the enforcement agency. Unlike many other services, there is no easy mechanism for identifying people who are using a television without paying; nor is there any means of cutting off the supply to those who are in default.

13   Transfer of responsibility for TV licence cases from the courts to an independent adjudication body would also be problematic. The cost and bureaucracy of such a body would be substantial given the need for national coverage and facilities for local hearings. I have already indicated that the vast majority of defendants charged with using a television without a licence plead guilty by post. The advantage of using an approach similar to that adopted by the London Parking Appeals Service[3], would be that these cases could be dealt with by way of a penalty charge notice. However, the same benefit can be achieved without creating an entirely new body to deal with the tiny minority of contested cases. The extension of the fixed penalty scheme to include television licence offences would both reduce magistrates' courts' workload and introduce consistency in treatment of offenders. Where enforcement staff had evidence that an individual was using a television without a licence they could serve a fixed penalty notice requiring purchase of a licence and payment of a penalty (discounted for prompt compliance) within a fixed period. Those few people who wanted to contest the case could request a hearing in the magistrates' court as now. Fixed penalties and any penalties imposed after conviction at court would be recoverable as fines in the normal way.

---

[3] see para 9 above

I recommend that the use of a television without a licence should remain a criminal offence, but that it should be dealt with in the first instance by a fixed penalty notice discounted for prompt purchase of a licence and payment of penalty, and subject to the defendant's right to dispute guilt in court.

Vehicle excise duty evasion

14   Similar considerations arise for the offence of using or keeping a motor vehicle without a vehicle excise licence. It is an offence of strict liability, with a maximum penalty of a level 3 fine (currently £1,000) or five times the chargeable duty, whichever is greater.[4] Unlike the lesser offence of using or keeping a vehicle without *exhibiting* a licence,[5] it is not capable of being dealt with under the fixed penalty provisions of the Road Traffic Offenders Act 1988.[6] Prosecutions are brought by the Driver Vehicle Licensing Authority (DVLA).   The DVLA is unusual amongst vehicle registration bodies in its combination of the functions of keeping the record, collecting the tax and prosecuting offences; in most other countries a Ministry of Justice deals with enforcement.   Despite the DVLA's considerable success in recent years in reducing evasion, the Revenue still loses almost £200 million a year.

15   The DVLA operates an out of court settlement scheme under which offenders can avoid prosecution on payment of back duty plus a penalty. This option is offered in all but the most serious cases (for example, repeat offenders or those who owe large sums). The DVLA deals with approximately 1,000,000 actionable offences a year. In 1999/2000 settlements were offered in about 700,000 cases and accepted in about 200,000. The DVLA prosecuted about 300,000 offenders and obtained a conviction in 98% of cases (the majority of defendants pleading guilty). The high level of prosecutions resulting in pleas of guilty has led the DVLA to refine its out of court settlement scheme. Under a revised procedure due to be introduced shortly, offenders will be given the opportunity to pay a reduced penalty provided that they respond within a specified time. Failure to pay will result in the full penalty becoming due and further reminder letters being sent before court action is considered. The DVLA hopes that introduction of the scheme will lead to a further reduction in the number of cases requiring prosecution.

---

[4] Vehicle Excise and Registration Act 1994, s 29

[5] ibid, s 33

[6] ibid, Sch 3

16   Failure to hold a vehicle excise licence often comes to light and is prosecuted with other offences, commonly using a vehicle without insurance or a motor test certificate, but also other more serious driving matters and offences of dishonesty. The DVLA makes an important contribution to the prevention and prosecution of crime generally by its provision of accurate vehicle records to the police, the most frequently used source of their information now that cameras are so widely used to collect evidence of road traffic and other offences. DVLA contractors also work with the police, the fire brigade and local authorities to find, clamp and remove cars belonging to or used by known criminals or causing a nuisance. Where other offences are also involved the police and the Crown Prosecution Service often take over and include the vehicle excise licence matter in the main prosecution. In my view, they should always do so.

17   The system of vehicle licensing and exaction of duty for it are separate, but complementary functions. The first is an aid to good public administration and crime prevention and detection; the second is the collection of revenue. A number of contributors to the Review have suggested that the collection and enforcement of payment of vehicle excise duty should be separated from vehicle registration by simply adding it to the tax on fuel. This is how a number of European countries deal with it, but they still charge a significant fee for registration to cover the costs of administration. There is also an argument that vehicle owners will not take the requirement to register seriously unless the fee is substantial. The Republic of Ireland experimented with a system of low cost registration and corresponding increase in fuel tax and found that it resulted in a less effective registration scheme. The Republic has now reinstated vehicle excise duty. In the light of this experience, the DVLA expresses concern at the prospect of any change which could be seen as 'downgrading' the importance of the obligation to license motor vehicles. This includes, not only its value as a means of tackling all forms of vehicle-related crime, but also of contributing to road safety through the licensing requirement for production of evidence of insurance and a roadworthiness certificate. The DVLA regards the ultimate threat of prosecution, with its maximum penalty of a £1,000 fine, as a vital tool in its task of reducing evasion.

18   Other contributors to the Review have suggested that failure to hold a vehicle excise licence should no longer be a criminal offence, but be dealt with by a separate penalty charge notice and adjudication scheme. It is difficult to see how that could work or what financial or other gain it would bring. First, it would not be straightforward to issue penalty charge notices on the street, as in the case of parking tickets, because registration details have to be checked and back duty calculated (although it might well be possible to overcome such practical difficulties by the use of new technology). Second, as I have said, many vehicle excise licence offences are dealt with by the courts as part of a wider prosecution. The establishment of a separate adjudication system could create unnecessary duplication of work and the potential for confusion since

two bodies could be charged with considering and responding to the same set of circumstances. And, any separate system, if it were to match the locality of provision of magistrates' courts, would be very costly and inefficient. Third, removal of the ultimate sanction of prosecution could weaken the registration system and its contribution to detection of crime, identification of offenders and road safety.

19   Accordingly, I do not consider that it would be helpful to anybody to decriminalise failure to hold a vehicle excise licence. In practice, the DVLA's out of court settlement scheme is broadly equivalent to a fixed penalty scheme (and the similarities will be even more marked once the discount for early payment is introduced). For that reason, I see no advantage in bringing vehicle excise licence offences into the fixed penalty schemes administered by magistrates' courts at this stage. I recommend below[7] that consideration should be given to the extension of the fixed penalty procedure to a wider range of legal infringements. If fixed penalty schemes were so extended, there could then be benefit in applying the standard approach to vehicle excise licence offences.

Other summary matters

20   There is some evidence that the existing fixed penalty provisions for minor road traffic offences[8] are not as widely used as they might be. It is for Chief Constables to decide in respect of which of the permitted offences they will employ the fixed penalty scheme. Contributors to the Review have suggested that it is not consistently used for offences that normally attract fairly standard penalties, such as excessive speed, driving in a bus lane and parking within the confines of a pedestrian crossing.

21   Whilst I acknowledge the importance of prosecutorial discretion as a generality, it seems to me that in cases of this sort it should normally be exercised in favour of use of the available fixed penalty system, unless there are particular circumstances requiring the offender to attend court, for example, in the case of a repeat offender or where the offence is related to another or others of greater seriousness not capable of disposal by way of fixed penalty.

22   Quite apart from under-use of the present statutory provision enabling fixed penalty criminal proceedings, there are a number of other relatively trivial infringements that could be dealt with in this way. I do not attempt an

---

[7] para 25
[8] Road Traffic Act 1988, Part III and Sch 3

exhaustive list, but mention, only as examples, some suggested by contributors in the Review: breaches of local or other public authority by-laws and regulations, for example unlicensed street trading, unlicensed fishing, prohibited smoking, unlawful movement of livestock and many consumer protection offences in the field of food safety, weights and measures and credit. During the course of the Review, the Home Office issued a consultation paper on the possible use of fixed penalties for certain public order offences[9] and, subsequently, inserted an enabling provision into the Police and Criminal Justice Bill, which received Royal Assent in May of this year. Ten additional offences (all falling within the broad category of 'disorderly conduct') are now capable of being dealt with by way of fixed penalty notice. The Home Office is preparing pilots for 2002. The Secretary of State has the power to add to the list of offences by statutory instrument subject to affirmative resolution.

23   Other offences might call for different treatment – but still within the criminal justice system – where the issues are too subjective to be readily amenable to determination by the criminal test of sureness of guilt, for example, whether a consumer was 'misled' by a credit advertisement or as to the legibility of a food label. Instead of seeking to prosecute such matters directly, they could be the subject of a notice to correct with which the person served could either comply or challenge by reference to the court.[10] Such a procedure would not remove all such difficult issues from the courts, but it should reduce the number of them.

24   The sheer number and variety of, and the many different prosecuting authorities for, all these sorts of offences make it difficult to recommend their removal from the criminal process altogether. Looking at many of them individually, it might be thought desirable to refer them to an alternative and knowledgeable forum in the field. For example, a recent report to the Food Advisory Committee draws attention to the ways in which the formality and rigour of the criminal process in food law can obstruct a satisfactory resolution of the main issue.[11] However, whilst suggesting some form of informed tribunal to resolve contentious issues without the trappings of criminal process, the report's authors acknowledge the need for a criminal law sanction where there are persistent breaches.

25   There is an obvious attraction in removing much specialist enforcement work of this sort from the criminal courts to separate, independent and expert tribunals. However, the relatively small number of prosecutions for infringement within each discipline and the great range of disciplines

---

[9] *Reducing Public Disorder: the role of fixed penalty notices*, (Home Office September 2000)

[10] cf the enforcement of planning restrictions, in the first instance by an enforcement notice which, if disregarded, becomes the subject of enforcement proceedings before magistrates.

[11] *The Food Advisory Committee Review of Food Labelling*, Food Standards Agency (2001 – in press)

involved would not justify the additional bureaucracy and cost of setting up a large number of alternative country-wide adjudication schemes as an alternative to the courts. The practical, and I believe principled, approach in such cases is not to remove them from the criminal justice system, but to reduce their impact on it by their inclusion in fixed penalty and notice of correction schemes.

> **I recommend:**
>
> - **the use of fixed penalty notices in respect of all offences provided for in the Road Traffic Offenders Act 1988, Part III and Schedule 3, unless there are special circumstances requiring the offender to attend court; and**
>
> - **a systematic review leading to similar fixed penalty and/or notice-to-correct schemes for a wider range of infringements that are presently the subject of criminal prosecution.**

SPECIALIST COURTS

26   There have been a number of calls in the Review for specialist criminal courts of one form or another. The term specialist court is used very imprecisely and in very different contexts. It has at least three different senses.

27   First, certain areas of criminal law may be so complex that the decision-makers need special expertise. Usually this specialist knowledge refers to technical issues for which the ordinary criminal procedures are ill-suited. This might mean that instead of a judge and jury there would be a judge and lay members chosen for their professional qualifications and/or experience as I have suggested for serious and complex fraud cases, or that only magistrates with appropriate training and expertise may sit, such as in the youth courts. Alternatively, it could refer to courts where the tribunal is not altered, but has access to specialist support workers who provide special sentencing options. Although not strictly concerned with diverting the offender from the criminal process, such a court may require the sentencer to have specialist knowledge of the sentencing regime.

28   Secondly, there are courts that depart so substantially from adversarial principles of justice as to amount to a different form of tribunal from the conventional criminal court. In the most extreme cases they might dispense with adversarial proceedings altogether, and take the form of arbitration, mediation or other form of dispute resolution. This type of court is usually suggested where the criminal process is so unsuitable to the nature of the

offence or offender as to fail in one or more of its main social functions. Consequently, the focus of its activities will shift from formal adjudication of facts and sentencing to 'restorative justice'. The objective is to obtain the offender's acknowledgement of 'responsibility' rather than to establish guilt, and to find an outcome that deals with the reasons for the offending behaviour. The focus is on problem-solving rather than punishment.

29   Finally, some people refer to a specialist court to denote one where a certain type of case is heard at a certain time, for administrative or court users' convenience, such as traffic courts, or night courts. In this instance, there is nothing specialist in the nature of the court, its personnel, or in the powers available to it. It is merely a concentration of work in one time and place that would otherwise have been heard in exactly the same manner at some other time or in some other court. In this sense there is nothing 'specialist' about the court at all; it is a convenience of listing.

30   I turn now to the main candidates suggested in the Review for specialist courts.

Drug courts

31   The success of drug courts in the United States, particularly those in Miami-Dade County, Florida and the New York City Drug Court, is much lauded. They follow different patterns in different States, but have common features. They are concerned exclusively with cases involving defendants who abuse drugs and offend as a result. They have specially trained and experienced judges who show a high degree of knowledge and commitment to the programme, and regularly review the progress of the individuals whom they sentence. The judges moreover have the advantage of the presence at court of drug workers with testing facilities, personnel from the main social services agencies who help prepare and evaluate the success of each defendant's treatment, and advanced information technology systems for the use of all involved. Their success, therefore, owes much both to the expertise of the judges and to the quality of sentencing support present in or at court.

32   Drug courts in the full United States' sense have not been established in this country, although drug testing and treatment orders (DTTOs)[12] introduced by the Crime and Disorder Act 1998 have incorporated some of their procedures and options for disposal.[13] These orders are a new type of community

---

[12] Crime and Disorder Act 1998, s 61

[13] a forerunner to DTTOs was the Substance misuse Treatment Enforcement Programme (STEP) project in West Yorkshire, an inter-agency initiative inspired by the United States' experience

disposal that came into force on 1 October 2000 which may be imposed provided that the offender is 16 or above at the date of conviction. They apply only to offences that would otherwise have been suitable for community penalties (thereby capping the level of seriousness), only to defendants who are dependent on or have a propensity to misuse drugs and where such dependency/ propensity requires and may be susceptible to treatment. Their duration may be from 6 months to 3 years (the 'testing and treatment period'). The order requires the offender to submit to treatment and to provide samples for the purpose of determining the presence of drugs in his body as and when required by the treatment provider. There will be supervision of progress at regular review hearings at which the offender must appear before the court, which must be at least once a month. It should be held by the sentencing bench where possible, although in practice this varies in different court centres. A breach of the order allows the court to sentence for the offence as if no order had been made.

33   The drug courts that I saw in the United States were in areas with high numbers of offenders, where there was sufficient turnover to justify the full-time allocation of a small number of judges to hear the cases, docketing of all cases to judges to ensure continuity, and, as I have said, presence at court of drug support workers and representatives of all the main social support agencies. These conditions ensure maximum expertise, commitment and immediate and continuous support from all involved in the process. There may be a demand for such a concentration of expertise in some of our major city centres where there are high levels of drug-related crime. If there is, to make specialist and adequate provision would be very expensive. The United States drug courts tend to be concentrated on major city centres and to enjoy special Federal funding.

34   It seems to me that, rather than attempt a separate drug court or dedicated drug courts in a few large centres, we should concentrate on developing the new drug testing and treatment order regime. However, the United States experience teaches us that, if it is to work as intended, it will need a move to the docketing of judges and magistrates to cases, to ensure continuity in the handling of those subject to the orders, and a major increase and permanent commitment to providing greater resources than it has at present. Home Office research shows that offenders respond to the praise and criticism of sentencers who show an interest in their progress.[14] Continuity has generally been possible in the Crown Court and with District Judges. It has been harder with magistrates, although there are geographical disparities, so that in Liverpool 68% of reviews were by the sentencing bench, while in Gloucestershire 76% of reviews were heard by a court with no previous involvement in the order.[15] It should be a priority everywhere now, when

---

[14] *Drug Treatment And Testing Orders – interim evaluation,* Home Office research findings No 106 by Paul Turnbull (1999)
[15] ibid

listing such matters, that review is conducted by the sentencers. This should be easier if my recommendations for the magistracy and for a new unified Criminal Court are adopted.

35   Substantially improved resources for the court should aim to ensure that there are sufficient and readily available places in treatment programmes so that the best sentencing option is not frustrated by lack of places. There should also be available at court experienced drug workers and, where appropriate, representatives of other involved agencies with detailed information about the offender's behaviour within the programme. Finally, there should be better information technology systems in court to allow the sentencer to view the defendant's history of compliance with the order, previous breaches and other relevant information at a glance.

36   Accordingly, I recommend at this stage making better use and support for what we have rather than the establishment of separate or dedicated drug courts. As we gain experience of the drug testing and treatment scheme, opportunities may suggest themselves for dedicated courts in individual centres.

Domestic Violence Courts

37   Any form of domestic violence is a criminal offence under the common law of assault, or the Offences Against the Person Act 1861, and varies from summary to indictable-only offences depending on the nature of the violence. The issue is usually one of fact rather than of law. If proved, the usual rules of sentencing apply, so that the severity of the assault will largely determine the sentence. The English courts do not, in the main, distinguish such cases from other offences of violence, and their sentencing options remain the same.

38   Yet, it is argued, there are some special features of domestic violence offences that make the court process unsuitable for the conventional courts. The victim's relationship with the offender makes the factual issues less straightforward. There may be suggestions that the allegation has been made in order to punish the defendant for some problem in the relationship. The victim may be under community or family pressure to drop the case, or feel guilt or fear about turning to the courts. Where there are children of the relationship, they may retain contact with the father and she will fear the inability of the courts effectively to protect her from further violence. Domestic violence is often repetitive, and the evidence suggests that it tends to escalate. If the victim takes the matter to court early, before it does so, there is unlikely to be a suitably deterrent penalty; but if she leaves it until later, the admissible evidence cannot usually reflect the history between the

parties and, therefore, the sentence may not reflect the true seriousness of the matter. There is also a tendency to regard such cases as less serious because they occur within the home, and with a possibility of reconciliation as a mitigating factor.

39   It has been suggested that domestic violence cases could be dealt with in a more informal setting, unconstrained by the need for admissible evidence and direct proof of guilt, which would help the parties to understand the causes of the violence and reach acceptable solutions. An example of this is the domestic violence court in Calgary, with its 'restorative justice' approach. The project, begun as a pilot in early 2000, aims to bring together many agencies, such as housing and social services, and to create a forum for discussion of appropriate treatment. The panel discusses the family circumstances and the reasons for the offending and seeks to produce an agreed solution, which might be a combination of community orders. The court oversees the process and can call the case in at any stage before sentencing. The project also aims to improve the speed of intervention and expertise about domestic violence in the core criminal justice system agencies. There is as yet no full evaluation of the pilot, but like other 'restorative' approaches that I saw in North America, its success appears to be, not so much in devising alternative procedures, but in gathering together the resources of a number of concerned agencies and focusing minds on the issue.

40   There is nothing similar in this country, although there are efforts to improve courts' response to domestic violence. A government interdepartmental working group on domestic violence has these issues under consideration. There is also much going on at the moment to improve inter-agency working as a result of the crime and disorder partnerships under the Crime and Disorder Act 1998. For example, the Leeds Domestic Violence Court project aims to ensure that, as far as possible, domestic violence cases are listed during specified slots within the court schedule to allow for a greater focus on the provision of background information to assist magistrates in making bail and sentencing decisions. A wide range of statutory and voluntary organisations are taking part in this project. I make no specific recommendations on domestic violence courts, but urge the need for all relevant agencies to match their stated policies with action.[16]

---

[16] note the CPS Inspectorate Report on Domestic Violence in 1998, which suggests a lack of rigour in applying and monitoring compliance with CPS policy.

ALTERNATIVE PROCEDURES

'Caution-plus'

41   'Caution plus' is a convenient heading for a variety of methods of disposal of criminal offences within the criminal justice system falling short of appearance and sentence in court. In England and Wales we have a system of cautioning by the police which is not generally conditional on offenders giving or complying with any undertakings. There are certain procedures that have some of the characteristics of caution plus. Most recently, the Crime and Disorder Act 1998 has replaced the old system of police caution for young offenders with a system of a reprimand and/or a final warning, the latter normally coupled with a requirement to participate in a rehabilitative programme.[17] There is also the long established ability of revenue authorities to 'compound' certain tax offences. But there is no general power in the police or the Crown Prosecution Service or other prosecutors to divert cases at an early stage from the criminal justice process by a combination of caution and, with the agreement of the offender, conditions as to his future behaviour.

42   In effect, our police caution amounts to an offender being 'let off' with a warning. In 1999, around 266,000 cautions were issued.[18]   This amounts to around 25% of all those found guilty or cautioned (i.e. the total number of 'solved' crimes). Many regard this as unsatisfactory, both in its lack of regard for the injury or insult to victims and in its lack of rigour as a response to criminality.   Concern has also been expressed that the police are under pressure to resolve crimes in this way (cautions are recorded as a 'clearance' and are therefore a relatively non-labour intensive method of contributing to one of the key measures of a force's performance).

43   Caution plus or conditional cautioning is widely used in other countries. The closest example from another jurisdiction is the 'fiscal fine' in Scotland, where the prosecutor fiscal, with the agreement of the offender, may administer a caution and impose a fine for a narrow range of minor offences as an alternative to court proceedings.[19]   Similar and more extensive provisions exist in many European countries. In Germany, for example, the public prosecutor may, with the consent of the court, caution for lesser offences, subject to the accused agreeing to one or more of four conditions: to pay compensation; to make a payment to a charitable organisation or to the Treasury; to do charitable work; and to provide support to someone or something. Other European countries have similar systems, some extending

---

[17] Crime and Disorder Act 1998, s 65

[18] these are apparently the most recent "confirmed" figures

[19] Criminal Procedure (Scotland) Act 1995, s 302

to wider ranges of offences and including other conditions, for example, the commission of no further offences within a set period.

44   As always, we should be cautious before drawing on other systems, particularly civil law jurisdictions with their very different jurisprudential cultures and forensic traditions. In continental systems there is no such thing as a conclusive plea of guilty; it would be regarded as contrary to the court's duty to establish the truth. So their development of the 'caution plus' option is, in part at least, a means of overcoming their inability to expedite matters by a plea of guilty once a case goes to court. Another important factor is that continental prosecutors, in general, have a different role and status from those of the Crown Prosecution Service in this country. They are closer professionally to the judiciary and there is, thus, more ready acceptance of their power to use the 'caution plus' system as a means of deciding the outcome of certain cases.

45   In my view, there is scope in England and Wales for the introduction of a more general, formalised and conditional cautioning system. I shall not attempt a detailed recommendation as to its form; that would require close examination and, no doubt, extensive consultation with a wide range of professionals and others experienced in the criminal process, criminology and sentencing. It could take the form of a discretionary power vested in the Crown Prosecution Service not to prosecute or to withdraw a prosecution on condition, for example, that the offender submitted to some form of penalty or supervision of his conduct and/or offered some form of redress and/or submitted to medical or other treatment. Failure to satisfy the condition could entitle the prosecutor to initiate or reinstate prosecution or to bring the offender before the court for breach of condition.

46   Any such scheme should, save for the most minor offences, be the responsibility of the Crown Prosecution Service and subject to the approval of the court. Without the protection of the court's approval, its use could be used or perceived as a 'cop-out' by the prosecution to avoid prosecuting cases that should be prosecuted, or of innocent criminals being at risk of pressure to accept onerous compromises to avoid prosecution, or of the rich being able to buy their way out of prosecutions when the poor could not.

47   Consideration of some such general scheme would need to take account of existing means of dealing with offenders within the criminal justice system without involving them in court proceedings or by minimising the content of such proceedings. If there is to be a further extension of this in the form of 'caution plus', it might be wiser to rationalise the whole system rather than just to add another variant. I have in mind: the relatively high proportion of vehicle related offences already dealt with by way of fixed penalty notices; the many minor offences capable of being dealt with by way of paper

proceedings; the existing powers of the revenue authorities to compound, often substantial, offences without reference to the courts; the increasing success of the courts, under the Narey provisions, in securing early hearings of defendants likely to plead guilty; and the many proposals now in the air for 'restorative justice'. I describe below[20] the various stages in the criminal process at which a restorative justice approach can be applied. A more structured, conditional cautioning system might well prove to be a valuable support for the use of such an approach in the early stages of the process, since it would provide a framework for ensuring compliance with any reparation agreed by the offender. I have recommended at paragraph 69 that a national strategy be developed for the use of restorative justice techniques across England and Wales. That recommendation should be considered alongside the recommendation below dealing with conditional cautioning.

> **I recommend that:**
>
> - **consideration should be given to the introduction of a conditional cautioning scheme over a wide range of minor offences, enabling the prosecutor with the consent of the offender and, where appropriate, with the approval of the court:**
>
>   **(a)   to caution him subject to his compliance with specified conditions; and**
>
>   **(b)   to bring the conditionally cautioned offender before the court in the event of his failure to comply with the conditions; and**
>
> - **in considering the introduction of such a scheme, regard should be had to its place alongside existing provisions for avoiding or modifying the criminal process and future developments in the form of 'restorative justice', with a view to over-all rationalisation into a single scheme.**

Regulatory enforcement

48   There is also scope for removal of certain matters from the criminal justice system at the upper end of the scale, notably for certain types of financial and regulatory offences. In considering offences as candidates for such a scheme, close attention would need to be paid to the widely expressed concern that it would enable the rich, but not the poor, to buy their way out of prosecution. The Runciman Royal Commission was alive to this concern. It welcomed the

---

[20] paras 58 - 69

possibility of the development of a separate regulatory regime,[21] but considered that it should be confined to 'technical' breaches rather than offences of dishonesty, that is:

> "[w]here the offence is of a technical nature, there has been no specific loss or risk to any member of the public (or if there has, where restitution can be made), and the predominant issue relates to the protection of the integrity of markets rather than to serious dishonesty ...".[22]

49   The Commission considered that this would be so in only "a handful of cases" and warned that, even then, penalties should be sufficiently severe so that it could not be said that 'white collar crime' was being dealt with more leniently than other equivalent offences.[23] It also recommended consideration of a procedure in appropriate cases for dropping or reducing a criminal charge in exchange for a defendant's acceptance of a sufficiently severe regulatory penalty[24] - an extension or modification of the compounding mechanism available to the revenue authorities.

50   I am not sure that the candidates for transfer to a regulatory process would today amount only to a 'handful of cases', or indeed that they would have done so at the time of the report of the Runciman Royal Commission. Certainly, there is now a proliferation of financial and market controls supported by criminal sanctions that might be more appropriately and better dealt with in a regulatory system tailored to meet the disciplines and understanding of individual markets. Often, the most serious penalty to the offender in such cases is the loss of his profession and/or the ability to continue to trade in the market that he has abused. That is a common-place part of any plea of mitigation in such cases in the criminal courts. The current Director of the Serious Fraud Office[25] favours decriminalisation of frauds, but only for regulatory offences, that is, "those that can be dealt with by, effectively, taking someone off the road by removing their licence".

51   The Runciman Royal Commission's recommendations produced little governmental response or scope for it until the establishment of the Financial Services Authority as part of the reforms contained in the Financial Services Act 1986. In June 1986 the Authority assumed responsibility for banking supervision. And, pursuant to the Financial Services and Markets Act 2000, it will shortly take over the investment services responsibilities of a number of

---

[21] then being considered by the Serious Fraud Office and the Securities and Investments Board

[22] Report, Ch 7, para 63

[23] ibid, para 63

[24] ibid, para 64

[25] Rosalind Wright

supervisory and regulatory bodies.[26] Once the Authority is fully established it should be become clearer what current criminal offences might fall more appropriately within its remit. I consider that it would be premature, and in any event, beyond the scope of this Review, for me to attempt to identify individual candidate offences for de-criminalisation in this field.

I recommend that once the Financial Services Authority has assumed full responsibility for supervision in the financial services field, consideration should be given to transferring appropriate financial and market infringements from the criminal justice process to its regulatory and disciplinary control.

Parallel proceedings

52   A number of agencies are responsible for the investigation and prosecution and/or regulation of allegations of financial irregularity. Investigations may result in criminal, regulatory and civil proceedings, all covering the same or similar allegations of misconduct. The different regimes and procedures have different standards of proof and disclosure requirements, which can cause serious difficulties in the criminal process for prosecutors and defendants.[27] Civil proceedings are normally stayed until after the conclusion of criminal proceedings, and in certain circumstances, regulatory proceedings will await the outcome of the criminal and/or civil matters. The resulting delays increase the likelihood of successful challenges under Article 6 of the European Convention of Human Rights.

53   Since criminal courts cannot normally deal with all the issues arising out of an allegation of financial irregularity, defendants are less likely to plead guilty at an early stage. Even where courts can, effectively, deal with all the important matters, for example, where, in addition to their normal powers of punishment, they can disqualify convicted defendants from continuing to act as a company director,[28] they are often reluctant to do so because of lack of familiarity with the jurisdiction.[29]

---

[26] viz Building Societies Commission, Friendly Societies Commission, Investment Management Regulatory Organisation, Personal Investment Authority, Register of Friendly Societies and Securities and Futures Authority

[27] see eg Saunders v UK (1997) 23 EHRR 313, ECHR

[28] under the Company Directors Disqualification Act 1986, s 2

[29] *Report on Parallel Proceedings*, p 17, The Society for Advanced Legal Studies Financial Regulation Working Group (December 1999)

54   The Lord Chancellor has proposed a form of unification of proceedings in such cases, but based in the criminal court.[30] The court would deal with issues of guilt and sentence as it does now. Present, but not participating in those proceedings, would be two expert assessors. At the end of the criminal proceedings the judge would discharge the jury and he and the two assessors would then deal with regulatory issues. The Society for Advanced Legal Studies' Financial Regulation Working Group did not favour the proposal,[31] giving three main reasons: first, it could lead to greater delay than at present because all regulatory proceedings would have to await the outcome of the criminal proceedings; second, acquittal in the criminal part of the proceedings might sit uneasily with any sanctions subsequently imposed in the regulatory part of the proceedings; and third, combining the procedures in this way could compromise the independence and effectiveness of regulatory processes.

55   With respect to the Working Group, I am not impressed by any of those arguments. As to the first, I do not see why the combination of the two procedures should lead to more delay than is now the norm where the criminal proceedings precede, as they normally do, further civil and/or regulatory procedures. As to the second, I do not see why acquittal in the criminal part of the proceedings should embarrass the partially differently constituted tribunal in the regulatory proceedings. To the extent that the regulatory infringement in question is the same as that of the criminal offence charged and the burden and standard of proof in both proceedings are the same, the judge and assessors would no doubt consider themselves bound by the finding of the jury. To the extent that there may be a difference as to the nature of the infringement in question or as to the manner of proof, the judge and assessors would be free to deal with the matter afresh as a regulatory tribunal. As to the third, I do not understand the basis for saying that commission of regulatory issues to a judge and expert assessors from the market or discipline in question could be said to 'compromise' the independence and efficiency of the regulatory process. In my view, this possible combination of criminal and regulatory processes in the hands of the court and expert assessors is worthy of further consideration. It might not be suitable for all cases of this kind, but some, depending on the regulatory traditions in question, might benefit considerably from the speed and combination of skills that such a 'one stop shop' might offer. I have recommended in Chapter 5 that in serious and complex fraud cases the nominated trial judge should be empowered to direct trial by himself sitting with lay members or, where the defendant has opted for trial by judge alone, the latter. In some cases, it might be possible and appropriate for lay members who sit with the judge in the criminal proceedings to be the same individuals who will act as expert assessors for the purpose of any regulatory proceedings. But for the reasons given in

---

[30] *The Feasibility of a Unified Approach to Proceedings arising out of Major City Fraud*, KPMG Lecture 1998
[31] *Report on Parallel Proceedings,* pp 10 - 13

paragraph 191 of that Chapter, the composition of the criminal tribunal in such cases should be approached with care.

I recommend consideration, for appropriate cases of parallel proceedings, of combining the criminal justice and regulatory processes, with a judge as the common president and with lay members or expert assessors for the second and regulatory part.

56   The Working Group recommended a more modest approach to reform which, so far as it goes, is favoured by the Serious Fraud Office. It amounts to encouraging the judge at the sentencing stage in criminal proceedings to consider exercising such regulatory type powers as he has and to giving him some more. Where there are, or may be such powers, the Working Group recommends that the Department of Trade and Industry should in appropriate cases instruct specialist counsel to make submissions at the sentencing stage as to the availability of such power and the desirability of exercising it. Though the latter might be thought contrary to our tradition of prosecuting counsel not seeking a particular penalty, it is not so very different from their accepted practice of seeking particular orders as adjuncts to the main sentence, i.e. confiscation, compensation, forfeiture or costs or, in offences concerning the management of a company, disqualification to act as a director or manager of a company.[32]   As to giving the courts some additional regulatory powers of this type, the Working Group suggested the ability to close down fraudulently run businesses, freezing of assets and imposing restrictions and disqualifications similar to those under Chapters V and VI of the Financial Services Act 1986 and wider powers of ordering compensation to victims. They also recommended further consideration of an open system of plea bargaining to enable a defendant to decide on his plea knowing the full range of sanctions he faces, a recommendation that the Director of Public Prosecutions strongly supports, and not just for offences of fraud.

57   In my view, to the extent that financial and regulatory matters remain the concern of criminal courts, there is sense in their exercising, wherever possible, their existing powers in that respect as part of their sentencing disposal. There is also sense in extending those powers where it is desirable and practicable to do so. I also agree that they should be assisted for the purpose, but I consider that it could be done by prosecuting and defence counsel, suitably instructed. I do not see why it should be necessary for a third party, say the Department of Trade and Industry in a case prosecuted by the Serious Fraud Office, to intervene for that purpose.

---

[32] Company Director Disqualification Act 1986, ss 1 and 2

I recommend that:

- **in cases of fraud and other financial offences courts should, wherever possible and appropriate, exercise their existing powers of a regulatory nature as part of their sentencing disposal;**

- **consideration should be given, in appropriate offences, to enlarging or extending the courts' conventional sentencing powers in this respect; and**

- **in the exercise of such powers courts should be assisted by counsel on behalf of the parties, properly instructed for the purpose.**

RESTORATIVE JUSTICE

58   I have always been of the view that we expect too much of the courts as a medium for reducing crime, for remedying wrongs to victims and society and for rehabilitating individual offenders. By the time criminal courts have reached the point of sentence, particularly with young offenders and when custody has become an option, the offender is often well established in a criminal life style. Previous responses to his criminality have failed for one reason or another, mostly because the causes of his crime were so overwhelming as not to be capable of resolution by the limited and under-resourced forms of disposal available. It is at this late stage, or when the offence is so serious that the court must mark society's disapproval by punishment or to protect it from further harm, that the courts are called on, as a backstop, to do the best they can. Before then, there is a wide range of offences and stages of offending which call for a more sensitive and sustained attention than most courts are presently equipped to give, if reduction in crime, rehabilitation and reparation are to have a chance.

59   These are trite sentiments. But they have been given fresh impetus and expression in recent years by exponents, world-wide, of 'Restorative Justice' - in part a modern version of a familiar concept of community involvement in the administration of justice. It is not within my remit or capability to examine so large a subject and its many variations and applications,[33] any more than it is to consider principles of sentencing or alternatives to it. It has been described as more a philosophy than a specific model.[34] Charles Pollard,

---

[33] see eg *'Restorative Justice' And Other New Penal Patterns*, an essay by Carolyn Hoyle on a conference at Ditchley Park, Oxfordshire, (June 2000)

[34] see *Restorative Justice in Yukon and Northern Canada*, Pierre Rousseau, a paper delivered at the Annual FPS Conference in Canada (September 2000)

the Chief Constable of the Thames Valley Police, a leading exponent and practitioner of the philosophy in this country, has described it as follows:[35]

> "Restorative Justice seeks to balance the personal/local needs of victims and communities with the broader goals for society of deterring criminality, punishing crime and reintegrating offenders. Thus it is an *inclusive* process, in which *all* the parties directly affected by the offending behaviour are involved in discussing its causes and consequences, how to prevent its reoccurrence and what should happen to the offender."

60   There is a vast body of contemporary literature, research and practical studies on the subject, and there are many well established versions of it world-wide. Interestingly, a number of these examples can be found in areas where indigenous people have suffered as a result of the imposition of western legal systems without common reference points.

61   As Charles Pollard has noted, most of the progress towards restorative justice in this country has been in the youth justice system. This has been given statutory impetus by the Crime and Disorder Act 1998, including its creations the Youth Justice Board and reparation orders, and the Youth Justice and Criminal Evidence Act 1999 enabling youth courts to make referral orders to youth panels to deal with matters on 'restorative principles'.

62   My purpose in mentioning restorative justice is simply to note that it embraces diversion in many different forms at different stages of the criminal process and that those responsible for considering any of the alternatives or minimising exposure to the criminal process that I mention in this Chapter should include it in their general consideration. Any initiatives in this field should be part of an over-all and principled reform aimed at removing from the courts matters for which they are not appropriate or necessary, while leaving them, in the main, to deal with matters for which they are well suited, in particular, marking society's disapproval and safeguarding public and private safety.

63   With that in mind, there seem to me to be at least six stages at which notions of restorative justice might be applied to a case as it approaches or makes its way through the criminal justice process.[36] I believe that general features of all or most of them are the offender's acceptance of guilt, his informed consent to the process, his recognition of the harm he has done and desire to make reparation for it, his rehabilitation, some involvement of the community

---

[35] in his submission in the Review; see also his article, *Victims and the Criminal Justice System: A New Vision* [2000] Crim LR pp 5 - 7

[36] cf Nova Scotia's Programme for Restorative Justice (June 1998), Department of Justice, Nova Scotia

and, where there is an individual victim, the victim's willing involvement in the process. The stages are:

- before charge, in cases identified by the police and/or prosecutor in accordance with general criteria or guidelines, and subject to return to the criminal justice system if the diversionary disposal fails;[37]

- between charge and first appearance in court, in cases identified by the prosecutor and, again, subject to return to the criminal justice system if the diversionary disposal fails;

- at or after the first appearance in court and during the pre-trial process, in cases identified by the parties and/or the court, and with the approval of the court;

- after conviction, in cases identified in the judicial process by the parties and Probation Service and/or other social service, by referring the matter of disposal to some non-court agency or agencies and/or involved persons, possibly including a conditional withdrawal of the conviction from the record;[38]

- in sentencing, as a complement or alternative to traditional court disposals; and

- after sentence, in cases identified by the parties and Probation and/or Prison Services and/or social services, through a judicial process of conditional vacating of the conviction and or sentence.

64   Whilst the mechanics of, and criteria for, intervention at any of those stages are likely to be different, there might be something to be said, as part of an exercise of over-all reform in this field, to put them under the oversight or direction of a single agency or joint body.

65   There are considerations, which others will have to evaluate, of the types and level of seriousness of the offences appropriate for some form of diversion, of the cost and the efficacy of various proposals when compared with forms of disposal now available and of the attitude of defendants, victims and of the public at large. As to the offences appropriate for some form of diversion from or in the course of the normal criminal justice process, even the most enthusiastic and experienced supporters of restorative justice recognise that there are limits. There are some cases that are just so serious and/or where the public needs protection and/or those which require to be publicly aired, that they will need to go through the court process at least some of the way.[39] However, I note that in New Zealand restorative justice procedures are used

---

[37] see, eg, the Thames Valley Police "restorative conference" scheme; and schemes for adults in Scotland provided by the Scottish Association for the Care and Resettlement of Offender

[38] eg the successful drug courts in the USA, the various forms of "circle sentencing" found in Canada, the Toronto Drug Treatment Court and the Yukon Family Court

[39] see *Mentally Disordered Offenders: Finding a Focus for Diversion*, p 294, Elizabeth Burney and Geoffrey Pearson, Blackwell Publishers Ltd (1995)

for serious and persistent offenders, though mainly in the youth justice system.[40]

66   There are three further points. The first is that restorative justice in the short term is expensive in the range and level of resources necessary to give it a chance of success. However, there is experience in Canada,[41] Australia, New Zealand, parts of the USA and other countries that proper investment can secure significant long-term and wide spread savings to the community in the reduction of crime.[42] Immediate and adequate commitment of resources by all the necessary agencies at the diversionary stage and maintenance of them thereafter is the key to successful restorative justice schemes. Lack of such immediacy and resources has blighted or impeded many initiatives already in the system. At the most basic level it has prevented the Probation Service from making more than it has of the various forms of community disposals that have been around for years. Similarly, schemes for psychiatric diversion of mentally disordered defendants, which have been set up in the last ten years or so in many magistrates' courts, are faltering for want of adequate planning, organisation and resources.[43] And, as is now well recognised but largely absent in the present working of the criminal justice system, such diversionary schemes are the shared responsibility of many agencies. These are not just those immediately concerned with the criminal justice process, but also other agencies vital to the success of the wide range of non-custodial responses already available and under consideration – notably those responsible for mental and physical health, housing, education and employment. There are models in the inter-agency panels in young offender cases, their strength lying in their responsibility for assessment, recommendation and implementation. I should mention in particular the recent introduction by the Youth Justice and Criminal Evidence Act 1999 of mandatory referral to a youth offender panel of all young offenders who plead guilty, unless the crime is serious enough to warrant custody or the court orders absolute discharge or a hospital order.[44]

67   Second, it is, in my view, important to have a machinery for symbolic and practical involvement of the courts as the representative and ultimate protector of society for this purpose, in:

• determining whether diversion from the traditional court process is appropriate;

• in protecting defendants and victims from bureaucratic oppression or insensitivity;

---

[40] *Victims and the Criminal Justice System: A New Vision,* Charles Pollard, [2000] Crim LR pp 5 - 17

[41] in particular, the drugs courts in many of the major centres

[42] including the reduction of court sittings and closure of penal institutions

[43] ibid, pp 293, 294, 296 and 308-9; and see *Court Diversion at 10 years: can it work, does it work and has it a future?*, David James, pp 507, Journal of Forensic Psychiatry, Vol 10 Mp 3 (December 1999)

[44] now consolidated in the Powers of Criminal Courts (Sentencing) Act 2000 and being piloted in a number of areas

- in ensuring that defendants and, where appropriate, victims are heard and that both are treated fairly;

- in monitoring and, where necessary, ensuring compliance with agreed forms of disposal;

- where there is default, in bringing the matter back to court; and

- over-all, in securing fair and proportionate outcomes.

68   The goal of fair and proportionate outcomes is important, particularly in the light of Article 6 requirements for a fair trial, given that restorative justice procedures can be a complementary part of or substitute for the criminal justice process. For example, out of court processes that may be determinative or highly influential as to outcome could be challengeable as unfair if the offender is not afforded adequate representation before or in the course of them, or access to documentation.

69   Third, it is plain that the courts, in particular, judges and magistrates – especially magistrates – will continue to have an important initiating, supervisory and fall-back enforcement role in the working of restorative justice in its developing and different forms. Some may take to it more readily than others. Most will require encouragement and training to make proper use of it. As it develops, the judiciary and magistracy should be closely consulted about it and trained in its possibilities and disciplines, as also should legal practitioners, court staff and those involved in the various criminal justice and social service agencies. Piloting of all new initiatives is obviously desirable. Care will also need to be taken to inform and persuade the public that it is a force for good, in particular crime prevention. Finally, it should be accompanied from the start by a practical and simple system of monitoring so that it can be seen whether it is such a force in all its aspects, including justice and fairness to all, reduction of crime and cost.

> **I recommend the development and implementation of a national strategy to ensure consistent, appropriate and effective use of restorative justice techniques across England and Wales**

ENFORCEMENT OF CIVIL DEBTS

70   I indicated at the beginning of this Chapter that council tax cases are one example of the use of the criminal courts to enforce civil debts. In addition to local authorities, the Inland Revenue and Customs and Excise are able to use proceedings in the magistrates' courts to pursue debtors. There are significant

variations in the procedures used by and the powers available to each of these bodies.

71   Local authorities faced with non-payment of council tax or non-domestic rates must first seek a liability order from a magistrates' court. Such summonses are issued in bulk, but only a minority of defaulters attend court. Nevertheless, many magistrates' courts devote a half day session monthly, or even fortnightly, to dealing with this work. The court is required to make a liability order if it is satisfied that the sum is payable and remains unpaid. The fact of non-payment is rarely in issue. Council tax payers have a right of appeal on a number of matters to a valuation tribunal, so there is very little of substance to be dealt with by the court at this stage. In the case of non-domestic rates the position at the liability order stage is different, since there is a much more limited right of appeal to a valuation tribunal. In such cases, magistrates may have to determine quite complicated issues, often involving large sums of money.

72   Once a local authority has obtained a liability order, it is entitled to take certain types of enforcement action including attachment of earnings, attachment of allowances and the distress and sale of goods. The magistrates' court is not involved in this action. If the debt remains unpaid, the local authority can seek committal, or suspended committal, of the defaulter to prison as a means of securing or encouraging payment. The court will only make such an order if it is satisfied that the non-payment is due to the defaulter's culpable neglect or wilful default and that there is no available alternative. However, the inquiry into the defaulter's means that such a process entails can be very slow, involving repeated, protracted and, often, distressing hearings for all concerned.

73   Unlike local authorities, the Inland Revenue has discretion whether to use summary proceedings to pursue debtors. Other options available to it are: distraint (carried out independently without the need for a warrant from a court); county court proceedings and proceedings in the High Court.[45] The Taxes Management Act 1970 limits summary proceedings to debts not exceeding £2,000, but the process tends to be used to recover amounts in the low hundreds. The Revenue submits complaints in bulk, prompting the issuing of summonses by the magistrates' court. If payment is not made by the hearing date, the court will grant an order for payment. For those who do not pay the sum adjudicated by the court, and where the execution of a distress warrant has not met it, the court can ultimately have the defaulter arrested and commit him for failure to comply with the order.[46] Though such

---

[45] Taxes Management Act 1970, ss 61, 65 - 68

[46] Magistrates' Courts Act 1980, s 96

power is rarely exercised, its existence is no doubt a powerful incentive to the defaulter to pay up.

74 The use of summary proceedings to recover civil debts is clearly effective. Local authorities report a high response rate to the threat of court action and achieve a council tax collection rate over-all of 95.6%. Similarly, the Revenue reports that 75% of defaulters clear their debt on receipt of a warning letter or of a magistrates' court summons. There would naturally be cause for concern if any change to procedures endangered these impressive performances, not least because of the negative impact on the public purse.

75 Nevertheless, I am troubled by the blurring of the distinction between two very different elements of the justice system which arises as a result of the use of criminal courts to enforce civil liabilities. Indeed, some contributors have suggested that it is precisely because defaulters are unable to make this distinction that the summary enforcement of civil debts proves so effective. The stigma and fear associated with the criminal courts may well be providing an additional incentive to defaulters to clear their debt and avoid court proceedings. While recognising that a degree of confusion might have practical benefits, I do not think it appropriate that the state should seek to profit from such misunderstanding.

76 The enforcement of civil debts in magistrates' courts brings with it one significant practical consequence. That is the possibility of imprisonment as a sanction for non-payment. Many magistrates, and various groups concerned with the liberty of the subject, are unhappy about the former's punitive role in support of tax collection against those in society usually least able to understand or cope with their civic obligations. There are also some practical difficulties as to how magistrates may or should exercise their discretion in individual cases which has given rise to some indigestible jurisprudence. It seems to me appropriate, therefore, to question the application of a serious criminal sanction to a civil and civic wrong.

77 It has been suggested to me that the county courts would struggle to cope with this enforcement work. There is obvious concern that county courts would not achieve the debt recovery rates currently secured by magistrates' courts. I acknowledge that moving the work would not be a straightforward matter. Much would need to be done to iron out differences in the processes used by each agency, to align those processes with existing county court practices and to ensure that outcomes would not suffer as a result of the move. However, the fact that considerable preparation would be required, is not sufficient reason to avoid proposing long term changes that should achieve clarity and consistency in the way that all civil debts are enforced. The enforcement review currently being undertaken by the Lord Chancellor's Department should result in improvements to the consistency and effectiveness with

which debts and orders are enforced generally. In due course, it seems to me appropriate that county courts should take over responsibility for enforcing any and all civil debts. Such enforcement could be carried out by way of bulk process as is the case with many of the high volume creditors who currently make use of county courts.

I recommend that preparatory work should be undertaken with a view to the removal, in due course, of all civil debt enforcement from courts exercising a criminal jurisdiction.

CHAPTER 10

PREPARING FOR TRIAL

INTRODUCTION

1   A wide misconception of the general public is that all or most of the criminal justice process takes place in court. But proceedings in court require preparation – much and by many. The trouble is that the process, by its very nature – fragmented among various government departments and agencies and adversarial as between prosecution and defendant – does not encourage joint and efficient preparation. There are constitutional and administrative divides, sharpened by separate budgets, that get in the way. There are limits to what can be expected of co-operation between the parties, particularly when the issue is as to guilt as well as sentence. Guilty defendants seeking to avoid conviction have not the same urgency as the public about the need for an efficient criminal justice system. Some innocent defendants, advised by their lawyers to keep their cards close to their chests, are equally unenthusiastic. And, as is now increasingly recognised, there are other individuals involved in the process, such as victims, witnesses and jurors whose interests need attention.

2   In all of these respects the process of criminal justice is a more difficult ground for orderly preparation by the parties and management by the court than in the case of civil disputes where the issue usually concerns two parties only, where legal protections for the defendant are less rigorous and where preparation for trial does not normally require input from public bodies. Unfortunately, the already infertile ground for efficient preparation of criminal cases - vital to just and efficient court proceedings - is aggravated by a number of unnecessary defects in the system. With will and resources, something can be done about them. There is now wide acceptance that there is scope for greater intervention by the court and various agencies, and for more vigour and co-operation by the parties without prejudice to their respective interests, in the preparation of cases for hearing.

3   Before considering areas for improvement, I should summarise the basic aims as I see them. Underlying them all is the truism that, although efficiency of the criminal justice process is an important end in its own right, it has a greater importance in its contribution to the overriding consideration in every case – a fair hearing leading to a just outcome.

4   First, the key to a just and efficient criminal process – good case preparation – is identification at the earliest possible moment of the likely plea and, if it is to be one of not guilty, the issues. There is a culture of last-minute decisions, which must be attacked if there is to be any significant improvement. Too often cases are warehoused between hearings, so that little is done until the next hearing is imminent. There should be active preparation for trial without constant recourse to the court. This depends in large part on the prosecution charging correctly at the outset, its timely and adequate disclosure of its proposed evidence and of all material otherwise relevant to the issues as it knows or believes them to be, and on the defence's early indication in response to such material of the issues it intends to take. The need for early and adequate identification of issues applies to proceedings in all courts, not just those to be tried by judge and jury; but, of course, the manner of securing it will depend on the proceeding and on the nature and complexity of the case.

5   In all this, regard must be had to the prosecution's obligation to make the court sure of guilt and the defendant's right of silence. But neither is threatened by requiring a defendant to identify with some precision the matters of fact and/or of law that he intends to put in issue. If his intention is to put the prosecution to proof of everything, or only to take issue on certain matters, he is, of course, entitled to do so when the matter reaches trial. But to delay telling the court and the prosecution what he challenges as a matter of tactics, has nothing to do with the burden and standard of proof or his right of silence. Those fundamental principles are there to protect the innocent defendant from wrongful conviction, not to enable the guilty defendant to engage in tactical manoeuvres designed to frustrate a fair hearing and just outcome on the issues he intends to take.

6   Second, the parties, not the court, are responsible for the preparation of their respective cases for trial and, as part of that, for informing each other of the issues, the scope of the evidence and points of law for resolution. Pre-trial hearings can be of great help if needed and held at the right time in the preparation for trial, but they should be reserved only for such matters as the parties cannot resolve informally between themselves. At present pre-trial hearings in their various forms,[1] in all but the most complex cases, are mostly unnecessary and misused. They are treated primarily as a means of bringing everybody together in court, to enable advocates to meet their clients (often

---

[1] see para 204 - 220 below

for the first time and to take instructions), theoretically to focus on the issues of law and fact and to make decisions as to the conduct of the case. Of course, it is a good thing to do all of that, but a pre-trial hearing in court is not the place or the means for it, save as a last resort. It is misused largely because of a mix of failures by the prosecution and defence, aggravated by lack of resources on both sides. Sometimes, the charges are unrealistic because the prosecution has failed to review its case at an early stage and/or it has not served its proposed evidence or made due disclosure. This in turn has encouraged the defence to delay in its preparation or prompted an unwillingness to indicate a plea or the issues it intends to take at trial. There is also little incentive for publicly funded defence solicitors and counsel to prepare early for trial because they are not paid a discrete fee for a conference with their client or for early preparation. And, as they are paid a derisory fee for attending a plea and directions or other form of pre-trial hearing, there is also little incentive to prepare properly for it or for the trial advocate to attend.

7   Third, where there is a need for a pre-trial hearing the court and the parties should take full advantage of it to resolve all outstanding issues as to the conduct of the trial and to deal with any preliminary issues of law or fact that will assist that resolution. This calls for the court to adopt a more interventionist and authoritative role than has been traditional in identifying the issues for trial and in securing the proper preparation by both parties to deal efficiently with them. This in turn requires adequate preparation, not only by the parties and their advocates, but also by the judge with the benefit of sufficient time out of court in which to do it.

8   Fourth, there is the problem to which I have referred, of the uncooperative or feckless defendant and/or his defence advocate who considers that the burden of proof and his client's right to silence justifies frustration of the orderly preparation of both sides' case for trial. Experience in this country and elsewhere in the Commonwealth[2] indicates that, in the main, court sanctions won't compel the sort of forensic discipline that efficient case preparation requires, that they could cause injustice one way or the other and could often delay trial and increase expense rather than the reverse. However, the Review has indicated some general themes for encouraging better preparation and compliance with any directions that the court might be called upon to give. They include the introduction of a discipline of formal written orders (commonplace in the civil jurisdiction), a combination of incentives and change in professional culture, the latter aided by a properly structured system of payment which rewards preparation for trial, professional management systems that are subject to regular audit and, in extreme and clear cases, by professional sanctions and/or of loss legal aid accreditation. Among the incentives for the defendant himself might be the introduction of a system of

---

[2] see para 231 below

advance indication of discounted sentence for a plea of guilty[3] and retention of bail or custodial privileges after a plea of guilty and before sentence.

9   Fifth, critical to a better system of preparation for trial is the development and introduction of a form of information technology that is common to all criminal courts, the various criminal justice agencies serving them and defence advocates. Such technology should enable each agency, prosecutor and defence advocate to make its or his appropriate input to a single case file, draw from it what it or he needs and it is appropriate for it or him to have, and for the ready transmission and updating of papers in the case. Coupled with this, there is scope, already being developed, for greater use of video-link technology to link courts and lawyers on both sides and defendants in or out of custody. With such facilities, it should be possible to do much of what is now the subject of wasteful and inefficient pre-trial hearings, including custody remand productions, and bail applications. In that electronic way, it should also be possible to recover some of the 'locality' of access to justice lost in the modern trend to concentration of courts into fewer larger centres. All of that requires common planning, management, commitment and pooling of resources by the courts, all the criminal justice agencies and also - and this is important – defence lawyers who will use and share the benefits of the new system. Hence the urgent need, to which I have referred throughout this Report, for a criminal justice system centrally planned, funded and directed.

10   Much of what I have said about the need for efficient case management was succinctly put by the Runciman Royal Commission, in 1993, summarising its intentions for its recommendations for change in the Crown Court, namely:

> "to ensure that cases arrive at the Crown Court with the defendant's plea, so far as possible, decided and disclosed in advance and, if the trial is to be contested, with issues in dispute clarified as far as practicable. This should enable cases to be listed on the basis of a more reliable estimate of the length of time that the trial is likely to take. Clarification of the issues should also ensure that the evidence is put before the jury in such a way that the risk of a miscarriage of justice from its verdict is kept to a minimum".[4]

---

[3] see paras 91-114 below

[4] Chapter 8, para 1

FOUR ESSENTIALS

11   Early identification of the issues, whatever form it takes, depends crucially on the ability and willingness of the prosecution and defence lawyers to do their respective jobs properly. There are four main essentials:

- a strong, independent and adequately resourced prosecutor in control of the case at least from the point of charge;

- an experienced, motivated defence lawyer or lawyers who are adequately paid for pre-trial preparation;

- ready access by defence lawyers to clients in custody; and

- a better system than at present of communicating and transmitting material between all involved in the criminal justice process and with the court.

A strong and independent prosecutor

12   The Crown Prosecution Service has still to fill its proper role which, in my view, should be closer to the more highly regarded Procurator Fiscal in Scotland or the Office of the Director of Public Prosecutions in Northern Ireland.   The Glidewell and Narey reforms have gone some way in this direction, but there is more to do. The prosecutor should take control of cases at the charge or, where appropriate, pre-charge, stage, fix on the right charges from the start and keep to them, assume a more direct role than at present on disclosure and develop a more proactive role in shaping the case for trial, communicating appropriately and promptly with all concerned.   For all this the Service needs greater legal powers, in particular the power to determine the initial charge, and considerably more resources, in particular trained staff and information technology, than it has had in the first fifteen years of its life and than presently proposed.[5] The Government has recently committed itself to provide "a better resourced, better performing Crown Prosecution Service, more effective in prosecuting crime and progressing good quality cases for court".[6] These are fine words, but are reminiscent of previous expressions of intent that were not implemented.

> **I recommend that the Crown Prosecution Service should be given greater legal powers, in particular the power to determine the initial charge, and sufficient resources to enable it to take full and effective control of cases from the charge or pre-charge stage, as appropriate.**

---

[5] see IBIS *Medium Term Strategic Plan,* Annex B (Home Office 1999)

[6] *Criminal Justice: The Way Ahead*, February 2001, CM 5074 paragraph 3.13

Efficient and properly paid defence lawyers

13   The contribution of defence lawyers to the just and efficient working of the system is equally critical. They too need to be properly resourced – paid – if they are to make a proper contribution consistent with their duty to their clients and the court. They also need to keep abreast of changes in law, procedure and technology through continued professional development. The basis and levels of their pay are not directly within my terms of reference. But I cannot ignore some of the effects of poor payment in publicly funded cases on the working of the criminal justice process.

14   Nearly all criminal defence work is publicly funded, accounting, in 2001-2002, for 7% of the total budget of £12.8 billion for the criminal justice system.[7] Publicly funded defence lawyers, the Bar and solicitors, need more support than they receive at the moment, in the form in which the prosecution case is presented to them and in proper pay for necessary preparatory work. There has been much change as to public funding in the course of the Review, and more is to come. The Legal Services Commission took over from the Legal Aid Board the public funding of defence work in April 2000.[8] And on 1st April 2001 the Criminal Defence Service was established under the aegis of the Commission to undertake piloting and research into a mixed system of public funding of criminal defence through salaried employees and contracted private practitioners.[9] A new system of franchising solicitors for publicly funded work in magistrates' courts was introduced in October 2000 as a preliminary to the implementation of a contractual scheme with the Criminal Defence Service on 2nd April 2001. There are similar proposals for franchising solicitors in the Crown Court from 2003.[10] Negotiations are also under way with the Bar Council over the extension of franchising arrangements to barristers' chambers.

15   Salaried public defenders will be introduced as part of a four year pilot starting in 2001/2002. Six offices will be established, each based in its own premises away from the Legal Service Commission's regional offices. The first pilot areas will be Birmingham, Liverpool, Middlesbrough and Swansea (with two more yet to be announced).[11] The intention is that the salaried and franchised services will operate alongside each other, with the work of the

---

[7] compared with 62% spent on the Police, 15% on the Prison Service, 4% on the Probation Service, 5% on the Crown and Magistrates' Courts, 3% on the CPS and SFO, 2% on the Criminal Injuries Compensation Scheme and Victim Support; see *The Criminal Justice System Strategic Plan 1999-2002*

[8] Access to Justice Act 1999 s 1

[9] ibid, s 12

[10] Legal Services Commission Corporate Plan 2001/02 – 2003/04 para 3.9 - 3.15

[11] ibid para 3.20

former being subjected to independent monitoring by outside researchers, who will publish comparative reports. All materials developed by the Criminal Defence Service in relation to public defenders will be made generally available on its website for the benefit of the whole profession.

16   As to public funding of private practitioners, this is not the place to examine in detail what has gone before or what is to replace it. To set the scene, however, I should mention the introduction in January 1997 of a graduated standard fees scheme, the system of calculating all defence advocates' fees, including those of QCs, for cases lasting up to ten days in the Crown Court. The Lord Chancellor has recently amended the scheme so as to extend it to cases lasting up to 25 days and has also reduced the level of fees so as to achieve parity between defence fee levels and those paid to prosecution advocates. In doing so the Lord Chancellor stated that his intention was to reduce the total cost of advocates' fees for Crown Court defence work by about 10%. The Bar Council supports standard fees in principle, but argues that these reductions have occurred over a period during which procedural burdens on them and the costs of practice have increased. And it claims that the true effect of the reductions cumulatively amount to at least 25% for the junior Bar, 36% for Queen's Counsel and 27.5% for the criminal Bar over-all.

17   Before summarising the fee structure itself I should record, with all the emphasis I can, that the general thrust of the criminal graduated fees scheme, and of the latest extension of it, is fundamentally flawed in that it does not provide an adequate reward or incentive for preparatory work. Quite apart from the interest of justice in securing a fair trial, the scope for savings and improvement in the efficiency of trial preparation are enormous. Yet the current fee structure, present and, seemingly, proposed, for publicly funded defence work perversely discourages, rather than encourages, efficient preparation.

18   In brief, the payment scheme in magistrates' courts is for a flat fee in all cases for a guilty plea and a graduated payment for most trials. These fees include a notional element for case preparation, but it is not separately identified. Longer and more complex cases are subject to the taxation procedure (i.e. scrutiny after the event by court staff of what has been done in the case). In magistrates' courts, the defence solicitor, who holds the budget, runs the case as he sees fit and, if he instructs counsel, pays him from that budget.

19   In the Crown Court, solicitors and barristers are paid separately. For guilty pleas and trials lasting up to two days, solicitors are paid standard fees which, again, include a notional element for preparation including securing proper prosecution disclosure, taking instructions from the defendant and preparation and service of the defence statement. For longer trials, solicitors' bills are subject to taxation, though the Lord Chancellor is considering other ways of

remunerating this work. In the very longest of trials (generally those lasting more than five weeks) the Criminal Defence Service enters into a specific contract with solicitors and counsel for the work that is to be undertaken.

20   As I have indicated, counsel is paid on the basis of standard graduated fees for trials lasting, now, up to 25 days. Though these fees contain notional elements for preparation, barristers receive no identifiable or discrete fee for any preparatory work, which ought in many cases to include advising on prosecution disclosure, holding a conference with the defendant (in prison, if he is in custody) and advising on the form of the defence statement, on evidence and the general conduct of the case. The one exception is an allowance of a flat fee of £75 (shortly to rise to £100) for preparing for and attending a plea and directions hearing – less than many a tradesman might charge for an hour or two's work even after the increase. The expectation is that counsel instructed for the trial will attend the plea and directions hearing. But such hearings are not listed to suit his availability and he is frequently engaged in another case when it takes place. The reality is that other – sometimes less experienced - counsel attend them. They will have had little or no part in such preparation of the case as there has been, and no authority to advise or commit the defendant to any critical matters needing resolution. It is no wonder that defendants, who have yet to see their trial counsel, are reluctant to enter pleas at that stage or to commit themselves to a firm strategy for the trial.

21   The problems of the inadequacy of payment for preparatory work and of the perverse structure discouraging rather than encouraging professional diligence at that critical stage of the process is common to proceedings in magistrates' courts and the Crown Court. But they are particularly pressing and costly in the latter. The perversities take two forms. The first, which is inherent in the system, is that the longer the trial the greater the brief fee. Poor preparation by one or both sides almost always lengthens trials and the system rewards them for it with additional fees. The second is where the defendant, for want of proper preparation by either or both sides or for some other reason such as lack of access to him in prison, initially pleads not guilty and only later changes his plea to guilty on the day of trial. In that event his lawyers receive more money in the form of a 'cracked trial' fee than they would have done if he had pleaded guilty from the outset.[12]

22   Those responsible in the Lord Chancellor's Department for devising an extension and modification of the existing graduated fee scheme are well aware of these features. In fact, many of the problems inherent in the standard fee system derive from the Lord Chancellor's Department's and the Legal Services Commission's concern about their own administrative and financial

---

[12] I am indebted to His Hon Judge David Mellor, the Resident Judge at Norwich, for this practical analysis

requirements, regardless of the consequences for other parts of the system. Standard fees suit both the Department and practitioners, since they are cheap to administer, predictable in quantity and quick to pay out. But they do not provide any incentive for adequate and timely preparation.

23   In my view, there is an urgent need for a change in the system of payment of defence lawyers to ensure that proper and timely preparation is encouraged by the payment of adequate fees for preparation. These fees could be calculable, whether on a percentage basis or otherwise, by reference to the over-all fee, and be deductible from it if want of proper preparation results in unnecessary pre-trial hearings and/or increases the length of trial. In the event of change of trial advocate, any difficulties as to entitlement to the preparatory fee should be capable of resolution by professional regulation. In addition, or alternatively, if my recommendations in paragraphs 221-228 below are adopted, in jury and other appropriate cases such a payment might be tied to the preparation of a case and issues summary.

24   A suggestion of His Honour Judge David Mellor, which I find attractive, focuses more sharply on the contribution of preparation to the process. It is that, in all but the largest cases requiring individual assessment or tender, the basic or 'core' fee should be a standard graduated fee for *preparation*. It would be on a graduated basis calculated according to weight and complexity. All other payments would be in the form of standard graduated uplifts on that figure, depending on whether the preparation results in a plea of guilty or a trial. There would be an enhanced uplift where it could be shown that preparation has shortened a trial, and daily payments ('refreshers') for trials lasting beyond one day.

25   For its part, the Legal Services Commission is proposing a system of 'quality assurance standards' for Criminal Defence Service contracted lawyers, but plans its introduction only after the outcome of its pilots to be conducted over the next four years.[13] The criteria for such a system should be selected so as to measure the *quality* of decisions as well as the achievement of staged targets, since the latter may not be a true measure of progress. Devising a system may not be easy; but there is already some experience in operating quality assurance standards in publicly funded work.[14] Contracts could provide for spot auditing of files and otherwise monitoring performance. In extreme cases, they could enable the Commission, subject to a right of appeal,[15] to remove or not renew the offending practitioner's contractual entitlement to undertake publicly funded work or to confine him to certain types or volume of work. An analogous regime could be devised for barristers' chambers, once franchising arrangements are extended to them.

---

[13] see the LCD Consultation Paper, *Criminal Defence Service: Choice of Representative*, June 2000, CP 10/00, para 4

[14] see eg *Legal Aid Franchise: Quality Assurance Standard*, Fourth Edition, April 2000, Legal Services Commission

[15] ibid, see eg Chapter 9

26   A third option would be to tie the judge's role in case preparation to triggering payment. It could build upon an interesting pilot project shortly to be undertaken at the Crown Court in Manchester Minshull Street under the supervision of His Honour Judge Woodward. Under the scheme, technological support has been provided to a dedicated Crown Prosecution Service team, four firms of defence solicitors and six sets of chambers and to the court. It will enable all the preparatory stages in criminal cases (excluding child abuse cases and those with more than four defendants) to be logged on a common access secure website, using forms derived from (but more detailed than) those used for plea and directions hearings. Protocols will set out what should be achieved by whom, and on what timescale. At a set point in time, the judge will interrogate the website, and if the case is ready, make the appropriate orders and allocate a trial date. Such "electronic" pre-trial case preparation is likely to have significant advantages over the present system. First, since a pre-trial hearing would not normally be required, it would be more convenient for trial advocates to attend properly to the preparation of their cases. Second, there would be significant savings in court time and in the accompanying expense and inconvenience. Third, it would be possible to tie the procedure to the payment of a realistic figure to defence lawyers if and when the case is certified by the judge as ready for listing. If the judge were to consider that a hearing is still necessary to bring the case to a stage of readiness, payment would depend upon the outcome of the hearing. If the case presented evidential or other difficulties which clearly merited an oral hearing, this could be indicated by the judge, and remunerated by an additional fee; but, if there were no such justification, it would not be payable. Such a system could, therefore, provide both incentives and sanctions.

27   I do not attempt more than to emphasise an urgent need to remove the perversities in the present system and to suggest possibilities for a better one. Those responsible should explore and develop a solution in close consultation with the Criminal Justice Council and the legal professions.

> **I recommend that urgent consideration should be given to changing the structure of public funding of defence fees in the criminal courts so as properly to reward and encourage adequate and timely preparation of cases for disposal on pleas of guilty or by trial, rather than discourage such preparation as it perversely does at present.**

Ready access by defence lawyers to their clients in custody

28   Critical to the process of preparation is early and ready access by defence lawyers to their clients. This should not be a problem where defendants are on bail, save for the unsatisfactory arrangements for payment for preparation, including conferences, to which I have referred. It is, however, a real problem where defendants are in custody. Defence lawyers often have great difficulty in gaining access to their clients in custody at times and for sufficient periods for them to take proper instructions and to advise. This is particularly so for pre-trial conferences in prison in the late afternoon or early evening, often the only time that busy practitioners can manage if they are engaged in court on other matters in the day. It is also a problem at court during trial, when it is frequently necessary to discuss the case before or after the day's proceedings and the defendant is brought to court late and returned promptly to prison.

29   There are no national standards or rules governing the access of unsentenced prisoners to their legal advisers. Practices as to prisoners' access to the telephone to talk to their advisers and for legal visits vary from prison to prison, and in some instances even from shift to shift within the same establishment. A recent thematic review by the Prison Inspectorate of the treatment and conditions of unsentenced prisoners[16] found that, over-all, remand prisoners, particularly those in custody for the first time, had difficulty in obtaining legal advice in prison and that prison officers were rarely proactive in helping them to do so. Here are some of the practical difficulties, most of which the Inspectorate highlighted:[17]

- often there is a problem in locating a defendant in custody; having found him, there is then considerable delay in getting through to the appropriate prison on the telephone to book a visit, a difficulty that the Prison Service have acknowledged, blaming it on lack of sufficient resources to fund additional telephone lines;

- prisoners cannot normally receive telephone calls from their solicitors;

- prisoners can only use the telephone by means of phone cards, the purchase of which can take up to six days to arrange after arrival in prison;

- the best time to contact solicitors by telephone is in the morning before court, but at that time prisoners are usually locked up in their cells or working;

- prisoners are most commonly given access to telephones in the evening when their solicitors' offices are closed;

- telephone calls in the main part of the day are on application only and not always granted because of staff shortages or other difficulties;

---

[16] *Unjust Deserts : A Thematic Review by HM Chief Inspector of Prisons of the Treatment and Conditions for Unsentenced Prisoners in England and Wales*, (Home Office, December 2000)

[17] ibid, para 4.25

- legal visits have to be booked in advance, which can take several days due to difficulties in telephonic communications or slow processing of mail (which is not conducive to the preparation of defence statements within 14 days of primary prosecution disclosure[18] as required by the Criminal Procedure and Investigations Act 1996);

- some prisons only allow legal visits in the evenings and, even then, allow insufficient time for them; and

- although prison officers should not open confidential correspondence, prisoners often find that letters from their solicitors have been opened.

30 It is not surprising that the Inspectorate found that Prison Governors frequently failed to discharge their responsibilities under Prison Service Rules to allow remand prisoners effective access to their legal advisers:

> "In our view the barriers to effective communication with legal advisers constitute an obstacle to the fair and just treatment of unsentenced prisoners which may well not stand up to legal challenge under the Human Rights Act, Article 6 which guarantees rights consistent with the proper preparation and conduct of a defence, including the right to consult with a lawyer prior to and during the trial. ...."[19]

31 I should not leave that finding without also referring to the undoubted reluctance of a significant proportion of both the Bar and solicitors to visit their clients on remand in prison, partly because of the difficulties it presents for them, but also because they are not paid properly for it. Quite apart from the injustice to defendants, those difficulties are another good example of one agency making relatively minor economies at the expense of a much greater cost to other agencies and individuals involved in the criminal justice process. If remand prisoners and their legal representatives could contact each other more readily, they could, together, prepare their defences more efficiently and earlier, and the need for defendants to attend pre-trial hearings simply in order to meet their legal representatives would go. It would also remove the need for many such hearings altogether. I should add that, in any event, many remand prisoners would prefer to remain at prison and participate in any preliminary court proceedings through video-link than endure the discomfort and other inconvenience of court attendance, which also puts them at risk of the upheaval of having to transfer to another cell on their return to prison.

32 There are a host of obvious answers to most of the difficulties that I have mentioned, which may involve large or relatively small initial expense to the Prison Service and other agencies, but which would almost certainly achieve

---

[18] see paras 127 – 140 below
[19] *Unjust Deserts* para 4.34

long-term savings for it and for the criminal justice system as a whole. For example, the arranging of legal visits could be expedited and eased by the basic means of installing dedicated telephone lines in prisons, and/or by the provision of a secure internet facility for on-line booking of visits, a facility at present only available in 2% of the country's prisons. Another and more significant improvement in its potential for savings in time and expense, would be the introduction of widespread video-conferencing arrangements between defence lawyers, operating from their own offices or a shared facility, and prisons. Such steps would remove the root causes of many of the difficulties in communication between remand prisoners and their legal advisers. With or without them, there is an urgent need for the formulation of national standards accompanied by protocols with others including the Bar Council, the Law Society and the Criminal Defence Service, to ensure that unsentenced prisoners in custody are at no disadvantage to those on bail in preparing their defences.

33   Accordingly, I warmly support the Prison Inspectorate's recommendation in its thematic review[20] that the Prison Service should introduce standards for access to due process for unsentenced prisoners which ensure that they experience no greater jeopardy than bailed defendants in preparing for their trial.

Better communication systems

34   Fundamental to all improvements in case preparation at the pre-trial stage is the need to harness advances in information and communications technology. In para 26 above, I have described the pilot exercise due to be undertaken in Manchester into electronic plea and directions 'hearings'. In my view, this points the way forward to a system in which prosecution and defence can exchange information quickly and cheaply, and in which the court can monitor progress without the need to call the parties in for a hearing. Video-conferencing also has an important part to play in allowing face to face communication without having to assemble everyone in the same room. The Lord Chancellor's Department is introducing discrete, secure audio-visual links from all magistrates' courts to the 'local' prison, to be used for remand hearings.[21] The use of these could be extended to solicitors who wish to take instructions from their clients. There need only be a simple booking system which might allow access to the facility even outside normal court hours. In the longer term, the recommendations I have made in Chapter 8 for electronic case files would allow all those involved in the case to work online, extracting the information they need and making their own contribution. The potential of such technologies for increasing the efficiency with which cases are prepared

---

[20] ibid para 4.35
[21] see paras 259-261 below

is very significant. Without them, case management systems for criminal cases will remain anchored in the last century.

IDENTIFYING THE ISSUES

The charge

35 A significant contributor to delays in the entering of pleas of guilty and in identifying issues for trial and, in consequence, the prolonged and disjointed nature of many criminal proceedings, is 'over-charging' by the police and failure by the Crown Prosecution Service to remedy it at an early stage. All too often the prosecutor does not review the case thoroughly or with a sufficiently realistic eye until late in the day. This results, as I have already noted, in the defence tendering and the prosecution accepting last minute changes of plea to lesser offences, including those of defendants in 'either-way' cases who only opt for trial with a view to securing a reduction in charges in the Crown Court. And, even where last minute reductions or changes in charges do not produce pleas of guilty, much time and money may have been spent by both sides in preparing for a bigger and more complex trial than in the event takes place. The Crown Prosecution Service Inspectorate, in its Annual Report for 1999-2000, noted that about 23% of all indictments in the Crown Court had to be amended before trial.

36 This pattern encourages defendants who believe, rightly or wrongly, that they have been overcharged to maintain tactical pleas of not guilty until the last minute. It can also give rise to hasty, ill-considered and inappropriate acceptances by the prosecution of pleas of guilty, which bewilder and distress victims, distort sentencing decisions, engender appeals against sentence and, sometimes, artificially prevent the Court of Appeal, from doing justice in the case. There are, of course, other reasons for last minute changes of plea, including a reluctance by defendants to face reality, a hope or expectation that proposed prosecution witnesses may not turn up to give evidence at the trial or simply a short-term consideration of retaining prison privileges or prolonging remand on bail for domestic reasons. Nevertheless, a mistaken decision as to charge at the start of the case can have a fundamental and damaging effect on the preparation by both sides for trial and in the court's attempts at efficient case management. In human terms, the effect of prolongation, repeated attendance at court and uncertainty of witnesses, victims, the accused himself, relatives and others concerned in the proceedings can be disruptive and distressing.

Public prosecutions

37   Much of the problem is due to the fact that the police, not the Crown Prosecution Service, initiate prosecutions. The police charge. The Crown Prosecution Service reviews the charge after the event; and, in doing so, it applies a more stringent test than that of the police, as I describe below.[22]

38   The police, in charging, act under the operational direction and policies of their individual Chief Constables, each subject to the oversight of his own police authority. In most cases they do not have the benefit of advice from the Crown Prosecution Service at this early stage. Its role has been almost wholly reactive – quite unlike that of the procurators fiscal in Scotland who have a grip on the case and what to charge from the very start. The Service is normally only brought into the picture for advice and review when the charge has been preferred or the summons issued, and the potential for damage created. The recent location of Crown Prosecution Service lawyers at police stations to be available to advise the police on charging and other matters has led to some improvement. However, the Crown Prosecution Service Inspectorate, in its Annual Report 1999-2000, still found that 22% of police charges relating to assault, public order and road traffic offences were incorrect.

39   We talk of 'the prosecution' as if it were a single entity. The Philips Royal Commission envisaged that, although the police and prosecutors would have separate and distinct responsibilities, the system would:

> "depend ... upon co-operation, with checks and balances operating within a framework in which all are seeking the same objectives. This unity of purpose, but independence of responsibility could be symbolised by providing that all cases ... brought by the police are brought in the name of the Crown and by designating the local prosecutor as 'the Crown prosecutor'.[23]

40   But there is no unified prosecution. The police and Crown prosecutor are institutionally, financially and culturally separate from and independent of each other. In recent years the Glidewell and Narey reforms have gone some way to encouraging greater unity of effort and to involve the prosecutor earlier in the process. Sir Iain Glidewell and his colleagues urged a shift in the centre of gravity of the Crown Prosecution Service's operations from magistrates' courts towards the Crown Court, a devolution of power from the Crown Prosecution Service headquarters to local Chief Crown Prosecutors,

---

[22] para 43

[23] *Report of the Royal Commission on Criminal Procedure*, (January 1981), Cmnd 8092, Ch 7, para 7.8

establishment of its 'proper role' as an integral part of the criminal justice system[24] and a clearer definition of the proper relationship and responsibilities of the police, the Service and the Courts.[25] As to the Service's relationship with the police, they recommended that the police should remain responsible for investigation and charging and the preliminary preparation of case papers, and that the Service should be responsible for the prosecution process immediately following charge, advising as to any further investigation and the preparation of the case file, arranging the initial hearing in the magistrates' court and witness availability, warning and care.[26] In the area for which both services would have a continuing role, the preparation of the case file, they recommended the creation of combined Crown Prosecution Service and police 'criminal justice' units headed by a Service lawyer, which were also to have sole conduct of fast-track cases and to be responsible for case management in magistrates' courts.[27] They also recommended the creation of what are now called criminal trial units consisting of lawyers with support staff, to be responsible for all prosecutions in the Crown Court and to act as advocates in trials of either way cases in magistrates' courts.[28] Martin Narey, in his Report,[29] also advocated the need to bring police and the Service closer together in the preparation of cases for trial by locating prosecutors in police stations to advise their administrative support units.[30]

41   Most of the Glidewell and Narey recommendations have been adopted and are being implemented after local pilots. Crown Prosecution Service staff are now increasingly located in or close to police stations working in liaison with the police in criminal justice units and are receiving papers for review shortly after charge. Although there are some difficulties in providing accommodation for them to work together in this way, early signs[31] are that the new system is producing some improvements in efficiency and savings, but not, in the main, in the accuracy of charging. An evaluation[32] of the pilot schemes to implement the Narey recommendations showed, for example, that, in six areas where a Service lawyer was 'on call' for 24 hours a day, there had only been twelve calls for advice on charging over a period of six months. Seemingly, police officers in those areas felt that they were capable of handling matters themselves or were content to wait for advice in normal working hours. Although the officers' assessment of the position may have been correct, the continuing large proportion of prosecution cases that are discontinued or proceed with reduced charges suggests that there is still much wrong with the system. The authors of the evaluation recommended other

---

[24] *A Report Of The Review of the Crown Prosecution Service,* (The Stationery Office, 1998) Ch 1 paras 26, 37, 61 and 65

[25] ibid Ch 7, paras 4 and 8

[26] ibid Ch 1, paras 27-28

[27] ibid Ch 8, paras 11 and 12

[28] ibid Ch 8, paras 21 and 22

[29] *Review of Delay in the Criminal Justice System,* Martin Narey, February (1997)

[30] ibid Ch 3, pp 10-11

[31] *An Early Assessment of Co-located Criminal Justice Units* a report by the Glidewell Working Group, January 2001 – available on the CPS website:www.cps.gov.uk

[32] *Reducing Delay in the Criminal Justice System: Evaluation of the Pilot Schemes* (Ernst and Young), (1999), Home Office

strategies to achieve more and earlier co-operation between police and the Crown Prosecution Service. This has been given added urgency since the abolition, from 15th January 2001, of committal proceedings for indictable-only offences,[33] resulting in the Crown Court receiving serious cases within days of charge. It will become even more pressing if my recommendations, in Chapters 5 and 7, for abolition of committal proceedings in 'either-way' offences and/or for the creation of a unified Criminal Court with three levels of jurisdiction are accepted.

42   The hope, expressed in the Philips Royal Commission Report,[34] that the expertise of the police in investigating would simply be supplemented by the legal expertise of Crown prosecutors failed to acknowledge that the scope and manner of investigation largely determine and shape the ensuing legal process.   Moreover, that Report was written against a very different procedural landscape. Notable changes have since combined to require more carefully prepared and faster prosecutions than before, for example: the Criminal Procedure and Investigations Act 1996, imposing on the prosecution rigorous and elaborate obligations of advance disclosure; the Crime and Disorder Act 1998, establishing simpler and faster procedures towards trial; the Human Rights Act 1998, introducing its potentially more testing Article 6 notion of a right to a fair hearing, including the right to prompt notification of the accusation; and Government initiatives to reduce delay.

43   As I have said, the police and the Crown Prosecution Service have different tests for charging. The Police and Criminal Evidence Act 1984 and its Code of Practice C[35] require an investigating officer, 'without delay' to bring a detained suspect before the custody officer for charging at the point where he considers that there is sufficient evidence for a successful prosecution and that the suspect has said all that he wishes to say about the offence. This test is different in one respect, and arguably different in another, from those governing the Service under the Code for Crown Prosecutors.[36] The Service may only continue a prosecution if it passes both an evidential test, expressed in the Code as whether "there is enough evidence to provide a realistic prospect of conviction", and also a public interest test.   As to the respective evidential tests, the police tend to apply a lower threshold of probability in considering whether there is sufficient evidence to charge than will satisfy the Service at the review stage of "a realistic prospect of conviction". This is commonly the case when determining specific charges in a range of options where certain evidence, for example, medical or other expert evidence, has yet to be obtained. And, as to the public interest test, not only is it not an express requirement for a police officer considering whether to charge, it is

---

[33] Crime and Disorder Act 1998, ss 51 and 52

[34] para 7.17

[35] para 16.1

[36] *Code for Crown Prosecutors,* fourth edition, issued in September 2000 by the Director of Public Prosecutions pursuant to the Prosecution of Offences Act 1985, s 10

hardly appropriate for him to shoulder that responsibility, especially in circumstances where the suspect is detained and he has to decide quickly.

44   In my view, consideration should be given to a move towards earlier and more influential involvement of the Crown Prosecution Service in the process to the point where, in all but minor, routine cases, or where there is a need for a holding charge, it should determine the charge and initiate the prosecution. The precise offences that could be left to the police without advance intervention by the Service could be provided by national guidelines contained within the Criminal Procedure Code that I have proposed. There would be nothing revolutionary or constitutionally difficult about such a shift. It would approximate to the arrangements of many other national and local prosecuting authorities in this country responsible for both investigation and prosecution of offences within their jurisdiction, including the Serious Fraud Office and various Government Departments, including the Departments of Trade and Industry, Health and the Revenue Departments. To my mind, since the Service has been given ultimate responsibility for the shape of the prosecution in its function of review of the charges and evidence supporting them after the start of proceedings, it would be logical and, certainly, more efficient to give it that control from the start. I note that the authors of the Review of the Criminal Justice System in Northern Ireland are of a similar view.[37]

45   Such a change, including correlation of the higher evidential and public interest tests at the stage of charge by the Crown Prosecution Service or, in minor, routine cases, by the police, would possibly require greater use of police bail to complete the investigation before charge. But this should be offset by: earlier involvement of the Service with the police in the investigation of the more serious cases; in consequence, a better understanding by the police of the evidential test governing decisions to prosecute; earlier pleas of guilty to properly investigated and charged prosecutions; a general increase in the speed with which cases proceed to trial; and greater confidence of victims, witnesses and the general public in the process as a result of fewer cases being discontinued after charge or continuing on reduced charges.

I recommend that:

- **the Crown Prosecution Service should determine the charge in all but minor, routine offences or where, because of the circumstances, there is a need for a holding charge before seeking the advice of the Service;**

---

[37] *Review of the Criminal Justice System in Northern Ireland,* (The Stationery Office, March 2000), paras 4.138-141

- in minor, routine cases in which the police charge without first having sought the advice of the Service, they should apply the same evidential test as that governing the Service in the Code for Crown Prosecutors;

- where the police have preferred a holding charge, and in other than minor, routine offences, a prosecutor should review and, if necessary, reformulate the charge at the earliest possible opportunity; and

- 'minor' or 'routine' offences for this purpose should be identified in the Criminal Procedure Code that I have recommended or in other primary or subsidiary legislation.

Private prosecutions

46   The English criminal law is, historically, founded on the basis that every citizen has the right to invoke it by private prosecution. The entitlement has survived the development in the 19th century of organised police forces, not least, as one contributor to the Review has observed, because of the absence until the introduction in 1986 of a national prosecuting authority in the form of the Crown Prosecution Service.[38]   Even now there is no single prosecuting authority for all matters. The Crown Prosecution Service, though by far the most comprehensive prosecutor on a national scale, coexists with a large number of other specialist national prosecutors, including the Serious Fraud Office, Customs and Excise and the Department of Trade and Industry, public agencies, such as the Driver Vehicle Licensing Authority, the Health and Safety Executive, and local authorities responsible for enforcing a wide range of environmental and consumer legislation and by-law control. Along with this mix of public prosecutors, the private prosecutor survives – just. The Philips Royal Commission in 1981 noted that, although the citizen had an almost unlimited right to issue proceedings, there were such severe restrictions on it in practice that it was very rarely used. This is still the case. The Prosecution of Offences Act 1985, which established the Crown Prosecution Service under the leadership of the Director of Public Prosecution, expressly preserved the right of private prosecution in cases not instituted by the police and certain other agencies, but it also empowered him to take over any private prosecution. Having done so, he may discontinue it where (though only where) he considers there is no evidential or legal case to answer.[39]   And, as mentioned at para 51 below, there are a number of offences in respect of which the Attorney General's or Director's consent to prosecution are, in any event, required. In addition, there are formidable

---

[38] SJ Wooler, Chief Inspector, CPS Inspectorate
[39] Prosecution of Offences Act 1985, s 6(2) and *R v DPP, ex p Duckenfield* [2000] 1 WLR 55

practical constraints on its exercise, including legal uncertainty as to the power to charge as distinct from laying an information for a summons or warrant for arrest, the need for some familiarity with legal process, the motivation to use it and the necessary financial resources.

47   A strong case has been advanced for abolition, or at least review, of the little that remains of an effective right of private prosecution.[40] The argument is that what might once have been a valuable safeguard against improper failure to prosecute has now been overtaken by other safeguards, and that even that limited use has a potential for expensive disruption of the system that is no longer justifiable. It is only in a very small number of cases that prosecutors wrongly decide against prosecution, leaving private individuals, successfully or not, to take up the baton.[41] And there have been some recent high profile cases where the Director, having taken the advice of experienced counsel, has decided not to prosecute, and ensuing private prosecutions have failed, sometimes after long trials mainly at the public's expense.

48   On the other hand, many feel that the right of private prosecution, though now largely a relic of our slow and incomplete move towards a single national prosecuting authority, may on occasion still operate as a necessary and effective safeguard against failure by public prosecutors properly and vigorously to enforce the criminal law. Like Burke's justification of the Royal Prerogative, its strength may lie in its availability when needed rather than in the extent of its use. For that reason, coupled with the relatively infrequent recourse to it, I am disinclined to recommend its abolition.

49   As a practical matter, there is clearly a need for an effective system for alerting the Director of Public Prosecutions to the initiation of private prosecutions, so that he may consider his power to intervene. There is no obligation on a private prosecutor to notify the Director before or within a specified time after he has begun a private prosecution, and no formal machinery by which the court concerned notifies him. In practice, the Director usually learns informally, if not through court staff, through the presence of Crown prosecutors in court at the time, or because the defendant asks him to take over the case and drop it. In my view, there should be a clear safeguard against private prosecution without merit, in the form of a duty on the court to inform the Director promptly of any private prosecution initiated before it.

50   The Philips Royal Commission's suggestion was that the would-be private prosecutor should first apply to the Crown prosecutor who, if satisfied, in accordance with his normal prosecuting criteria, that the matter should

---

[40] by, among others, the Chief Inspector of the CPS

[41] The Inspectorate Annual Report (1999-2000), noted that in 98.2% of cases checked, the CPS were correct in their assessment of evidence, and in 99.7% they were correct in their assessment of the public interest

proceed, should undertake the prosecution. The Commission recommended that if the Crown prosecutor declined to prosecute, the complainant should be entitled to apply to magistrates for leave to do so himself. At that hearing the prosecutor would be required to explain his decision. Since the Director does not apply a public interest test for allowing private prosecutions to continue, the effect of this proposal would have been to preserve, although in reduced form the limited right of private prosecution. But it would also have introduced a cumbrous form of pre-charge check and, in my view, an inappropriate forum for it. As the Law Commission recommended,[42] when considering this as an aspect of the regime of consents to prosecution, it would make a more efficient safeguard against abuse to require the court to notify the Director on receipt of the application for a summons. In my view, the only filter on private prosecutions should be the power of the Director to take over the conduct of proceedings and discontinue them. But I do not see why, in considering whether to discontinue, he should not apply his normal public interest test as well as the evidential test.

I recommend that:

- **the right of private prosecution should continue, subject to the power of the Director of Public Prosecutions, on learning of a private prosecution, to take it over and discontinue it;**

- **any court before which a private prosecution is initiated should be under a duty forthwith to notify the Director of it in writing; and**

- **the Director, in deciding whether to discontinue a private prosecution that he has taken over, should apply the public interest test as well as the evidential test set out in the Code for Crown Prosecutors.**

Consent to the charge

51   About 150 statutes creating criminal offences require the Attorney General's or Director of Public Prosecution's consent before proceedings are instituted. Most of these preceded the creation of an independent prosecuting agency in the form of the Crown Prosecution Service. In all cases where the Director's consent is required, it may be exercised by any Crown prosecutor,[43] which, given their general power to review and to discontinue prosecutions, effectively renders the requirement otiose. The Attorney General has not delegated his powers of consent, save to the Solicitor General.[44] Thus, the

---

[42] *Consents to Prosecution* Law Comm No 255, para 7.4-7.8

[43] Prosecution of Offences Act 1985, s 1(7)

[44] Law Officers Act 1997, s 1(1)

involvement in most public prosecutions of consequence of the Director, through the Crown Prosecution Service, or of the Director of the Serious Fraud Office, removes the need for most consent provisions where the decision is whether to continue, or, if my recommendation above is accepted, to initiate a prosecution.

52   The Law Commission has recently examined and reported on the continued justification for this check on public prosecutions.[45] The Government has not yet taken action on its recommendations. The Commission found that consent to prosecution is required in a wide variety of cases[46] and that it was difficult to discern a principled or otherwise rational basis for the inclusion of many of them. However, some are clearly offences in respect of which the decision to charge could involve particularly sensitive issues of public interest or of national security, for example, alleged breaches of security or public order, or offences of terrorism or corruption of a public official or public morals, such as publication of obscene material. The Commission recommended that the requirement of consent of the Attorney General or the Director of Public Prosecutions should be removed in all cases except for specified categories in which the requirement clearly protected the public interest.   I support that recommendation.

I recommend the adoption of the Law Commission's recommendation to remove the requirement for the Attorney General's or Director of Public Prosecution's consent to prosecution, save in those categories of case where its retention clearly protects the public interest.

Mechanics of charging

53   There are two main ways of starting a prosecution. The first is by laying an information seeking the issue of a summons to an accused requiring him to attend a magistrates' court to answer the information, the second, by charge, normally at a police station. The summons procedure accounted for 54% of all prosecutions in 1999.[47] It is used by the police and other bodies when they have no power of arrest, or where that power was not exercised, and by individuals seeking to initiate a private prosecution. The application, which may be oral or in writing, is made ex parte before a magistrate - who may grant it if he considers it a proper case for process. The summons may then be given to the applicant to serve on the accused, or the court may do so on his behalf. Although, the decision whether to issue a summons is judicial,

---

[45] *Consents to Prosecution,* Law Comm No 255

[46] including a number of those prosecuted by various Government Departments

[47] Table 8.2, Criminal Statistics in England and Wales 1999, Home Office, Cmnd 5001

there is not normally a preliminary hearing. And, because of the large numbers of prosecutions begun in this way, magistrates' consideration of each information or batch of them is necessarily perfunctory. The majority of informations are in writing, often many dozens or even hundreds of them at a time before individual courts. Almost all road traffic prosecutions are begun in this way.

54 Turning to the second method of initiating a prosecution, police officers and other prosecuting authorities with power to initiate prosecutions may charge a suspect where they have reasonable grounds to believe that there is sufficient evidence for a successful prosecution against him. They may do so whether or not he is in custody. Most charges are made by police officers of suspects in their custody. In which event, the station custody officer is responsible for determining whether there is sufficient evidence to charge the suspect for the offence for which he was arrested and, if so, to charge him, remand him in custody or release him on bail and set a date for his first attendance at court. An accused in custody must normally be brought before a court within 24 hours.[48] And, under the Narey procedures,[49] an accused on bail is now likely to attend court within days, possibly hours, after being charged. Private prosecutors, for example those who have effected a 'citizen's arrest' and taken the suspect to the police, were thought to have a power to charge, but the law is not clear on the point, especially having regard to the station custody officer regime introduced by section 37 of the Police and Criminal Evidence Act 1984.[50]

55 In comparing the two methods of initiating a prosecution, two matters stand out. The first is the anomaly that, in the most serious cases, the police may do so by charging a suspect without the intervention of the court, yet not in the far greater volumes of lesser offences, where the process is by summons. The second is that the court's role in the summons procedure is now, perforce, exercised in so notional a manner as to make it unnecessary. And, as to the setting of the first date for attendance at court, there is no reason why the police should not have similar powers in a summoning process to those that they already have for the more serious cases in which they charge the suspect.[51] In my view, the time has come to introduce a common form for the commencement of public prosecutions and to remove from the mass of less serious ones the unnecessary, cumbersome and delaying involvement of the court. The involvement of the station custody officer in the more serious cases is primarily to protect the suspect who is in custody. The courts are well equipped in all cases to determine at an early stage after the

---

[48] Police and Criminal Evidence Act 1984, s 46, which requires suspects to be brought to court no later than the first sitting after charge

[49] Police and Criminal Evidence Act 1984, s 47(3A), as amended by the Crime and Disorder Act 1998, s 46

[50] see *R v Ealing Justices, ex p Dixon* [1990] 2 QB 91; not followed *in R v Stafford Justices, ex p Customs and Excise Commissioners* [1991] 2 QB 339 *and R v Croydon Justices, ex p, Holmberg* (1993) 157 JP 277

[51] Police and Criminal Evidence Act 1984, ss 46 and 47A as amended by the Crime and Disorder Act 1998

commencement of the case the legal propriety of the charge. In addition, with the earlier involvement of the Crown Prosecution Service that is taking place and that I recommend,[52] there should be less, not more, scope for misguided or baseless prosecutions.

56   The need for change of this sort was identified as long ago as 1981 by the Philips Royal Commission, which recommended[53] the replacement of the alternative methods of initiating a prosecution, which it described as "the relics of the mid-nineteenth century system". It observed that the then procedure for charging had no statutory basis[54] and that, in practice, there was little effective magisterial scrutiny in the summons procedure. It recommended that there should be a single procedure for starting public prosecutions, one in which responsibility passed from the police to the prosecutor, that it should be called an 'accusation' and that it should not be subject to any magisterial scrutiny. This is my own view save for the suggested use of the word 'accusation' which, I believe, could be confusing. The word 'charge' conveys more accurately the notion of formal commencement of proceedings and is widely understood in that sense.

57   The common form of procedure for public prosecutions that I have in mind is a charge administered orally, coupled with manual service of a written copy, or by postal service of a written charge, coupled with a statutory requirement to attend court on a specified date on pain of arrest on warrant for failure to do so, as presently required with some summonses.[55] In either case the court should be provided with a written copy of the charge at the same time. The same system could apply to private prosecutions, save that it would be wise to retain the court as a filter for frivolous or vexatious attempts at prosecution by requiring the private prosecutor first to obtain permission from the court to make a charge. Even then it should be administered in written form only by manual or postal service. Existing provisions for listing, whether on prosecution by summons or in charging, should be standardised and extended to other smaller prosecution authorities who initiate their own proceedings. With the development of an integrated system of information technology for the whole of the criminal justice system, the booking of a court time on an 'on-line' court diary should become a simple matter for all prosecuting bodies.

58   I should comment briefly on the procedure of commencing a prosecution by way of a voluntary bill of indictment.[56] Under this procedure the prosecutor may seek the consent of a High Court Judge to prefer an indictment at the

---

[52] see para 44 above

[53] paras 8.3-4 and 10.10

[54] see now Police and Criminal Evidence Act 1984, Code C, para 16.1-16.8

[55] for a fuller discussion of this subject, see paras 61-63 below

[56] see Indictments (Procedure) Rules 1971, r 6

Crown Court without the defendant having been committed, transferred or sent there on the charge the subject of the Bill, or where magistrates have declined to commit him for trial. The procedure had its origin in a Victorian statute,[57] and until the statutory innovations, starting in 1987, of 'transferring' and 'sending' cases to the Crown Court, was the only way[58] of by-passing committal proceedings, or overcoming refusal of magistrates to commit. Its main, albeit exceptional, use was where committal proceedings had been frustrated by the defence or, where there had been a valid committal, to secure the trial of connected matters based on evidence not available at the committal, or to join a defendant who had been separately committed for trial. There seems little point now in retaining a procedure the main rationale of which was to provide an exceptional alternative to committal proceedings, themselves being overtaken by direct access to the Crown Court, and subject to control by the Crown Prosecution Service as to the evidential and public interest merits of prosecution. In my view, the voluntary bill procedure should be abolished and such safeguards as to its use as were provided by a High Court Judge should be built into the common form for public prosecution, final abolition of committal proceedings as a route to trial on indictment and a system of allocation of cases for trial that I recommend.

59   When a case reaches the Crown Court, the original charge or summons is withdrawn and replaced by an indictment. An indictment is no more than a written accusation of the crime after its signature, usually, by a member of court staff. No matter how a case is commenced, the Crown Court cannot try it unless this has occurred. Yet, an indictment normally does little more than re-state in different form the contents of a charge or summons. Although indictments, charges and summonses are governed by similar considerations as to particularity of accusation, duplicity, accuracy and so on, the formalities of drafting and preferring an indictment are peculiar to the Crown Court, in the main contained in the Indictments Act 1915 and the Indictment Rules issued under it.

60   The thousands of indictments that are prepared, lodged and signed each year amount to a significant administrative burden for the prosecution and courts to administer. The strongest argument in favour of the present system, that it acts as a check on the legal basis of the prosecution case, does not withstand examination, since neither by law or practice does the signatory normally consider the contents of the indictment. That is left for the judge at the plea and directions, or other pre-trial hearing. Indictments merely highlight the gap between the Crown Court and magistrates' courts, and further mystify the court process to 'outsiders'. It would be far simpler and more logical to maintain the same form of charge throughout the case and subject it to the same procedural and drafting requirements in all Divisions of the Court. To

---

[57] Vexatious Indictments Act 1859

[58] save for two other rarely used procedures; see *R v Raymond* [1981] 1 QB 910, CA, per Watkins LJ, giving the judgment of the Court at 914F-915C

signify the final settlement of the prosecution case, the prosecution should be required to serve on the court and all parties at the latest by the pre-trial assessment date[59] a final trial copy of the charges on which it will rely. Thereafter, further amendments or alterations should be permissible only with the leave of the trial court.

Warrants

61 The technical requirements for the issue of warrants is complex and detailed, and I do not propose to set them out here, except as necessary to illustrate the problems they present in respect of defendants who fail to appear in response to a summons. At present, failure to attend court on a summons does not automatically result in the issue of a warrant of arrest; the court must first be satisfied that the summons has been served. Assuming that the summons was for a summary-only offence, and was not issued on the basis of information sworn on oath (which the majority will not have been), a police officer, or other suitable person must go to court to swear on oath that the information contained in the summons is true to the best of their knowledge. The court may then issue a warrant for failure to attend.[60] If the matter is indictable, a warrant may be issued without the information being sworn.[61.]

62 I believe that these procedures are unnecessarily complex. There seems little logic in requiring a sworn information in summary-only cases, but not in indictable cases. It is supposed to act as a safeguard, since summonses that are posted may not have come to the notice of the person to whom they are addressed. But if a defendant has not received a postal summons, the procedure of swearing an information on oath does not overcome the problem. It might be intended to be a safeguard against abuse, yet it also fails on that count too, since there is no pretence of testing the witness. Indeed, the Act does not even require that a person with first hand knowledge of the offence swears the information. In many instances it is a wholly unrelated officer who will swear a number of informations at a time, or one who just happens to be available.

63 The procedure is, therefore, expensive and ineffective. I recommend that failure to attend court after a posted charge should enable the court, in its discretion, to issue a warrant for the defendant's arrest. The court could refuse to issue a warrant if there appears to be a defect on the papers, or other material irregularity. The procedure could take place in open court in order to

---

[59] see paras 221-228 below
[60] see Magistrates' Courts Act 1980, s 13
[61] ibid, s 1

ensure open justice, but without the attendance of police officers, merely on their paper application.

I recommend that:

- all public prosecutions should take the form of a charge, issued without reference to the courts, which should remain the basis of the accusation against the defendant throughout all stages of the case, irrespective of the level of court in which it is tried;

- the charge may be oral or in writing, a written copy or original, as the case may be, being served manually or by postal service;

- in either case, under arrangements with the court's administration, the charge should specify the date of first attendance at court on pain of arrest on warrant;

- the present procedure for application for a warrant, by swearing an oath as to service of process, in summary offences should be abolished and replaced by paper application considered and determined in open court;

- the same regime for commencing proceedings should apply to private prosecutions, save that: 1) the charge should only be administered in writing; 2) it should be subject to the prior permission of the court; 3) the permission should be endorsed on the charge sheet by an officer of the court; and 4) the court, before listing the matter should notify the Director of Public Prosecutions;

- the voluntary bill of indictment should be abolished and, to the extent necessary under new procedures of allocation of work in a unified Criminal Court, safeguards should be introduced to secure the interests of justice by Criminal Procedure Rules;

- the form of charge should be common to summary and indictable offences; and

- the prosecution should be entitled to amend the charge up to the pre-trial assessment date (or in a summary trial without such an assessment, up to a date to be specified), but thereafter only with the permission of the trial court.

'Dropping' the prosecution

64 The Crown Prosecution Service and other prosecuting authorities may and should stop a prosecution at any stage if there is insufficient evidence to proceed or the public interest no longer favours a prosecution.[62] There are three main ways of doing so, dependent on the court dealing with the matter and/or the stage of proceedings. The choice is important since on it depends whether the prosecution may later be reinstated. The first is discontinuance on notice. This may be done in a magistrates' court before hearing evidence for the prosecution in summary proceedings, and before committal or 'transfer' for trial in the case of an indictable offence. If the case is 'sent' rather than committed or 'transferred' for trial, the prosecution may discontinue at any time before the indictment is preferred. Subject to the accused's right to insist on continuance to enable him to secure an acquittal and thus bar any further prosecution, the prosecution may later reinstate the prosecution, say, if further evidence becomes available.[63] The second is withdrawal at the hearing in the magistrates' court, again permitting later reinstatement, but without the safeguard to the defendant of enabling him to insist on continuance to enable him to secure an acquittal. The third, the only way in which the prosecution can drop the case in the Crown Court after the indictment is preferred, is the common law device of offering no evidence, resulting in an acquittal and thus, no possibility of further proceedings for the same offence.[64]

65 The Runciman Royal Commission commented on the unnecessary complexity of these different forms and recommended[65] that the prosecution should be given the same power to discontinue cases in the Crown Court as before magistrates. However, the Government declined to follow this, and instead there is a new administrative procedure, available after arraignment and before the defendant is put in charge of a jury, enabling the offering of no evidence and entry of a verdict of not guilty by prior written consent and in the absence of the parties. I agree with the Runciman recommendation. It is clearly sensible to have a single and common form for stopping a case at the prosecution's behest, no matter what level of court or stage of the proceedings the case has reached.

66 Such a simplification is important now that indictable-only cases are reaching the Crown Court more quickly. It will be essential if my recommendations are adopted for abolishing committal proceedings in 'either-way' cases, for a unified Criminal Court and for a common form of charging and allocation of

---

[62] see *Raymond v Attorney General* [1982] QB 398, CA; and see the Code for Crown Prosecutors, which also governs the Serious Fraud Office and is voluntarily applied, with some modifications by other prosecution authorities
[63] Prosecution of Offences Act 1985, ss 23(9), and s 23A(5)
[64] subject to the procedure of leaving a matter 'to lie on the file', (see para 67 below)
[65] *Report Of The Royal Commission On Criminal Justice*, Cmnd 2263, (1993, HMSO),Ch 5, para 37 and recommendation 97

work to the appropriate level of court within it.[66] It is for consideration whether the common form should be of the discontinuance or offering no evidence variety. In either case the defendant can secure a verdict of not guilty, though in the case of discontinuance it is only by dint of insisting on the prosecution continuing, and taking the risk of conviction. In the case of offering no evidence, the decision is almost always ultimately for the prosecution, but can engage the time of the judge if asked, as he frequently is, to approve the prosecutor's decision.

67   In my view, the answer would be to combine the convenience of one procedure with the discipline of the other by enabling the prosecutor to discontinue the proceedings at any stage, up to and including the pre-trial assessment[67] without requiring the consent of the defendant or the approval of the court. This would enable a reinstatement in appropriate cases. The advantage of this procedure would be reduction of paperwork, and avoidance of the need for a hearing in the early stages of a case. But once the pre-trial assessment date has passed, the prosecution would be expected to have properly prepared its case, so that normally there should be no occasion for it to change its mind. If it then decides to drop the case, it should be entered as an acquittal. There would be no court hearing in either case unless required for consequential matters such as costs or return of property. As a safeguard, the prosecution should be able, even after the pre-trial assessment date, to apply to the court to leave the matter to 'lie on the file', but only where it could demonstrate good reason for the late decision, and the judge is satisfied that it is in the public interest. In those cases that would not have a pre-trial assessment date (generally the less serious cases), the defence should be entitled to apply for a formal acquittal upon receipt of the discontinuance notice after a stage specified in Criminal Procedure Rules.

68   Objections that a purely paper or administrative procedure would deprive interested parties, in particular, victims, of learning about the matter in a public hearing could be met by requiring the prosecutor to notify and explain the decision to them in advance of the notice of discontinuance. The Crown Prosecution Service already does this; and I return to that aspect later in the Chapter.[68] I see no danger or injustice to the parties or to any victim in removing from the procedure what remains of the courts' power to influence the outcome. The decision is now in the hands of the Crown Prosecution Service who should have the same competence and a proper regard for the public interest in deciding whether to stop as well as to continue a prosecution.

---

[66] see Ch 7 paras 36 – 40, and paras 200-202 below

[67] see paras 221-228 below

[68] see paras 239-255 below

I recommend that:

- the law should be amended to provide a form of procedure common to all courts to enable a prosecutor, without the consent of the defendant or the approval of the court, to discontinue proceedings at any stage before close of the prosecution case on trial;

- in the event of the prosecution discontinuing at any time before pre-trial assessment or, where there is no pre-trial assessment, before a stage to be specified, the prosecution should be entitled to reinstate the prosecution, subject to the court's power to stay it as an abuse of process;

- in the event of the prosecution discontinuing after that stage, the defendant should be entitled to an acquittal, save where the court for good reason permits the prosecution to 'lie on the file'; and

- there should be common provision for all courts, subject to their approval and the agreement of the parties, to give formal effect to such discontinuance and, where appropriate, acquittal in the absence of the parties.

BAIL

69 A defendant's qualified right to bail must now be considered in the light of Strasbourg jurisprudence on the European Convention of Human Rights. The relevant provisions of the Convention are Article 5(1) and (3) and (4), providing for the right to liberty and security of the person, including entitlement to bail and to court proceedings to enforce it, and also Article 6(2), providing that a person charged with a criminal offence must be presumed innocent until proved guilty. Wherever possible, the courts must also read and give effect to legislation in a way that is compatible with Convention rights. The Law Commission, in a consultation paper in 1999,[69] identified three statutory provisions which, in its provisional view, should be repealed or amended because of a serious risk of non-compliance and consequent risk of claims to compensation. However, in its recent Report *Bail and the Human Rights Act 1998*,[70] it expressed the view that our law of

---

[69] Consultation Paper, Law Comm, No 157, 19th December 1999

[70] Law Comm Report No 269, 21st June 2001

bail is generally compliant with the Convention. More precisely, it concluded:

> "1.9. … there are no provisions which, upon analysis, cannot be interpreted and applied compatibly, or which, given appropriate training, decision-makers would be likely to apply in a way which would violate Convention rights.
>
> 1.10. This does not mean that we have given the law of bail in England and Wales an unequivocal 'clean bill of health' in the sense of being incapable of improvement following a general review…".[71]

The present system

70   After the police have arrested a suspect they may release him on bail or keep him in custody. In the latter event, they must charge him within 24 hours and bring him before a court as soon as possible, normally within 24 hours.[72] If they have not charged him, but wish to hold him while they make further enquiries, and they are investigating a serious arrestable offence, they may extend the period of custody to a maximum of 96 hours with regular scrutiny and warrants of detention from the magistrates' court.[73]

71   At an accused's first appearance before a court, both parties may make representations on the issue of bail and the court must decide whether to remand him on bail or in custody. Initial decisions may be made on inadequate or incorrect information, and defendants wrongly refused bail should have ready access to advice and help on the matter on their remand to prison. The Prison Service has a duty to assist in providing this access and, since September 1999, all remand prisons have been required and funded to provide bail information schemes.[74] Each establishment should have a bail information officer to interview prisoners, assess their cases and assemble information for the courts. Similarly, the Prison Service is obliged to ensure prisoners access to legal advice if they want it,[75] and each establishment should have an officer, known as a Legal Service Officer, for the purpose. The Prison Inspectorate's recent thematic report on the treatment and conditions of remand prisoners recorded wide variation in performance by establishments throughout the country, but over-all performance was pretty poor.[76] The Inspectorate acknowledged that the Prison Service was in a state

---

[71] ibid, paras 1.9-1.10

[72] Police and Criminal Evidence Act 1984, s 41

[73] there are strict criteria for determining whether detention should be authorised; ibid s 42 and 43

[74] Prison Service Orders 6100 and 6101

[75] Prison Service Order 2605

[76] *Unjust Deserts*, paras 4.09-4.17

of transition in the provision of these services and that it was too early to evaluate performance. But it urged effective monitoring by each establishment of their ready availability, and consideration of national monitoring as a key performance target for the Service as a whole.[77] This is clearly another area in which there should be national standards and, probably, protocols to which other agencies, including the Probation Service, the Legal Services Commission, the Bar Council and the Law Society should contribute and be parties.

72   In all cases the magistrates' court is the first court to consider bail. The starting point set out in the Bail Act 1976 is that all defendants charged with an imprisonable offence have a right to bail, save those charged with homicide or rape, previously convicted of such an offence.[78] It is only where the court is satisfied that the defendant falls into one or more of a number of limited exceptions that it "need not" grant bail. I stress the words 'need not', because they preserve the court's discretion or, more accurately, its ability and duty to decide the matter in accordance with the individual circumstances of each case. And, even in cases of homicide and rape, the courts retain an element of discretion since they may still allow bail "if there are exceptional circumstances".[79] The exceptions to the right to bail include where:

- there are substantial grounds for believing that a defendant, if released on bail with or without conditions, would fail to surrender to custody when required, or commit an offence while on bail, or interfere with witnesses or otherwise obstruct the course of justice;

- in a case triable on indictment, the defendant was on bail at the date of the alleged offence;[80]

- he should be kept in custody for his own protection or, if he is a child or a young person, for his own welfare;

- it has not been practicable to obtain sufficient information for the purpose of taking the decision because of the shortness of time since the institution of the proceedings; and

- if, having been granted bail in the present proceedings, the defendant has been arrested for absconding or breaching a bail condition.

73   In deciding these questions, the court is required to have regard to: the nature and seriousness of the alleged offence and the probable sentence for it if the defendant is convicted; his character, associations and community ties; his

---

[77] ibid, paras 4.18 and 4.19

[78] s 4; and Criminal Justice and Public Order Act 1994, s25

[79] introduced by amendment by the Crime and Disorder Act 1998, s 56 following the decision of the European Court in *Caballero v UK* [2000] Crim LR 587

[80] The Law Commission have recommended amendment of the Act so as to relegate this to one of the factors which the court may take into account when considering whether a defendant comes within any of the main statutory exceptions; Report, para 4.11

previous bail record, if any; and, except where the case is adjourned for inquiries or a report, the strength of the prosecution case.[81]

74 Where the court is minded to grant bail, it may do so subject to requiring the defendant to provide a surety or sureties or to give a security for his surrender and/or to imposing such conditions as appear to be necessary to meet the various contingencies against which it might otherwise refuse bail. [82]

Criteria

75 Deciding whether to grant or refuse bail is a difficult exercise, based as it is on predictions about future behaviour. Grant of bail may enable a defendant rightly to retain his liberty and his job or wrongly to commit an offence whilst on bail. A refusal may unnecessarily deprive him of his liberty or rightly prevent him from committing offences that he would have committed if on bail. The main criteria in the 1976 Act that I have mentioned are designed to balance the right of an innocent person, or one who should not in any event merit a custodial sentence, from being wrongfully deprived of his liberty and the need to protect the public from a person awaiting trial with a propensity to commit offences during that time. As I have said, the Law Commission is of the view that the criteria and the statutory scheme of which they form part are capable of being applied in a manner compliant with the Convention. Quite apart from the Convention, the general tenor of submissions in the Review has been that they are about as good a formulation as can be devised to strike a fair balance between the two interests.

Quality and inconsistency of bail decisions

76 The problem is rather the way in which many courts interpret and apply the criteria. The consequence of 'wrong' grants of bail can be serious and far-reaching. The most recent Home Office research suggests that persons responsible for a large proportion of offences are not being identified and restrained early enough in the criminal justice process, particularly at the stage of consideration of bail.[83] The research indicated that in 1998 24% of a sample of 1,283 alleged offenders granted bail were subsequently convicted or cautioned for an offence committed whilst on bail. For cases within that sample of vehicle crime and shop lifting, the percentage rose to over 40%.

---

[81] Bail Act 1976, Sched 1 Part I, para 9

[82] ibid s 4 and Schedule 1, Part I, paras 2, 2A, 3 and 5 and 6; the Law Commission have recommended that the Act should be amended to make clear that the court must be satisfied that there are substantial grounds for believing that the defendant, if released on bail, would commit further offences, fail to surrender to bail, interfere with witnesses or otherwise obstruct the course of justice. See Report para 7.35

[83] *Offending on Bail and Police Use of Conditional Bail,* Home Office Research Findings, No 72

Unsurprisingly, the longer the period of bail, the more likelihood there was of offending in the course of it. Thus, nearly 30% of those on bail for over six months offended in the course of it, compared to nearly 15% of those brought to trial within two months.

77 The Home Office figures also indicated that 30% of young offenders breached their conditions of bail and that their rate of offending was over double that of adults. In many instances, continuation of bail notwithstanding, breaches of the original bail resulted in further breaches. As the Association of Chief Police Officers have pointed out,[84] the courts are handicapped in the case of persistent young offenders. By section 23 of the Children and Young Persons Act 1969, they cannot require them to be remanded in secure accommodation unless they are of the opinion that "only such a requirement would be adequate to protect the public from serious harm" from them. There is evidence, from the police and others, that many courts seemingly do not regard driving stolen vehicles at speed, house burglary (unless accompanied by violence) or street robbery as representing 'serious harm' for this purpose. Perhaps the answer would be to amend section 23 to allow custody for persistent young offenders in cases where previous grants of custody have failed.

78 There is much criticism of the quality and of the lack of consistency of bail decisions.[85] The criticism falls more heavily on magistrates' courts than the Crown Court, because magistrates deal with most bail applications, often in the course of a crowded list and with insufficient information. A recent study of two London Magistrates' Courts showed an average length for bail proceedings of six minutes.[86] As to information, despite the introduction in 1988 of bail information schemes, it is often incomplete and for that and other reasons inaccurate. A research study for the Home Office in 1998[87] commented on the lack of ready availability to the police, prosecutors and magistrates of the defendant's criminal record and other relevant information, the need for training of magistrates and police custody officers in risk assessment, more and better bail information and support schemes, simplification of bail notices to defendants so that they know exactly what is required of them and changes in listing to enable more communication between the responsible agencies before the first remand hearing.

79 Another problem is that lay magistrates, who often sit in differently constituted panels, are, understandably, less consistent than their professional

---

[84] in their submission in the Review

[85] see generally: Morgan and Henderson, *Remand Decisions and Offending on Bail: Evaluation of the Bail Process Project* 1998, Home Office Research Study No 184; Dhami and Ayton, *Bailing and Jailing the Fast and Frugal Way*, (2001) Journal of Behavioural Decision Making

[86] Dhami and Ayton, ibid

[87] Morgan and Henderson, op cit

colleagues, the District Judges who sit full time. The problem should not be overstated. The quest is for consistency in approach and general outcomes, not uniformity of individual decisions. In such a difficult predictive exercise, balancing the interests of the defendant against those of the public, where decisions have to be made quickly, and often with insufficient information, it is to be expected that seemingly similar cases sometimes result in different decisions.

80   However, the degree, or perceived degree, of inconsistency in magistrates' bail decisions is capable of undermining public confidence in the criminal justice system, and there should be no let up in attempts to reduce significant inconsistencies. With the advent of Convention rights to our law, it is even more important that magistrates and judges should persist in this endeavour. The Law Commission, has urged that they should be provided with appropriate training and guidance on the making of bail decisions, with Article 5 particularly in mind. It also proposed, as a practical aid to correctness and consistency that all courts should record their decisions in such a way as to indicate clearly how they had been reached. I strongly support those proposals.

81   There is also some evidence of a laxness on the part of the Crown Prosecution Service and the courts to breaches of conditions of bail, the outcome often being a relaxation of the conditions. ACPO has observed:

> "... Bail conditions rarely inhibit recidivists from committing further crime and police efforts to enforce bail are generally regarded with indifference by the courts. We should underline here that the complaint from police forces right across the country was unremitting, that when arrests were made for breach of bail, conditions were usually relaxed.
>
> ... Advancing applications for remands in custody and dealing with defence applications for bail is not an issue which the Crown Prosecution Service generally take on with any zeal.... [I]t is an almost universal observation of operational police officers that the Crown Prosecution Service are generally 'lukewarm' to this procedure".[88]

82   Such figures and descriptions, the latter replicated in many individual submissions in the Review, suggest that, however appropriate the criteria for balancing defendants' and the public interest, the manner of their application, particularly in the case of young recidivists, often frustrates the central aim of the criminal justice system – crime control. This defect is all too public. It is of understandable concern to victims of such crimes and the public generally

---

[88] in its submission in the Review

who look to the courts to fulfil their role in that over-all objective. It is also dispiriting to police officers in their task of catching criminals and bringing them to justice.

I recommend that:

- magistrates and judges in all courts should take more time to consider matters of bail;

- listing practices should reflect the necessity to devote due time to bail applications and allow the flexibility required for all parties to gather sufficient information for the court to make an appropriate decision;

- courts, the police, prosecutors and defence representatives should be provided with better information for the task than they are at present, in particular, complete and up-to-date information of the defendant's record held on the Police National Computer, relevant probation or other social service records, if any, verified information about home living conditions and employment, if any, and sufficient information about the alleged offence and its relationship, if any, to his record so as to indicate whether there is a pattern of offending;

- courts and all relevant agencies should be equipped with a common system of information technology, as recommended in Chapter 8, to facilitate the ready availability to all who need it of the above information;

- there should be appropriate training for magistrates and judges in the making of bail decisions, with Article 5 ECHR and risk assessment particularly in mind, as the Law Commission has proposed;

- all courts should be provided with an efficient bail information and support scheme;

- bail notices should be couched in plain English, printed and given to the defendant as a formal court order when the bail decision is made, so that he understands exactly what is required of him and appreciates the seriousness of the grant of bail and of any attached conditions; and

- all courts should be diligent in adopting the Law Commission's proposals that they should record their bail decisions in such a way as to indicate clearly how they have been reached.

Appeals

83   Contributors to the Review have raised three main issues about appeals from bail decisions: first, the relationship between a defendant's right of appeal to the Crown Court against refusal and his right of recourse to a High Court Judge; second, as to the need for a right of appeal against conditions; and third, as to the extent of the prosecution's right of appeal against the grant of bail.

Appeal to the Crown Court and application to a High Court Judge

84   A defendant has a right of appeal to the Crown Court from a refusal to grant bail, but not against conditions magistrates have imposed on its grant.[89] There, the chain of appeal ends, though anomalously there is a statutory right in all cases to apply to a High Court Judge against magistrates' refusal of bail or the imposition of conditions in the grant of bail, empowering the judge, save in cases of homicide or rape, to grant bail or vary the conditions.[90] And a High Court Judge, sitting in chambers, also has an inherent and distinct power from that when sitting in the Crown Court, to grant bail before and after a case is committed or sent to the Crown Court.[91] This jurisdiction overlaps the original and appellate jurisdiction of the Crown Court.   If nothing else, there are question marks about the right of defendants refused bail by a Crown Court judge in the exercise of his original or appellate jurisdiction, being able to renew the same application to a High Court Judge and, in the case of a conditional grant of leave by magistrates, to challenge the imposition of those conditions before a High Court Judge, but not by way of appeal to the Crown Court.

85   This is all a bit of a muddle and wasteful duplication of process.   There may long have been a good reason for keeping the High Court Judge as a long-stop in support of the liberty of the subject.   But there is less of an imperative for it now. We have a permanently manned Crown Court all over the country which can deal with the matter by way of appeal, and those detained in custody no longer have to await the next visit on circuit of the High Court Judge or apply to a judge in Chambers in London to seek release.   It is a separate and parallel, not appellate, jurisdiction.

86   In my view, there is no longer any need for a High Court Judge to consider afresh the grant of bail after refusal by a magistrates' court or the Crown

---

[89] Supreme Court Act 1981, s 81(1)(g)

[90] Criminal Justice Act 1967, s 22(1)

[91] *R v Reading Crown Court, ex p Malik* [1981] QB 451 72 Cr App R 146, DC

Court. If the magistrates' court and a Crown Court judge, the latter on an original application or appeal by way of re-hearing, acting within the proper bounds of their discretion, have refused bail, it is an anomaly that another judge, albeit a High Court Judge, is entitled to exercise a further discretion in the matter. It seems to me more in accord with principle, and a better use of judicial resources, to confine any reopening of a bail decision in the Crown Court, to an appeal to a High Court Judge on a point of law. There should be an initial application in writing for leave to appeal. It should identify with precision the point of law involved, which should not include complaints about the exercise of discretion dressed up as points of law. If the High Court Judge, on examination of the application, considers that there is an arguable point of law, he should grant leave for an appeal by way of oral hearing.

87   The Law Commission have concluded that our bail procedures are in practice unlikely to breach Article 5(4) or such procedural requirements of Article 6 as are appropriate to bail applications.[92] I do not believe that the reform that I propose would breach those rights. What is required is 'judicial supervision' of a decision to remand in custody, which, the European Court has held, implies certain characteristics, namely that the defendant must be able to participate in the proceedings, that they must be adversarial in nature and possibly, if the defendant so requires, that they must be in public. It does not require, in addition, a right of appeal, or where, as here the Crown Court has dealt with the matter on appeal from magistrates, a further right of appeal.

I recommend the removal of the right of application to a High Court Judge for bail after determination by any criminal court exercising its original or appellate jurisdiction, and the substitution therefor of a right of appeal from the District Division or Crown Division (Crown Court) on a point of law only.

Conditions

88   Conditional bail is permitted by Article 5(3) of the Convention. And the lack of provision for a defendant to appeal to the Crown Court against conditions imposed on the grant of bail does not appear to infringe Article 5(4).[93] Quite independently of compliance with the Convention, it seems to me sensible, in general, to restrict a defendant's right of appeal against conditional grant of bail. Otherwise the appellate process could be corrupted by endless wrangling over conditions that in most cases should be manageable for the defendant. There are two possible exceptions in the case of conditional bail granted in the magistrates' courts. The first is where he cannot comply with a

---

[92] op cit, Part XI; and see *De Wilde, Ooms and Versyp v Belgium* (No 1) A12 1971 1 EHRR 373, overruling its earlier decision in *Neumeister v Austria* (No 1) A 8 (1968) 1 EHRR 91, para 24

[93] see para 87

condition of residence away from the area of the alleged offence or the home of a victim or witness and there is no suitable bail hostel placement. The second is a requirement to provide sureties or to give a security. In my view, there is a strong case in those instances for allowing an appeal from magistrates or a district judge to the Crown Division of a new unified Criminal Court (Crown Court).

I recommend that defendants should have a right of appeal against conditional grants of bail from the Magistrates' Division (magistrates' courts) to the Crown Division (Crown Court) in respect of conditions imposed as to their residence away from home and/or to the provision of a surety or sureties or the giving of security.

Prosecution appeals

89   There is also an issue about the prosecution right of appeal against the grant of bail. It has a limited right of appeal to the Crown Court against magistrates' grant of bail, but not against any attached conditions. The Bail (Amendment) Act 1993[94] confers a right of appeal only where the alleged offence is punishable with imprisonment for five years or more or is an offence of taking a vehicle without authority or of aggravated vehicle taking. And there are strict procedural safeguards to control the exercise of the right.[95] In addition, the Crown Prosecution Service's internal guidance for prosecutors urges them to do so "judiciously and responsibly" and only in cases of "grave concern". As is plain, the number of cases in which the prosecution may appeal are relatively small, and it has exercised the right in very few cases.

90   Given the difficulty for magistrates and judges deciding the matter at first instance of assessing the risk of (further) offending by those to whom they grant bail and to the potentially enormous damage to the public if they get it wrong, there is a strong case for removing the high threshold for prosecution appeals. Why, in any event, should it be limited to offences attracting custodial sentences of five years or more if the Service's criterion is 'grave concern'? And, if the test is to be one of 'grave concern', or something like it, it does not follow that the yardstick should be the seriousness of the offence, at whatever level that is pitched. Widespread or day-to-day commission of relatively less serious crimes justify similar provision. Some may amount to what are called in North America, 'quality of life' crimes and, regardless of their individual seriousness, can have a powerful impact on the local community's sense of security. In my view, the right should be extended to all cases that may attract custodial or part custodial sentences, subject to the same or similar procedural safeguards as those provided in the 1993 Act and

---

[94] s 1
[95] s 1(3) –(8) and Magistrates' Courts Rules 1981, r 93A

guidance to prosecutors that it is to be used with great care and only in exceptional cases.

I recommend that the prosecution should have a right of appeal to the Crown Division (Crown Court) against the grant of bail by the Magistrates' Division (magistrates' courts) in respect of all offences that would, on conviction, be punishable by a custodial, or partly custodial sentence.

ADVANCE INDICATION OF SENTENCE

91   I have called this section 'Advance indication of sentence' to underline its distinction from what is commonly called 'plea' or 'charge bargaining'. In this country, where the prosecutor has no responsibility for seeking or recommending a particular sentence, the bargaining mainly takes the form of his agreeing to drop certain charges or proceed on lesser ones in exchange for pleas of guilty to other or lesser charges. The advantage to the prosecutor, as representing the public, is that it avoids the need for a trial and consequent ordeal for victims and witnesses; and the benefit to the defendant is that he can expect a discount on sentence for his plea of guilty. The court is not a party to the agreement. The prosecuting advocate is not obliged to seek its approval, but if he does, he must abide by its view. If he does not seek the court's view, he should nevertheless inform it of what he intends to do and, if it volunteers its disapproval, he should take the view of the Director of Public Prosecutions before continuing.[96] In either event, there is no question of any agreement with or undertaking by the court as to sentence, save that it is constrained by the sentencing limits for the offence to which the defendant has pleaded guilty and should reflect the plea by a sentencing discount appropriate in the circumstances. This form of plea bargaining, though involving questions of high principle as to the sentencing process and the role in it of a sentencing discount for pleas of guilty, has not been the main focus of contributions in this area to the Review.

92   The possibility of advance indication by the court of sentence for a plea of guilty, which is not presently permitted, has attracted greater attention. Unlike plea or charge bargaining, it would not amount to a reduction of charge in exchange for a plea of guilty, but it would introduce an element of a bargain between the defendant and the court as to sentence in the event of a plea of guilty. If introduced, it would enable a defendant to know in advance where he would stand as to sentence if he pleaded guilty.

---

[96] see the Report of a Committee chaired by Lord Justice Farquharson, (Counsel Magazine May 1986) and *R v Jenkins* (1986) 83 Cr App R 152l

93 The issue arises for discussion because of the now well established practice of judges and, more recently, of magistrates, of discounting the 'normal' severity of sentence because of a plea of guilty, a practice now statutorily recognised.[97] The extent of the discount, for which there is still no set common law or statutory tariff, is usually within a range of 25% to 30%.[98] But it may be lower or higher than that range depending on special factors in the case. The main factors influencing the extent of the discount are how early the plea was proffered, whether its effect was to spare witnesses from the trauma of having to give evidence, whether the defendant has assisted the police, say, in the recovery of property, and also whether the defendant had little option but to plead guilty at some stage because of the strength of the prosecution case.[99] The rationale for this practice is to encourage guilty defendants to plead guilty early and thereby save public expense and private disturbance and anxiety that would otherwise have resulted from a trial. Those are usually the matters to which judges refer in their sentencing remarks when commenting on and justifying the discount, though sometimes they also talk of the plea of guilty as evidence of the defendant's 'remorse'.

94 Given the existence of such a sentencing practice, it is to be expected that a guilty defendant may wish to know what sentence he is likely to receive if he pleads guilty as against that to which he is at risk if he goes to trial. Formerly, although the practice of judges and courts varied, the defendant's counsel could seek and obtain an indication from the judge about this in his room. However, in 1970 the Court of Appeal, in *R v Turner*, sought to put an end to private meetings of this sort with the judge, save in exceptional cases.[100] The Court held that, even in such exceptional cases, the judge should not indicate the sentence he was minded to impose, save where he intended, whatever the plea, to impose or not impose a particular sentence. There are indications, despite the Court's ruling in *Turner* and its several subsequent and emphatic reminders of it, some judges and defence advocates have continued to breach it in different ways. They have no doubt been motivated for the best, for example, to secure the best possible outcome for defendants minded to acknowledge their guilt, to save vulnerable witnesses from the distress and trauma of giving evidence and to avoid great public expense of a long trial.

95 In 1993 the Runciman Royal Commission recommended that there should be a more clearly articulated system of graduated discounts so that, other things being equal, the earlier the plea the higher the discount. It also proposed a relaxation of the *Turner* rule to permit the judge, at the defendant's request, to

---

[97] Powers of Criminal Courts (Sentencing) Act 2000, s 152, reproducing the Criminal Justice and Public Order Act 1994, s 48 as amended by the Crime (Sentences) Act 1997
[98] See eg *R v Buffrey* (1993) 14 Cr App R (S) 511, CA
[99] see eg *R v Hollington and Emmens* (1985) 7 Cr App R 364, CA
[100] 54 Cr App R 322, CA

indicate in advance the highest sentence he would impose for a plea at that stage. It did not recommend that the judge should be permitted to indicate what sentence he would impose as compared with that which he might impose on conviction after a trial, because it considered that it could put pressure on some defendants who were not guilty to plead guilty for fear of being convicted and receiving the higher sentence.[101]

96   The National Audit Office, in its Report, *Criminal Justice: Working Together*, noted that information on the use of sentence discounts was not routinely collected and that a Court Service review had found that defendants often did not believe they would be given sufficient credit for an early plea. It recommended that the Home Office and Lord Chancellor's Department should: collect information on the use of sentence discounts; evaluate their impact on defendant behaviour; and review whether the system could be improved to encourage those defendants who plead guilty to do so as early as possible.[102] Governmental response to those recommendations has so far been muted, seemingly because of expected resistance from the bench to any requirement that they should identify, when sentencing, the sentence discount given for a plea in isolation from other mitigating factors.

97   Many of the judiciary and most criminal practitioners would like to see a return to the pre-*Turner* regime, albeit conducted in a more formal manner. They regard the matter pragmatically – given the existence of a system of sentence discounts for pleas of guilty – as a means of encouraging defendants to face up to their guilt at an early stage and before putting the public, victims and others involved to the expense and trouble of an unnecessary trial. Put another way, it would reduce the number of 'cracked trials', that is, of guilty defendants only pleading guilty at the last minute, and of guilty defendants taking their chance with a trial hoping that something may just save them from conviction. There are, of course, other reasons why defendants do not face up to their guilt earlier, including overcharging, inadequate and late preparation of the case by one or both sides and short-term considerations of retaining as long as possible their right to bail or their privileges as unconvicted remand prisoners.

98   The Bar Council and many others have urged a relaxation of the *Turner* rules. They propose a system of advance indication of sentence in the event of a possible plea of guilty, but without commitment as to the likely sentence in the event of a trial. They suggest that that such a system should have the following features:

  • a publicly well defined and consistently applied scale of minimum discounts according to the stage in the proceedings that the plea is offered;

---

[101] Chapter 7, paras 41-58 and recommendations 156-163

[102] HC 29 Session 1999-00, 1st December 2000, paras 5.26-5.28 and recommendation 48

- the discounts should be such as to secure for the defendant a significant reduction in sentence;

- the level of discount above the appropriate minimum would remain a matter for the judge's discretion, but in exercising it, he should disregard the strength of the prosecution case since otherwise that could undermine the incentive to a defendant to enter an early plea;

- the judge should indicate the sentence he would give in the event of a plea of guilty and what his sentence *might* be if the matter went to trial;

- the present disincentive to early pleas of guilty of loss of bail or change of status for remand prisoners should be removed; and

- the procedure should be subject to review by the Court of Appeal on a reference by the Attorney General, but without power to the Court of Appeal to increase individual sentences.

99   The Bar Council suggests the following procedure. It would be for the defendant, through his advocate, to initiate it by requesting an advance indication of sentence from the judge. Before doing so, his advocate should advise him firmly that he should not plead guilty unless he is guilty. The application would be made formally in court, though sitting in private, in the presence of the defendant and his legal advisers and of the prosecution advocate. The proceedings would be recorded. The judge should satisfy himself through canvassing the matter with both advocates as to the mental competence and emotional state of the defendant and as to whether he might be under any pressure falsely to admit guilt. He should firmly warn the defendant that he should not plead guilty unless he is guilty. If satisfied as to those matters and as to the sufficiency of the information before him of the circumstances of the offence, the judge should indicate the maximum sentence he would give in the event of a plea of guilty

100   Arrayed against that seemingly just and pragmatic solution to the long-standing problems of 'cracked' and unnecessary trials and the advantage to defendants in knowing where they stand, there are powerful arguments of principle voiced in the main by leading academics.[103] They are directed, not so much against a clearer articulation of the system of sentence discounting for a plea of guilty or the relaxation of the *Turner* rule, but at the very existence of pleas of guilty as part of our criminal justice process and, in any event, against the practice of discounting sentence for a plea of guilty.

101   As to the former, Professor Ashworth and others have referred to the general absence in European jurisdictions of a procedure for pleading guilty and have

---

[103] see, in particular, Andrew Ashworth, *The Criminal Process: An Evaluative Study*, (OUP, 1998, 2nd ed), pp 276-297, and Penny Darbyshire, *The Mischief of Plea Bargaining and Sentencing Rewards* [2000] Crim LR 895 and the many sources there cited

urged consideration of abolition of the guilty plea itself, say, in indictable cases. They suggest replacing it with some form of judicial scrutiny of the acknowledgement of guilt. However, Professor Ashworth rightly acknowledges that "there would be tremendous difficulties in such a great cultural change".[104] I have to confess to timidity about such a radical approach given the state of development of our sentencing law and practice. There would be obvious problems in devising a new criminal justice system equipped to subject every serious criminal case to judicial scrutiny of some sort to test an acknowledgement of guilt against all the other evidence, in order to evaluate the fact of guilt and the extent of it. I cannot see in what practical way it would improve the quality or administration of justice or what significant, if any, advantage the public or defendants would gain from it. The comparison, often made in this context, with bench trials in Philadelphia, is unhelpful. There, they have earned the description of 'slow pleas of guilty' to meet those cases in which, under that State's plea bargaining system, the prosecutor and defendant have been unable to make a bargain as to the disposal of the case, and the defendant opts instead for trial by judge alone in the hope of persuading him of the level of culpability for which he contends.

102   As to the challenge to our present system of discounting sentence for a plea of guilty, Professor Ashworth's and others' arguments include the following: [105]

- defendants who plead guilty, and by that means secure a lower sentence than would have been imposed on conviction, receive a benefit that they do not deserve, since a plea of guilty does not reduce their culpability or need for punishment and/or containment;

- it is contrary to the presumption of innocence and, by implication, the defendant's entitlement to require the prosecution to prove his guilt, that, as a result of requiring it to do so, he should receive a more severe sentence than if he had admitted guilt;

- although a defendant can waive that entitlement, a system of discounting sentences is an incentive and, therefore capable of amounting to an improper pressure on him to do so;

- in other jurisdictions, for example, Scotland, no discount is given for a plea and to do so would be regarded as an improper inducement; and in many European countries, at least formally, admission of guilt is not a mitigating factor for the purpose of determining sentence;

- victims, though relieved of the ordeal of having to give evidence, may be unhappy about the lower sentence secured by the plea and untested mitigation; and

- discounting sentence for pleas of guilty indirectly discriminates against defendants from ethnic minorities who, regardless of their guilt or innocence,

---

[104] op cit, p 295

[105] op cit p 276-297

tend to maintain a plea of not guilty and, in consequence on conviction, face a greater risk of custody and longer sentences than white offenders.[106]

103   As to the effect, or lack of effect, of a plea of guilty on culpability, admission of guilt may not significantly reduce a defendant's blameworthiness for the offence at the time he committed it. But it flies in the face of reason to reject the admission as a relevant factor when later sentencing him, along with other circumstances which, similarly, may not bear directly on culpability such as presence or absence of previous convictions, age or current state of health, prospect of rehabilitation and the making of reparation. Given the fact of guilt, it must be a mitigating factor to admit it and an aggravating factor to persist in denying it. It is a shame that the Court of Appeal, in developing and articulating the practice of discounting sentences for guilty pleas, has not faced up to this. It has persisted in encouraging judges openly to reduce sentence for pleas of guilty while illogically enjoining them not to be open about imposing a heavier sentence (than would have been imposed on a plea of guilty) because they have persisted in denying guilt. As Professor Ashworth has noted, depending on which way you look at it, a 30% discount for a plea is equivalent to a 50% increase in sentence for unsuccessfully maintaining a plea of not guilty.[107] In my view, once guilt has been established, there is no logical reason why a dishonest plea of not guilty should not be openly treated as an aggravating factor just as an honest plea of guilty is treated and rewarded as a mitigating factor.

104   As to the argument of the effect of a sentence discount on the presumption of innocence, it only gets off the ground, and then not very far, if one equates the presumption of innocence with a right of a man subsequently found to be guilty to have put the prosecution to proof of his guilt. In my view, it is an incident of the presumption of innocence and criminal burden of proof that a defendant facing a criminal charge can require the prosecution to prove it, but that falls far short of saying that, once guilt has been established in one manner or other, that his sentence should be the same regardless. Neither our domestic law before the advent of the European Human Rights, nor the Convention itself, in particular Article 6(2), in terms or in spirit goes that far.

105   As to a system of sentence discount amounting to an improper inducement or pressure on a defendant to plead guilty when he is not guilty,[108] it is by this route, if at all, that the presumption of innocence as articulated in Article 6 and other Convention protections might enter the scene. Of course, if the present discounting practice operated in a fashion likely to induce significant numbers of innocent defendants to plead guilty when they are not, there might

---

[106] see Roger Hood, *Race and Sentencing: A Study in the Crown Court*, Oxford, 1992; and see the Runciman Royal Commission Report, Chapter 7, para 58

[107] *The Criminal Process: An Evaluative Study* p 288

[108] ibid pp 292-297

be a cause for concern. But the mere availability of a discount for a plea of guilty as one of a number of matters of mitigation, when coupled with a system requiring defendants to be properly advised, does not, in my view, justify characterising it as an improper inducement or pressure on an innocent defendant wrongly to admit guilt. For the reasons I have given in the last paragraph, I again distinguish between the innocent defendant and the defendant who knows he is guilty and might be minded to put the prosecution to proof of his guilt. A sentencing system should not be tailored or modified to encourage the latter to try his luck; or at least it should not reward him with the same sentence he would have received if he had not done so. Of course, no system can guarantee that individual defendants, however innocent, will not regard the likelihood of a lesser sentence as an incentive to trade it for the risk of conviction and a more serious sentence, or that lawyers will not sometimes advise their clients badly. But those are not reasons for rejecting a sentencing practice if in general it serves a proper sentencing purpose, operates justly and assists the efficient administration of justice.

106 As to the interests of victims, as I say in Chapter 11,[109] it is vital that they should be fully informed of the course of a case concerning them, that they should have an opportunity to indicate to the court the effect on them of the crime and that they should be told the reasons for its outcome. The present sentence discounting system does not affect any of those imperatives or the improving provision now being made for them, except possibly when the *Turner* rules are not observed. The proposals to bring greater openness and clarity to the exercise of sentence discounting for pleas of guilty should remove that problem and secure more effective recognition of their interest when proceedings take this turn

107 Finally, there is the argument that discounting sentences for pleas of guilty indirectly discriminates against ethnic minority offenders because they tend to plead not guilty more than white offenders and thus, when convicted, face a greater risk of custody and longer sentences than white offenders. This argument, like the earlier ones, depends largely on the equation of the presumption of innocence with the right of a guilty man to put the prosecution to proof of his guilt. The fact that, statistically, ethnic minority offenders may suffer more severe punishment than their white counterparts is a feature of the adversarial system, of which, if the research referred to is correct, they have chosen to take greater advantage. As in all adversarial systems someone has to lose, and the consequence of a defendant's loss in this one is that the presumption of his innocence has been rebutted. He, therefore, faces the sentencing consequences of all offenders who have taken the same route. Whether or not this nevertheless justifies the description of indirect discrimination, it is one that is self inflicted, for whatever reason. If the reason is one of perception - perception of discrimination in the workings of

---

[109] para 72

the justice system - the answer, as I have said before, is to remove any malfunctioning of that sort and adequately to inform the public of it, not to skew the system generally to meet one element of society's perceptions of it.

108   However, to conclude this difficult subject on that level of generality would be unsatisfactory and not particularly constructive. It is important to discover why one group of defendants, distinguished only by their ethnicity, should behave differently from others when faced with the same choices. There are two possible explanations. First, maybe we are not comparing like with like; perhaps, proportionately more innocent ethnic minority defendants are charged and prosecuted than innocent white defendants. Or second, all things being equal, ethnic minorities may behave differently from white defendants because of their perception of the treatment they will receive. It might of course be both of these possibilities. But we need to know, because if there is a malaise it needs to be identified and treated. On the information obtained in the Review, I cannot say that discrimination, direct or indirect, exists in this respect. And I do not consider that removal of the discount for a guilty plea because of these different behavioural patterns would be necessary or, in itself, sufficient to remove any discrimination that may exist. The matter needs to be thoroughly researched and monitored, aided by suitable information technology, to gather and analyse all relevant data. A priority, I suggest, for the Criminal Justice Board, the establishment of which I have recommended.[110]

109   Turning to the proposals for reform of our present system, like the Runciman Royal Commission, I do not see how clearer articulation of the well known principle of greater discounts for earlier pleas, or relaxation of the *Turner* rule to permit judges formally to indicate a maximum sentence in the event of a plea, would increase the risk of defendants pleading guilty to offences that they have not committed. As to how such reforms should be introduced, there are difficulties in doing it by statute, with the draftsman's tendency to be overly prescriptive. Apart from anything else, there would be difficulty in isolating graduated discounts for early pleas of guilty from other elements of mitigation. The Runciman formula of graduated discounts, *other things being equal*, might be the way, but would not lend itself readily to statutory formulation. Perhaps the answer would be for the Court of Appeal, in consultation with the Sentencing Advisory Board to devise a scheme for expression by the Court in a Sentencing Guideline, which could subsequently be embodied in a Sentencing Code.[111]

110   As to relaxation of the *Turner* rule, at whatever stage a defendant considers pleading guilty in the expectation of a lesser sentence for doing so, it is, of course, vital that he is properly and firmly advised by his advisers and left to

---

[110] see the Runciman Royal Commission Report, Chapter 7, para 58, and recommendation 163
[111] see Chapter 11, para 198

make his own choice. The fact that he may seek an indication from the judge of the likely maximum sentence before doing so, would not, it seems to me, materially increase the risk of untrue pleas of guilty. On the question of possible ethnic disadvantage because those from ethnic minorities are less likely to plead guilty, to the extent that it exists I do not see why it should be materially aggravated by clearer articulation of an existing sentencing practice or by relaxation of the *Turner* rule to allow a defendant who wishes to know where he stands, being told.

111   In my view, the proposed reforms would be of appropriate benefit to guilty defendants, to others, in particular victims and witnesses, involved in criminal proceedings and to the system in general in the reduction of 'cracked' and unnecessary trials. As to the problem of 'cracked' trials, the reforms should be supported, as the Runciman Royal Commission recommended, by retention of bail by those on bail and extension to convicted prisoners awaiting sentence privileges enjoyed by unconvicted prisoners.[112]

112   I do not agree with the Runciman Royal Commission that a system under which a judge informs a defendant both of the maximum sentence on a plea of guilty and the possible sentence on conviction after trial would amount to unacceptable pressure on him. That comparison is precisely what a defendant considering admitting his guilt wants to know. He knows and will, in any event, be advised by his lawyer that a plea of guilty can attract a lesser sentence and broadly what the possible outcomes are, depending on his plea. So what possible additional pressure, unacceptable or otherwise, can there be in the judge, whom he has requested to tell him where he stands, indicating more precisely the alternatives? As Douglas Day, QC, put it in a persuasive address to the Millenium Bar Conference in 2000, an open system under which a defendant "can know the sentencing options will put no more pressure on him than firm advice, in ignorance of the reality, from his legal advisers".[113]

113   In my view, the judge should tell a defendant who wishes to know the maximum sentence he would receive in the event of a plea of guilty as compared with the possible sentence on conviction after trial. Such indication, coupled with the clearer public articulation of graduated discounts for advance pleas of guilty, would enable the guilty defendant and those advising him to evaluate the judge's indication and assess the advantage or otherwise of proceeding with a plea. Where there are co-defendants and only one of them seeks an advance indication of sentence on a plea of guilty, the judge

---

[112] in response to a request from the Senior Presiding Judge, the Lord Chancellor in early 2000 reopened with the Home Office the issue of loss of immediate loss of remand privileges on entering a plea of guilty. I say 'reopened' the issue because earlier approaches on the subject had been opposed by the Prison Service because of operational reasons and cost. So far as I am aware, those reasons continue to prevail

[113] *Plea Bargaining,* 14th October 2000

would have to decide whether his role and culpability were sufficiently identifiable at that stage to enable him to give an indication or whether he could not do so until all the evidence had been heard. Such a system, which formally and openly involves the defendant and his advisers throughout would not, I believe, violate Article 6 ECHR. Indeed, it should be fairer than the present one since it would enable a defendant who might wish to benefit from an early plea to do so on a far better informed basis.

114   The mechanics are important. The procedure should only be initiated by the defendant after taking advice from his lawyers, which advice should include a firm warning that he should not plead guilty unless he is guilty. The request should be made formally in court, sitting in private, and should be fully recorded. It should be made in the presence of the prosecution and the defendant and his advisers. Both parties should be equipped to put before the judge all relevant information about the offence and the defendant to enable the judge to give an indication. This may not always be possible straightaway, for example, if a pre-sentence report is not available, as it mostly won't be if the defendant has hitherto pleaded or indicated a plea of not guilty. Once the judge is satisfied that he has enough information and that it is appropriate to do so, he should indicate the maximum sentence on a plea at that stage and the possible sentence on conviction after trial. If the defendant, in the light of that indication, indicates his wish to plead guilty, the judge should, by questioning him direct, satisfy himself that he understands the effect of his proposed plea, that it is true and that it is voluntary. The judge's indication should be binding on any other judge before whom the defendant may appear for sentence on the consequent plea of guilty.

Accordingly, I recommend that:

- **there should be introduced, by way of a judicial sentencing guideline for later incorporation in a Sentencing Code, a system of sentencing discounts graduated so that the earlier the tender of plea of guilty the higher the discount for it, coupled with a system of advance indication of sentence for a defendant considering pleading guilty;**

- **on the request of a defendant, through his advocate, the judge should be entitled, formally to indicate the maximum sentence in the event of a plea of guilty at that stage and the possible sentence on conviction following a trial;**

- **the request to the judge and all related subsequent proceedings should be in court, in the presence of the prosecution, the defendant and his advisers and a court reporter, but otherwise in private, and should be fully recorded;**

- the judge should enquire, by canvassing the matter with both advocates, as to the mental competence and emotional state of the defendant and as to whether he might be under any pressure falsely to admit guilt;

- the prosecution and defence should be equipped to put before the judge all relevant information about the offence(s) and the defendant, including any pre-sentence or other reports and any victim impact statement, to enable the judge to give an indication;

- the judge should only give an indication if and when he is satisfied that he has sufficient information and if he considers it appropriate to do so;

- where, as a result of such an indication, a defendant's advocate indicates to the judge that he wishes to plead guilty, the judge should, by questioning the defendant direct, satisfy himself that the defendant understands the effect of his proposed plea, that it would be true and that it would be voluntary; and

- the judge should be bound by his indication, as should any other judge before whom the defendant may appear for sentence, on the consequent plea of guilty.

DISCLOSURE

115   Advance disclosure by the prosecution serves two main purposes. The first is its contribution to a fair trial looked at as a whole.[114]   The second is its contribution to the efficiency, including the speed, of the pre-trial and trial process and to considerate treatment of all involved in it.   There are two categories of material held by the prosecution: the first is 'evidence', ie that upon which the prosecution will rely to prove its case. The second is 'unused material' which encompasses all other information and material that the prosecution has seen or collected. Early and full disclosure of all material in the first category and of relevant material in the second is vital for good preparation for trial, narrowing disputed issues, and most importantly to ensuring a fair trial. If the prosecution knows of or has information in its possession which it is not using but which may help the defence secure an acquittal, justice obviously demands disclosure. Failure of the prosecution to disclose such material has been a major factor in overturning convictions, often after the defendant has spent many years in jail, so it is imperative that the right decision on disclosure is made by the prosecution.

---

[114] for the purposes of Article 6, see *Benendenoun v France* 18 EHRR 54

116   Assuming that the prosecution has correctly charged the accused at the outset, there is a firm framework on which both sides can prepare for court. Critical to this exercise is a scheme of mutual disclosure. The burden of disclosure lies more heavily on the prosecution than on the defence, rightly so, for the prosecution brings the charge and must prove it. The defence need not admit or prove anything, but where it intends to put matters in issue, it should indicate them at an early stage so that both sides can concentrate on those issues in their preparation for court. The law attempts to give effect to that approach in the following manner. In indictable cases, and increasingly in summary matters too,[115] it requires the prosecution to disclose in advance the evidence and/or case upon which it intends to rely, other unused material which may be relevant to the issues that it contemplates or of which the defence inform it and copies of the defendant's custody record and record of search, if any. The defendant is required to make advance disclosure of the general nature of his defence and of any expert evidence upon which he proposes to rely. I deal briefly below with the obligation on the prosecutor to disclose his proposed evidence and, in more detail with his obligation to disclose unused material and with the corresponding and dependent obligation of the defendant to disclose the general nature of his defence.

Advance disclosure by prosecution of its proposed case and/or evidence

117   The law is somewhat muddled in its provision for advance notification of the prosecution case and/or evidence, but reasonably satisfactory in its operation. In brief, in indictable-only and 'either-way' cases there are no statutory obligations to provide copies of the proposed evidence at any earlier stage than, respectively, in cases 'sent' to the Crown Court 42 days after the first preliminary hearing there or at which the prosecution seeks committal proceedings in the magistrates' court.[116] In 'either-way' cases there is a statutory requirement on the prosecution to provide the defence, on request and before the court considers mode of trial, with copies of the parts of the witness statements on which it proposes to rely or a summary of the prosecution case.[117] The main purpose of this requirement is to enable the defence to determine its stance on the issue of mode of trial, but it also serves a useful purpose in notifying it of the nature of the case it has to meet.

118   In summary-only matters the prosecution, anomalously, has a statutory duty to make advance disclosure of unused material, but not written witness statements. And, until the issue of guidelines by the Attorney General on 29th November 2000, the latter was left to the discretion of individual prosecutors. However, those guidelines, directed at ensuring compliance with a

---

[115] Attorney General's Guidelines on Prosecution Disclosure, 29th November 2000; and the Criminal Procedure and Investigations Act 1996

[116] Magistrates' Courts Act 1980, s 5B(2)(c)

[117] Magistrates' Courts (Advance Information) Rules 1985, SI 1985 No 601, r 4

defendant's right to a fair trial in this respect,[118] require,[119] in addition to advance disclosure of unused material, advance provision to the defence of all proposed prosecution evidence in 'sufficient time' to allow proper consideration of it before it is called. Also, the Court of Appeal has recognised a residual common law duty on prosecutors to serve proposed evidence earlier, where it is in the interests of justice to do so, for example, where it might assist the defendant in an application for bail or for a stay of the proceedings as an abuse of process.[120]

119   Thus, in all cases there is a legal duty on or a practical requirement for a prosecutor to supply its proposed evidence in advance of the hearing. But it is still a bit of a muddle and not as rigorous as today's culture of speedy progress to hearing requires. Even the new 'fast-track' procedures allow the service of proposed evidence weeks after charge. That period between charge and service is largely 'dead-time' in the life of the case, time for completing investigation and preparation of papers which, with a more prescriptive regime, earlier involvement of the Crown Prosecution Service and the provision of adequate resources to it and the police, could often have been undertaken earlier. Whilst the effect of such delay could be lessened, on some defendants at least, by alignment of the police evidential test for charging with that of the Service[121] and proper use of their power to bail a suspect pending charge,[122] the delay in progressing cases over-all would remain much the same.

120   The Philips Royal Commission recommended the introduction of a formal and comprehensive framework of rules for advance prosecution disclosure of proposed evidence in all courts, but no rules were made.[123] The Runciman Royal Commission dealt briefly with the topic, simply stressing the need for disclosure of all prosecution evidence and unused material before the defence disclosure that it proposed.[124] In my view, there is a need for certainty and clarity of the law and, in a climate of cases moving more speedily to hearing, for the introduction of an appropriate sense of rigour to this important obligation on the prosecution to inform the defence in good time of the case it has to meet. For these purposes there should be a single set of rules providing, so far as possible, a common machinery for all levels of jurisdiction, the only practicable solution in any event if a unified Criminal Court replaces the present dual structure of courts. This could be achieved, as the Philips Royal Commission recommended, by imposing a statutory duty on the prosecution, in all cases where guilt is in issue, to provide its proposed

[118] see *R v Stratford Justices, ex p Imbert* [1999] 2 Cr App R, DC, per Collins J at pp 282-3 and Buxton LJ at p 286

[119] Attorney General's guidelines, para 43

[120] *R v DPP ex pLee* [1999] 2 All ER 737, DC

[121] see para 43 above

[122] Police and Criminal Evidence Act 1984, s 37(1)

[123] paras 8.13-14

[124] Chapter 6, paras 33, et seq

evidence in sufficient time before hearing to enable the defence to prepare for trial. The precise timescale would be prescribed by rules.

> **I recommend that there should be a single set of statutory rules imposing on the prosecution in all cases a duty to provide its proposed evidence in sufficient time to enable the defence adequately to prepare for trial, the precise timescale to be prescribed by rules.**

Disclosure of unused material and defence statement

121 In 1997 the Criminal Procedure and Investigations Act 1996 replaced the common law rules of prosecution disclosure of unused material, introducing a staged procedure of primary prosecution disclosure, defence disclosure of the issues taken with the prosecution case and then additional and secondary prosecution disclosure informed by the defence identification of the issues. The 1996 Act has not worked well, prompting two lively questions in the Review. First, should the statutory scheme be abolished and be replaced by some other and, if so, what, scheme? Second, should and could the statutory scheme be made to work better, in particular, by the wider use of information technology for speedier collation, transmission and examination of documents?

122 The scheme is set out, repetitiously and confusingly, in a number of instruments, including: the 1996 Act, Disclosure Rules,[125] the Code of Practice issued under Part II of the Act,[126] recent Guidelines of the Attorney General[127] and Rules issued under the Crime and Disorder Act 1998. The scheme applies in its entirety to cases tried on indictment in the Crown Court and partially to summary trials in magistrates' courts. It provides for two stages and, respectively, two different levels of prosecution disclosure.

- Primary disclosure - In both jurisdictions it imposes duties on a police officer known as a disclosure officer, usually drawn from the investigating team: to record and retain all information gathered or generated in the investigation and which may be relevant to it; to prepare a descriptive schedule of the material for the prosecutor; to draw to the prosecutor's attention any material that "might undermine" the prosecution case or in respect of which he is in doubt; and to certify that he has complied with all his duties under the Code. The prosecutor must then make his own determination whether the disclosure

---

[125] Crown Court (Criminal Procedure and Investigations Act 1996) (Disclosure) Rules 1997 (SI 1997 No 696), made by the Crown Court Rule Committee

[126] Code of Practice under Part II

[127] *Attorney General's Guidelines: Disclosure Of Information In Criminal Proceedings*, 29th November 2000; see also *Joint Operational Instructions - Disclosure of Unused Material*, issued by ACPO and the CPS in March 1997

officer has listed all unused material in compliance with the Code and disclose to the defence all such material that, in his opinion, "might undermine" the prosecution case.[128] He must then serve such material "as soon as is reasonably practicable" after committal or after service of the evidence in 'sent' cases. In the magistrates' court, he must do so "as soon as is reasonably practicable" after the defendant has pleaded not guilty.[129]

- Defence statement - In the Crown Court the defence must and, in the magistrates' court, may, within 14 days of the prosecutor's compliance or purported compliance with the duty of primary disclosure, give to the court and the prosecutor a written statement setting out in general terms the nature of the defence. This should set out the matters on which issue is taken with the prosecution and in the case of each issue, why, and, if one of the issues is an alibi, particulars of it.

- Secondary disclosure - In all cases, where a defence statement has been served, the disclosure officer must reconsider the extent of any unused material and draw the prosecutor's attention to any that "might be reasonably expected to assist" the defence as disclosed in the defence statement, and further certify his compliance with the Code. The prosecutor, again exercising his own judgment, must then, within 21 days of receipt of the statement, disclose any such further material, unless the court on his application orders that it is not in the public interest to disclose it.

123   The level and machinery of prosecution disclosure of unused material has been a thorny issue for many years and has prompted many submissions in the Review. There are two main conflicting considerations: first, the requirement of justice that a defendant should have full disclosure of all material relevant or potentially relevant to the case he has to meet; and second, the administrative and financial burden on the police, prosecution and third parties of over-wide and potentially irrelevant disclosure.

124   In the mid 1990s the courts, taking as their starting point guidelines on disclosure issued by the Attorney General in 1981, [130] held that the defence was generally entitled to disclosure of matter that "has or might have, some bearing on the offences charged".[131] The result, described by some as close to "opening the police file to the defence", was seen by many as unnecessarily generous to the defence, too burdensome on prosecutors in having first to vet the whole file for sensitive material and costly to the criminal justice process as a whole. There were also concerns that defendants were using their new entitlement to go on 'fishing trips' to uncover relatively peripheral material

---

[128] subject to special provisions for 'protected material' in sexual cases under the Sexual Offences (Protected Material) Act 1997

[129] Criminal Procedure and Investigations Act 1996, s 13

[130] Guidelines for the disclosure of 'unused material' to the defence in cases to be tried on indictment (1982) 74 Cr App R 302

[131] R v Saunders & Ors , unreported, September 29, 1990, CCC; R v Ward (1993) 96 Cr App R 1, CA; R v Davis, Johnson and Rowe (1993) 97 Cr App R 110; R v Keane (1994) 99 Cr App R 1, CA; and R v Brown (Winston) [1995] 1 Cr App R 191, CA

and to facilitate the 'manufacture' of defences. The Runciman Royal Commission, reporting in 1993, felt that the courts' decisions had swung the pendulum too far in favour of the defence:[132]

> "... the decisions have created burdens for the prosecution that go beyond what is reasonable. At present the prosecution can be required to disclose the existence of matters whose potential relevance is speculative in the extreme. Moreover, the sheer bulk of the material involved in many cases makes it wholly impracticable for every one of what may be hundreds of thousands of individual transactions to be disclosed".

125   It was to overcome this perceived imbalance that the Royal Commission recommended the two stage regime of disclosure, which became a feature of the 1996 Act scheme.[133]   However, Parliament did not adopt the Royal Commission's recommendations of the same test for disclosure at both stages, namely of "all material relevant to the offence, the offender or to the surrounding circumstances".[134]   Nor did it adopt the Royal Commission's recommendation that, at the second stage, after defence disclosure of "the substance of its case", relevance was to be informed by the defence disclosure and the defence had to establish it.

126   Some consider that the present system would be fair and workable if only it were properly resourced. Most, however, are of the view that the present system is unworkable, though not all for the same reasons. I turn first to the mechanics of the 1996 Act scheme and then to the vexed question of its different tests for prosecution, primary and secondary disclosure.

Primary disclosure

127   Some consider that the system operates unfairly against defendants at the most critical, the primary, stage, for two main reasons. First, they say that the test, material that "might undermine" the prosecution case, is too narrow and that, if there is to be a test at all, it should simply be one of relevance or potential relevance to issues in the case and common to both stages of disclosure, as the Runciman Royal Commission recommended. Many go further and suggest that there should be no filtering test for disclosure and that the prosecutor should disclose everything gathered or engendered by the

---

[132] Chapter 6, para 49
[133] Chapter 6, para 51
[134] Chapter 6, para 52

police in the course of their investigation,[135] much as happens in many continental jurisdictions where the defence are entitled to see the prosecution 'dossier'.[136]

128   Second, critics say that it is wrong and unfair to defendants and the police to consign to, mostly, poorly trained junior police officers the heavy responsibility, often in large and complex cases, of identifying all the unused material and the candidates from it of potentially disclosable documents. Joyce Plotnikoff and Richard Woolfson, in a recent study for the Home Office, noted[137] that most police forces regard the training that they provide on disclosure as inadequate; the average length of training given to disclosure in volume and serious crime cases is less than a day. Moreover, the exercise is rapidly becoming more onerous and difficult with the wide ranging and sophisticated use by the police and other investigative bodies of information technology in the investigation of crime, often drawing on considerable banks of intelligence built up over long periods.

129   The Code and the Attorney General's Guidelines require the disclosure officer and the prosecutor to work together in the process of primary disclosure. The disclosure officer should, where necessary, seek help from the prosecutor in the preparation of the schedule of unused material and those documents in it that he considers to be disclosable. And the prosecutor should check for himself the completeness of the scheduled material and what is potentially disclosable. However, the prosecutor, for good practical reasons and his own professional commitments, is largely in the hands of the officer in the basic exercise of identification of all unused material, potentially disclosable or not. Surveys undertaken by the Criminal Bar Association in conjunction with the British Academy of Forensic Science and the Law Society in 1999, a Thematic Review of The CPS Inspectorate in March 2000,[138] the Plotnikoff and Woolfson Study and submissions in the Review all indicate that this is a fundamental failure in the system. All too often disclosure officers are late in providing schedules and material to prosecutors, leaving them little time for adequate review of the documents. Frequently the officers do not provide them with complete and accurate documentation to enable them adequately to review the schedules, or to make sound decisions as to disclosability. But even when the disclosure officer provides full, accurate and timely documentation, many prosecutors still do not have time to examine it properly to satisfy themselves of the officer's compliance and assessment as to disclosability. The seriousness of this inability is illustrated by the fact that

---

[135] including the Criminal Bar Association in submissions in the consultation process leading to the Attorney General's Guidelines on Disclosure of 29th November 2000

[136] however, the common and civil law systems are not readily comparable, since in the latter the 'dossier' is usually judicially compiled and may not be complete

[137] Joyce Plotnikoff and Richard Woolfson *A Fair Balance? Evaluation of the Operation of Disclosure Law* Home Office, (2001) (as yet unpublished), p 11

[138] Crown Prosecution Service Inspectorate *Report on the Thematic Review of the Disclosure of Unused Material*, 2/2000, (March 2000)

when they do examine the material, they often disagree with the assessment of the disclosure officers.

130   The police themselves recognise these weaknesses in the system. At least one force, the Kent County Constabulary, has felt the need to employ direct a number of lawyers to assist it with its heavy and growing burden of disclosure. Whilst such initiative is to be commended as a response to a failing system, the statutory responsibility for disclosure lies with the prosecutor. It is a task critical to his forensic role. Involvement by the police of other lawyers would encourage, in practical terms, shedding of some of that responsibility or at best unnecessary and costly duplication of effort. In my view, the proper answer is to provide a better system in which: police are properly resourced and trained to gather and schedule the unused material; prosecutors are provided in sufficient numbers to examine it and make disclosure decisions; and both are equipped with common information technology systems for the collation, scanning, transmission and reading of documents to ease their respective tasks.

131   The Narey reforms may go some way to achieving a better system over-all. Changes are already under way to provide new systems for the preparation and submission of files, the establishment of criminal justice units working in close co-operation with the police to support most of the casework in magistrates' courts, and trial units to handle the Crown Court work.[139] However, as a recent evaluation by the Trial Issues Group of co-located criminal justice units has reported,[140] it is not yet evident whether it will improve prosecution disclosure.

132   As I have indicated, the time limits for primary disclosure are loose and imprecise according to different procedures.[141] The result is that the decisions are often left until late in the day, and by the time the material is given to the defence there are only a few weeks to trial. Many delays and ineffective hearings are caused by ill-considered and late disclosure, which is probably why many practitioners and judges urge the introduction of more specific and rigorous time limits for primary disclosure. There is much force in this argument, especially as the defence is permitted only 14 days thereafter for service of its defence statement.

133   I favour a clear timetable for prosecution disclosure at an early stage in the case. In the Crown Court, the service of the prosecution case within 42 days of first preliminary hearing as it now is, and in the unified Crown and District

[139] CPS Inspectorate, Chief Inspector's Annual Report 1999-2000

[140] *An Early Assessment of Co-located Criminal Justice Units* a report by the Glidewell Working Group, January 2001 – available on the CPS website:www.cps.gov.uk

[141] see para 122 above

Divisions of a Criminal Court within 42 days of the allocation hearing as it would be, should whenever practicable, carry with it primary disclosure of unused material. Failing that, it should be in sufficient time to enable completion of mutual disclosure by the pre-trial assessment[142] where there is one, according to a standard timetable unless the court orders otherwise. In summary cases, which would not normally require a pre-trial assessment, there should still be primary disclosure where appropriate by reference to a clear timetable, which I suggest should be between two to three weeks after a plea of not guilty has been entered, unless the court orders otherwise. In all such cases, the standard timetable should also cover the giving of a defence statement and secondary disclosure.

134   Not surprisingly, the problems of primary disclosure give rise to many disputes, some of them requiring resolution by the courts, as to its adequacy and timeliness, the defence asking for more, and the police and prosecutors seeking to keep it within reasonable bounds. Quite apart from the disadvantages of such pre-trial wrangling between the parties, they can contribute significantly to delays and the costs of preparation for trial, and sometimes spill over into the trial itself. On occasion, they emerge for the first time on appeal when the Court of Appeal is asked to rule on the disclosability of documents not disclosed at the trial. However, I should record that, in large and serious cases, where advocates of experience are instructed by the prosecutor and on behalf of the defendant, there is often less difficulty than in the smaller cases. Both sides co-operate in early identification of the issues and tailor their respective preparation for trial without rigid adherence to the formulae of the 1996 Act. And, in all cases, the Director of Public Prosecutions has encouraged his prosecutors to short-circuit some of the problems by taking a generous view of their obligations as to materiality at the primary stage.[143] Many prosecutors, counsel and judges have gone further and have respectively advised or directed, as a matter of routine, primary disclosure of certain categories of documents, for example, crime reports, incident report books, police officers' notebooks and draft versions of witness statements where the draft differs from the final version. Many judges also direct disclosure of any material requested if it is not unreasonable to do so.

135   The Crown Prosecution Service Inspectorate noted such practices in its Thematic Review Report. It guardedly and partially accepted them as permissible, but only at the secondary stage and in relation to crime reports and logs of messages, and then only as a 'fail-safe' for all non-sensitive unused material if the police were not confident that they were able to make informed decisions about disclosure.[144] Plotnikoff and Woolfson, in their

---

[142] see paras 221 – 228 below

[143] *The Prosecuting Authority's Role: Disclosure under the CPIA 1996* British Academy of Forensic Science's Seminar, Gray's Inn, 1st December 1999

[144] op cit, paras 4.54-75 and 9.13

report,[145] noted that, although there is not yet a national consensus, an increasing number of police forces and Chief Crown Prosecutors, including those in the London area, have agreed on a system of routine revelation of certain categories of documents. Other prosecuting authorities, notably the Serious Fraud Office and the Commissioners of Customs and Excise also commonly provide routine disclosure, the former doing so by scanning both evidential and unused material and providing it to the defence on CD-ROM.

136   All such practices, though sensible devices to make the system work, are outside the legislation, which confines disclosability to material satisfying one or other of the two tests. Also, because not all courts have the same approach, geographical inconsistencies have developed, which further undermine the credibility of the legislation.[146] Further, if the law were amended to provide for general disclosure by the prosecution of all non-sensitive unused material, it might simply substitute for much of the present costs of police and prosecutors in determining disclosability, increased copying and transmission charges and a burgeoning of defence legal aid claims for reading vast quantities of irrelevant documents.

137   Many of the most significant practical difficulties associated with disclosure concern the volume of paperwork that modern police investigation generates. The basic production costs of photocopies have fallen steadily as technology has developed, but these are by no means the only costs involved. As any visitor to a courtroom can see, the trial process requires the assembly and maintenance of large paper files in ever-increasing numbers. All this paper has to be produced, transported (often incurring delay and significant postal and/or delivery charges), managed and stored.

138   This is an area in which modern communication technology has the potential to secure significant savings. In the recent Scottish "Lockerbie" trial at Kamp van Zeist in the Netherlands, 28,000 pages of written exhibits were scanned and stored on a bespoke database system.[147] The physical process of creating the scanned images was not that different from producing photocopies. But once the process was complete, it was no longer necessary to produce hard paper copies, since the scanned images could be grouped into case files and sent electronically to the defence and others involved or entitled to see them. If, at a later stage, others needed to be given access to all or part of the files, it could be done by further electronic transmission or by copying to a floppy disc. Nor was there any need for the parties and their lawyers to store or manage the security of 28,000 sheets of paper.

---

[145] *A Fair Balance?* pp 6 and 11

[146] see *The Report of the CPS Inspectorate's Thematic Review of Disclosure*, 2/2000

[147] see the discussion of some of the technological issues by Donna E Arzt in *The Scotsman*, 8 January 2001, p 15

139 Use of this technology could significantly speed and make more manageable and less expensive the process of disclosure over the whole range of cases. Once the prosecutor indicates to the police disclosure officer the items to be disclosed, they can be scanned onto an electronic case file, transmitted to the defence, and held available by the prosecution for disclosure to the court when necessary. Although originals of scanned documents would be available for production and examination if required, for most purposes the scanned images should suffice, both for the purpose of disclosure and, when the courts are suitably equipped, for use at trial.

140 The system that I have described would be a signal advance, but it would only be a first step. As the use of information technology widens, most documents required in any case are likely to have originated electronically. If my recommendations are accepted for a single electronic case file to which all involved have access, subject to appropriate security safeguards,[148] even initial scanning of documents would not be necessary. Disclosure would not be a matter of sending or transmitting material at all, but simply a means of the parties obtaining appropriate access to the material on the file.

The defence statement

141 The 1996 Act requires a defendant in proceedings on indictment, and enables him in summary proceedings, to serve a written defence statement on the court and the prosecutor: "(a) setting out in general terms the nature of ... [his] defence;" "(b) indicating the matters on which he takes issue with the prosecution"; and "(c) stating, in the case of each such matter, the reason why he takes issue with the prosecution"; and, if the statement discloses an alibi, particulars of it, including, if known to the defendant, the name and address of every proposed alibi witness, or, if not known, any information the defendant can give that would help to find them.[149]

142 These requirements go beyond simply putting in issue prosecution assertions of primary fact. They require a defendant to challenge allegations of secondary fact and to identify issues of law, including ECHR challenges. going to the root of the charge. They also include any positive defences, for example, provocation, self-defence or diminished responsibility upon which he proposes to rely. They do not, however, require him to reveal his proposed evidence at trial, save to the extent indicated where the defence is alibi.[150] And they do not require him to state how he proposes to controvert the

---

[148] eg through adherence to the *BSI Code of Practice for Legal Admissibility and Evidential Weight of Information Stored Electronically*, BSI, (1999)

[149] s 5(6)

[150] note also the separate provision for advance notification by either side of any expert evidence on which it proposes to rely in the Crown Court (Advance Notice of Expert Evidence) Rules 1987 and corresponding Rules for magistrates' courts.

prosecution's case. In my view, the requirements are a logical and fair way of identifying the issues likely to engage the court at trial, of helping the prosecutor to identify any further unused material that may be of assistance to the defendant in the determination of those issues and in assisting both parties to focus on the evidence needed for that determination.

143 The function of the defence statement in the 1996 Act's scheme of mutual disclosure raises three main questions: first, as to the fairness of making secondary prosecution disclosure conditional on it; second, the particularity of the information about the defence case that it should give; and third, what, if any, proper and effective sanctions there should and could be for failure to serve it.

144 It has been argued that the linking of a defendant's right to full prosecution disclosure with his disclosure of the issues he intends to take in his defence violates his right to a fair trial under Article 6.[151] Plotnikoff and Woolfson[152] questioned the fairness of the scheme in this respect. They referred to "widespread dislike of the legislation and rejection of the idea" that there should be such linkage, "often manifested in unwillingness of the defence to submit meaningful defence statements and judicial reluctance to deny defence applications to see unused material". They commented that these attitudes frustrated the working of the scheme regardless of the performance of the police and the Crown Prosecution Service. That process of reasoning led them to urge a debate "on whether the principles upon which the Act is based remain valid and compatible with the European Convention of Human Rights". They hoped that the outcome might produce a consensus on what it is reasonable, as distinct from practicable, to require by way of defence disclosure. There are, it seems to me, at least two obstacles to this Utopian goal. First, there is the natural reluctance of many criminals seeking to avoid just conviction to co-operate with a system that would fairly and efficiently secure it. Second, there are many defence practitioners with an imprecise view of the principle of the defendant's right of silence as it applies in this context. The courts may well be asked to consider the matter before long. But the limited and somewhat general observations on the subject from Strasbourg so far,[153] do not, in my view, amount to condemnation of a system linking and limiting prosecution disclosure to the issues in play. Provided that the issues or likely issues in a criminal case are broadly interpreted, I see no canon of fairness, Article 6 or otherwise, for not tying disclosure to materiality.

---

[151] see, eg Tim Owen, QC, *The Requirements of the ECHR and the PII Problem,* a paper given at a Justice Seminar on 12th June 2000 for the Review

[152] *A Fair Balance?* op cit

[153] see eg the Commission's assertion in *Jespers v Belgium* 27 DR 61, at paras 51-56 of the accused's right to know of the results of investigations "throughout the proceedings" and wide-ranging third party disclosure; and *Bendenoun v France* 18 EHRR 54; cf *R v Brown (Winston)* [1998] AC 367, per Lord Hope at pp 374F – 377F

145   It is difficult to pin down what, in practice, the 'right of silence' is for this purpose. Lord Mustill, in his illuminating analysis of the expression in *R v DSFO, ex p Smith*,[154] said that it "arouses strong but unfocused feelings" but does not "denote any single right; rather it refers to a disparate group of immunities, which differ in nature, origin, incidence and importance, and also as to the extent to which they have already been encroached upon by statute". The Philips Royal Commission considered the question[155] and a number of options, one of which was for the judge to determine, on the application of the defence, what should be disclosed. However, it felt unable to recommend it:

> "... if the judge were to be able to determine what would be relevant or useful the defence would first have to disclose its case. Such a requirement seems to us inconsistent with the central feature of the accusatorial system that it is for the prosecution to prove guilt without assistance from the defence".[156]

146   For the same reason of principle, and also of practicability, the Philips Royal Commission rejected any formal obligation of general disclosure by the defence. But it did recommend the extension of requirement of advance notification applicable to alibi to other specific defences, such as those depending on medical or other scientific evidence, which, as a result of taking the prosecution by surprise, would otherwise cause inconvenience and expense of adjournments to enable the prosecution to investigate them.[157]

147   The Philips Royal Commission's solution was that the prosecution should take responsibility for disclosure, adopting as the test whether the material would "have some bearing" on the alleged offences or surrounding circumstances.[158] However, it observed in the concluding paragraph of its treatment of the subject:

> "Our concern with disclosure has been partly motivated by our wish to improve the efficiency of the prosecution process. And in this context we believe that the defence may be more willing to make elements of their case known once a system for fuller and more certain prosecution disclosure has developed."[159]

---

[154] [1993] AC 1, HL, at 30E

[155] paras 8.14-8.23

[156] para 8.19

[157] paras 8.20-8.22

[158] paras 8.14-8.19 and 9.11

[159] para 8.23

148   The Runciman Royal Commission, by a majority, took the same line as the Philips Royal Commission on an accused's right to silence when questioned by the police.[160]   But it was more robust in its approach to the question of some disclosure of the defence in indictable cases.[161]   It set out its stall at an early stage of the Report,[162] namely that it regarded as fundamental to both adversarial and inquisitorial systems that the prosecution had the burden of proving guilt, but did not regard that as incompatible with requiring a defendant to disclose at an early stage an outline of his proposed defence and/or to indicate that he would not call any evidence. It said:[163]

> "... it is when but only when the prosecution case has been fully disclosed that defendants should be required to offer an answer to the charges made against them at the risk of adverse comment at trial on any new defence they then disclose or on any departure from the defence which they previously disclosed."

It added:[164]

> "Disclosure of the substance of the defence at an earlier stage will no more incriminate the defendant nor help prove the case against him or her than it does when it is given in evidence at the hearing. The burden of proof remains on the prosecution and the defence remains free to decide what its case will be."

> "If all the parties had in advance an indication of what the defence would be, this would not only encourage earlier and better preparation of cases but might well result in the prosecution being dropped in the light of the defence disclosure, an earlier resolution through a plea of guilty or the fixing of an earlier trial date. The length of the trial could also be more readily estimated, leading to a better use of the time both of the court and of those involved in the trial; and there would be kept to a minimum those cases where the defendant withholds his defence until the last possible moment in the hope of confusing the jury or evading investigation of a fabricated defence."

149   Such a procedure had long applied to alibi defences.[165] Shortly before, it had been extended to require notification of any proposed defence expert

---

[160] Chapter 4 para 22

[161] with the exception of Professor Zander, for whose note of dissent, see pp 221--235

[162] para 15

[163] Chapter 4, para 24

[164] Chapter 6, paras 2 and 59

[165] Criminal Justice Act 1967, s 11; now subsumed in the defence statement requirements of the 1996 Act

evidence.[166] And, in serious fraud cases, if the judge so orders, a defendant must give the court and the prosecution a statement of general nature of the defence and the principal issues raised.[167]

150   Professor Michael Zander, the dissenting member of the Runciman Royal Commission on this and two other matters, considered that to require a defendant to indicate the general nature of his defence was wrong in principle and, given the way the system works, would cause inefficiency.   As to principle, his view appears to have depended on his equation of a defendant's right of silence to a right, not only to make the prosecution prove all or some of its case, but to leave it guessing until the last minute precisely what parts he requires it to prove.   He said:

> "1. The most important objection to defence disclosure is that it is contrary to principle for the defendant to be made to respond to the prosecution's case until it has been presented at the trial.   The defendant should be required to respond to the case the prosecution makes, not to the case it says is going to make.   They are often significantly different.
>
> 2. The fundamental issue at stake is that the burden of proof lies throughout on the prosecution.   Defence disclosure is designed to be helpful to the prosecution and more generally, to the system.   But it is not the job of the defendant to be helpful either to the prosecution or to the system.   His task, if he chooses to put the prosecution to proof, is simply to defend himself.   Rules requiring advance disclosure of alibis and expert evidence are reasonable exceptions to this general principle.   But, in my view, it is wrong to require the defendant to be helpful by giving advance notice of his defence and to penalise him by adverse comment if he fails to do so."[168]

151   As to efficiency, his argument was that there was little or nothing that could be done to improve case management measures of this sort because of defence counsel's inefficient ways of working and their likely uncooperative attitude to any such reform, and because of a reluctance by the judiciary to enforce it. But even in 1993 both of those stands had a certain period flavour to them, treating the defendant's right to silence more as a right of non co-operation with the criminal justice process than of putting the prosecution to proof of his guilt, and a defeatist attitude[169] to the advantages to all, including the defendant, of efficient and speedy preparation for trial.

---

[166] Police and Criminal Evidence Act 1984, s 81 and the Crown Court (Advance Notice of Expert Evidence) Rules 1987

[167] Criminal Justice Act 1987, ss 9 and 10

[168] Note of Dissent, paras 1 and 2, p 221

[169] later manifested again in relation to Lord Woolf's Civil Justice reforms

152 The Runciman Royal Commission, however, had in mind only the barest outline when it spoke of defence disclosure, that is, a simple ticking of a form containing a number of standard defences, such as 'accident', 'self-defence', 'no dishonest intent' etc, though it allowed for the possible need for more tailored indications in complex cases.[170] However, it considered that the disclosure requirements of the 1987 Act for serious fraud cases, namely a written statement setting out the general nature of the defence and the principal issues taken, were too sparse, and recommended more detailed information in the form of a certified statement of what facts in the prosecution statement were denied or admitted and what facts were neither denied nor admitted in advance of proof. It recommended, in addition to costs sanctions where defence lawyers were at fault, the use, where appropriate, of contempt powers against the defendant personally.

153 It seems to me that the 1996 Act was logical in principle in treating the test of ultimate prosecution disclosure as dependent on its materiality to the issues in the case. Only the defendant knows for sure what issues he is going to take. They may be obvious enough to the prosecution at the stage of primary disclosure or they may be a mystery to all until the defendant gives some post-charge indication. I do not see it as an attack on the prosecution's obligation to prove its case and the defendant's right of silence that he should be required to identify the allegations or facts that he intends to put in issue. It does not require him to set out his defence other than by reference to what he disputes. If he intends to put the prosecution to proof of everything, he is entitled to do so. But if his intention is, or may be, to take issue only on certain matters, the sooner he tells the court and the prosecutor the better, so that both sides knows the battleground and its extent.

154 Whilst acknowledging the apparent logic of such an approach, some contributors to the Review argued that it is naïve and that the interests of justice justify a right of defence by ambush as a protection against abuse of public authority. In particular, they suggested that a defendant may be justified in holding back his defence since it may give the prosecution an opportunity before trial to strengthen or change a weak case[171] or to fabricate or falsify evidence to overcome it. To the extent that the prosecution may legitimately wish to fill possible holes in its case once issues have been identified by the defence statement, I can understand why, as a matter of tactics, a defendant might prefer to keep his case close to his chest. But that is not a valid reason for preventing a full and fair hearing on the issues canvassed at the trial. A criminal trial is not a game under which a guilty defendant should be provided with a sporting chance. It is a search for truth in accordance with the twin principles that the prosecution must prove its case

[170] Chapter 6, para 68

[171] considered by the Runciman Royal Commission, Ch 6, paras 61-62 and 65

and that a defendant is not obliged to inculpate himself, the object being to convict the guilty and acquit the innocent. Requiring a defendant to indicate in advance what he disputes about the prosecution case offends neither of those principles. Equally untenable is the suggestion that defence by ambush is a permissible protection against the possibility of dishonesty of police and/or prosecutors in the conduct of the prosecution. It may not be "the function of law to trust those who exercise lawful powers."[172] But a criminal justice process cannot sensibly be designed on a general premise that those responsible for law are likely to break it. In those cases where, unfortunately, the police or other public officers are dishonest, the criminal trial process itself is the medium for protection and exposure.

155   Another argument is that failure to provide all non-sensitive unused material from the start may deprive an innocent defendant of a legitimate defence where, because of his ignorance of what has occurred, he cannot advance an explanation of the prosecution evidence consistent with innocence.[173]   But such argument confuses the nature of the defence, in the sense of why the defendant says he is not guilty, with the means available to him to advance that plea. In most cases the defendant knows why he says he is not guilty and the issues that he will take in his forthcoming trial. Even in the rare case where a defendant may not know from the start whether he has committed the offence, he can properly take broad issue with the prosecution case in his defence statement. The broader the issue the more secondary disclosure to which it will entitle him.

156   In my view, there is a sound need for a defence statement as an aid to early identification of the issues and, in consequence, an efficient process and one that is fair both to the defence and to the prosecution as the representative of the public interest. Whether it is seen as a condition of further disclosure and thus, as a means of securing a defendant's co-operation in the trial process, or simply as a logical step in the identification of the issues in the case and hence of the materiality of any as yet undisclosed material, is an arid debate. Looked at in that light, there is no good reason for the unease expressed by some at the statutory link between prosecution and defence disclosure. The unease, it seems to me, owes less to that logical link than to the perceived difference in the tests of primary and secondary disclosure, that is, the notion that primary disclosure is a limited first instalment and that secondary disclosure is a full entitlement that the defendant has to earn by co-operating with the system.

157   The Act provides, in section 11, a sanction for failure or where he seeks to advance a defence at trial inconsistent with that indicated in his defence

---

[172] *pace* Roger Leng, *Disclosure: A Flawed Procedure,* in a paper at a Justice Seminar on 12th June 2000 for the Criminal Courts Review
[173] ibid

statement. The court or jury may draw such inferences from it as appear proper on the issue of guilt, though not seemingly on the issue whether there is a case to answer. However, the court or jury may not convict him solely on the strength of such inference. Where the defendant advances a defence inconsistent with his defence statement, the court must have regard to the extent of the inconsistency and any justification for it.

158   As I have indicated, the reality is that many defence statements do not comply with the requirements of the 1996 Act. They do not set out in general terms the nature of the defence or the matters on which issue is taken with the prosecution case and why. Often defence statements amount to little more than a denial, accompanying a list of material that the defence wish to see and without explanation for its potential relevance to any issues in the trial. Most judges, Crown Prosecution Service representatives or practitioners who have commented on the matter in the Review and to the Plotnikoff and Woolfson Study,[174] have said that the statements, in the form in which they are generally furnished, do little to narrow the issues at, or otherwise assist preparation for, trial. Even when a request for secondary disclosure is accompanied by some semblance of a defence statement, this may be an occasion for further wrangling over disclosure, followed by recourse to the court. More often, and for a quiet life, prosecutors provide, and judges suggest that they should provide, the further material requested even though the prosecution cannot see how it could possibly assist the defence case.

159   The 1996 Act places the responsibility for giving a defence statement on the defendant, not on his legal representative acting on his instructions. However, the time limit of 14 days from receipt of primary disclosure is tight, and the norm is for his solicitor, possibly without consulting counsel, to draft it on the defendant's behalf, often with only the barest of instructions. There is thus little scope for use of the sanction of adverse inference to encourage proper use of the defence statement. Even with the best of defence intentions, primary disclosure by the prosecution may have been defective or late; defendants, for all sorts of reasons, may not give their solicitors any or sufficient instructions, or do so in time; their solicitors may misunderstand their instructions;[175] and neither may focus sufficiently on the issues in the case. Judges are likely to be cautious before permitting a jury to draw adverse inferences where such circumstances are suggested or, at the very least, hedge their permission with emphatic warnings. And, as the editors of the current edition of Blackstone's Criminal Practice observe,[176] there is the added complication in the case of an inconsistent defence of the likely need for a

[174] *A Fair Balance?* p 13
[175] see eg *R v Wheeler* (2000) 164 JP 565, CA
[176] 2001 edition, para D6.10

'Lucas' direction as to whether the defendant deliberately lied in his defence statement.[177]

160   More effective might be a known willingness on the part of the court to adjourn a trial for the period necessary to enable the prosecution to meet any surprise defence.   But this is not always easy when there are a jury and witnesses and others to consider, and it is also expensive.   Of course, if the surprise defence surfaces only after the close of the prosecution case, the prosecution, with the leave of the court, may deal with it by calling evidence in rebuttal.

Secondary disclosure

161   There is much criticism of the different tests for primary and secondary disclosure. The difference between material that "might undermine" the prosecution case and that which "might reasonably be expected to assist" the defence is largely a matter of semantics. At the primary stage the prosecution knows what its own case is and what may undermine it. It may or may not have a good idea of the defence case, but cannot, until it is told, be sure of it. The test of materiality in each case should be the same; only the factual basis upon which it is determined is different.   However, the words in the statutory test[178] for primary disclosure, "might undermine", invite a search only for material that might have a fundamental effect on the prosecution case. It is true that the apparent rigour of the test has been softened in the Code of Practice[179] and Attorney General's Guidelines[180] to encompass any material that might cast doubt on the prosecution case, or any part of it, or have an adverse effect on its strength. However, the word 'undermine' in the statutory formulation of the test has tended to mislead disclosure officers and prosecutors into taking too narrow a view of what should be disclosed at that stage and wrongly to withhold information on that account.

162   This tendency has been aggravated by the belief, fostered by the fact that only the secondary disclosure test includes the word 'reasonably', that the test at the primary stage is subjective whereas at the secondary stage it is objective. But fairness and common sense demand that the decision as to disclosure, at whatever stage and in whatever terms, should be reasonably based in the light of the knowledge of the disclosure officer and prosecutor as to what might be material to the issues as then known or contemplated.   The fact that they may have less knowledge about that at the primary stage should not relieve them

---

[177] *R v Lucas* [1981] QB 720, 73 Cr App R 159, CA ; and *R v Burge and Pegg* [1996] 1 Cr App R 163, CA
[178] 1996 Act, s 3(1)(a)
[179] para 7.3
[180] paras 36-38

from an obligation to act reasonably in their light of that knowledge. In my view, the differently formulated tests for disclosure, suggesting a subjective and narrow approach at the primary stage and a broader and objective one at the secondary stage, are logically indefensible, confusing and the cause of much unnecessary pre-trial dispute and delay. They are widely condemned by judges, practising and academic criminal lawyers and many others involved or interested in the pre-trial process.

Defects of the present system

163   The Crown Prosecution Service Inspectorate, in its Thematic Review of the Disclosure of Unused Material found that the 1996 Act was not working as Parliament intended and that its operation did not command the confidence of criminal practitioners. It highlighted: the failure of police disclosure officers to prepare full and reliable schedules of unused material; undue reliance by the prosecutors on disclosure officers' schedules and assessment of what should be disclosed; and "the awkward split of responsibilities, in particular between the police and the Crown Prosecution Service",[181] in the task of determining what should be disclosed. The Inspectorate's principal recommendations were for greater involvement of prosecutors in the collation and examination of unused material and, from the start, in deciding on what should be disclosed; more involvement of counsel in the prosecution's duty of continuing review of unused material; and firmer reaction by prosecutors to no or inadequate defence statements. In making those recommendations, the Inspectorate acknowledged that, if implemented, they would have "very significant resource implications" for the Crown Prosecution Service and the police. More prosecutors would be needed to spend more time examining more material and deciding on disclosability, and police officers would have to copy more material than they do at present.

164   Plotnikoff and Woolfson, covering much the same ground, confirmed most of these all too apparent defects. In their opening conclusion they said:

> "Our findings confirmed the conclusion of the CPS Inspectorate's Thematic Review that poor practice in relation to disclosure was widespread. The study also revealed a mutual lack of trust between the participants in the disclosure process and fundamental differences of approach to the principles that underpin the CPIA. There is enormous scope to improve and monitor the working practices of all those involved…".[182]

---

[181] para 13.2
[182] *A Fair Balance?* p19

165   They found that government objectives for improvement in efficiency had not
       been achieved; that, in the Crown Court, the average length of trial had not
       fallen as hoped and that the scheme was expensive. It had been expected that
       it would be 'cost-neutral' for the criminal justice system, but in fact it was so
       resource intensive that it cost the Crown Prosecution Service as much or more
       than it saved the police and produced no identifiable, significant savings for
       the courts. To remedy its inadequacies would, they noted, require spending a
       lot more money on training and other resources. Despite their finding of
       widespread shortcomings in disclosure officers' unused material schedules,
       they disagreed with the Inspectorate's recommendation of concentrating more
       responsibility on prosecutors for examination of unused material and
       determination of its disclosability:

       "... we believe that it would be a backward step to remove
       responsibility from the police for decisions on disclosability
       .... The Code sets out for the first time the investigator's
       responsibility to pursue all reasonable lines of enquiry
       whether these point towards or away from the suspect. The
       ability to recognise material which may undermine the
       prosecution or support the defence is fundamental to this
       duty. Understanding relevance is crucial in deciding what
       items should be retained and recorded in the first place,
       surely a task that will fall to the police whatever disclosure
       regime is in place".[183]

166   And they estimated that, if the Crown Prosecution Service were to undertake
       the examination of all unused material, it could or would cost an additional
       £30 million a year and that, if defence lawyers also were to do so, it would
       cost the legal aid fund at least as much again.[184] Their solutions were to
       subject trained police personnel "to checks and balances in the form of proper
       quality assurance within the force, meaningful review by the Crown
       Prosecution Service and scrutiny in the courts...,formal feedback when things
       go wrong and training regimes...[to] rectify poor practice when it appears".[185]

167   To summarise, the main concerns about the disclosure provisions of the 1996
       Act are: a lack of common understanding within the Crown Prosecution
       Service and among police forces of the extent of disclosure required,
       particularly at the primary stage; the conflict between the need for a
       disclosure officer sufficiently familiar with the case to make a proper
       evaluation of what is or may be disclosable and one sufficiently independent
       of the investigation to make an objective judgement about it; the consignment
       of the responsibility to relatively junior officers who are poorly trained for the
       task; general lack of staffing and training for the task in the police or the

---

[183] p 19
[184] pp 12 and 23
[185] p 19

464

Crown Prosecution Service for what is an increasingly onerous and sophisticated exercise; in consequence, frequent inadequate and late provision by the prosecution of primary disclosure; failure by defendants and their legal representatives to comply with the Act's requirements for giving the court and the prosecutor adequate and/or timely defence statements and lack of effective means of enforcement of those requirements; seemingly and confusingly different tests for primary and secondary prosecution disclosure; and the whole scheme, whether operated efficiently or otherwise, is time-consuming and otherwise expensive for all involved. The outcome for the criminal justice process is frequent failure to exchange adequate disclosure at an early stage to enable both parties to prepare for trial efficiently and in a timely way.

Possibilities for reform

168   Reform is needed, but it is clear that there is no consensus as to what form it should take. One suggestion is for a reversion to the common law position immediately before the 1996 Act of more extensive prosecution disclosure. Another, and more widely supported, suggestion is for automatic disclosure by prosecutors of all non-sensitive unused material held by the prosecution or to which it has access. This is strongly advocated by the Criminal Bar Association,[186] at least at the stage of secondary disclosure when a lawful defence has been indicated. It is also supported by many judges, the Law Society and JUSTICE as a pragmatic solution to the often difficult and – if it is done properly – time-consuming task for the police and the prosecutor of determining disclosability on the known and expected issues in the case. For those reasons, as I have mentioned, there has been a move in many areas towards informal and automatic disclosure of certain categories of documents, regardless of their potential materiality. And the Attorney General, in his recent Guidelines, has recommended blanket disclosure of large quantities of material seized by the police as a precautionary measure but unlikely, because of its source, general nature or for other reasons, ever to be relevant and therefore left unexamined.[187]

169   Routine partial disclosure may achieve ready savings in time and other efficiencies in relatively straightforward cases, but it still leaves considerable scope for present difficulties where material falls outside the categories for automatic disclosure, especially in large and complex cases involving wide-ranging and sophisticated investigation. Automatic disclosure of the police investigation "file", apart from sensitive material, in every case could involve enormous and unnecessary cost for the police and prosecutors, particularly in large cases where the "file" may be spread among a number of computers and between various agencies whose assistance the police may have sought. Such

---

[186] in its submission to the Review
[187] para 9

between various agencies whose assistance the police may have sought. Such savings as might be made in the present task of identifying documents disclosable by reason of their potential materiality would in many instances be eclipsed by the costs of compilation by the prosecution and of examination by the defence of vast volumes of irrelevant material.

170 In my view, there is scope for an adoption of partial routine disclosure of non-sensitive unused material, but at the primary stage rather than, as recommended by the Crown Prosecution Service Inspectorate[188] at the secondary stage. It could include certain common categories of document, for example, crime reports, incident report books, police officers' notebooks, custody records, draft versions of witness statements where the draft differs from the final version and experts' reports. It could also include, as the Criminal Bar Association have suggested,[189] certain types of material by reference to their subject matter as distinct from the category of document on which it is recorded.

171 For material outside the categories for routine disclosure, I favour building on and improving the present system of two stage prosecution disclosure of information relevant to the issues in the case, coupled with a defence statement identifying those issues to the extent that they are not otherwise apparent to the prosecutor at the outset. The principle of the scheme is logical and fair – logical in that relevance of information depends on what is to be in issue – fair in that all that is required of the defendant is to say what he puts in issue. However, for the reasons I have given, the present differently expressed tests of relevance for the two stages of disclosure are not logical and are capable, in their application, of being unfair. They should be replaced with a common test. The precise formulation of the test would be for others, but I suggest that it should be more precise than that suggested by the Runciman Royal Commission of "all material relevant to the offence, the offender or to the surrounding circumstances".[190] I believe that it should be anchored to the issues in the case as the police and prosecutor know or believe them to be, for example, "material that, in the prosecutor's opinion, might reasonably affect the determination of any issue in the case of which he knows or should reasonably expect". A more readily understood, though tautologous way of putting it, would be "material which in the prosecutor's opinion might reasonably weaken the prosecution case or assist that of the defence". [191] Such a test could be supplemented by a non-exhaustive list of illustrations of its application of the sort presently contained in the Attorney General's Guidelines,[192] including for example, whether it might assist in cross-examination of prosecution witnesses or in applications to exclude

[188] *Thematic Review of Disclosure*, para 475
[189] p 12 of its submission to the Review
[190] Chapter 6 para 51
[191] ie reflecting the present glosses on the statutory test provided in the Code of Practice and the Attorney General's Guidelines
[192] paras 37 and 40

evidence or for a stay of the proceedings, or indicate a line of enquiry that might not otherwise have occurred to the defence.

172   There remains the problem of who is to have effective control - as well as ultimate responsibility, which already lies with the prosecutor - for determination of what is disclosable. As I have said, the system could be coupled with automatic disclosure of a wide range of categories of documents common to most prosecutions and already covered in the many existing informal initiatives. However, that would still leave a need: 1) for honest and competent recording and retention by the police of all unused material gathered and generated in the investigation; and 2) competent and independent evaluation of material requiring disclosure at each stage.

173   As to the former, there are many who believe that one of the greatest flaws of the scheme of disclosure continued in the 1996 Act is the trust that it reposes in the honesty, independence and competence of investigating police officers. Roger Leng, in a contribution to the Review, observed that "there is no historical justification for investing police and prosecutors with this degree of trust, if it can be avoided".[193] However, as he acknowledged, in the task of recording and retention of material collected in the course of investigation, there is little practical alternative. It is difficult to see how it can be taken away from the police or an officer involved in the particular investigation, whatever may said about the next stage, decisions about disclosability. To bring in some person from outside the police or the investigation team for this purpose or to involve the court routinely in some sort of examination of its own, as some have suggested,[194] could considerably delay and encumber trials. And it would be impractical and expensive and would duplicate the role for which an independent prosecuting authority, if properly resourced, is best suited.

174   Nevertheless, failure of the police, for whatever reason, to identify for the prosecutor all available and potentially disclosable material is a great danger to justice. The Court of Appeal, in a public interest immunity case last year, which had gone badly wrong for that reason, stressed the need for scrupulous accuracy in the information provided by the police.[195] Before considering 'farming out' the exercise to some body independent of the police or of the investigation team, with all the practical difficulties that that would involve, I believe that the present system is capable of significant tightening up in a number of ways. First, there should be statutory guidelines for recording,

---

[193] see eg Roger Leng, *Disclosure: A Flawed Procedure*, a paper given at a Justice Seminar on 12th June 2000 for the Criminal Courts Review
[194] see eg John Epp, *Encouraging Police Compliance with the Law of Disclosure*, [2001] 5 E & P, 147
[195] see editorial comment on *R v Jackson* [2000] Crim LR 377, at 379

retention and collation of material arising in an investigation as it proceeds.[196] Second there should be a nationally approved or agreed system of thorough training for that purpose. Third, there should be a rigorous system of spot 'audits' by HM Inspectorates of Constabulary and/or of the Crown Prosecution Service to encourage compliance. Fourth, this should be supplemented by prosecutors' rigorous observance of their own professional duty to check the police schedules against the witness statements and unused material for any likely categories of material that may have been omitted. A major part of this exercise would be, as the Criminal Bar Association has put it,[197] to test the comprehensiveness of the material against the categories a prosecutor would expect to find scheduled, given the known circumstances of the case and its background. And, fifth, failure of the police properly to schedule and to make available to the prosecutor all unused material could be a police disciplinary offence.

175   The increasing use of logging all material gathered or generated in the course of an investigation should remove some of the difficulties in this essentially mechanical but hitherto burdensome job for busy policemen. Whilst they should have an appreciation of the importance of their task to questions of disclosability, that need not be part of their responsibility as it is at present. For that reason I suggest that the officer in the case given this responsibility should no longer be called a 'disclosure' officer, but a 'collation' officer. The prosecutor, if given the time as well as the responsibility for assessing the completeness of the investigation material collated and scheduled by the police, should be as efficient as any other body within or outside the police, or the court, in making an independent check.

176   It follows that, despite the view to the contrary of Plotnikoff and Woolfson,[198] and the assistance given by the Attorney General in his recent Guidelines, I consider that there should be a shift in initial, as well as ultimate, responsibility from the police to prosecutors for determination of disclosability. Assessing the materiality of information to issues or likely issues in a criminal trial - as distinct from gathering and scheduling all unused material in an investigation - is a lawyer's task, not that of an, often relatively inexperienced investigative officer perfunctorily trained for the purpose. It is one of the most critical tasks in the preparation of a case for trial, and one that will call for a much more sure and speedy touch with the quicker pre-trial process of cases at all levels now under way. It is also essential for the prosecutor's fair conduct of the prosecution case before and at trial, not least because of his continuing duty to review the adequacy of disclosure.[199] He

---

[196] The Joint Operational Police Instructions (JOPI) and the 1996 Act Code of Practice; the CPS Inspectorate's Report on Disclosure, at para 3.26 et seq, stated that was non-observance of JOPI and their ambiguity as non-statutory guidelines which led to most of the failings

[197] in its Response in the consultation process on the draft Attorney General's Guidelines on Disclosure

[198] see para 165 - 166 above

[199] 1996 Act, s9

should also take steps, through a clearly and simply devised procedure, of which he should keep a record, to obtain and examine and/or otherwise identify with the degree of detail appropriate to the material and the case, all unused material, including in the examination an assessment of its likely completeness having regard to the known extent of the investigation. Whilst I consider the making of a record important as a routine discipline and working reference, I do not think he need be asked to certify it.

177   I should pause to say something of the critical role of the prosecuting advocate as adviser and, as appropriate, decision-maker at the outset of and throughout the progress of a criminal prosecution. His responsibility which, crucially, continues throughout the trial, includes attention to what the justice of the case demands by way of disclosure to the defence. As the Criminal Bar Association have noted in their submission in the Review, he can only discharge that responsibility if he is aware of the existence of potentially disclosable material as previously known issues are developed evidentially and new ones appear in the course of the trial. He must also have this information if he is to comply with his duty under paragraph 3.4 of the Code to advise on further lines of enquiry, for example, as to material held by third parties. He should be instructed and involved in any decisions as to disclosure at an early stage, especially in cases where there are difficult disclosure issues. He should also be asked to advise on the adequacy of the defence statement with a view to securing appropriate secondary disclosure and to seek further particulars where it is plainly inadequate. As in the case of the Crown Prosecution Service or other prosecuting authority, I do not consider that prosecuting advocates should be required to certify their compliance with what are essentially part of their professional obligations.

178   I have not ignored more radical suggestions that the initial decision as to disclosability should be taken out of the hands of the prosecutor, as well as those of the police. Roger Leng suggested, for example, that it should be the responsibility of the defence lawyer and that to leave it with the prosecution violates Article 6(3)(b) and (c) ECHR, which entitle a defendant to "adequate time and facilities for the preparation of his defence" and to "legal assistance of his own choosing".[200] I do not consider that it is possible to draw from Article 6 an absolute defence right to prosecution disclosure of all material, relevant or not, by conflating in that way two separate provisions of the Article. The House of Lords have recently emphasised[201] that the courts should not parse each element of Article 6 and apply it individually to each stage of procedure. The test is the over-all fairness of the process and, in applying that test the courts are entitled to have regard to proportionality.

---

[200] *Disclosure: A Flawed Procedure*
[201] see *R v Lambert* [2001] 3 WLR 206, HL, per Lord Clyde at 259, para 159

179   In my view, the police and prosecutors should continue to work together where necessary, but the prosecutor should examine the file and the material at the earliest possible time and make the initial decisions as to disclosability, rather than, as now, spend much time in reviewing and, often, overruling those of the officer. Although, as Plotnikoff and Woolfson have pointed out, the police would necessarily retain prime responsibility for assembling the file, that is, for retaining and recording all material gathered or generated in the investigation, they should be relieved of the additional and initial responsibility of determining what is disclosable. Although Plotnikoff and Woolfson suggest that the likely additional cost of such concentration of disclosure responsibility in the hands of the prosecutor would be an additional £60 million a year in prosecution costs and defence legal aid fees, they do not indicate the basis for that estimate. And, as I have said, the whole exercise could in the long run be significantly simplified and made less expensive by use of information technology – and that includes transmission of the material to and examination of it by the defence. Whatever the accuracy of the Plotnikoff and Woolfson figures, the likely efficiency savings to the criminal justice system as a whole and release of police officers to concentrate more on their investigative function would be significant. In any event, full and timely prosecution disclosure is so fundamental to the fairness and efficiency of the criminal justice process that if it costs more to do it properly, it is a price well worth paying.

180   As to the defence statement, I have already indicated that the present requirements, if observed, seem to be adequate to enable identification of the issues, not only for the purpose of securing disclosure of any, so far, undisclosed unused material that might be relevant, but also for the purpose of determining the scope and form of prosecution evidence required for trial.[202] I have considered whether to recommend any additional requirements, for example, a general obligation to identify defence witnesses and the content of their expected evidence similar to that where the defence is alibi or it is intended to call expert evidence for the defence. Whilst, as a matter of efficiency, there is much to be said for them, many would find them objectionable as going beyond definition of the issues and requiring a defendant to set out, in advance, an affirmative case. And they would be difficult to enforce.

181   But what if the prosecution moves the goal posts by amending the charge late in the day? The most recent Crown Prosecution Service Inspectorate Report found frequent weaknesses in the Services' review of cases going to the Crown Court, in particular, that the quality of instructions to counsel was generally low, that too many indictments needed amendment and that there had been little improvement in the management of its files.[203] And what if the

---

[202] paras 141-160 above
[203] Chief Inspector's Annual Report 1999-2000, paras 3.9 and 3.12

prosecution does not provide adequate or timely primary disclosure, or if, regardless of the form and time of it, the defence still do not comply with their obligations in this respect? The courts can and do penalise the prosecution in costs for their failure. But where the failure lies with the defence, as it does in many cases,[204] few prosecuting counsel are asked to advise on the non-compliance and few raise it with the court. There can be no question of the court punishing a defendant by depriving him at trial of the right to advance an unannounced defence and, as I have said, rarely by the drawing of adverse inferences of guilt. It would often be difficult to determine whether it was the defendant's or his lawyers' failure to comply and, where the issue is as to adequacy of a served defence statement, the matter could degenerate into a 'pleading' point.

182   As to financial penalties, it could be unfair and potentially prejudicial to the proper conduct of the defence, to penalise the lawyer, say by way of a wasted costs order or reduction in publicly funded fees,[205] for what might be his client's neglect or refusal to take advice. And to seek to punish a defendant in this way, say by fining or imprisoning him for contempt of court, would in most cases be both impractical and counterproductive to the fairness and efficiency of the trial process. Attempting, save in extreme cases, to solve the problem by imposing penalties on defence lawyers or defendants personally would also encourage satellite litigation. In either case the question of fault for the court could also be muddied by defence complaints of inadequacy of primary prosecution disclosure or change of charge hindering the provision of an adequate defence statement.

183   There are other and better avenues to making the defence statement requirement effective. Though even they are limited in this imperfect field of criminal litigation, with many defendants incapable or unwilling to co-operate with the system and whose hard pressed lawyers often have difficulty in obtaining instructions and, where publicly funded, are inadequately paid for preparatory work.[206] The first, as I have urged, is to provide full and timely prosecution disclosure, aided with modern communications technology. The second, as I have also urged, is to pay publicly funded defence lawyers a proper and discrete fee for preparatory work, including taking instructions from the defendant whether in custody or on bail, and the drafting of a defence statement. This may sound a basic requirement, but, for the reasons I have given, is not the case today.[207] The third is to make defendants on remand in custody more accessible to their lawyers than they are now. As I have shown earlier,[208] the limited visiting times are often difficult for busy criminal advocates and the visiting periods too short for taking adequate

---

[204] in Plotnikoff and Woolfson's study about 40% of the defence statements contained only a denial of guilt

[205] the latter would also be discriminatory in that no such penalty would be available in private paid defences

[206] see paras 13 - 27 above

[207] see Guidance of the Professional Conduct and Complaints Committee of the Bar Council of 24th September 1997

[208] see paras 28-33 above

instructions, a product largely of Prison Service budgetary constraints taking priority over the needs of the criminal justice system as a whole. Much could be done to meet this problem by the introduction of lawyer to prison video-conferencing facilities.[209] The fourth is for the prosecuting advocate, routinely, to advise on the adequacy of the defence statement and, where he considers it is inadequate, to request particulars of it, seeking a direction from the court if necessary. The fifth is, through professional conduct rules and guidance, training and, in the rare cases where it might be appropriate, discipline, to inculcate in criminal defence practitioners and, through them, their clients the principle that a defendant's right of silence is not a right to conceal in advance of trial the issues he is going to take at it. Its purpose is to protect the innocent from wrongly incriminating themselves, not to enable the guilty, by fouling up the criminal process, to make it as procedurally difficult as possible for the prosecution to prove their guilt regardless of cost and disruption to others involved.

184   Finally, reform of the law should be in the form of a single and simply expressed instrument. The present combination of the cumbrously drafted 1996 Act and Rules, the Code, the Attorney General's Guidelines and the Joint Operational Police Instructions is confusing and hard work for anyone to master, not least busy policemen and prosecutors. This is another job for a Criminal Procedure Rules Committee.

Accordingly, I recommend:

- **retention of the present 1996 Act scheme of material disclosure in particular, of two stages of prosecution disclosure under which the second stage is informed by and conditional on a defence statement indicating the issues that the defendant proposes to take at trial;**

- **replacement of the present mix of primary and subsidiary legislation, Code, Guidelines and Instructions by a single and simply expressed instrument setting out clearly the duties and rights of all parties involved;**

- **the same test of disclosability for both stages of prosecution disclosure providing in substance and, for example, for the disclosure of "material which, in the prosecutor's opinion, might reasonably affect the determination of any issue in the case of which he knows or should reasonably expect" or, more simply but tautologically, "material which in the prosecutor's opinion might weaken the prosecution case or assist that of the defence";**

---

[209] see paras 259-261 below

- in addition, automatic primary disclosure in all or certain types of cases of certain common categories of documents and/or of documents by reference to certain subject matters;

- retention by the police of responsibility for retaining, collating and recording any material gathered or inspected in the course of the investigation; police officers should be better trained for what, in many cases, may be an extensive and difficult exercise regardless of issues of disclosability, and subject, in their exercise of it to statutory guidelines and a rigorous system of 'spot audits' by HM Inspectorates of Constabulary and/or of the Crown Prosecution Service;

- removal from the police to the prosecutor such responsibility as they have for identifying and considering all potentially disclosable material;

- the prosecutor should retain ultimate responsibility for the completeness of the material recorded by the police and assume sole responsibility for primary and all subsequent disclosure;

- the requirement for a defence statement should remain as at present, as should the requirement for particulars where the defence is alibi and/or the defence propose to adduce expert evidence;

- there should be more effective use of defence statements facilitated by the general improvements to the system for preparation for trial that I have recommended, and encouraged through professional conduct rules, training and, in the rare cases where it might be appropriate, discipline, to inculcate in criminal defence practitioners the propriety of and need for compliance with the requirements;

- a clearly defined timetable for each level of jurisdiction for all stages of mutual disclosure unless the court in any individual case orders otherwise; and

- the Prison Service should introduce national standards for access to due process for remand prisoners that ensure that they experience no greater difficulty than bailed defendants in preparing for their trials.

Third party disclosure

185   The prosecutor's obligation under the 1996 Act is to disclose material "which is in his possession, and came into his possession in connection with the case for the prosecution against the accused" or which he has inspected in connection with that case.[210] In the case of material not in the possession of the police but which they or the prosecutor believe to be in the possession of a third party and of possible relevance, the Attorney General's Guidelines require them to take reasonable steps to identify and consider it.[211] Where such material is with Government departments or other Crown bodies, there are established procedures for them to co-operate in this respect.[212]

186   In the case of other third parties, agencies and individuals, for example local authorities, schools, hospitals and doctors, the guidance is that prosecutors and/or defendants should seek the co-operation of the third party concerned. This may involve extensive enquiries and considerable expense to third parties, in particular local authorities and various social services in child abuse cases, both in identifying relevant or possibly relevant material, and in considering its sensitivity. Commendably, in many areas the police have agreed protocols with all local social services departments[213] for fair and efficient working of what can be very complicated exercises in co-operation to secure informal disclosure of third party material. The Crown Prosecution Service Inspectorate, in its Report on its recent Thematic Review of Disclosure, recommended national or local protocols wherever possible.[214]

187   A major problem is late and unspecific requests by the defence for disclosure of third party material. Compliance is often difficult or impossible because of the short time available, the volume of material involved and the fact that those searching often do not know exactly what to look for because they do not know to what issues the request relates.

188   Failing agreement between the parties and third parties as to what should or can be disclosed (which may be because the third party is unwilling to go to the expense of what seems an extensive and pointless exercise and/or for reasons of public interest), the parties must seek the assistance of the court. But the only means of doing this is under the Criminal Procedure (Attendance of Witnesses) Act 1965 for securing the production of documents as evidence at court, a procedure that has been grafted onto the 1996 Act scheme of pre-trial disclosure of unused material. The applicant (prosecutor or defendant) must obtain a witness summons requiring the third party to attend and to produce document(s) at trial which the applicant believes are likely to be

---

[210] CPIA 1996, s 3
[211] paras 29-33
[212] *Giving Evidence or Information About Suspected Crimes: Guidance for Departments and Investigators*, Cabinet Office (March 1997)
[213] Plotnikoff and Woolfson, *A Fair Balance?* p 10
[214] para 8.32

material evidence. Such a summons can now, as a result of amendment made by the 1996 Act, also require production of the document(s) for inspection in advance of trial. If, on inspection, the applicant considers that they are not likely to be material evidence he can ask the court to discharge the summons. If he considers that the documents are likely to be material evidence, then, subject to provisions enabling the third party to challenge the validity of the summons or the likely materiality of the document(s), or to argue that they are not disclosable on public interest grounds, the summons remains in force and the third party must attend court with the documents. Such issues, though ostensibly about 'likely' material evidence, are, before trial, only about disclosure of documents to see if they are such or have some other forensic use. These issues should be put before the court at the earliest opportunity. All too often they surface late in the day, resulting in costly and disruptive delay for all concerned.

189   The problem with this adaptation of the 1965 Act procedure is that it is a mix of two quite separate requirements, namely a duty on a body or individual to attend court and produce as evidence documents considered to be "likely material evidence" with the prosecution's earlier obligation to disclose to the defence documents which it does not seek to adduce as evidence but which may be material to an issue in the case.[215] Its materiality could be such that the defence would wish to put the documents in evidence, but not necessarily; they could be material in suggesting a line of cross-examination of prosecution witnesses or of further enquiries. No doubt prosecutors, who use this procedure as an aid to discharging their duty of advance disclosure of unused material, interpret the term "likely material evidence" broadly, but it is unsatisfactory to require them to bend the words of the Act in that way.

190   In my view, statutory provision should be made for disclosure of third party documents potentially material to an issue in the case, regardless of their likely evidential character. Such an additional restriction on access to relevant matter in the hands of third parties is plainly inappropriate. No doubt, that is why the 1965 Act procedures, even as amended, are little used, and the police and concerned local agencies have turned instead to local protocols. Careful consideration should be given to devising a new statutory scheme for third party disclosure, including its cost implications, alongside and more consistently with the general provisions for disclosure of unused material. No doubt, its mechanics could be guided by the local protocols. Again, I suggest this is a task for a Criminal Procedure Rules Committee.

I recommend consideration of a new statutory scheme for third party disclosure, including its costs implications to all concerned, to operate alongside and more consistently

---

[215] see *R v Stratford Justices, ex p Imbert* [1999] 2 Cr App R 276, at pp 279-280

with the general provisions for disclosure of unused material.

Public interest immunity

191   The doctrine of public interest immunity enables the prosecution to withhold disclosure of material where, in the court's view, the public's interest in non-disclosure outweighs the defendant's interest in having full access to all relevant material. In reaching its decision the court must examine the material and consider the nature of the immunity claimed, the likely effect of its disclosure on the public interest, the sensitivity of the information in question and the degree to which it may assist the defence – the so-called "balancing exercise".[216] The public interest in the fair administration of justice always outweighs that of preserving the secrecy of sensitive material where its non-disclosure may lead to a miscarriage of justice.[217] That fundamental and well known common law test is reflected in the 1996 Act scheme of disclosure in its provision: "Material must not be disclosed … to the extent that the court, on an application by the prosecutor, concludes it is not in the public interest to disclose it and orders accordingly".[218]

192   The 1996 Act, reproducing the common law,[219] makes the court, not the prosecutor, the arbiter of what may be withheld from disclosure on the ground of the public interest or, as the Runciman Royal Commission recommended[220] and the 1996 Act Code of Practice describes and lists it, "sensitive material".[221] Where the prosecutor is not prepared, or is uncertain whether, to make voluntary disclosure because of the sensitivity of the material, the statutory procedure takes one of three possible forms.[222] First, and whenever possible, he should notify the defence of his intention to apply to the court for a ruling, and indicate at least the category of material in question. The court then holds a hearing at which both parties may make representations. Second, where the prosecutor considers that disclosure of the category of material would reveal what it would be contrary to the public interest to reveal, he should notify the defence of his intention to make an application, but not of the category of material the subject of it. The court then holds a hearing in the absence of the defence to determine whether they should be present and, if not, rules on the application. Third, in a highly exceptional case in which the prosecutor considers that even notification of an intention to make an

[216] see Archbold, (2001 edition) para 12-44e

[217] see *R v Keane* (1994) 99 Cr App R 1, at 6

[218] in ss 3(6), 7(5), 8(5) and 9(8)

[219] *R v Davis, Johnson and Rowe* ; *R v Ward* ; and *R v Keane*

[220] Chapter 6, para 47

[221] paras 6.12-14

[222] s21(2) and the Crown Court (Criminal Procedure and Investigations Act 1996) (Disclosure) Rules 1997 (SI 1997 No 698), reproducing the procedure laid down by Taylor LJ in *R v Davis, Johnson and Rowe*, at 114

application would reveal too much to the defence, the prosecutor should apply to the court in the absence of, and without notice to, the defence. The court then considers whether either of the first two procedures should have been adopted and, if not, considers whether to order non-disclosure. Whichever of the three procedures is adopted, the court, if it orders non-disclosure, must keep its decision under review as the case progresses. In the magistrates' courts, the conflation of roles of magistrates as triers of fact and law has necessitated a variation of the scheme. An application by the prosecution to withhold material, if granted, may lead to the bench being disqualified and a new bench hearing the trial. But apart from that difference, the procedure is the same as that in the Crown Court.

193 The scheme that I have described is an improvement on what went before and has been generally welcomed on that account. But there is widespread concern in the legal professions about lack of representation of the defendant's interest in the second and third of the three forms of application, and anecdotal and reported instances of resultant unfairness to the defence.[223] This concern has been fuelled by the clear unease of the European Court of Justice as to whether, in the absence of the defence, hearings for such purpose are Article 6 compliant.[224] A suggestion, argued on behalf of applicants in Strasbourg[225] and widely supported in the Review, is that the exclusion of the defendant from the procedure should be counterbalanced by the introduction of a "special independent counsel". He would represent the interest of the defendant at first instance and, where necessary, on appeal on a number of issues: first, as to the relevance of the undisclosed material if and to the extent that it has not already been resolved in favour of disclosure but for a public interest immunity claim; second, on the strength of the claim to public interest immunity; third, on how helpful the material might be to the defence; and fourth, generally to safeguard against the risk of judicial error or bias.

194 In my view, there is much to be said for such a proposal, regardless of the vulnerability or otherwise of the present procedures to Article 6. Tim Owen QC, in a paper prepared for the Review,[226] has argued powerfully in favour of it. It would restore some adversarial testing of the issues presently absent in the determination of these often critical and finely balanced applications. It should not be generally necessary for special counsel to be present throughout the trial. Mostly the matter should be capable of resolution by the court before trial and, if any question about it arises during trial, he could be asked to return. If, because of the great number of public interest immunity issues now being taken in the courts, the instruction of special counsel for each would be

---

[223] see eg the report of a survey of the Criminal Bar Association and the Law Society, published in 1999 reporting serious failings in the system

[224] see *Rowe and Davis v UK* (2000) 30 EHRR 1; and *Fitt and Jasper v UK* (2000) 30 EHRR 441, in which the ECHR held, only by a narrow margin of 9 to 8 that ex parte hearings to determine PII claims do not violate Article 6

[225] in *Rowe & Davis v UK*

[226] *The Requirements Of The ECHR and The PII Problem* paras 20-22

costly, it simply indicates, as Owen has commented, the scale of the problem and is not an argument against securing a fair solution.

195   The role would be similar to that of an *amicus curiae* brought in to give independent assistance to a court, albeit mostly on appeal. In rape cases, where an unrepresented defendant seeks to cross-examine a complainant, the court must inform him that he may not do so, and should he refuse to instruct counsel, the court will appoint and instruct one.[227] After the decisions of the European Court of Human Rights in *Chahal* and *Tinnelly*,[228] the Government introduced such a procedure in immigration cases involving national security. Although such cases are extremely rare, it is sufficient that the principle of a 'third' or 'special' counsel being instructed on behalf of a defendant has been conceded in a number of areas.

196   The introduction of a system of special independent counsel could, as Owen has also noted,[229] in part fill a lacuna in the law as to public interest immunity hearings in the absence of a defendant appellant in the Court of Appeal, to which the 1996 Act and supporting Rules do not apply. Where there has been a breach of Article 6 because a trial judge did not conduct a public interest immunity hearing due to the emergence of the material only after conviction, the European Court of Human Rights has held that the breach cannot be cured by a hearing before the Court of Appeal in the absence of the appellant.[230] The Court's reasons for so holding were that the appeals court is confined to examining the effect of non-disclosure on the trial ex post facto and could possibly be unconsciously influenced by the jury's verdict into underestimating the significance of the undisclosed material.

197   However, even the introduction of special counsel to such hearings would not solve the root problem to which I have referred of police failure, whether out of incompetence or dishonesty, to indicate to the prosecutor the existence of critical information. Unless, as I have recommended, the police significantly improve their performance in that basic exercise, there will be no solid foundation for whatever following safeguards are introduced into the system.

I recommend the introduction of a scheme for instruction by the court of special independent counsel to represent the interests of the defendant in those cases at first instance and on appeal where the court now considers prosecution applications in the absence of the defence in respect of the non-disclosure of sensitive material.

---

[227] Youth Justice and Criminal Evidence Act 1999, ss 34-40

[228] *Chahal v UK* (1996) 23 EHRR 413 and *Tinelly and Sons Ltd, & Ors v UK* (1998) 27 EHRR 249

[229] *The Requirements of the ECHR and the PII problem,* paras 24-28

[230] *Rowe and Davis v UK*

CASE MANAGEMENT

198   Case management has different and overlapping meanings. They include:

- what each side does to prepare its case for trial;

- what both parties do in the preparation of their respective cases, jointly and severally to identify and inform the court and others of the issues, the nature and forms of evidence that will be necessary at trial to determine those issues, the likely length of trial and any special requirements; and

- the involvement of the court to assist and, where necessary, resolve any difficulties in those processes, including listing the case for trial and keeping all involved informed.

199   The major impediments to correct charging and giving parties the information they need to prepare cases for hearing, should be significantly reduced by the improvements to the charging and disclosure procedures that I have recommended. But the second and third elements of case preparation must also be made to work properly. In a unified Criminal Court, many of the present procedures in the criminal justice system could be rationalised, and would contribute to better case management. The first is to simplify and speed the allocation of cases to the appropriate level of court.

Case allocation

200   At present, there are six different procedures for moving a case from magistrates' courts to the Crown Court:

- Committal for trial under section 6(2) of the Magistrates' Courts Act 1980 without consideration of the evidence – now available only for offences triable 'either-way'. The vast majority of committals occur under this procedure. Any defendant charged with an 'either-way' offence which is to be tried at the Crown Court must be committed for trial. In practice this is something of a hollow ritual, as any observer at court can see. It entails nothing more than the prosecution providing a copy of the papers and the court formally pronouncing the matter committed;

- Committal with consideration of the evidence under section 6(1) of the 1980 Act – also now available only for 'either-way' offences. Although in the past this was an opportunity for the defence to require the prosecution to call its witnesses and to challenge the evidence, that has now gone as a result of recommendations made by the Runciman Royal Commission. The procedure now consists of a reading of the papers, and legal argument before the magistrates. This is a relatively rare occurrence and even rarer are the times when the bench will find for the defence, and refuse to commit a defendant for trial;

- Voluntary bills of indictment. As I have described earlier,[231] this is an alternative method of commencing cases in the Crown Court;

- Transfer under section 4 of the Criminal Justice Act 1987. This applies to serious and complex fraud cases. The prosecution may transfer the case direct to the Crown Court by giving 'notice of transfer' to the magistrates' court;

- Transfer under section 53 of the Criminal Justice Act 1991. This applies to certain offences of a violent or sexual nature, where there is a child witness, and allows transfer at the instigation of the prosecutor in appropriate cases; and

- 'Sending' under section 51 of the Crime and Disorder Act 1998. Where defendants are charged with indictable-only offences, they must be sent to the Crown Court forthwith after the first appearance before the magistrates. The defence has no right to challenge the sufficiency of the evidence at the sending stage, although it may do so after the prosecution serves its evidence, which it must do within 42 days of the case reaching the Crown court.[232] This procedure is likely to account for a large proportion of all cases going to the Crown Court.[233]

201   As can be seen, there is little over-all coherence or consistency in these procedures, which are a product of piecemeal reforms over the years. Some procedures allow the defence a challenge before the matter goes to the Crown Court and some do not. And there are slightly different procedures for each course. A simple form of procedure common to all cases should be found.

202   Under my recommendations in Chapter 7 for a new unified Criminal Court and for allocation and moving cases to the appropriate level of court, all cases would start in the Magistrates' Division and stay there or move by allocation to one of the other two Divisions after the first hearing. There would be wide power in all Divisions for an early hearing as to whether, on the prosecution papers, the evidence is sufficient for the court properly to convict.

I recommend that:

- **under the present system of our criminal courts, a single simple form of procedure for the movement of cases from magistrates' courts to the Crown Court should be substituted for the present mix of**

---

[231] see para 58 above

[232] Crime and Disorder Act 1998 (Dismissal of Sent Cases) Rules 2000

[233] in 1999- indictable-only cases accounted for about 34% of all Crown Court cases.

procedures of committal, voluntary bill, transfer and sending; and

- **if my recommendations for a unified Criminal Court are adopted, a similar procedure should govern the movement of cases, after allocation, from the Magistrates' Division to the District or Crown Divisions.**

203   It may be convenient for me to refer here to the recommendations I made in Chapter 7 about the allocation of cases involving linked offences of different levels of seriousness and linked defendants. First, all cases based on the same or similar facts or committed by the same defendant or defendants which, in the interests of justice should be heard together, should be allocated to the Division to which the most serious has been allocated. Second, once a case has been allocated under these arrangements to a higher Division than would otherwise have been the case, it should deal with it, subject only to its sentencing power being limited to that of the lower Division to which it would otherwise have gone.

Pre-trial hearings

204   In recent years, and given added momentum by the Civil Justice Reforms, the role of the court in case management has come to the fore. For many, the sooner the court takes hold of the case at an early preliminary stage, the better. The rationale for this is that the parties are not preparing their respective cases for trial as speedily or otherwise as efficiently as they should, and are not co-operating appropriately with each other on disclosure and identification of the issues. Accordingly, so the thinking goes, the police, prosecutors and professional lawyers need the goad of the court to make them do their jobs properly, and the defendant needs it to encourage him to focus on the nature of his defence, if any. The vehicle for the application of the goad is a pre-trial hearing of some sort. In magistrates' courts in cases where it is needed. it is called a 'pre-trial review'. In the Crown Court, there are four separate, but largely similar, forms of procedure. First, there is the traditional non-statutory 'plea and directions hearing', in which the judge can make non-binding rulings before the start of trial.[234] Second, there is a statutory 'pre-trial hearing' under Part IV of the Criminal Procedure and Investigations Act 1996 in which the judge can make binding rulings.[235] Third is the now well established statutory procedures of 'preparatory hearings', as the start and part of the trial; for serious or complex fraud cases under the Criminal Justice Act 1987, in which the judge can make binding rulings.[236] Fourth is the similar

---

[234] *Practice Direction (Crown Court: Plea and Directions Hearings)* [1995] 1 WLR 1318
[235] ss 39-43
[236] ss 7-10

and parallel form of 'preparatory hearings' for other cases of complexity or length introduced by Part III of the 1996 Act.[237]

205 Magistrates' courts also have several different types of pre-trial hearing. First, 'early first hearings' are listed for a case which is likely to be an early guilty plea. If it turns out not to be so, the court will put it over to an 'early administrative hearing'. Second, at an early administrative hearing the court takes a plea before venue, determines mode of trial and sets pre-trial review and trial dates as necessary. Where the matter is indictable-only the court deals with it as part of an ordinary remand hearing. Finally, where a case has been set down for summary trial, a pre-trial review is held where needed to assess the state of readiness. Theoretically it should perform the same function as a plea and directions hearing in the Crown Court, but usually fails to do so. That is because of lack of targets, lack of enforceable sanctions for failure to achieve them, lack of clarity about the aims of the hearing and local variations in practice.

206 Pre-trial reviews in magistrates' courts have developed piecemeal, and differ from area to area. They may be heard by one, two or three magistrates, or a justices' clerk or a combination of magistrates and justices' clerk. They may be oral or written, required in all cases or never. The form and practice is a matter for each local bench, the different forms being developed and distinguished for ease of listing, so that cases may be block listed in busy court centres. Many courts would otherwise list all of them in their remand list and deal with them as they came up. The hearings are not necessarily the first hearing in the case; they are sometimes the second or even third, so the terms 'early' or 'first' may lead to confusion.

207 For many – perhaps most – cases tried summarily and in the Crown Court, the charge(s) and the issue(s) are clear from the outset, there is obviously not much point in elaborate prosecution disclosure, and case management in the sense of seeking the court's assistance or directions is not, or should not, be necessary. But for as long as most veteran criminal court judges and practitioners can remember, preparing the more complex cases so as to keep them within their proper bounds and avoid unnecessary public and private expense and inconvenience has been a problem. The most often voiced criticisms of the various forms of pre-trial hearings over the years is that the parties are not paid to prepare cases properly and the courts have no effective sanctions to make them do so. Nevertheless, it is to the credit of prosecutors and defence lawyers that they have instinctively and increasingly looked for the help of the courts in this regard. One of the earliest examples was the Central Criminal Court's practice direction, reproduced in many editions of Archbold in the 1960s and 1970s as a guide for general use in heavy cases

---

[237] ss 28-38

that called for it. In 1993 the majority of the Runciman Royal Commission recommended a system of 'preparatory hearings', but only for long and complex cases. It considered that in the majority of cases reliance on informal consultation between the parties was the better course.[238] The system it suggested was similar in some respects to that of preparatory hearings for serious and complex frauds already in being.

208   Whilst the Runciman Royal Commission was working on its report, the Government had begun experimenting with a recommendation of its Working Group on Pre-Trial Issues[239] for the holding of an early plea and directions hearing in all cases committed to the Crown Court. The Working Group's proposal prevailed, and a scheme now embodied in a practice direction issued by Lord Taylor CJ in 1995[240] provides for the holding of a plea and directions hearing in all cases, (other than serious fraud and otherwise complex or long cases for which statutory preparatory hearings are appropriate). The primary function of these hearings is for the pleas to be taken and, in contested cases, for the prosecution and the defence "to assist the judge in identifying the key issues, and to provide any additional information required for the proper listing of the case". The Lord Chancellor's Department has also issued a standard check-list of questions, called the 'Judge's Questionnaire', for the judge and the parties to consider at the hearings.[241]

209   The system of plea and directions hearings has been the subject of much local experimentation and adaptation. There are mixed views among the judiciary and practitioners as to their value. Much depends on the style and vigour of individual Resident Judges and other judges in the conduct of the hearings and on the local culture of criminal court practitioners. Often, the hearings amount to little more than the judge asking the parties' representatives, by reference to the standard check-list, about the progress of their preparation for trial and what, if any, issues still require resolution. Part of the exercise is also to inform the court of the likely shape, including the main issues, and length of trial, and availability of those involved so as to enable the court to fix a trial date. In the main, they are perfunctory proceedings. As many as 30 to 40 may be listed a day in some of the larger centres, taking the form of a report on progress, good or bad, and the fixing of a trial date or the judge chivvying the parties into getting on with basic matters of preparation and to resolving issues that they may or may not have discussed before then.

210   In more complex cases, where there are issues on which the parties cannot or will not agree, there may be more substance to the hearings. But often such cases have the benefit of more experienced and better resourced legal

---

[238] Chapter 7, paras 4, 11 and 16

[239] in a report issued, but not published, in November 1990

[240] see Appendix B in the 2001 edition of Archbold.

[241] for the latest version see Appendix C in supplement no 3 to the 2001 edition of Archbold

representatives who have been able to resolve all or most matters informally among themselves and are there simply to inform the court of that. In large part, therefore, the involvement of the judge is to monitor progress and to chase the parties in their preparation for trial. As to the latter, all courts now have 'case progression officers' whose function is to remind the parties of imminent deadlines in the timetable of preparation and to initiate action by the court when they fail to meet them. Depending on the size of the centre and the relationship that the officer can build up with local prosecutors and defence solicitors, this can be a valuable additional spur to efficient and timely case preparation. But, like the plea and direction system itself, it can also lead to parties waiting for the 'wake-up' call of the hearing or the telephone call or letter of reminder.

211   As I have indicated, there are no fewer than four separate, but largely similar forms of preliminary hearing for Crown Court cases. They are a good example of the unsystematic and overlapping way in which the legislature, when it intervenes in matters of criminal law, burdens and confuses its procedures. In all of them arraignment may take place and, if there is an acceptable plea of guilty and the case is ready for it, the judge can proceed to sentence. Where the matter is to be contested and there are substantial outstanding issues, the hearings can be of real utility, for example as to the adequacy of mutual or third party disclosure or in ruling on claims of public interest immunity or on matters of law on agreed facts. But in all of them, there is little difference in effect between the 'binding' orders made in the statutory procedures and those made in the non-statutory plea and directions hearings. And, in all of them the court has little effective sanction to enforce its directions if the parties are unable or unwilling to comply.

212   There are also problems in tailoring the time-tabling of pre-trial hearings to the parties' progress, or lack of it in preparing for trial. The regime for plea and directions hearings, of within four weeks after committal or, in "sent" cases, service of evidence when the defendant is in custody and within six weeks if on bail, is no doubt a reassuring target for the Court Service with its own targets and key performance indicators in mind and for the Government with its commendable aim of speeding the criminal justice process. For cases not needing such a hearing, it is an unnecessary and expensive intrusion in getting the case to trial. For cases needing a plea and directions hearing, the timing is often too tight. For example, when a defendant is in custody, the time taken to complete mutual disclosure often results in the plea and directions hearing taking place before the defendant has given a defence statement. And it is rare, even in bail cases, for the prosecution to have given secondary disclosure within the six weeks allowed for the hearing. The result is, that by the time of the initial plea and directions hearing, the parties are often nowhere near identification of the issues or assessment of the evidential and other requirements for trial, far less a realistic joint estimate of the likely length of the case to enable the Court to fix a firm date for listing. In many cases one or more further costly plea and directions hearings may be

necessary. Or the parties may commit themselves to a trial date when they do not yet know the precise issues in the case, what evidence they require to deal with them and what other pre-trial complications may emerge.

213   The result is that this well-intentioned, but rigid time-table, accompanied by equally insistent Court Service targets for trial dates, achieves the reverse of what is intended, because the parties become committed to a trial for which they may not be ready. It can generate, rather than reduce, last minute changes of plea ('cracked trials') or inability to start the trial on the day listed for it ('ineffective trials'), all because the timetable of disclosure and for preliminary hearings is not consistent or sufficiently flexible to meet the different circumstances of individual cases.

214   Some judges and legal practitioners consider that pre-trial hearings of one sort or another are a useful means of getting the parties together to focus on the matter of the plea and, in the event of a contest, the issues and the likely evidence required. There is also the convenience to defence practitioners of having defendants in custody brought from prison to court for a conference. Frequently, the last factor is the most important in the exercise. For reasons that I have given,[242] defence lawyers are often unable – and sometimes unwilling – to visit and take instructions from clients in custody. In my view, this is a major blot on our system of criminal justice. It should be a fundamental entitlement of every defendant, whether in custody or on bail, to meet at least one of his defence lawyers in order to give him instructions and to receive advice at an early stage of the preparation of his case for trial, and certainly before a pre-trial hearing.

215   Consideration should also be given to the unnecessary expense and disruption to the prison system and to the physical and mental well-being of prisoners in ferrying them to and from court for this purpose. In many instances, this involves long uncomfortable journeys and tedious hours of waiting before and after a conference with legal advisers and the proceedings in court. Prison governors and prisoners alike complain about the lateness of return from court, a particular problem in the case of young prisoners and adult women who, because of the fewer establishments accommodating them, generally face longer journeys. Astonishingly, as the Prison Inspectorate's Report on its Thematic Review on the Treatment and Conditions of Unsentenced Prisoners indicates,[243] this results in high numbers of prisoners being locked out from their prisons and having to be housed at short notice overnight in police cells. These unpleasant side effects of the plea and direction system for prisoners awaiting trial result from a combination of factors, including: excessive travel distances from prison to court as a result of the large catchment areas of

---

[242] see para 29 above
[243] paras 5.01-5.05

courts and prisons; general contractual arrangements between the Prison Service and prison escort contractors; inability of the contractors to collect prisoners before a certain time in the mornings; contractual constraints making it necessary for the contractors to make the maximum use of their vehicles by using them to make deliveries of prisoners to a number of different courts in the course of a single and sometimes long and tortuous journey; and the individual evening locking out times of different prisons. Conference and other conditions at court, particularly in magistrates' courts,[244] can be bad. And there is the highly unsettling effect on a remand prisoner of returning from court to a different cell and, often, a different cell-mate, a feature which the Prison Service Inspectorate regarded as of considerable importance for those newly brought into custody.[245] These unnecessary consequences can be eliminated by using available communications technology to enable prisoners to give instructions and participate in court hearings from a video-link (see paragraph 259 below for a detailed account of the possibilities and advantages of this technology).

216 Another important instance of the unsuitability of an unbending approach to plea and directions hearings is where civil and criminal matters arise out of the same or similar facts, particularly in cases involving neglect or abuse of children, where the needs of a family case may conflict with the criminal proceedings. A useful initiative to reduce this tension has been a system of joint plea and directions hearings conducted by one judge. These were successfully piloted in Norwich, Liverpool and then London and are now established as needed all over the country. They have proved to be particularly valuable in early identification of the issues, obtaining co-operation of all the parties and agencies concerned, so facilitating and simplifying third party disclosure and obtaining earlier dates of hearings in both jurisdictions than might otherwise have been the case. His Honour Judge Hyam QC, the Recorder of London, who has conducted a number of these hearings has commented on the procedure:

> "...its most striking feature is the fact that the parties, when gathered together, seem much more inclined to be co-operative than when they attend ordinary pre-trial hearings".[246]

217 In my view, this initiative is to be commended and should be given full support as a permanent feature in whatever form of case management of criminal cases that results from my recommendations. In the pre-trial assessment scheme that I recommend below, these cases are likely to be

---

[244] see *A Review of Custody Arrangements in Magistrates' Courts, London* Report of HM Magistrates' Courts Service Inspectorate (2000)
[245] *Thematic Review Of Treatment And Conditions Of Unsentenced Prisoners* paras 5.23 -5.24
[246] in a paper submitted in the Review

among those that will most often require an early pre-trial hearing as part of the scheme.

218 However, apart from such special cases, my view is that oral pre-trial hearings should become the exception rather than the rule. They should take place only in cases which, because of their complexity or particular difficulty, require them. In the majority of cases they are unnecessary, expensive, time-consuming and, often, because of their timing and the failure of trial advocates to attend, ineffective. Paradoxically, for the reasons I have given, they also often serve to delay rather than speed disposal of cases on pleas of guilty or by trial. Martin Narey felt unable, on the material before him, to reach a conclusion on their efficacy and recommended that the Trial Issues Group should examine whether they should be held in every case.[247] TIG did not do so, but, as I mention below, the Court Service is now piloting 'paper' plea and directions procedures.

219 Now that indictable-only cases are sent straight to the Crown Court – and, if my recommendations are adopted all cases will, after allocation, start at their appropriate level in a unified Criminal Court – the pace of preparation of cases from charge to trial should increase considerably.[248] It will become more important to provide a flexible system for tying together, in a tailor-made fashion for each case, mutual disclosure and such pre-trial involvement of the Court as the case may need. In this, recourse to the court by way of an oral preliminary hearing, other than an initial preliminary hearing, should be a last recourse rather than an early and automatic incident of the process. In this respect, it should be more like the system for pre-trial hearings in the magistrates' courts, only held where the case requires it.

220 In courts at all levels the main players – the police, prosecutors and defence lawyers – should take the primary responsibility for moving the case on. They should concentrate on improving the quality of the preparation for trial rather than trying to compensate for its poor quality by indulging in a cumbrous and expensive system of, often unnecessary and counterproductive court hearings. The way to do this, as I have urged in this and other Chapters in this Report, is by adequate organising and resourcing of the police, prosecutors, defence practitioners and the courts, including the provision of a common system of information technology for all of them and the Prison and Probation Services.

---

[247] *Narey Report* Ch 7, pp 38-41
[248] plea and directions hearings in 'sent' cases at present take place about eight to ten weeks after the first preliminary hearing, which approximates broadly to present target periods for committed cases

Pre-trial assessment

221 In many cases it may be plain from the outset how much or little time may be required for mutual disclosure and other preparations for trial and whether it will be necessary to trouble the parties or the court with a pre-trial hearing. In cases of size and/or complexity which look as if they will be contested, that would normally be the time to assign a judge of an appropriate level to manage and try it. But in all cases in the upper two Divisions, and as appropriate in the Magistrates' Division, the court and the parties should set a provisional time-table by reference to a suitably adapted standard check-list or case-management questionnaire, including a date before which trial should start. There is already a basis for this in the standard time-table issued by the Trial Issues Group as a guidance for the Crown Court and magistrates' courts. Thereafter, the parties should liaise with each other, informally communicating progress, or lack of it, on key tasks to the court and any others involved. In such a system, depending on the size or complications of the case, case progression officers could assume a wider role, not only chasing progress where required, but also involving themselves in arrangements for listing and, where appropriate, obtaining and transmitting written directions of the judge. In the event of failure of liaison of that sort between the parties and the court to achieve progress in accordance with a provisional or modified time-table, or in accordance with a requested or acknowledged need, say for a ruling on third party disclosure or a matter of law or evidence, the matter could be listed for a pre-trial hearing.

222 The Bar Council have suggested a more formal model of what I have in mind, in the form of a 'paper' plea and directions hearing coupled with front-loading of fees to cover preparatory work. It would build upon the Judges' Questionnaire and requirement for a defence statement by requiring the defence advocate to advise on evidence and as to a trial plan. There would be a fixed date for a paper hearing, based on the parties' answers to a supplementary or extended form of questionnaire served on the court and on each other, say, seven days before the date fixed for it. The matter would then proceed without an oral hearing unless the defendant indicates a plea of guilty, or either side require an oral hearing or the judge directs it. The defence advocate would be entitled to a fee for his preparatory work based on a percentage or percentages of the basic fee for plea of guilty or trial, plus a fee for a plea and directions hearing. The fee would be payable whether or not there is an oral hearing, thus providing an incentive to prepare properly and avoid it unless it is necessary.

223 A system of 'paper' or 'flexible' plea and directions hearings in straightforward cases is being piloted at three centres by the Court Service, following unofficial trials at two others. The criteria for determining whether a case is suitable for the procedure is left to each court to decide and a judge will make the determination on a case by case basis. I warmly commend this

initiative, but express caution as to its use as a marker for general use unless it is supported by the other mechanisms and resources, to which I have referred, necessary to improve the parties' performance in preparing for trial.

224   In my view, the time has come to replace the present mix of overlapping pre-trial procedures with a single statutory, but flexible, system of the sort that I have suggested and/or as advanced by the Bar Council. I would call it preparation by the parties for trial culminating in a 'pre-trial assessment' of the case by them and the court as to its state of readiness for trial. In most cases the assessment would be a paper exercise, the parties signifying in writing to each other and the court their readiness or otherwise for trial and the court responding in writing as appropriate. In those cases where outstanding matters could not be resolved by written directions, and an oral hearing is required, it should be called simply a pre-trial hearing and conducted at court. When the defendant is in custody and consents, he should participate in the hearing to the extent necessary by video-link from prison. Any cases likely to require an oral pre-trial hearing or substantial paper directions should, wherever possible, be allocated the trial judge who should assume responsibility for oversight of the parties' preparation for trial. Such a system of 'docketing' judges for the heavier cases should become more feasible if my recommendations for a move to fixed listing of such cases,[249] and more efficient use of judicial and everybody's time in case preparation, outside as well as inside the courtroom, are adopted.

225   If an oral pre-trial hearing becomes necessary, it should enable the judge to give binding rulings on substantive law, and procedure and evidence before the trial which may speed and simplify or otherwise shape it, subject to variation or discharge at trial as justice might require. Such hearings, particularly in indictable cases, should have two main functions: first to confine the trial and the evidence called at it to the issues of substance on which the case will turn; and second, so far as possible to resolve in advance all legal, procedural and evidential issues material to the outcome of the trial, so as to enable it to proceed smoothly and speedily without frequent interruptions for legal argument.

226   It is clearly vital that trial advocates should attend any pre-trial hearings. It should be a professional requirement that they should do their utmost to do so. Courts should do their best to list the hearings to accommodate their other professional commitments, if necessary by sitting earlier or later than the normal court working day.[250]

---

[249] see para 237 below

[250] see Chapter 11 para 177

227 Unlike Civil Courts, the Crown Court and magistrates' courts do not generally issue interlocutory orders to the parties in writing. The clerk of the court keeps a hand-written log of the proceedings, which should, but does not always, include all rulings, orders and directions. It is not normally checked by the judge or magistrates or the parties' representatives. The result is that frequently a judge or magistrates cannot readily tell from the file what orders were made on the last occasion the matter was before the Court for directions, the reasons given for earlier adjournments or relevant comments made from the bench. In the Crown Court it is not uncommon for there to be dispute between the parties as to what was directed on a previous occasion and for a debate to take place with the judge or his clerk in which the latter's record conflicts with what counsel have recorded on their briefs.

228 Such a casual culture of recording and disseminating courts' directions does not encourage proper respect for or compliance with them. There are exceptions. One is the Crown Court at Norwich, which routinely issues to the parties a computer print-out of the judge's order, including a 'trial by' date, a practice which, according to the Resident Judge, Judge Mellor,[251] "has significantly improved compliance rates". In my view, all rulings, orders and directions, at all pre-trial hearings, whatever their form, should be routinely recorded and, immediately or within a short time, issued to the parties in writing. If the courts were provided with the equipment, this could be done on the spot as it is in urgent cases in the County Court, and increasingly in magistrates' courts and in many of the criminal courts in the USA that I visited in the course of the Review. Or it could be done shortly afterwards by electronic transmission. Unfortunately, the CREST computer system used in the Crown Court does not have this basic facility.

Sanctions

229 I have mentioned the lack of effective sanctions and the need for better incentives to encourage all concerned in the preparation of criminal cases for trial to co-operate where they reasonably can and to get on with it. Orders of costs, wasted costs orders, the drawing of adverse inferences or depriving one or other side of the opportunity of advancing all or part of its case at trial are not, in the main, apt means of encouraging and enforcing compliance with criminal pre-trial procedures. In these respects criminal courts have much less control than civil courts. In civil disputes there is not the same tension between justice and efficiency in the preparation of cases for trial. One of both of the parties may not be willing litigants, but mostly they have a common aim in keeping costs down and thus in efficient and timely preparation for trial. There is a costs sanction available and routinely exercised against, not only the loser of the issue, but also against either party for procedurally culpable conduct causing unnecessary expense. Moreover, it

---

[251] in his submission in the Review

can be, and is imposed, except against a publicly funded litigant, without regard to his ability to pay.[252]

230   In criminal cases an order for costs against a defendant personally[253] is rarely an option because of his lack of means and because it may be hard to apportion fault as between him and his legal representatives. And there are problems about the fairness of a trial if a defendant is under threat of a sanction of that or other sorts if he, or his representatives misjudge the extent of their obligations to co-operate with pre-trial procedures. An order for costs against the prosecution for procedural default is possible and sometimes imposed. But, though it serves as a mark of the court's disfavour and dents a departmental budget, judges are disinclined in publicly funded defence cases to order what amounts to a transfer of funds from one public body to another. The third possible financial sanction is to make a wasted costs order against the legal representatives on one side or another. But again there are often practical limitations on the court of identifying who is at fault - on the prosecution side, counsel, those instructing him or the police - and on the defence side, counsel, his solicitor or the defendant. And wide use of such cumbrous satellite proceedings would be both an impractical and expensive way of achieving efficient preparation for trial, whether instituted before or after trial. Again, there are considerations of public interest, including the fairness of the trial, in too ready a use of this weapon as a threat and means of enforcing compliance with procedural requirements in criminal proceedings. The same applies to any possible extension of present powers of the courts to draw adverse inferences against one side or the other or to any attempt at importation from the civil process of the notion of 'strike-out', for example, by depriving a defendant from advancing all or part of his defence, or by too ready a use of the court's power to stay a prosecution for abuse of process.

231   Throughout the Review I have anxiously searched here and abroad for just and efficient sanctions and incentives to encourage better preparation for trial. A study of a number of recent and current reviews in other Commonwealth countries and in the USA shows that we are not alone in this search and that, as to sanctions at any rate, it is largely in vain. In a recent report, the Standing Committee of Attorneys General in Australia commented:

> "... the primary aim is to encourage co-operation with pre-trial procedures. There are inherent practical and philosophical difficulties associated with sanctions for non-co-operation".[254]

---

[252] Access to Justice Act 1999, s 11 (replacing the former procedure for legally aided parties)

[253] at present only possible on conviction; see Prosecution of Offences Act 1985, s 18(1)

[254] Report of the Standing Committee of Australian Attorneys-General, September 1999, p43; see also *Deliberative Forum on Criminal Trial Reform*, Report of the Standing Committee of Australian Attorneys-General, June 2000, Ch 4, p52 and recommendation 25

232   For the reasons I have given, I have concluded that there is little scope for improving on existing sanctions against the parties or their representatives for failure to prepare efficiently for trial save in two respects.

233   The first turns on adoption of my recommendations for equipping and resourcing both sides to shoulder the primary responsibility for the task, having recourse to a pre-trial hearing only if and when there are matters that they cannot reasonably resolve between them. Unnecessary recourse to or 'call-in' by the court could be met by a direction, as appropriate, that prosecuting counsel or publicly funded defence counsel and/or solicitors should not be paid for the appearance or, as the Bar Council have put it, should not be paid any more for the hearing than they would have been paid without it. And/or the matter could be dealt with by a judicial reprimand which could be recorded and used as part of the monitoring, inspection and assessment process to which public prosecutors and defenders, and defence lawyers franchised to undertake publicly funded defence work are or should be subject.

234   The second is to encourage professional bodies, in the main the Bar Council and the Law Society, to incorporate more stringent and detailed rules in their codes of conduct about preparation for trial. These should be accompanied by clear guidance as to the seriousness with which the court will view professional failures in this respect.

235   At or after the pre-trial assessment, or any necessary and final pre-trial hearing, the parties should be required to certify their readiness for trial. The date for such certification should be prescribed in the appropriate standard timetable or, directed by the trial court. Thereafter, in all cases tried in the Crown Division the parties' representatives should agree a form of case and issues summary for use by the judge in introducing the case to the jury and by the jury as an aide-memoire throughout the trial. I say more about this in Chapter 11, but emphasise here that the sort of document I have in mind should be neutral in its presentation and, in most cases, consist of a brief summary of only a few pages.

Accordingly, I recommend that:

- **In the preparation for trial in all criminal courts, there should be a move away from plea and directions hearings and other forms of pre-trial hearings to co-operation between the parties according to standard or adapted timetables, whenever necessary supplemented by written directions from the court;**

- **there should be national standard timetables and lists of key actions for preparation for trial in each of the** three Divisions of the new unified Criminal Court, with suitable variations to meet categories of case of different nature and complexity;

- the Magistrates' Division, when allocating cases to the Crown or District Divisions and, where appropriate, in summary cases at an early administrative hearing, should issue the parties with the appropriate standard timetable and list, including dates for mutual disclosure and a date within a short period after secondary disclosure for 'pre-trial assessment';

- the parties, by agreement or on notice to each other, should be at liberty to seek in writing leave from the trial court to vary the standard timetable;

- the parties should endeavour to prepare for trial in accordance with the timetable and list of key actions appropriate to the case and to resolve between themselves any issues of law, procedure or evidence that may shape and/or affect the length of the trial and when it can start;

- the timetable in each case should set a date for the 'pre-trial assessment' that is, an assessment, by the parties and the court as to the state of readiness for trial;

- by the pre-trial assessment date the parties should complete and send to the trial court a check-list showing progress in preparation and as to readiness, for trial, and seeking, if appropriate, written directions;

- only if the court or the parties consider it is necessary for the timely and otherwise efficient preparation for, and conduct of, the trial should there be a 'pre-trial hearing', for example where one or other of the parties cannot comply with the timetable or where there are unresolved issues affecting the efficient preparation for or conduct of the trial, or when the case is sufficiently serious or complex to require the guidance of the court;

- where there is a pre-trial hearing, and the defendant is in custody and consents, he should not be brought to court, but should participate in it to the extent necessary by video-link with the prison in which he is housed;

- a judge or magistrates conducting an oral pre-trial hearing should be empowered to give binding directions or rulings subject to subsequent variation or discharge if justice requires it;

- where a pre-trial hearing is necessitated by one or other or both parties' failure without good cause to comply with the time-table or other directions of the court, or to resolve issues of procedure, law or fact between them, the court should have power:

  - to make such order as to payment of a publicly funded defence advocate for his attendance at the hearing as may be appropriate in the circumstances; and/or publicly to reprimand either party's advocate or those instructing them as appropriate; any such public reprimand to be communicated to and taken into account by the professional body of the person reprimanded and, where the person is franchised for publicly funded defence work, by the Legal Services Commission; and/or

  - to make such order of costs against one or other or both sides as may be appropriate;

- all interlocutory court rulings, orders or directions in criminal courts as presently structured or in a new unified Criminal Court should be expressed in writing as a formal document of the court and served forthwith or shortly afterwards on all parties.

Listing and docketing

Responsibility for listing

236   Listing is said to be a judicial function. A better description is that it is a judicial responsibility. In the nature of things a listing officer has a better grasp both of the long-term, 'strategic' shape and needs of the list and the day-to-day programming and contingencies. The Resident Judge should maintain a general oversight of the listing at his court, but should not bury himself in the detail. Often his function is to decide or advise when a crisis has arisen on which the listing officer needs help. Of course, every judge has a closer involvement in cases in his own list and those cases assigned to him for future trial, but he must always keep an eye on the potential effects on other cases of his listing decision. Some have suggested that there should be a definition or re-definition of accountability as between the judiciary and listing officers. But I see no pressing need for it and cannot, in any event, feel able, with confidence, to suggest a better system. So much depends, in any event, on personalities and style and on the fluidity of demands on court time.

Close liaison between judges and their listing officer is the key, and, in my experience, it usually works very well.

Fixed trial dates

237   However, I consider that there should be a move to give fixed trial dates to cases of any substance. If case preparation improves this should occasion less risk of 'wasting court time' through cracked or ineffective trials and should enable judges to undertake a greater amount of case management as their contribution to better preparation. There is inevitably a tension between, on the one hand, the certainty, efficiency and convenience to all of a fixed system of listing in appropriate cases and, on the other, the need for flexibility to make optimum use of courts and judges. But the tension is not so evident if in providing greater certainty as to trial dates, it results in greater consideration to all involved in the criminal justice process, not just the courts and the judges.

Docketing

238   Those cases that will inevitably require judicial 'hands-on' management, including a pre-trial hearing, should be assigned at the outset to a particular judge for management and trial. It is a waste of resources for more than one judge to have to read and familiarise himself with issues and matters for pre-trial resolution. And a judge who knows that he is going to try the case is likely to take a closer interest in it and the task that it will pose for him and the parties. Docketing of such cases goes with fixed listing of them and the risks and compensations of the latter to which I referred in the last paragraph.

I recommend that:

- **there should be a move to greater use of fixed trial dates in cases of substance; and**

- **there should be a corresponding move to early allocation of such cases to a judge for case management and trial.**

VICTIMS

239   From time to time in the course of this Report I have mentioned the increasingly recognised role of victims in the criminal justice process. It arises at at least three stages: first, between the time of the alleged offence and the plea of guilty or trial; second, if the case is contested, at the trial; and, third, during the sentencing process. In the event of an appeal there is a fourth stage.

240   In this chapter, I am concerned just with the pre-trial stage, but I should begin with some general remarks. For almost every criminal there is a victim - and often also indirect victims in the form of bereaved, upset or closely involved relatives and friends. Yet, until recently, the focus has been on the criminal, or alleged criminal, leaving the victim, or alleged victim, with only a walk-on part – 'the forgotten party' - in the criminal justice system. 74% of those questioned in the British Crime Survey 2000 "felt" or "were not confident" that the criminal justice system met the needs of victims.

241   However, there has been a gathering momentum in recognition of the importance of victims in the system. It was initiated in the mid-70s by Victim Support, a national charitable organisation, and carried forward by it and, more recently, by JUSTICE, an all-party organisation dedicated to assist victims of miscarriage of justice. But it is only in the last few years that government has turned its mind to the more formal involvement and rights of the victim in all stages of the criminal process. In 1996, after a process of consultation with, among others, Victim Support, the Home Office introduced a non-statutory Victim's Charter[255] and guidance in the form of National Standards of Witness Care covering, among other things, listing, waiting times and witnesses' needs for information and protection. And there is now a proposal for a Victim's Bill of Rights of the sort promulgated in the United States, and for a Victims' Ombudsman.[256]

242   The primary role of Victim Support has been to comfort and support victims in the aftermath of the offences of which they have complained and to advise them in general terms of what any ensuing prosecution may require of them. Victim Support also runs the Witness Service, which is well established in every Crown Court Centre in the country. There, usually in dedicated accommodation within the court-building, trained volunteers offer support and information to witnesses, victims and their families before, during and after hearings. This includes pre-trial familiarisation visits to courts and provision of a leaflet of advice in most languages, *Going to Court*.[257] It is an impressive and valuable service conducted with financial support from government. Magistrates' courts though, as I have said, dealing with about 95% of all criminal prosecutions in the country, have had to depend, until now, on modest local initiatives by the courts themselves. However, a recent increase in government funding has enabled Victim Support to embark on a programme to provide, by early 2002, witness support services at every magistrates' court in the country.

---

[255] a successor to the Home Office Victim's Charter of 1990, and itself in process of being reviewed, and, according to *Criminal Justice: The Way Ahead*, Cm 5074 (Feb 2001) para 3.99, to be implemented in November 2001
[256] see *The Way Ahead* paras 3.104-3.105
[257] available in every language likely to be required

243   There is also much governmental examination of specific measures to increase the formal involvement of victims in the criminal process. This flows from pilot projects prompted by the 1996 Charter, the Glidewell and the Narey reports into the way in which prosecutions are prepared for trial[258] and the MacPherson report.[259]

244   All this is a belated recognition that, whilst it is for the state to prosecute crime and for victims and others to assist it in doing so, there would be no effective criminal justice system without the ready co-operation of victims in reporting and assisting in the prosecution of offenders.[260] It is in everybody's interest, and the entitlement of the victim, that he should be treated in a civilised manner and with due regard to his special needs at every stage of the process. This is not just a matter of expediency for the efficient prosecution of crime. It is, as JUSTICE has put it,[261] one of 'integrity' in the criminal justice system itself.

245   In addition, there are a number of practical reasons for giving victims, whether or not they are witnesses, more involvement and recognition in the system. They include: first, to inform the court of the effect of the offence on the victim so as to enable it to match the sentence to the seriousness of the offence; second, to inform the court of the victim's vulnerability to further injury from the offender or others so as to alert it to the need for his future protection, whether by sentence or otherwise; third, to equip the court publicly to acknowledge the wrong done to the victim and the need, where appropriate, for treatment; fourth, to enable the victim to have his say especially where a plea of guilty has deprived him of the opportunity of doing so in the trial; and fifth, to enable the court to assess and order compensation.

246   The English criminal justice system is most open to criticism in the information, or lack of it, given to victims and witnesses about the arrangements for hearings and their progress and outcome. By far the greatest number of complaints from lay people in the Review have come from those who have been called to give evidence in criminal trials. Many of them have said "Never again" or words to that effect. This may not be representative of the attitude of all or most victims who have been involved with the courts, since those who have suffered bad treatment are more likely to complain than those who have not. However, there are enough of them to confirm a similar picture emerging from other studies, and with it a serious risk of alienation of the public, victims in particular, as a result of their bad experience of the criminal justice system.

---

[258] *Review of the Crown Prosecution Service,* and the *Narey Report*

[259] *The Stephen Lawrence Inquiry,* CM 4262-1, February 1999

[260] as observed by JUSTICE in its 1998 Report *Victims in Criminal Justice,* p 22

[261] ibid pp 5 and 30 - 31

247   The complaints are straightforward enough and are vouched for by many who work in the criminal courts, including police, prosecuting and defending advocates and representatives of Witness Support. They are of: long delays after victims have made witness statements without information as to whether and when a prosecution is to be undertaken or of its progress after commencement; abortive attendances at court because of last minute adjournments or because of late decisions that their evidence is unnecessary or is agreed; failure to inform them of the outcome of the proceedings or to explain it; and failure to inform them of an appeal, when it is to be heard and of its outcome. These shortcomings are more serious where victims need support, particularly in the early stages or where, because of their relationship with the alleged offender or the nature of the offence, they feel vulnerable and in need of protection or, at least, of reassurance.

248   Then there is the treatment of witnesses who, on attending court to give evidence - often their first exposure to such an experience and at some personal and emotional cost - have to wait for long periods, sometimes for over a day, before being called into the witness box. Sometimes too there is bewilderment, in the absence of explanation, at the course a trial may take, for example, an acceptance by the prosecution of a change of plea to a lesser offence or the matter being removed from the jury at the close of the prosecution case or at some other stage.

249   There are, of course, great difficulties in time-tabling the forensic process, however well planned it may be. But all too often these ordeals for witnesses result from a combination of inadequate preparation by the parties and/or case management by the court, and almost always by a failure to keep them sufficiently informed of what is going on. For witnesses who are not victims, it is bad enough; for those who are - those who rightly consider the process to be in part a vindication of their suffering - it must be worse.

250   As I have indicated, efficient preparation for trial has as one of its important objects the reduction of uncertainties in listing and in the planned progress of cases so as to avoid waste of time and money and inconvenience and distress to many, including victims who are witnesses. Such uncertainties result from 'cracked trials' - late pleas of guilty in cases listed for trial and from 'ineffective trials' - trials not proceeding on their listed commencement dates for one last minute reason or another.

251   For the sake of victims and witnesses too there is a need for a significant improvement in the efficient preparation of cases for trial so that the trial process runs more closely to plan than it does now, and a better system of informing them and all others concerned of the state of progress, the outcome

and the reason for it. No single agency has responsibility for the care of victims and witnesses. Traditionally, the police have kept them informed; Police National Guidelines impose the responsibility on the officer in charge of the case, but he is not always best placed to do that once the prosecutor has the conduct of it. Even if, which may be difficult, liaison between the two is good, it is undesirable for the police, or more likely some civilian assistant, to relay information about developments for which the prosecutor may be responsible. Under new and developing practices prompted largely by the Glidewell and Narey Reviews, prosecutors, together with the police in special units, are beginning to share the responsibility. In my view, there should be a clear understanding between them at the start of each case involving a victim, who is to keep him informed, of what and how. At the point when such decisions are made there should be a clear understanding, to be noted on the file, as to whose responsibility it is to communicate the decision to the victim.

252   Beyond a few basics, I doubt whether this division or sharing of responsibility is susceptible to national guidelines or to an overly prescriptive approach, because the circumstances of each case and the concerns of the victim are different. However, there are some decisions of the prosecutor that are or may have such an important effect on the victim that I consider the prosecutor should personally inform him of them, for example, the substitution for the original charge of a lesser one, the acceptance of a plea of guilty to a lesser charge and a dropping of the whole prosecution. I am pleased to see that the police and Crown Prosecution Service are already making arrangements for such a shift of responsibility, and these will be finalised by October 2002. In addition, in every case victims and witnesses should be given at the outset a point of contact and, wherever possible, the name of the person whom they can ask for information or advice. They should also be given an indication of the extent and timing of information that they can expect, so that they do not have unrealistic expectations, and the contact point of a senior person to whom they can complain if they are dissatisfied with the information they receive.

253   There is also a suggestion that once a prosecution has reached the courts, court staff should be responsible for keeping everyone, including victims and witnesses informed of the progress, listing and outcome of the case. This suggestion may become stronger and more realisable as and when the criminal justice system as a whole is properly served with a common system of information technology. A first step could be an automatic telephone 'bulletin board'.

254   I should emphasis that my proposals are directed towards information of, not consultation with, victims, for example as to the charges, discontinuance or as to the level of court for trial. There are a number of reasons why the victim should not be part of a consultative process, all or most of which are acknowledged by Victim Support:

- in many instances, at the pre-trial and trial stages of the process it has yet to be established whether the alleged victim is in truth a victim;

- he would not normally have the necessary knowledge or experience;

- he would be unlikely in most cases to have the necessary objectivity and would expose the criminal justice process to the risk or at least the perception of prosecuting decisions being influenced by the vengefulness of victims, hardly a recipe for fairness or consistency in the enforcement of the law;

- it could create false expectations if his view were not acted upon;

- if it were thought that victims could influence the dropping of prosecutions, it would expose them to intimidation or pressure to urge it in individual cases; and

- it would place a heavy responsibility on them that they might not wish, or be psychologically prepared, to bear.

255 All these and other associated questions have been the subject of many reviews, national and local initiatives and pilot studies over the last few years. This Review is the broadest, but only one, of a number of current searches for improvement of the system.

INFORMATION TECHNOLOGY

Case management

256 Professor Richard Susskind has identified[262] four different senses in which the phrase 'Case Management' is used to describe the way information and communications technology could transform the way cases are prepared for trial:

- management information systems – to monitor the work and performance of the courts;

- case administration systems – to support and automate the back office, administrative work of court staff;

- judicial case management – comprising case tracking, case planning, telephone and video conferencing and document management; judicial case management support systems - systems used by court staff in support of judges who are involved with case management; and

---

[262] Richard Susskind, *Transforming the Law* (OUP 2000) p 239

- non-judicial case management – to help court staff progress cases which do not, in the event, proceed to trial.

257 In Chapter 8, I have recommended the introduction of a single electronic case file with information accessible to each of the main criminal justice agencies. The implementation of an integrated information technology system of this kind would radically improve case management in the first two of these senses, by allowing the prosecution, defence and the court to communicate online, extracting information from and adding information to, the same body of data. There are, however, also very significant improvements which can be made to the way the courts assist the judiciary once they have the benefit of support which modern technology can offer. There are at least four ways in which the court could use these technologies:

- case tracking systems – to produce daily reminders, progress reports, lists of outstanding tasks and notices of who has responsibility for further actions, thus supporting judges in supervising, monitoring and controlling their cases from start to finish;

- case planning systems – PC-based project management software to enable judges to generate their own plans for complex cases, depicting timescales, key events and activities;

- telephone and video conferencing – enabling judges to monitor the progress of cases and to keep in direct contact with parties' legal representatives where formal hearings with parties physically present are unnecessary; and

- document retrieval systems – allowing judges access to documents to cases for which they are responsible and to retrieve them.

258 Once these functions are available (and, as I have noted in Chapter 8 this is not yet the case even in our civil courts), the way would be clear for a step change in the way cases are organised, scheduled and managed by the criminal courts. A simple example will suffice to illustrate this point. At present, if a judge (for example a Resident judge) wishes to survey progress on a group of cases listed for trial on a particular day, he (or a court clerk acting on his behalf) would first have to locate the relevant paper files, and then seek the assistance of court staff in making enquiries by e-mail, fax or telephone of those involved. To undertake such an exercise for a batch of twenty cases might take a whole morning, and might result in little more than a list of unanswered questions. But in a world in which all case information could be available to the judge online via a central electronic file, the judge could survey each case himself in a matter of minutes or seconds and could concentrate on prompting or directing any necessary action rather than merely seeking to find out what is going on.

The virtual courtroom

259   Technology also has the potential to transform processes by which judicial decisions are taken at each stage in of a criminal case. Live video links can provide real-time, two-way transmission of images and sound between two or more locations. Parliament has recently provided for the use of video-link participation by defendants in custody in pre-trial hearings,[263] and by vulnerable or intimidated witnesses, in trials.[264] As to the former, pilot courts were established in 1998/99 in magistrates' courts in Bristol, Swindon and, Manchester, and at Manchester Crown Court. An evaluation[265] of the pilots showed that the introduction of live video-links had been a considerable success and was generally popular with the majority of remanded defendants. However, many expressed concern about the confidentiality of parallel arrangements made for telephone and video consultations with their representatives. Some lawyers objected in principle to the use of the link for bail applications. Others felt that their clients' chance of being granted bail was adversely affected when they were not physically present at the court. But this was not borne out by the evaluation data,[266] which showed no difference in the proportion of bail applications granted before and during the pilot. As to the cost of national provision of these facilities, it should be borne in mind that the present costs of transporting prisoners between prisons and courts are substantial (and rise exponentially with the security classification of the prisoner). In addition, the one-off capital cost of such links would quickly be balanced by savings of time and money, not only in transportation costs but also in solicitors' and counsels' travelling time, and court time in waiting for prison vans. Routine use of video-links for most pre-trial hearings, including the taking of pleas and applications for bail, with the consent of the defendant, would be welcomed by the Prison Service, defence lawyers and many defendants for their different reasons. Naturally, defendants would have to have ready and secure video-link or telephone communication with their lawyers before, during and after the hearings and otherwise to safeguard their position. The evaluation concluded that the favourable outcome of the pilots clearly justified the extension of these facilities. And the Government announced in its policy paper, *The Way Ahead*, [267] that every prison handling remand prisoners will have a video link to a magistrates' court by March 2002.

---

[263] Crime and Disorder Act 1998, s57

[264] Youth Justice and Criminal Evidence Act 1999, Part II

[265] Plotnikoff and Woolfson *Video Link Pilot Evaluation* (Home Office 1999) and *Evaluation of Information Video Link Pilot Project at Manchester Crown Court,* (Court Service and HM Prison Service, 2000)

[266] see *Video Link Pilot Evaluation*

[267] Cmnd 5074 p 107

260   However, the Government's commitment relates only to magistrates' courts. In my view, and for the reasons I have given, there is an equally compelling case for extending this facility to all pre-trial hearings in the Crown Court, and/or in the Crown and District Divisions of the new unified Criminal Court that I have recommended. In addition, as I have stated, I would like the links to become more than a resource for court hearings. They should also be available to enable representatives to speak to their clients and take instructions during the course of the preparation of the case. This could significantly improve the speed of preparation.

261   One of the problems encountered during the pilot exercises concerned cases with co-defendants. The number of co-defendants who can be accommodated with the present video-link equipment is limited by the camera field of view at both the courthouse and in the prison. This is because the single telecom link requires all co-defendants to be present in the same room in the prison. In addition, the use of point to point fixed links means that there are inevitable limitations on the number of prisons which can be linked up to each court, so that there might still have to be movement of prisoners between prisons, if not from prisons to court, as use of video links became more widespread. With the increasing use of special lines,[268] more prisons should be able to link up with courts; and the substitution of internet technologies for fixed telecom links would clearly improve and accelerate matters considerably Links could then be combined from a number of sources simultaneously, provided adequate levels of security could be assured.   As Professor Susskind has pointed out,[269] techniques to ensure that web transmissions can be secure, confidential and capable of an authentication are already in prospect and will lead to an enormous increase in telecommunications capacity.   The courts should be ready to take early advantage of these technologies.

I recommend that the present provision for the use of video-link with prisons in pre-trial hearings in magistrates' courts should be extended to all such hearings in all criminal courts and, as technology develops, consideration should be given to the use of web technologies for them.

Time limits

Over-all time limits

262   Although there are no over-all time limits governing prosecutions in indictable cases for England and Wales, the courts have jurisdiction to stay

---

[268] ISDN and ADSL
[269] *Transforming the Law* (OUP 2000) p 127

unduly delayed proceedings where they amount to an abuse of process, a jurisdiction now underlined by a defendant's right under Articles 5(3) and 6(1) of the European Convention of Human Rights to trial within a reasonable time. There is a six months' limitation on the prosecution of summary offences in magistrates' courts begun by information or complaint, running from the date of the alleged offence to the laying of the information or making of the complaint, a constraint which, at that level seems to operate reasonably well.[270]

263   Experience in other jurisdictions suggests that rigid or vigorously applied over-all time limits can be counterproductive. In Scotland, for example, a jury trial must normally proceed within 110 days of committal if the accused is in custody (subject to the court's discretionary power to extend) and within a year of commencement of proceedings, if on bail. On the expiry of either deadline, the prosecution is stayed and the defendant is released from custody or his bail obligation as the case may be. However, the availability of these time limits does not, in general, contribute to the aim of efficient and speedy preparation for trial. To comply with them, procurators fiscal frequently have to list the cases for trial even when they are not, or may not be, ready and then seek repeated adjournments while the parties continue to prepare for trial. Not only does such necessity defeat the purpose of the time limits, but it also causes much waste of time and other inconvenience to defendants, witnesses, victims and all others involved in the process. In Canada a decision of the Supreme Court,[271] interpreting the constitutional right of defendants charged with serious offences to trial within a reasonable time, led to so many motions to stay, that the prosecution dropped thousands of cases awaiting trial. The resultant public outcry contributed eventually to the legislature reclassifying a broad range of offences so as to take them outside that relatively loose time bar.

264   Similar experiences in other jurisdictions suggest that the Secretary of State has been well advised in not introducing over-all time limits here.[272] Compliance with arbitrary and rigid time limits is likely to give only an illusion of speedy preparation for trial, hiding the reality of injustice in substantive and procedural compromises that they may impose on the criminal justice process. At their worst, they may prevent conviction of the guilty whilst doing little to speed the trial of both the guilty and innocent. Neither is conducive to public confidence in the system. In my view, the provisions for bail, custody time limits and power of the courts to stay cases where delay amounts to an abuse of process are adequate legal safeguards against undue delay in bringing cases to trial. Accordingly, I do not recommend the introduction of over-all time limits for the conduct of

---

[270] Magistrates' Courts Act 1980, s 127

[271] *R v Askov* (1990) 79 CR (3rd) 273, 56 CCC (3d) 449 (SCC)

[272] as he has power to do under the Prosecution of Offences Act 1985, s 22(1)(a)

prosecutions of indictable offences or for variation of the six months' limitation on summary prosecutions in Magistrates' Courts brought by information or complaint.

Custody time limits

265   There has been little comment in the Review about the value and broad effect of the custody time limits. But because of my recommendation for the establishment of a unified Criminal Court, and a number of problems in their practical application, I refer to them in a little more detail than might otherwise be thought necessary. In summary-only and 'either-way' cases, the maximum custody period from first appearance to trial or mode of trial hearing, as the case may be, is 56 days, and, for 'either-way' cases, to trial or committal, 70 days. In the Crown Court the maximum custody period is 112 days from committal and 182 (less any time spent in custody while in the magistrates' court) from sending or transfer,[273] to start of trial.

266   Under a unified court structure, or even without it, if my recommendation for abolition of committals in either-way offences is adopted, there would be no need for staged custody time limits pegged to the times of allocation and committal. All cases should have a single maximum custody period from first appearance to start of trial. I have received no submissions in the Review to persuade me that the present maxima from first hearing to trial of 56 days in summary cases or 182 days in those tried on indictment should change. And, for those cases allocated to the District Division, 182 days would also appear to be suitable.

Accordingly, I recommend that the present maximum custody periods should continue, save that, in the event of abolition of committal proceedings for 'either-way' offences and/or of the establishment of a unified Criminal Court, the periods should be 56 days for cases tried summarily (whether summary-only or 'either-way') and 182 for those tried otherwise.

Extension of custody time limit

267   A court may extend the custody time limit if it is satisfied that the need for it is due to "some … good and sufficient cause" and "that the prosecution has acted with all due diligence and expedition".[274] There has been much jurisprudence on these two criteria, focusing on the need to establish both of

---

[273] Crime and Disorder Act 1998, ss 51 and 52;and Criminal Justice Act 1987, ss 4 and 5
[274] Prosecution of Offences Act 1985, s 22(3)

them and on the application of the first, in particular, that inability to list the case because of lack of a judge or a court is not normally "a good and sufficient cause".[275] ACPO have criticised the outcome that, despite due diligence on the part of the police and prosecutor, an inability on the part of the court system, for whatever reason, to provide a judge or a court could nevertheless result in refusal of an extension. I can understand the police frustration about this. On first impression, it seemed to me that the observation of Lloyd LJ in *R v Governor of Winchester Prison, ex p Roddie*, in relation to the duty of the prosecution to proceed with all due expedition, that Parliament having willed the speedy trial of defendants in custody "must also will the means", might also apply to the provision of a judge or a courtroom to try the case.[276] However, such or any other causes have, in the words of the statute, to be "sufficient" as well as "good", which is its way of ensuring that that they are not used to subvert its purpose of speedy trial for those in custody. Courts must examine such claims rigorously and, in the end, decide each on its own facts to see whether it is both "good" and "sufficient". It follows that, depending on the circumstances, unavailability of a judge or a courtroom may be held to justify an extension. In that state of the law, I see no justification for recommending amendment of the 1985 Act in this respect.

268   The consequence of expiry of the custody time limit where, because of a slip, the prosecution has not before then sought an extension, can be serious. A defendant is only held in custody where there are substantial grounds for believing that he would abscond, or commit an offence while on bail or obstruct the course of justice. But the courts can only extend the limit on application made before its expiry.[277] And even where a magistrates' court or the Crown Court have considered and wrongly refused an extension before the expiry of the period, their decision cannot be corrected on application to the Divisional Court after its expiry.[278] This is aggravated by the anomaly that a prosecution appeal to the Crown Court from a magistrates' court's refusal to extend the time limit will not be deemed to expire until the appeal has been determined. Yet, in a prosecution appeal from the Crown Court to the Divisional Court, the time limit takes effect despite the pending proceedings. Thus, as a result of a procedural slip an accused person may be let free to wreak havoc of one or other of those sorts. Equally, where one or other court has wrongly granted an extension, the defendant is without remedy unless he can get his case before the Divisional Court within the period. The right of appeal in either case is often academic by the time the appeal is listed for hearing. An application may be made "at any time before the expiry of a time limit", but a further application within the period on essentially the same basis would ordinarily be an abuse of process. It has been held that, where the court has refused an extension because of "a fundamental error of fact", it would be

---

[275] for a review of the authorities and general statement of the law, see *R v Manchester Crown Court, ex p McDonald* [1999] 1 Cr App R 409, DC, per Bingham LCJ, giving the judgment of the Court

[276] ibid at 415D-416B

[277] *R v Sheffield JJ, ex p Turner* [1991] 2 QB 472, 93 Cr App R 180, DC

[278] *R v Croydon Crown Court, ex p Comnrs Of Customs and Excise* [1997] 8 Archbold News 1, DC

permissible to re-apply to the same court on the true facts.[279] However, that is a very restricted basis of challenge and does not overcome the absence in most cases of an effective remedy by way of appeal.

269 In my view, some provision should be made for enabling a criminal court at any level to consider and grant an extension outside the period and for an effective right of appeal outside the period against a refusal within the period. Because of the fundamental nature of the presumption in favour of a defendant's liberty while awaiting trial, any relaxation of that sort would have to be tightly circumscribed. For example, there could be a limit on the further period during which the matter could be raised. But the central criterion, I suggest, should be that a first instance court should only exercise the power to extend after expiry of the time limit where it is satisfied that there is a compelling public interest for doing so.

270 It has been suggested[280] that many of the difficulties of overrunning the custody time limits in the Crown Court could be overcome by holding an early pre-trial hearing at which a date is set for trial before expiry of the limit or, if that is not practicable, at which a direction is given that it should be tried within a "window of time" before expiry and re-listed for directions in good time if there is any problem about it.[281] That is undoubtedly one way of doing it, but potentially wasteful in the number of pre-trial or mentions hearings which it may require. An early pre-trial hearing, as I have said, is rarely good use of the court's or the parties' time; in many cases, mutual disclosure will not have taken place and the likely shape and length of the trial cannot be reliably estimated. What is needed is an automatic system by which the court and the prosecution register from the outset the relevant maximum custody period and which they can set as an alert as time moves on. In my view, a better practical and more efficient safeguard against the risk of the prosecution overlooking the imminence of expiry of custody time limits would be greater use by courts of information technology in their case management systems. Both the courts and the prosecutors could have built into their case files in custody cases 'landmark' dates to trigger the need for timely applications for extension if appropriate. Such 'landmarks' should also be of assistance in identifying priorities for listing of cases for trial.

I recommend:

- **amendment of section 22 of the Prosecution of Offences Act 1985 to enable a court to consider and grant an extension of the custody time limit after its expiry, but only if such power is closely**

---

[279] *R v Bradford Crown Court, ex p Crossing* [2000] 1 Cr App R 463, DC

[280] see the 2001 edition of Archbold, para 1-270a

[281] *R v Sheffield Crown Court, ex p Headily* [2000] 2 Cr App R 1, DC; and *R v Worcester Crown Court, ex p Norman* [2000] 2 Cr App R 33, DC

circumscribed, including a provision that the court should only grant an extension where it is satisfied that there is a compelling public interest in doing so; and

- the provision of an effective right of appeal outside the period against the refusal of an extension within the period.

A CODE OF CRIMINAL PROCEDURE

271   Fairness, efficiency and effectiveness of the criminal justice system demand that its procedures should be simple, accessible and, so far as practicable, the same for every level and type of criminal jurisdiction. There are many features of criminal procedure that are common to summary proceedings and those on indictment, yet at present they are separately provided for in each jurisdiction and in a multiplicity of instruments and, often, in quite different language. Such a mix of different provisions providing for common procedural needs is an impediment to understanding by courts, legal practitioners, parties and others of the workings of the courts, and thus to the accessibility of the law. A unitary court, whilst not essential to the establishment of a common code, would ease its introduction and the task of all who have recourse or are exposed to the criminal process.

272   There has been an enormous increase in the growth in and pace of change to our substantive and procedural criminal law in recent years. Scarcely a year passes without one, or some times two, pieces of criminal justice legislation, introducing in a disjointed way fundamental changes to the work of the criminal courts. There were Criminal Justice Acts in 1982, 1987, 1988, 1991 and 1993. They were followed by the Criminal Justice and Public Order Act 1994, the Criminal Procedure and Investigations Act 1996 and the Crime and Disorder Act 1998. Most of these enactments made fundamental changes to the law, and they represent only a proportion of the legislative unrest of recent years. Such legislation is usually accompanied by secondary legislation. There are also common-law rules, judicial practice directions and statutory and non-statutory codes of practice. The Law Commission, in a survey for this Review in early 2000, found: 207 Acts of Parliament devoted to criminal procedure and/or evidence, the earliest enacted in 1795; 64 pieces of secondary legislation containing rules that differed according to whether they governed summary proceedings or those on indictment - 271 different sources of law, procedure and evidence, not including case law or guidance from the Lord Chief Justice or the Attorney General. Few of these sources, standing on their own, represent the whole law or the current law on any particular aspect, many of them being subject to piecemeal amendment, often by several more recent instruments. In short, there is no definitive, simple and ordered

statement of the law governing either the separate procedures of the two jurisdictions, still less the procedures common to both.

273   Finding the right source or sources can be a time-taking and confusing task for judges and experienced criminal law practitioners. And, having found them, the content is often impenetrable and sometimes leads to conflicting decisions. What can it be like for lay magistrates, dependent on the advice of their often over-pressed court legal adviser in the middle of a busy list, still more for the often unrepresented defendant in the magistrates' courts, equally dependent on help from the court staff or even the prosecutor's goodwill? Complexity and uncertainty such as this increases cost. Little attention is paid to it because it is hidden. It causes expensive delays and mistakes in the legal process at all levels; it spreads beyond the courtroom itself in the training and - with each new piece of legislation – re-training in one form or another of many involved in the criminal justice process. There are significant costs to all this – in the form of injustice and loss of public confidence and a financial cost to the public who have to pay the bill. For a characteristically entertaining, but also depressing, account of the mess we are in, I commend Professor John Spencer's recent paper, *The Case for a Code of Criminal Procedure*.[282]

274   What is needed is, not a consolidation of all relevant current provisions, but a concise and simply expressed statement of the current statutory and common law procedural rules and the product of the present overlay of practice directions, codes of guidance and the like. It should be in a single instrument and laid out in such a form that it, the Code, can be readily amended without constant recourse to primary legislation and without changing the 'geography' or the familiar paragraph and section numbers governing each topic. There is nothing new in an instrument formulating, as distinct from merely consolidating, the law from time to time, and doing so within a constant framework. In the procedural sphere Civil law countries took as an early model the Napoleonic Code d'Instruction Criminelle of 1808,[283] drawing as the French did, on common as well as civil law traditions. The United States of America have developed codification of primary and secondary legislation and jurisprudence into a fine art in both state and federal jurisdictions. And, as Lord Bingham memorably said in a speech some three years' ago:

> "For 25 Canadian dollars Canadian citizens can buy a small paperback which contains a comprehensive and comprehensible statement of everything he, and the policeman, and the judge, need to know about the substantive

---

[282] presented to a meeting of the Statute Law Society in October 1999 , now published in [2000] Crim LR 519

[283] see now the French *Code de Procedure Penale*, which dates from 1958

criminal law, evidence, procedural and sentencing in Canada."[284]

275 In the more modest form of statutory consolidation, Commonwealth countries have done much the same for two or more centuries. There is a good practical example of the latter close at hand in Scotland's consolidation, starting in 1975, of its statutory laws of criminal procedure.[285]

276 As Professor Spencer has suggested,[286] we should proceed in two stages. First, there should be an exercise in consolidation of primary and secondary legislation coupled, possibly, with some codification of the more important and uncontroversial common law rules. This would be a valuable exercise in ground clearing, in identifying the inconsistencies and the anomalies and in searching for and identifying some broad and overriding principles. The Law Commission would probably be best suited for the task of preparing a draft Bill, the passage of which into legislation could be swift and uncontroversial, as in Scotland.

277 A start could then be made on codification, an exercise of both systematic restatement and reform, with the aim of producing a single corpus of rules for a unified Criminal Court. That instrument should begin with a clear statement of purpose and general rules of application and interpretation, as successfully pioneered in the Civil Justice Rules flowing from Lord Woolf's reforms of the civil law. It should combine the various sources into a concise summary of rules, reducing them so far as possible into a discipline common to all levels of jurisdiction, using the same language and prescribing the same forms. It should make separate provision only insofar as necessary to allow for procedural differences at each level flowing from the court's composition and nature and volume of its work. It should be capable of ready and orderly amendment, by secondary legislation along the lines of that enabling the Lord Chancellor to amend the Civil Procedure Rules, subject to the negative or positive resolution procedure.[287] The boundary between procedure and substantive law is often ill-defined and there will no doubt continue to be changes of important principle that may require primary legislation. In that event, if the integrity of a new convenient and concise code of procedure drawing on all relevant sources is to be maintained, some method would need to be devised for convenient and orderly amendment of it. I emphasise that I am talking about codification of all procedural sources, that is, statutory, case law, custom and judicial practice directions and other guidance.

---

[284] delivered at a dinner for HM Judges at the Mansion House, London on 22nd July 1998; now published in his selected essays and speeches, *The Business of Judging* (OUP, 2000), p 295, under the heading: *A Criminal Code: Must We Wait For Ever?*
[285] Criminal Procedure (Scotland) Act 1975, itself included in further consolidation in the Criminal Procedure (Scotland) Act 1995;
[286] *The Case for a Code of Criminal Procedure* pp 529-531
[287] see Civil Procedure Act 1997, s 4

278   Codification of procedure would, however, be a substantial task and would need to be carried out by a body with a specific remit and particular expertise. As the Law Commission have observed,[288] some matters of procedure involve questions of general principle requiring primary or secondary legislation on which it could advise, if asked, for example, questions of bail, disclosure, joinder and rules of evidence. But the bulk of the work, whether of principle or practicality, in proposing and formulating provisions of the Code and, subsequently, their amendment would have to be consigned to a separate, standing body specially constituted for the purpose, such as a statutory rules committee. It should be closer in form and function to the Civil Procedure Rules Committee[289] the function of which is to make rules subject to the Lord Chancellor allowing them, rather than to the much smaller Crown Court and Magistrates' Courts' Rules Committees which do not meet as committees and which, in the main, simply react in correspondence to drafts prepared by the Home Office and Lord Chancellor's Department.[290] Its initial role would be to draft the code and thereafter to maintain it, taking into account new and projected legislation and draft Bills produced by the Law Commission. It should have a power to propose change as well as to advise on changes proposed by others, or likely to be made necessary by legislation, case law or other developments. There should be a complementary duty on government to seek the Committee's advice at an early stage on all proposed procedural innovation or change.

279   I suggest that the body entrusted with this important task should be statutory and have a status similar to that of the Civil Procedure Rules Committee. It should be called **The Criminal Procedure Rules Committee**. In my view, it should be chaired by the Lord Chief Justice and should include judges from each level of the Criminal Court, including the Vice President of the Court of Appeal, (Criminal Division), the Senior Presiding Judge, at least two High Court Judges and two Circuit Judges sitting in crime, together with an appropriate number of District Judges, magistrates and justices' clerks. It should also contain a number of experienced criminal practitioners from both branches of the profession, and at least one academic specialising in the field, together with appropriate representatives of voluntary organisations with a direct interest in the work of the criminal courts. And it should be supported by a full-time staff of lawyers and administrators with similar experience.

280   In Chapter 8 I recommended the creation of a statutory Criminal Justice Council to act as a standing advisory body to the Government on the criminal justice system and to provide general oversight of the programme and structures for codification of the criminal law. I believe that such a body

---

[288] in a submission in the Review

[289] Civil Procedure Act 1997, s 2

[290] Supreme Court Act 1981, s 86; Magistrates' Courts Act 1980, ss 144 and 145

would have an important role in advising on and co-ordinating the process of change flowing from this Review but also more generally in its role of keeping the criminal justice system under review. For these purposes, I believe that the Council should have over-all oversight of the work of the Criminal Procedure Rules Committee.

I recommend that:

- **the law of criminal procedure should be codified, but in two stages;**

  - **first, the Law Commission should be requested to draft legislation consolidating existing primary and secondary legislation coupled, possibly, with some codification of the more important and uncontroversial common law rules;**

  - **second, a statutory Criminal Procedure Rules Committee should be established to draft a single procedural code for a unified Criminal Court, restating and reforming as necessary statute and common law, custom, judicial practice directions and other guidance;**

- **the code, which should be expressed concisely and in simple English and Welsh, should provide, so far as practicable, a common set of rules for all levels of jurisdiction, and different rules only to the extent that they are necessary for different forensic processes;**

- **the draft code should be enacted in primary and subsidiary legislation, and the Committee should, thereafter maintain it, proposing amendments where necessary for the Lord Chancellor's approval and initiation of amendment by secondary legislation subject to negative or positive resolution as may be appropriate;**

- **in all its activities, the Committee should be under the general oversight of the Criminal Justice Council;**

- **the Government should be under a statutory duty to refer to the Committee all proposals for amendment of the law of criminal procedure;**

- **the Criminal Procedure Rules Committee should be chaired by the Lord Chief Justice and its membership should also include: the Vice-President of the Court of Appeal (Criminal Division), the Senior Presiding Judge, at least two High Court Judges and two Circuit Judges sitting in crime, together with an appropriate number of District Judges, magistrates and justices'** clerks, a number of experienced criminal practitioners from both branches of the profession and at least one academic specialising in the field, together with appropriate representatives of voluntary organisations with a direct interest in the work of the criminal courts; and

- the Committee should be supported by a full-time staff of lawyers and administrators experienced in the work of the criminal courts.

CHAPTER 11

THE TRIAL: PROCEDURES AND EVIDENCE

INTRODUCTION

1   Trial by ordeal, common throughout Europe in the Middle Ages, gave way in England to an accusatorial system based on trial by jury of a citizen's complaint, and in much of Europe to an inquisition by some trusted person. Eventually the two systems developed respectively into our system of trial by judge and jury, with a private or public prosecutor, and the continental inquisition in which, in its early stages at least, a judge acted also as prosecutor.

2   The shaping of the accusatorial process by jury trial as it developed towards its present form over the centuries is brought home by the realisation that until the middle of the eighteenth century almost all criminal cases were tried before a jury, and guilty pleas and summary trials as we know them today were rare. The trial, the setting for a public confrontation between accuser and accused and the court's first involvement in the matter, was, until well into the nineteenth century, often a very summary affair. In Europe on the other hand, the judiciary, in their inquisitorial role, spent much time before the formal trial process, privately interrogating witnesses and the defendant and building up a case file (*dossier*).

3   The contrast between our accusatorial system and the continental system has survived in large part until today, but as Professor John Spencer has put it:

> "the borrowings between the two have been so extensive that
> it is no longer possible to classify any of the criminal justice

systems in Western Europe as wholly accusatorial or wholly inquisitorial".[1]

4   Napoleon's Code d'Instruction Criminelle of 1808,[2] which formed the basis of or influenced many European countries' codes of criminal procedure, introduced a mixed system of a juge d'instruction who investigated the matter in private followed by a public trial before different judges sitting, in serious cases, with a jury. However, the role of the juge d'instruction has begun to wane or has disappeared in a number of countries; and juries, where they are part of the process, in general bear little resemblance in composition or role to those of the English jury.

5   Equally, English law, with the advent in the 19th century of local police forces and a Director of Public Prosecutions and, in the late 20th century of a centralised service of full-time prosecutors in the form of the Crown Prosecution Service,[3] has gradually focused courts' attention more and more on the manner of investigation and drawn them into pre-trial procedures. The result has been a longer pre-trial and trial process in jury cases, widespread use of pleas of guilty as a route to conviction and, since the mid 19th century, a remorseless increase in summary work to its present level of about 95% of all criminal cases.

6   The point of this short historical comparison is to draw attention to the relationship between the composition of the tribunal and its procedural and evidential rules and practices. Many aspects of a system developed over the centuries to introduce safeguards against the forensically primitive jury trials and harsh penal regimes of the time may not fit, or be necessary for, modern trials, whether by judge or jury or in some other form.[4]

7   A notable feature of the Review has been the widespread acceptance of the basic structure of the English criminal trial. It is shaped by the twin principles that the prosecution, as the complainant, has the task of making the tribunal sure of guilt and that the defendant has the choice of answering the prosecution case or remaining silent. The trial process is a contest between two parties, though, in some respects, it is no longer entirely adversarial. In it, the parties deploy their respective cases before a tribunal the role of which is primarily to listen, intervene only when necessary to ensure a fair and efficient trial and, at the end, to decide the issue of guilt. It is a continuous and public process in which the prosecution orally explains its case and still relies mainly on oral evidence to support it. The defence tests and challenges

---

[1] In preparing this outline analysis, I have drawn heavily on the assistance of Professor John Spencer.
[2] replaced in 1958 by the Code de Procedure Penale, which, much modified is still in force
[3] of which the Director of Public Prosecutions became head
[4] see Report of the Philips Royal Commission, para 1.15, citing Radzinowicz, *History of English Criminal Law*, Vol 1, App 3, pp 699 - 726

the prosecution case by cross-examining prosecution witnesses as appropriate and/or by submissions of law or as to the inadequacy of the evidence. If the defendant wishes, he may in turn give oral evidence and call witnesses in his support. Thus, our system of trial is dominated by the principle of orality, namely that evidence as to matters in issue should normally be given by oral testimony of witnesses in court, speaking of their own direct knowledge.

8   I have to record that, on the topics of trial procedure and evidence, I have received few proposals for fundamental reform in either the Crown Court or magistrates' courts. The general theme, particularly from judges, magistrates, the Bar and solicitors, is that, while there is scope for some improvement, the trial process is basically sound and should not be disturbed – often expressed in the hackneyed phrase "if it ain't broke, don't fix it".

9   Others were not so relaxed about the system. The Association of Chief Police Officers, in a comprehensive and powerful submission, set out a number of fundamental criticisms, the underlying theme of which was that pre-trial and trial procedures and rules of evidence are artificially and unfairly slanted in favour of defendants. In their view: the adversarial procedure relegates the court to a reactive role when it should have far greater direction and control of the way in which the issues and the evidence are put before it; fact-finders are wrongly denied access to material relevant to their findings of fact; procedural law – 'due process' – dominates substantive law to the extent of creating, rather than preventing, injustice, resulting in a loss of public confidence in the courts' contribution to the control of crime; the 'adversarial dialectic' and the 'principle of orality' have been elevated to ends in themselves rather than means to get at the truth and also, as a result, discourage modern and more efficient ways of putting evidence before the courts; and the criminal justice system over-all is not equipped to bring to trial and or try effectively those engaged in highly sophisticated and organised crime.

10   The police are not alone in criticising the system. Many distinguished academics with a close working knowledge of it have, in various studies, papers and articles in recent years been powerful advocates for procedural reform. Also, some judges of great experience in this field are impatient for principled reform of the trial process. Both complain of the piecemeal and muddled nature of our rules of procedure and evidence and the lack of an over-all philosophy in our consideration of the need for, and shape of, possible reform.

11   The fundamentals of the trial process are the same for trial by judge and jury as they are for the magistrates' courts. Yet, when most people, lawyers included, talk of trial procedures they think of trial by judge and jury. That is forgivable since, as I have mentioned, that is how most trials used to be. With the burgeoning of summary jurisdiction from the mid-19th century on, it was

no doubt instinctive to borrow and adapt for its use much of the structure and procedures of trial by judge and jury. With Parliament's corresponding increase in provision for the trial of offences 'either-way' that I have described in Chapter 5, it was important to retain as much as possible of that commonality of procedures and rules of evidence. Subject to the necessary differences between trial with and without a jury, the aim must have been to stick to one concept of a fair trial whatever the composition of the tribunal conducting it. The result is a lumping together of the two jurisdictions when discussing criminal procedures and evidence, though usually in the context of trial by judge and jury because that's where most of the problems arise. In magistrates' courts, in the nature of things, trials are generally shorter, faster and simpler than they are in the Crown Court. I have, therefore, some sympathy for the Runciman Royal Commission for its focus on the trial procedures of the Crown Court and apparent disregard - for which it has been criticised - of those in the magistrates' courts. It is an imbalance I have sought, not always successfully, to avoid throughout the Review.

12   I have attempted to identify what is not working well and what major candidates there may be for change. In doing so, I have taken into account, not only the many submissions in the Review and academic and judicial writings on the subject, but also a large number of past and present studies and reviews of procedure and evidence in this and other common law jurisdictions. In all of this, it is important to keep in mind that different forms of tribunal may administer justice with efficiency in different ways. This has particular significance to my proposal for a unified Criminal Court consisting of various forms of tribunal, namely: judge and jury, judge alone, judge and lay members (in serious fraud cases), judge and magistrates (District Division), and magistrates on their own.

13   In terms of studies and reviews, this is well-worn and relatively recent trodden ground. The Philips Royal Commission, which reported in 1981, was directed by its terms of reference to examine pre-trial procedure. However, as it observed,[5] "it is the nature of the trial itself which largely determines the pre-trial procedure". Lord Roskill's Committee's Report in 1986, which, though focused on fraud trials, said much that was of application to trial generally. And the Runciman Royal Commission, appointed in the wake of mounting public concern over a number of high profile miscarriages of justice, was charged with a wide-ranging review of the manner and supervision of police investigations, the role of the prosecutor, expert evidence, pre-trial and trial procedures, evidence, the role of the court and other machinery in correcting miscarriages of justice. In its Report in 1993 it made a large number of recommendations, some of which were adopted and some not.

---

[5] ibid para 1.6

TRIAL BY JUDGE AND JURY

General

14   I start with trial by judge and jury because, as I have said, that is where most of our features of trial have their origin and in which, because of the partnership of judge and jury there are particular problems. Some of these are to be found in greater or less degree, according to the composition of tribunal, in the magistrates' courts. I return to them and other forms of tribunal below, but briefly.[6] I see the problem, not so much as speeding up the trial once it has started; much of the scope for saving of trial time lies in efficient preparation for it. If, in advance, the issues of fact have been identified, the issues of law and admissibility of evidence, have, so far as practicable, been resolved and the evidence of both sides has been pared down to deal only with the issues, the stage should be set for an orderly and expeditious trial. Putting aside unforeseen contingencies that can delay or interrupt any trial, the manner in which the case proceeds is then in the hands of the parties, their advocates and the judge. If the advocates are properly prepared and competent and the judge intervenes suitably to move the case on when they are prolix, repetitious or moving away from the issues, the case should make reasonable progress to its conclusion within present procedural constraints. For the moment, I want to look at the effect of the procedures on the fairness and simplicity of the process and, on jurors and other outsiders to it, as to its comprehensibility. I do so by following the passage of a trial from its beginning to its end.

The start of a jury trial

15   I wrote in Chapter 5 of the need to give potential jurors advance and adequate information in writing of what to expect before attending court to sit on a jury. I also referred to the need for more informative guidance on their arrival than the instruction video and talk from the jury usher that is now provided. But not all persons summoned for jury service have the inclination or mental rigour to do their homework before the first day of attendance. Some of them may be late on the first day because of difficulties in finding their way around and miss the video and/or introductory talk. Some may be distracted by the disruption of their work or domestic obligations. Many will be nervous about what is expected of them and bemused by the unfamiliar court environment. Before they have had time to become acclimatised, they are taken to a courtroom with strangely dressed judge and advocates and, often, a full public gallery. Almost immediately they are thrust into the limelight, as they are

---

[6] see paras 57 - 67

individually called forward into the witness box and asked to stand and swear the juror's oath.

16   Within a short time of all that novelty and after a few explanatory words from the judge, they are expected to listen, take in and remember from the prosecuting advocate's speech what the case is all about. Conventionally, such an opening is a fairly - sometimes a very - detailed exposition of the constituents of the charge or charges, the issues to the extent that the defence may have indicated them and the proposed prosecution evidence. They may be provided during the opening with copies of documentary exhibits, schedules, photographs or plans as required. In large and complex cases, the judge may give juries a more extended explanation of what they are in for, and the prosecution may provide them at the outset with more elaborate documentary aides-memoires. But, in all cases the jury's introduction to the case is essentially oral, a telling of a story by the prosecuting advocate from the prosecution's point of view.

17   Whilst jurors are told by judges that they may take notes and are provided with the materials to do so, the pace of the prosecution advocate's opening and their own unfamiliarity with such a technique may not encourage it. Yet, somehow, these strangers to the forensic process are expected to absorb, unaided, in the main, by a written summary or reference to key issues and allegations and counter-allegations relating to them, the prosecution advocate's framework of what is to follow. The reality is, of course, that most of them cannot, and cannot reasonably be expected to, retain all that detail. The system's answer to that is repetition, and the promise of it. Often a judge, in his short introductory remarks before the prosecuting advocate's opening, tries to reassure a jury by telling them that they need not worry about taking in and remembering all the detail straightaway because they will hear it all again many times - in the evidence in chief and cross-examination of witnesses, in the advocates' closing speeches and in his summing-up at the end of the case. And, as in the case of students preparing for examinations or actors learning their lines, sheer repetition, no doubt, eventually fixes the memory of at least some of them.

18   To anyone other than lawyers steeped in the procedural traditions of the criminal courts, this must seem a strange way to expect jurors, upon whose understanding and judgment so much depends, to do justice in the case. When they embark upon it they are given no objective and convenient outline in oral or written form of its essentials, the nature of the allegation, what facts have to be proved, what facts are in issue and what questions they are there to decide. And, mostly they have little in the way of a written aide-memoire to which they can have recourse as the case unfolds to relate the evidence to such questions. Any experienced court observer has only to note the exhaustion, and sometimes the distress, of jurors as a case of some length or complexity moves towards its end and the enormity and complications of their

decision-making task is belatedly brought home to them. Trevor Grove, in his informative and entertaining book, *"The Juryman's Tale"*, quotes an American Judge who said that it was like "telling jurors to watch a baseball game and decide who won without telling them what the rules are until the end of the game".

19   Depending on the case, on the nature, volume and detail of the evidence and on the aptitude of individual jurors to absorb it, the repetitive nature of the process may be helpful or become tedious in the extreme. But it is commonplace for juries, having retired to consider their verdict, to return to court to ask the judge to be reminded of what a witness has said and, often, for a copy of his written witness statement. In most instances they know that there is such a statement because the advocates and the judge were plainly following their copies of it as he gave his evidence, the witness may have referred to it, or the advocates may have cross-examined and re-examined him by reference to it. All the leading players in the courtroom have a copy, but not the jury. If no point was taken on the statement, they are left to their recollection and the reminders of the advocates and the judge of what the witness said. If a point was taken about the difference between his evidence and the statement, they are dependent on what the advocates and the judge have told them of the contents of the statement as it compares with the witness's oral evidence. Either way, they are not allowed to see the document.

20   What more natural request - in any setting but that of a criminal court - than to have access to a witness's written statement made shortly after the event, when considering his oral evidence long after it? Putting aside for a moment the rule that such a statement or part of it is not admissible evidence, save by reference if a witness confirms it in cross-examination, the main rationale for not allowing juries to see it, is that, even with a proper warning and further reminder by the judge of the witness's oral evidence, they would be likely to give the statement more weight than their recollection of what he said. There is a similar problem in the case of evidence in chief of young children recorded on video-tape, even if, when the jury are permitted to view it for a second time, it is accompanied by a reminder of the cross-examination and re-examination.[7] So, what more could and should be done at the start of and throughout trial to assist the jury's understanding of the trial process, the case in hand, what they are there to decide and to assist them in their task?

21   First, there is the indictment (or charge as I have recommended it should be called in future). To the extent that it does not happen already, each juror should routinely be provided in all cases with a copy of the charge or charges at the outset. I say "all cases" because under my proposal for allocation of work in a new unified Criminal Court, all cases tried by judge and jury are

---

[7] *R v Rawlings and Broadbent* [1995] 2 Cr App R 222, CA; *R v M (J)* [1996] 2 Cr App R 56, CA

likely to be of some substance. In Scotland, each potential juror is handed a copy of the indictment as he enters the jury box.

22   Second, I am strongly of the view that the time has come for the judge to give the jury at the start of all cases a fuller introduction to their task as jurors than is presently conventional, including: the structure and practical features of a trial as it may affect them, a word or two about their own manner of working, for example note-taking, early selection of a foreman and his role, asking questions, time and manner of deliberation etc. He should also give them an objective summary of the case and the questions they are there to decide, supported with a written aide-memoire. I have referred to this in Chapter 10 as a "case and issues summary". The parties' advocates should prepare and agree the summary in draft before the trial (and be paid for doing so) for the judge's approval and use by him, them and the jury throughout the trial. The summary should identify:

- the nature of the charges;

- as part of a brief narrative, the evidence agreed, reflecting the admissions of either side at the appropriate point in the story (not leaving them to be read or provided in written form to the jury then or at some later stage simply as a list of admissions);

- also as part of the narrative, the matters of fact in issue; and

- with no, or minimal, reference to the law, a list of the likely questions for their decision.[8]

23   There is little new in the proposal of a short introduction by the judge to the jury of the case and the issues they are there to decide. Some judges in England and Wales do it. Scottish judges often do it by reference to the narrative indictment which is customary in their jurisdiction. And the practice is well established in the United States. As I have seen, it serves as an impressive and effective objective introduction to the jury of the task ahead of them. If and to the extent that the issues narrow or widen in the course of the trial, the case and issues summary should be amended and fresh copies provided to the judge and jury as an update of the matters on which they have to focus. At the end of the trial, it should also serve as a common point of reference for the judge and advocates when considering any matters of difficulty before speeches, and also for the jury during speeches and the summing-up. Now that most judges and practitioners use word processors as a normal working tool, creating and maintaining such a running and useful aide-memoire is not the burden it might have been only a few years ago.

---

[8] see paras 43 – 45 below

24   I know that many criminal practitioners may not initially welcome this proposal, one that requires the advocates on both sides to co-operate in providing a basic document for the use of the judge and the jury as well as themselves. They may believe that it would be impracticable in the hurly-burly of their life, preparing cases for trial - often in the cracks of the day while engaged in the trial of other cases. However, equally busy civil and family practitioners have become accustomed to the discipline of advance and concise identification for the courts of the issues and as part of their own preparation for trial, in documents setting out the agreed facts, those in dispute and the issues for determination. I recognise that in those jurisdictions such documents are primarily skeleton arguments rather than a common aide-memoire. I recognise too that in criminal cases there are special considerations of the liberty of the subject and the safeguards of the prosecution's heavy burden of proof and the defendant's right of silence. But I am not proposing routine exchange and provision to the court of skeleton arguments or pleadings, simply a neutral and summary document derived from the sort of analyses that competent advocates on both sides would, in any event, need as part of their own preparation for trials of substance, which, under my proposals, would in future be the sole or main candidates for trial by judge and jury. I should note that in serious and complex frauds there is already provision for the judge to direct both sides to provide the court and each other with a 'case statement' setting the sort of matters that I have in mind for this purpose.[9] If there are improvements in the manner of preparation for trial, as I have recommended in Chapter 10, the task should not be too onerous and would serve as a valuable checklist for all in the course of the trial.

I recommend that in all cases tried by judge and jury:

- **each juror should be provided at the start of the trial with a copy of the charge or charges;**

- **the judge at the start of the trial should address the jury, introducing them generally to their task as jurors and giving them an objective outline of the case and the questions they are there to decide;**

- **the judge should supplement his opening address with, and provide a copy to each juror of, a written case and issues summary prepared by the parties' advocates and approved by him;**

- **the judge, in the course of his introductory address, and the case and issues summary, should identify:**

  - **the nature of the charges;**

---

[9] Criminal Justice Act 1987, s 9(4) and (5)

- *as part of a brief narrative*, the evidence agreed, reflecting the admissions of either side at the appropriate point in the story;

- *also as part of the narrative*, the matters of fact in issue; and

- with no, or minimal, reference to the law, a list of likely questions for their decision; and

- if and to the extent that the issues narrow or widen in the course of the trial, the case and issues summary should be amended and fresh copies provided to the judge and jury.

Time estimates

25   Under the present plea and directions system, trial advocates are required to inform the court of their estimates of the likely length of the trial and to keep it informed of any variation in it. Normally, the judge asks them about it on the first day of trial. In cases of any length it has long been good practice for the prosecuting advocate to prepare in good time before trial a provisional list of the order in which he will call prosecution witnesses. This enables arrangements to be made, so far as possible, for staging their attendance at court and, by supplying a copy to the defence and the court, advance indication of the order of subject matter of the evidence. Normally the prosecuting advocate does not attempt to estimate, other than by reference to the number of witnesses to be warned for each day, how long each will take, and the court does not require it. The same applies with the defence.

26   I am generally against any attempt to introduce rigid time limits for various stages of a criminal trial. However, in cases that have required careful and detailed preparation, a joint estimate of how long the principal witnesses would take to give their evidence assists in the more accurate staging of their evidence and should introduce a useful discipline for advocates in their respective questioning of them. There is provision for this in the judge's questionnaire for use in the plea and directions hearing, though there are indications that advocates could give it more careful consideration than the time taken at trial suggests they do. Such a system seems to work better in children's cases in the Family Courts where, pursuant to guidance given by the President,[10] advocates on both or all sides at the pre-trial review submit a schedule to the court indicating how long each will spend with each witness. Of course, such estimates are likely to be rough and ready approximations; much will depend on the manner and content of the witnesses' response to

---

[10] *MD & TD (Children's Cases:Time Estimates)* [1994] 2 FCR 94

questions and where the questioning leads. But they are useful as a rough guide to planning and some reminder to the advocates, where practicable and consistent with the proper conduct of their cases, to try to keep to them.

> **I recommend that advocates should regard it as of the highest importance to attempt accurate estimates of the likely length of their principal witnesses' evidence, including a review of them as the issues become clearer in the course of preparation for trial.**

Opening speeches

27 Refinement of the issues, confinement of the proposed evidence to the issues and an introduction from the judge, coupled with a case and issues summary, as I have recommended, should reduce the need in many cases for a long opening prosecution speech. In Scotland, they manage to do without a prosecution speech altogether. I write this with pangs of nostalgia because there are few pleasures at the criminal bar greater than opening an enthralling prosecution case to a jury. But the time and best use for advocacy is later as the evidence begins to unfold. I do not go so far as the Runciman Royal Commission in suggesting a presumptive time limit for the prosecution advocate's opening unless the judge has given leave for longer.[11] But I do endorse its general recommendation against overloading the jury in the opening with the detail of the proposed evidence or of the law unless it is essential to their understanding of the task ahead.[12]

28 I have always been puzzled at the lack of any formal provision for a short opening defence speech at the beginning of a criminal trial and at the general reluctance of defence advocates to make one, even when the judge informally invites them to do so. No doubt there are tactical reasons for the latter where the defence is weak or uncertain or dependent on the appearance or performance of critical prosecution witnesses. But in many cases it would be of strategic advantage to the defendant as well as of assistance to the jury for his advocate to balance the prosecution's opening by underlining the nature of his defence at that stage.

> **I endorse the Runciman Royal Commission's recommendation[13] that a defence advocate should be entitled to make a short opening speech to the jury**

---

[11] Chapter 8, para 8, recommending a presumptive time limit of 15 minutes
[12] Chapter 8, paras 8 and 9
[13] Chapter 8, para 10

immediately after that of the prosecution advocate, but normally of no more than a few minutes.

Evidence in chief

The art of examination in chief

29 Getting the witness to give a clear, orderly and relevant account, but in his own words - and its contribution to the pace of a trial – are often under-estimated. Two major causes of delay in the progress of trials under our present system are the manner in which witnesses are required to give their evidence in chief and the interruption of it by technical and often arid disputes as to its admissibility. As to the manner of giving evidence, it can be an extremely slow and difficult business to elicit from a witness an orderly, comprehensive and accurate account of the matter on which he is there to give evidence. The advocate examining him is not permitted to lead him – ask him questions that suggest the answers. And, unless the witness is a police officer or other experienced witness, he may be nervous, or he may lack the ability to give a clear account, or he may not remember all or some of the important detail. Sometimes the opposing advocate may assist on those parts of the evidence not in dispute by indicating to the judge that he does not object to the witness being led. Sometimes, in the hope that the witness may not come up to proof, he may not assist in that way.

30 As if those impediments to presenting a brisk and clear account to the court are not enough, the verbal gymnastics involved in seeking to overcome them often lead to distracting and off-putting interruptions to the witness. The advocate examining him will be alert to prevent him from breaching the rules of evidence, mostly the rule against hearsay, before his opponent rises to his feet to object. There are thus constant breaks in the flow of the story while the witness is warned - to his bewilderment and that of the jury - why he cannot give his account as he would in any other setting. In that way, as Professor IH Dennis has recently written, the adversarial nature of the process can also distort the witness's account from that which he would have given, if left to himself:[14]

> "... witnesses will not generally be questioned by anyone involved in the proceedings in a spirit of free impartial inquiry. Partisan, controlled questioning is the norm, and free report by the witness is the exception. This point helps to explain why some witnesses find the process of testifying at best bewildering, because they are unable to tell their story in their own way, or at worst traumatic, because of 'robust'

---

[14] *The Law of Evidence* (Sweet and Maxwell, 1999), p 428

cross-examination which may have the effect of making them feel that they themselves are on trial".

31   There are frequent skirmishes, signalled or played out in the jury's presence as to the form of the examining advocate's questions or as to whether and in what form the witness may be allowed to refresh his memory from written material. These are unedifying and, in my view, disfiguring aspects of our trial process. They are prompted in the main by archaic and inappropriate rules of evidence, giving unrealistic primacy to the oral over the written word and causing confusion and anomaly where common sense suggests another course. The rules make the truthful witness's evidence a test of his memory rather than ensure its truthfulness and accuracy, and they do little to expose the dishonest witness's lies. In my view, something should be done to enable a witness's evidence in chief to be put before a tribunal more cleanly than is now the case. I have in mind general reform of the rule against hearsay and, in particular, widening the category of documents from which he may refresh his memory while giving evidence or, possibly, by allowing an earlier written statement or audio or video-recorded record of questioning to stand as his evidence in chief. I discuss these possibilities in more detail under the heading of Evidence below.[15]

The use of information technology

32   Information technology, in various forms, could be of great value in simplifying and making more effective the presentation of evidence. Just as there could be a single electronic case file for the use of all involved agencies and parties in preparation for trial, so also, in cases meriting it, there could be a single electronic trial file to which all involved in court, including the judge and jury, could have access on screen.[16] This could enable documents to be presented on screen, whether as electronic text or a scanned image, the use of photographic three dimensional images of exhibits, and computer generated drawings, simulations and animations.

33   There are, of course, risks associated with the use of these new technologies before a jury. A well prepared computer animation could be a very powerful exhibit, and overshadow other evidence in the minds of jurors.[17] And the use of information technology may not be appropriate or necessary in the presentation of evidence in many cases. But in the right cases its potential for assisting the jury should not be underestimated. Also, if evidence is being

---

[15] see paras 81 - 94

[16] this technique was used with considerable success in the Lockerbie Trial; see the Lockerbie Trial Media Pack (Scottish Court Service, 2000)

[17] Siemer, Deanne C, *Tangible Evidence, How to use exhibits at deposition and trial,* third edition (Nita, 1996)

presented on screen to the jury, arrangements should be made so that those in the public gallery and press box are also able to see it.

I recommend that screens and projection equipment should be more widely available to enable electronic presentation of evidence in appropriate cases.

Cross-examination

34   The Runciman Royal Commission was concerned about prolongation of trials and unfairness to witnesses by the incompetence or overbearing behaviour of advocates, and about the failure on occasion of judges to control such conduct.   In the intervening eight years the Bar and solicitors have done much, by way of continuation training and the promulgation of codes of conduct,[18] to improve the general quality of advocacy.   With encouragement from the Court of Appeal, (Criminal Division), and greater emphasis in training, judges and magistrates are now more alert than formerly to their power and duty to intervene to prevent repetitious or otherwise unnecessary evidence and to control prolix, irrelevant or oppressive questioning of witnesses.   There is still room for improvement in advocates' conduct of trials, particularly at the junior and inexperienced end of the professions, resulting all too often in costly appeals with little benefit to the defendant/appellant or to justice.   And there are still the odd cases when a judge has not acted as firmly as he might have done to prevent incompetence or misconduct.   Often the decision when to intervene is a difficult one, and it is not aided by the developing tension between Article 6, in its focus on due process, and the safety of the conviction.   There may also be a difficulty for a judge in a long trial to assess the impact of individual rulings on the fairness of the trial over-all.   These are, in the end, matters of judgment in individual cases, some of which can be troublesome to the Court of Appeal when the matter reaches them.   I do not believe that legislation of the sort urged by the Runciman Royal Commission[19] is necessary as an encouragement to judges to be robust in their control of proceedings or a practical aid in keeping them within proper bounds.   But the Court of Appeal should support them.

---

[18] see Code of Conduct of The Bar of England and Wales, 31st July 2000, Part 7, para 708, and *The Guide To The Professional Conduct Of Solicitors,* Part V, eighth edition (Law Society Publishing, 1999) as updated periodically in the professional standards bulletins of the Law Society

[19] Report, Chapter 8, para 13

The defence case

35   If, as I have recommended, the judge at the outset of the case introduces the jury to the issues they have to decide with the assistance of a case and issues summary, and if the defence advocate has made a short opening speech after the prosecution opening, there should normally be no need for the defence to open the case at the close of the prosecution case. However, whether or not the defence advocate has made an earlier short opening speech, he should be entitled to make one at this stage, and I do not see why that entitlement should continue to depend on whether he is intending to call a witness as to fact other than the defendant. That limitation was introduced in 1898[20] to curb what had formerly been an unlimited right to a defence opening granted in 1865[21] when a defendant was not entitled to give evidence on his own behalf.

I recommend that:

- **a defence advocate who makes a short opening speech immediately after the prosecution opening should not thereby forfeit his right to make an opening speech at the beginning of the defence case; and**

- **a defence advocate's entitlement to make an opening speech at the start of the defence case should no longer depend on whether he intends to call a witness as to fact other than the defendant.**

Judges' power to call witnesses

36   The power of judges to call witnesses undoubtedly exists, though the established weight of authority – most of it before the Runciman Royal Commission Report in 1993[22] - is that it should be used sparingly and only to achieve the ends of justice and fairness. Certainly, a judge should not undertake the role of the prosecutor, for example by calling further prosecution witnesses in order to pursue a case that the prosecuting advocate has decided it is not proper to pursue.[23] However, he may cause to be called, or himself call, a witness not called by the prosecution or defence, and without the consent of either, if he considers it necessary in the interests of justice. The Runciman Royal Commission urged judges, in appropriate cases, to make more use of this power or to suspend a trial to enable further investigations to take place.[24] So far as I can tell, judges here continued to be

---

[20] Criminal Evidence Act 1898, s 2

[21] Criminal Procedure Act 1865, s 2

[22] see the authorities set out in paras 4-345 and 4-346 in Archbold, (2001 edition)

[23] *R v Grafton* (1993) 96 Cr App R 156, CA

[24] Chapter 8, para 18

sparing in their use of such powers. The arrival in the intervening years of a system of mutual advance disclosure, earlier identification of issues and greater involvement of judges in overseeing the preparation of cases for trial should have equipped them better to identify in the course of trial whether justice requires the calling of a witness whom neither side has considered or wishes to call. Nevertheless, so long as we retain our essentially adversarial system, I consider that judges should use this power only in exceptional cases, where justice demands it. Even then they should be cautious about its use because one or other side may have very good reasons, that they cannot divulge, consistent with justice and in the interests of a fair trial, for not calling the witness themselves. There is also a danger, where the witness is thought to be possibly adverse to the defence case, in the judge assuming what might be perceived as the role of an auxiliary prosecutor. In the main, judges should be able to rely, on the one hand, on the competence and sense of public duty of the prosecutor to protect the public interest and, on the other, on the defence advocate to know what is in the best interest of the defendant.

Taking stock

37   It is vital that the judge and the advocates, in the absence of the jury, should take stock of the case at the close of all the evidence and before speeches and the summing-up. This should take two forms. First, this is the time for the judge and advocates finally to review the case and issues summary and, if necessary, to amend it for the jury. The case may have taken a different turn as the evidence unfolded or as unexpected legal points emerged, removing some factual issues or introducing new ones. Second, if there appear to the judge or the advocates any points of difficulty as to the manner in which he should apply the law or as to his treatment of the evidence in his directions and summing-up to the jury, he and they should discuss and, if possible, resolve, them. Similarly, if he intends to supplement his oral directions and/or the case and issues summary with a written list of directions or questions, he should also show that to the advocates for comment at this stage. It is vital that they should be able to fashion their speeches knowing how he is going to put the matter to the jury. It is also a useful exercise for judge and advocates together to remove in advance any misunderstanding and, so far as possible, scope for error. There is nothing new about such an exercise. Over the last ten or so years the Court of Appeal has urged it in case after case, many of them reported and mentioned in successive editions of Archbold.[25] But the Court of Appeal is still frequently troubled with errors resulting from failure to take this basic and common sense precaution. In my view, it is of such importance that it should be considered for inclusion in the Criminal Procedure Code that I have recommended and, in the meantime, for consideration by the Lord Chief Justice in a special practice direction.

---

[25] see paras 4-355 and 4-356 in the 2001 edition

I recommend that:

- **at the close of evidence and before speeches, the judge and advocates, in the absence of the jury, should finally review the case and issues summary and, if necessary, amend it for the jury; and**

- **such a procedure, along with those already established by the Court of Appeal for review of evidential and legal issues at this stage of a trial, should be considered for express inclusion in the Criminal Procedure Code that I have recommended and, in the meantime, by the Lord Chief Justice for a special practice direction.**

38   There is another and connected matter that I consider needs urgent clarification. A prosecuting advocate has a positive duty, before or after the judge sums up the case to the jury, to draw to his attention any prospective or actual errors of law. He is also obliged to ensure that the judge's directions and summing-up contain all the essential ingredients. However, there appears to be some uncertainty, both as a matter of law and professional conduct rules, as to the corresponding duty of the defence advocate. It stems from an obiter observation of James LJ in *R v Cocks* in 1976[26] that "a defending counsel owes a duty to his client and it is not his duty to correct the judge if a judge has gone wrong". Robert Goff LJ (as he then was), when presiding in the Court of Appeal in a subsequent case not calling for decision on the proposition, was clearly uneasy about it.[27] It is said[28] that the Code of Conduct of the Bar of England and Wales does not specifically deal with the matter in that it merely states counsel's general duty to inform the court of all relevant decisions and legislative provisions of which he is aware, whether favourable or not to his case, and to inform the court of any procedural irregularity during the hearing, and not reserve it for appeal.[29]   The relevant provisions of the Code in force at the time of the Runciman Royal Commission were the same or similar, and the Commission found them unsatisfactory as to the extent of defence counsel's duty. It recommended clarification to require him to intervene where the judge had plainly overlooked or misinterpreted a legal matter.[30]

39   In my view, if and to the extent that the law and professional codes of conduct do not require a defending as well as a prosecuting advocate to seek to correct any error of law, or for that matter, of material fact, of the judge of which he

---

[26] 63 Cr App R 79, CA at 82

[27] *R v Edwards (NW)* (1983) 77 Cr App R 5, CA, at 8

[28] see para 4-373 of Archbold (Sweet and Maxwell, 2001)

[29] see now 7th edition of the Code, July 2000, Part VII, para 708 (c) and (d)

[30] Chapter 8, para 24

becomes aware, both the law and the codes should be changed to require it. A defendant's right to a fair trial, including the twin requirements that the prosecution must prove his guilt and that he can remain silent, do not entitle him to ignore the error hoping for a better chance of acquittal or in the hope, if there is a conviction, of getting it quashed in the Court of Appeal. As Professor Sir John Smith has commented:

> "... counsel owes a duty to the court. Should not that duty extend to the correction of an obvious slip on the part of the judge? By doing so, he ensures that his client gets a fair trial instead of an unfair one. A client aware of the possible tactic of silence might not like it; but his right is to a fair trial and, if gets that, he should have no complaint."[31]

I recommend that if, and to the extent that, the law and professional codes of conduct do not require a defending, as well as a prosecuting, advocate to seek to correct a judge's error of law or of material fact of which he becomes aware, both the law and the codes should be changed to require it.

Closing speeches

40   I do not, as the Runciman Royal Commission did,[32] recommend any normal limit of time on closing speeches and/or consideration by the judge of costs sanctions against advocates who, he considers, have unjustifiably exceeded it. I believe that it would be wrong and, in any event, impracticable to attempt such prescription. It would be wrong to subject advocates at so critical a stage of the case to the additional strain and, in many cases, distracting pressure of an arbitrary time limit. I also believe that it would be capable of seriously prejudicing one or other party in any but the most simple cases. And, if strictly enforced it could be vulnerable to an Article 6 challenge. As to practicability, cases vary enormously in the time that advocates may require to open or close them to a tribunal. To attempt a norm (the Royal Commission suggested 30 minutes) is about as unhelpful as fixing on an average. Whatever reduction in the length of closing speeches such a norm might achieve could be lost in many cases in submissions as to the need to exceed it and/or as to the appropriateness of a costs sanction for exceeding it. However, the absence of formal time limits does not mean that judges are or should be without power to intervene to control prolixity, for example, where the advocate is repetitious or advancing irrelevant arguments. As always in such circumstances, the Court of Appeal should support them.

---

[31] see his commentary on *R v Holden* [1991] Crim LR 478, at 480

[32] Chapter 8, para 19

Judge's directions on law and summing-up

41   I have considered how the judge's directions to the jury on the law and his summing-up of the evidence could better assist juries in their task and, thereby, improve the quality of their decisions. As I have said, I believe that, under our present procedures and rules of evidence, we expect too much of juries, particularly in longer and more complicated cases.[33]   If my recommendation for a case and issues summary is adopted, future juries will have a head start on their present day predecessors. When the judge at last turns towards them to begin his summing-up, they will have those, by then, familiar aides-memoire before them. The judge can use them as the framework for his directions and reminder of the issues and evidence on both sides material to them. If the case and issues summary has been updated, he may not need to consider providing them with any further written list of questions. But he should do so if the summary needs supplementing and they are so numerous and/or complicated as would suggest a need for them. As now, the judge should use such of those documents provided to the jury as an integral part of his summing-up, referring to the points in them, one by one, as he deals with them orally[34] - much in the way that other public speakers use a power-point machine to illustrate and pace their delivery at a speed that the audience can follow. I have already mentioned the way in which modern information technology could enable some categories of evidence to be more effectively presented to a jury by electronic rather than by conventional means. Judges also should make use of it where appropriate, provided that they keep it simple.[35]

42   The case law is well established as to judges' incorporation into their summings-up of written or other visual aids, and I believe is generally followed. However, to mark the importance of the new case and issues summary, I believe that consideration should be given to including it in the Code of Criminal Procedure that I have recommended and, in the meantime, in a direction of the Lord Chief Justice.

> **I recommend that:**
>
> - **consideration should be given to including in the Code of Criminal Procedure that I have recommended and, in the meantime in a practice direction of the Lord Chief Justice, a requirement**

---

[33] paras 15 – 19 above

[34] *R v McKechnie, and others* (1992) 94 Cr App R, 51, CA;

[35] See Her Honour Judge Mary Ann Yeates, *Using PowerPoint In Charging Juries* (Conference paper at Technology for Justice 2000 in Melbourne)

that a judge should use a case and issues summary
and any other written or visual aid provided to a
jury, as an integral part of his summing-up, referring
to the points in them, one by one, as he deals with
them orally; and

- courts should equip judges with, and in cases
  meriting it they should consider using, other visual
  aids to their summings-up, such as PowerPoint and
  evolving forms of presentational soft-ware.

43   So much for the means of presentation of the directions and summing-up.
What about the content? At present it has four main elements: first, a broad
identification of the issues; second, directions of law of a general nature and
as to the elements of the charges; third, how the matters of law bear on the
issues; and fourth, an account of the material evidence on both sides bearing
on the issues, including guidance on any inference that the jury may draw
from them.

44   Under the scheme I propose. the judge would still start with a broad
identification of the issues, referring the jury, as I have said, to the case and
issues summary and any supplemental written list of questions for them to
answer. Under the present system he would then normally tell them about the
law, apply it to the issues and then turn to the facts. This is often a long and
burdensome journey for judge and jury alike. In my view, there is a better
way for both of them, and one that is true to their partnership in the trial of
crime. The judge should no longer direct the jury on the law or sum-up
evidence in the detail that he now does. In one sense, as Professor Edward
Griew, a distinguished academic criminal lawyer pointed out some years ago,
the law is nothing to do with the jury— "It should be the function of the judge
to protect the jury from the law rather than to direct them on it".[36] And, save
in particularly complex or long cases, or where the evidence has not been put
before them in a manageable way, he should not need to remind the jury in
great detail of the evidence. Scotland, with its narrative indictment and no
prosecution opening seems to manage well enough without the
comprehensive judicial survey of the evidence that is commonplace here.
And most jurisdictions in the United States combine the judge's fairly
extensive introduction of the case to the jury at its start with little or no
mention of the evidence in his 'charge' to them at the end.   Whilst the
American system is not without its critics, its jury system retains a central role
in the administration of justice in both Federal and State courts and in both
criminal and civil jurisdictions.

---

[36] Professor Edward Griew, *Summing Up the Law* [1989] Crim LR 768, at 779

45   As to directions of law, our present system is to burden the jury with often highly technical and detailed propositions of law – lots of them. Many are prolix and complicated, often subject to qualifications and in some instances barely comprehensible to criminal practitioners never mind those who may never have heard them before. They have become worse in all of these respects over recent years, in part as a piecemeal response to rulings of the Court of Appeal refining and qualifying the law on which the earlier forms of direction were based. Not surprisingly, judges need a crib for these directions when preparing their summings-up; and one is provided for them by the Judicial Studies Board in the form of a Bench Book containing specimen directions. The start of most summings-up consists in the judge reading or rehearsing adapted versions of the appropriate specimen directions to the jury, who are expected to take them all in and retain them in their mind for their later deliberations. Many judges and practitioners accept the system because that is how they have always known it, though they recognise it has become vastly more complicated for them and the jury than it was. For many others the process is, frankly, an embarrassment in its complexity and in its unreality as an aid to jurors in returning a just verdict. To return to Professor Griew and the passage from which the above quotation came:

> "… a more radical simplification of the summing up should be achieved by freeing it of any implications of the theory that the jury are concerned with the law as well as the facts. It should be the function of the judge to protect the jury from the law rather than to direct them on it. The judge does in practice typically tell the jury that the law is for him and facts are for them. This should become more profoundly true than it now is. A brief statement of the law will be unavoidable if the case is to be intelligible. But what is said should not be by way of formal instruction. When it comes to instructing the jury on their task, the job of the judge should be to filter out the law. He should simply identify for the jury the facts which, if found by them, will render the defendant guilty according to the law of the offence charged and of any available defence".

46   As to the facts, like the Runciman Royal Commission,[37] I consider that judges should continue to remind the jury of the issues and, save in the most simple cases,[38] the evidence relevant to them, and should always give the jury an adequate account of the defence. But they should do it in more summary form than is now common; and, again, the Court of Appeal should support them. Whilst each case calls for its own treatment, they should, in the main, refer only to evidence which bears on the issues.

---

[37] Chapter 8, paras 20 and 21
[38] see eg *R v Wilson* [1991] Crim LR 838

47   Such an approach should remove or significantly reduce the scope for judicial comment in summings-up; though judges now rarely deserve Serjeant Sullivan's barb at the end of an Old Bailey trial that the jury should be asked whether they found for the defendant or his Lordship.[39] And it would significantly reduce the scope for time-consuming appeals to the Court of Appeal which routinely include complaints, rightly or wrongly, that the trial judge has summed-up the evidence unfairly or commented on it in a manner unduly prejudicial to the defendant.

48   The scheme that I have proposed should mean that, when the judge begins to address the jury, they should already be familiar, in an organised way, with the essential issues and evidence relevant to them and will have at their finger tips a convenient aide-memoire in the form of the case and issues summary. Thus aided, the judge should find it easier to achieve Lord Hailsham LC's memorably described model of:

> "a succinct but accurate summary of the issues of fact as to which a decision is required, a correct but concise summary of the evidence and arguments on both sides and a correct statement of the inferences which the jury are entitled to draw from their particular conclusions about the primary facts".[40]

49   I believe that simplification of the way in which judges direct and sum up to juries is essential for the future well-being of our system of trial by judge and jury. I recognise, however, that the task of extricating us from our present tradition would be formidable. The Court of Appeal bears ultimate responsibility for the elaborate and complex structure now enshrined in the Judicial Studies Board's specimen directions. What is needed is a fundamental, and practical review of the structure and necessary content of a summing-up with a view to shedding rather than incorporating the law and to framing simple factual questions that take it into account. Perhaps a body drawn from the judiciary and the Judicial Studies Board could be given a blank sheet of paper and charged with the task.

50   Under the simpler scheme that I have in mind, the judge's prime function would be to put a series of written factual questions to the jury, the answers to which could logically lead only to a verdict of guilty or not guilty. The questions would correspond with those in the up-dated case and issues summary, supplemented as necessary in a separate written list prepared for the purpose. Each question would be tailored to the law as the judge knows it to be and to the issues and evidence in the case. One likely objection to that course would be the time taken in preparing the written questions and inviting the advocates' comments on them. But much of the work would have

---

[39] *The Last Serjeant*, 1952, p 288
[40] *R v Lawrence* [1982] AC 510, HL, at 519

been done in the preparation of the case and issues summary. And, in any event, it is an exercise that in one form or another provides the bones of a conventional summing-up and also of lists of written questions for the jury that are now commonplace in cases of any complexity. And there should be significant savings of time in shorter summings-up, swifter verdicts and the avoidance of lengthy consideration by the Court of Appeal of challenges to the minutiae of judges' directions of law and treatment of the evidence and the merits. If the procedure that I have so far recommended finds favour, there are then two options for the next stage of the trial, the jury's verdict.

51 The first option is the easy one, namely leave the jury to answer the questions with a single answer as now - a verdict of guilty or not guilty - based on a reasonable belief that the new procedure would be more helpful than the present in assisting them to reach a just verdict.

52 The second is the logical one, though it has considerable 'political' difficulties and problems of expediency, both of them going to the root of our traditions of trial by judge and jury. The judge could, if he considers it appropriate, require the jury publicly to answer each question. The verdict, which he would require them to declare would flow logically from their answers to his questions. There would be nothing novel about the machinery, save in its modern day application to criminal cases. That is how it operates in some civil cases tried by a judge and jury where the judge gives judgment in the light of the jury's individual findings of fact.[41] It is still possible in criminal cases in the form of a 'special verdict', though a judge has no power to compel a jury to find a special verdict, and the procedure has been barely used since the 19th century. It may be a 'rusty' weapon, as Dr Glanville Williams has described it,[42] but perhaps it is time to polish it up and use it again. In my view, as I have said in Chapter 5,[43] the time has come for judges, where they consider it appropriate, to require juries to identify their process of reasoning by seeking from them answers to specific questions fashioned to the particular circumstances of the case. And I see no reason why the jury should not be required to return a special verdict or verdicts if directed by the judge, whatever the present state of the law about that.[44]

53 A return to special verdicts where appropriate would have a number of important advantages. First, it would be a convenient way of producing a publicly reasoned verdict whilst also removing some of the Article 6 restlessness about the present form of jury verdicts. Second, it would

---

[41] eg claims of false imprisonment or malicious prosecution

[42] Williams, G *The Proof of Guilt: a study of the English criminal trial* (Hamlyn lecture series, No 7 1963), p201, and see eg *R v Hendrick* (1921) 15 CrApp R 149, CCA; and *R v Bourne* (1952) 36 Cr App R 125, CA "special verdicts ought to be found only in the most exceptional cases"

[43] para 97

[44] see eg *R v Allude* (1837) 8 C & P 136

significantly reduce the ability of a jury to return a perverse verdict, whether of not guilty or guilty. Third, it would be a more honest and open system of justice. Fourth, it should induce a more structured debate in the jury room, thus reducing the chance of prejudice influencing the outcome. Fifth, it could identify the impact on the verdict of "controversially admissible" evidence admitted in the trial. And sixth, it would lead to better informed decisions in the Court of Appeal.

54   Despite all those advantages, I can foresee great opposition by the many and fervent supporters of the jury system to a public particularisation of a jury's verdict in that way. As I have said, it would go some way to removing from the jury its ability, which many cherish, to enter a perverse verdict. Though a determined and sufficiently conspiratorial jury could still manage it in their answers to one or more of the individual questions of fact. There is also the objection of expediency, likely to be articulated by many experienced criminal judges and practitioners, that it would be harder to secure unanimous verdicts because different jurors are likely to take different views on different questions, whereas, under the present system, all or an acceptable majority can agree on the final verdict. (I have referred in Chapter 5 to the rule that judges must direct juries that they can only convict if they agree on every ingredient necessary to constitute the offence charged.[45]) But the premise of that objection is that the jury system may not be working as it should do and that requiring juries to particularise their verdicts would reveal that.

55   I find both those arguments unattractive in their lack of logic and their apparent determination to preserve an ancient institution without matching its performance to modern needs. My conclusion, which I have already expressed in more general terms in Chapter 5,[46] is that a judge, where he considers it appropriate, should be able to require a jury to justify their verdict by answering publicly each of his questions.

I recommend that:

- **so far as possible, the judge should not direct the jury on the law, save by implication in the questions of fact that he puts to them for decision;**

- **the judge should continue to remind the jury of the issues and, save in the most simple cases, the evidence relevant to them, and should always give the jury an adequate account of the defence; but he should do it in more summary form than is now common;**

---

[45] see *R v Brown (K)* (1984) 79 Cr App R 115, CA and the voluminous and confusing jurisprudence it has engendered, noted in Archbold, (2001 ed) paras 4-391 – 4-393

[46] para 97

- the judge should devise and put to the jury a series of written factual questions, the answers to which could logically lead only to a verdict of guilty or not guilty; the questions should correspond with those in the updated case and issues summary, supplemented as necessary in a separate written list prepared for the purpose; and each question should be tailored to the law as the judge knows it to be and to the issues and evidence in the case; and

- the judge, where he considers it appropriate, should be permitted to require a jury to answer publicly each of his questions and to declare a verdict in accordance with those answers.

Trial by Judge alone

56 Trial by judge alone would have much of the structure but, necessarily, many differences in procedure and evidence from that of trial by judge and jury. The role of the judge should not be considered as if it were something in isolation. Without a jury it becomes more than that of an umpire and distiller of law and facts for a separate fact finding body; he is also the fact-finder. He is inevitably more interventionist, testing and probing the issues of law and fact as they are canvassed before him. There is a greater dialectic between him and the advocates. And there is less of a role or need for procedural and evidential constraints designed to insulate lay fact finders from potentially unfairly prejudicial evidence. This is not the place to analyse the many differences in the two forms of trial procedure. As I have said in Chapter 5, there are many well established models of trial by judge alone in the United States and several Commonwealth countries, and we have it nearer to home in the Diplock Courts in Northern Ireland and in our magistrates' courts when presided over by a District Judge. For a useful examination of the possibilities and practicalities of this mode of trial I can do no better than refer the reader to the writings of Professors Jackson and Doran and other authors mentioned in Chapter 5.

Trial by judge and magistrates in the District Division

57 As with trial by judge alone, the main structure of the trial process would be the same as with trial by judge and jury. I have already summarised in

Chapter 7 how the District Division could work.[47]   For the sake of convenience I repeat part of that summary here.

58   I propose that the District Division bench would consist of a judge, normally a District Judge, and two magistrates. However, the District Judge should be able to make binding preliminary rulings on his own at pre-trial hearings as would a Crown Division judge. At the trial the judge would be the arbiter of all matters of law, procedure and the admissibility of evidence. He would rule on such matters in the absence of his lay colleagues wherever he considered it would be potentially unfairly prejudicial to the defendant to do it in their presence. As to the facts, he and the magistrates would each have an equal say, and the decision of the court when not unanimous could be by a majority of any two of them.

The case and issues summary

59   It should not normally be necessary to have a case and issues summary in the District Division. However, in cases of complexity, the judge should be able to direct it if it will assist him or his colleagues on the bench. In that event, he should also, where appropriate, discuss and amend it with the advocates in the course of the trial and/or just before closing speeches.

Speeches

60   The prosecuting advocate's opening statement should ensure that the court has sufficient information about the issues in cases where there is no need for a case and issues summary. The same order of speeches should apply as in the Crown Court. I have considered, but have rejected, proposing that the prosecuting advocate should not have a right to make a closing speech save to correct defence errors of fact on law, or with the permission of the court in cases of particular complexity. The sole justification for doing so would be to remove some of the scope for repetition of evidence which is a feature of jury cases. However, it would not be an even-handed way of shortening the proceedings and, I believe, would not shorten them very much. Often the prosecuting advocate's closing speech is much shorter than that of the defending advocate. And before this tribunal the likelihood is that the judge would be better placed and more justified than a judge sitting with a jury to keep the whole proceedings within a tight rein, including both sides' closing speeches. After speeches the judge and magistrates would retire to consider their decision. Whether unanimous or by a majority, the judge on their return

---

[47] paras 29 - 32

to court would deliver a fully reasoned judgment of the court. It follows that I see no need for the judge publicly to sum up the case before he and his colleagues retire. Any outstanding issues of law and the issues of fact at that stage can and should be publicly resolved in the court's judgment.

Sentencing

61 Sentencing would be a matter for the judge alone, for the reasons I have given in Chapter 7,[48] though there is no reason why the magistrates should not remain on the bench while he deals with it.

I recommend that in the District Division:

- **the judge should be the sole judge of law;**

- **the judge and the magistrates should together be the judges of facts, each having an equal vote;**

- **the judge should normally conduct any pre-trial hearings on his own;**

- **the judge should be empowered to make binding pre-trial rulings as would a Crown Division judge;**

- **the judge should rule on matters of law, procedure and the admissibility of evidence in the absence of the magistrates whenever he considers it would be potentially unfairly prejudicial to the defendant to do so in their presence;**

- **the same order of speeches and structure of trial should apply as in the Crown Division;**

- **the judge should not sum up the case to the magistrates, but, after retiring with them to consider the court's decision, should give a publicly reasoned judgment of the court; and**

- **the judge should be solely responsible for sentence.**

---

[48] para 31

Trial in the Magistrates' Division

62 The magistrates' courts are peculiar in having a body of laymen who, together, are judges of both law and fact. Magistrates are assisted in the performance of their functions by legal advisers (who are often qualified solicitors or barristers). In many respects the latter's function resembles that of a judge, giving advice on matters where in trial on indictment the jury would receive direction or warning. However, the legal adviser has specific duties and responsibilities to the magistrates and parties which reflect the special regime that applies to summary level proceedings. For example, they provide advice on matters of mixed fact and law, practice and procedure in open court, participate in the proceedings to the extent of asking questions in order to clarify evidence and issues, and assist the magistrates in the formulation and recording or reasons.[49]

63 I see no overwhelming case for any major change in the general structure and procedures of summary trial as they are today. They combine reasonably well fairness and speed appropriate to the trial of summary offences. Particular strengths are the legal adviser's public statement of advice he has given to the magistrates on matters of law, procedure or evidence and their move to giving publicly reasoned decisions.

64 There is, however, the much canvassed problem of magistrates, as judges of law, having to rule on the admissibility of evidence which could potentially unfairly prejudice them against the defendant in their capacity as judges of fact. Short of radical change in the judicial composition of magistrates' courts – for example by making the legal adviser, the sole judge of law, procedure and admissibility of evidence – which I have not recommended, the best answer lies in the reform of the law of evidence for judges, magistrates and jurors alike. If, as I propose,[50] there is a move away from orality and rules of inadmissibility to trusting fact finders to assess the weight of the evidence for themselves, there would be no need for the present artificial procedure. And if there were to be some relaxation of present restrictions on admitting evidence of previous convictions, it would be for the magistrates to assess their relevance and weight to the issues before them.

---

[49] see *Practice Direction (Justices: Clerk to Court)* [2000] 4 All ER 895

[50] paras 80 - 81 below et seq

Accordingly, I recommend that the structure and procedures of trial in the Magistrates' Division of a new unified Criminal Court should broadly follow those of the present magistrates' courts.

Abbreviated procedures

65   Summary trial and guilty pleas are two examples of abbreviated procedures in English law. Historically, both were ways of abridging the normal form of criminal procedure. Another possibility is an abbreviated form of summary procedure in mostly minor cases where guilt is clear, such as that used in Germany (Strafbefehlsverfahren) and France (ordonnance pénale) under which the prosecutor invites the court to deal with the matter on paper and proposes a punishment, leaving it for the defendant to object and, in any event, for the court to agree. In the event of objection or the court's non-agreement, the matter proceeds to court in the normal way. In Germany this procedure applies to the lower of two categories of crime (Vergehen) and extends to offences carrying custodial penalties of up to 12 months where the defendant is legally represented, and accounts for 30% of the work of the lower courts. In France the procedure is more restricted, applicable only to *contraventions*, the least serious of its three classes of criminal offence and punishable only by fines and confiscation.[51]

66   In England and Wales there are two main procedures which magistrates' courts use to dispose of certain straightforward summary cases expeditiously. The first affects trial procedure, and the second, to which I refer in more detail at paragraphs 217-219 below, relates to sentencing. They both apply to a defendant charged with offences not imprisonable for more than 3 months nor specified by statutory instrument.[52]

67   Where the prosecution has served witness statements on a defendant with the summons and the defendant does not send a plea of guilty by post, it may then prove the case in his absence or in his presence on the first hearing on the basis of the statements. Where the prosecution has made use of the procedure, there has been a significant reduction in time and work for operational police officers, the Crown Prosecution Service and the courts. There has been a fall in the number of adjournments previously caused by the widespread failure of defendants to respond to summonses and a corresponding increase in the proportion of cases finalised on the first hearing. It also safeguards the rights

---

[51] Barbara Huber, in Hatchard, Huber and Vogler, *Comparative Criminal Procedure*, (BIICL, 1996), pp 158-159

[52] Magistrates' Courts Act 1980, s 12 as amended by the Magistrates' Courts (Procedure) Act 1998, s 1

of defendants who attend the hearing and only then object to the absence of the witness, since the court may then allow an adjournment. The trouble is that not all areas have made use of the procedure. A recent Joint Inspectorate Report[53] showed that only 40% of police forces were fully using it and that 50% were using it in part or planned its implementation. The main reason for the incomplete and/or slow take-up of such an obviously worthwhile scheme is lack of co-operation between the various agencies. The Trial Issues Group, through the Local Trial Issues Groups, have recently urged local criminal justice agencies to take full advantage of it. The use of such a procedure has obvious advantages. It significantly reduces the administrative burdens for the police and prosecuting authorities and inconvenience to witnesses and saves court time. In the many cases of defendants failing to respond to summonses it is a speedy and efficient means of overcoming such disregard.

I recommend use in all areas and by all prosecuting authorities of the present provisions of section 12 of the Magistrates' Courts Act 1980, as amended, for disposal of cases on pleas of guilty or on proof of guilt in the absence of the defendant.

The role of the victim

68   The Government, in its recent policy paper *The Way Ahead*, records a number of measures already introduced or planned to improve the lot of victims and witnesses in the criminal justice process.[54] I have referred in Chapter 10 to a number of them at the pre-trial stage. Those concerned with the trial stage include: protection of alleged victims of rape from being cross-examined by defendants in person, or as to their previous sexual history;[55] new statutory protection of vulnerable or intimidated witnesses when giving evidence;[56] the extension of the Witness Service to all magistrates' courts, the introduction of victim personal statements (in which victims, in their own words can say how the alleged crime has affected their lives) for use throughout the criminal justice process; requiring the Crown Prosecution Service to inform victims about certain key casework decisions[57] and requiring the Probation Service to consult, and subsequently to inform, victims of serious violent and sexual crimes about offenders' release and conditions. The Government also proposes: a new Victims' Charter, possibly including statutory rights and a Victims' Ombudsman; better court facilities to secure separation of

---

[53] *The Implementation of Section 1 of the Magistrates' Courts (Procedure) Act 1998* A joint study by HM Magistrates' Courts Service Inspectorate, HM Inspectorate of Constabulary and the Crown Prosecution Service Inspectorate, November 2000

[54] *Criminal Justice: The Way Ahead*, 26th February 2001, CM 5074, pp 69-75

[55] Youth Justice and Criminal Evidence Act 1999, ss 34-43

[56] Youth Justice and Criminal Evidence Act 1999, Part II

[57] implementing the recommendations of Sir Iain Glidewell's Review and the Stephen Lawrence Inquiry

prosecution and defence witnesses and their families; provision of information about the progress of cases by internet technology; a significant increase in compensation for victims of rape and child abuse and for bereaved families in fatal cases;[58] and generally better facilities for the care of and information to victims. However, these latter proposals are, in the main, concerned with better treatment of victims, rather than with their role at the trial.

69   The *Way Ahead* Paper makes no mention of a number of other, more radical, suggestions that have been mooted by Ministers and others from time to time. One is that a victim, actual or alleged, and/or his family should be permitted to be a party to a criminal prosecution, as in most Continental systems, including, famously, the French *partie civile*, or even 'an auxiliary prosecutor', as in a few countries, notably, Germany.   Sir William Macpherson in his Report on the Stephen Lawrence Inquiry,[59] recommended consideration of the former as an addition to the existing right in English law of private individuals to initiate their own criminal proceedings.   In a conference considering these and other proposals in 1999 the weight of informed opinion seems to have been against the introduction of either system.[60]

70   The '*partie civile*' or 'adhesion procedure', which carries with it rights of information as well as the right to participate in the trial, is not considered to confer much practical advantage in either respect over the English system. As a means of obtaining adequate or any compensation, continental experience suggests that it is too complicated for those who have no legal representation or advice.   Free legal aid is limited.   For those who can afford legal representation, the net recovery is often not worth the outlay.   And European criminal court judges are, seemingly, reluctant to rule on the victim's claim, often referring it to the civil court.   Even if a victim secures a compensation order in the criminal court, he is left with the often hopeless task of having to enforce it against the offender.   An English victim has the same problem.   As most offenders are poor he can mostly only expect to receive his compensation in instalments, often extending over a year and exceptionally for up to three years. If the offender does not pay and the court is unable to enforce the order, the victim remains without compensation.

71   Similar considerations apply to a system enabling the victim to participate in a criminal trial as an auxiliary prosecutor and also to claim compensation.   In the few continental jurisdictions that provide for it, he is entitled to free legal aid for the purpose.   However, the role, in the way it is exercised, is largely symbolic and passive, the conduct of the prosecution being left entirely or

---

[58] subject to approval by Parliament and the Scottish Executive

[59] February 1999, CM 4262-1

[60] see the Report of the Conference held by the Home Office's Special Conferences Unit in September 1999 *The Role of Victims in the Criminal Justice Process.*

almost entirely to the public prosecutor. As in the *partie civile* procedure, there are important benefits to the victim in knowing at each stage what is going on and in the opportunity to make representations, either direct or indirect.

72 One view is that rights of information and effective compensation could be secured without the victim's participation in the process in either of those ways. As to information, there needs to be clear definition of who is responsible for informing the victim/witness of the progress, listing and outcome of the prosecution and provision of resources, in particular, information technology, to do it.[61] The Government, according to its *Way Ahead* Paper clearly has these matters in mind. As to compensation and recognition of the victim's role in the case, there is undoubtedly scope for improving the manner in which the Court is informed of the impact of the crime on him.[62]

73 Victim Support has suggested that the victim should have a more prominent role in the process. I believe that it had in mind giving the victim, whether witness or not, some formal or special status in the proceedings at trial and at sentence. This seemingly would have included permitting him or his representative to intervene to ask questions or to tell of the injury done to him to the extent that he had not already done so in evidence as a prosecution witness. Another suggestion is that he should at least have some clearly indicated place in court and one sufficiently close to the prosecutor to enable him to confer with him, for example, to enable him to contradict any misrepresentation by the defence.

74 It is difficult to see how such a scheme would fit our adversarial system, in which there are only two parties and the hearing is a substitute for private vengeance not an expression of it. To put an alleged victim whose account the defendant challenges - as will often be the case - in the ostensibly privileged role of an auxiliary prosecutor would be unfair. Whilst the current concern for the plight of victims in the criminal justice process and the steps being taken to right it are thoroughly justified, care must be taken, in particular when there is an issue as to guilt, not to treat him in a way that appears to prejudge the resolution of that issue.

75 I warmly commend the important contribution that Victim Support has made to improving the recognition and care of victims in the criminal justice process and the steps that the Government has proposed to further those ends. However, I recommend against giving victims, as some have suggested, a formal role in the trial process similar to that of the continental *partie civile* or

---

[61] see Chapter 10, paras 239 - 255

[62] see paras 220 – 223 below

auxiliary prosecutor, or any outwardly special position in relation to the prosecutor.

EVIDENCE

General principles

76   My terms of reference require me to examine the fairness and efficiency of the rules of evidence in the criminal justice process. That is an enormous subject in its own right, suffering, as Professor Colin Tapper has put it, from a 'blight' in the law of evidence as a whole. It is a blight that he and many distinguished academics have long attributed to incoherence, confusion and conflict in the aims and policy of the law of evidence. This is in large part due to our tradition of sporadic and piecemeal statutory reform and constantly evolving overlay of judge-made law softening its edges.[63] It also suffers from a neglect of the needs of summary trial. Rules devised in the main for, or which have their origin in, jury trial are often far too complex or artificial for application in the fast moving list of magistrates' courts. Magistrates, who undertake the bulk of summary work, or their advisers, cannot be expected to grapple with the minutiae and refinements devised principally for the more leisurely proceedings in the Crown Court.[64]   Indeed, I suspect that District Judges, with their equally long and arduous lists, have little time or patience for fine evidential points.

77   For these reasons there is an urgent need for a comprehensive review of the whole law of criminal evidence to make it a simple and an efficient agent for ensuring that all criminal courts are told all and only what they need to know. I believe that an important part of this exercise should be an examination of the justice and feasibility of a general move away from rules of inadmissibility to trusting fact finders to give relevant evidence the weight it deserves. It is no part of this Review to attempt a comprehensive study or to make detailed recommendations for reform in this field. As I have indicated in Chapter 1, that should be part of a principled and comprehensive exercise in the reform and codification of the criminal law, to be undertaken by a standing body working under the oversight of the Criminal Justice Council.[65] In the meantime, I have tried to identify those areas where I see the greatest need for, and potential benefits from, change and to suggest, in the broadest terms, possible lines of reform. To provide a framework for that task I have

---

[63] *Hearsay in Criminal Cases: An Overview of Law Commission Report No 245,* [1997] Crim LR 771

[64] see Penny Darbyshire,*Previous Misconduct and the Magistrates' Courts – Some Tales from the Real World* [1997] Crim LR 105

[65] see Chapter 8, paras 78 - 84

accepted a number of features of our criminal process as given and have adopted a number of general principles, I have taken as given:

- a continuation of a trial procedure that is in the main adversarial and that relies largely on oral evidence and argument;

- the involvement of juries and lay magistrates as the main fact finders on the issue of guilt;

- the criminal burden of proof and the defendant's right to silence in its present qualified form;

- relevance as a threshold of admissibility; and

- fairness as a criterion for admission.

78   Within those constraints, rules of evidence should aid, not hinder, the search for truth; be such as to promote a fair trial for the defendant; be clear; be simple to apply; and, so far as is consistent with those principles, secure an efficient trial process. A common theme of all my recommendations under this section is the view I have just expressed, that we should, in general, move away from technical rules of inadmissibility and focus more on the weight of evidence. I express the theme here as a recommendation in its own right.

> **I recommend that the English law of criminal evidence should, in general, move away from technical rules of inadmissibility to trusting judicial and lay fact-finders to give relevant evidence the weight it deserves.**

Orality

79   A common justification for our system of orality of evidence, including the rule against hearsay, is that seeing the demeanour and hearing the evidence of a witness in the witness box is the best means of getting at the truth. But there is much judicial, academic and psychological scepticism about the weight that even seasoned observers of witnesses should attach to the impressions they form of them in the witness box.[66] It may be a factor, depending on the witness and what he has to say and on the experience and good judgment of the fact finder. But it is only one factor and I respectfully agree with the Law Commission that it is not of such significance, on its own, as to justify the exclusion of hearsay.[67] I would go further and join Lord Bingham and a

---

[66] Law Commission Consultation Paper, *Evidence in Criminal Proceedings: Hearsay and Related Topics,* 1995, Law Comm 138, para 6.1

[67] ibid para 6.30

growing band of other distinguished jurists who, on the whole, doubt the demeanour of a witness as a reliable pointer to his honesty.[68]

80   Nevertheless, I can see no well-founded argument for a general move away from orality of evidence in criminal proceedings where there is an issue of the reliability or credibility of a witness's account on a material matter. For there are features other than the demeanour of the witness which make it a convenient way of testing the truthfulness of his evidence, in particular its external and internal consistency, consistency with what he has said previously, and matters going to credit. And, in issues not turning on truthfulness, but accuracy or reliability of memory, there is clear advantage in an oral process, at least for the purpose of testing the strength of the evidence in cross examination. The witness box (or by way of video-tape or video-link) is the place for such critical evidence to be tested and, if necessary, challenged. But there are some rules of evidence surrounding this tradition that, in my view, deserve urgent review. In one form or another, they are an expression or consequence of the rule against hearsay. Professor John Spencer in his contribution to the Law Commission's consultation process on the reform of the law of hearsay, wrote that the weakness of the principle of relying solely or mainly on oral testimony is that it requires us:

> "to accept two remarkable scientific propositions: first, that memory improves with time; and secondly, that stress enhances a person's powers of recall".[69]

'Refreshing memory'/ Witness Statements

81   A witness may refresh his memory in the witness box from a 'contemporaneous' document, namely a note that he made or verified when his memory was clear.[70] However, the exercise is often, not one of 'refreshing memory', but of permitting a witness to substitute for his evidence the reading of a note of matters of which he has little or no memory.[71] Every day, in courts all over the country, police officers are permitted to give evidence by reference to their notebooks of matters of which they could not possibly be expected to have any independent recollection. Often, they freely acknowledge their total dependence on their note when the point is put to them by way or as a result of a challenge from the defence advocate. Yet, they are still expected, when giving evidence, to go through the charade of seemingly not reading their notebooks, but only glancing at them from time to

---

[68] Lord Bingham of Cornhill, The Business of Judging, (OUP, 2000), *The Judge as Juror: The Judicial Determination of Factual Issues,* at pp 7-13

[69] see Law Comm 245, para 10.31; see also his article *Hearsay Reform: A Bridge Not Far Enough* [1996] Crim LR29, at 32-33

[70] see *Attorney General's Reference (no 3 of 1979)* 63 Cr App R 411, CA, per Lord Widgery CJ at 414; see also *R v Richardson (D)* [1971] 2 QB 484, at 490, 55 Cr App R 244, at 251, CA

[71] see eg *R v Bryant and Dickson* (1931) Cr App R 146, at 150

time when their memory needs jogging. The understandable reality is, of course, that they have usually spent time, shortly before going into the witness box, reading and re-reading their notes so that, at best, their evidence is a test of their short-term memory of what they have just read. So, for all practical purposes, the note, though not physically admissible, becomes the evidence in chief. The absurdity of all this is aggravated by the usual and recognised practice that a witness may also refresh his memory shortly before going into the witness box by reading a non-contemporaneous written statement if he has made one.[72]

82   In recent years the courts have attempted to loosen the rules for refreshing memory so as to accord more with reality. In 1990, in *R v Da Silva* the Court of Appeal held that, in the exercise of a judge's discretion, a witness who has begun to give evidence could be permitted to read, for the purpose of refreshing his memory, a statement made near to the time of the events in question subject to a number of provisos: 1) that he cannot remember the events because of the lapse of time; 2) that when he made the statement it represented his recollection at the time; 3) that he has not read the statement before coming into the witness box; 4) that he wishes to read the statement before continuing with his evidence; and 5) that, having read the statement he should then continue his evidence without further reference to it.[73] In 1996 in *R v South Ribble Magistrates, ex p Cochrane*[74] the Divisional Court held that the Court of Appeal in *Da Silva* had not intended to confine the discretion of a court by reference to those provisos and that there was strong discretion in the court to permit a witness to refresh his memory from a non-contemporaneous document, applying the requirements of fairness and justice. On that approach, the Court held: that it did not matter whether the witness had not read the statement before coming into the witness box or had done so but had not taken it in for some reason; and that in some cases it could be appropriate to permit the witness to refresh his memory from the witness statement while giving evidence.

83   As the editors of the 2001 edition of Archbold indicate,[75] these decisions could lead to the routine use of witness statements as memory refreshers. They suggest that the rule should be re-cast to avoid altogether the test of contemporaneity and to make the only condition of use of a document that there is good reason to believe that the witness would have been significantly better able to recall the events in question when he made or verified the statement than at the time of giving evidence. That would permit most witness statements made much nearer the time to be used as memory refreshers. The editors of Archbold mention two features in all this to which the courts should

---

[72] see Home Office Circular 82/1969; *R v Richardson* (1971) 55 Cr App R 244 at 250, per Sachs LJ; see also *Lau Pak Ngam v R* [1966] Crim L R 443, Supreme Court of Hong Kong
[73] (1990) 90 Cr App R 233, CA
[74] [1996] 2 Cr App R 544, CA
[75] para 8-76

have regard. The first is that a witness with his statement in the witness box tends to use it as a script. But that has long been the reality in the use of contemporaneous records as memory refreshers. The second is that a witness statement often bears little relationship to a witness's evidence. But inconsistency between a witness's statement and his evidence may have a number of causes, including: fallibility of the witness's recollection without it; incorrect drafting by a police officer not corrected at the time by the witness; and lies in the statement, possibly in collusion with other witnesses; or lies in the evidence. The first of those is a reason for allowing the witness to see the statement; in the second and third the defence will usually ensure that he sees it and that the court is made aware of the conflict; only where, by dint of the witness's good memory or lies, there is consistency between the two, does the statement tend to remain unused as a memory refresher or tool for cross-examination.

84   In my view, the suggested new rule would be a clearer and more principled way of recognising the reality of the Da Silva approach, namely that testimony should be an exercise in truthfulness rather than a test of long or short term memory. At present the rules seem to me to have more to do with gamesmanship than the criminal burden of proof or the reliability of evidence. In their application to prosecution witnesses, in respect of whose evidence the point mostly arises, the defence may do their best to deprive a witness of access to his statement in the witness box in the hope that he will not keep to it, whereupon they will confront him with the inconsistency and make much of it with the jury. If, notwithstanding such denial of access to his witness statement, the witness does keep to it, the defence can keep the consistency from the jury. In either case, his credibility or accuracy falls to be tested by what he said nearer the event alongside what he says in the witness box. If he has had the opportunity to read his statement before going into the witness box, he will tell the truth or lie as he did in the witness statement; if the former, the only casualty of justice may be the weakness of his short term memory. The suggested new rule would also clear away more cleanly the pre-Da Silva anomaly that a witness may refresh his memory from a witness statement before going into the witness box but not use it as a memory refresher when in the box.

85   But, whether such a useful but small step would remove the mostly time-wasting – and to the witness and jury, mystifying – procedural wrangling as to whether the witness needs or should be permitted to refresh his memory from the document in question, I have some doubt. There would still be scope for defence advocates to take points as to whether the defendant has indicated a need to refresh his memory and, if so, whether the memory refreshing document originated at a time when his memory was much clearer. Nevertheless, as a starting point in a line of reasoning and on the road to a longer goal:

I recommend consideration of making the only condition for a witness's use of a written statement for refreshing memory that there is good reason to believe that he would have been significantly better able to recall the events in question when he made or verified it than at the time of giving evidence.

Prior witness statements as evidence

86   The present rule – 'the rule against narrative' – excludes evidence of a witness's previous witness statements except where they contradict his testimony, when they may be used to challenge his truthfulness or reliability. If we reach the stage when witnesses may have recourse in the witness box to a broader range of memory refreshing documents and may largely read them, would it not be more sensible, expeditious and helpful to the tribunal, to a jury in particular, to invite the witness to put in the document as his evidence in chief, as in civil or family cases and ask him simply to confirm and, if required, add to it orally.   He could then be cross-examined both as to his written statement and as to any additional oral evidence in the ordinary way. It would also remove the present nonsensical requirement for juries, magistrates and judicial fact finders, when previous statements are presently admitted as a result of cross-examination, to treat them as relevant only to the credibility of the witness and not as evidence supportive of his account of the facts.

87   As long ago as 1972 the Criminal Law Revision Committee recommended the admission in evidence of previous statements, expressing the view that if a witness is honest, what he said soon after the event is likely to be at least as reliable as his evidence at the trial, and probably more so; and if he is dishonest his evidence can still be tested in cross-examination.[76] In Scotland a witness's prior statement is admissible as evidence of any matter stated in it if it was contained in a 'document' and sufficiently authenticated by the witness prior to the trial, provided that the witness was competent when making it, that he confirms having made it and adopts it as his evidence.[77] Other Commonwealth jurisdictions have, in various ways, shown more flexibility about this than we have, tending to adopt an inclusionary rather than exclusionary approach to such hearsay, and trusting juries to give it the weight it deserves.[78]

---

[76] Eleventh Report, Evidence (General), Cmnd 4991, para 239 and Clause 31 of its Draft Bill
[77] Criminal Justice (Scotland) Act 1995, s 18, and Criminal Procedure (Scotland) Act 1995, s 260
[78] Law Comm 138, para 13.40 and Appendix B

88   The Law Commission, in its 1997 Report, *Evidence in Criminal Proceedings: Hearsay and Related Topics* , was not prepared to go that far.[79] It expressly rejected the option that any previous statement should be admissible regardless of the ability of the witness to remember the details in it or of their freshness in his memory at the time he made it. The Law Commission did so because it feared that it would allow the admission of many previous consistent statements, adding little or nothing and distracting fact-finders from more important evidence. It also considered that defendants would be tempted to make many denial statements in the hope that their volume would impress a lay tribunal. It acknowledged the ability and readiness of judges to exclude material which is purely repetitious and for that reason irrelevant and that, in practice, only statements adding value to a witness's statement or enhancing his credibility would become admissible. However, it foresaw long arguments on the relevance of documents and a focus on statements in documents at the expense of oral evidence, the latter of particular concern because of doubts as to the general quality of witness statements taken by police officers. For those reasons it rejected this option.[80]

89   Those concerns seem to me to give insufficient weight to the ability of the criminal courts to restrict where appropriate the use of unhelpful or simply repetitious hearsay by the mechanism of judicial permission, as applies in civil proceedings.[81] Disputes about the grant of permission should not interrupt or delay trials once under way; the proper place for resolution of such matters is before trial as part of the process leading to pre-trial assessment and, if necessary, pre-trial hearing. In the result, the Law Commission recommended the admissibility of a witness's previous statement as evidence of fact where the witness: first, does not, and cannot reasonably be expected to, remember a matter well enough to be able to give oral evidence of it; second, he has made a statement about it when it was fresh in his memory; and third, he indicates in evidence that it is his statement and that to the best of his belief it is true.[82] As the Law Commission states, for most purposes such a rule would remove the necessity for witnesses to have recourse to statements to refresh their memory because the statement would stand as part of their evidence. The only possible use for it as a memory refresher would be where a witness has a partial recollection which genuinely needs jogging by his witness statement.

90   However, there is little logic in distinguishing between no independent recollection and partial recollection for this purpose. And, as the Law Commission points out, under the present law, the use that can be made of the statement, if the witness is cross-examined on it, varies according to whether it is regarded as evidence or a memory refreshing document – in the former,

[79] Law Comm 245
[80] ibid, paras 10.30-10.34
[81] Civil Evidence Act 1995, s 6(2)
[82] Law Comm No 245, para 10.80

evidence of the facts, in the latter going only to consistency. In my view, the answer is not to maintain the two possible uses of witness statements and give them the status of evidence of fact, as suggested by the Law Commission.[83] Instead, all previous statements should be admissible regardless of the existence or extent of the witness's memory, leaving their weight, along with the oral evidence of the witness after testing in cross-examination, a matter for determination by the tribunal. I draw strength from the following argument of the Scottish Law Commission in its Report in 1995, giving rise to the present Scottish law admitting prior witness statements:

> "7.14 ... First, if a prior statement by a witness is of such a nature that its reliability may be accurately assessed by a properly directed jury, it should be admissible not only to support or undermine the witness's credibility, but also as evidence of the truth of its contents, whatever the witness may say in court about the matters dealt with in the statement.... That would simplify the law and render admissible reliable evidence which, under the present law, is inadmissible for that purpose.

> 7.15 Secondly, if a witness finds it difficult to give evidence in court – whether because his or her memory of events is no longer accurate, or because he or she is under considerable stress ... for any ... reason – a prior statement by him ... should be admissible provided that ... the witness accepts that he ... made a statement and adopts it as his ... evidence.

> 7.16 ... the effect of our recommendations is that the prior statement would be no more than an admissible item of evidence for the jury's consideration. The witness could be examined and cross-examined as to the truth of its contents and the circumstances in which it was made, and contradictory evidence could be led about the matters dealt with in the statement. Further, we propose that any objection which could have been properly taken if the contents of the statement had been given orally may be taken to the statement or any part of it, or to any question which is recorded as having been put to the witness".[84]

91   Such an approach would also be more of a piece with the Law Commission's recommendation to extend the present exception to the hearsay rule of recent complaint in sexual cases to all offences and to treat it as evidence of the facts complained of, not (to the extent that any difference is discernible) simply of the witness's credibility.[85] And, as Professor John Spencer has pointed out in a consultation paper for the Review, it would merely be a reversion to English

---

[83] ibid para 10.82

[84] *Evidence: Report on Hearsay Evidence in Criminal Proceedings*, Edinburgh, 22nd February 1995, Scot Law Comm No 149, at para 7.14

[85] Law Comm No 245, paras 10.22-10.26 and 10.53-10.61.

law as it was until the 19th century[86] and incorporated by Stephen as late as 1872 into the Indian Evidence Act.[87] The rule as to the admissibility of complaints as relevant only to consistency was peculiar to complaints in sexual cases and had its origin in a strong presumption against the truthfulness of a woman complainant in such a matter if she had made no complaint at or shortly after the sexual assault of which she complained.[88] The rationale for singling out sexual allegations in this way was the unavailability of independent evidence in most such cases.[89] But the same is true of many offences; and the law now no longer penalises complainants in sexual offence cases by requiring corroboration of their evidence.[90] I agree, for the reasons I have given, that a witness's previous statement in written, audio-recorded or video-recorded form, consistent or inconsistent, should be capable of being put in evidence, and that the rule should be extended to all cases. I also agree with the Criminal Law Revision Committee[91], the Law Commission[92] and, I suspect, just about every judge sitting today that it is unrealistic to tell a jury, as the law currently requires, that a recent complaint in a sexual offence case only goes to the truthfulness of the complainant not as to whether the complaint itself was true. The complaint, if admitted in evidence, should be regarded as evidence of the truth of its contents, challengeable in the same way as the witness's oral evidence.

92   Accordingly, and as further step on the road to ultimate reform,

> **I recommend consideration of amendment of the law as to admissibility of witness statements so that:**
>
> - **where a witness has made a prior statement, in written or recorded form, it should be admissible as evidence of any matter stated in it of which his direct oral evidence in the proceedings would be admissible provided that he authenticates it as his statement;**
>
> - **an integral part of the new rule should be that a defendant's previous statement should in principle be admissible whether it supports or damages his case and the fact that it may appear to be self-serving should go only to weight; and**
>
> - **the witness should be permitted, where appropriate, to adopt the statement in the witness box as his evidence in chief.**

---

[86] Hawkins, *Pleas of the Crown* (7th ed, 1795) Vol 4, p 427

[87] s 157

[88] see Hawkins' *Pleas of the Crown,* bk I C 41, s 9, cited by Hawkins J in *R v Lillyman* [1896] 2 QB 167, CCR, at 170-171

[89] Law Comm No 245, para 10.22

[90] or accomplices.

[91] Eleventh Report, Evidence (General), Cmnd 4991 para 232

[92] Law Comm para 10.57

93   But that is not the end of that story. There is the danger, to which I have referred, of a statement, whether in documentary, audio-recorded or video-recorded form, carrying much greater authority with a lay fact finder than in the impermanent forms of hearing the statement read and/or seeing it in the course of the evidence and/or in oral reminders of it by the advocates and the judge. If, for example, a jury were left to take a prosecution witness's statement to their retiring room when considering their decision with only oral reminders of the judge in his summing-up of the defence inroads on it in cross-examination, there is a danger that the printed words in front of them would carry more weight. [93] This danger also arises in relation to evidence presented by electronic means, such as computer graphics or virtual reality simulations. One way of dealing with it would be to make the reading of the statement or the playing of the recording in the course of the trial evidence of the facts to which it relates, but not to permit the jury to have it in any permanent form. This is the solution adopted in the United States Federal Rules of Evidence, which admit prior statements into evidence, subject to certain conditions, but by 'reading it into evidence' and not by way of an exhibit unless offered by an adverse party, the object being to deny the jury the statement in their jury room during deliberation.[94]

94   This may become less of a problem with the march of science when all courts are equipped with facilities for the transcription, searching and ready production in electronic or hard copy form of oral evidence, but that is not likely to be achievable everywhere for some time. There would also be the danger, to which the Law Commission referred, of swamping juries with much unnecessary material. An alternative, also in the long-term, would be to improve and to refine the practices of the police when taking witness statements and for the recording of interviews with witnesses as for suspects.[95] Sir Anthony Hooper, who has recently written of the need for a comprehensive reform of the manner in which the evidence of witnesses is taken and presented,[96] cited the recent extension of provision for the use of video recorded evidence of children to all vulnerable witnesses[97] as examples of 'sticking plaster culture', and urged its extension, for serious crime at least, to the evidence of all witnesses. Such a system, he argued, could be subject to the sort of safeguards provided by Police and Criminal Evidence Act 1984 and its Codes in the interview of suspects. It would enable the witness to give his account in his own words at a time when it is fresh in his mind, thus avoiding the distortions of incompetent or subjectively over zealous statement

---

[93] see for comparable problems arising in evidence by video-link: *R –v- Rawlings & Broadbent* [1995] 2 Cr AppR222, CA; *R – v- M(J)* [1996] 2 CrApp R 54, CA; and *R v Morris* [1998] Crim LR 754 CA

[94] Rule 803(5)

[95] as urged by, among others, Anthony Heaton-Armstrong and David Wolchover, *Analysing Witness Testimony* (Blackstone, 1999)

[96] *The Investigation And Trial Of Criminal Offences In The New Century – The Need For A Radical* Change, (1999) 21 Liverpool Law Review, 131, at 136-138

[97] Part II of the Youth Justice and Criminal Evidence Act 1999

taking by the police. Inadmissible material could be edited out later. Such recordings, accompanied by transcripts or written summaries, would become, or form part of, the witness's evidence in chief at the trial whether or not he then confirmed it, any inconsistency and the reason given for it going to weight.[98] In my view, such a scheme deserves serious consideration. It would be likely to make demands in terms of skill and manpower on the police for which they are not presently equipped, but with the increasing use of video technology in the investigation and prosecution of crime, coupled with ready editing mechanisms, the long term benefits in cost to, and justice administered by, the criminal justice system as a whole could be worth it.

> **Accordingly, I recommend consideration in the long term of extending the present provisions for the use of video-recorded evidence to the evidence of all critical witnesses in cases of serious crime, coupled with provision where required of a record and/or transcripts or summaries of such evidence and also of that in cross-examination and re-examination.**

Hearsay[99]

95 The rule against hearsay in criminal proceedings, like many other past and present rules of inadmissibility in that jurisdiction, has its origin in the late 18th and early 19th centuries when the cards at trial were so stacked against defendants that judges felt the need to even the odds. The classic definition of hearsay is " an assertion other than one made by a person while giving oral evidence in the proceedings as evidence of any fact asserted".[100] It is an exclusionary rule of evidence, albeit subject to a number of wide statutory[101] and common law exceptions. In civil matters it has been abolished completely.[102] At its most basic, the rule confines a witness to giving evidence orally and only about matters of which he has direct or personal knowledge. It excludes four main categories of evidence: first, that which I have just considered, an earlier statement of a witness proffered in support of his oral evidence; second, written, tape-recorded or filmed evidence proffered as a substitute for oral evidence; third, an oral account by a witness of what someone else told him; and fourth, reliance on a written record to prove a disputed fact. On one view, it tends to exclude weak evidence and to ensure that a defendant may question his accusers, thus preserving the oral character

---

[98] see footnote 96

[99] I am much indebted to Professor John Spencer, in his capacity as a Consultant to the Review, for his contribution to much of the analysis in this section

[100] *Cross and Tapper On Evidence*, eighth edition (Butterworths, 1995) p 46

[101] eg the 'documentary hearsay' provisions of the Criminal Justice Act 1988, ss 23-26, and the 'deposition' provisions of the Criminal Procedure and Investigations Act 1996, s 68 and Sch 2

[102] Civil Evidence Act 1995, s 1

of the English trial. On the other, it is capable of being too restrictive so as to work injustice either way and, in its artificiality, interferes with the smooth running of the trial process.

96   It is common ground that the present law is unsatisfactory and needs reform. It is complicated, unprincipled and arbitrary in the application of a number of the many exceptions. It can exclude cogent and let in weak evidence. It wastes court time in requiring it to receive oral evidence when written evidence would do. And it confuses witnesses and prevents them from giving their accounts in their own way.

97   There is a strong case for reversing the rule so as to render all relevant hearsay admissible, leaving its weight for determination by the tribunal. The Runciman Royal Commission, while recognising the complexity of the law on this matter and the need for examination by the Law Commission, favoured that approach:

> "We think that, in general, the fact that a statement is hearsay should mean that the court places rather less weight on it, but not that it should be inadmissible in the first place. We believe that the probative value of relevant evidence should in principle be decided by the jury for themselves, and we therefore recommend that hearsay evidence should be admitted to a greater extent than at present."[103]

98   Much, of course, depends on the quality of the fact finders, who are mostly jurors or magistrates. Many are of the view that both are already more competent than we give them credit for in assessing the weight of evidence, including hearsay evidence presently admitted under the various exceptions to the rule. If the recommendations that I have made in Chapters 4, 5, 6 and 7 are adopted, future fact finders in our tribunals should improve in quality.

99   However, the Law Commission, in its recent Report,[104] recommended continuation of the exclusionary hearsay rule, with specified exceptions.[105] These were to consist of three categories of automatically admissible hearsay, namely unavailability of the declarant, reliable hearsay and admissions and confessions, and two categories of hearsay admissible at the discretion of the court, namely where required in the interests of justice and in the case of frightened witnesses. The Law Commission described the first of the two discretionary categories, as a "limited inclusionary discretion" or a "safety-valve", for use where, "despite the difficulties in challenging the statement, its

---

[103] *Runciman Royal Commission Report,* Chapter 8, paras 26 - 28

[104] Law Comm No 245

[105] in this broad respect, its approach was the same as Scottish Law Commission in its Report, *Evidence: Report on Hearsay Evidence in Criminal Proceedings,* 1995, Edinburgh HMSO, Scot Law Comm No 149, see in particular, paras. 4.47-4.48

probative value is such that the interests of justice require it to be admissible".[106]

100   A number of contributors to the Review have suggested that those recommendations do not go far enough in their relaxation of the rule. And there is much distinguished academic support, past and present, for substituting for the present, exclusionary rule subject to exceptions, an inclusionary approach, leaving the fact finders to assess its weight – also the approach, as I have indicated, of the Runciman Royal Commission. Professor John Spencer, as a consultant to the Law Commission in preparing its consultation paper and to this Review, is among them. Praying in aid the views of such eminent writers in the common law world as Jeremy Bentham, JB Thayer, CT McCormick and Glanville Williams,[107] he has argued that there should be a generally inclusionary system subject to a "best available evidence" principle. That is, each side would be obliged to produce the original source of the information if the source is still available. He also suggested as part of that solution, the establishment of some regular means of deposing witnesses who, for one reason or another, it is thought might not be available to give evidence at trial. Professor John Jackson and the Standing Advisory Committee on Human Rights are of a similar view, arguing that the Law Commission "should … have approached the subject on the basis that relevant hearsay should be admissible except where there is good reason for exclusion".[108]

101   The Law Commission considered the 'best available evidence' principle as its third option for reform, likening it to the approach of the German Courts which have a duty to search for the truth and in which the directness of the evidence goes to its weight and not to its admissibility.[109] It rejected the option principally on the ground that, whilst it might suit an inquisitorial system like that in Germany, it would not work in our adversarial system where the parties, not the tribunal, are responsible for seeking out and calling the evidence. In doing so, it was plainly much influenced by the weight of the opposition to it from most of its respondents, in the main judges and practitioners, but also the Society of Public Teachers of Law. It concluded its discussion with these words:

> "… we are troubled by the change of attitude that this option would require on the part of practitioners and judges. It would be necessary for them to change the habits of a life-time and be re-educated. We do not underestimate this task,

---

[106] ibid. para. 1.39

[107] see also his article, *Hearsay Reform: A Bridge Not Far Enough* [1996] Crim LR 29, at p 30

[108] see also Adrian Zuckerman, *The Principles of Criminal Evidence* (Clarendon , 1989), p 216; and *The Futility of Hearsay* [1996] Crim LR 4; Andrew L-T Choo, *Hearsay and Confrontation in Criminal Trials* (Clarendon, 1996), and Professor Richard D Friedman, *Thoughts from Across the Water on Hearsay and Confrontation* [1998] Crim LR 697, particularly at 700-701

[109] paras, 6.17-6.32

and this consideration fortifies the conclusion that we had already reached".[110]

102   The Law Commission's proposals for relaxation of the rule against hearsay, looked at individually, represent useful improvements on the present law.[111] They relax some of the rigidity of the present rule through a widening of the exceptions and the introduction of the limited inclusionary discretion. However, their implementation would not significantly change the present landscape nor, I believe, remove much of the scope for dispute that disfigures and interrupts our present trial process. Within a short time the new scheme, as Professor Spencer has put it, would "generate a new crop of case law interpreting the limits of the definition and exceptions, leaving us essentially in the position we are in today".[112] In my view, this difficult subject should be looked at again, I suggest by the body that I have recommended should be established to undertake the reform and codification of our law of criminal evidence. It would also have the benefit of the impressive Report in 1999 of New Zealand Law Commission and its Draft Code for criminal and civil evidence.[113] That body took as its two main criteria the reliability of the proposed statement and the unavailability of the person who made it, adopting the following proposition of Lamer CJ:[114]

> "[H]earsay evidence of statements made by a person who is not available to give evidence at trial ought generally to be admissible, where the circumstances under which the statements were made satisfy the criteria of necessity and reliability … and subject to the residual discretion of the trial judge to exclude the evidence when its probative value is slight and undue prejudice might extend to the accused. Properly cautioned by the trial judge, juries are perfectly capable of determining what weight ought to be attached to such evidence, and of drawing reasonable inferences therefrom."

103   In advance of over-all reform of the law of criminal evidence, I make the following obvious points. The need and form of reform of the rule against hearsay should be approached from the fundamental standpoints that rules of evidence should facilitate rather than obstruct the search for truth and should simplify rather than complicate the trial process. Inherent in a search for truth is fairness to the defendant and his protection from wrongful conviction – but

---

[110] paras 6.22 and 6.31

[111] see Professor Colin Tapper, *Hearsay in Criminal Cases: An Overview of Law Commission Report No 245* [1997] Crim LR 771

[112] in a consultation paper prepared for the Review

[113] Report No 55, Evidence, Vol 1, pp 13-20 and Vol 2, p 53 setting out section 19 of the Commission's Draft Code covering hearsay in criminal proceedings

[114] *R v Smith* (1992) 15 CR (4th) 133 SCC, at 152

it should not be forgotten that the present rule can operate unfairly against a defendant as well as the prosecution.

104   As to the Law Commission's view that an inclusionary approach based on the best evidence principle might not suit our adversarial system, I share Professor Spencer's view that, if our courts are expected to police an exclusionary system hedged with exceptions, they could surely do the same with a system based on the availability of the witness. As I said at the beginning of this chapter, the boundaries between the adversarial and inquisitorial systems of trial are blurring; our judges and magistrates are already assuming an increasingly active role in the preparation of cases for trial and becoming more interventionist in the course of it than has been traditional. If they do not already have authority to secure the production of the best available evidence, they can be invested with it, without prejudice to the defendant's right to put the prosecution to proof of his guilt. Whilst due respect should be given to the views of judges and practitioners trained in and with long experience of the present system, their resistance to a particular form of change should not hold sway if there is otherwise a compelling case for it.

I recommend:

- **further consideration of the reform of the rule against hearsay, in particular with a view to making hearsay generally admissible subject to the principle of best evidence, rather than generally inadmissible subject to specified exceptions as proposed by the Law Commission; and**

- **in this respect, as with evidence in criminal cases generally, moving away from rules of inadmissibility to trusting fact finders to assess the weight of the evidence.**

Unfair evidence

105   There is a mix of broadly overlapping statutory and common law rules designed to protect defendants from the admission of evidence that is unfair to them. They are directed at the reliability of the evidence in question and whether admission of it will prejudice a fair trial. Alleged confessions of a defendant may be excluded under no less than four main rules, two of which also apply to evidence generally. First, under section 76(2)(a) of the Police and Criminal Evidence Act 1984, a court *must* exclude a confession unless it is sure that it was not obtained by oppression of the defendant. Second, under section 76(2)(b) of the 1984 Act, a Court *must* exclude a confession unless it

is sure that it was not obtained in consequence of anything said or done which was likely, in the circumstances existing at the time, to render unreliable any confession which he might have made in consequence of it. Third, under section 78(1), a Court *may* exclude any evidence upon which the prosecution proposes to rely if it appears that, having regard to all the circumstances, including those in which the evidence was obtained, the admission of the evidence would have such an adverse effect on the fairness of the proceedings that it ought not to admit it. Fourth, pursuant to section 82(3) of the 1984 Act preserving the common law, a court *may in its discretion,* exclude evidence so as to protect a defendant from an unfair trial.

106   There is a separate but, some would say, closely related jurisdiction in the courts to stay proceedings for abuse of process, which may include improper police activity or illegally obtained evidence. There is a 'disciplinary' element in the exercise of this jurisdiction. It is not restricted to cases where a fair trial is impossible, but is also exercisable where it would be contrary to the public interest in the integrity of the criminal justice system that a trial should take place. However, the jurisdiction can only be exercised to stay the prosecution, not to exclude the offending evidence and permit a trial to continue.

107   The 1984 Act statutory provisions had their origin in the Philips Royal Commission Report of 1981.[115] The Commission had considered the 'reliability' principle as expressed by Lord Diplock in *R v Sang*,[116] namely whether evidence, by virtue of its nature and quality, was arguably reliable, and the 'disciplinary' principle of exclusion well established in the United States of America, namely whether, despite its arguable reliability and cogency, the court may exclude it because it does not like the manner in which it was obtained.[117] The Commission had commented on the ineffectiveness of the latter as a deterrent to police misconduct, drawing on the experience of the United States and citing Chief Justice Burger's powerful observation:

> "We can well ponder whether any community is entitled to call itself an 'organised society' if it can find no way to solve the problem except by suppression of truth in search of truth."[118]

It had concluded that the solution was to be found in police supervisory and disciplinary procedures coupled with a discretion in the court to exclude or

---

[115] paras 4.123 –4.135 and 5.18
[116] [1980] AC 402, HL 402, at 436F-437C
[117] paras 4.123-134
[118] Warren Burger, *Who Will Watch the Watchman?,* American University Law Review 14.1, pp 11-12 and 23

admit evidence obtained in breach of those procedures, where the breach was relevant to its reliability.[119]

108   The Runciman Royal Commission, in 1993, expressed general satisfaction with the working of the resultant provisions in the 1984 Act.[120] However, it is only since then that the size of the problem in their application, has become apparent. Not only is there a confusing overlap between the various provisions, there is much uncertainty as to the ambit of section 78(1) and the common law power to exclude and as to their relationship one with another. The central problem is whether under section 78 and at common law the courts are generally[121] confined to excluding evidence only on the ground of its quality, the "reliability" principle of exclusion. An associated question, on which there is a division of judicial and academic views, is whether section 78, in requiring the court to have regard to "all the circumstances, including the circumstances in which the evidence was obtained", widened the common law so as to require consideration of the propriety of obtaining of evidence as well as or regardless of its reliability.[122] Of course, in those cases where the impropriety may affect the reliability of the evidence, there is no difficulty. The problem arises where the evidence, despite the impropriety, is potentially reliable and cogent. Quite apart from the question of construction of section 78 and the effect of the authorities, there is an argument that evidence, however reliable, which should never have been before the court because of the way in which it was obtained, may for that reason violate Article 6.

109   A further question is the overlap between the courts' increasing exercise of its jurisdiction to stay proceedings for abuse of process, which, as I have said, clearly does include a disciplinary as well as a reliability function, and its statutory or common law power to exclude evidence, which, in general, arguably only includes the latter. As academic commentators have observed,[123] if there is such difference in the two jurisdictions, then, where the tainted evidence in question is not the only or even crucial prosecution evidence, it would be anomalous if the court were confined to the drastic measure of staying the prosecution and could not simply exclude the evidence. The answer to this question may affect in turn the statutory power

---

[119] para 5.18

[120] *Runciman Royal Commission Report,* Ch 4, paras 33-40

[121] that is, save in the case of admissions, confessions and evidence obtained from the accused after the commission of the offence

[122] authorities in favour of the reliability principle include: [1980] AC 402, HL 402, at 436F-437C *R v Mason* [1988] 1 WLR 139, CA; *R v Christou and Wright* (1992) 95 Cr App R 264, CA, per Taylor JCJ at 269; *R v Khan (Sultan)* [1997] AC 558, per Lord Nolan at 582B-C; and *R v Chalkley and Jeffries,* supra (but see Professor IH Dennis's powerful critical analysis of this case in his book, *The Law of Evidence,* (Sweet and Maxwell 1999), at pp 74-77); and *Attorney General's Reference (No 3 of 1999)* [2001] All E R 577, HL per Lord Steyn at 585h-j. Authorities said to support the disciplinary principle, see *R v Horseferry Road Magistrates' Court, ex p Bennett* [1994] 1 AC 42, per Lord Griffiths obiter at 61A; *R v Smurthwaite (1994)* 98 Cr App R 437, CA, per Taylor LCJ at 440; R v Cooke [1995] 1 Cr App R 318, per Glidewell LJ at 328; *R v Mullen (1999)* 2 Cr App R 143, CA; *Mohammed (Allie) v The State* 2 AC 111, PC; and *R v Togher and Ors* [2001] 3 All ER 463 CA

[123] Andrew L-T Choo and Susan Nash, *What's the Matter with Section 78?* [1999] Crim LR 929, p 933

of the Court of Appeal, as it is presently stated, only to quash a conviction if it is 'unsafe'.[124]

110 It may be, as the editors of the 2001 edition of Archbold suggest, that the effect of the Human Rights Act 1998 is to require courts' approach to section 78 to be more 'rights based'. Perhaps, as Professor I.H. Dennis[125] and others[126] have argued, the answer lies in the opening words of section 78. "In any proceedings", indicating that the court in its assessment of the fairness of admitting evidence is concerned with more than the trial and that:

> "[t]he fairness of the proceedings as a whole may be adversely affected if admission of the prosecution evidence in question means that the prosecution have an advantage which is inconsistent with the fundamental moral and political values of the criminal justice system."

111 Whatever the true position, the sooner the law in this field is clarified and simplified the better. In my view, consideration should be given, as part of the reform and codification exercise that I have recommended, to rationalising, possibly by combining, and certainly by simplifying, the various forms of jurisdiction for exclusion of evidence and that of staying a prosecution for abuse of process on account of improperly obtained evidence.

> **I recommend, as part of the over-all reform of the law of criminal evidence that I have recommended, consideration of rationalising and simplifying the various forms of statutory and common law rules for exclusion of evidence because of its unfairness and that of staying a prosecution for abuse of process on account of improperly obtained evidence.**

Previous misconduct of a defendant/ Similar fact evidence

112 The general rule in England and Wales is that evidence of a defendant's criminal record or any other evidence that he has a tendency to commit the offence charged or offences in general is inadmissible in evidence against him. The main reasons advanced for the rule are that such evidence is generally irrelevant and that, in any event, its prejudicial effect is likely to outweigh its probative effect. There are three exceptions to the general rule: first, where it would be admissible to prove he is guilty of the offence

---

[124] see further Chapter 12 paras 8 - 10

[125] *The Law Of Evidence*, pp. 81-82

[126] Andrew Choo and Susan Nas, *What's the Matter with Section 78?*, p 940

charged, in the main similar fact evidence,[127] but also including evidence under various statutes; second, where he has sought to establish that he is of good character or has attacked the character of a prosecution witness or a deceased victim; and third, where he has given evidence against a co-defendant in the proceedings.[128]

113   It has long been acknowledged that the law in this area is highly unsatisfactory in its complexity and uncertainty.[129]   The Criminal Law Revision Committee in 1972,[130] and the Runciman Royal Commission in 1973[131] recommended continuation of the scheme of general exclusion, but subject to slightly different exceptions, the latter also recommending that the Law Commission should consider it. In 1994 the Law Commission was asked to do so; it produced a consultation paper in 1996[132] and is shortly to produce its final report. In the meantime, the Government, in its recent policy paper, *The Way Ahead*,[133] mentioned as a possibility for 'simplification' of the law, the admission of evidence of previous convictions where relevant, providing that their prejudicial effect does not outweigh their probative value.   The Labour Party, in its election manifesto in May 2001 stated that it saw "a strong case for a new presumption" to that effect.

114   Before I continue, I should acknowledge my long held resistance, both at the Bar and as a judge, to putting a defendant's previous convictions before a jury as part of the proof of guilt even under the present statutory regime. It has always seemed to me that it is a poor prosecution case that needs to rely on a man's previous convictions in order to convict him. If the case is strong, why bother? If the case is weak, it is unfair. That is still my instinct, which my examination of the matter in this Review has not shaken. However, the reality of the present law is that it mostly does not conceal from the tribunal of fact that a defendant has some – though not precisely what – criminal record. In the resultant scope for speculation, it is thus capable of engendering as much or more prejudice against him. And it is not an honest system in that it does not do what it is claimed to do.

115   This is a complex issue, for which there are no straightforward answers. It has been widely accepted for some time that reform is needed, but much dispute as to the form it should take. As the Law Commission is about to

---

[127] which is capable of including evidence of complainants in previous cases resulting in acquittals; see *R v Z* [2000] 3 WLR 117, HL

[128] Criminal Evidence Act 1898, s 1

[129] for helpful and close analyses of the problems, see the trilogy of articles in [1997] Crim LR at 75 – 115: (1) Paul Roberts; *All the Usual Suspects: A Critical Appraisal of Law Commission Consultation Paper No 141,* (2) Jenny McEwan *Law Commission Dodges the Nettles in Consultation Paper No 141,* and (3) Penny Darbyshire *Previous Misconduct and Magistrates' Courts – Some Tales from the Real World*

[130] Eleventh Report: Evidence (General), Cmnd 4991, at para 78

[131] Report, Chapter 8, paras 29-34

[132] Law Comm No 141

[133] CM 5074, para 3.51

publish its final report on the matter, I do not think it appropriate for me to venture any firm recommendation. However, given the Government's indication of interest in introducing a general rule of admissibility of relevant evidence where its prejudicial effect does not outweigh its probative value, I should touch briefly on the two broad opposing approaches of general admissibility or non-admissibility, each qualified either by specified exceptions or a balancing of probative value and prejudicial effect.

116   The main advantage claimed for a general exclusionary rule, subject either to specified exceptions as at present or a balancing of probative value and prejudicial effect, is that it leans against admission of evidence unfairly prejudicial to a defendant. The main advantages of subjecting a general exclusionary rule only to a general exception based on balancing probative value over prejudicial effect are said to be simplicity and more focus on the relevance of the evidence. There is no doubt that the present system, with its mix of statutory and common law, is unduly complex, difficult to apply, particularly in the case of similar fact evidence. And it often fails to distinguish between relevant and irrelevant evidence and – some would say – leaves too much discretion to individual judges.[134] If it were to be replaced by a test of balancing proof against prejudice, the imprecision of the exercise applied on a case by case basis might in the early days substitute uncertainty for complexity, only to succumb again to complexity as it became overlain with case law. In either form of general exclusionary rule, there is the practical problem of keeping from the tribunal of fact that a defendant who does not put his character in evidence is likely to have a bad one.

117   A general inclusionary rule subject to one or other form of exception might or might not, depending on the extent and bases of the exceptions, expose the previous bad character of more defendants. But there would be the same practical difficulty of keeping it from the fact finders even when the court excludes it.

118   Professor John Spencer has long been of the view that there is an entirely different and better avenue for reform, a view that he has advanced as consultant to the Law Commission in the preparation of its consultation paper and as consultant to this Review. In brief, he considers that the present law, both in its form and application by the judges, is unreasonably favourable to defendants and is, in any event, ineffective as a protection to them where they are entitled to it. His proposals are: first, in order to remove the scope for possibly prejudicial speculation by a jury or lay magistrates when a defendant's character is not mentioned, his criminal record should be put in evidence quietly and in a matter of fact manner at the start of every trial; second, the prosecution should be allowed to treat it as supportive of the

---

[134] see in particular, the considerable body of case law on similar fact evidence

565

defendant's guilt where it goes beyond showing he has a general tendency to break the law and is relevant - that is, probative; and third, where there is no other substantial evidence of guilt, the court should normally be required to stop the case. The Law Commission, in its consultation paper, considered this with other options for reform and rejected it. Its arguments were that it would involve the admission of irrelevant and prejudicial material for no very clear purpose.[135] It provisionally favoured continuation of a system similar to the present exclusionary rule subject to exceptions.[136]

119   There is no doubt that the admission of all convictions as a matter of course at the beginning of the case, even if not relied upon as supportive of guilt, could result in the admission of irrelevant and unfairly prejudicial material. Dr Sally Lloyd-Bostock's research on the effect of bad character evidence on mock jurors ('the Oxford Study')[137] indicated that a jury would be more likely to convict if they know that the defendant either had a conviction for a similar offence or for indecent assault (irrespective of the offence charged).   As against that, Professor Spencer and others have advanced the following arguments:

- it is illogical for the law to allow a defendant to put in his good character to indicate lack of propensity but to deny the prosecution the opportunity to establish the converse when he has a bad one;

- jurors rapidly learn and magistrates and judges know that if there is no mention of a defendant's good character, he probably has a bad one, and so it permits the tribunal of fact to guess what it is not officially allowed to know;[138]

- magistrates, in any event, soon recognise the regular offenders in their court;

- in the case of the exception where a defendant's character goes in because he has wrongly sought to establish his own good character or attacked a prosecution witness, the requirement on the judge to tell a jury that it goes only to credibility, not to propensity, is confusing and unreal;[139]

- evidence showing that a defendant has committed offences of a similar type before statistically and logically suggests that he is more likely than those without such a record to commit such offences again, and should for that reason be regarded as relevant evidence - and some propensities can be more significant than others;[140]

---

[135] paras 9.15-9.23

[136] paras 9.72-9.73

[137] commissioned by the Home Office in 1995 and later partly replicated with a sample of magistrates; see Sally Lloyd-Bostock, *The Effects on Juries of Hearing about the Defendant's Previous Criminal Record: A Simulation Study*, [2000] Crim LR 734

[138] see also Penny Darbyshire, *Previous Misconduct and the Magistrates' Courts – Some Tales from the Real World* [1997] Crim LR 105, at 109-110

[139] see also Paul Roberts, *All the Usual Suspects: A Critical Appraisal of Law Commission Paper Consultation Paper No 141* [1997] Crim LR 75; and Jenny McEwan, *Law Commission Dodges the Nettles in Consultation Paper No 141* [1997] Crim LR 93, at 102-103

[140] see also Jenny McEwan, *Law Commission Dodges The Nettles In Consultation Paper 141*, at 95 - 98

- though studies have shown that juries would be influenced to some extent[141] by knowledge that the defendant has a criminal record, they do not show that juries would be *unduly* influenced by it;

- to remove the scope for possibly prejudicial speculation, fact-finders should be informed at the start of the trial whether the defendant has a criminal record and, if so, what it is;

- we should substitute weight for admissibility, confining the prosecutor to making active use of the criminal record or bad tendencies where they appear to be relevant to some disputed element in the case, and we should trust jurors and other fact finders to give it the weight it deserves; [142]

- adequate safeguards against juries and other fact finders giving unduly prejudicial weight to such evidence would be to prevent prosecutors inflating its importance and to prohibit a conviction when there is no other prosecution evidence of substance;[143] and

- such a system would be simpler and more honest.

120   Those are powerful pointers to the futility of a rule, whatever its form, for rendering inadmissible prejudicial matter inferential knowledge of which cannot and arguably need not be kept from fact finders. As I have said, magistrates will know,[144] and so will most jurors - if not the first time they sit on a jury, the second time - that silence about a defendant's character probably means he has a criminal record. They may not know what it is, but they can speculate about it. Professional judges, sitting as fact finders in the magistrates' courts or on appeal in the Crown Court usually cannot avoid knowing the full details if an issue arises before them as to character. Prominent among the reasons for retaining a lay element in the administration of criminal justice is a belief in their worldly judgment and common sense. Magistrates and jurors are seemingly trusted now, where as a result of the conduct of a defendant's case his previous bad character goes in, to distinguish between its relevance to his credibility but not to his propensity, a distinction which must be incomprehensible to most jurors and, possibly to many magistrates. Yet they are not to be trusted as a generality to assess such evidence for themselves. In my view, there is much to be said for a more radical view than has so far found favour with the Law Commission, for placing more trust in the fact finders and for introducing some reality into this complex corner of the law.[145] Whilst judgment should be reserved until publication of the Law Commission's final report, there is a strong case for

---

[141] Sally Lloyd-Bostock *The Effects on Juries of Hearing about the Defendant's Previous Criminal Record: A Simulation Study*, [2000] Crim LR 734

[142] see also Penny Darbyshire, *Previous Misconduct and the Magistrates' Courts – Some Tales from the Real World* [1997] Crim LR 105, at 115

[143] cf similar suggestions supported by some members of the Criminal Law Revision Committee, in its Eleventh Report, see para 90

[144] see Martin Wasik, *Magistrates: Knowledge of Previous Convictions* [1996] Crim LR, 851; and Penny Darbyshire, *Previous Misconduct and the Magistrates' Courts* at 109 -110

[145] see per Lord Griffiths in R H [1995] 2 WLR 737, HL, at 750

considering its recommendation in a wider review of the law of criminal evidence as a whole.

I recommend consideration of the Law Commission's imminent final report on evidence in criminal proceedings of a defendant's misconduct in the context of a wider review of the law of criminal evidence, having regard, in particular, to the illogicality, ineffectiveness and complexity of any rule, whatever its form, directed to keeping a defendant's previous convictions from lay, but not professional, fact finders.

Evidence of children

121 This is a vast and difficult subject on which a great deal of work has been, and is being, done within and without government agencies. Childline and the NSPCC, under the guidance of Professor Spencer, in a joint submission, provided me with an evaluation of the changes in the rules of evidence and procedure since the 1980s, with a view to considering possible reforms. More research is a necessary pre-condition of legislative and policy changes, more perhaps than in any other area of criminal law. The interrelation of law, psychology, child welfare and fair trial considerations make this very delicate terrain, and it has not been feasible for me to undertake detailed research in the course of this Review. But, in deference to the many submissions that I have received (and with acknowledgements to Professor Spencer), I shall mention, without making any recommendations, some of the possible areas for reform.

122 The major area of concern is in child abuse cases, but it is not confined to them. At the heart of the problem are the strongly conflicting interests of the need for sensitive and supportive treatment for children, both as alleged victims and witnesses, and of the requirement of the criminal justice process that the prosecution must prove the defendant's guilt to a high standard. It is clearly in child witnesses' interest that the proceedings should be got over as quickly and painlessly for them as possible. Defendants, on the other hand are entitled to the protection of a fully disclosed prosecution case to enable them properly to prepare their defence, and to the opportunity, to test in cross-examination, the child's evidence. There is also a frequently expressed concern that a child's evidence should not be 'tainted' in the meantime as a result of interviews with him or her as part of care proceedings and/or by way of therapy, such concerns often resulting in delays in resolving the child's future and the start of any necessary therapy. A solution that does full justice to those conflicting interests is likely to remain elusive, though, as I have

noted in Chapter 10, a recent initiative for joint plea and directions hearings has had promising results.[146]

123   A fundamental concern is whether trial by judge and jury – which is the normal forum for most child abuse matters – is suitable for cases in which children are required to give evidence. First, there is the, possibly damaging, ordeal for the child witness, only partly mitigated by his or her being able to give evidence by video-tape and video-link. Second, many feel a real unease in entrusting assessment of a child's evidence to a randomly selected body of twelve people, most of whom will have little experience of assessing evidence at all let alone children's accounts of such traumatic matters. It is certainly strange when one considers that Circuit Judges have to be specially trained and authorised to try rape and other serious sexual offences or to exercise care jurisdiction in family work, and that magistrates must reach a certain level of experience and training once elected to a youth court panel. Alternatives suggested by contributors to the Review are for trial in such cases by judge alone or by judge and two magistrates drawn from the youth court panel. However, given the heavy penalties that convictions for child abuse often attract, many would consider it wrong to deprive defendants of the opportunity to defend themselves in front of a jury. Yet, as I have indicated in Chapter 5,[147] it is in just such cases that defendants often waive jury trial, in jurisdictions providing for it, because of their concern at the possible emotional response or outrage of juries to the horrific nature of the allegations. My recommendation that defendants should have an opportunity, subject to the consent of the court, to opt for trial by judge alone, should go some way to meeting the concern of many, including defendants, that juries are not the appropriate fact finders in such cases. It would not, however, be an answer in cases in which defendants did not exercise the option. If jury trial is to continue, it may be that some thought should be given by psychologists and lawyers alike as to what, if any, special guidance might, in fairness to both sides, be provided to juries in such cases. It could possibly take the form of a court appointed expert and/or of a special direction from the judge.

124   As to the timing and means by which children give evidence, a start was made in 1989 with the much applauded report of the Pigot Committee,[148] the main thrust of which was to start and complete a child complainant's evidence in sex cases on video-tape well before the trial so as to remove from him or her the strain of the proceedings at the earliest possible stage and to enable the start of any necessary therapy. The Committee specifically recommended that cross-examination should take place as soon as possible after the initial video

---

[146] para 216

[147] para 112

[148] The Home Office Advisory Group on Video Evidence, chaired by His Honour Judge Pigot, then the Common Serjeant of London (Home Office, 1989); see also the Report of the Scottish Law Commission: *The Evidence of Children and other Potentially Vulnerable Witnesses* (SLC No125)

interview and any subsequent police interview of the defendant. The Committee's recommendations were only partly adopted, and then only in piecemeal form.

125   The Criminal Justice Act 1991[149] introduced a scheme under which the evidence in chief of children could take the form of a video-taped interview before the trial, but the child still had to attend trial for cross-examination, either through a video-link system or in court if thought suitable. Now, under the 'special measures' provisions of the Youth Justice and Criminal Evidence Act 1999,[150] provision is to be made effectively requiring the evidence of persons under 17 to be given by video-tape and live video-link and, where the prosecution is for a sexual offence, for the evidence to be given entirely on video-tape, thus replacing 'live' cross-examination at trial with a pre-recorded cross-examination unless the witness wishes to give live evidence.[151] However, these new provisions still fall short of the Pigot Committee's recommendations in that they will not ensure that video-recording of the cross-examination of the child takes place shortly after the initial video-taped interview (save possibly without exceptionally vigorous pre-trial control of the case by the judge). The reality is that most video-taped cross-examinations will take place shortly before the trial, namely not much earlier than now. That is because cross-examination cannot take place until after disclosure, including any third party/local authority disclosure and the defence advocate has been fully instructed. Even then, the cross-examination is likely to be at a court centre unless and until alternative facilities are provided.

126   I leave these statutory provisions with three further comments. First, they and the other special measures provisions in Part II of the 1999 Act are extraordinarily complicated and prescriptive. I can only assume that those drafting them have no idea of what judges and criminal practitioners have to cope with in their daily work of preparing for and conducting a criminal trial or of what they need as practical working tools for the job. Simple and more flexible rules of court are what are needed – another task I suggest, for a Criminal Procedure Rules Committee. Second, the Court Service will need to do better than it has done so far to provide enough courtrooms equipped for showing video evidence, so as to avoid delays in the speedy trial of child abuse cases. Third, there is a striking difference between the care for children as witnesses in these provisions and the lack of any corresponding provision for them when they are accused of grave crime in the Crown Court, a disparity that concerns many judges. The proposals that I make for young defendants to be tried in a youth court appropriately constituted for different categories of case should ensure that the formalities of Crown Court trial are no

---

[149] s 54, which added section 32A to the Criminal Justice Act 1988

[150] Chapter 1, Pt II, but not as yet implemented nor given a date for implementation

[151] s 21

longer a problem, but that will not resolve the lack of provision of 'remote' and video evidence facilities for them.

127   Moving to the content of children's evidence, I have said that there is a general illogicality and impracticality in our law of confining a witness's evidence in chief to what they say in the witness box and leaving it to the defence, if they wish, to draw attention to previous statements in the course of cross-examination. This is a particular defect in the case of the evidence of young children where it could be vital in the interest of justice to know the circumstances of and terms in which the complaint was first made and how it was dealt with up until the time of the video-recording of his evidence in chief. If my recommendation under paragraphs 86 – 92 above, that prior witness statements should be admissible as evidence of fact, is accepted, it would remove some of the difficulties for fact finders in assessing the truthfulness and reliability of young children's evidence. Another possibility would be the use of court appointed experts, as is done in family and care cases where similar issues arise, but this is not a matter on which I am equipped to make any positive recommendation.

128   There are other problems. One, to which I have referred in Chapter 10, is third party/local authority disclosure, which is a particular difficulty in child abuse cases.[152] Another – seemingly insoluble – is minimising the trauma to the child witness of cross-examination whilst ensuring that the defendant's advocate can thoroughly test his evidence. Of course, the defence advocate can do this quietly and circumspectly, and if he doesn't the judge can intervene to restore fairness. But often advocates overdo it, making what may amount to a 'third speech', and the judge may not intervene soon enough in an excess of caution about the defendant's right to a fair trial. The result can be both damaging to the child and cause him, out of confusion or a desire to please, to distort his evidence or to break down so that he is unable to complete it. One possibility would be for a testing of the evidence of very young children by some neutral person, say the judge, or a court appointed expert or a special counsel. However, as I have said, all such suggestions should await the outcome of more wide-ranging and detailed research on the best way to balance the rights of the child and of the defendant.

Expert evidence

129   As with Lord Woolf's work on Civil Justice, the subject of expert evidence has featured strongly in the Review. The main topics covered were: the

---

[152] paras 185 - 190

competence and objectivity of those who put themselves forward as expert witnesses; the suitability of calling expert evidence; simplification of the manner of presentation of their evidence; inequality of arms between prosecution and defence experts; delays in obtaining expert evidence; the effect of listing practices on busy forensic practitioners; and poor pay for publicly funded defence experts. Although many of these issues concern preparation for trial as well as the trial itself, it seems to me more convenient to deal with than all together here.

Competence

130   The competence of an expert witness is governed by the common law. Whether, in any particular case, a witness is qualified to give expert evidence is for the judge. However, there is no single or comprehensive guide to the courts in the form of a professional register of accreditation to which they or parties may have recourse when considering the suitability of proposed expert witnesses. Although the Runciman Royal Commission did not recommend any fundamental changes on the subject of expert evidence, it gave detailed consideration to this question. It recommended the establishment of a Forensic Science Advisory Council to oversee matters including accreditation, performance evaluation and professional development, with a view to the possible introduction of an enforceable code of conduct for all forensic scientists.[153] Although the Government did not implement that recommendation, it supported the principle of development of standards, training and accreditation by a non-statutory body or bodies. The Forensic Science Society and the Academy of Experts[154] were already in the being, each with its draft code of practice. Since then the field has become more crowded. In 1995, the Society of Expert Witnesses and in 1996 the Expert Witness Institute were founded, each producing its own Code of Practice and maintaining a membership list. And most recently, in early 2000, the Council for the Registration of Forensic Practitioners, a company limited by guarantee was established with financial support from the Government. The Law Society maintains an annual Directory of Expert Witnesses and there are also other associations of experts from particular disciplines.

131   It seems to me that it would be sensible, make better use of resources and be of more value to users and the Courts, if the work of all these bodies could be concentrated in one. It could then set, or oversee the setting of, standards, maintain a register of accredited forensic scientists in all disciplines and regulate their compliance with those standards. I do not suggest that it should be a statutory or governmental body, for I believe that professional self-regulation, albeit with governmental encouragement and financial help to the

---

[153] Chapter 9, paras 33 - 36
[154] then the British Academy of Experts

extent that it may be necessary in the early days, is the better way forward. The Council for the Registration of Forensic Practitioners, although only recently established looks a strong candidate for such a role. It is an independent body of forensic practitioners, their managers and bodies and people who use their services, including the police, lawyers and judges. Its Register, which it opened in the Spring of this year will include forensic practitioners of all kinds. Entry to the Register, which is voluntary, is by peer review of current competence against agreed criteria, with revalidation every four years to ensure that practitioners maintain their skills and keep up to date. The Council has underpinned the Register with a Code of Conduct which includes the principle that a forensic practitioner's overriding duty is to the court and the administration of justice and that his findings and evidence must be presented fairly and impartially. There will be procedures to deal with complaints of professional misconduct, poor performance or ill health, with the ultimate disciplinary sanction of removal from the Register. It is hoped that the courts will regard entry on the Register as an indicator of competence, though of course they will retain the power to determine whether a witness is qualified to give expert evidence on a case by case basis. The Crown Prosecution Service and other prosecuting bodies, legal practitioners and the courts should, in their various ways, encourage and support the Council in its work.

I recommend that:

- **consideration should be given to concentrating in one self-governing professional body within England and Wales the role of setting, or overseeing the setting, of standards and of conduct for forensic scientists of all disciplines, the maintenance of a register of accreditation for them and the regulation of their compliance with its conditions of accreditation; and**

- **for those purposes, the several existing expert witness bodies providing for all or most forensic science disciplines should consider amalgamation with, or concentration of their resources in, the Council for the Registration of Forensic Practitioners.**

Objectivity

132   All the inter-disciplinary bodies to which I have referred and, I am sure, all others accept the principle that the overriding duty of their members is to provide the court with objective evidence. The same applies to government agencies, such as the Forensic Science Service and to every forensic scientist individually contributing to the Review. Indeed, they positively welcome it as

a protection against being drawn into the adversarial mode of some of those instructing them. In my view, this consensus should be given the same formal recognition in new Criminal Procedure Rules as it has been given in the civil jurisdiction by Civil Procedure Rules, Part 35.3, which reads:

> "(1) It is the duty of an expert to help the court on the matters within his expertise.
>
> (2) This duty overrides any obligation to the person from whom he has received instructions or by whom he is paid".

It would also be a useful reminder to all expert witnesses about to give evidence – and to their clients – to require them to include a declaration to like effect at the start of their witness statements or reports.

I recommend that:

- **the new Criminal Procedure Rules that I recommend should contain a rule in the same or similar terms to that in Part 35.3 of the Civil Procedure Rules that an expert witness's overriding duty is to the court; and**

- **any witness statement or report prepared by an expert witness for the assistance of the court should contain at its head a signed declaration to that effect.**

Suitability of expert evidence

133   An expert witness is different from other witnesses in a number of respects, an important one of which is that he is permitted to express an opinion on the issue to which his evidence relates. But, at common law, it is for the judge to decide in each case whether the issue is one which is suitable for opinion evidence. Often the issue clearly does justify the calling of an expert. However, there is an increasing tendency, particularly in the criminal courts, for parties to seek to call opinion evidence masquerading as expert evidence on or very close to the factual decision that it is for the court to make. It is for the judges or magistrates to determine whether an issue truly is susceptible to and justifies the calling of expert evidence, in particular whether a proffered expert is likely to be any more expert than anyone else in forming an opinion on separately established facts. In the Crown Court the judge normally directs or indicates at the pre-trial stage whether any particular issue justifies the calling of expert evidence and, if so, of what nature.

134   There is a side effect to this when the defence seek to call an expert and need legal aid to pay for it. If the judge directs or indicates that it is a suitable case for a defence expert, it is still for the Legal Services Commission to decide whether to fund it. That body can and sometimes does effectively second

guess the judge's direction by declining to authorise the instruction of an expert. Even when it agrees with the judge, the need to obtain, and the slowness in grant, of its authorisation is a frequent cause of substantial delay in the preparation of cases for trial. One has only to consider how much has to be done following the grant of authorisation to see why this is so. The expert has then to be instructed, he must be provided with all relevant papers and prosecution forensic science reports, and possibly be given access to original prosecution exhibits. Then he has to prepare his report and, often confer with those instructing him.

135 Whenever there is a possible need for the instruction of expert witnesses on either side, the decision is for the court. It should be taken at the earliest possible stage and, in my strong view, in publicly funded cases, it should not be subject to further authorisation by the Legal Services Commission. Once a judge has directed that expert evidence is appropriate in a particular case, I cannot see upon what basis that body is competent to take a different view.

136 In my view, criminal courts' power to control the admission of experts' evidence should be formalised in the new Criminal Procedure Rules that I have recommended and put on a similar footing to that for the civil courts as set out in the Civil Procedure Rules, Part 35, 1 and 4, namely by imposing upon them a duty, and declaring their power, to restrict expert evidence to that which is reasonably required to resolve any issue of importance in the proceedings.

I recommend that:

- **criminal courts' power to control the admission of experts' evidence should be formalised in the new Criminal Procedure Rules that I have recommended, and put on a similar footing to that for the Civil Courts as set out in the Civil Procedure Rules, Part 35. 1 and 4, namely by imposing upon them a duty, and declaring their power, to restrict expert evidence to that which is reasonably required to resolve any issue of importance in the proceedings;**

- **judges and magistrates should rigorously apply the test governing that power and duty, and the Court of Appeal should support them; and**

- **in publicly funded defence cases, where a judge or magistrates' court has directed that it would be justifiable to call a defence expert, that direction should constitute authorisation for the expenditure of public money on an expert at a specified rate.**

137   At the heart of this question is the seeming absurdity in our present system of entrusting to a tribunal, whether judge, magistrates or jury, unversed in a particular discipline the task of determining which of two conflicting experts is right. However, to hand over the decision to a single expert or body of experts would remove that part, possibly the crucial part, of the decision-making from the court. Lord Justice May ruminated on this central dilemma in an address to last year's Annual Conference of the Expert Witness Institute,[155] when citing the following passage from a seminal article of Judge Learned Hand in 1901:

> "The trouble with all this is that it is setting the jury to decide, where doctors disagree. The whole object of the expert is to tell the jury, not facts, as we have seen, but general truths derived from his specialised experience. But how can the jury judge between two statements each founded upon an experience confessedly foreign in kind to their own? It is just because they are incompetent for such a task that the expert is necessary at all.... If you would get at the truth in such cases, it must be through someone competent to decide".

That conviction of Judge Learned Hand led him to stop short, but only just, of removing the decision from the court. He turned instead to a removal of adversarial expert evidence, replacing it with a board of experts or a single expert on the assumption that, in all but exceptional cases, the court would adopt its or his advice in reaching its conclusion.

138   The same dilemma, most acutely present in an adversarial and jury system, and at its sharpest in criminal trials, has remained the subject of debate ever since, and is still unresolved. It has given rise to a large number of submissions in the Review, as it did in Lord Woolf's Review of Civil Justice. Short of providing specialist courts of one sort or another for every discipline in which expert evidence may be required, the search is to find some compromise by which the court more closely controls the way in which expert evidence is put before it. It could be done by the court appointing or selecting a single expert or body of experts to advise it, or by more closely controlling the parties in the manner in which they deploy their own expert evidence.

139   A number of contributors to the Review have suggested that criminal courts should have power to appoint a court expert to give evidence to the exclusion of expert evidence on each side. Lord Woolf made such a recommendation in his interim report,[156] but it did not find general support and he did not pursue it

---

[155] EWI Conference: *The Expert Witness –Present issues and future challenges*, 12th October 2000

[156] Chapter 23, paras 20 - 23

in his final report. Others have suggested that criminal courts should have similar power to that in fact introduced in the Civil Procedure Rules, that the court should have power to direct that evidence is to be given by a single joint expert, leaving it only with a residual power of selection of the expert where the parties cannot agree who it should be.[157] Where a civil court exercises that power, the practice is for the preparation of the joint expert's report to be treated as the first step and, if one or other party is dissatisfied with it, then, subject to the court's discretion, he should be allowed to call his own expert evidence.[158] The rule is, I believe, increasingly used. A recent survey of 500 experts[159] has indicated that a single joint expert is being appointed in about 40% of cases. In the civil jurisdiction there may not be any Article 6 difficulties in a system of court appointed or directed and selected experts, save that our adversarial process would probably entitle both sides to be actively involved in the process by which he prepares his report, for example, in submitting to interviews and having access to documents on which the report is based.[160]

140   Interestingly, the Runciman Royal Commission, despite its drive to introduce a more inquisitorial flavour to the pre-trial stage, showed little interest in court appointed experts in criminal proceedings, either to the exclusion of parties' experts or in addition to them.[161] The overwhelming majority of the many contributors to this Review were against it. Where the court has directed that expert evidence is appropriate, I too cannot see any scope for introduction to criminal trials of a system of court appointed experts to the exclusion, even in the court's discretion, of the right of each party to call its own expert evidence. Even without Article 6, it seems to me that there are fundamental difficulties in denying a criminal defendant that entitlement, particularly where the issue is highly controversial and central to the case and - I would add with Lord Bingham[162] - whatever the weight of the case. He would have to instruct an expert to obtain advice as to whether to accept the court expert's view and, if not, he would probably need his assistance for the purpose of cross-examination of the court expert. Yet he would be unable, unless permitted by the judge, to call him to justify the points put in cross-examination or to give his contrary view on which they were based. To leave it to the judge's discretion, as under the Civil Procedure Rules, would, I believe, result in most judges allowing the defendant, or the prosecution for that matter, to call their own expert witness – effectively making the provision a dead letter. Otherwise, the court appointed or selected expert would

---

[157] CPR Part 35.7

[158] *Daniels v Walker* [2000] 1 WLR 1382; CA; *Cosgrove v Pattison*, the Times, 13 February 2001, Neuberger J

[159] conducted by Bond Solon Training

[160] *Mantovanelli v France* (1997) 24 EHRR 370, ECHR

[161] Chapter 9, paras 67 and 74

[162] *Forensic Experts: The Past Present and Future*, an address to the Expert Witness Institute's first Annual Conference on 29th September 1999

effectively decide the issue and, depending on its importance, possibly the case.[163]

141 Nor do I believe that it would be helpful for the court to appoint its own expert in addition to any expert witnesses called by the parties, since, in jury cases, the very nature of his appointment might suggest to a jury a greater authority than one or other or both of the parties' experts. Accordingly, where there is an issue on a matter of importance on which expert evidence is required, I can see no justification for empowering the court to appoint or select an expert, whether or not it excludes either party from calling its own expert evidence. Of course, where there is no issue or one in which the parties are content that the matter should be resolved by a single expert, they should be encouraged to deal with it in that way, agreeing his report or a summary of it as part of the evidence in the case.

I recommend that:

• **where there is an issue on a matter of importance on which expert evidence is required, the court should not have a power to appoint or select an expert, whether or not it excludes either party from calling its own expert evidence; and**

• **where there is no issue, there is or one in which the parties are content that the matter should be resolved by a single expert, they should be encouraged to deal with it in that way, agreeing his report or a summary of it as part of the evidence in the case.**

142 Two other, less controversial, aspects of simplifying the presentation of expert evidence to courts are advance mutual disclosure of experts' reports and pre-trial meetings between them to identify and narrow what is in issue.

143 As to mutual disclosure, there is already detailed provision for it in rules made under section 81 of the Police Criminal Evidence Act 1984,[164]corresponding broadly to Part 35,10 and 13 of the Civil Procedure Rules. However, slowness in prosecution disclosure of expert evidence is a major cause of delay in many criminal trials. Until it is provided, the defence expert cannot get on with or complete his work, the preparation of the defence statement may have to be wait and, in turn, secondary prosecution disclosure. The

---

[163] In addition, such a system might violate Article 6(3)(d) ECHR which guarantees the right of the accused, not only to cross-examine witnesses, but to call and examine his own under the same conditions as the prosecution witnesses; see *Bonisch v Austria* (1985) 9 EHRR 191, Ecomm, HR However, the counter argument is that there is parity between them if, as would be the case under this approach, the prosecution is also excluded from calling expert evidence

[164] Crown Court (Advance Notice of Expert Evidence) Rules 1987; and Magistrates' Courts (Advance Notice of Expert Evidence) Rules 1987

delays are in large part due to poor co-ordination between the police, the Crown Prosecution Service and the Forensic Science Service, the Government agency responsible for providing prosecution expert witnesses. A second factor is the tendency of the police not to refer matters to the Forensic Science Service for examination unless and until they are sure the case is to be contested, a saving in money for the police but a negation of the advance disclosure system the object of which is to inform the defendant at the earliest of the nature and strength of the case he has to meet. A third factor is the time taken by the Forensic Science Service itself to prepare its reports. In fairness to the Service, the tight time constraints imposed by the present pre-trial programme and the increasing demands on its services do not help. But the result of all these factors is often serious delay to the mutual disclosure regime, unreadiness of both parties for the plea and directions hearing, necessitating a second hearing and a generally disorderly preparation for trial.

144   Under the present regime, it is not easy to find a sure solution. A start is the theme that permeates this Report, the need for closer co-ordination and less sectionalism among the various agencies responsible for the process of a case through the courts, in this case the police the Crown Prosecution Service and the Forensic Science Service. To be fair to them they have attempted, within the constraints of their individual budgets, to do something about it by entering into a tripartite agreement in June 1999 for better co-ordination of their working practices in this respect. Another step is to speed the flow of communication by greater use of electronic transfer of documents and for providing ready access to defence experts of original exhibits where required. Greater co-operation and joint efficiency at some individual cost at this stage of the proceedings could produce significant savings for all in the quicker resolution of issues and smoother progress to trial.

145   As to pre-trial meetings between experts, this occasionally takes place on an informal basis with the agreement of both parties, but I believe it to be the exception rather than the rule. If the views expressed in the Review are representative, the reluctance to arrange such meetings comes mainly from the defence, not the prosecution or the expert witnesses themselves, both of whom urge it. Subject to proper safeguards of confidentiality as to undisclosable information on both sides, I strongly encourage it. It is obviously of great assistance to the court in the simplification of the expert evidence over-all. And it can give no improper advantage to either party if they can discuss and identify in advance the extent of the likely issue between them when the matter goes to court. It is of particular importance where one side is proposing to use information technology for the presentation of some of its evidence, since there will need to be discussion of the system to be used, as well as of content of the evidence.

146   Two further questions are whether the court should be given a power to direct such discussion, which could be in person or over the telephone or by video-

conferencing, similar to that which civil courts have under paragraph 35.12 of the Civil Procedure Rules, and who, if anyone, should be present at or party to it in addition to the experts. As to the former, I consider that the court should have power to direct such discussions and, normally, to exercise it. It could be subject to the sort of conditions set out in CPR Part 35, 12, that the content of the discussions would not be divulged at the trial or the parties be bound by any agreement reached unless they, the parties, agree. As to who, if anyone, should be at such discussions in addition to the experts, I do not think it necessary or wise to be too prescriptive; much may depend on the nature and circumstances of the over-all issue or issues and the relationship to them of the proposed expert evidence. I note that this has been the subject of much debate in the civil jurisdiction but, as yet, there is no all-purpose solution.[165] It may be that this could be left for the specific direction of the judge in each case after hearing representations from both sides, as the Runciman Royal Commission appears to have considered when making a similar recommendation.[166]

I recommend that:

- **the prosecution and defence should normally arrange for their experts to discuss and jointly to identify at the earliest possible stage before the trial those issues on which they agree and those on which they do not agree, and to prepare a joint statement for use in evidence indicating the measure of their agreement and a summary of the reasons for their disagreement; and**

- **failing such arrangement, the court should have power to direct such a discussion and identification of issues and preparation of a joint statement for use in evidence and to make any consequential directions as may be appropriate in each case.**

147   I have suggested a wide ranging reconsideration of the rule against hearsay in criminal matters. It is of particular relevance to scientific evidence with its increasing reliance on the build-up of conclusions from electronic records and reports by others of their work. Most advocates co-operate sensibly on matters of continuity of treatment of exhibits and as to various stages of testing and/or analysis that have gone into producing a final report. There is provision of a conditional nature for the admission of such hearsay material in the Advance Notice of Evidence Rules[167] and of the final reports themselves under section 30(1) Criminal Justice Act 1988; and the Runciman Royal Commission and the Law Commission have proposed some extension of it.[168]

---

[165] see the White Book, (2001)Vol 1, para 35.12.1

[166] *Runciman Royal Commission Report,* Ch 9, para 63

[167] see footnote 164 above

[168] *Runciman Royal Commission Report,* Chapter 9, para 78; Law Comm No 245, paras, 1.42- 1.43

Nevertheless, points, good and bad, can be taken on such minutiae, and unrepresented defendants have been known to spin out trials for weeks unjustifiably putting the prosecution to proof of everything in sight. The wide-ranging and fast-moving developments in information technology will have a particular impact in the field of expert evidence, its preparation and the way it is given. Just one of the matters for attention will be the admissibility, where the point is taken, of electronically transmitted certificates or other documents bearing a scanned copy of a signature. I am sure that there will be many others.

148   Other facilities of modern technology that are already well established are video-conferencing and the giving of evidence by video-link or, increasingly, via the internet. As they become more widely available, these new techniques should be used wherever possible for instructing and conferring with experts. And the law should be developed and facilities provided nationally to enable experts in appropriate cases to give evidence via one or other of these technologies at locations remote from the court and more convenient to them, for example, where their evidence is self-contained and does not turn on possible developments in other evidence in the course of the trial. Expert witnesses are particularly exposed to the vagaries of our listing system, which result in them committing themselves to court fixtures that are cancelled or delayed at the last moment, or which require them to spend much wasted time waiting around at court to give evidence. Anything that can be done, by more efficient preparation of cases for trial, greater use of fixed listing dates and by shorter or alternative ways of giving evidence will make for better use of busy professionals' time and a more respectable trial process.

> I recommend:
>
> • close attention in any further and general review of the rule against hearsay to the increasing reliance of forensic science laboratories and of many experts in certain disciplines on electronic recording, analysis and transmission of data;
>
> • greater use by legal practitioners of video-conferencing and other developing new technology for communicating and conferring with experts in preparation for trial; and
>
> • development of the law and the provision of national facilities to enable experts to give evidence by video-link or other new technologies in appropriate cases.

149   I leave the subject of experts by commenting, without recommendation, on a few miscellaneous matters that have prompted many submissions. The first is the practice of some defence solicitors of 'shopping around' for an expert who

will support the defence case and not disclosing the reports of those who have reported unfavourably to it. The problem arises mainly in the cases of privately funded defences, not in the vast bulk of cases where the defence is publicly funded and there are tight financial constraints on such expenditure. There have been suggestions that the defence should be required to disclose all 'unused' expert reports of this sort. So long as our system remains adversarial, I can see no proper basis upon which the defence should be required to disclose material of this or any sort that is unfavourable to their case. There is undoubtedly a lack of parity between the prosecution and the defence in this respect, but that is a necessary consequence of where the burden of proof lies.

150   The second matter that has been the subject of considerable complaint by defence solicitors and experts is the low level of publicly funded experts' fees. I have had a look at the current scales, and, without going into detail on the figures, they are meagre for professional men in any discipline. I am not surprised that solicitors complain that they have often had difficulty in finding experts of good calibre who are prepared to accept instructions for such poor return. The best expert witness in most cases is likely to be one who practises, as well as giving expert evidence, in his discipline, rather than the 'professional' expert witness – one who does little else. Justice is best served by attracting persons of a high level of competence and experience to this work. If we expect them to acknowledge an overriding duty to the court and to develop and maintain high standards of accreditation, they should be properly paid for the job. I hope that the Legal Services Commission will take an early opportunity to review and raise appropriately the levels of their publicly funded remuneration.

151   Finally, I state the obvious in urging the judiciary, magistracy and criminal practitioners to maintain and, where possible, improve their familiarity with the more common aspects of forensic science that engage the courts. If we expect experts to raise their act in the manner of presentation of their evidence, the least we can do is complement and assist their task by ensuring a basic level of understanding of what they are talking about. I am conscious that much is already being done in this field, most recently, for example, in presentations by the Forensic Science Society on DNA evidence to the Judicial Studies Board and publication of a guide on the subject.

THE COURT AT WORK

Respecting Diversity

152   An important feature of a modern court should be its ability to respond flexibly to the differing needs and concerns of the wide variety of people who participate in its proceedings. Much work has been done in recent years to raise awareness of diversity issues (race, gender and disability issues in particular) amongst judges, magistrates and court staff. In August 1999, building on earlier guidance about equal treatment of ethnic minorities, the Judicial Studies Board published an Equal Treatment Bench Book providing detailed guidance to judges in all courts and tribunals on a variety of topics that might lead litigants, victims, witnesses or legal representatives to feel disadvantaged in dealing with our legal system. At the same time, the Board published *Race and the Courts*, a companion leaflet to the Bench Book designed to be used by judges as a practical working guide. The Board has also produced a training pack containing guidance, information and exercises for equal treatment training events for magistrates.[169] The third competence of the Magistrates New Training Initiative framework covers magistrates' commitment to a non-discriminatory approach implicit in the judicial oath, impartiality of their decision-making and their ability to ensure fair and equal treatment. Once the Training Initiative is fully implemented, all magistrates will be appraised regularly against these criteria and, where appropriate, will undertake relevant training and development activities.

153   In 2000 the Magistrates' Courts Service Joint Liaison Group (whose membership is drawn from the main representative organisations) set up a Race Issues Group to consider the implications for the service of Sir William Macpherson's report of the Stephen Lawrence Inquiry.[170] The Group produced *Justice in Action*, a report that drew on examples of good practice from a number of magistrates' courts committee areas and proposed further action.

154   Notwithstanding these and other initiatives, there is more to be done. In its submission in the Review, the Bar Council's Disability Committee gave a number of practical examples where people with disabilities had been offended or had felt themselves to be disadvantaged by ignorance or prejudice displayed by judges or other court personnel. Other minority groups could, no doubt, provide similar examples. A new unified Criminal Court would

---

[169] Equal Treatment Training for Lay Magistrates Handbook, (JSB and NACRO), March 1998.

[170] February 1999, CM 4262-1

bring with it greater scope to drive forward national initiatives, develop common standards of good practice and monitor performance. At the same time, the emphasis I have placed on devolved decision-making at a local level, would allow court managers to work with their local communities to ensure that the service is responsive to their particular needs.

Interpreters

155   The Runciman Royal Commission commented on the difficulties of obtaining good quality interpreters at police stations and at court. They made a number of recommendations, in particular, for their better training and remuneration.[171]

156   There have been considerable improvements since then. From 1998 the courts have been responsible for securing the attendance of suitable interpreters for defendants.[172] The parties remain responsible for providing interpreters for their own witnesses. In 1993 a National Register of Public Service Interpreters was established, which provided for a system of accreditation, guaranteeing that all its members were properly trained, conformed to professional standards and were subject to monitoring and disciplinary procedures.[173] Similarly, *The Council for the Advancement of Communication with Deaf People Directory* provides a list of accredited interpreters which conform to the same quality standards. Those two National Registers are the main sources for selection of interpreters required for all the criminal justice system agencies It is intended by the Trial Issues Group that by the beginning of 2002 all agencies will be able to rely exclusively on them when selecting interpreters for criminal investigations and court proceedings. However, there are continuing difficulties in the distribution and variable standards of interpreters, resulting in a somewhat patchy provision of services country-wide. In some areas where there are few non-English speakers, there would normally be a correspondingly low demand for interpreters at local police stations and courts. But there will always be occasions when there is a demand that cannot readily be met, one that may be aggravated by surges of asylum-seekers from different countries and the high levels of competence now required of interpreters.

157   The establishment of the National Registers is a welcome improvement, but more needs to be done, particularly as the Human Rights Act 1998 may require a greater guarantee of the competence of interpreters than before. A

---

[171] Chapter 3, paras 41- 45 and Chapter 8, paras 48 - 51

[172] as agreed with TIG. It is not covered by the Crown Court or Magistrates, Courts Rules or Practice Direction, and is not the subject of any primary legislation

[173] as a result of the work of the Interpreters Working Group, a Trial Issues Group sub-group

recent attempt by a sub-group of the Trial Issues Group[174] to produce a national needs analysis on which to base further planning and work was thwarted by poor response from many local Trial Issues Groups.[175] The national Group, working on the responses available, found that shortages of interpreters in various languages had necessitated significant recourse to non-accredited interpreters, for example, to meet the recent increase in the number of immigrants from the Balkan States. As I understand it, the Trial Issues Group has attempted, with the National Register and the Institute of Linguists, to meet this problem, but its efforts have not been matched by government funding for wider and better local training where needed.

158   There are a number of other bodies or associations, with overlapping memberships or registration involved in accreditation and maintaining public registers of interpreters' services. These include: the Institute of Translation and Interpreting, the Association of Police and Court Interpreters, the Institute of Linguists and the Association of Sign Language Interpreters. This seems to me a wasteful spread and duplication of resources for the various bodies and their members, and an inefficient way of providing a comprehensive national and local service to the courts. In my view, it would be sensible, make much better use of resources and provide a better service to those involved in or exposed to criminal investigation and the courts, if the work of all these bodies were concentrated, as appropriate in one or other of the two national Registers, preferably by some form of amalgamation. At the very least, they should all meet the same standards of accreditation as the two National Registers.

159   There are signs in some of the local Trial Issues Group analyses that a number of nationally registered language interpreters and sign language interpreters do not wish to work in the courts because of the nature of the work, poor pay and the criticism of their work. Some of them also have a sense of isolation on attendance at court. They are, for the occasion, officers of the court yet have no accommodation or facilities there and are obliged to mingle in the public area, possibly in the vicinity of parties on one side or another. In my view, it would be a proper recognition of their official status and independence from the parties if they could have access and be welcomed to, say, a staff common room while waiting to interpret in court or during adjournments.

I recommend that:

- **the Government should continue to encourage the concentration in the two national Registers as**

---

[174] the Interpreters Working Group

[175] a notable exception was the West Midlands Trials Group who produced a useful analysis of needs and a number of good practical suggestions for improvement

appropriate of the role of oversight of national training, accreditation and monitoring of performance of interpreters, with a view to providing an adequate national and local coverage of suitably qualified interpreters;

- training and accreditation of all interpreters should include coverage of the basics of criminal investigation and court procedures, and should provide for changing and different geographic demands for linguists;

- the Government should consider central funding of further education establishments to equip them, where necessary, to provide courses in lesser known languages for the Diploma in Public Service Interpreting;

- the Government should undertake a national publicity campaign in further education establishments and other colleges in support of the two national Registers;

- there should be a review of the levels of payment to interpreters with a view to encouraging more and the best qualified to undertake this work and to establishing a national scale of pay; and

- interpreters should be provided with facilities appropriate to an officer of the court when attending court to provide their services.

160   The parties should inform the court at the earliest possible moment whether any of their witnesses will require an interpreter. The Trial Issues Group, in 1998, issued guidance to police forces for the early booking of interpreters. This guidance was largely ignored in many police areas with the result that courts had to make hurried arrangements on the day of the hearing. The latest (agreed, but as yet unpublished) version of the Group's national guidelines will require the police to book interpreters for the first hearing where it takes place only a few days after charge. Otherwise the police are reminded to inform the court early of the need for an interpreter and the details of the language.

161   In cases involving much documentation, or of a technical or otherwise complex nature, it would enable interpreters to perform their task more efficiently if they had access beforehand to papers relevant to the evidence for which their services are required. This should normally be capable of resolution between the parties without reference to the court. But, if there is a problem, the judge should be asked to give a direction in writing or at a pre-trial hearing if it is necessary. In doing so, he should have regard to any need for confidentiality and security of documents and to the arrangements for the

interpreter to familiarise himself with them. In addition, I consider, that an interpreter should be entitled where necessary to apply direct to the court for such access.

I recommend that:

- **the standard check-list for agreement or directions leading to the pre-trial assessment should require all parties to indicate to the court in good time before the trial date the need for an interpreter, identifying the party or witness for whom he is required and the language;**

- **the check list should also require the parties to agree or, failing agreement, to seek the court's directions for making available to the interpreter in good time before trial, any documents likely to assist him in his task at court;**

- **an engaged interpreter should be entitled to apply direct to the Court for such access; and**

- **in all cases where an interpreter is provided with or given access to such documents, it should be in circumstances under which he undertakes to preserve their confidentiality until trial or otherwise in conditions of security directed by the court.**

162   A further aid to interpreters would be to provide them with adequate, visible and audible working positions for their work in court. Many present courtroom layouts require an interpreter to stand uncomfortably next to the witness in a confined, and sometimes precarious, space next to the witness box. Sometimes, the geography of the courtroom is such that they cannot always hear, or be seen or heard by, others in the court. This can be a particular problem for interpreters assisting a defendant in the dock, where sight lines and audibility may be obstructed by high dock partitions or glass screens. The Institute of Translation and Interpreting have raised, in addition to problems of visibility and audibility, concerns about intimidation, particularly when interpreting in the dock for a defendant when some may perceive them as acting for him. They suggest that interpreters should be provided with a set position away from the defendant and means of communication with him by portable radio microphones and headsets. Wherever feasible, existing courtrooms should be adapted and equipped to take account of these concerns. They are not yet a consideration in the design of new court buildings. In my view, they should become part of the design brief. Those responsible should consult with a suitably experienced and representative body of interpreters drawn, say, from the two National Registers, to establish standards of best practice for this purpose.

I recommend the establishment of standards of best practice in the design of new court buildings and the adaptation of equipment in existing courtrooms for the provision of adequate accommodation and facilities to interpreters.

Information about the court

163   The growth in information technology will make it easier for the public to obtain information about the criminal courts. The internet is often the first place people look now; I have been impressed with the information I have been able to obtain in this way during the course of the Review. Some magistrates' courts have already developed their own web pages, though the quality is variable. Every court centre should be able to set up its own website in a relatively short space of time, and at relatively little cost. A website could provide useful information to all involved in a case, or to members of the public who are more generally interested in the work of the court.

164   Each court website could include cases listed for future hearing and their fixed or estimated hearing dates, the cases listed on each day and their individual progress. The Court Service is already looking at the use of such technology, as well as more basic aids, such as electronic bulletin boards at court and automated telephone information services. These information services should be standard provision for all court centres in the new unified Criminal Court that I have recommended and for the Court of Appeal (Criminal Division). In addition to the service that they will provide for all involved in individual trials, they will be a valuable source of information for the media. A court website could also give details of the advice and support services available at each court centre, its other facilities and information about the area, including travel arrangements, eating places, shopping facilities etc.. However, not everyone will have access to information technology. It should, therefore, be matched with more basic communication and information aids such as an automated telephone information system, giving like information.

I recommend that early progress should be made to equip each court centre or group of court centres, as appropriate, with:

- **its own website containing information of cases listed for future hearing and their fixed or estimated**

hearing dates, daily listings of cases and information as to their progress; and general information about the court centre, travel to it and local facilities; and

- **an automated telephone information system giving like information.**

165   Strangers to courts can be unfamiliar with and intimidated by their geography. Much can be done to make the court building, and the courtroom, a more open and less intimidating place. Proper signs around the court should be standard; there are still many centres where directions are confusing or non-existent. Each court centre should have, as a minimum, a reception desk, after any security arrangements, where those attending can obtain information.

166   Once inside the courtroom, the furniture and layout can also be intimidating and confusing. While there is usually an usher on hand to offer assistance, that is not always so. Some courts have helpful diagrams of the layout of courtrooms in the waiting areas outside. Some magistrates' court centres have signs in each of their courtrooms giving the same information. The Witness Service is, of course, of great help, its members showing prospective witnesses around the courtroom when not in use and pointing out who sits where. In the Crown Court, familiarisation visits are often arranged for young or vulnerable witnesses, but not for the vast majority of those who are asked to come to court. In my view, all courts should have a layout diagram in the waiting area outside each courtroom, or group of courtrooms if they are similar. This would help to remove much of the mystery before people enter the courtroom. It would also be helpful to have function plates inside the courtroom, to clarify for witnesses, jurors and members of the public the role of each person present.

167   I have already indicated that the Court Service is experimenting with electronic bulletin boards. These are a considerable improvement on the paper copies of the daily lists that are pinned up in most court centres each day, and amended by hand when the usher has time as the day progresses. The bulletin boards, which would be placed in the public areas of the court and outside each courtroom, would provide up-to-date information on the progress of each case – information that it should also be possible to provide to the court websites when they are more widely and fully developed.

I recommend that early progress should also be made to equip each court centre with:

- **electronic bulletin boards indicating the progress of cases listed each day; and**

- **diagrams in waiting areas of the layout of courtrooms and corresponding signs inside each courtroom.**

168   In many courtrooms it is still difficult for those present other than the main participants to hear what is being said. Modern court design has the judge and the advocates facing each other at fairly close range, the witness to one side of them facing across to the jury on the other side of them. Those outside that 'inner square' often have difficulty following the proceedings. The speakers are naturally modulating their speech to their group and, because the advocates have their backs to those instructing them, the defendant in the dock and the public gallery, others tend to feel excluded. Having spent much time observing in most Crown Court centres in England and Wales and in many magistrates' courts, I can vouch for the common scene of members of the public, defendants and even those sitting behind the advocates, straining forward trying to hear what is being said. The answer to this practical impediment to open justice is simple, though no doubt expensive. All courtrooms should be equipped with suitable sound amplification systems to ensure that everyone in court can hear what is going on.

Sitting times

169   An issue in the Review has been whether Courts should sit for longer than they do. Conventional sitting hours for magistrates courts are Monday to Friday 10 am to 1 pm and 2pm to about 4.30 pm or earlier or later according to the list. Sitting hours in the Crown Court and the Court of Appeal (Criminal Division), are much the same, though 10.30 am is a more common starting time. However, many Crown Court judges and High Court judges sitting in the Court of Appeal will start earlier to deal with interlocutory matters, bail applications and for other urgent reasons. Some magistrates' courts sit on Saturdays and Bank Holidays, particularly in the larger metropolitan areas. Magistrates' courts may also sit at abnormal hours on special occasions to deal with emergencies and surges of work occasioned by particular events.

170   Many contributors to the Review – mostly those who are not directly or regularly involved in the criminal justice process – have argued that courts should routinely sit for longer hours. On the face of it, they have an arguable case. 10.30 am or even 10 am to about 4.30pm is a short working day. And, like shops before they were allowed to open late in the evenings and on Sundays, courts do not cater for those who work a full working day, whether it be to attend a hearing, pay a fine or simply to seek advice or information from court staff. For that reason witnesses of crimes may be reluctant to put themselves forward, and accused persons who are in work may be seriously inconvenienced or prejudiced if they have to seek time off work to attend court.

171 The Government, in its recent policy paper, *The Way Ahead*,[176] signalled its interest in longer court opening hours and weekend sittings to improve the courts' service to the public, reduce delays, deter criminals and reassure local communities. It proposed two pilot schemes, one in a high crime area and another in a low crime area. Such pilots should be devised so as to enable a confident assessment of how extended hours might meet a significant demand, for what types of work, where and at what cost and benefit to all concerned.

172 First, there is the question whether such extended sitting times would relieve present pressures of listing and reduce delays. I assume that magistrates' courts are the main candidate for late evening, night and weekend courts. There has been no serious proposal that courts above that level should effectively move over to shift work, and the costs of it would be formidable. Whatever the level of courts involved, there is no point in using them as remand courts for those arrested late in the afternoon or at night-time. Police officers are already required to bring an arrested person before a court within 24 hours. Presumably the main work in high and serious crime areas, apart from remands, would be dealing with pleas of guilty. But, if evening or night courts are going to dispose of cases straightaway, or even attempt directions for their disposal, they will need the assistance of lawyers, probation and welfare agencies responsible for advising on and arranging community disposals and prison or custody contractors. Given the sort of work that the courts might attract in high crime areas, there would also be a need for ready access to medical support, drug-testing facilities and a strong security presence. In short, unless evening and night courts are to serve only as remand courts or for speedy disposal of trivial offences (as is mostly the role of night courts in high crime areas in the United States[177]), there is a strong likelihood that they would cost a lot of money for relatively small benefits to the system.

173 Evening or night courts in low and less serious crime areas, probably catering in the main for traffic and relatively minor offences, might be less labour intensive and provide a valuable service to those who could not, for one reason or another, conveniently attend court in normal working hours. However, with the present move to greater use by magistrates' courts of postal pleas of guilty and paper proceedings, to which I have referred,[178] it remains to be seen how much demand there would be for out-of-normal-hours sittings for minor cases of this sort.

---

[176] CM 5074, paras 3.82-84

[177] much of the demand for which, for example, in New York, stems from a dramatic increase in the work of inner city courts as a result of policies of zero-tolerance leading to many arrests for very trivial offences

174   As to extension of sitting hours generally, it is a mistake to regard the working day of judges, magistrates, court staff and all others who are involved in their proceedings as confined to the sitting hours of the court. All court work needs much daily preparation and follow-up. Judges and, to an increasing extent, magistrates, need to familiarise themselves with the papers and the issues of fact and law with which they may have to deal. Judges need the beginnings and the ends of the day to keep up with their current trial, including the preparation of rulings and their summings-up, and to cope with their increasing burden of case management of future cases. For the more senior judges, there are also daily administrative tasks requiring close liaison with court staff. And court staff too have a correspondingly heavy daily round of work to service the sittings and to draw up and transmit orders and directions.

175   Lawyers engaged in court have the same problem. They have to cram all their preparatory, advisory and administrative work into the cracks of the day when the courts are not sitting. Prosecutors have much to do to ensure an orderly start to the day and the days ahead if trials are to run smoothly and without interruption. Defence lawyers need time to confer with their clients, to contact witnesses, to turn round their correspondence and generally to attend to the daily responsibilities of their practices. The same will apply to the Criminal Defence Service when it is in operation. Police too have patterns of working and responsibilities outside the individual cases in which they attend court as witnesses. Prisons contractors have to bring prisoners to court early in the morning and take them back in the late afternoon or evening, often involving long, tortuous and, for the prisoners, uncomfortable journeys. The prisons and the contractors between them already find it difficult to provide a timely delivery of prisoners to and from court. The Probation Service, Witness Support and various other agencies vital to the efficient running all have to be considered. The Probation Service is already under great pressure to provide a speedy and efficient service to the courts, split as they are between their responsibilities of assessing and supervising offenders and their reporting and advisory work in the Courts.

176   In short, I believe that any general and significant extension of court working hours would be very costly and would demand a massive increase in resources if the courts and all who serve them were to be adequately equipped to make good use of the extra time. This has been the experience of the much publicised night courts in the United States, confined, as they are, in the main, to particular problem areas in major metropolitan centres and supported by special Federal funding.

177   There may be more scope for providing a better service to everyone, and at little or no extra cost, in various initiatives already undertaken by judges,

---

[178] paras 65 and 67 above

magistrates and court staffs, and with the willing co-operation of those involved in the trial process. I mention some of them only to commend them and pay tribute to those involved in the day to day work of the courts who have found solutions for particular patterns and types of work and who are flexible in response to the needs of particular cases. No national targets or standards or key performance indicators were, or are, needed to monitor their success. These include the introduction of 'Maxwell'[179] sitting hours in long and complicated jury cases, the judge sitting with the jury from about 9:30 am to 1.30 pm, with only a short break mid-morning, leaving the afternoon for the judge and the parties to deal with matters of law or procedure not requiring the jury or, in their different ways, to keep on top of the case. Another is the readiness of judges and court staff where necessary to hold pre-trial hearings of one sort or another out of normal court hours to enable the trial advocates, currently engaged in other case, to attend them. Other initiatives, with local variations, are in the arrangements for more considerate staging of the evidence of witnesses, enabling them to be called to court at short notice and by providing waiting jurors with pagers to absent themselves from the court building for short periods to do their shopping or attend to other domestic needs.

178   However, I can see advantages both to the public and to the courts' administration in the provision of out-of-hours access to court staff for the purpose of advice or information about individual cases or court procedures and payment of fines and the like. These facilities could be provided on the premises by a duty clerk and/or over the telephone and/or by internet facilities. As I have said, it should be possible, as technology develops and its use becomes more wide-spread, for inquirers to obtain information from court electronic bulletin boards of the progress of cases, hearing dates etc, and of general information and on common points of procedure.

Accordingly, I recommend that:

- **there should be thorough examination of the need for and the costs/benefits of extending court working hours, including the use of evening, night and weekend courts, whether as a general provision or for areas with a concentration of serious and/or minor crime; and**

- **out-of-hours provision should be made for administrative assistance to court users through the medium of help-desks, the telephone and electronic means for obtaining advice or information, paying fines, obtaining forms etc.**

---

[179] so-called because Phillips LJ, as he then was, adopted this pattern in his trial of the Maxwell brothers in 1996

Court dress

179   Court dress is presently governed by a 1994 Practice Direction of Lord Mackay of Clashfern LC.[180] Although it was prompted by the Courts and Legal Services Act 1990's extension to solicitor and other higher court advocates of rights of audience in the Supreme Court, it confirmed the long-standing practice and difference in court dress for the Bar and solicitors. Queen's Counsel wear a wig and silk or stuff gown, with wing collar and bands, over a court coat. Junior counsel wear a wig and stuff gown with wing collar and bands. And solicitors wear a black stuff gown with wing collar and bands, but no wig. The Practice Direction concluded by stating that the Lord Chancellor proposed to consult further "with a view to reaching a long-term decision". I have received many submissions about the court dress of judges and advocates, suggesting variously its retention or modification or abolition. The interesting feature of the different options is that each has a broad mix of support from a wide range of persons involved in the trial process. Many judges want to retain wigs and gowns, but many do not. The same division of views applies to jurors, witnesses and past defendants. However, most of the members of the Bar and solicitors who have expressed a view on the subject tend to favour retention of some special court dress, the latter making a strong case that solicitor-advocates in the higher courts should wear the same as the Bar.

180   The main arguments advanced for retention of formal dress for judges and advocates in the higher courts are that it assists to maintain the authority, formality and dignity of the court, and that it bestows a degree of anonymity on the wearers, both 'de-personalising' their roles and protecting them from identification outside court. Arguments against retention are that wigs and gowns are old fashioned, too formal and intimidating. Arguments for modification are primarily for abolition of the 18th century style wigs, wing collars and bands, but retention of a simple gown, which, it is said, would still serve to maintain the special dignity and authority of court proceedings. Such modification would also remove an appearance of a difference in standing between the Bar and solicitor-advocates in the higher courts.

181   The issue of court dress has surfaced from time to time over the last two or three decades. In 1992, shortly before the Practice Direction, the Court Service undertook a survey of a range court users, including judges, members of both legal professions, witnesses, jurors, court staff, prison officers, and even defendants. The result was a substantial majority in favour of retention of wigs and gowns. In a poll of jurors conducted, as part of that survey, by His Hon. Judge Giles Rooke, QC, at the Crown Court in Canterbury, only a small minority of them, before sitting on a jury regarded court dress as undesirable,

---

[180] *Practice Direction (Court Dress)* [1995] 1 Cr App R 13; as varied by *Practice Direction (Court Dress) (No 3)* of Lord Irvine of Lairg, LC [1999] 1Cr App R336

a minority that fell by about two thirds after they had completed their jury service.

182   There is, I believe, something to be said for the view that judicial uniform, and to a lesser extent, advocates' uniforms, give a proper sense of authority and formality to the proceedings of a criminal court. The same may not be so important in civil and family courts where it is more common in certain proceedings for the judge and the parties' advocates to conduct matters without such formal trappings. Court dress is also useful as a distinguishing mark for those attending courts who are unfamiliar with their personnel and ways of working, just as it is to identify the ushers by their gowns or a policeman by his uniform or in other contexts, a clergyman by his collar or a doctor in a hospital by his white coat. And a gown has at least some practical advantage as a protective working garment, saving suits from becoming shiny through wear and giving warmth in winter in cold and draughty courtrooms. Most courts all over the world retain some special uniform of that sort for judges and advocates.

183   However, I believe that, in the Crown Court, and possibly all the Superior Courts, we should consider dispensing with some of the present highly inconvenient garb as we enter the 21st century. Perhaps the answer would be to modify court dress for judges and advocates by discarding wigs, wing collars and bands. Judges could continue to wear gowns distinctive of their judicial status and of their level within the judicial hierarchy, possibly also including District Judges whether sitting on their own in magistrates' courts or as chairmen of mixed tribunals in the District Division of the new Unified Court.[181]   Barristers and solicitors could also continue to wear gowns. Queen's Counsel could continue to wear one distinctive of the status, which is now achievable by solicitors as well as junior counsel. But junior counsel and solicitor higher court advocates could wear the same type of gown to give them parity in appearance as well in their rights of audience.

184   Wherever formal authority lies in the matter, I do not consider that Parliament or the Government should be the arbiter of change. Nor do I consider that change, if it occurs, should take place only in the criminal courts or without reference to the civil and family jurisdictions. It seems to me that the Higher Judiciary should consider the question for each of the jurisdictions and after consultation with all levels of judges, the legal professions and any other bodies they consider appropriate, should advise the Lord Chancellor.

I recommend that the Higher Judiciary, in consultation with all levels of the judiciary, the legal professions and

---

[181] I believe that District Judges in Hull, by long tradition, sit robed

any other appropriate bodies, should consider and advise the Lord Chancellor on what, if any, formal court dress judges, barristers and solicitors should wear in future in the Supreme Court of Justice and the County Court.

Forms of address

185   Similar considerations should apply to present forms of addressing judges. Judges of the Court of Appeal and High Court Judges are addressed as 'My Lord' (or 'Your Lordship') or 'My Lady' (or 'Your Ladyship'). Circuit Judges are addressed as 'Your Honour',[182] District Judges are called 'Sir' or 'Madam', and so are magistrates when addressed individually; but collectively and in the third person as 'the Court' or, less usually nowadays, 'Your Worships'.

186   Judges, including Lords Justices of Appeal, are not Lords; the title is a remnant of a bygone legal age and is now purely honorific and not usually used outside courts or their immediate precincts. Circuit Judges, though deserving respect, no longer need an 18th or 19th century handle to engender it. And magistrates, equally worthy of respect, do not need it garnished with veneration. Many contributors to the Review have argued that the time has come to remove these anachronistic forms of address from what is supposed to be a modern criminal justice system. Others cling to familiar traditions and arguments that such formality, like present court dress, is a practical reminder of the authority and dignity of the court.

187   There is something to be said for courts not becoming so 'user-friendly' as to lose their appearance of authority. However, forms of address in the Superior Courts identifying the judicial function would command just as much or more respect than the quaint unprofessional forms at present in use. Why not 'Judge' used vocatively for all professional judges? I see no need to distinguish between their level of appointment in this respect; it need not affect their various judicial titles or roles. As to magistrates, the only probable need for change is the already diminishing use of the collective 'Your Worships' in favour of a vocative 'the Court' used in the third person. However, as in the case of court dress, any change of this sort could not be made in isolation from the civil and family jurisdictions of the Supreme Court. It is no doubt a matter for the Lord Chancellor after consulting the Higher Judiciary who, before advising him should consult with all levels of the judiciary, magistracy, legal professions and any other bodies they consider appropriate.

---

[182] with some exceptions such as the Recorder and Common Serjeant of London, and any judge whilst sitting at the Central Criminal Court.

Accordingly, I recommend that the Higher Judiciary, in consultation with all levels of the judiciary, the magistracy, the legal professions and any other appropriate bodies, should consider and advise the Lord Chancellor on future forms of address in all courts.

Court language

188   It is important that the criminal justice process as it unfolds in court, as well as in its pre-trial rules and procedures, should be comprehensible to all involved in or exposed to it. Plain English, and/or, in Wales, Welsh, should be the norm. And whatever is said as part of the trial should be audible to everyone in court. Both those considerations are vital to the principle of open justice and proper understanding by all of what is going on. There is much improvement on the old days when the proceedings had more the feel of a private colloquy between the judge, counsel and the witness, not only difficult for many to hear because of the geography of the courtroom, but also difficult to follow when heard because of the unfamiliarity of legal language.

189   Drawing on Lord Woolf's recommendations in his Access to Justice Reports on the civil justice system,[183] I believe that there should be a thrust throughout the criminal justice process for the use of plain and simple English and, where appropriate, Welsh so that it is understandable by lawyer and non-lawyer alike. However, where technical expressions are conveniently concise and have an established and important legal meaning, it may be counterproductive and lead to legal uncertainty to attempt some alternative description. There are far fewer Latin expressions in use in the criminal courts than was the case in the civil jurisdiction. Many technical terms are, in any event, well understood by many outside the judiciary and the legal professions and are the common coin of television programmes about the police, courts and criminals. Simplification of language, both in procedural rules and forms and in court proceedings should be one of the tasks for early consideration by a Criminal Procedure Rules Committee, the establishment of which I have recommended.

I recommend that a Criminal Procedure Rules Committee should examine all court procedures, forms and terms with a view simplifying their language and content.

Oaths and affirmations

190   The subject of oaths and affirmations extends well beyond the criminal law and, if there is to be attempt at reform, it should be looked at in the broadest context. It is of concern to all jurisdictions, not just the criminal courts. It is closely related to questions of the competence and compellability of witnesses, as Parliament has recently underlined.[184]   And any significant change would have considerable knock-on effects, notably in the law of perjury. The current position is that oral testimony of a competent witness is not admissible unless the witness has been sworn or has asked to, or been required by the court, to affirm[185] or is a child under the age of 14.[186]

191   This is not the place to attempt a review of the law of competence and compellability, particularly in relation to the evidence of children, where – partly for want of implementation of sections 53 to 57 of the Youth Justice and Criminal Evidence Act 1999 - it remains in a statutory mess.[187] My main enquiry, and that of the few contributors to the Review who have commented on the subject of oaths and affirmations, is whether they should be abolished and replaced by a simple and solemn promise to tell the truth.

192   A Christian taking the oath is required to hold the New Testament, and a person of the Jewish faith, the Old Testament, in his uplifted hand and say, or repeat after the court officer administering the oath "I swear by Almighty God that I shall tell the truth, the whole truth and nothing but the truth".[188]   For other religions the law simply requires that the oath shall be administered "in any lawful manner", the critical matters being whether the oath appears to the court to be binding on the conscience of the witness and, if so, whether the witness himself regards it as so binding.[189] Witnesses in the youth court and children and young persons in any court swear the same oath save that it begins with the words "I promise before Almighty God...".[190]   A witness affirming says "I, ... do solemnly, sincerely declare and affirm", and then continues with the words of the oath prescribed by law, omitting any words of imprecation or calling to witness.[191]

---

[183] Interim Report, June 1995, Chapter 26, paras 32-36; and Final Report, July 1996, Section V, paras 13 - 16.

[184] Youth Justice and Criminal Evidence Act 1999, ss 55 and 56, yet to be brought into effect.

[185] Oaths Act 1978, ss 5 and 6

[186] Criminal Justice Act 1988, s 33A(1)

[187] see Archbold, (2001 edition) paras 8-32 – 8-35c. And for a compelling historical account and analysis of the role of the oath in court proceedings and, in relation to the evidence of children in particular, see J R Spencer and Rhona Flin, *The Evidence of Children: The Law and The Psychology*, 1993, 2nd ed, pp 46-65

[188] Oaths Act 1978, s 1

[189] ibid s 1(3) and *R v Kemble* 91 Cr App R 178, CA

[190] Children and Young Persons Act 1963, s 28

[191] Oaths Act 1978, ss 5 and 6

193   The general rule requiring witnesses to give evidence on oath has a relatively recent history by common law standards, developing only in the 18th century. By the late 19th century judges seem to have regarded its significance as an acknowledgement by the witness of his belief that, if he did not keep to it, he would suffer "some kind of divine punishment, although it need not be as bad as hell-fire".[192]   Since then, as Professor John Spencer has put it, "the oath gradually became little more than a solemn promise to tell the truth with a reference to God attached".[193] Bridge LJ observed in the Court of Appeal in 1977, that the reality in society by then was that most adults probably did not recognise the divine sanction of the oath.[194] Today, I suspect that many, if not most, witnesses regard its administration as a quaint court ritual which has little bearing on the evidence they are going to give; they will have resolved by then whether to tell the truth or to lie. For some, however, it may remain an important manifestation of the religious imperative upon them to tell the truth.

194   In my view, there is a need to mark the beginning of a witness's evidence with a solemn reminder of the importance of telling the truth and to require him expressly and publicly to commit himself to do so. However, for many – both witnesses and those observing them – the combination of archaic words invoking God as the guarantor of the proposed evidence and the perfunctory manner in which they are usually uttered detracts from, rather than underlines, the solemnity of the undertaking. I consider that it should now be enough to mark the beginning of a witness's evidence and to acknowledge the great diversity of religious or non-religious beliefs, by requiring him simply to promise to tell the truth.   If greater solemnity or emphasis is thought necessary, the oath could be administered by the judge.

I recommend that the witness's oath and affirmation should be replaced by a solemn promise to tell the truth.

195   Much the same considerations apply to a juror's oath or affirmation. The words of the oath are "I swear by Almighty God that I will faithfully try the defendant[s] and give [a] true verdict[s] according to the evidence".   The affirmation begins "I do solemnly, sincerely and truly affirm", and continues in the same form.   It seems to me that a single undertaking for all in simpler language could usefully replace the present two forms. For some jurors, to have to stand up and speak in public, usually within minutes of their first introduction to a court at work, can be an ordeal, and they often stumble with embarrassment over the unfamiliar mantra. I suggest that an undertaking in the following, or a similar form would be better, "I promise to try the defendant and to decide on the evidence whether he is guilty or not".

---

[192] Spencer and Flin, *The Evidence Of Children* p 51, citing Brett MR in *Attorney General v Bradlaugh* (1885) 14 QBD 667
[193] ibid
[194] *R v Hayes* 64 Cr App R 194, CA, at 196

196   But for one factor, I would commend the Scottish practice, in which the judge administers the oath, collectively, to the jurors once they have all been called into the witness box. Sometimes a potential juror's difficulty in reading the oath is the only and last opportunity for the court to determine whether he is sufficiently literate to cope with a trial involving much documentary evidence. If it is obvious that the juror will have difficulty, the judge can diplomatically and quietly excuse him or the prosecution advocate can ask for him to stand by. It is an inappropriate and embarrassing way of ensuring that jurors have sufficient command of written English to follow the evidence. But, as I have indicated in Chapter 5,[195] short of the even more invidious option of introducing a literacy test and of the complications and expense of administering it in advance, I can see no alternative.

> **I recommend that the juror's oath and affirmation should be replaced with a promise in the following or similar form: "I promise to try the defendant and to decide on the evidence whether he is guilty or not".**

SENTENCING

Introduction

197   In the event of conviction of a defendant, a court is required to impose a sentence that will do one or more or all of the following: punish him; mark the degree of harm to the victim and to society; deter others from similar offending, and assist him to mend his ways. This Report is not concerned with the practical or jurisprudential framework of sentencing. That is the subject of a recent Review by John Halliday CB.[196] But I believe my terms of reference do require me briefly to mention some matters: first, the need for a sentencing code; second, the means by which the sentence, and what it means, is communicated in court to the defendant, the victim, and those in the public gallery; and third, the way information is provided to judges and magistrates to inform their decision, above and beyond the evidence in the trial itself. I also comment on John Halliday's proposals for courts to be more actively engaged in reviewing the effectiveness of their sentences, pleas of guilty in summary matters and the involvement of victims in the sentencing process.

---

[195] para 49 - 50

[196] *Making Punishments Work: Report of the Review of the Sentencing Framework for England and Wales* (Home Office, July 2001)

A sentencing code

198   I start with a familiar refrain - the complexity of the law governing sentencing and the urgent need for the law to be brought together and maintained in a single and comprehensible Code. Although sentencing legislation has recently been consolidated in the Powers of Criminal Courts (Sentencing) Act 2000, it is not a code, and, as a consolidating instrument, the ink was barely dry on it before it was amended by the Criminal Justice and Court Services Act 2000. As I recommend in Chapters 1 and 12, codification and its maintenance should become the task of a standing body, under the general oversight of the Criminal Justice Council.[197]

Honesty and simplicity in sentencing

199   As to the sentencing process, the present complexity in the law places judges and magistrates in an invidious position. Their aim in passing sentence should be to communicate clearly to the offender, to the victim and to those in the public gallery both what the sentence is and what it will mean in practice. The intricacies of the current law make these two objectives hard to reconcile in practice. I make no recommendation but urge: first, 'honesty and sentencing' in that the sentence pronounced should be the sentence served; and second, that judges should be freed from legislative mantra so that they can pronounce sentence simply and shortly, addressing the defendant rather than the Court of Appeal.

Sentencing information

200   As to the provision of sentencing information to the court, there is more to say. Lord Lane CJ observed: "Sentencing consists in trying to reconcile a number of totally irreconcilable facts. Judges receive little help in this difficult matter."[198] The problem facing a judge passing sentence, even when it is possible to infer what facts the jury has found, is to weigh the various elements of a criminal's behaviour against a body of decided cases, evidence about what course of action offers the best balance of deterrence, retribution and of rehabilitation in the instant case, and what options are actually available. The problem has been well summarised as follows:

> "In certain ways, it seems that the judges currently have the worst of all possible worlds: they have too little information in an easily usable form, and too much of it in a form that

---

[197] Chapter 1, para 36 and Chapter 12, paras110 - 111
[198] HL Deb, Vol 486, Col 1295

cannot be used effectively. Thus they might have no systematic, organised and easily accessible information, but will have hundreds of reports of cases scattered across volumes of law reports".[199]

201　The most important support to judges and magistrates in the courtroom comes from those who have had responsibility for the supervision and/or welfare of the defendant or who have assessed him for the purpose of advising the court as to sentence. There is also an important role for information technology. In sharp contrast to this country, a number of other jurisdictions have made striking uses of it. There are essentially two models. Diagnostic systems take the sentencer through the formal steps required to reach a valid sentence, according to the presence and seriousness of a range of factors prescribed by law. These systems, mainly in use in the USA, in the form of so-called 'Grid Sentencing', turn the exercise into a mechanical process, and have not found favour in this country or most other Commonwealth jurisdictions. In contrast, information systems provide sentencers with sophisticated means of analysing the case before them, and of obtaining access to comparative and other data in a form that will assist them in reaching a decision. These data relate principally to: sentences passed by other courts in similar cases; information on appropriate principles of sentencing; and about options for rehabilitative and other programmes.

202　So far, sentencing information systems in other jurisdictions have been developed to assist sentencers in four separate, but complementary ways:

- consistency – to provide judges with legal, factual and statistical data. The purpose of the system is not to curtail discretion, but better to inform it, and so achieve consistency of approach;[200]

- exercise of discretion – to support the decision-taking process;

- availability of sentencing facilities – to inform judges of the availability of facilities for any sentencing options they may be considering; and

- public understanding – to secure timely and adequate information to the public of sentencing decisions and the reasons for them.

203　I give four examples of the many well-established or developing sentence support systems in other jurisdictions.

204　Scotland –The Scottish system, introduced in the High Court in the early 1990s on the initiative of Lord Ross (then the Lord Justice Clerk) and

---

[199] Doob, AN and Park, NW *Computerised Sentencing Information for Judges* (1987) Criminal Law Quarterly 30, 54-72

[200] Stein Schjølberg: *Judicial Decision Support Systems From A Judge's Perspective* International Journal of Law and Information Technology, vol 6, No 2, 93-98

researchers at Strathclyde University, contains information on all sentences passed by the High Court in the previous seven years. It allows the judge to enter into his computer the characteristics of the offence and the offender in the instant case, and to obtain from it the range and quantum of penalties imposed by the courts for similar cases. The system was developed in close consultation with the Senior Judiciary, and has been developed so as to be easily used, particularly by judges who are not experts in computing.[201] It is widely used and a much valued tool in the Court of Session.

205 <u>New South Wales</u> – The New South Wales system is one of the most sophisticated yet unobtrusive systems of its kind in the world.[202] It consists of: a database of over 3,500 full text judgments from the Court of Criminal Appeal in New South Wales from 1st January 1990; a database of 2,500 case summaries providing efficient means of finding cases of similar facts and their sentencing outcomes; a principles database consisting of an electronic textbook on sentencing; a statistical database which allows a judge to analyse aggregate sentencing outcomes for defendants displaying a wide range of behaviours and characteristics; a facilities database containing information about the availability of various services for both adult and juvenile offenders, cross-referenced by geographic location and type of service; a help desk; and a variety of information of interest to other court users and the general public. It is probably the world leader in this field.

206 <u>British Columbia</u> – British Columbia has a well-established sentencing information system which was developed in the mid-1980s. It was designed under the guidance of a Judicial Steering Committee and has a highly practical focus. Initially it contained first instance sentencing decisions in five Canadian Provinces (British Columbia, Saskatchewan, Manitoba, Prince Edward Island and Newfoundland), decisions of provincial Courts of Appeal being added later. The database allows sentencing decisions across a range of common offences to be analysed and interrogated according to six factors: seriousness of the offence; involvement of the offender; criminal record; aggravating/mitigating circumstances; impact on the victim; and the prevalence of the offence in the community.

207 <u>The Netherlands</u> – The development of sentencing support systems is not confined to the common law world. In the Netherlands, the NOSTRA system is at an early stage of development, but concentrates on those offences which come before the courts in the greatest number, and is based upon offence descriptions as used in legal practice rather upon strict legal classifications. The system will enable the judge to compare a pending case to comparable ones in the system. The judge will be able to enter case features to compose

---

[201] see Potos, *Judicial Information Research System :A Resume of Progress* NSW Judicial Offices Bulletin Vol II No6

[202] see Hutton, Patteson, Tata & Wilson, *Decision Support for Sentencing in a Common Law Jurisdiction* (Fifth International Conference on Artificial Intelligence and Law) Washington DC: ACM Press

an offence profile corresponding to the pending case. The statistical presentations will show him how many cases with these characteristics resulted in imprisonment, fines or community service orders, and the sentencing ranges.

208   Thus, the use of information technology in support of judicial sentencing is feasible and well tried and tested. England and Wales are significantly behind the game. In my view, urgent steps should be taken to rectify this. A sentencing information system should be introduced to meet the objectives I have mentioned: consistency; improved decision-making in the exercise of discretion; the provision of information of available local sentencing facilities and wider and better public access to sentencing information.

Administration of the system

209   If a sentencing information system is to be established, who should design and administer it? In the jurisdictions I have mentioned, there are different approaches. In Scotland, the database is administered by a university faculty. In New South Wales, it is one of the statutory responsibilities of the Judicial Commission of New South Wales.[203] In the Netherlands, the system is administered by the Ministry of Justice. I doubt whether any of those solutions would work here. The independence of judicial decision-taking in sentencing is a cornerstone of our system, and I do not think our judges or practitioners would be comfortable with a database administered by the Executive. Clearly the use of an academic law faculty would present neither of these difficulties, but the database I have in mind would be substantially larger than that which exists in Scotland, not only because of the difference in size between our two jurisdictions but also because the Scottish system includes only decisions of the High Court. In order to be of practical value, a database for England and Wales would need to cover cases in all our criminal courts, including the Court of Appeal, together with other functions that the Scottish system does not provide.

210   One option would be for the Sentencing Advisory Panel established by the Crime and Disorder Act 1998 to administer the database as part of its responsibilities for providing advice to the Court of Appeal to assist it in framing sentencing guidelines. But, this would involve a significant extension of the work of the Panel that might impede the discharge of its core functions. And, as a matter of principle, I consider it important that the administration of the database should be under judicial control, as it is in New South Wales. I do not believe that the Judicial Technology Group as currently constituted would be in a position to sponsor and operate such a

---

[203] Judicial Officers Act 1986 (NSW) Section 8

system. In the absence of a Judicial Commission on the Australian or Canadian models (covering also questions of appointment, conditions of service and complaints against the judiciary), the most appropriate body would be the Judicial Studies Board, as part of its wider remit to provide training materials and information to the judiciary. It would require significant additional resources to devise, implement and maintain such a project. But it does have experience of providing information and materials to judges online, via its website, and is under the control of a Board the majority of whose members are judges.

I recommend

- **early establishment of an online sentencing information service for all full- and part-time judges. The system should include:**

  - **a statistical record of sentences imposed in criminal courts at all levels, analysed according to key case features;**

  - **a statement of sentencing principles and the text of judgments in key cases via an online sentencing textbook; and**

  - **online and up-to-date information about the availability of sentencing and related facilities.**

- **the sentencing information system should be available online to members of the public and the media, and should be designed with their needs also in mind; and**

- **consideration should be given to charging the Judicial Studies Board with the responsibility for establishing and administering a sentencing information system, resourcing it sufficiently for the purpose.**

'Making Punishments Work'

211 Finally, I consider briefly the recommendations in the Halliday Sentencing Review[204] for development of the courts' sentencing role, and in particular that of sentence review. The main proposals are to involve the courts more closely in the implementation of their sentences in four main respects:

- action following breaches of community sentences;

---

[204] *Making Punishments Work* Report of the Review of the Sentencing Framework for England and Wales (Home Office, July 2001)

- appeals against recall to prison;

- pre-release planning (in relation to the new structure for community penalties recommended in the Halliday Report); and

- reviewing progress of the proposed new community or custody plus sentences, and deciding whether to vary their intensity.[205]

212   I support the principle of sentence review. At the moment, judges and magistrates are required to take a single decision at a particular time (often well after the offence to which the proceedings relate) to meet the objectives of retribution, deterrence and rehabilitation. Having done so, the same tribunal may not hear of the matter again, even in the event of breach proceedings for failure to comply with its order or of conviction of a further offence. In the latter event, the previous conviction is added to the tally, and the court repeats the one-off sentencing exercise. The suggestion is that the court might learn more and do more good by viewing a continuous film rather than just seeing an unconnected series of snapshots.

213   I start from the proposition that the expertise of judges lies in the law, the application of law to facts, and in trial and case management. Judges do not, in general, have qualifications or experience in psychology, sociology or social work. Articles 5 and 6 of the European Convention of Human Rights effectively require criminal sanctions to be imposed only by judges and magistrates. But in doing so they are entitled to all the help they can get. I believe that the introduction of a sentence review jurisdiction would be welcomed by many judges and magistrates, and that it would considerably strengthen their expertise in sentencing.

214   However, there are two main difficulties. The first is practicality. As the Halliday Report acknowledges,[206] it would be unrealistic to expect a sentence review always to be carried out by the original sentencing judge or magistrates Thus, those carrying out the review would not always have the same knowledge of, or personal involvement in, the case. It would be necessary to create and maintain more detailed records than at present of sentencing reasons and expectations. This would, of course, be a great deal easier if there were a common information technology system based upon a shared electronic case file, but it would still have significant resource implications.

215   The second difficulty is cost. The Halliday Report estimate[207] for the basic cost of instituting review hearings is £28m a year. These are merely the costs

---

[205] ibid para 7.26

[206] ibid para 7.27

[207] ibid para 9.15 and para 27 of Appendix 7

of conducting the hearings, and take no account of the significant training required for all judges and magistrates exercising the review jurisdiction. Consideration would also have to be given to the over-all capacity of the system to assimilate change. If the recommendations in this Report are implemented, then judges and magistrates will already have to adapt to new case management procedures, new rules of evidence, a new jurisdictional structure, different trial procedures and a different system of judicial management.

I support the recommendation in the Halliday Sentencing Review Report for the creation of a sentence review jurisdiction for the criminal courts, provided that resource and practical difficulties can be overcome.

Sentencing in the magistrates' court

216   A defendant on whom a short statement of facts has been served may plead guilty by post. On receipt of a postal plea of guilty in such cases the court may sentence in the absence of the prosecutor and the defendant on the basis of the copy of the statement of facts read to it by their clerk. This is widely used for less serious traffic offences, and assists both the court and the defendant in enabling cases to be concluded swiftly and fairly. These cases are usually dealt with en bloc in open court, often empty at the time apart from the magistrates and their clerk, and the prosecutor.

217   Some contributors to the Review have suggested that such formality could be dispensed with and that postal pleas should be dealt with in chambers and the outcomes posted in an open register, court bulletin and/or on a website. I do not see what would be gained by moving the proceedings into chambers. On the contrary, I can see little procedural or administrative advantage in them being conducted in private, and I think that there could be much to lose. I also believe that it would go against the grain of the time and Article 6 for the material upon which decisions are made and their pronouncement to be behind closed doors, whatever the manner of subsequent publication. Disposal of such matters in open court is an important discipline and a mark of due process, one to which the public, the press, interested parties and defendants, who may wish to turn up after all, should have ready access.

218   Greater use of the procedure is to be encouraged and there is no reason why it should not be extended to allow a plea of guilty by fax or by e-mail. However, there are clear limits to the nature of cases which can be dealt with in this way. The requirements of open justice run counter to extending the procedure to cases where other parties may have been injured, or there is any

possibility of a sentence greater than a fine, or where other public interest demands the defendant's attendance.

Participation by the victim in the sentencing process

219   A major area of concern for victims in the criminal justice system is the relevance of their suffering to the sentencing function and how the court is informed of it. For some years there had been an informal, but generally followed, practice in cases of violent crime by which the prosecuting advocate provided such information. Mostly this had been gleaned from the victim's witness statement taken shortly after the offence, sometimes supplemented by up-to-date information from a police officer at the time of the sentencing. However, the system had not been uniform and often left the sentencing tribunal with incomplete information, particularly where the effects were long-term and not readily measurable. A recent innovation is a victim 'impact' or 'personal' statement in which victims (including bereaved relatives in homicide cases) can give an account in their own words of how the crime has affected them. This is a welcome development, but care will have to be taken in the use of victim statements not to give victims false expectations of their role in the sentencing process.[208]

220   Judges have always regarded information on the effect of the crime on the victim as a relevant factor in assessing the seriousness of the offence and, where appropriate, as to whether and in what amount to order compensation. But Victim Support's view is that it is an imprecise tool for those purposes since no court can assess with confidence the full and possible long-term effect on the victim of an offence and of its aftermath. Victim Support regards such information more as a means of equipping the court openly to acknowledge the harm done to the victim, his contribution to the process and of identifying and securing protection and/or treatment and/or other help to him.

221   Whatever the mix of purposes of victim personal statements and their relative importance in the sentencing process, the Government has now decided to extend their use to every case and court in the country. Their purpose is not simply to provide information at the sentencing stage, but also to inform earlier decisions of the police, the prosecution and the courts as to bail and compensation and to identify any necessary support and protection to victims and, where appropriate, their relatives. The Government has not adopted a suggestion of some that victims should be permitted at the sentencing stage to

---

[208] for recent discussion of the pros and cons of the use of such statements in an adversarial system, see Edna Erez, *Who's Afraid of the Big Bad Victim? Victim Impact Statements as Victim Empowerment and Enhancement of Justice.* [1999] Crim LR 545; see A Ashworth *Victim's Rights, Defendants' Rights and Criminal Procedure* in Crawford and Goodey (eds) *Integrating Victims' Perspectives in Criminal Justice* (2000); and Sanders & Ors, *Victim Impact Statements: Don't Work, Can't Work* [2000] Crim LR 447.

give oral evidence of the harm they claim to have suffered or that they or representatives instructed for the purpose should be entitled to address the court or cross-examine the offender on the matter.

222   The greater prominence now given to the effect of the crime on the victim is undoubtedly an improvement and long overdue. However, it carries with it some practical problems. Often an offender or his representative will make serious allegations against the complainant/victim as part of his mitigation. These allegations may be unsubstantiated and incapable, or not readily capable, of independent verification or refutation. The allegations, if untrue, can be hurtful to the victim and, if given publicity, damaging to his or her reputation, particularly in the case of violent or sexual offences. The prosecution advocate, if properly instructed on the matter, has a duty to refute such allegations and, if they are likely to affect the sentencing decision, the court should order a Newton hearing[209] to determine the facts. Such a hearing, depending on the defence allegations, could well result in a victim giving evidence. Fairness requires that the victim should have some opportunity to refute what he or she claims to be unfounded allegations. How this can be achieved without the criminal process descending into a detailed and public trading of allegations between victim and accused will require careful thought. It may be that at the sentencing stage there is something to be said for Victim Support's proposal that the victim should be allotted a place in court close to the prosecutor to enable the latter as part of his public function to refute where possible, or simply put in issue, unsubstantiated allegations of that sort.

223   The English criminal courts have long had a power to award compensation when imposing sentence in certain cases[210] and, there is a wider statutory scheme for the compensation of victims of crime administered, independently of the courts, by the Criminal Injuries Compensation Authority.[211] However, there is a concern – not just of Victim Support – that these mechanisms do not always achieve for the victim the compensation he deserves and do not, in any event, formally or adequately recognise his central role in the process. I have already noted that the perceived advantages of the *partie civile* in France are often illusory, particularly when it comes to compensation and that an English victim has the same problem.[212]

224   The problems of delayed payment and non-payment of awards of compensation could and, many say, should be resolved by requiring the State to pay the victim the whole amount awarded immediately and leaving it to

---

[209] see *R v Newton* (1983) 77 Cr App R 13 CA

[210] Powers of Criminal Courts Act 1973, s 35

[211] Criminal Injuries Compensation Act 1995

[212] this is not so under the wider scheme for compensation awarded under the Criminal Injuries Compensation Scheme, where the State, not the victim, assumes responsibility for payment.

recover and/or enforce the award against the offender. I note from the Government's *Way Ahead* policy paper [213] that it is considering the possibility of a Victim's Fund "to ensure that every victim receives immediate payment of any compensation order" leaving the courts to pursue defaulters. Whilst, at first sight, that seems a sensible and humane proposal, there are some counter considerations. First, such a scheme would amount to the State lending the offender money or, in the event of default, underwriting his obligation to pay. Second, if the recent transfer of enforcement functions from the police to the courts results in a general improvement in the recovery of fines and compensation, there would not be the same imperative for the State to underwrite recovery in this way. Third, it could be seen as an extension of the Criminal Injuries Compensation Scheme, and an inconsistent one at that, since the level of compensation would depend on what the courts consider the offender could afford to pay and not according to the nature and extent of the injury or damage as under the Scheme. Fourth, it could encourage victims or alleged victims to exaggerate or fabricate their complaint with a view to securing greater compensation and engender challenges to their credibility in cross-examination as compensation seekers.

225   I am conscious that I have raised more questions in this section than I have answered. But, I hope that it may have been useful, at least to highlight some of the practical issues for the courts, even though my terms of reference do not require me to answer them.

---

[213] para 3.118

CHAPTER 12

APPEALS

INTRODUCTION

Purposes and principles of a good appellate system

1   Lord Woolf wrote, in his Report, *Access to Justice*,[1] that there are two main purposes of appeals. The first is the private one of doing justice in individual cases by correcting wrong decisions. The second is the public one of engendering public confidence in the administration of justice by making those corrections and in clarifying and developing the law.

2   With those two purposes in mind it seems to me that the main criteria of a good criminal appellate system are that:

- it should do justice to individual defendants and to the public as represented principally by the prosecution;

- it should bring finality to the criminal process, subject to the need to safeguard either side from clear and serious injustice and such as would damage the integrity of the criminal justice system;

- it should be readily accessible, consistently with a proper balance of the interest of individual defendants and that of the public;

- it should be clear and simple in its structure and procedures;

- it should be efficient and effective in its use of judges and other resources in righting injustice and in declaring and applying the law; and

- it should be speedy.

3   In this chapter I have attempted to apply those various criteria to all levels and main forms of criminal appeal below the Appellate Committee of the House

---

[1] *Access to Justice* Final Report, p 153

of Lords. The practices and procedures of the Appellate Committee have not been at the centre of my Review and I have received few submissions about them. I have not, in any event, thought it appropriate for me to enquire closely into the Committee's composition or workings or make recommendations for its possible reform.

4   The system is notable for its mixed and overlapping appellate routes and remedies and lack of clarity in jurisdiction and procedure. There are also procedural impediments to its ability both to do justice in individual cases and adequately to protect the public interest. In what follows I summarise briefly the present appellate structures and jurisdictions, indicate how well or badly they meet the above criteria and recommend improvements. In formulating my recommendations, my main aims have been to improve justice and efficiency by:

- establishing, so far as practicable, broadly similar grounds of appeal at each jurisdictional level;

- replacing the several and overlapping appellate procedures and jurisdictions with a single procedural strand from the lowest to the highest level; and

- better matching of the appellate tribunal to the seriousness and complexity of the case.

Most of the recommendations that I make would benefit the present structure of the courts as well as the three tiered unified court structure that I propose. However, to make clear what I have in mind, I express them in terms of my recommended structure relating it in parentheses to present courts.

THE APPELLATE TESTS

5   The test that I have in mind for defendants' challenges of conviction at all levels is broadly based on the statutory jurisdiction of and restriction on the Court of Appeal (Criminal Division) to allow appeals against conviction only where it thinks they are 'unsafe'. The interpretation of that word is, so far, to be found wholly in the jurisprudence of the Court. There is judicial and academic disagreement about it, to which I shall return.

6   The Court of Criminal Appeal, on its establishment in 1907, was empowered to quash a verdict where it was wrong in law or unreasonable, or could not be supported having regard to the evidence or, on any ground, that there was a miscarriage of justice.[2] Its successor, the Court of Appeal (Criminal Division), shortly after its establishment in 1996, was given very much the same criteria, though expressed differently, namely whether the conviction

---

[2] Criminal Appeal Act 1907, s 4

612

was wrong in law, "unsafe or unsatisfactory" or there was "a material irregularity" in the course of the trial, but all subject to an express proviso that, even if the appellant established any of those complaints, the Court could still dismiss his appeal if it considered that "no miscarriage of justice" had occurred.[3] Given that proviso, the unsafety of the conviction was in practice the paramount consideration, and the Court rarely had to spend long considering what it should do if it was of the view that there had been something unsatisfactory about the proceedings in the form of a material irregularity or otherwise, but that the conviction was nevertheless safe on the evidence. It applied the proviso and dismissed the appeal.

7   Clearly, the Court could not apply the proviso if it was of the view that the conviction was 'unsafe', because that would have been a miscarriage of justice. But that did not necessarily follow if it was, in some way not giving rise to unsafety, 'unsatisfactory' or followed a material irregularity in the course of the trial. Because the existence and use of the proviso effectively cancelled the two criteria of an unsatisfactory conviction and a material irregularity in the absence of unsafety, Parliament, by amendment of the 1968 Act in 1995,[4] simplified the formula by confining the Court's power and duty to quash a conviction by reference to the single criterion of its 'unsafety'. The intention was clearly to make no substantial change in the law.

8   Unhappily, there is some dispute as to the effect of the old law that remained unchanged. Some, while agreeing that there has been no change, take the restrictive view that the Court has, and always has had, a power to quash a conviction only where it was unsafe in the sense of a doubt as to its 'correctness' – that is, as to the proof of its commission by admissible evidence - and that the words 'unsafe' and 'unsatisfactory' in the old test had been used interchangeably.[5] Despite the exiguous use by the Court before the 1995 amendment of the criterion of 'unsatisfactoriness' as distinct from 'unsafety',[6] many others maintain that there was a difference between the two which has been preserved in their replacement with the single word 'unsafe'. They argue, on that basis alone, that it is open to the Court to take the view that, however 'correct' the conviction may be in terms of the cogency of the evidence supporting it, it might yet be considered unsafe because of some unsatisfactory feature before or at the trial giving rise to it. Such reasoning has gathered strength from the greater use by courts over recent years of their long-standing power to stay prosecutions for abuse of process, regardless of the effect of the abuse on the safety of the conviction in pure evidential terms. This development has gone hand in hand with an increasing

---

[3] Criminal Appeal Act 1968, s 2(1)

[4] Criminal Appeal Act 1995, s 2(1)

[5] see: *R v Graham and ors* [1997] 1 Cr App R 302, Lord Bingham CJ at 308A-309E; and *R v Chalkley and Jeffries* [1998] QB 848, CA, at 867H-868H, citing, as an example of interchangeable use of the terms, *R v McIllkenny* [1991] 93 Cr App R, 287

[6] there are only one or two reported instances of it; see eg *R v Llewellyn* [1978] 67 Cr App R 149, and *R v Heston Francois* [1984] QB 278

acknowledgement of the importance of due process in the criminal justice system, encouraged and now firmly ushered into our law in its Human Rights form.[7]

9   The logic of such a development where there has been abuse of process in bringing a defendant to trial is unassailable. As Lord Justice Rose has recently put it, "for a conviction to be safe, it must be lawful; and if it results from a trial which should never have taken place, it can hardly be regarded as safe".[8] But the position is not quite so clear where the abuse or lack of due process has occurred in the trial process. The European Court of Human Rights has ruled that the test of safety of a conviction is not the same as the question whether a defendant has had a fair trial.[9] However, the Court of Appeal, while acknowledging the separateness of the two tests, has in practice, where they have both been in play as to the conduct of a trial, so elided them as to suggest that unfairness is only an operative consideration on appeal where it may have affected the safety of the conviction.[10] That entirely logical, though not precisely formulated approach, may not satisfy many who believe that serious failures of due process, whatever their effect on the safety of a conviction, should be punished by an acquittal.

10   There is thus much uncertainty as to the relationship of the notions of a fair trial and a safe conviction, in particular as to whether unfairness not affecting the safety, in the sense of 'correctness', of a conviction, requires the Court of Appeal to quash it. The point has yet to be directly considered by the House of Lords,[11] but would it not be better to clarify in statutory form the Court of Appeal's power and duty in this respect? In my view, consideration should be given to amendment of the present statutory test to make clear whether and to what extent it is to apply to convictions that would be regarded as safe in the ordinary sense of that word but follow want of due process before or during trial.

---

[7] see *Condron v United Kingdom* (2000) 31 EHRR 1; [2000] Crim LR 679, ECHR

[8] see eg *R v Mullen* [2000] QB 520, CA, at 540D-E; see also *R v Smith* [1999] 2 Cr App R 238, CA

[9] see *footnote 7*

[10] see eg *R v Davis* [2001] Cr App R 115, CA, per Mantell LJ at 134-135, paras 64 and 65 ; *R v Francom* [2001] Cr App R 237, CA, per Woolf LCJ at pp 250-25, paras 49-51; and *R v Togher* [2001] Cr App R 457. CA, per Woolf LJ at .467-468, paras 29 and 30; and see Lord Bingham's discussion of the word 'unsafe' in *R v Criminal Cases Review Commission, ex p. Pearson* [2000] Cr App R 141, at 146F-147A

[11] it was considered only peripherally in *R v Martin* [1968] 1 Cr App R 347, HL

Appeals against sentence

11   The test that I have in mind for appeals against sentence at all levels is again broadly based on that developed by the Court of Appeal. It is whether the sentence is legally permissible, or imposed on a wrong factual basis, or on irrelevant matters or without regard to relevant matters, or wrong in principle either because it is the wrong sort of disposal in the circumstances or, depending on whether the defendant or the prosecutor is the appellant, whether it is far too severe ('manifestly excessive') or far too lenient ('unduly lenient').

> **I recommend that:**
>
> - **there should be the same tests for appeal against conviction and sentence respectively at all levels of appeal below the Appellate Committee of the House of Lords, namely those applicable to the Court of Appeal; and**
>
> - **consideration should be given to amendment of the statutory test of unsafety as the ground for quashing a conviction so as to clarify whether and to what extent it is to apply to convictions that would be regarded as safe in the ordinary sense, but that follow want of due process before or during trial.**

12   The test for prosecution appeals against acquittal, I leave for later detailed discussion, but its core element should be a well founded belief, by whatever level of appellate court is concerned, that a guilty man has probably been wrongly acquitted and that the public interest requires the matter to be re-opened. In addition, in certain circumstances, the Attorney General should be entitled, in the public interest and for the guidance of the courts, to seek a ruling of law arising out of a criminal proceeding without it affecting the final decision in that proceeding.

13   With the above principles and core criteria for appeal in mind, I now give an outline of the present appeal structures and respective criteria for appeal or challenge in order to identify and illustrate the need for change.

APPEALS FROM MAGISTRATES' COURTS

14   There are two routes of appeal from magistrates' courts. The first is to the Crown Court by way of rehearing and thence to the Divisional Court of the Queen's Bench Division on matters of law or jurisdiction on appeal by way of case stated or judicial review. The second is direct to the Divisional Court by one or other of those procedures. Whichever route is chosen, either side may then, with leave, take the matter direct from the Divisional Court to the House of Lords. The main issues raised in the Review on appeals from magistrates' courts were: first, whether appeal to the Crown Court or its successor should continue to be by way of rehearing; second, if not, what criteria should govern the success or failure of appeal, for example, should it be the same as those in the Court of Appeal; third, if so, should there be a requirement of leave; fourth, what court or courts should hear appeals from magistrates' courts and what judges should sit in them; and fifth, should appeals by way of case stated and challenge by judicial review continue in criminal matters or should they be subsumed in appeals to the Crown Court and/or to the Court of Appeal? Before looking at these questions, I should say that there was strong support in the contributions in the Review for removal of the right of appeal to the Crown Court by way of rehearing, for the introduction at that level of the same or similar grounds of appeal to those for the Court of Appeal and for merging the present remedies of appeal by way of case stated and judicial review into a single form of criminal appeal to the Court of Appeal. There was little support for conferring an appellate jurisdiction in crime on a District Judge, sitting with or without lay magistrates, in a new District Division, or on a High Court Judge sitting singly as such.

Appeals to the Crown Court

15   A person found guilty in the magistrates' courts may appeal as of right against conviction or against sentence to the Crown Court composed of a Circuit Judge or Recorder sitting with at least two lay magistrates not involved in the case below.[12] The prosecution has no corresponding right of appeal to the Crown Court against acquittal or sentence. The procedure is the same as that for a summary trial and the parties are not limited to, or bound to call all, the evidence called before the magistrates' court. An appeal against sentence also follows the same format as that before the magistrates' court. The Crown Court may reverse, affirm or amend the magistrates' decision, or may remit

---

[12] Magistrates' Courts Act 1980, s 108

the matter back to them giving its opinion for its disposal.[13] Thus, the Crown Court may consider points of law as well as decide matters of fact and may impose its own sentence, though not one greater than the magistrates could have passed. In the main, appeals to the Crown Court are on matters of fact.

16   Few of those convicted and sentenced in the magistrates' courts take the matter to appeal, even by way of rehearing as of right in the Crown Court. In 2000, there were nearly 14,000 appeals against conviction and/or sentence to the Crown Court, 125 appeals by way of case stated to the Divisional Court and 336 claims of judicial review in criminal cases to the Divisional Court. Expressed in percentage terms, less than 1% of magistrates' courts' decisions are appealed. By any standards, those are very low levels of appeal.

17   The right of appeal from magistrates' courts by way of rehearing must have its origin in a general lack of confidence in the impartiality and competence of the old 'police courts', mostly manned by local worthies with little knowledge of the law, little or no training and not obliged, unless required to state a case, to explain their decisions. Quite apart from the greater number of District Judges now sharing magistrates' jurisdiction, their standing and function today bear little comparison with those of the old police courts. I have referred in Chapter 4 to their increasingly thorough training, the advice and support that they receive from their full-time legal advisers, the valuable national guidance provided by the Magistrates' Association and, not least, their recent move to give reasons for their decisions. I have also made a number of recommendations, which, if implemented, should further improve their performance. In those circumstances, it is hard to see what is left of the original justification for permitting another tribunal, even one presided over by a judge, to re-hear the case.

Appeals by way of case stated

18   Both sides also have a right of appeal from a final decision of a magistrates' court,[14] or from the Crown Court on appeal from the magistrates' court,[15] direct to the Divisional Court of the Queen's Bench Division on points of law by way of case stated. Under this procedure, one or other party or both may challenge a decision or other proceeding of the magistrates on the ground that it is wrong in law or in excess of jurisdiction. Application is made to the magistrates to state a case for the opinion of the High Court. As in the case of a notice of appeal to the Crown Court, the application must be made within 21 days of the order of which complaint is made. Despite this appellate route

---

[13] Supreme Court Act 1981, s 48

[14] except where there is a separate statutory right of appeal to the High Court or where an enactment makes the magistrates' decision final

[15] Supreme Court Act 1981, s 28

being confined to points of law, there is potential for some overlap between law and fact in the ability to challenge a finding of fact on the basis that there was no evidence to support it or, put another way, one which no reasonable bench of magistrates could have made. Similarly, this procedure may be used to challenge a sentence that is so harsh or oppressive, or so far outside the normal discretionary sentencing limits, as to be regarded as an error of law. A defendant who applies to appeal straight from a magistrates' court to the Divisional Court by way of case stated loses his right of appeal to the Crown Court. But, as I have said, if he goes first to the Crown Court he can then challenge the Crown Court's decision by way of case stated.

19   It is important to note that this avenue of appeal is only available where the magistrates have exercised their jurisdiction, reached a final decision and have agreed to state a case. So, for example, where magistrates dismiss a charge for want of jurisdiction or where a defendant is given no opportunity of meeting a charge so that there is a breach of natural justice, the remedy is by way of judicial review. Magistrates may refuse to state a case, (save for an application by the Attorney General) where they are opinion that it is 'frivolous', that is, futile, misconceived, hopeless or academic. If an applicant seeks to challenge that refusal, he can do so by judicial review.

20   The procedure is rooted in the days when magistrates' decisions, like those of a jury, were oracular. They were not required, as they are now, publicly to give reasons for their decisions when they announced them. Thus, the content of a case stated should include the facts found (but not the evidence upon which the findings were based), the question or questions of law on which the opinion of the High Court is sought, the contentions of the parties and the opinion or decision of the magistrates.[16] When the matter reaches the High Court, it is heard by a single judge or a Divisional Court comprising a Lord Justice and a Queen's Bench Division Judge. The magistrates are not normally parties to the appeal unless joined as a party or accused of misconduct. But the court may consider any affidavits filed by them or on their behalf and may, if it considers it necessary, ask the Attorney General to appoint an amicus. Otherwise, no new evidence is called. However, new points of law can be raised. As in the case of an appeal to the Crown Court, the High Court may reverse, affirm or amend the magistrates' decision, or may remit the matter to them to take action in accordance with its opinion. This may include substituting an acquittal or a conviction or a more lenient sentence for a 'harsh and oppressive' one. It may also order a re-trial and direct, for example, that certain matters should be ruled admissible or non-admissible on the re-trial.

---

[16] see Practice Direction [1972] 1 W.L.R. 4, and also Magistrates' Courts Rules, 1981 rr 76-81

Judicial Review[17]

21 Both prosecution and defence may also challenge magistrates' courts' decisions, or decisions of the Crown Court on appeal from the magistrates, in the Divisional Court by way of the discretionary remedy of a claim for judicial review.[18] Judicial review is concerned with failure to exercise or excess of jurisdiction, regularity of the decision-making process and, through it, the legality, including the rationality, of the decision itself. Where there is an overlap between the case stated jurisdiction and this, a party should normally proceed by way of case stated. The court may decline to consider an application for judicial review if he has not done so. Judicial review takes three main forms, derived from the old prerogative writs: certiorari, enabling the court to quash a summary conviction and, exceptionally, an acquittal; mandamus, requiring magistrates to carry out their duty, for example to try an information or to state a case for the Divisional Court; and prohibition, to require them to not to do something, for example, not to act in excess of their jurisdiction.

22 A claim for judicial review can only be made with permission. A request for permission must be made to a single judge of the High Court promptly and in any event within three months of the decision complained of (thus, capable, depending on the circumstances, of being a more generous time limit than the 21 days allowed for appeal to the Crown Court or by way of case stated). It is made in a written claim form, served on the defendant, and normally determined in writing. If permission is refused the request may be renewed within seven days before a Divisional Court. If permission is granted the claim is heard, on notice to all persons directly affected, by the same court that hears appeals by way of case stated, a Divisional Court of the Queen's Bench Division. Evidence may be received in these proceedings, usually on affidavit. The court may remit the matter to the lower court for decision in accordance with its judgment or take the decision itself.

23 Although judicial review lies in circumstances where appeal by way of case stated is not possible, there is a considerable overlap between the two jurisdictions, including the extent to which the court may exercise discretion in the grant of relief. It is generally more appropriate to go to the Crown Court if the question is essentially one of fact and, by way of case stated to the High Court, when magistrates have acted within their jurisdiction but have made a mistake in law.

---

[17] see Supreme Court Act 1981, ss 29 – 31 and Civil Procedure Rules, Part 52
[18] ibid, s 29(3)

Unsatisfactory features of the system

24   There are a number of unsatisfactory features of the present system. First, there are the three partially overlapping routes of appeal. Depending on the matter challenged, a defendant can take his point of law to the Crown Court by way of rehearing or by one of two different procedures to the same tribunal in the High Court. Depending on the selection made, a convicted defendant may make his way on a point of law to the High Court via a rehearing in the Crown Court or lose his right to such a rehearing if he proceeds straight to the High Court. Choosing the most appropriate route and form of relief in the High Court is not always straightforward.

25   Second, it is anomalous that there should be an appeal as of right capable of turning on points of law from a magistrates' court to the Crown Court when the two other forms of challenges on points of law going to the High Court require some form of judicial filter.

26   Third, it is equally anomalous that there should be a right of appeal on issues of fact, by way of rehearing from a magistrates' court to the Crown Court. As I have said, District Judges and increasingly well trained magistrates now give reasons for their decision which require them to justify why and on what evidence they decided the matter and, where there was a conflict of evidence, why they preferred one version to the other. Where magistrates have taken the decision, the appeal is heard by a similarly constituted tribunal, save only that one of its fact finders is a judge. Where the appeal is from a District Judge, it is equally anomalous that a defendant should then be able to repeat the process before a mixed tribunal of professional and lay judges. It is also an unsatisfactory feature of a normal appeal process, particularly one exercisable by a defendant as of right, that witnesses should have to attend court twice to give evidence.

27   Fourth, there seems little point in retaining two distinct and partially overlapping procedures for challenging magistrates' courts' jurisdictional and other legal errors in the same tribunal in the High Court.

28   Fifth, depending on the form of challenge chosen, different time limits apply either to the start of the process or the stages by which it reaches hearing.

Proposed changes

29   All this is very confusing and makes for duplicity of proceedings, much unnecessary jurisprudence on the extent of and differences between the respective jurisdictions, both as to which should be used and in what order. In

my view, there should be one avenue and form of appeal for each court, including the new middle tier that I have proposed.

30   In my view, the only avenue of direct appeal from the Magistrates' Division (magistrates' courts) should be to the Crown Division (Crown Court), and should be subject to permission from a judge of the Crown Division (Crown Court). The corollary of such a restriction would be a removal of the present direct access from a decision of magistrates to the supervisory jurisdiction of the High Court by appeal by way of case stated and judicial review. However, as I recommend below, that supervisory jurisdiction should in substance be exercisable in criminal matters by the Court of Appeal on appeal from the Crown Division (Crown Court). The effect would be, not to deny access to the High Court Bench for this purpose, but to limit it to a second stage of appeal to High Court Judges and above sitting in a different court. And, of course, there would still be scope in appropriate cases for direct access to a High Court Judge presiding as a judge of the Crown Division (Crown Court) on appeal from the Magistrates' Division (magistrates' courts).

31   I have considered and rejected the possibility of an appeal from the Magistrates' Division to the new District Division that I have proposed. It would be wrong, divisive and lack authority to subject District Judges' and magistrates' first instance decisions to the scrutiny of their peers on appeal who, when sitting in the Magistrates' Division, would exercise exactly the same jurisdiction and would mostly come from the same or neighbouring courts and benches. So, under my proposals for a three tier court structure, the District Division would have no appellate function.

32   Applications for permission to appeal from the Magistrates' Division (magistrates' courts) to the Crown Division (Crown Court) would be in writing, as would the judge's decision, unless for any reason of urgency, including bail, the application should be made orally. In the event of refusal, the applicant would have an opportunity to renew his application orally. The appeal would be heard by a judge sitting alone who, depending on the nature and importance of the case, could be a High Court Judge, Circuit Judge or Recorder. It would no longer be by way of rehearing, either on conviction or on sentence, but of law and on other grounds that now make a conviction 'unsafe' or a sentence unlawful, wrong in principle or manifestly excessive in the Court of Appeal.

33   I should record that I considered recommending, in the case of appeals against sentence, retention of the present form of rehearing before a judge sitting, as now, with magistrates. I had in mind the experience of magistrates in sentencing at summary level and the mutual benefit to the judge and them in exercising this appellate function together. However, it makes no more sense to re-run an essentially factual exercise as to sentence of a District Judge *or*

magistrates before a tribunal constituted by a judge *and* magistrates than it does to re-run the issue of guilt. The critical question should be, as it is in the case of Crown Court sentences, whether they are permitted by law or are wrong in principle because they are the wrong sort or far too severe. Those are questions that a judge is well able to determine on his own. Circuit Judges already have considerable experience of summary sentencing levels in their appellate capacity and through statutory provisions permitting them to deal with summary offences associated with indictable offences before them.[19] They would have even more in the event of adoption of my recommendation (in Chapter 7) that courts at every level should have jurisdiction to try and sentence all cases brought before them, say as part of a group of matters heard together, some of which would normally have been determined by a lower court.

34   If, as I recommend, appeals against conviction were confined to a judge alone, it would, in any event, be impracticable for magistrates to sit on many sentence appeals. In combined appeals, against conviction and sentence, they would have to spend much time waiting around, presumably as little more than passive observers of the conviction proceedings, before becoming part of the constitution of the court for the purpose of sentence. In my view, magistrates would have a far greater contribution to make as first instance judges in the important District Division that I have recommended.

35   In conviction appeals the Crown Division (Crown Court), sitting in this appellate capacity, should be in better position than the Court of Appeal on appeals from it under the present system of jury trial, because it would have a reasoned decision from the magistrates on the law and the facts. The Court of Appeal presently has to do the best it can with the judge's direction and the jury's unreasoned verdict (though that distinction would disappear if my recommendation for a reasoned jury verdict were to find favour*).*

Accordingly, I recommend that:

- **a defendant's right of appeal against conviction and/or sentence in the magistrates' court to the Crown Court by way of re-hearing should be abolished;**

- **it should be replaced by a right of appeal to the Crown Division (Crown Court), with leave from that court, on the same grounds that would support appeal from the Crown Division (Crown Court), sitting in its original capacity, to the Court of Appeal;**

- **the constitution of the Crown Division (Crown Court) for this purpose should be a judge sitting alone who,**

---

[19] eg under the Criminal Justice Act 1988, ss 40 and 41

depending on the nature and importance of the appeal, could be a High Court Judge, Circuit Judge or Recorder; and

- **there should be no right of appeal from the Magistrates' Division (magistrates' courts) to the High Court by an appeal by way of case stated or by a claim for judicial review.**

APPEALS FROM THE CROWN COURT

36   This section concerns appeals from the Crown Court as an appellate court and as a court of first instance.

In its appellate capacity

37   As to appeal from a decision of the Crown Court in its appellate capacity, I can see no more justification for maintaining the present two overlapping forms of recourse on law and jurisdiction to the High Court by an appeal by way of case stated and judicial review than in the case of challenges to magistrates' decisions. In my view, there should be a single form of appeal and procedure combining the best of both jurisdictions. The only question is to what court should it go? For reasons that are reinforced below when considering appeals from the Crown Court as a court of first instance,[20] my view is that it should go to the Court of Appeal suitably constituted for the purpose. The Court should be invested as far as necessary for this purpose with the High Court's present powers on appeal by way of case stated or judicial review. It is not as if there is any difference in judicial personnel between the two Courts to justify the present complicated and overlapping procedures and separate courts for essentially the same exercise. Both are constituted, as necessary, by Lords Justices and Queen's Bench Judges. Thus, from the Crown Division (Crown Court), sitting as an appeal court from the Magistrates' Division (magistrates' courts), an appeal would lie to the Court of Appeal, but only with the permission of that Court and in special circumstances. I have in mind a similar principle in criminal appeals to that formulated by the Bowman Committee for civil appeals, and already applicable to appeals from the Crown Court sitting as a court of first instance, namely that only one level of appeal should be the norm. Thus, criteria for a second appeal in Magistrates' Division (magistrates' courts') decisions to the Court of Appeal could be similar to those for civil appeals from the High Court sitting on appeal from the county court, namely that the appeal would have to raise an important point of principle or practice or that there is some

---

[20] see paras 38-44 below

other compelling reason for the Court of Appeal to hear it.[21] The second criterion of some other compelling reason would be a vital safety valve in the interest of justice, including the liberty of the subject in each individual case. For that reason, and also in recognition that the first level of appeal in crime would be to the Crown Division (Crown Court) – save that an appeal could be listed before a High Court Judge sitting as a judge of the Crown Division (Crown Court) - it should fall to be interpreted more widely than its counterpart in the civil sphere. It could include, for example, where the single judge of the Court of Appeal considers that an appeal would have a high prospect of success and/or that there is a risk of the 'lurking doubt'[22] variety that a serious injustice has been done.

> **Accordingly, I recommend that where it is sought to challenge the decision of the Crown Division (Crown Court) sitting in its appellate capacity:**
>
> - **there should be no right of challenge to the High Court by appeal by way of case stated or by claim for judicial review;**
>
> - **instead, appeal should lie to the Court of Appeal under its general appellate jurisdiction enlarged, if and as necessary, to cover matters presently provided by the remedies of appeal by way of case stated or claim for judicial review – and for which the Court should be suitably constituted; and**
>
> - **all such appeals should be subject to the permission of the Court of Appeal, which it should only give in a case involving an important point of principle or practice or where there is some other compelling reason for the Court to hear it.**

As a court of first instance

38   The main avenue of appeal from the Crown Court as a court of first instance is to the Court of Appeal. Between April 2000 and March 2001, there were 2029 applications for leave to appeal against conviction, of which 430 were granted leave, and 5545 applications for leave to appeal against sentence, of which 1426 went to appeal. The percentage rates of success on appeal were 30% for conviction appeals and nearly 68% for sentence appeals.

---

[21] Access to Justice Act, s 55(1) and Civil Procedure Rules Part 52.13
[22] see *R v Cooper* [1969] 1 QB 267, CA

39   The main issues raised by contributors to the Review on the question of appeal at this level were: first, whether challenges by way of case stated or judicial review to the Crown Court's decisions, when acting as a court of first instance, should be subsumed in a general right of appeal to the Court of Appeal; second, as to the composition of the Court of Appeal, in particular, whether it should it be composed differently according to the seriousness and difficulty of appeals; third, whether a single judge of the Court of Appeal, who normally deals with applications for leave to appeal, should be given greater powers of 'case management'; and fourth, whether there should be changes in the Court's working practices and procedures.

40   Appeals from the Crown Court "in matters relating to trial on indictment" lie to the Court of Appeal (Criminal Division), either on the certificate of the trial judge that the case is "fit for appeal" or, more usually, with the leave of a single judge of the appellate court. On the hearing of the appeal, the 'Full Court' normally consists of a Lord Justice, who presides, and two High Court Judges of the Queen's Bench Division or a Lord Justice, a High Court Judge and Circuit Judge acting as a Judge of the Court.[23] From time to time when the list consists entirely of short sentence appeals the Court may be constituted by two High Court Judges or one High Court Judge and one Circuit Judge appointed to act as a Judge of the Court.

41   Challenges to Crown Court decisions in matters not "relating to trial on indictment" cannot presently be made to the Court of Appeal, but go the High Court on appeal by way of case stated or judicial review. As I have indicated, those are also the present procedures for challenging decisions of the Crown Court in its appellate capacity.[24] However, when the Crown Court sits as a court of first instance, there are sometimes difficulties in drawing the line between matters that do and do not relate to a trial on indictment. In *Re Smalley* in 1985[25] Lord Bridge of Harwich stated that matters that relate to a trial on indictment extend beyond decisions taken during the actual course of a trial on indictment and cover all decisions "affecting the conduct of the trial", including those taken at a pre-trial stage.

42   The intention seems to have been that the course of trials on indictment should not be interrupted or delayed by recourse to the High Court in respect of decisions relating to them, but should await determination by the Court of Appeal on appeal against conviction or sentence.[26] However, a large body of case law has built up as to what and what does not satisfy the test, engaging the House of Lords in a number of cases. For example, a decision not to

---

[23] under the Supreme Court Act 1981, s 9

[24] Supreme Court Act 1981, ss 28 and 31

[25] *Re Smalley*, [1985] A.C. 622

[26] *R. v Manchester Crown Court and others, ex p DPP* (1994) 98 Cr App R 461, per Lord Browne-Wilkinson at pp 463-467

prosecute, a forfeiture of a surety's recognisance for bail, binding over an acquitted person to keep the peace or discharging a restriction on publication of material that might lead to the identification of a juvenile do not satisfy it because they have no bearing on the conduct of trial and are, therefore, amenable to challenge by judicial review. On the other hand, an order that an indictment should lie on the file or direction as to the order of trials do satisfy the test and are challengeable only by appeal to the Court of Appeal. The law on this matter is needlessly imprecise and the Divisional Court has recently called for its reconsideration by Parliament.[27]

43   In my view, appeals from the Crown Division (Crown Court) in all criminal matters, whether relating to trial on indictment or not, should go where they properly belong, to the Court of Appeal. The same should apply to appeals from the District Division. As I have recommended, the Court of Appeal for this purpose, should be invested, so far as is necessary, with the High Court's powers on appeals by way of case stated or judicial review. Under my proposals, therefore, appeals would lie to the Court of Appeal from the new District and Crown Divisions, on their certification or with leave from the Court under broadly the same regime as it now hears appeals from the Crown Court.

44   I should add that, just as I considered and rejected the possibility of an appeal from the Magistrates' Division to the District Division, so also have I considered and rejected the notion of an appeal from the District Division to the Crown Division. That is because they would both have a first instance jurisdiction in indictable cases. And, under the flexible use of judges in the new three tier system of jurisdiction I propose, they could in certain cases be presided over by the same level of judge. Thus, according to the seriousness of the case, including grave offences by young offenders, the presiding judge in a District Division court could be a High Court Judge, Circuit Judge, Recorder or District Judge. With such contiguity of jurisdiction and judicial overlap, it is clear that appeal from the District Division should lie only to the Court of Appeal.

> **Accordingly, I recommend that where it is sought to challenge the decision of the Crown Division (Crown Court) as a court of first instance or of the District Division:**
>
> - **there should be no right of challenge to the High Court by appeal by way of case stated or claim for judicial review; and**
>
> - **instead, appeal should lie only to the Court of Appeal under its general appellate jurisdiction enlarged, if**

---

[27] *R. v Manchester Crown Court, ex p H and D* [2000] Cr App R 262, DC

and as necessary, to cover matters presently provided by the remedies of appeal by way of case stated or of claim for judicial review - and for which the Court should be suitably constituted.

Defendants' appeals

45 The vast majority of appeals are defendants' appeals against conviction or sentence. As I have said, the sole ground on which the Court can and must allow an appeal against conviction is if they think it is "unsafe". If not, they must dismiss it.[28] If the Court allows an appeal by quashing a conviction they may order a retrial where the interests of justice require it.[29]

46 On an appeal against sentence the Court, "if they consider that the appellant should be sentenced differently" from below, may quash the sentence and substitute for it such sentence or order "as they think appropriate for the case". This power is subject to two qualifications, the substituted sentence or order must be one that the court below would have had power to impose and, "taking the case as a whole" must not be more severe than the sentence or order appealed against. As I have said, the Court may allow an appeal against sentence in four circumstances: where it was wrong in law; where it was passed on a wrong factual basis; where the court below improperly took certain matters into account or did not take into account matters then before it, or which have subsequently emerged; or when it was wrong in principle or "manifestly excessive". The last is the most common complaint.

Prosecution rights of appeal

47 There is no general prosecution right of appeal against acquittals, rulings staying prosecution as an abuse of process or, as they occur, rulings of law or of inadmissibility of evidence likely to result in an acquittal. The only three current instances of the prosecution's right to appeal decisions adverse to it are: with leave, rulings of law or as to the admissibility of evidence in preparatory hearings in serious fraud cases or other long or complicated cases,[30] against 'tainted' acquittals, that is, where a person is convicted of interference with or intimidation of a juror or witness in the trial leading to the acquittal,[31] and, by Attorney General's reference, against unduly lenient

---

[28] Criminal Appeal Act 1968, s 2(1)

[29] ibid, s 7

[30] Criminal Justice Act 1987, s 9(11) and Criminal Procedure and Investigations Act 1996, s 35(1)

[31] Criminal Procedure and Investigations Act 1996, ss 54 –57; a provision which, since its introduction on 15 April 1997 has remained un-used

sentences.[32] The Attorney General may also refer an acquittal or removal of a case from the jury to the Court of Appeal for its opinion, or for reference to the House of Lords, on a point of law.[33]

48 The Runciman Royal Commission, rejected, rather cursorily, the notion of any general right of appeal against acquittals.[34] Sir William Macpherson of Cluny in his Report on the Stephen Lawrence Inquiry, recommended that consideration be given to empowering the Court of Appeal to permit prosecution appeals after acquittal where "fresh and viable" evidence is presented.[35] The Home Affairs Committee of the House of Commons, in its Third Report of the 1999-2000 session, expressed the view that there was a strong case for relaxation of the double jeopardy rule in two circumstances: first, where there is new evidence that makes the previous acquittal unsafe; and second, where the offence is sufficiently serious for a life penalty to be available on conviction and where the Attorney General considers it in the public interest to apply for the acquittal to be quashed.[36]

49 The Law Commission, in its recent report, *Double Jeopardy and Prosecution Appeals*,[37] has proposed statutory reform, as part of a codification exercise, to give the Court of Appeal power to set aside an acquittal, but for murder only,[38] in cases where there is apparently reliable and compelling new evidence of guilt and it is in the interests of justice to do so. It also recommended that the prosecution, in the more serious types of case,[39] should be able to appeal rulings before trial, during the hearing of the prosecution case and of no case to answer under the first limb of the rule in *R v Galbraith*,[40] which have resulted in termination of the trial ('terminating rulings'). It recommended the preservation of, and certain extensions to, the existing rights of appeal enjoyed by both sides in preparatory hearings in serious fraud and other long or complex cases, whether or not they are terminating rulings, and some changes to the tainted acquittal procedure. The Law Commission expressly excluded from its recommendations a prosecutor's right of appeal against judicial misdirections that may result in acquittal by a jury. The Government, in its February 2001 policy paper, *The Way Ahead*, published a few days before the Law Commission's Report, expressed interest in prosecution rights of appeal against acquittal and

---

[32] see paras 69-72 below

[33] see para 68 below

[34] *Royal Commission on Criminal Justice*, Chapter 10, paras 75 and 76

[35] *Report on the Stephen Lawrence Inquiry*, recommendation 38

[36] see its *Third Report for the 1999-2000 Session*, (The Stationery Office), paras 39-41 and 21-24

[37] March 2001, Law Com No 267, recommendation 1, p 122

[38] also genocide consisting in the killing of a person, and (if and when the Law Commission's recommendations on involuntary manslaughter are implemented) reckless manslaughter

[39] ie all indictable-only cases and such other offences as are or may be prescribed by order for the purpose an unduly lenient sentence reference; see paras 7.79-7.85

[40] (1981) 73 Cr App R 124, CA; namely that the prosecution has called no evidence of one or more elements of the offence

terminating rulings and an enhanced prosecution role in sentencing procedures, including appeals.[41]

50   The Law Commission's proposals, if implemented, would make inroads on our hallowed common law doctrine of *autrefois acquit* or, as it is more commonly called, the rule against double jeopardy, under which no-one may be put in peril of conviction twice for the same offence. Like many of our principles of criminal law, it has its origin in harsher times when trials were crude affairs affording accused persons little effective means of defending themselves or of appeal, and when the consequence of conviction was often death. Thus, in Hawkins' *Pleas of the Crown*[42] it is said that it is founded on the maxim "that a man shall not be brought into danger of his life for one and the same offence more than once".

51   The doctrine, in its application to an acquittal, is not absolute and, as a matter of common sense, should not be so. As I have said in Chapter 1, adopting Professor Ashworth's analysis, the general justifying aim of the administration of criminal justice is to control crime by detecting, convicting and duly sentencing the guilty. It is not part of that aim, simply a necessary incident of it, that the system should acquit those not proved to be guilty. If there is compelling evidence, say in the form of DNA or other scientific analysis or of an unguarded admission, that an acquitted person is after all guilty of a serious offence, then, subject to stringent safeguards of the sort proposed by the Law Commission, what basis in logic or justice can there be for preventing proof of that criminality?[43] And what of the public confidence in a system that allows it to happen?

52   To permit reopening of an acquittal in such a circumstance is not inconsistent with the International Covenant on Civil and Political Rights 1966[44] or with the European Convention of Human Rights.[45] Both provide that no-one shall be tried a second time for an offence of which he has been 'finally' convicted or acquitted "in accordance with the law and penal procedure" of each state. And both accommodate the reopening of criminal proceedings in exceptional circumstances. Indeed, the ECHR expressly provides for the reopening of cases in accordance with provisions of domestic law where there is evidence of newly discovered facts or if there was a fundamental defect in the proceedings, which could affect the outcome of the case.

---

[41] *The Way Ahead*, paras 3.53-3.56

[42] 7th ed, Vol IV, p 311

[43] for a powerful expression of the thought behind this question, see Professor Ian Dennis, *Rethinking Double Jeopardy: Justice and Finality in the Criminal Process* [2000] Crim L R 933, at 945

[44] Article 14(7)

[45] Protocol 7, Article 4; the Government has not yet ratified Protocol 7, but has expressed its intention to do so

53   There are also a number of Commonwealth statutory precedents for
        prosecution appeals from trials on a point of law and against decisions to stay
        proceedings or to quash indictments.[46]   And, as I have mentioned, in this
        country there are already some inroads on the principle, if not always in the
        formal expression of the rule. There may be a re-trial in a magistrates' court
        following a successful prosecution appeal to the Divisional Court by way of
        case stated or, exceptionally, by way of judicial review. Where the defendant
        initially sets the appeal process in motion, the House of Lords may restore a
        conviction or order a re-trial following a conviction that it has set aside and
        annulled.[47]   And the prosecution may appeal a 'tainted' acquittal where a
        person is convicted of interference with or intimidation of a juror or witness in
        the trial leading to the acquittal.

54   I support the general thrust of the Law Commission's proposals for statutory
        reform and codification of the law of double jeopardy. They seem to me to
        give proper weight to justice in individual cases whilst, in the criterion of
        exceptionality, to take account of and reasonably limit their impact on the
        principle of 'finality' of decisions and the anxiety and insecurity to defendants
        and others involved in the process. Indeed, in the last respect, they seem to
        me to involve no greater burden than is already a feature of retrial after jury
        disagreement or when ordered on appeal against conviction. I also support
        the Law Commission's view that the decision whether fresh evidence justifies
        reopening the prosecution should be for the Court of Appeal, as it is in
        appeals against conviction based on fresh evidence received under section 23
        of the Criminal Appeal Act 1968.

55   Some have expressed concern that such a relaxation of the general rule might
        encourage laxity of police investigation because investigators would rely on
        the prospect of a second trial if the first went badly.   I doubt whether
        investigating police officers would regard the possibility of a second trial as a
        reason for not trying hard enough the first time. In any event, as Professor Ian
        Dennis has written, whilst that may be part of the rationale for the general
        rule, it is no reason for not considering a tightly drawn exception to it.[48] And,
        as the Law Commission observed, want of due diligence in investigation is
        one of the factors that the Court can take into account in deciding whether to
        grant leave to appeal.[49]

56   Concern has also been expressed that a re-trial following an acquittal could be
        unfair, given that jurors or some of them might know that the Court of Appeal
        had only directed it because it considered that new evidence against the

---

[46] see Rosemary Pattenden, *Prosecution Appeals Against Judges' Rulings,* [2000] Crim L R. 971, at 972 and 973,
referring to M. Friedland, *Double Jeopardy,* Oxford, (1969), p 979
[47] Criminal Appeal Act 1968, s.33; and see Rosemary Pattenden, ibid,p 293
[48] *Rethinking Double Jeopardy*, at 951
[49] *Double Jeopardy and Prosecution Appeals*, para 4.83

defendant was apparently reliable and compelling[50] or, as the Law Commission put it, because it made it "highly probable that the defendant was guilty".[51] The Home Affairs Committee suggested that a better way to deal with this problem would be to concentrate on the unsafety of the previous acquittal, rather than appear to prejudge the outcome of any new trial by making it conditional on the appearance of probability of a conviction.[52] However, this seems to me largely a matter of semantics or presentation, for only prima facie compelling new evidence should be enough to unseat an acquittal.

57 This is a familiar enough problem. It could be mitigated by enabling the Court of Appeal to impose reporting restrictions on its decision to quash an acquittal, as the Law Commission has recommended.[53] Re-trials take place today without juries being told that they are re-trials. They also take place where, because of great national publicity given to the first trial and related appeal, it cannot be kept from jurors that a previous jury have disagreed or have convicted and their verdict has been set aside. Courts and juries, in the public interest as well as the interests of defendants in individual cases, are expected to cope with it. They do - and juries often acquit despite what has gone before, as the Director of Public Prosecutions noted in his evidence to the Home Affairs Committee.[54] As in many other circumstances where the jury are exposed to potentially prejudicial and inadmissible material, the retrial judge could suitably direct them. In the end, it would be for the jury to determine how compelling the new evidence is, along with all the other evidence in the retrial. I wonder to what extent they would, at the end of the day, be influenced in that exercise by drawing some inference as to why they were there so engaged. It should be remembered too that the retrial judge would also have the power to stay the prosecution if he was of the view that, despite all those considerations, there had been such publicity as would make a fair trial in the particular case impossible.

58 I have, however, two reservations of substance on this part of the Law Commission's proposals. The first is its concept of the public interest, leading it to limit a prosecution right of appeal to cases of murder. It considered public interest both in relation to a right of appeal against an acquittal and against rulings. This is what it said in the latter context in its final Report,[55] referring to its consultation paper, *Prosecution Appeals Against Judges' Rulings*:

---

[50] Professor Ian Dennis in *Rethinking Double Jeopardy*, at 939, has effectively despatched other suggestions of possible unfairness
[51] *Double Jeopardy and Prosecution Appeals*, para 4.69
[52] *Third Report for the 1999-2000 Session*, para 41
[53] *Double Jeopardy and Prosecution Appeals*, para 4.103
[54] *Third Report for the 1999-2000 Session*, para 43; for a recent example of this in Scotland, see the convictions following the decision of the Privy Council in *Montgomery & Coulter v HM Advocate*, The Times, December 6, 2000, PC
[55] *Double Jeopardy and Prosecution Appeals*, para 7.12

"... we tried to identify the main principles and aims which have a bearing on the question whether it would be fair to extend the prosecution's existing rights of appeal. We distinguished two aims of the criminal justice system. One such aim, which we called *accuracy of outcome*, is to ensure, as far as possible, that those who are guilty are convicted and those who are not guilty are acquitted. On the other hand, we pointed out, there is also a *process aim* in ensuring that the system shows respect for the fundamental rights and freedoms of the individual. Accuracy of outcome can benefit either the prosecution or the defendant, depending on whether the defendant is guilty or innocent. **By contrast, process aims by their nature work only in favour of the defendant. They arise out of the relationship between the citizen and the state, and regulate what the state can properly do to the citizen. They reflect society's valuation of the citizen's autonomy and entitlement to be treated with dignity and respect."** *[my emphasis]* [56]

59   The Law Commission clung to that approach in its final Report, whilst acknowledging the prosecution role and that of others, such as complainants, in representing the public interest. It also asserted a need to balance competing interests so as to secure a fair trial, seemingly by balancing the interests of justice with what would achieve a fair trial for the defendant. [57] I am not quite sure what to make of that analysis. But I feel bound to express concern at the Law Commission's seeming confinement of the public interest in its definition of *process aims* to the protection of defendants. [58] The public too have an interest in seeing that the criminal justice system - which is also there to protect them – works, and that it is not all just a procedural game. I believe that the Law Commission's approach in this respect led it to be unduly cautious in ultimately limiting its main proposal to cases of murder.

60   In its consultation paper, the Law Commission had provisionally suggested that the proposal should apply to all cases in which the sentence would be likely to be at least three years' imprisonment. However, it finally confined it to murder for two main reasons. First, it was concerned about the lack of finality and consequent uncertainty and distress that its provisional proposal, if implemented, could have caused to a large number of acquitted defendants. Second, it was uneasy about making too big an inroad on a principle so fundamental to the public's confidence in the criminal justice system as a whole. [59] However, as I have indicated, it appears to have considered that the

---

[56] Law Commission CP 158, Part III

[57] *Double Jeopardy and Prosecution Appeals*, paras 7.18 and 7.19

[58] drawing in part on an eloquent passage in an article by Paul Roberts, *Acquitted Misconduct Evidence and Double Jeopardy Principles, From Sambasivam to Z* [2000] Crim L R pp 952-970, at 954

[59] *Double Jeopardy and Prosecution Appeals*, paras 4.11- 4.22

only or primary interest in this connection is that of defendants. In my view, the Law Commission's retreat, for these reasons, to murder as the sole exception where there is new and apparently reliable and compelling evidence of guilt is hard to justify. What principled distinction, for individual justice or having regard to the integrity of the system as a whole, is there between murder and other serious offences capable of attracting sentences that may in practice be as severe as the mandatory life sentence? Why should an alleged violent rapist or robber, who leaves his victim near dead, or a large scale importer of hard drugs, dealing in death, against whom new compelling evidence of guilt emerges, not be answerable to the law in the same way as an alleged murderer?

61   I can see why the likely three years custody sentence criterion could, in its uncertainty, have been difficult to apply and that, in any event, it was almost certainly too low. As the Home Affairs Committee observed,[60] in theory a relaxation of the double jeopardy rule could apply to all cases, but in practice the public interest in securing conviction of the guilty depends on the seriousness of the offence. My inclination is the same as that of the Committee and the majority of the respondents to the Law Commission's first consultation paper, namely to fix on some objective and clear criterion of seriousness for this purpose, for example, by reference to the type of offence or the maximum sentence available for it. A suitable level of seriousness of offence and clarity of application might be to include in the exception all offences punishable with life imprisonment, as suggested by the Home Affairs Committee,[61] and/or to sentences up to a specified maximum. Professor Ian Dennis has pointed out that the list would then include, in addition to murder, such offences as rape, arson, robbery and wounding with intent to do grievous bodily harm, just the sort of offences "from which victims may justifiably demand the greatest degree of protection, and which figure most often in discussion about the merits of a new exception".[62] It would be for Parliament to decide and specify the offences to which it would apply. I sympathise with the Law Commission's unease about identifying the line between those offences that do and those that do not qualify, but such an exercise is commonplace in the criminal law and is capable of a broadly principled approach.

62   For the reasons I have given, I regret to say that I do not understand the Law Commission's reliance on the public interest test, as it has defined it, for confining to murder its proposed exception to the *autrefois acquit* rule. Nor do I see any logic in distinguishing, for this purpose, murder from all other offences, simply because of a "widespread perception" that it is "not just more serious than other offences but qualitatively different".[63] There may be all

---

[60] *Third Report for the 1999-2000 Session*, para 21
[61] ibid, para 24
[62] [2000] Crim L R at 948; see also the editorial in [1999] Crim L R at 927
[63] *Double Jeopardy and Prosecution Appeals*, para 4.30; and see further paras 4.31 – 4.36

sorts or reasons for giving - and legal contexts in which murder should be given special treatment. But that is not a reason for excluding other serious offences from a procedure capable of removing grave injustice in their cases too.

63 The Law Commission has usefully recommended that the personal consent of the Director of Public Prosecutions should be obtained before applying to the Court of Appeal for an acquittal to be quashed on the grounds of new evidence.[64] A number of contributors to the Home Affairs Committee's proceedings, to the Law Commission's consultation exercise and to the Review, have expressed concern about any inroad on the double jeopardy rule enabling police authorities, disappointed with acquittals, to harass those acquitted with further investigations. The fact that they might come to nothing, or not produce fresh evidence that would prompt the Director of Public Prosecutions to challenge an acquittal or the Court to quash it, would not detract from the anxiety and uncertainty that abortive fresh investigations could cause. There is force in those concerns. Adopting with slight variation a suggestion of the Law Society to the Home Affairs Committee, I believe they could and should be dealt with by requiring the consent of the Director of Public Prosecution to the reopening of an investigation and, if he so recommends, by a different police force.

> **Accordingly, whilst I also support the general thrust of the Law Commission's recommendation for the introduction of statutory exceptions to the double jeopardy rule, I recommend that:**
>
> - **the exceptions should not be limited to murder and allied offences, but should extend to other grave offences punishable with life and/or long terms of imprisonment as Parliament might specify; and**
>
> - **there should be no reopening of an investigation of a case following an acquittal without the Director of Public Prosecution's prior, personal consent and recommendation as to which police force should conduct it.**

64 Subject to my recommendations in Chapter 10 for rationalisation of the various present forms of pre-trial procedures, I also support the Law Commission's arguments for extension of the preparatory hearing regime to include appealable rulings on potentially terminating matters such as severance, joinder and applications to quash or stay proceeding as an abuse of

---

[64] ibid, paras 4.98 and 4.99

process.[65] Equally, I support its proposals for a prosecution right to appeal before the close of the prosecution case against terminating rulings and to extending it in this instance to all indictable-only cases and to such other offences as are or may be prescribed by order for the purpose of an unduly lenient sentence reference. There is no good reason that I can see why a defendant should be able to take advantage of a judge's error of law that can be quickly corrected on appeal. If the error is left to go uncorrected and the defendant is convicted and successfully appeals, he and others involved in the case face the possibility and ordeal of an unnecessary re-trial. And if the error is left to go uncorrected and, as a result, he is acquitted, justice is not done. Also, as Professor Rosemary Pattenden has observed,[66] judges at first instance are at present unaccountable to the Court of Appeal for errors that they may make in directing acquittals and other rulings that wrongly abort trials. This can engender a laxity of approach on their part that is damaging for the public interest in that it can encourage them to err on the side of safety against later challenge by defendants of their rulings.

65 Some have expressed concern about the potential for delay of trials if there were widespread use of such an extended right of appeal against judges' pre-trial and trial directions. But if these measures are justified, the fact that they may be well used is an argument in support of meeting a need rather than an argument against doing so.[67] They should all, in any event, be subject to the filter of leave by the Court of Appeal. Appeals against rulings in preparatory hearings do not appear to have caused undue delays in serious fraud cases. The important matter is to ensure that procedures are devised and that the Court of Appeal and its staff are staffed, organised and equipped to deal quickly with challenges to pre-trial and trial rulings and directions so as not unduly to delay or interrupt trials.

Accordingly, I also support the general thrust of the Law Commission's recommendations for:

- **extending the present preparatory bearing regime to include appealable rulings on potentially terminating matters such as severance, joinder, quashing the indictment or staying the prosecution as an abuse of process;**

- **giving the prosecution a right of appeal against an acquittal in certain cases arising from a terminating**

---

[65] for a recent example of problems arising from the present restrictive nature of the power, see *R v G & Ors* The Times, March 30 2001, CA

[66] *Prosecution Appeals Against Judges' Rulings*, at 985

[67] research conducted for the Runciman Royal Commission in the early 1990s showed that acquittals of over half of arraigned defendants who have pleaded not guilty result from an order or direction of the judge; see Rosemary Pattenden, *ibid*, citing 1993 research reported in [1993] Crim L R 95

> ruling during the trial up to the close of the prosecution case; and

- giving the prosecution a right of appeal against an acquittal arising from a ruling of no case to answer under the first limb of the rule in R v Galbraith.

Appeals against perverse verdicts

66   In Chapter 11 I have recommended that, in appropriate cases in the Crown Division (Crown Court), judges should be entitled to require juries to return a special verdict, that is, to answer publicly a number of questions fashioned by the judge to the issues in the case. If that recommendation is accepted, the reasoning of the jury would be exposed to judicial and public scrutiny in a way that it is not now. For reasons that I have given, I believe that that would be good for justice and would lead to a system in which the public could have greater confidence. One consequence would be that the open reasoning of juries in their special verdicts could, on occasion, reveal what is mostly undiscoverable now, namely perverse verdicts. These could be verdicts of guilty or not guilty.

67   In those circumstances, it would be vital in the interests of individual justice and public confidence in the system that the defence or the prosecution, as the case may be, should be able to challenge the verdict on the ground of perversity on its terms. This could include, not only internal inconsistencies in the jury's individual answers to the judge's questions, but also inconsistency with the issues or agreed facts in the case. In my view, in such cases, which I would expect to be limited, both the defence and prosecution should have a right of appeal, subject to the usual filter of leave, to the Court of Appeal. There is no great novelty about this in our system. Perverse decisions of magistrates have always been open to scrutiny on appeal, either of the defence or the prosecution, by way of case stated to the Divisional Court. And, now that magistrates are required to give reasons for their decisions, their vulnerability to such scrutiny will increase, whatever the procedural nature of the appeal. Why should juries' verdicts be treated differently?

> **Accordingly, I recommend that where any special verdict of a jury reveals on its terms that it is perverse:**
>
> - **if the verdict is guilty, the defence should have a right of appeal to the Court of Appeal, subject to the usual leave procedure, on the ground that the perversity renders the conviction unsafe; and**

- **if the verdict is not guilty, the prosecution should have a right of appeal to the Court of Appeal, also subject to leave, on the ground that the perversity indicates that the verdict is probably untrue or unfair and such as to merit a re-trial.**

Attorney General's reference on a point of law

68   The Attorney General, following an acquittal or where the trial judge has removed the case from the jury, may refer a case to the Court of Appeal for its opinion, or for reference by it to the House of Lords, on a point of law.[68] However, whatever the outcome of the reference, it does not affect the acquittal. The purpose of the procedure is to clarify the law for future cases. It is limited to cases tried on indictment and has been sparingly used.[69] Its limitation to indictable cases is no doubt in part a recognition of the prosecutor's ability to appeal a summary acquittal by way of case stated to the Divisional Court and, thence, if necessary, direct to the House of Lords. Under the revised appellate structure that I have recommended, the prosecutor would retain this ability. If the separate forms of appeal to the High Court by way of case stated and judicial review and to the Court of Appeal were to remain as they are, I would see no reason for removal of the limitation in section 36. However, if, as I have recommended, the three forms of appeal are rationalised and channelled to the Court of Appeal suitably constituted for the purpose, the limitation should be removed so as to preserve and concentrate such prosecution rights of challenge in that procedure.

Attorney General's reference of an unduly lenient sentence

69   The Attorney General may also, with leave of the Court of Appeal, refer to it a sentence of the Crown Court that appears to have been 'unduly lenient', including one not authorised or required by law.[70] This procedure applies to offences triable only on indictment, or to triable 'either-way' offences specified by the Home Secretary.[71] The Court may quash the sentence and substitute a sentence which it considers 'appropriate' and which the court below had power to impose.[72] The Attorney General has made considerable use of this power to refer, and the Court more often than not substitutes a higher sentence.

---

[68] Criminal Justice Act 1972, s 36

[69] see the Law Commission's Report, *Double Jeopardy And Prosecution Appeals*

[70] Criminal Justice Act 1988, s 36

[71] the latter include offences of indecent assault, threats to kill, cruelty to a person under 16 and serious fraud

[72] Criminal Justice Act 1988, s 36

70   On the whole, this procedure appears to be working well, though a significant number of Court of Appeal judges consider that the Attorney General should make more sparing use of the power, reserving it for points of principle of real public interest. In appropriate cases it is a flexible and sensitive way of monitoring undue leniency and giving general guidance to sentencing judges - far preferable to the alternative of introducing highly prescriptive statutory constraints in the form of statutory minima, however qualified.

71   There have been suggestions for extension of the power to *all* offences triable 'either-way' and those triable summarily-only.[73] That suggestion should be considered against the Court's criterion for intervention, namely that there should be some error of principle in the sentence such that public confidence would be damaged if it were not altered. Regard should also be had to the significant discount that the Court allows in any sentence that it substitutes, for the ordeal to the defendant of being brought back before a court a second time. Given both those considerations, I doubt whether there would be much scope for the exercise of such power in lesser offences, given the narrower range of custodial sentencing options available. It might have some application to fines but, as they are always bounded by the defendant's ability to pay, the individual circumstances of the offender would often intrude on any exercise of comparing the fine imposed with some notional 'right' level of fine.

72   It seems to me that the better course is to look to the general levels of sentencing in such cases established or approved by the Court of Appeal, to the Judicial Studies Board in its training of judges and magistrates and to the Magistrates' Association in their sentencing guidelines to influence on a general basis any obvious under-sentencing in lesser offences. I advise strongly against any attempt to deal with the question by further statutory prescription, setting tariffs of minimum sentences and the like. Accordingly, I do not recommend extension of the Attorney General's power to refer to the Court of Appeal sentences that he considers are unduly lenient to *all* offences triable 'either-way' and/or those triable summarily-only.

---

[73] Penny Darbyshire, *An Essay on the Importance and Neglect of the Magistracy* [1997] Crim L R 627, at 634

PROCEDURE ON APPEALS TO THE COURT OF APPEAL[74]

Obtaining leave and preparing for appeal

73   Leave must be sought for appeals to the Court of Appeal, initially to a single judge of the Queen's Bench and usually in writing. If the single judge refuses leave the applicant may renew his application orally, or in writing if unrepresented, to the Full Court who, if they grant leave, may continue with the hearing as the determination of the appeal. The test for the grant of leave to appeal against conviction or sentence is whether the single judge, or the Full Court as may be, consider that the appeal is 'reasonably arguable'. In the case of an appeal against conviction this is sometimes put as whether the Court feels there is a need to hear the prosecution on the merits. A notice of appeal or of application for leave to appeal must be given within 28 days of the determination appealed against, a period that the Court or the Registrar may extend before or after its expiry.[75]

74   Each Queen's Bench Judge who sits in the Court of Appeal has a regular allotment of paper applications for leave to appeal - normally about 14 a month. This is an essential and invaluable filter to the work of the Full Court. The applications may vary considerably in complexity. Some may take a half an hour or so to read and to write a short determination; others, in particular, appeals against conviction in long and complex trials, could take up to a day or more. With the advent of human rights as a backcloth to many appeals, this filtering process is likely to become more demanding and important. The judges are required to do this work out of normal court sitting hours and in addition to their preparatory work for each day's sitting. Sometimes there is time to do them in the cracks of the day when a case 'goes short', but the norm is that they do them in the evenings, sometimes over the weekend and during vacation periods. In my view, they should be allowed time to deal with them in chambers as part of their regular sitting plan.

I recommend that single judges of the Court of Appeal should be allowed time to consider and determine written applications for leave to appeal against conviction or sentence in chambers as part of their regular sitting plan.

---

[74] see generally the Criminal Appeal Office's *Guide To Proceedings In The Court Of Appeal (Criminal Division)* February 1997
[75] Criminal Appeal Act 1968, ss 18 and 31A, as amended by Criminal Appeal Act 1995, s 6

75   In addition to the grant of leave, each single judge has a number of other, but limited, powers to give directions connected with the appeal, including extension of time for service of notice of appeal or of application for leave to appeal, to allow an appellant to be present at any proceedings, to order a witness to attend for examination, to grant, vary or revoke bail pending appeal and for removal of the anonymity of a complainant in a sexual offence.[76] There is a strong case for reviewing and extending the powers exercisable by the single judge; too many matters of a procedural nature are left unnecessarily to the Full Court. These include a power to give directions to enable proper consideration of the application, for example, in a potential appeal concerning the conduct of or towards jurors outside their deliberations, or for the hearing of the appeal. However, even under such extended powers, there should be a right of renewal to the Full Court.

> **I recommend that a judge of the Court of Appeal should be empowered, when considering applications for leave to appeal, to give procedural directions for the hearing of the application or of the appeal that need not trouble the Full Court, subject to a right on the part of the applicant or the prosecution, as the case may be, to renew the application to the Full Court.**

76   Before or once leave has been granted, the advocate for the appellant may, if necessary, 'perfect' the grounds of appeal by reference to the transcript of the relevant proceedings in the court below. The Criminal Appeal Office prepares a case summary for the use of the Court, the factual contents of which are copied to the parties. In appeals against conviction a Practice Direction requires the appellant's advocate to lodge a skeleton argument with the Registrar of Criminal Appeals and to serve it on the prosecuting authority within 14 days of receipt of notification of leave to appeal. And the prosecuting authority is required to respond within 14 days after receipt of the appellant's skeleton. In both cases, the Registrar or the Court may direct a longer period.[77] As I mention below, this Direction is honoured more in its breach than its observance.

77   The effect of all these requirements is to produce much repetition of material for the Full Court on the hearing of the appeal. Included in each judge's case papers filed on behalf of the appellant, there are or should be: his advocate's positive advice on appeal; initial or draft grounds of appeal; in most cases also 'perfected' grounds of appeal; a skeleton argument; sometimes a supplemental or amended skeleton argument; and the Registry's case summary incorporating in outline some of that material. In large and

[76] ibid s 31; and see s 31A which empowers the Registrar of Criminal Appeals to direct extensions of time, order a witness to attend for examination and, where the respondent does not object, vary conditions of bail
[77] Lord Chief Justice's Practice Direction on 15th December 1998 [1999] 1 All ER 669

complicated cases those documents, with their overlapping and varying forms of presentation and accounts of the appellant's case, are time consuming to read and potentially confusing to follow when his advocate refers variously to them in the course of his oral submissions. I believe that it would simplify both the Court's and advocates' task of preparation and conduct of appeals if some of this repetitious and sometimes inconsistent documentation could be reduced to one master appellant's 'brief' for the Court, coupled with an amalgamation of the time limits for service of notice of appeal and skeleton arguments. I have in mind a document that could combine the grounds of appeal and skeleton argument, along the lines now provided for in the Civil Division of the Court of Appeal.[78] Under those provisions a notice of appeal must be accompanied by, or include, a skeleton argument or the skeleton argument must be served within 14 days of filing the notice. But, ideally, the skeleton argument should stand as the grounds of appeal.

I recommend that consideration should be given to combining, or more closely associating in content and time, appellants' grounds of appeal and skeleton arguments, and to making appropriate adjustments to time limits for their filing and service.

Composition and working methods of the Court

78   The Lord Chief Justice is the President of the Court of Appeal (Criminal Division). In addition, there are a Vice-President, 19 Lords Justices and about 46 High Court Judges mostly drawn from the Queen's Bench Division who regularly sit in the Court. There are also about 26 experienced Circuit Judges who are requested to act as judges of the Court, usually for a three week period once a year.[79] As I have said, the normal constitution of the Court is three, the Lord Chief Justice or the Vice-President or a Lord Justice presiding and sitting either with two High Court Judges or with one High Court Judge and one Circuit Judge. Sometimes the Court sits as a two judge court for short sentence appeals, usually consisting of two High Court Judges. None of the judges of the Court has any dedicated legal assistance for the purpose of research, analysis of legal and factual issues or in the preparation of judgments. In this respect, they lack the legal support of judges of most appellate courts of corresponding jurisdiction in the United States or major Commonwealth countries – usually in the form of law graduates of high academic standing acting as their 'law clerks' for a period of one or two years at a time. In the last year or so, some judges have had assistance on a temporary or ad hoc basis from one of a few judicial assistants seconded from the Bar or solicitors firms for short periods, but that is all.

---

[78] see Civil Procedure Rules, 52 PD-016 and 017
[79] under the Supreme Court Act 1981, s 9

79 The Court sits mostly in the Royal Courts of Justice in London. But in recent years it has increasingly sat for short periods around the country in the major cities on circuit. In London the Court sits continuously throughout the year, drawing on judges in rotation in up to six constitutions of three judges at a time. Save for Circuit Judge members of the Court, each of its judges normally sits three times a year for about four weeks at a time. Each constitution normally sits on average about four days a week. The fifth day is intended to give them time to read the papers and prepare judgments for the other four days work in court. It is not enough for those purposes. The average daily list for each constitution is two to three appeals against conviction (depending on their length and complexity), four to six appeals against sentence and a number of renewed applications for leave to appeal against conviction and/or sentence. If the day's list consists entirely of appeals against sentence, between twelve and sixteen are listed. For each judge, to prepare for each day involves much preparatory work, since the norm is for one or other of them, according to an allocation made by the Registry with the agreement of the Presiding Lord Justice, to give an extempore judgement of the Court. Five or six hours preparation a day in addition to normal sitting hours, sometimes longer, and much of the weekend is not unusual.

80 Thanks to the encouragement of Lords Chief Justices of the day and the hard work of the judges and the Registrar and staff of the Court, there has been a fall in waiting times for criminal appeals over the last decade. In the early 1990s, a 22 months' wait for hearing of an appeal against conviction was not uncommon. And appeals against sentence frequently waited for 15 months, sometimes being heard after the appellant had been released from custody. The average waiting time for conviction appeals is now between eight and nine months, including miscarriage of justice cases referred to the Court by the Criminal Cases Review Commission, and for sentence appeals, about five months or a shorter period if the sentence is very short. To many unfamiliar with the system and, even more so with appellate systems of other countries, these averages may still seem too long – and so they are for the wrongly convicted or sentenced appellant.

81 A further significant increase in the number of Lords Justices or High Court Judges and supporting staff to increase the capacity of the Court of Appeal – even if it were feasible to find enough sufficiently qualified and experienced for the task – is not the answer. [80] Nor, as I hope I have shown, would it be possible to speed the Court's work by sitting for longer hours. In my view, rationalisation of the work and working patterns of the judges manning the Court so as better to match their skills and experience to the work in hand is

---

[80] in the last ten years, the numbers of Lords Justices and Queen's Bench Division Judges have risen respectively from 27 and 54 to 35 and 73

what is required. Some of the recommendations that I have made in Chapter 6 for more flexible deployment of Queen's Bench Judges trying crime on circuit should enable many of them to spend longer in London and to give more time to the Court of Appeal. The proposals that I make below for reorganisation of the constitutions and working practices of the Court should, if adopted, make more appropriate use of judicial resources and, over-all, speed its work. In some respects, they may slow it, but with potentially long-term benefits of reducing the number of unnecessary appeals.

82   Before I turn to proposals for change, I should say a little more about the practices of the Court as it is now organised. The judges of each constitution of the Court usually receive their hearing papers from the Criminal Appeal Office Registry about a week before the appeals are listed for hearing. They are expected to read and digest them thoroughly before sitting on the appeals. It is no secret that the judge allotted the task of giving the judgment of the Court in each case will often need to prepare in advance some provisional notes of the relevant facts, issues and law as a reference for his judgment. The volume and speed of the work is such that the judges could not cope if they did not do that. In this task they are helped by the Registry's case summary, which, as I have mentioned, summarises the essential facts of the case, its procedural history, the matters of which complaint is made, the grounds of appeal, any arguments that timely skeleton arguments may have disclosed and brief references to any relevant law. The quality of the summaries is generally very good, but it is not unusual for the judges to have to prepare provisional notes of their own to match the issues as they see them and as developed in skeleton arguments, many of which are served on the Court after the case summary has been prepared.

83   The appeal papers are often incomplete, largely because the parties do not file their papers on time. They may contain differently numbered or composed bundles of case documents, mostly because the parties have not co-operated to provide a single paginated bundle. Late papers and late skeleton arguments or supplemental skeleton arguments, are common, often delivered to the judges shortly before they go into court on the day listed for the appeal. There is rarely any advance notification that a ground or grounds of appeal will be abandoned, though the judges may have spent a considerable time considering it or them as part of their preparation for the hearing.

84   Despite all this, I believe that the judges of the Court manage well in the circumstances, exhibiting a familiarity with the facts and the points of law in issue and despatching the appeals with speed, courtesy and, in general, sound judgments on the law as applied to the cases in hand. However, there are obvious disadvantages in the system that I have described. The first is that working at such speed gives the judges of the Court little time to focus on anything but the application of the law to the particular facts before them. They usually meet for the first time to discuss each day's list for about a

quarter of an hour before going into court to hear and deal with it. It is thus difficult for them to apply and develop the law in a principled and consistent manner. Despite the Registrar's introduction of machinery to alert one constitution of the Court to similar points that have arisen or are about to arise in another constitution, inconsistencies arise or anomalies develop because of the piecemeal and focused way in which the judges have to work. The system is capable, because of these inconsistencies and anomalies, of engendering wrong decisions at first instance and otherwise unnecessary appeals. This is a serious shortcoming in the main judicial institution in this country responsible for declaring and developing the criminal law as well as for applying it. In all but a small minority of cases, the Court is effectively the final appellate criminal court; in the last three years the number of criminal appeals to the House of Lords has averaged only about three a year. I say that without disrespect to the contribution of the House of Lords to criminal jurisprudence, but its coverage of the criminal law, though of great principle and impact where matters reach it, is necessarily patchy.

85   Second, the performance of the judges of the Court of Appeal, in their obvious familiarity with the facts and issues of law in the cases before them, and in the speed with which they despatch them, often suggests to those in court that they have made up their minds before hearing argument in the matter. I believe that, despite the rush, the judges are anxious to allow advocates to make their points and, if the points are good, are prepared to reconsider whatever provisional views they may have formed. But it does not always sound or feel like that to an unsuccessful advocate who has not been given an opportunity to develop his argument or to his client who may feel that his case has not received a full hearing.

86   Third, the Court, as it is presently constituted and in the volume of its work, is plainly overloaded. Even though its judges can cope – just – I do not see why they or those appearing in front of them or their respective clients should have to put up with it.

Reorganisation and reconstitution of the Court of Appeal

87   For all those reasons, I consider that the Court should be reorganised and reconstituted to enable it: first, to concentrate on cases of general significance in which it can declare and develop the criminal law in a principled and more reflective way, so as to provide useful guidance to the courts below; and, second, to apply well established principles or rules of law in a more consistent manner to correct errors and to ensure justice in individual cases.

88   To meet the various criticisms I have levelled at the manner of working of the Court, I consider that it needs reorganising and reconstituting in the following manner. First, the present 'standard' constitution of the Lord Chief Justice or the Vice-President or a Lord Justice and two High Court Judges should be reserved for cases where there is a point of law of general public importance or of particular complexity or public interest. Such cases would also include sentencing appeals calling for guidelines or involving some other point of general principle or very long custodial sentences, over which the Lord Chief Justice or the Vice-President would normally preside. In particularly important and high profile cases, the rare practice of convening a court presided over by the Lord Chief Justice or the Vice-President and two or more Lords Justices and/or High Court Judges should continue to be an option.[81]

89   In addition, I believe that in cases of exceptional legal importance and complexity, the contribution of the Court to criminal jurisprudence could on occasion be strengthened by the involvement in its process of a distinguished legal academic with specialist knowledge and expertise in the subject matter of the appeal. This could be done in one of two ways as appropriate in any particular case: either by appointing an academic to sit ad hoc as a judge of the Court under a suitably amended section 9 of the Supreme Court Act 1981; or by inviting him to submit a written brief to the Court on the point(s) in issue with copies to the parties. In the latter role, his function might be similar to that of an academic lawyer retained by the Law Commission to prepare a consultation paper for its consultative process, or to that of an advocate general in the Court of Justice of the European Court, Luxembourg.

90   For 'straightforward' appeals against conviction or in respect of short sentences, where the law, procedures and principles are clear and the only issue is whether the trial judge has correctly followed them, or where the issue turns on his treatment of the facts, I believe that the Court should be differently and less 'heavily' constituted, in particular, without a Lord Justice. There would be nothing new about that. The present Court's predecessor, the Court of Criminal Appeal, frequently sat as a constitution of three High Court Judges, and the present Court is often composed of High Court Judges in straightforward sentence appeals. Many of the appeals from the Crown Division (Crown Court) and the District Division would be likely to come within this category, as would many cases presently the subject of recourse to the Divisional Court on appeal by way of case stated or claim for judicial review.

91   Some have suggested for this purpose a three judge court consisting of three High Court Judges, or two High Court Judges and one Circuit Judge or one

---

[81] the most recent example of such a constitution was in 1988; *R v Watson & Ors* 87 Cr App R 1, CA (on the 'give and take' direction to a jury)

High Court Judge and two Circuit Judges. Whichever of those combinations might be considered, they would be at least as well qualified by their current trial experience, to deal with matters of practice and procedure as the present Full Court. But, in my view, there would still be an over-provision of judicial talent for the types of appeal that I have in mind. Both High Court Judges and experienced Circuit Judges are a valuable and scarce judicial resource, upon whom many other important calls are made. The former, in addition to trying heavy criminal work on circuit, have other equally demanding responsibilities in their civil jurisdiction and in specialist courts, including the Administrative or Commercial Courts. As to the latter, the 26 Circuit Judges who presently sit in the Court are the most experienced Circuit Judges in the country. All of them are authorised to try murder and rape and many of them are Senior Circuit Judges and Resident Judges. For all those reasons, they are much needed in their own courts and could not reasonably be asked to give more time to the Court of Appeal than they do.

92   Others have suggested there should be a two judge court consisting of two High Court Judges or one High Court Judge and a Circuit Judge requested to act as a judge of the Court. In my view, this would be a more appropriate match of judges for relatively straightforward appeals from Circuit Judges sitting in the Crown Division (Crown Court) and from the District Division.[82] And they could convene on circuit more readily than is now possible, thus reducing the cost and time to the parties of bringing many appeals to London.

93   There are three possible obstacles to the option of a two judge court, but none of them is insurmountable. The first is that that the law does not permit two judge courts in conviction appeals,[83] but if the proposal is otherwise acceptable, that is curable by legislation. Second, some have suggested that there could on occasion be listing difficulties where the Court consists of a High Court Judge and a Circuit Judge and the appeal is from a High Court Judge. By statute a Circuit Judge may not sit on an appeal from a conviction before or a sentence imposed by a High Court Judge.[84] Whilst it might be acceptable to amend the law to enable a Circuit Judge to sit in a three judge court on appeal from a High Court Judge, it would be less so in a two judge court. But I believe that in practice this would not be much of a listing problem. Most two judge court appeals, by their very nature, would come from a District Judge and two magistrates sitting in the District Division, or from a Circuit Judge, rather than a High Court Judge, sitting in the Crown Division (Crown Court). Third, there is the possibility of judges disagreeing,

---

[82] cf the similar suggestion in the Bowman *Report of the Review of the Court of Appeal (Civil Division)*, pp 57-58
[83] Supreme Court Act 1981, s 55(4)(a)(i)
[84] Supreme Court Act 1981, s 56A, as inserted by the Criminal Justice and Public Order Act 1994, s 52

but in that event, the Court could be given statutory power to re-list the matter before a three judge court.[85]

94   The section 31 Judge should be responsible for allocation of cases to the Full Court as variously constituted under these proposals. I do not consider that his decision should be amenable to a formal process of appeal, but the Full Court, if it considers it necessary, should be able to review the allocation before or during the hearing of the appeal.

I recommend that:

- **the Court of Appeal should be variously constituted according to the nature, legal importance and complexity of its work:**

  - **in cases where there is a point of law of general public importance or of particular complexity or public interest, including sentencing cases calling for guidelines or involving some other point of general principle or very long custodial sentences, the Court should consist of the Lord Chief Justice or the Vice-President or a Lord Justice and two High Court Judges;**

  - **in straightforward appeals against conviction, or in respect of short sentences where the law and procedures are clear and the only issue is whether the trial judge has correctly followed them, or where the issue turns on his treatment of the facts, the Court should consist of two High Court Judges or one High Court Judge and one Circuit Judge; and**

  - **consideration should be given to introducing a system under which, in cases of exceptional legal importance and complexity, a distinguished academic could either be appointed ad hoc to act as a judge of the Court or be invited to submit a written brief to the Court on the point(s) in issue.**

- **a single judge of the Court should be responsible for allocation of appeals to the Full Court as variously constituted under these recommendations, subject to review by the Full Court before or during the hearing of the appeal.**

---

[85] as the Court attempted, unsuccessfully, to do in *R v Shama* (1990) 91 Cr App R 138, CA

Practice and procedure

95   For the reasons I have given in paragraphs 78 - 86 above, I consider that the Court, however it is constituted, should 'slow down'. More preparation and judgment writing time should be allowed to the judges as part of their sitting plan. More time should be allowed to advocates to deploy their arguments and to the judges to consider the issues *together* in an unhurried way before and after argument. And, as part of that more orderly approach to the work of the Court, tighter and more rigorously enforced practice requirements should be made of appellants and respondents in their preparation of appeal papers. The Criminal Appeal Rules 1968 and the Registry's valuable *Guide to Proceedings in the Court of Appeal (Criminal Division)* issued in 1997 provide a clear and detailed indication of the procedural steps from notice to hearing.[86] But they say little about court bundles, pre-trial directions and final advance notification to the Court of the 'live' issues in the appeal.

96   In my view, what is needed, initially in the form of a Practice Direction but ultimately in a Code of Criminal Procedure, is a clear statement of what the Court requires in the structure, content and pagination etc. of bundles and the provision of common bundles to the extent possible. I have in mind something like the Practice Directions on court bundles in the civil and family jurisdictions.[87] In appeals of any complexity, there should be provision for pre-appeal hearings for directions before the single judge who granted leave or the Registrar as may be appropriate. And, in all cases the appellant's advocate should be required, not less than, say, ten days before the hearing, to provide the Court with a certificate indicating whether there are any last minute changes that may affect the content or duration of the appeal, for example, whether any grounds of appeal are to be abandoned or additional authorities are to be relied upon. This is all more work for advocates and those instructing them, but it is a discipline to which their counterparts in the civil and family jurisdictions are well used, and no less should be expected of criminal practitioners. They should be properly paid for the additional work; this is another area in which additional cost of preparatory work could produce enormous efficiency savings in court time.

97   Whilst a slowing down of the pace of court work may ease the present heavy workload of the Registrar and his staff, it may also increase it in the greater sophistication in listing and support arrangements that would be necessary for the Court variously constituted according to the nature of its work. In general the Registry has coped remarkably well with the increasing demands made on it in recent years, but from time to time the strain has shown and administrative problems have hindered the work of the Court. It is vital that

---

[86] the Registry proposes to issue a revised edition in early 2002
[87] Civil Procedure Rules, Part 39.5.3 and Practice Direction 52 on *Appeals* (February 2001); and the President of the Family Division's Practice Direction on *Court Bundles* of 10th March 2000

close attention is paid to the staffing needs of the Registry in its work of supporting the Court whatever changes lie ahead, especially having regard to the, as yet, uncertain effect of the Human Rights Act 1998 on its work load.

98   I repeat what I have said in other contexts in this Report: in conviction appeals the Court should support trial judges' robust case management and control of the trial, so long as it has not prejudiced the fairness of the trial over-all and thereby put the safety of the conviction at risk.

99   In appeals against sentence that do not involve any points of law or significant mistakes of fact or as to relevance of facts, the Court, however constituted, should draw back from its present tendency to 'tinker' with sentences passed below.   I say this notwithstanding the present well known criteria for intervention, that a sentence should be 'wrong in principle' or 'manifestly excessive'.   Part of the problem is that when the case has passed the leave threshold and is before the Court, it is too easy for it to slip into an exercise of attempting to determine the 'right' sentence, rather than of concentrating on whether the sentence below is seriously wrong.   The high percentage of successful sentence appeals of nearly 70% that I mentioned in paragraph 38 above may be illustrative of this tendency.   There is also an over-reporting of sentence appeals, which tends to encourage advocates – and the Court if it is not careful - to rely on fine factual distinctions from other reported cases. And there is the manner in which the present Government, and its recent predecessors, have sought consistency – sometimes confused with uniformity – of sentences.   I believe that sentencing is not apt for fine prescription, imposing rigid and potentially unjust sentencing brackets for cases with, often, very different circumstances.   And that is so, whether the prescription comes from Parliament or is attempted by the Court of Appeal itself.   I believe too that more credit should be given than is sometimes done at present to the experience and judgment of first instance judges and magistrates, and also to the greater time and thoroughness they give to their sentencing decisions than is often possible in the Court of Appeal.   With those thoughts in mind, I take the opportunity of citing the following passage from the Halliday Sentencing Review Report.

"Consistency can be recognised through like cases resulting in like outcomes.   The variety of circumstance in criminal cases, however, makes this an incomplete definition, and one which can result in undesirable priority being given to apparently uniform outcomes, regardless of circumstances.   A better approach is to seek consistent application of explicit principles and standards, recognising that these may result in justifiably disparate outcomes.   The goal is consistency of approach not uniformity of outcomes. This makes consistency difficult to monitor but not impossible."[88]

100   There have been a number of suggestions for change. One is for a different formulation of the test for intervention by the Court, for example, that it should only do so where the sentence "is well outside the permissible bracket or general sentencing level for the particular offence". But that is essentially the test that the Court presently applies, or should apply, and has the same elasticity. Another is that the Court should only intervene when it considers that the sentence is at least, say, 25% or 33.3% higher that it should have been. But a rule that the Court should not intervene unless a sentence is at least X% higher than it should have been, would hardly engender public confidence in the system and, depending on the length or severity of the sentence, could operate disproportionately against some offenders. To stop tinkering is probably more a matter of judicial appellate culture that needs firm general guidance and regular reminder from the Lord Chief Justice and/or the Vice-President. In short, the Court should be vigilant not to 'tinker' with the sentence of the court below, but only to intervene where it is wrong in principle, that is of the wrong sort or far too long.

101   A frequent problem for the Court of Appeal on sentence is when an issue of fact arises as to the circumstances of the offence or as to what happened in the court below or since sentence. The prosecution is not normally represented on sentence appeals, and the Court is often hampered by its uncertainty as to the accuracy of matters put to it by the appellant's advocate on his lay client's instructions. In my view, the Crown Prosecution Service should consider on a case by case basis whether to appear on the hearing of an appeal against sentence so as to be able to assist the Court, if required, on matters of fact, including the effect on any victim, or of law.

I recommend that:

- **the Court, however it is constituted, should 'slow down' - its judges should be allowed more time for preparation and judgment writing as part of their sitting plan, and appeal hearings should be less rushed so as to allow advocates adequate time to deploy their arguments and judges to consider them;**

- **the Lord Chief Justice should consider issuing a Practice Direction for the better conduct by the parties of their preparation for hearing, including provision for pre-appeal directions hearings in complex cases, the form and contents of appeal**

---

[88] *Making Punishments Work: Report of a Review of the Sentencing Framework for England and Wales*, (Home Office, July 2001) para 2.21

bundles and advance notification to the Court of last minute changes likely to affect the content or duration of the appeal;

- criminal practitioners should provide a standard of service to the Court of the same level as is presently required of their counterparts in the Court of Appeal (Civil Division) and they should be paid properly for it;

- in conviction appeals the Court should support trial judges' robust case management and control of the trial, so long as it has not prejudiced the fairness of the trial over-all and thereby put the safety of the conviction at risk;

- in sentence appeals the Court should be vigilant not to 'tinker' with the sentence of the court below, but only to intervene where it is wrong in principle, that is, of the wrong sort or far too long in the circumstances; and

- the Crown Prosecution Service should consider on a case by case basis whether to appear on the hearing of an appeal against sentence so as to be able to assist the Court, if required, on matters of fact, including the effect on any victim, or of law.

CRIMINAL CASES REVIEW COMMISSION

102   The Commission, a non-departmental public body, was established in 1997 to review alleged miscarriages of justice in England, Wales and Northern Ireland.[89] It has assumed the former responsibilities in this respect of the Home Office and the Northern Ireland Office.   It is concerned with miscarriages of justice in summary cases as well as those triable on indictment, and refers them to the appropriate court of appeal where it considers that there is a 'real possibility' that a conviction would not be upheld on account of some argument or evidence or, in the case of sentence, some information not raised in the proceedings giving rise to it.   It investigates and reports to the Court of Appeal on any matter in an appeal referred to it by the Court. And it considers and advises the Secretary of State on any matter referred to it as to the exercise of the Queen's prerogative of mercy.

---

[89] established by the Criminal Appeal Act 1995, s 8

103 Four main points about the Commission's work have been raised in the Review: first, the inability of the Court of Appeal to direct the Commission to investigate and report to it on any matter in an application for leave to appeal, as distinct from an appeal itself; second, delays in its handling of the many applications made to it after its establishment, and in the Court of Appeal in hearing and determining references; third, its power to refer old cases; and fourth, its power to refer comparatively trivial cases.

104 Section 23A of the Criminal Appeal Act 1968 empowers the Court of Appeal on an appeal against conviction, but not on an application for leave to appeal against conviction, to direct the Commission to investigate and report to the Court on any matter relevant to the determination of the case and likely to assist in resolving it. There may be instances where the Court might require such assistance at the application stage, and without it, may be obliged to deny leave. In my view, this is a gap in the provision of justice that should be filled by extending the ambit of section 23A to applications for leave to appeal against conviction.

105 As to the question of delay, one has only to read the Annual Report of the Commission for 1999-2000, to see what it has been up against - an enormous number of applications following its establishment and insufficient staff to cope with them. Under the vigorous leadership of its Chairman, Sir Frederick Crawford, it has reduced its initial considerable backlog of work, partly through acquiring more staff, partly through setting appropriate priorities and systems and partly, in the last year or so, as a result of a decrease in the number of applications for a reference. The general tenor of comment in the Review has been that the Commission has been a success. So far, it has referred 128 cases to the Court of Appeal, over 65 of which the Court has considered and, in 47 cases, quashed the conviction or reduced the sentence. However, the Court is barely keeping up with the cases that the Commission refers to it. As I have mentioned earlier in this Chapter, the average period between referral and judgment is similar to that for ordinary conviction appeals, nine months, which is far too long, especially for cases that have come to the Court by such a route. If my recommendations for reorganisation of the Court are adopted, it should be better equipped to reduce this lengthy waiting time.

106 As to the age of some of the cases that the Commission has referred, the Court of Appeal has recently called for urgent consideration of the ambit of the Commission's power to refer a conviction whenever it had taken place.[90] Once a reference has been made to the Court it has no option, however old the case, but to declare the conviction unsafe if it results from a change in the common law since trial deemed on judgment to be retrospective, as distinct in

---

[90] *R v Kansal*, The Times, 11th June 2001

the ordinary way from statutory changes or of a breach of convention rights before the Human Rights Act 1998 came into force.[91] The problem for the Court of Appeal is that its established law and practice until now has been not to reopen convictions because of a change in the law since trial. The answer may be, as some contributors to the Review have suggested, to amend the 1995 Act to introduce a time limit or simply to require application of the law in force at the time of conviction. The latter seems to me the more logical course.

107 As to the ability of the Commission to refer cases however trivial, there have been one or two examples of that recently, and some concern has been expressed whether it is an appropriate use of the Commission's or appellate courts' stretched resources given the Commission's own declared priorities in favour of those in custody, those who are old or in ill-health where there is a possibility of deterioration of evidence and cases believed to be of particular significance for the criminal justice system.[92] However, the Commission has a wide statutory discretion to refer convictions of offences tried on indictment and summarily[93] and is better placed than I am to assess priorities over that range and in individual cases. I do not think it appropriate for me even to attempt to form a view on this issue.

I recommend that:

- **section 23A of the Criminal Appeal Act 1968 should be amended to extend the Court of Appeal's power to direct the Criminal Cases Review Commission to investigate and report on a matter on appeal, to a matter in an application for leave to appeal; and**

- **on any reference by the Commission to the Court of Appeal or the Crown Court of a conviction or sentence, those courts should apply the law in force at the time of conviction or sentence as the case may be.**

SENTENCING ADVISORY PANEL

108 The Panel was established under sections 80 and 81 of the Crime and Disorder Act 1998 and began work in July 1999. It is an independent, advisory and consultative non-departmental public body sponsored by the Home Office and the Lord Chancellor's Department. Its Chairman is Professor Martin Wasik and there are about 12 other members drawn from

---

[91] *R v Lambert* [2001] UKHL, 5th July 2001, not following *R v DPP, ex p Kebilene* [2000] 2 AC 326
[92] *Criminal Cases Review Commission Annual Report 1999-2000*, p 22
[93] Criminal Appeal Act1995, ss 9 and 11

academe and various disciplines serving the criminal justice system. The Act empowers the Panel to make proposals to the Court of Appeal of its own choice as well as in response to a reference from the Court or a direction from the Home Secretary, but only in relation to "a particular category of offence". The Act requires the Court, when framing or revising sentencing guidelines, to have regard, *inter alia*, to the Panel's views and to frame and include any resultant guidelines in a judgment of the Court in a case under appeal.

109   As the Panel has itself observed,[94] one of the reasons for its establishment was to provide a broader input into sentencing guidelines through the experience and expertise of its members and also through its own consultative process. The Panel has made a good start, albeit that the majority of its proposals to date have been on its own initiative since, with or without the provisions of the 1998 Act, the Court of Appeal can only issue sentencing guidelines through the medium of a judgment in an appropriate case on appeal before it. The Panel has made proposals on the following categories of offences: environmental offences (on which the Court of Appeal has decided not to issue a guideline); offences involving offensive weapons (not yet the subject of guideline); importation and possession of opium (now part of a Court of Appeal guideline judgment); racially aggravated offences (adopted in a Court of Appeal guideline judgment); and handling stolen goods (adopted in a Court of Appeal guideline judgment). And it is now in the course of preparing final proposals for domestic burglary.

110   Despite this good start, my view is that the remit of the Panel, limited as it is to proposing guidelines for particular categories of offences, is too narrow and fails to make full use of its talents and consultative machinery. I consider that it should have a wider responsibility, enabling it to consider and advise on general principles of sentencing, in particular as to the courts' use of the various sentencing options available to them regardless of the category of offence. I also consider that the Court of Appeal would be able to work more closely with and respond more speedily to the Panel's advice if it were empowered to issue guidelines without having to tie them to a specific appeal before it. In Chapter 1, I have proposed that we should build on the Law Commission's recent initiative in consolidating sentencing legislation by general codification of our sentencing law and practice, and have suggested that a standing body should be responsible for undertaking this work, under the oversight of the Criminal Justice Council. I believe that we should make a start by amending the law to allow the Panel and the Court a freer rein in devising, as part of the codification exercise, some general principles and guidelines for categories of cases and sentencing options across the full range of offences.[95]

---

[94] *Annual Report for 1 April 2000 – 31 March 2001*, p 7
[95] this is a personal view, first expressed in a paper given at the 19th Annual Conference of the Statute Law Society, 17th October 1999, *Do We Need A Sentencing Code?*

111   It follows that I strongly support the recommendation in the Halliday Sentencing Review[96] for a statutory framework in the form of a Penal Code, the incorporation into it of sentencing guidelines, the establishment of a new body for the purpose and widening the remit of the Sentencing Advisory Panel to provide more general advice on sentencing issues, including draft guidelines.

Accordingly, I recommend that:

- **the law should be amended to widen the remit of the Sentencing Advisory Panel to include general principles of sentencing, in particular as to the courts' use of the various sentencing options available to them regardless of the category of offence; and**

- **the law should be amended, to enable the Court of Appeal to work more closely with and respond more speedily to the Panel's advice, by empowering it to issue guidelines without having to tie them to a specific appeal before it.**

APPEALS TO THE HOUSE OF LORDS

112   As I have said, the composition and the workings of the Appellate Committee of the House of Lords have not been at the centre of the Review, and I have not felt it appropriate for me to look closely at them in the context of only part of its jurisdiction – and a small part at that. In the years 1998 to 2000 it dealt with only ten criminal appeals against 183 civil appeals. The Judicial Committee of the Privy Council has dealt with many more criminal cases from the Commonwealth. As the authors of a study in 2000 have observed, the combination of recent legislation in the form of the Human Rights and 'Devolution' Acts are likely to increase the case load for the common membership of the Appellate and Judicial Committees, and reform of either will necessarily affect the other.[97] Consideration of such fundamental constitutional reform is for others.[98] There are, however, a few matters of practicality that have arisen in the Review that it may be helpful for me to record and, on some of which, to make recommendations.

---

[96] *Making Punishments Work* paras 0.22-023 and recommendations 41 - 43
[97] *What Do the Top Courts Do?*, Andrew Le Sueur and Richard Cornes, School of Public Policy, University College London, (June 2000)
[98] a start is being made by the above authors, funded by the Economic and Social Research Council and the British Academy with a view to developing a detailed and costed outline for a new structure for the United Kingdom's 'top courts'

113 First, a basic summary of the Appellate Committee's criminal jurisdiction. An appeal lies from the Court of Appeal, (Criminal Division) to the House of Lords at the instance of a defendant or a prosecutor where the Court has certified a point of law of general public importance and where either the Court or the House grants leave.[99] Similar provision is made for an appeal from the Divisional Court in a criminal cause or matter direct to the House of Lords. The Committee hears no criminal appeals from Scotland, where the Inner House is the final court of appeal.

Academic assistance to the Appellate Committee

114 As in the case of the Court of Appeal, I believe consideration should be given to introducing a system under which, in cases of exceptional legal importance and complexity, a distinguished academic in the field of criminal law in question could be invited to assist an Appellate Committee, say, by the submission of a written brief with copies to the parties. But for the present requirement that membership of this 'top court' should be combined with membership of the House of Lords, I would also recommend, as I have done for the Court of Appeal, legislation to enable an academic to sit as an ad hoc member of it where appropriate. If the Court of Appeal is to have such assistance then so should the ultimate appellate tribunal if it requires it.

The ratio of House of Lords judgments

115 A number of contributors to the Review have expressed concern about the difficulty of determining the ratio of the Appellate Committee's decisions. This is because of the modern tendency for them to be contained in a number of speeches which, even when unanimous or in a majority, may use different or differently nuanced routes to the same end. It would clearly assist the clarity of the criminal law and its application in the courts if there were to be a single speech, if not on behalf of the whole Committee then at least for the majority. The dissentients, if any, should, of course, continue to express their own views. As Lord Justice Rose has noted, in a copy letter provided in the Review, the need for such clarity has given rise to the long-standing practice for the Court of Appeal (Criminal Division) to give only one judgment. Until recently, the Judicial Committee of the Privy Council did the same. And, in the House of Lords, until the last decade or so, most of the 20th century landmark decisions were contained in one or, at most, two speeches. I respectfully record and adopt Lord Justice Rose's concern, and Lord Bingham's view expressed in the Review, that rules made at this level "should be as clear and short and simple as possible" and that "[t]his will be more

---

[99] Criminal Appeal Act 1968, s 33

readily achieved if the majority speak with one voice (or if more than one voice) to the same effect".

'Leap-frog' applications for leave

116 On points of law of general public importance where there are conflicting decisions of the Court of Appeal, or where the law on them is otherwise in such an unsatisfactory state that only the House of Lords can resolve it, there may be a case for introducing some form of 'fast-track' appeal to it from the Crown Division (Crown Court). I have in mind a procedure similar to the 'leap-frog' provisions for civil appeals direct from the High Court to the House of Lords provided by Part II of the Administration of Justice Act 1969. Under such procedure a High Court Judge may, if he considers it an appropriate case and all the parties consent, certify the case fit for an application to the House for leave to appeal. Any of the parties may then apply direct to the House of Lords for leave, and the House determines the application in writing. In criminal cases, to ensure a rigorous filter, the task of certification could be restricted to the trial judge, where he is a High Court Judge, or otherwise to a single judge of the Court of Appeal. I shall not explore the procedural minutiae of this possibility any further, but commend it in principle for further consideration.

Time limits

117 There is a disparity between a defendant and a prosecutor as to operation of the time limits within which each may petition the House of Lords for leave to appeal where the Court of Appeal, having certified a point of law of general public importance, has refused it. Both have 14 days from the decision of the Court of Appeal to apply to it for leave and, if leave is refused by the Court, a further 14 days from the date of refusal.[100] Whilst the House or the Court have power at any time to extend a defendant's time for application for leave, neither has power to do so if the prosecutor wishes leave but fails to apply within time.[101] I do not understand why there should be such disparity and consider that the law should be changed to permit the same flexibility to prosecutors.

I recommend that:

---

[101] Criminal Appeal Act s 34(2); and see *R v Weir*, The Independent, 14th February 2001, in which Lord Bingham expressed puzzlement at the disparity

- consideration should be given to introducing a system under which, in cases of exceptional legal importance and complexity, a distinguished academic could be invited to assist an Appellate Committee, say, by the submission of a written brief, with copies to the parties, on the point(s) at issue;

- on points of law of general public importance, where there are conflicting decisions of the Court of Appeal or the law on them is otherwise in such an unsatisfactory state that only the House of Lords can resolve it, consideration should be given to introducing a form of 'leap-frog' appeal from the Crown Division (Crown Court) to the House of Lords, similar to that provided for civil appeals by Part II of the Administration of Justice Act 1969; and

- section 34(2) of the Criminal Appeal Act 1968 should be amended to empower the House of Lords and Court of Appeal, as the case may be, to extend the time within which a prosecutor may apply for leave to appeal, as it does in the case of a defendant.

APPENDIX I

LIST OF CONTRIBUTORS - INDIVIDUALS

Mr M R Adamson
Mr N Addison
Mr R Ager
The Hon Mr Justice Aikens
Mr W T Alden
Mr H C Alexander
Mr S S Allen
Professor A Allot
Mr C Amos
Mr M A Ansell
Mrs J Anstis
Mr F Apfel
Ms P Appleby JP
Mr I E Argyle
Ms A Arnold
Ms G Ashworth, JP
The Hon Mr Justice Astill
Mr B Atherton
Mr M Auchincloss
Miss R Auld
Mr R Bailey
His Honour John A Baker, DL
Mr A Baker
Mr D Baker
Mr L E Baker
Mr S Baker
The Hon Mr Justice Scott Baker
Professor J Baldwin
Mr R Barker
Mr R J Batchelor
HHJ Bathurst Norman (on behalf of
Southwark Crown Court Judges)
Mr M J Batt
Mr K Bayman
Mr B Beard
His Honour Judge Beashel
Mr A Beck
Mrs V Bell
The Hon Mr Justice Bell
Dr R Benians
Mr S Best
Mr D Bethlehem
Lady C Bett
Lord Bingham of Cornhill
Mr D Birrell
Mr J Blackwell
Mr P W Blackwell
Dr R Blenkinsop
The Hon Mr Justice Blofeld
Ms V J Boddington
Mr M L Boland
G C Bond

Mr P D Bradley
Mr P W Bridge
Professor L Bridges
Mr M V Bridgewater
Mr T Bright
Mrs M A J Brockbank
His Honour Judge Brodrick
The Rt Hon Lord Justice Brooke
Mr D Brooks
Mr T G M Brooks
Mr D Brown
Mr K Brown
Mr D Browning
Mr P Brudenell
Ms L Bryan-Brown
The Hon Mr Justice Buckley
Mr J T Bulled
His Honour Judge Burford QC
Mr R Burriss
Mr J Burrows
Mr A J P Butler
Mr I E M Buttress
Mrs L J Buxton
Mr M Cadman
Mr D Calvert–Smith QC
Mr G Carey
Mr G Carey QC
The Hon Mr Justice Carnwath CVO
The Hon N H Carruthers
Professor H Carty
Mr R J Castle
Mrs S C J Cawley
Mr R Chadwick
Lt Colonel Aubrey Chalmers
Mr M Chance
DJ C Chandler
His Honour Judge Chapman
Mr J W Cheeseman
Ms L Chillingworth
Mr G Claeys
Mr R Clancy
Mr T A Clark
His Honour Judge David Clarke QC
Dr K M Clews
Mr J Clucas
Dr J Coker
Mr V Coles
Mr J M Collins
The Hon Mr Justice Connell
Mr A Conrad QC
Mr J Cook
Mr R W Cook

Mr P Cooke
Mrs C A Cooke
Mr B Cooper
Mr G A Cooper
Mr M Cooper
Sir Louis Blom Cooper QC
Mr S G Cornford
Mr R Cory
The Hon Mr Justice Cresswell
Mr M Critchley
M Crookes
Mr M F Crosby
Mr C Cross
Dr K J Cross
Mr R Crosskey
Mr E Crowther
Mr R C Curry OBE TD
Ms S Curtis
The Hon Mr Justice Curtis
Mr F Dacros
Mr J Daly
Miss P Dann
Ms P Darbyshire
Baroness Darcy de Knayth
Mr P W Davidson
Mr B G Davies
Mr G Davies
His Honour Judge Sir Rhys Davies QC
Professor G Davis
Mr J S Davison
Ms M Davison
Mr D De Coteau
Mr C Dehn QC
Ms M C Dellor
His Honour Judge Devaux
Mr R Dobbelstein
Mr P R Douglas-Jones
Mr P Doyle
The Hon J Doyle
Mr D R Drew
Mr J V Duckett
Ms M Dyer
The Hon Mr Justice Eady
Mrs S J Eagle
Mrs J M Earle
Mrs M L Edgecombe
Mrs H Edmonds
Dr M Edwards
His Honour Judge Elgan Edwards
Mr J Edwards
Miss J Eeles
Mr D A Elliot
Mr C W Elston
Mr C Elstub
Mr H Elwes
Mr G M England
Mr J A Epp
Dr Z Erzinclioglu
Mr A J Evans

His Honour Judge Fabyan Evans
The Hon Mr Justice Roderick Evans
Mr D Faulkner
Ms D Fear
Mr A S Ferguson
Mr B Ferris
Mrs G Fielding
Mr M Firman
Mr P J Firth
Mrs K Fish
Mr D R Fletcher
Mr F Flin
Mrs A Foot
Mr T W Ford
Mr R Forrest
Mr A Foster
Mr M Foster
Mr M Fowler
His Honour Judge Fox QC
Mrs L Fox
Mr B France
Mr E J Franklin
Mr C Fraser
Mr R Frey
The Hon Mr Justice Gage
Mr G E G Galletly
Mr D Gammage
Mr J Gammon
Mr C Gardner
The Hon Mr Justice Garland
Mr E S Germaine
Ms F Gibb
The Hon Mr Justice Gibbs
Mr T Gilbert
Mr E Giles
Mr B Gill
The Hon Constance R Glube
Her Honour Judge Goddard
His Honour Judge Goldsack QC
Mr D W Gorman
Mr P S Gourlay
Mr R J Gourlay
His Honour John Gower
Mr M P Green
His Honour Judge David Griffiths
Mr M Griffiths
Dr S Gul
Mrs J M Gulliver
Mr K M Hack
Mr G W Hall
Mr J Hall
Dr S Halliday
Ms P Hamilton Bird
Mr R Hamilton
His Honour Judge Hammond
Mr B Hancock
Mrs M Hanley
Mr J A Hanson
The Hon J Harber-Phillips

Mrs N Harlow
Mrs J Harper
Mr B Harris OBE QC
Mr M Harris
Mr N H Harris
Mr G M J Harrison
Mr J R G Hawes
Miss S Hawkins
Mr N Hayes
Mr R J Haynes
Mr C Headley
Mr A Heaton-Armstrong
Mr K Hellawell QPM
Mr I J Henderson MP
His Honour Judge Heppel QC
Mr G Herrick
DJ P Hewitt
Mr R J Hibbert
Mr M Hill QC
Mr T Hillier
Mrs E L Hine
Mr S Hockman QC
His Honour Judge Hodson
Mr A R Hogg
Mr M Holden
The Hon Mr Justice Holland
Mrs S C Holman
Mr J G Holton
T J Horton
Mr B Houlder QC
Miss S Howard
Mr J J A Howath
The Hon Mr Justice Hughes
Mr A G Hunt
Dr M A Hunter
Mr P T Hurst
His Honour Judge Hyam
Dr A R Hyett
His Honour Hywel ap Robert
His Honour Judge Issard-Davies
His Honour Judge Dr Jackson
The Hon Mr Justice Jackson
Mr A Jacob
Mr G E James
Miss S A Jefford
Mr L Jerman
Mr S John
Mrs J Johnson
The Hon Mr Justice Johnson
Mr G Jones
Mr R L Jones
Mrs A Judge
The Rt Hon Lord Justice Judge
Mr H Karnac
The Hon Mr Justice Keene
Mr A Keily
Mr T C Kellett
Sir Ludovic Kennedy
The Hon Mr Justice Ian Kennedy

Mr I M Kenny
Mr J Kenny
Dr C Kent-Johnson
Mr G Kenure
The Hon Mr Justice Kirkwood
Mr S E Kisbee
Mr D Knight
Mrs E Knight
Mr P Knowles
Mr D Labdon
Mrs C L Lane
Mrs D Lawal
Miss S Lawrence
Ms P Lawrence
Lady Caroline Lay
Mrs A Lee
Mr G L Leigh
Mr S J Leighton
The Hon P J LeSage
His Honour Judge Levy
Dr H B M Lewis
Mr A Lewis
Mr A Linacre
Mr R V Lister
Mrs I Little
Mr A Lloyd Jones
Mr B E Lloyd
Dr S Lloyd-Bostock
Mrs H M Longbottom
The Hon Mr Justice Longmore
Dr J H Loose
Mr J Lord
Mr M Lovett
Ms E Low
Mr A Lowery
Mr C Luckhurst
The Rt Hon Sir Nicholas Lyell QC
Mr A J W Lynch
Mr P Lynch
Mr T J MacAndrews
Mr G Mackenzie
The Hon D K Macpherson
Mr N A MacRae
Mr H Malins CBE MP
His Honour Judge Mander
Mr R Manley
Mr R Marshall-Andrews QC MP
The Hon Justice B F Martin
Mr T Marwood
Mr D B Mash
His Honour Judge Matthews
Mr J Matthews
Miss K May
Mr C May
His Honour Judge McCarthy
The Hon A McEachern
His Honour Judge McElrea
Mr R McFarland
Master McKenzie CB QC

The Hon Beverly McLachlin
The Hon M McMurdo
Mr J Meads
His Honour Judge Mellor
Mr L Messer
Ms J Millan
Dame Barbara Mills DBE QC
Mr P Mitchell
Dr E R Moerman
Mrs M Moon
Dr J M Moore
Mr B Moore
Mr J Moore
The Hon Mr Justice Moore-Bick
Miss I Morgan
Professor R Morgan
His Honour Judge Morris
Professor N Morris
Mr N Moss
Dr K Murray
His Honour Judge Neligan
Mr J Nemes
Mr C Nevick
Mr S J D Newell
Mr A S Noble
Mr K Norman
Mr E F Northcote
Mr P Nyles
Mr P P Oakes
Mr D O'Brien
Mr C P O'Connor
Mr P O'Connor QC
Mr J O'Donnell
Mr F O'Donoghue
Mr W O'Leary
Sir Michael Ogden QC
Mr M Oldman
Mr C R Orchard
His Honour Judge Orde
Mr N Orton
Mrs R Palmer
Mr G E Parkinson
Mr C Parry QC
Mr J D Parry
Chief Justice Paul de Jersey
Mr R Paul-Jones
Mr G R Pearce
Her Honour Judge Pearlman
Mrs P Pearson
Mrs S Pearson
Mr F Pedley
Mr J Penny
Ms J Perry
Mr I Persuad
Mr A Peterson
Mrs M Peterson
Lord Phillips of Sudbury
His Honour Judge Philpot
The Rt Hon Lord Justice Pill

Mr N Pletchy
Mr M Podmore
Mr C Pollard QPM
Mr R Pond
The Hon Mr Justice Poole
Miss A M Pope
Jean, Tony & Louise Pratt
Mr T Price
Mrs L Price
Mr C Pritchard
Mr R Purchas
Mr C Purdy
Mr R Quaife
Mr M Quantrill
Mr D Radlett
Sir David Ramsbotham GCB CBE
Miss T Ranson
Mr D Raspin
Mr B A Rathmell
Baroness Rawlings
Mr J M Rawnsley
Ms M Read
Dr P Reed
The Hon Mr Justice Richards
Mr C S Richenberg
Mr J Rickard
Mr H Riddle
Mr S Rippon
His Honour Judge Rivlin QC
Dr K J B Rix
Mr F Roads
Dr P Robertshaw
Mr W Robertson
Mr D Robinson
Mr R K Robinson
Ms G Robson
His Honour Judge Rodwell QC
Mr J M F Rogers
His Honour Judge Rooke TD QC
Mr A Rosato
The Rt Hon Lord Justice Rose
The Hon Mr Justice Rougier
Mr M Routh
Mr I B Rowan
Mr I Rowing
Mr B Rowland
Mr M Rowley
Mr J Rozenberg
Mrs J H Sagi
Mr Saguall
His Honour Judge Samuels QC
Mr A Samuels
Mr N Sanders
Mr C R Sanderson
Professor I Scott
Mr R Scott-Duhig
Ms J Seal Stewart
Ms H Seddon
Mr P B Setterfield

Mr C R Seymour
Mr R Shallcroft
Mr B Sharp
Mr M Shaw
Ms A Shipp
Dame Helena Shovelton
Ms M Shuttleworh
The Hon Mr Justice Silber
Mr C T Silverthorne
Mr R Simmons
Mr J M Simon
Mrs D M Simpkins
Mr M Simpson
Dr R Simpson-White
Mr F Sinclair
Mr K Singh
Ms M Skilling
Mr W A Smart
Mr B Smith
Mr C J Smith
Mr M Smith
His Honour Judge Smith
Professor Sir John Smith
Mr J Snell
Mrs S Somjee
Ms M Spence
Mr C Stanley
Mr G Staple
Mr R I Starkey
The Hon Mr Justice David Steel
Mr A Stephens
Mr A Stevens
Ms J Stevens
Dr A Stevenson
Mr H Stevenson
Mr J W Stevenson
Mr N Stewart-Lack
Mrs M C Storey
Mr J Suffield
Mrs S Sullivan
The Hon Mr Justice Sullivan
The Hon Mr Justice Sumner
Mr L C Sutherland
Mr J Swan
The Hon Mr Justice C F Tallis
Mr J A Tanner
Ms J Tapley
Mr C Taylor
Mr S Taylor
Mrs M Taylor
T P Taylor
Mrs M Thacker
Mr D L Thomas
Mr W D Thomas
The Hon Mr Justice Thomas
The Rt Hon Lord Justice Swinton Thomas
Mr B Thompson
Mr T J Thompson

Mr P Thornley
His Honour Judge Thorpe
Mr N Thorpe
Mr R M Thorpe
Mr M Tildesley
Mr R Titheridge QC
Ms R Titley
Mrs B M Todd
Mr S Tombs
Mr A R Tomison
The Hon Mr Justice Toulson
The Hon Mr Justice Tucker
Senior Master Turner
Mr D K Uffindall
Mr W J Usher
Mr B Uttley
Mr J A Vagler
Mr R Walduck
Mr A A Walker
Mr K C Walker
Professor C Walker
Mr C G Wall
The Rt Hon Lord Justice Waller
Mr K F Walters
Mr G Ward
Mrs V Ward
The Rt Hon Lord Justice Ward
His Honour Judge Watling QC (on behalf of
Chelmsford Crown Court Judges)
Mr D Watters
Mr D Watts
The Hon C K Wells
Mr T Welsh
Mr M Whincup
Mr G Whitburn QC
Mr I Whitby
Mr P Whitehouse QPM
Mr M Wi
Mr D Wilding
Mr M Wiles
Mrs A Wilkes
Mr J Williams
Ms P Williams
His Honour Judge Wilson
Mr J A Wilson
Ms P Wojciechowski
Mr D Wolchover
Mr R Wong
The Hon Mr Justice J Wood
Mrs D Worlock
Mr D Wornham
Mr T P Wragg
Mrs C J Wurr
Ms J Wynne
Mr H Young
Professor W Young
Professor Zander

APPENDIX I

LIST OF CONTRIBUTORS – ORGANISATIONS

Association of Chief Officers of Probation
Association of Chief Police Officers
Association of District Judges (Magistrates' Courts)
Association of Guardian ad Litem and Reporting Office Panel Managers
Association of Justices' Chief Executives
Association of Magisterial Officers
Association of Police and Court Interpreters
Association of Police Surgeons
Association of Sign Language Interpreters Legal Task Group
Australian Institute of Judicial Administration and the Standing Committee of Attorneys General
Barnado's, Policy, Planning and Research Unit
Barnet Bench
Bath & Wansdyke Bench
Bedfordshire Police
Berkshire Magistrates' Association
Bexley Magistrates' Courts Committee
Birmingham Bench
Brent Borough Criminal Justice Operational Group
Bristol Bench
Bristol Law Society
British Association in Forensic Medicine
British Computer Society
British False Memory Society
British Institute of Verbatim Reporters
British Juvenile and Family Courts Society
British Security Industry Association
British Standards Institute
British Transport Police
Bromley Bench
Bromley Magistrates' Courts Committee
Calderdale Bench
CambridgeshireProbation Service
Campaign For A National Legal Service
Canterbury and St Augustine Bench
Cardiff Bench
Central Council of Magistrates' Courts Committee
Central Buckinghamshire Bench Committee
Centre For Criminological Research and Probation Studies Unit, University of Oxford
Channel Bench East Kent
Chelmsford Crown Court Judges
Cheshire Constabulary
Cheshire Magistrates' Courts Committee
Children's Society
Children's Society, The Wales Advocacy Unit

City of London Magistrates' Courts Committee
City of London Police HQ
Cleveland Magistrates' Courts Committee
Cleveland Police HQ
Commission for Racial Equality
Consultative Committee West Dorset Bench
Council For Registration of Forensic Practitioners
Council of HMCircuit Judges
Court of Appeal New Zealand
Court Service, Bristol Group
Court Service, Chelmsford Group
Court Service, Exeter Group Managers
Court Service, London Crown Court Group
Court Service, Midland and Oxford Circuit
Court Service, Newcastle Group, (Manager's Office)
Court Service, North Eastern Circuit
Court Service, Teesside Group Staff and Judges
Criminal Bar Association
Crown Prosecution Service, Association of Senior Civil Servants
Crown Prosecution Service, HQ
Crown Prosecution Service, Inspectorate
Crown Prosecution Service, Maidstone
Croydon Magistrates' Courts Committee
Department of Justice, Canada
Department of Trade and Industry
Derbyshire Dales District Council
Document Evidence Ltd
Dorset Bench
Dorset Probation Service
Drayton Petty Sessional Division
Dunheved and Stratton Bench
Dyfed Probation Committee
Ealing Bench
East Central Division, Inner London Magistrates'Courts Service Justices
East Derbyshire Bench
East Sussex Magistrates' Association
Embassy of the Federal Republic
Enfield Bench
Enfield Petty Sessional Area Justices
Equal Treatment Advisory Committee of the Judicial Studies Board
Essex Magistrates' Courts Committee
Expert Witness Institute
Forensic Science Society
Forensic Science Service
Formedecon Ltd
Furnival Chambers

General Council of the Bar
General Council of the Bar, Disability
Committee
General Council of the Bar, Sex
Discrimination Committee
General Council of the Bar, Race Relations
Committee
General Council of the Bar, Young Barristers'
Committee
General London Lay Observers Panel
Gloucestershire Magistrates' Courts
Committee
Gloucestershire Magistrates' Courts Service
Gloucestershire Probation Service
Gough Square Chambers
Greater Manchester Campaign Against
Domestic Violence
Greater Manchester Police
Greater Manchester Probation Service
Halsey Meyer Higgins Solicitors
Hampshire Magistrates' Courts Committee
Hampshire Probation Service
Haringey Magistrates' Courts Committee
Herefordshire Fine Enforcement Panel
Hertfordshire Magistrates' Association
Hertfordshire Magistrates' Courts 'Committee
Hillingdon Magistrates' Courts Committee
HM Customs and Excise
HM Magistrates' Courts Service Inspectorate
HM Prison Service
Hodgsons Chartered Accountants
Home Office Inspectorate of Probation
Hounslow Magistrates' Courts Committee
Howard League for Penal Reform
Humberside Police HQ
Humberside Probation Committee
Inner London and City Family Panel
Inner London Magistrates' Courts Committee
Inner London Probation Service
Inner London Youth Panel
Institute of Legal Executives
Institute of Linguists
Institute of Translation and Interpreting
Ipswich Magistrates' Courts Committee
Isle of Man Courts of Justice
Joint Council of Stipendiary Magistrates
Judicial Studies Board
JUSTICE
Justices' Clerks' Society
Kent Magistrates' Courts Committee
Kent Magistrates' Courts Service
Kent Probation Committee
Kirklees Council
Lancashire Bench
Lancashire Constabulary
Lancashire Probation Committee
Law Commission
Law Commission, New Zealand
Law Society

Law Society, Criminal Law Committee
Leeds District Magistrates Court
Legal Action Group
Leicestershire Bench
Leicestershire Magistrates' Courts Committee
Liberty
Lincolnshire Police
Local Government Association
Magistrates' Association
Manchester Magistrates' Courts Committee
Mansfield Bench
Market Bosworth Bench
Marten Walsh Cherer Ltd
McCullochs Solicitors
Media Training Centre
Mediation UK
Merseyside Local Authority
Merseyside Magistrates' Courts Committee
Merseyside Probation Service
Metropolitan Police Service, Strategic
Development, New Scotland Yard
Mid Glamorgan Probation Service
Ministry of Defence Police, Wethersfield,
Braintree
Naborro Nathanson
National Assembly for Wales
National Association for the Care and
Resettlement of Offenders
National Association of Citizens Advice
Bureau
National Association of Probation Officers
National Plant and Equipment Register
National Society for the Prevention of Cruelty
to Children
National Working Group on Fraud
Newcastle Upon Tyne Bench
Newspaper Society
Norfolk Magistrates' Courts Committee
North and West Greater Manchester
Magistrates' Courts Committee
North Port Talbot Bench
North Wales Magistrates' Courts Committee
North Westminster Bench
North Yorkshire Magistrates' Courts
Committee
Northamptonshire Police
Northern Oxfordshire Bench
Nottingham City Council
Nottinghamshire Magistrates' Courts
Committee
Nottinghamshire Magistrates' Courts Service
NSPCC
Oxford and Southern Oxfordshire
Magistrates' Divisions
Oxfordshire and Buckinghamshire Probation
Service
PA Consulting Group
Parole Board
Payback

Police Federation of England and Wales
Powys Magistrates' Courts Committee
Queensland Criminal Justice Commission
Rotherham Magistrates' Courts Committee
Scottish Law Commission
Sentencing Advisory Panel
Serious Fraud Office
Sheffield Magistrates' CourtsCommittee
Shepherd, Harris and Co Solicitors
Shrewsbury Bench
Smith Bernal Court Reporters
Society for Advanced Legal Studies
Society of Conservative Lawyers, Criminal Justice Sub-Committee
Society of Editors
Society of Labour Lawyers
Somerset Magistrates' Association
Sorene Court Reporting and Training Services
South Cumbria Magistrates' Courts Committee
South Hants, Magistrates' Executive Committee of the Petty Sessional Division
South Wales Magistrates' Courts Committee
South Wales Police
South West London Probation Service
South Yorkshire Police, Sexual Offences and Child Abuse Unit
Southampton Bench
Stockport Magistrates' Courts Committee
Stopping Convictions On No Evidence
Suffolk Constabulary
Suffolk Magistrates' Courts Committee
Support After Murder and Manslaughter Centre, Merseyside
Supreme Court Costs Office
Taunton Deane Bench

Teesside Probation Service
Telford Bench
Thames Valley Magistrates' Courts Committee
The Office of the Legal Services Commissioner
Trafford Magistrates' Courts Committee
TV Edwards Solicitors
Uxbridge Bench
Vale of Glamorgan Bench
Values Into Action
Victim Support
Wason and Associates Verbatim Reporters
West Allerdale and Keswick Bench
West Midlands Magistrates' Courts Service
Westgate Chambers
Wigan Magistrates General Purposes Committee
Wiltshire Magistrates' Association
Wiltshire Magistrates' Courts Service
Winchester Bar
Worcestershire Magistrates' Association
Youth At Risk Impact Centre
Youth Justice Board

APPENDIX II

INFORMATION AND RESEARCH PROJECTS FROM OTHER JURISDICTIONS

Australia

Managing complex criminal trials: reform of the rules of evidence and procedure: Mark Aronson, The Australian Institute of Judicial Administration Incorporate, 1992

Jury management in New South Wales, Mark Findlay, The Australian Institute of Judicial Administration Incorporate,1994

Criminal Trial Reform Conference, The Australian Institute of Judicial Administration Incorporate and The Standing Committee of Attorneys General, 24/25 March 2000 (Conference Papers)

Reform of Court Rules and Procedures in Criminal Trials, The Australian Institute of Judicial Administration Incorporate Conference paper, 3-4 July 1998

Anatomy of Long Criminal Trials, Dr Chris Corns, The Australian Institute of Judicial Administration Incorporate, 1997

Shorter Trials Committee: report on criminal trials, PA Sallman, The Australian Institute of Judicial Administration Incorporate and the Victoria Bar, 1985

The conduct of complex criminal trials, The Australian Institute of Judicial Administration Incorporate Report No. 10, October 1989

Australian Judicial perspectives on expert evidence: an empirical study, Dr Ian Freckelton, The Australian Institute of Judicial Administration Incorporate, 1999

Pleading guilty: issues and practices, Kathy Mach, The Australian Institute of Judicial Administration Incorporate, 1995

Information technology in complex trials, Graham Greenleaf & Andrew Mowbray, The Australian Institute of Judicial Administration Incorporate, 1993

Committals Review Committee: report, New South Wales, March 1999

Law Foundation of New South Wales: Annual Report 1999

Review of the Criminal and Civil Justice System in Western Australia, Project 92, Final Report, Law Reform Commission of Western Australia, September 1999

Adducing evidence under privilege: new perspectives on Uniform Evidence Act, 1998, Anthony Lo Surdo, 36(6) Law Society Journal (New South Wales)

Submission to the Honourable Attorney General concerning complex criminal trials, JA Nader QC, New South Wales, 1993

Annual Reports 1997-98 and 1998-99, The Office of the Legal Services Commissioner

Working Group on criminal trial procedure: report, Standing Committees of Attorney General, September 1999

Criminal Trial Reform Conference, discussion paper, Professor Warren Young

Uniform evidence Law – Third Edition, Stephen Odgers, Faculty of Law, Sydney University

The NSW Barristers' Rules, Bar Brief, Special Edition February 2000

Managing complex criminal trials – reform of the rules of evidence & procedure, The Australian Institute of Judicial Administration Incorporate

Incorporating criminal trial reform – joint national commission, The Australian Institute of Judicial Administration Incorporate & Standing Committee of Attorney Generals, March 2000

Deliberation forum on criminal trial reform Report, The Standing Committee of Attorneys General, June 2000

Managing Trial Court Delay: An Analysis of Trial Case Processing in the NSW District Criminal Court, Don Weatherburn & Joanne Baker, NSW Bureau of Criminal Statistics & Research, 2000

Review of the Criminal & Civil Justice System in Western Australia, Submissions Summary, Law Reform Commission of Western Australia

Receipt of evidence by Queensland Courts: the evidence of children, Report No.55 Part 1, Queensland Law Reform Commission, June 2000

Law Reform Commission of Western Australia Annual Report 1998–1999

Review of Criminal & Civil Justice Consultation Drafts, Vols 1 & 2, Law Reform Commission of Western Australia, June 1999

Canada

Setting Judicial compensation: multi disciplinary perspectives, Law Commission of Canada, 1999

Special Commission on Court Restructuring, Report of the Ontario Supreme Court Judges' Association, June 2000

Report of the Criminal Justice Review Commission, February 1999

Ontario Specimen Jury Instructions – Preliminary Instructions, Mid-Trial Instructions 1-17 and Final Instructions 1-41

Criminal Rules of the Supreme Court of British Columbia

Criminal Law Practice Direction (consolidated), Chief Justice Dohm, Supreme Court British Columbia

Criminal Appeal Rules, British Columbia Court of Appeal, 1986

Court of Appeal Rules, Saskatchewan

New Zealand

Changes in international and domestic law which are critical to a borderless world of electronic commerce: an update, Hon Justice Baragwanath, 6 September 1999

Electric commerce part 2, New Zealand Law Commission Report No 58

Magistrates in the District Court, paper by Cabinet Committee on Health & Social Policy, 27 March 1997

Community Magistrates' Bill 1998

Chief Justice of New Zealand: Practice Notes:

- Criminal jury trials caseflow management.

- Sexual offences involving child complainants & child defendants.

- Criminal law: preliminary hearings.

- Serious Fraud Office prosecutions

Criminal Prosecution Report, Law Commission of New Zealand, December 1999

Consultation paper regarding preliminary hearings and criminal disclosure, Ministry of Justice, 27th October 1997

Selection and qualification for jury duty, New Zealand Law Commission

Juries in Criminal Trials Part 2 - Volume 1: a discussion paper and *Volume 2: a summary of research findings,* New Zealand Law Commission, November 1999

Evidence: Volume 1: reform of the Law and *Volume 2: Evidence code and commentary,* New Zealand Law Commission, Report 55, August 1999

Victims' Rights Bill: draft, 29 September 1999

Criminal Prosecution Report, December 1999

Northern Ireland

A new beginning: policing in Northern Ireland, The Independent Commission on Policing for Northern Ireland, September 1999

Review of the Criminal Justice System in Northern Ireland – A Progress Report, Criminal Justice Review Group, April 1999

Review of the Criminal Justice System in Northern Ireland, Criminal Justice Review Group, March 2000

Northern Ireland Court Service Annual Report 1999/2000

Scotland

Charging the Jury: Some notes for the guidance of Judges and Sheriffs, Judicial Studies in Scotland, January 2000

Law Commission Reports on Evidence Nos 78, 93, 120, 125 & 137

Law of Incest, Law Commission Report No. 69

Charging the Jury, Judicial Studies Board Scotland, January 2000

Isle of Man

Summary Jurisdiction Act 1989

Germany

The German code of Criminal Procedure, April 1987

Vietnam

Comparative Legal Exchange Visit – Vietnam, 19th November to 2nd December 2000

The Law On the Organisations of People's Procuratorates, Socialist Republic of Vietnam

United States of America

The Jury Project – Report to the Chief Judge of the State of New York, 31st March 1994

APPENDIX III

CURRENT RESEARCH PROJECTS – ENGLAND AND WALES

Current government research projects and pilots

Accommodation

Internal review of estate and accommodation: Lord Chancellor's Department

Review of judges' lodgings: The Court Service

Pathfinder: A model courtroom: The Crown Court Programme, The Court Service

Case management

Pilots on case progression: The Crown Court Programme, The Court Service

Case management perspectives: the views of judges across jurisdictions in England and Wales, Lord Chancellor's Department research by Joyce Plotnikoff and Richard Woolfson (report expected in 2001)

The applicability to other adjudicative settings of organisational arrangements at the London Parking Service, Lord Chancellor's Department research by John Raine and Stephanie Snape (report expected in 2001)

Children

Electronically monitored curfew for 10 to 15 year olds – report of the pilot, Robin Elliott, Jennifer Airs, Claire Easton and Ruth Lewis. Home Office Occasional Paper, 2000

Evaluation of the Youth Court Demonstration Project, Charlotte Allen, Iain Crow and Michael Cavadino. Home Office Research Study 214, 2000

New strategies to address youth offending: the national evaluation of then pilot youth offending teams, S Holdaway, M Davidson, J Dignan, R Hammersley, J Hine and P Marsh. Home Office Occasional Paper, No69, 2001

Delay

Reducing delay in the criminal justice system: evaluation of the indictable only initiative, Ernst and Young. Home Office Occasional Paper, 2000

Reducing delays in the magistrates' courts, David Brown. Home Office Research Findings 131, 2000

Evaluation of statutory time limits in the Youth Court pilot, Home Office research by a team from Sheffield University, due to report at the beginning of 2002

Drugs

Drug Treatment And Testing Orders – the 18-Month evaluation, Paul Turnbull, Tim McSweeney and Mike Hough. Home Office Research Findings 128, 2000

Drug Treatment and Testing Orders - final evaluation report, Paul J Turnbull, Tim McSweeney, Russell Webster, Mark Edmunds and Mike Hough. Home Office Research Study 212, 2000

Drugs and crime: the results of the second developmental stage of the NEW-ADAM programme, Trevor Bennett. Home Office Research Study 205, 2000

Problem drug use and probation in London, Ian Hearnden and Alex Harcopos. Home Office Research Findings 112, 2000

Human Rights

The impact on courts and the administration of justice of the Human Rights Act 1998, Lord Chancellor's Department research by John Raine and Clive Walker (on-going)

The Judiciary

The effects on magistrates of learning that the defendant has a previous conviction, Sally Lloyd-Bostock, Lord Chancellor's Department research series, 2000

Review of research and secretariat support, House of Lords Appellate Committee

New public management and the administration of justice in the magistrates' court, Lord Chancellor's Department research by Ben Fitzpatrick, Peter Seago and David Wall (report expected in 2001)

The judiciary in the magistrates' courts, Rod Morgan and Neil Russell. Home Office and LCD Occasional Paper 66, 2000

Legislation

An evaluation of the use and effectiveness of the Protection from Harassment Act 1997, Jessica Harris. Home Office Research Study 203, 2000

The Protection from Harassment Act 1997 – An Evaluation of its use and effectiveness, Jessica Harris. Home Office Research Findings 130, 2000

Assessment of Anti-Social Behaviour Orders, Home Office research due to be completed in autumn 2001

New measures for fine defaulters, persistent petty offenders and others: reports of the Crime (Sentences) Act 1997 pilots, Robin Elliott and Jennifer Airs. Home Office Research Findings, 2000

The right of silence: the impact of the Criminal Justice Act 1994, Tom Bucke, Robert Street and David Brown. Home Office Research Study 199, 2000

Procedure and evidence

A study of requests for disclosure of evidence to third parties in contested trials, Alan Mackie and John Burrows. Home Office Research Findings 134, 2000

Evaluation of the operation of disclosure law, Home Office research by Joyce Plotnikoff and Richard Woolfson (final report due for publication in 2001)

Public confidence

Attitudes to crime and criminal justice: findings from the 1998 British Crime Survey, Joanna Mattinson and Catriona Mirrlees-Black. Home Office Research Study 200 and Research Findings 111, 2000

Pilots on provision of information to the public and court users: The Crown Court Programme, The Court Service

The 2000 British Crime Survey, Home Office Statistical Bulletin 18/00

Confidence in the criminal justice system: findings from the 2000 British Crime Survey, Catriona Mirrlees-Black, Home Office Research Findings 137, 2001

Race

Problems of perception and lack of trust, Roger Hood and Stephen Shute. On-going part of LCD Race and the Courts Research Programme

Sentencing

Effectiveness of 1991 Road Traffic Act - sentencing of careless and dangerous driving offenders, Department of the Environment, Transport and the Regions

Enforcement of financial penalties, An LCD/Home Office project to identify best practice in fine enforcement due to report in autumn 2001

Mentally disordered offenders, England and Wales, Home Office Statistical Bulletin 21/00

Professional awareness in sentencers, Ongoing Home Office research

Restorative Justice, An initial review of seven such schemes in England will be published by the Home Office in 2001. (The Youth Justice Board is also evaluating a number of new schemes for juvenile offenders)

Making punishments work: report of a review of the sentencing framework for England and Wales, John Halliday. Home Office, July 2001

Technology

Electronically monitored curfew as a condition of bail – report of the pilot, Jennifer Airs, Robin Elliott and Esther Conrad. Home Office Occasional Paper, 2000

Home Detention Curfew – the first year of operation Kath Dodson and Ed Mortimer. Home Office Research Findings 110, 2000

Pilots on in-court technology (in-court workstation, digital audio recording, voice enhancement for witnesses, electronic presentation of evidence): The Crown Court Programme, The Court Service

Forensic science & technology, Home Office research programme (on-going)

Victims

CPS victim liaison pilots

Public perceptions and victims' experiences of Victim Support: findings from the 1998 British Crime Survey Mike Maguire and Jocelyn Kynch. Home Office, Occasional Paper 2000

The impact of measures recommended in the report 'Speaking Up For Justice' to assist vulnerable and intimidated witnesses give best evidence, research by Liverpool John Moores and Manchester Universities, in conjunction with BMRB Social Research. A date for a final report of the Home Office sponsored project is to be agreed once implementation dates for the measures are decided

Victim and witness intimidation: key findings from the British Crime Survey, Roger Tarling, Lizanne Dowds and Tracey Budd. Home Office Research Findings 124, 2000

Victim Support: findings from the 1998 British Crime Survey, Mike Maguire and Jocelyn Kynch. Home Office Research Findings 117, 2000

Key findings from the witness satisfaction survey 2000, Emmy Whitehead, Home Office Research Findings 133, 2001 (a full Home Office report of survey will be available in 2001)

Research commissioned for the Criminal Courts Review

Evaluation of the composition of juries based on surveys from Liverpool, Nottingham and Durham Crown Court centres

The criminal standard of proof – how sure is sure, Michael Zander

What Can the English Legal System learn from jury research published up to 2000?, Andy Maughan, Angus Stewart and Penny Darbyshire

APPENDIX IV

THE CURRENT WORKLOAD OF THE CRIMINAL COURTS

Overall caseloads

1 In 1999, the courts of England and Wales dealt with nearly two million criminal cases. All of these cases had at least one hearing in a magistrates' court. A minority were subsequently committed, transferred or sent to the Crown Court. The table below shows the level of court at which cases were completed:

Crown Court	97,000[1]	5%
Magistrates' Court	1,789,000[2]	95%

[NB all figures in this appendix have been rounded to the nearest 1,000. Any apparent discrepancies between tables, have arisen because cases are measured at the point at which they are completed by the relevant court. Cases completed by the Crown Court during 1999 may well have been committed or sent there by a magistrates' court in 1998 (or earlier). Also, the category of such a case may change after it has been recorded as leaving the magistrates' court.]

Categorisation of offences

2 All criminal offences currently fall into one of three categories. **Summary offences**, which include most motoring offences and other relatively minor matters such as drunkenness, common assault and prostitution, are triable only in a magistrates' court. **'Either-way' offences**, including theft, drugs offences and some involving violence against the person, are triable either by a magistrates' court or by the Crown Court. And **indictable only offences**, such as murder, rape and robbery, must be tried by the Crown Court. The 1999 caseload (measured at the point at which cases left or were dealt with by a magistrates' court) breaks down as follows:

Summary	'Either-way'	Indictable only
1,369,000[3]	480,000[4]	33,000[5]
73%	25%	2%

---

[1] criminal statistics 1999, Supplementary table S2.1(A) (total for trial + total convicted at magistrates' court)
[2] criminal statistics 1999, Supplementary table S1.1(A) (total proceeded against - committed for trial or sentence)
[3] criminal statistics 1999, Supplementary table S1.1(A) (total proceeded against)
[4] figures provide by RDS (IRS 6599)
[5] figures provided by RDS (IRS 6599)

Summary cases

3   The table below shows the outcomes of the summary cases dealt with by magistrates' courts during 1999:[6]

Defendants proceeded against	Case terminated in advance of trial	Found not guilty after trial	Convicted
1,369,000	281,000	24,000	1,064,000

4   Firm data are not available on the number of defendants who plead guilty in summary cases. Sampling exercises carried out by magistrates' courts and reported to the Lord Chancellor's department during 1999 suggest a guilty plea is entered in around 55% of summary cases.[7] It should be noted that the Crown Prosecution Service, working from a different base, puts the figure substantially higher.

'Either-way' cases

5   Almost half a million 'either-way' cases were dealt with by magistrates' courts in 1999. The outcomes of these cases were as follows:[8]

Defendants proceeded against	Case terminated in advance of trial	Committed to Crown Court for trial	Found not guilty after summary trial	Convicted and sentenced by summary court	Convicted by summary court and committed to Crown Court for sentence
480,000	133,000	51,000	11,000	266,000	19,000

6   Firm data are not available on the number of those defendants who pleaded guilty while the case remained in the magistrates' court. Estimates based on sampling exercises carried out by magistrates' courts and reported to the Lord Chancellor's department during 1999 suggest that this is the outcome in around 50% of 'either-way' cases. It should be noted that the Crown Prosecution Service, working from a different base, puts the figure substantially higher. As explained in paragraph 9, additional guilty pleas were entered later in respect of those cases committed to the Crown Court for trial.

7   As the above table illustrates, around 11% of all 'either-way' cases were committed to the Crown Court for trial. In the majority of these cases (nearly 70% according to CPS statistics[9]), magistrates declined jurisdiction on the basis that their sentencing powers would be insufficient if the defendant was convicted. In the remainder of these cases (ie just over 30%), magistrates

---

[6] criminal statistics 1999, Supplementary table S1.1(E)+(F)
[7] estimated using 1999 Time Interval Statistics
[8] criminal statistics 1999, Supplementary table S1.1(E)+(F)
[9] CPS Annual Report 1999/00

were content to accept jurisdiction, but the defendants elected trial by judge and jury. Overall, therefore, less than 4% of defendants charged with an 'either-way' offence elected to be tried in the Crown Court.

8 The following table shows the outcomes of 'either-way' cases completed during 1999 after being committed to the Crown Court for trial:

Defendants in 'either-way' cases committed to Crown Court for trial	Case terminated in advance of trial	Not convicted (inc jury acquittals and judge ordered/ directed acquittals)	Convicted
58,000[10]	2,000	13,000	43,000

9 62% of defendants committed to the Crown Court for trial subsequently entered a guilty plea. Of the approximately 20,000 defendants who pleaded not guilty and were tried, 64% were acquitted.

10 The following table[11] sets out the penalties imposed on defendants charged with 'either-way' offences and sentenced in the Crown Court during 1999. Of the defendants convicted after being committed for trial, over 55% received a sentence which was within the powers of a magistrates' court. Magistrates' decided to commit about 20,000 defendants to the Crown Court for sentence. Nearly 60% of these defendants received a sentence which was within the powers of a magistrates' court.

	Defendants sentenced in Crown Court for 'either-way' offences	Non-custodial sentence	6 months and under	Over 6 months and up to 12	Over 12 months and up to 18	Over 18 months and up to 24	Over 24 months and up to 60	Over 60 months
Committed for trial	43,000	19,000	5,000	6,000	4,000	3,000	5,000	1,000
Committed for sentence	20,000	7,000	5,000	4,000	2,000	1,000	1,000	<100

---

[10] figures provided by RDS (IRS 6519c)
[11] figures provided by RDS (IRS 6519c for trials, 6519b for sentences)

Indictable only cases

11   In 1999, in addition to the 'either-way' cases committed for trial or sentence, the Crown Court dealt with just under 17,000 defendants charged with indictable only offences. The table below shows the outcomes of those cases:

Total proceeded against	Case terminated in advance of trial	Not convicted (inc jury acquittals and judge ordered/ directed acquittals)	Convicted
17,000	<500	5,000	12,000

12   52% of indictable only defendants pleaded guilty. Of the approximately 8,000 defendants who pleaded not guilty and were tried, 62% were acquitted.

Review of the

CRIMINAL

COURTS

OF ENGLAND AND WALES

REPORT

OCTOBER 2001

By the Right Honourable
LORD JUSTICE AULD

ISBN 0 11 702547 X

CORRECTION

Pages 680-682 are missing. The pages are included in this addendum slip.

APPENDIX V

BIBLIOGRAPHY FOR RESEARCH PAPER WHAT CAN THE ENGLISH LEGAL SYSTEM LEARN FROM RESEARCH PUBLISHED UP TO 2000?

PENNY DARBYSHIRE, ANDY MAUGHAN & ANGUS STEWART

Jury Excusal and Deferral: J Airs and A Shaw, Home Office Research and Statistics Directorate Research Study No. 102, 1999

Jury service: a personal observation, Anon., Legal Action Group Bulletin, December 1979, 278, referred to throughout as the LAG psychologist.

Why I despair for British Justice, Anon., Daily Mail, 27th December, 1990

Evidence evaluation in jury decision-making, R Arce, Handbook of Psychology in Legal Contexts (Bull & Carson eds.) 1995

The criminal process – an evaluative study, A Ashworth, (2nd ed.,) Oxford, 1998

Jury trial,s J Baldwin and M McConville, Clarendon Press, 1979

The jury and reality, Z Bankowski,

The Jury Under Attack (Findlay & Duff eds.) 1998

Members of the jury, D Barber and G Gordon, Wildwood House, London 1974

The jury is still out: the role of jury science in the modern American courtroom, J W Barber, J W Barber, 31 Am Crim L Rev 1225, 1994

Miscarriages of justice in potentially capital cases, H A Bedau & M Radelet, 40 Stan. L. Rev. 21, 1987

Twelve men and true! Bah humbug, A Bell, 147 NLJ 1857, 1997

Jury selection and bias: debunking invidious stereotypes through science, M J Bonazzoli, 18 *Quinnipiac Law Review* 247, 1998

Jury decision making; an empirical study based on actual felony trials, D L Bridgeman and D Marlowe, 64 *Journal of Applied Psychology* No 2, 91-98, 1979

How to make jury verdicts less hit and miss, P Brock, The Times 23rd April 1980

The University of Chicago jury project, D W Broeder, 38 Nebraska L.R. 744, 1959

Carlton, Darbyshire, Harris, Hodgetts and Robbins, in separate articles 140 N.L.J. 1264-1276, 1990

Making legal language understandable, R Charrow & V Charrow, 79 Colum.L.Rev.1306, 1979

The law of the other, M Constable, University of Chicago Press, 1964

Contempt of Court Act, 1981

The Jury, W. R. Cornish, Allen Lane, 1970

Learning lessons and speaking rights. Creating educated and democratic juries, B M Dann, 68 IndLJ 1229, 1993

The Lamp That Shows That Freedom Lives: Is it Worth the Candle?, P Darbyshire, CrimLR 740, 1991

For the New Lord Chancellor – Some Causes of Concern About Magistrates, P Darbyshire, CrimLR 861, 1997

The Judge, Devlin

Serving as a juryman in Britain, E Devons, 28 MLR 561, 1964

The case for jury waiver, S Doran & J Jackson, Crim LR 155, 1997

The Scottish criminal jury: a very peculiar institution, P Duff, 62 Law & Contemporary Problems 173, 1999

Anyone know what the Judge is on about?, C Dyer, The Guardian 17th July 2000

Hard Cases Make Bad Law, Editorial,142 NLJ 1293, 1992

A jurors tale, R Eldin, 138 NLJ 37, 1998

Some steps between attitudes and verdicts, P C Ellsworth, in R Hastie, ed., *Inside the Juror,* Cambridge University Press, 1993

Report of the Departmental Committee on jury service, Cmnd 2627, 1965

Making jury instructions understandable, A Elwork, B D Sales and J J Alfini, Charlottesville, VA: Michie, 1982

A ceiling or consistency effect for the comprehension of jury instructions, P W English & B D Sales, 3 Psychol Pub Pol'y & L 381, 1997

Multi racial juries, S Enright, 141 NLJ 992, 1991

Jury research in America, H S Erlanger, 4 *Law & Society Review* 345, 1970

The juror under attack, M Findlay & P Duff (eds), Butterworths, 1998

Common sense justice: jurors' notions of the law, N J Finkel, Cambridge, MA: Harvard University Press, 1995

Race and the jury: racial disenfranchisement and the search for justice, H Fukurai, Edward W Butler and Richard Krooth, Plenum Press, 1993

Cross-sectional jury representation or systematic representation? Simple random and Cluster Sampling Strategies in Jury Selection, H Fukurai, E Butler & R Krooth, 19 *Journal of Criminal Justice* 31-48, 1991

Race, social class and jury participation: new dimensions for evaluating discrimination in jury service and jury selection, H Fukurai, 24 *Journal of Criminal Justice* No1, 71-88, 1996

The representative jury requirement: jury representatives and cross sectional participation from beginning to the end of the jury selection process, H Fukurai, 23 International Journal of Comparative and Applied Criminal Justice, No1, 55-90, 1999

Social de-construction of race and affirmative action in jury selection, H. Fukurai, 11 La Raza LJ 17, 1999

The myths and realities of attorney jury selection folklore and scientific jury selection: what works?, S M. Fulero and S D Penrod, 17 Ohio NUI Rev 229, 1990

Explaining the verdict, J Gibbons, 147 N.L.J. 1454, 1997

The Juryman's Tale, T Grove, 1998

Sec. 12 of the Canada Evidence Act and the deliberation of simulated juries, V P Hans & A N Doob, 18 Crim. Law q235, 1976

*The Arizona jury reform permitting civil jury trial discussions: The views of trial participants, judges and jurors ,*V P Hans, P L Hannaford and G T Munsterman, 32 U Mich. JL Ref 349, 1999

Judging the Jury, V P Hans & N Vidmar, New York: Plenum Press, 1986

Why the middle class is a trial, J Harlow, The Sunday Times, 11th February 1990

Inside the Juror, R Hastie (ed), Cambridge University Press, 1993

Inside the Jury, R Hastie, S D Penrod & N Pennington, Harvard University Press, 1983

Magistrates Court or Crown Court? Mode of trial decisions and sentencing, C Hedderman & D Moxon, Home Office Research Study no125, 1992

Racism, impartiality and juries, P Herbert, 145 New Law Journal 1138, 1995

Instructing jurors: a field experiment with written and preliminary instructions, L Heuer & S D Penrod, *Law and Human Behaviour,* 13 at 409, 1989

The effect of jury nullification instruction on verdicts and jury functioning in criminal trials, I A Horowitz, 9 Law and Human Behaviour 25, 1985

The value of jury trial, J Jackson, in *Criminal Justice* (Attwood & Goldberg eds) pp87-93, 1995

Judge without jury: Diplock trials in the adversarial system, J Jackson & S Doran, Oxford, 1995

The Jury System in Contemporary Ireland: In the Shadow of a Troubled Past, J Jackson, K Quinn & T O'Malley, 62 Law & Contemporary Problems 203, 1999

Black innocence and the white jury, S L Johnson, 83 Mich.L.R. 1611, 1985

Judicial Studies Board

Defining the standard of proof in jury instructions, D K Kagehiro, *Psychological Science* 194, 1990

Jury Representativeness: A Mandate for Multiple Source Lists, D Kairys, J Kadane and J P Lehoczky, 65 *California Law Review* 776-827, 1977

The American Jury, H Kalven & H Zeisel, Little Brown & Company, Boston, 1966

Reducing the effects of juror bias, M F Kaplan & L E Miller, *In The Jury Box* (Wrightsman, Kassin and Willis eds) p114

Dirty tricks of cross-examinations, S M Kassin et al,. 14 Law & Hum Behav 373, 1990

Final Report of the Blue Ribbon Commission on Jury System Improvement, J Clark Kelso, 47 Hastings L J 1433, 1996

The Route to Clear Jury Instructions, J Kimble, 78 *Michigan Bar Journal* 1406, 1999

Postconviction review of jury discrimination: measuring the effects of juror race on juror decisions, NJ King, 92 MichLR 63, 1993

The American criminal jury, N J King, 62 Law & Contemporary Problems 41, 1999

Stratified juror selection: cross section by design, N King and G T Munsterman, 79 *Judicature* No5, 273, 1996

Deliberating juror pre-deliberation discussions: should California follow the Arizona model?, N K Lakamp, 45 UCLA Law Review 845, 1998

Lawtel

D Leigh and R Lustig, in two articles in The Observer, 23rd August 1981

Telling tales in court: trial procedure and the story model, R Lempert, Cardoza LR vol.13:559, 1991

What social science teaches us about the jury instruction process, J D Lieberman & B D Sales, 3 PsycholPubPol'y & L 589, 1997

The effects on juries of hearing about the defendant's previous criminal record: a simulation study, S Lloyd-Bostock, Crim LR 734, 2000

Decline of the 'Little Parliament': juries and jury reform in England and Wales, S Lloyd-Bostock & C Thomas, 62 Law & Contemporary Problems 7, 1999

The trials of a UK juryman, S Lofthouse, 142 NLJ 561, 1992

Reducing the Trials of Jury Service, Lord Chancellor's Department, Press Release, 31st August 2000

Jury research in England and the United States, S McCabe, 14 BJ Crim 276, 1974

The Shadow Jury at Work, S McCabe & Robert Purves, Oxford University Penal Research Unit, 1972

R v McCalla, CrimLR 335, 1986

Burdens of proof, degrees of belief, quanta of evidence, or Constitutional guarantees?, C M A McCauliff, 35 Vand.L.Rev 1293, 1982

Criminal justice in crisis, M McConville and L Bridges, Edward Elgar, 1994

The system in black and white: exploring the connections between race, crime and justice, (Markowitz & Jones-Brown, eds) Praeger, 2000

Jury selection in the United States: are there lessons to be learned?, R May, CrimLR 270, 1998

Juror characteristics: to what extent are they related to jury verdicts?, C J Mills and W E Bohannon, 64 Judicature Number 1, June/July 1980, 23-31, 1980

The psychology of jury persuasion, M O Miller & T A Mauet, 22 Am J Trial Advoc. 549, 1999

*The criminal standard of proof ,*J W Montgomery, 148 NLJ 582, 1998

Scientific juror selection: sex as a moderator of demographic and personality predictors of empanelled felony juror behaviour, Moran and Comfort, 43 Journal of Personality and Social Psychology, No5, 1982

The Jury and the Legal System, G Mungham and Z Bankowski, in P Carlen, *The Sociology of Law,* P Carlen, University of Keele, Staffordshire, 1976

A Brief History of State Jury Reform Efforts, G T Munsterman, 79 Judicature, Number 5, March-April, 1996

The search for jury representativeness, G T Munsterman & J T Munsterman, 11 Justice System Journal (1) 59-78, 1986

Criminal Justice Process, N Padfield, (2nd ed) Butterworths, 1999

A cognitive theory of juror decision making: the story model, N Pennington & R Hastie, Cardoza LR vol 13:519, 1991

Statistics on race and the criminal justice system – the 1995 British Crime Survey, Percy, Home Office Publications, 1998

Reasonable and other doubts: the problem of jury instructions, R C Power, 67 Tenn L R 45, 1999

Practice Note, 3 All ER 240, 1988

Jury deliberations, voting and verdict trends, JP Reed, 45 Social Scene Quarterly 361 370, 1965

Judge and jury: the Crown Court in action, P Robertshaw, Dartmouth Publishing Company, 1995

The Roskill Report, Fraud Trials Committee Report, London, HMSO, 1986

Social psychology in court, Saks and Hastie, Van Nostrand Reinhold Company, 1978

What do jury experiments tell us about how juries (should) make decisions?, M J Saks, 6 S Cal Interdisciplinary LJ 1, 1997

Jurors and their Verdicts, A P Sealy and W R Cornish, 36 Modern Law Review 496, 1973

The vanishing juror: why are there not enough available jurors?, R Seltzer, 20 The Justice System Journal No3 203-218, 1999

Improving the ability of jurors to comprehend and apply criminal jury instructions, L J Severance & E F Loftus, Law & Society Review, 17, 1982

A more active jury: has Arizona set the standard for reform with its new jury rules?, J E Shtabsky, 28 AZSLJ 1009, 1996

The Jury and The Defence of Insanity, R J Simon, Little, Brown and co Boston

The jury system in America: a critical overview, R J Simon (ed), Sage Publications, 1975

Commensurability: understanding jury research and juror information processing, M S Sobus, 65 Def Couns J 408, 1998

Where is justice for the jury?, L Spence, The Times 6th August 1991

Jury instructions: a persistent failure to communicate , W W Steele & E G Thornbug, 67 NCLRev 77, 1988

The psychology of criminal justice, G M Stephenson, Blackwell-Oxford, 1992

Procedural justice: a psychological analysis, J Thibaut & L Walker, 1975

Jury selection procedures, Van Dyke, Ballinger Publishing Company, 1977

Evidence and outcome: a comparison of contested trials in the magistrates' courts and the Crown Court, J Vennard, Home Office Research Unit, London, 1986

The use of peremptory challenge and stand by of jurors and their relationship with trial outcome, J Vennard and David Riley, Crim LR 723, 1998

World jury systems, N Vidmar (ed) Oxford, 2000

The Canadian criminal jury, N Vidmar, 62 Law & Contemporary Problems 141, 1999

Juries and expert evidence: social framework testimony, N Vidmar & R A Schuller, 52 Law & Contemp Probs 133, 1989

Juror decision making: the importance of evidence, C A Visher, 11 *Law and Human Behaviour,* No1, 1-17, 1987

Criminal Justice – Text & Materials, M Wasik & T Gibbons, Addison Wesley Longman, 1998

Westlaw

Beauty and the Beast: physical appearance discrimination in American criminal trials, D L Wiley, 27 St, Mary's LJ 193, 1995

Jury source representativeness and the use of voter registration list,s C Williams, New York University Law Review, 590, 1990

On the inefficacy of limiting instructions, R Wissler & M Saks, 9 Law & Hum Behav 37, 1986

Criminal trials: curtailing the judge's summing-up function, D Wolchover, The Law Society Gazette at p363, 5th Feb 1986

Should judges sum up the facts?, D Wolchover, Crim LR 784, 1989

In the jury box, L S Wrightsman, S M Kassin, C E Willis (eds), Sage, 1987

Colour blindness in the jury room, P Wynn Davis, The Independent, 29th June 1990

Juries in criminal trials, W Young, N Cameron and Y Tinsley, New Zealand Law Commission Preliminary Paper no 37, 1999

Cases and materials on the English legal system, M Zander, (8th ed.) Butterworths, 1999

The Royal Commission on Criminal Justice, Research Study no 19: Crown Court Study, M Zander & P Henderson, HMSO, 1993

'Convincing empirical evidence' on the six member jury, H Zeisel & S Steadman Diamond, 41 University of Chicago Law Review 281, 1974

The effect of peremptory challenges on jury and verdict: an experiment in a Federal District Court, H Zeisel and S Seidman Diamond, 30 Stanford Law Review 491-531, 1978

The jury on trial, H B Zobel, July-Aug. Am Heritage at 42, reported in 105 Yale LJ 2285, 1995